Garfield

FAT CAT 3-PACK

VOLUME 2

BY
JIM DAVIS

BALLANTINE BOOKS · NEW YORK

Published in the United States by Ballantine Books, an imprint of Random House, a division of
Penguin Random House LLC, New York.

BALLANTINE and the HOUSE colophon are registered trademarks of Penguin Random House LLC.

NICKELDOLEON is a Trademark of Viacom International, Inc.

GARFIELD WEIGHS IN was published separately by Ballantine Books, an imprint of Random House,
a division of Penguin Random House LLC, in 1982 and 2002. GARFIELD TAKES THE CAKE was
published separately by Ballantine Books, and imprint of Random House, a division of Penguin Random
House LLC, in 1982 and 2003. GARFIELD EATS HIS HEART OUT was published separately by
Ballantine Books, an imprint of Random House, a division of Penguin Random House LLC, in 1983 and
2004.

Library of Congress Control Number: 2003105484

ISBN: 978-0-345-46465-1

Printed in China

randomhousebooks.com

22

BY JIM DAVIS

Ballantine Books • New York

A GARFIELD MORNING

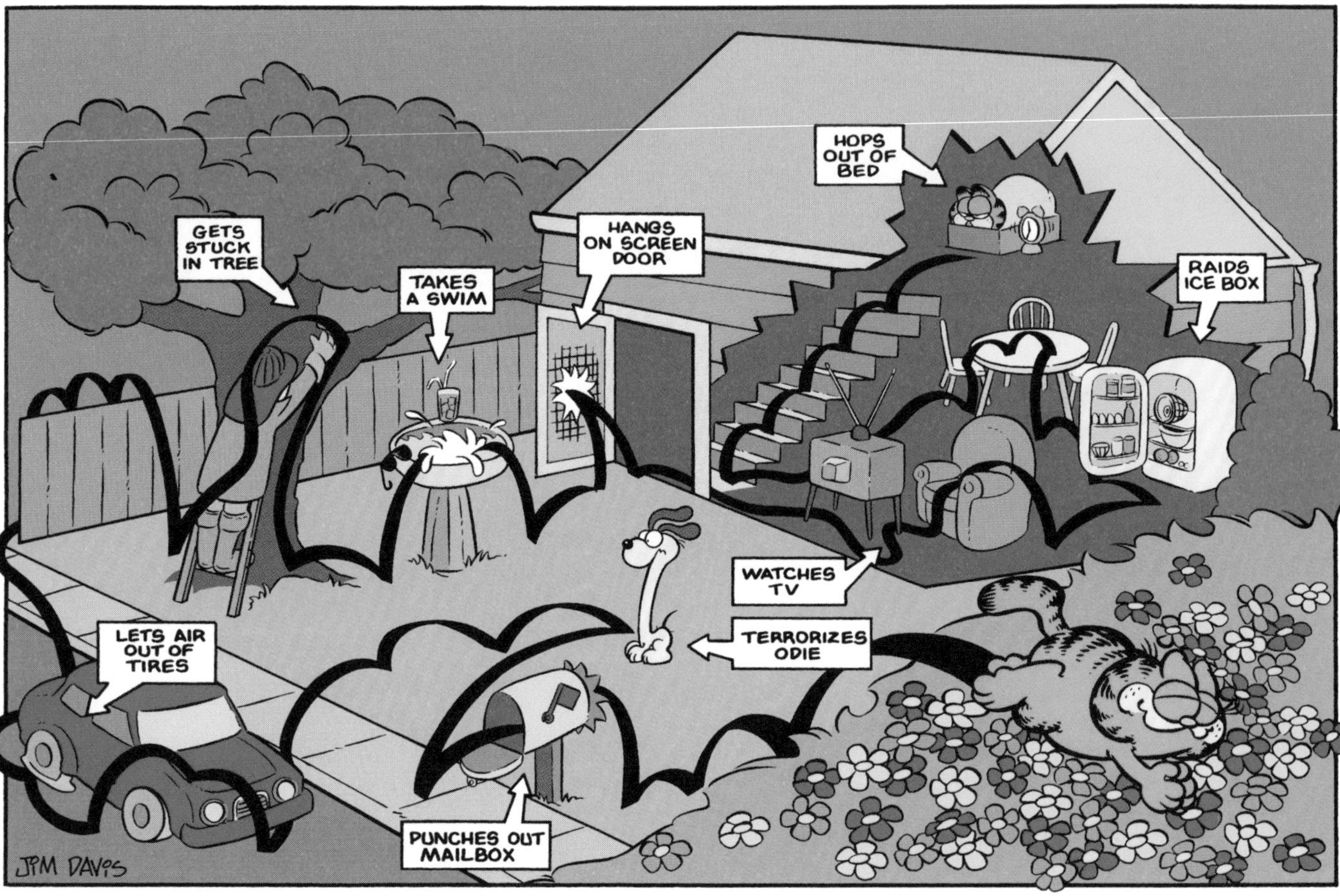
HOPS OUT OF BED
GETS STUCK IN TREE
TAKES A SWIM
HANGS ON SCREEN DOOR
RAIDS ICE BOX
WATCHES TV
LETS AIR OUT OF TIRES
TERRORIZES ODIE
PUNCHES OUT MAILBOX
JIM DAVIS

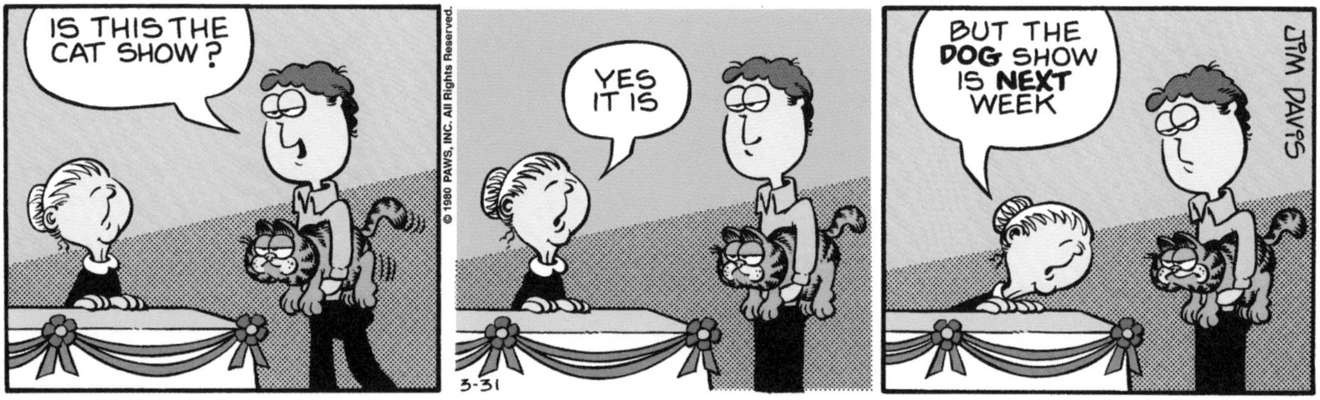
IS THIS THE CAT SHOW?
© 1980 PAWS, INC. All Rights Reserved.
YES IT IS
3-31
BUT THE **DOG** SHOW IS **NEXT** WEEK
JIM DAVIS

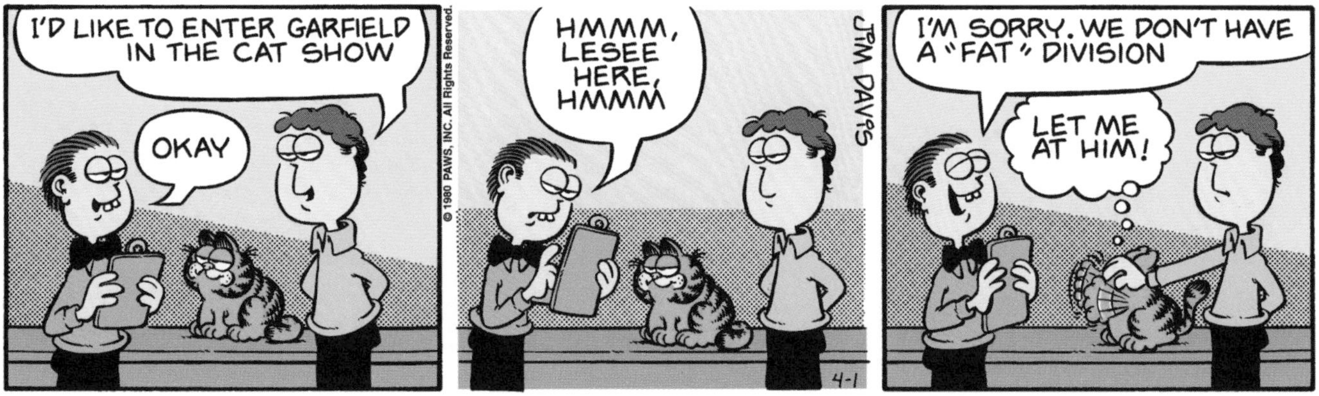
I'D LIKE TO ENTER GARFIELD IN THE CAT SHOW
OKAY
© 1980 PAWS, INC. All Rights Reserved.
HMMM, LESEE HERE, HMMM
JIM DAVIS
4-1
I'M SORRY. WE DON'T HAVE A "FAT" DIVISION
LET ME AT HIM!

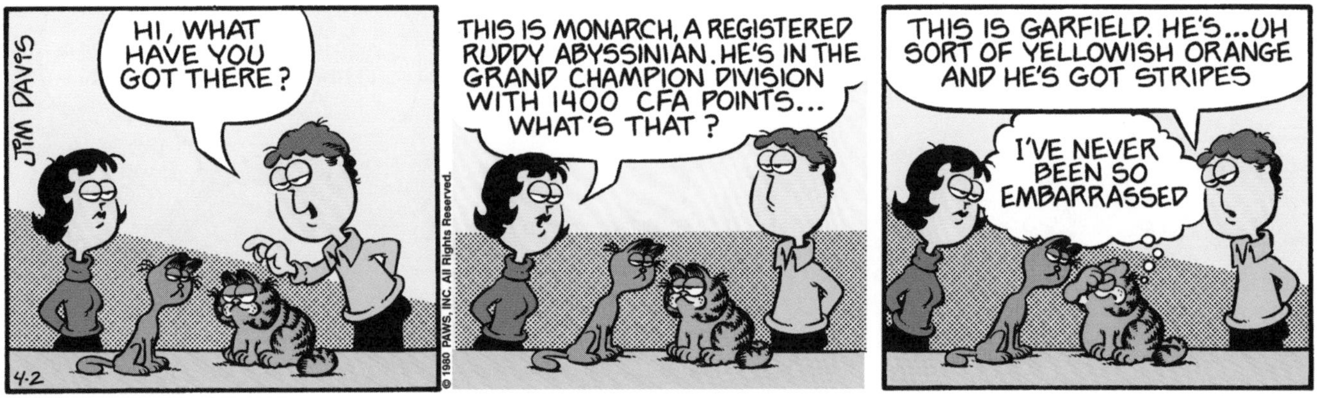
JIM DAVIS
HI, WHAT HAVE YOU GOT THERE?
4-2
© 1980 PAWS, INC. All Rights Reserved.
THIS IS MONARCH, A REGISTERED RUDDY ABYSSINIAN. HE'S IN THE GRAND CHAMPION DIVISION WITH 1400 CFA POINTS... WHAT'S THAT?
THIS IS GARFIELD. HE'S...UH SORT OF YELLOWISH ORANGE AND HE'S GOT STRIPES
I'VE NEVER BEEN SO EMBARRASSED

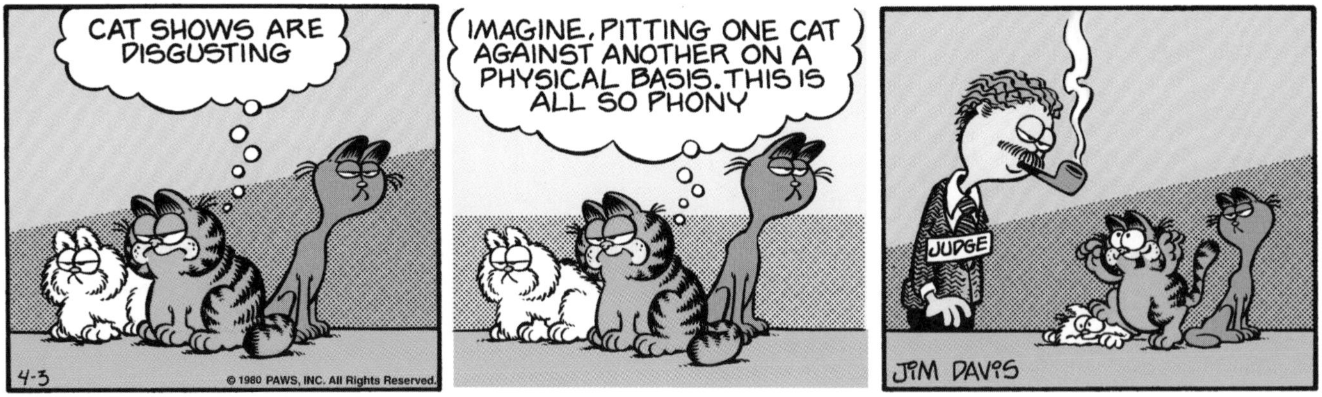
CAT SHOWS ARE DISGUSTING
4-3
© 1980 PAWS, INC. All Rights Reserved.
IMAGINE, PITTING ONE CAT AGAINST ANOTHER ON A PHYSICAL BASIS. THIS IS ALL SO PHONY
JUDGE
JIM DAVIS

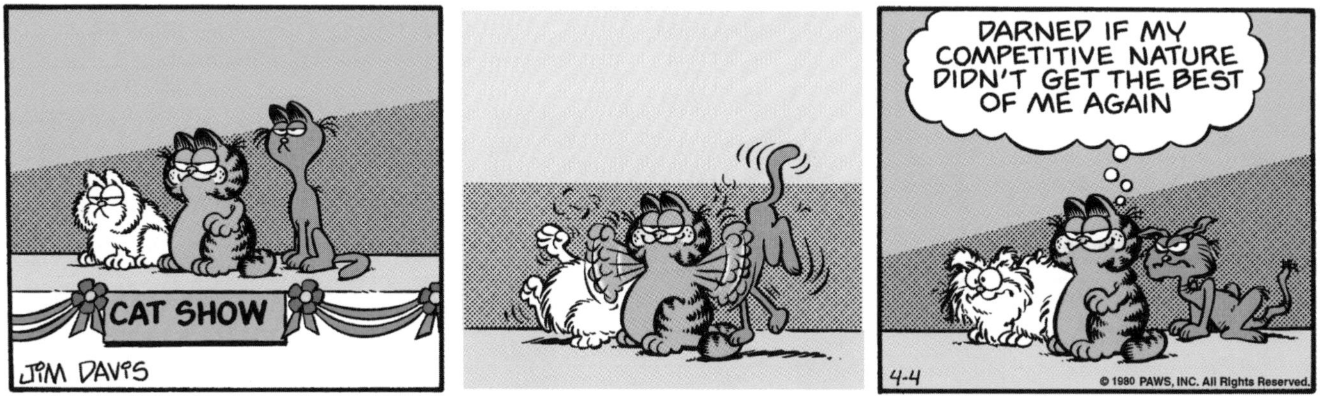
CAT SHOW
JIM DAVIS
DARNED IF MY COMPETITIVE NATURE DIDN'T GET THE BEST OF ME AGAIN
4-4
© 1980 PAWS, INC. All Rights Reserved.

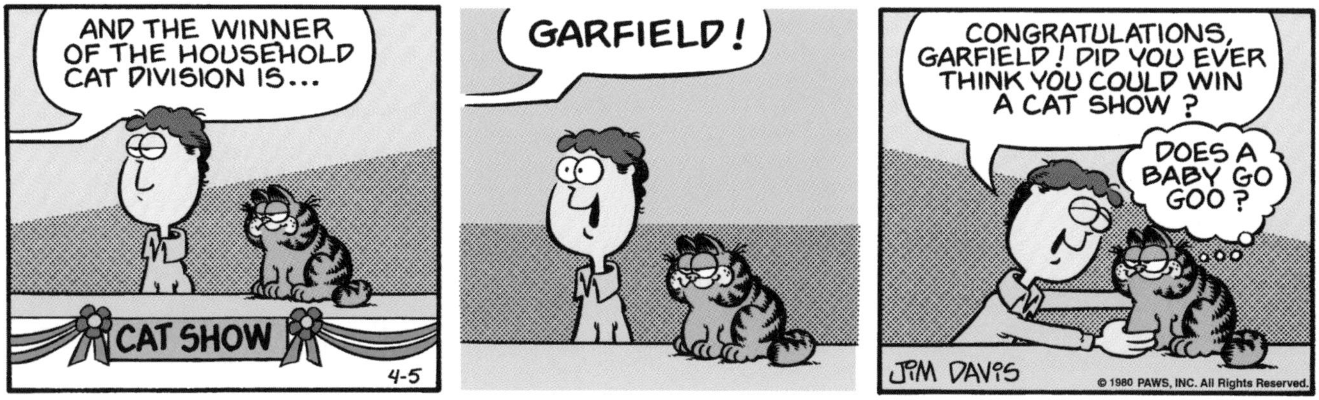
AND THE WINNER OF THE HOUSEHOLD CAT DIVISION IS...
CAT SHOW
4-5
GARFIELD!
CONGRATULATIONS, GARFIELD! DID YOU EVER THINK YOU COULD WIN A CAT SHOW?
DOES A BABY GO GOO?
JIM DAVIS
© 1980 PAWS, INC. All Rights Reserved.

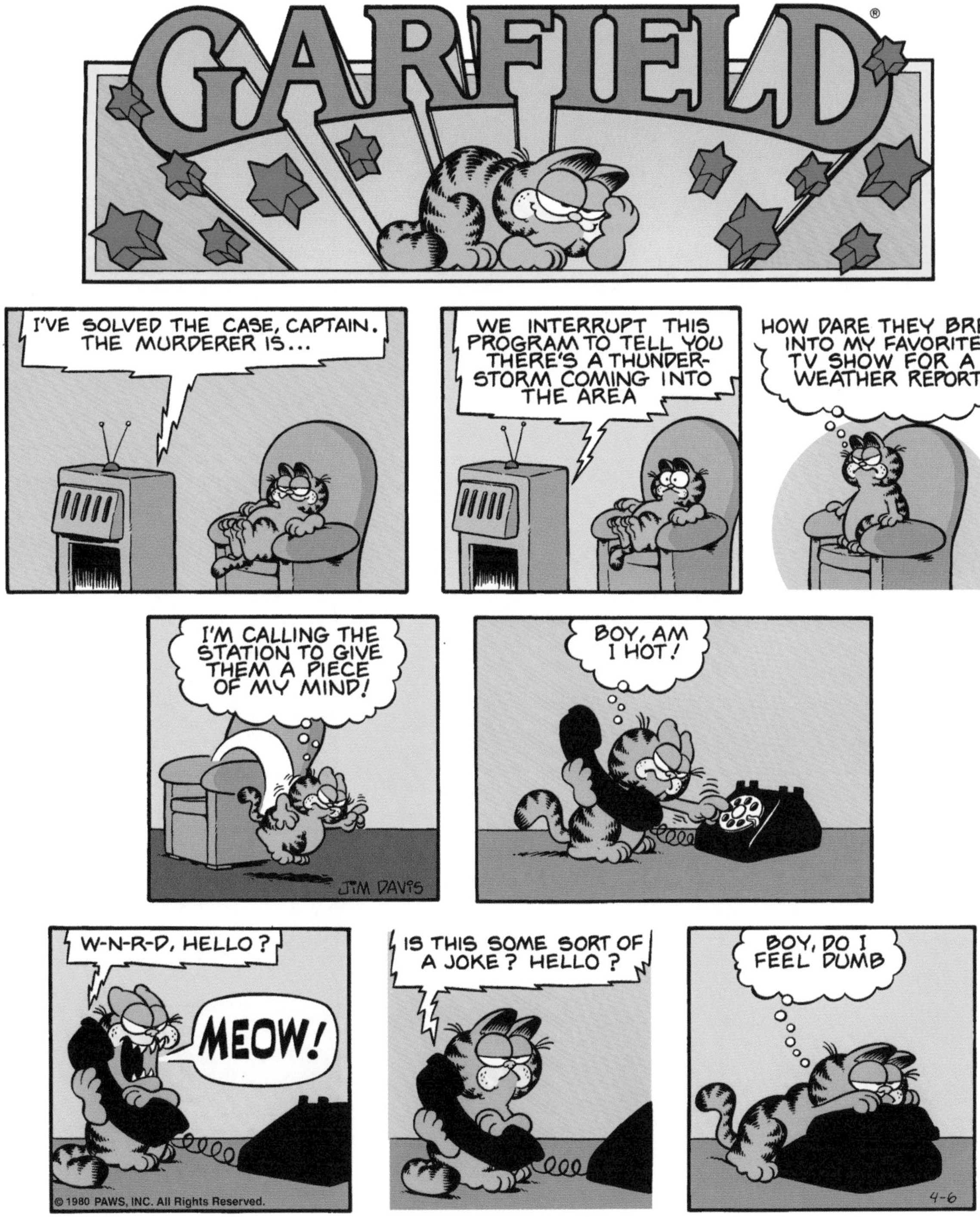
GARFIELD
I'VE SOLVED THE CASE, CAPTAIN. THE MURDERER IS...
WE INTERRUPT THIS PROGRAM TO TELL YOU THERE'S A THUNDER-STORM COMING INTO THE AREA
HOW DARE THEY BREAK INTO MY FAVORITE TV SHOW FOR A WEATHER REPORT!
I'M CALLING THE STATION TO GIVE THEM A PIECE OF MY MIND!
JIM DAVIS
BOY, AM I HOT!
W-N-R-D, HELLO?
MEOW!
IS THIS SOME SORT OF A JOKE? HELLO?
BOY, DO I FEEL DUMB
4-6

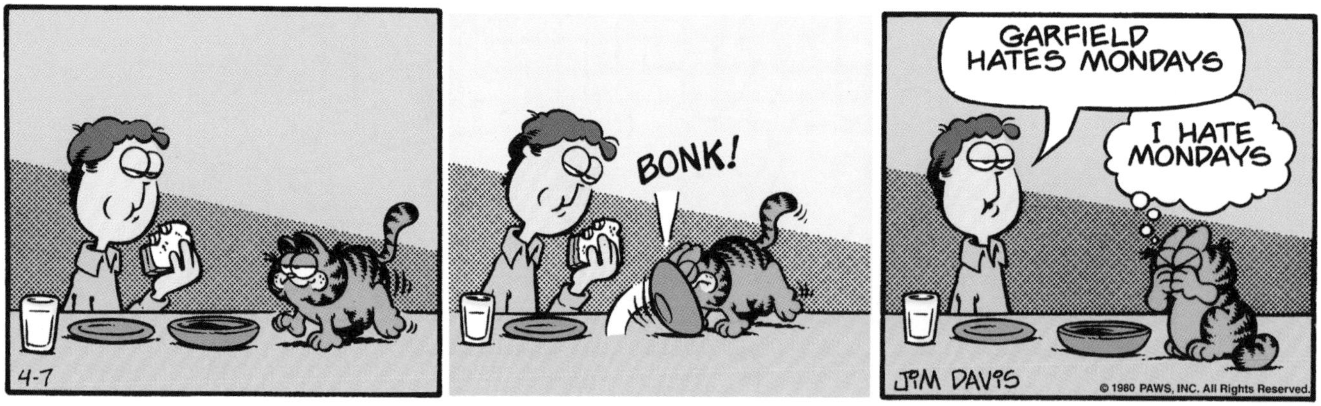
4-7
BONK!
GARFIELD HATES MONDAYS
I HATE MONDAYS
JIM DAVIS
© 1980 PAWS, INC. All Rights Reserved.

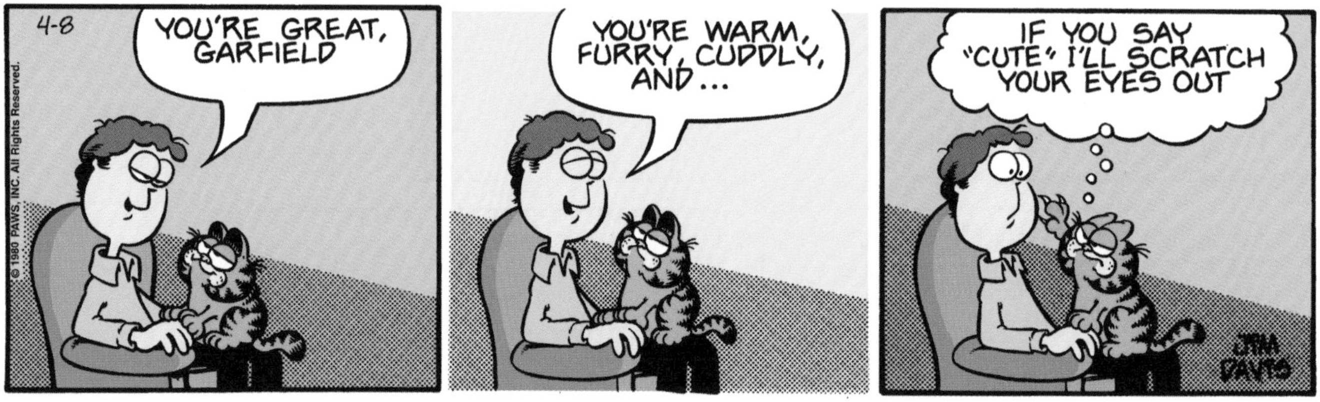
4-8
© 1980 PAWS, INC. All Rights Reserved.
YOU'RE GREAT, GARFIELD
YOU'RE WARM, FURRY, CUDDLY, AND...
IF YOU SAY "CUTE" I'LL SCRATCH YOUR EYES OUT
JIM DAVIS

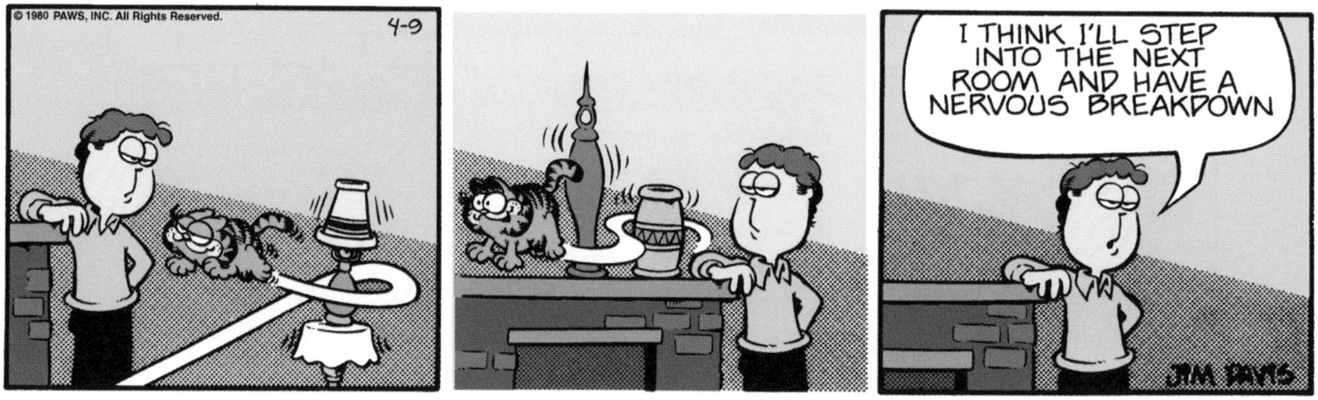
© 1980 PAWS, INC. All Rights Reserved.
4-9
I THINK I'LL STEP INTO THE NEXT ROOM AND HAVE A NERVOUS BREAKDOWN
JIM DAVIS

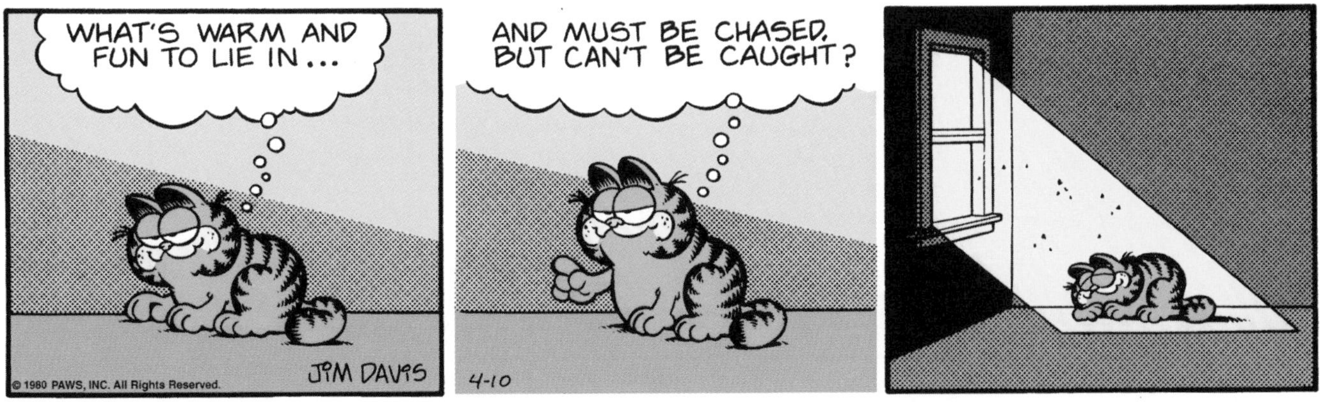
WHAT'S WARM AND FUN TO LIE IN...
© 1980 PAWS, INC. All Rights Reserved.
JIM DAVIS
AND MUST BE CHASED, BUT CAN'T BE CAUGHT?
4-10

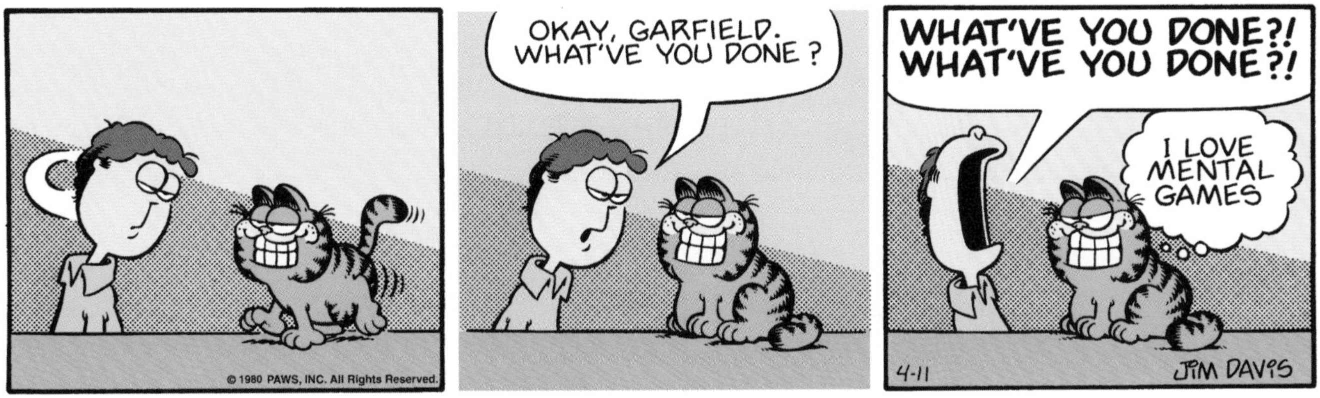
© 1980 PAWS, INC. All Rights Reserved.
OKAY, GARFIELD. WHAT'VE YOU DONE?
WHAT'VE YOU DONE?! WHAT'VE YOU DONE?!
I LOVE MENTAL GAMES
4-11
JIM DAVIS

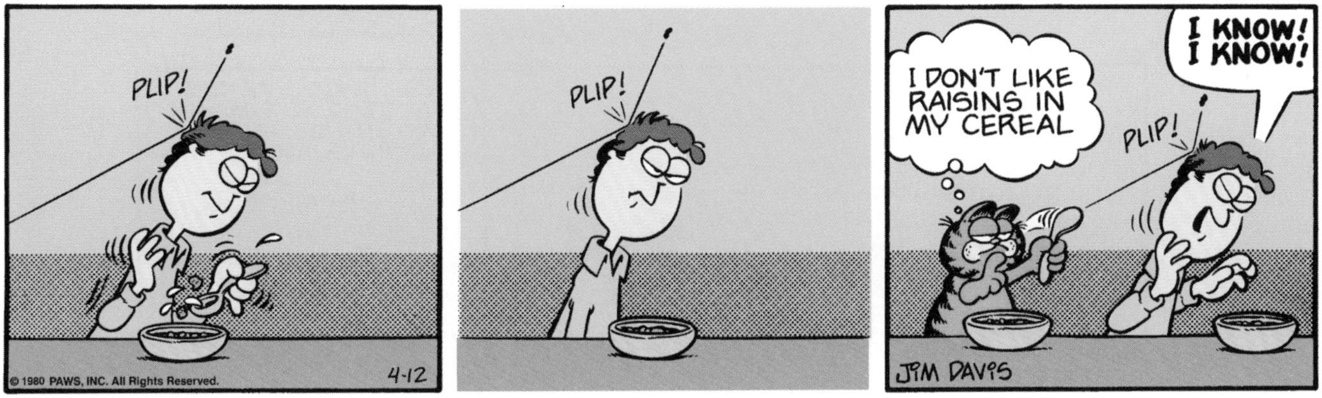
PLIP!
© 1980 PAWS, INC. All Rights Reserved.
4-12
PLIP!
I DON'T LIKE RAISINS IN MY CEREAL
PLIP!
I KNOW! I KNOW!
JIM DAVIS

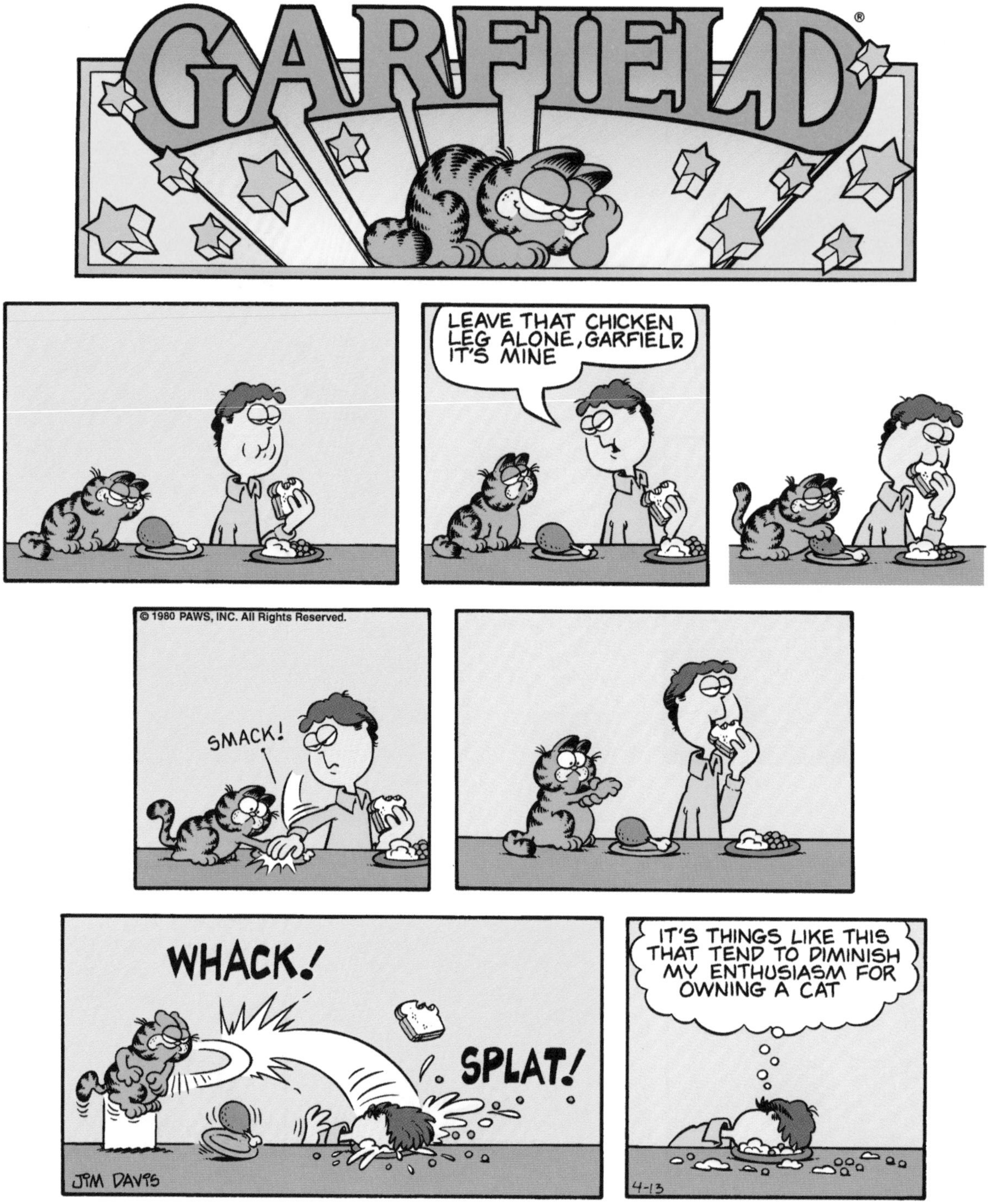
GARFIELD®
LEAVE THAT CHICKEN LEG ALONE, GARFIELD. IT'S MINE
© 1980 PAWS, INC. All Rights Reserved.
SMACK!
WHACK!
SPLAT!
JIM DAVIS
IT'S THINGS LIKE THIS THAT TEND TO DIMINISH MY ENTHUSIASM FOR OWNING A CAT
4-13

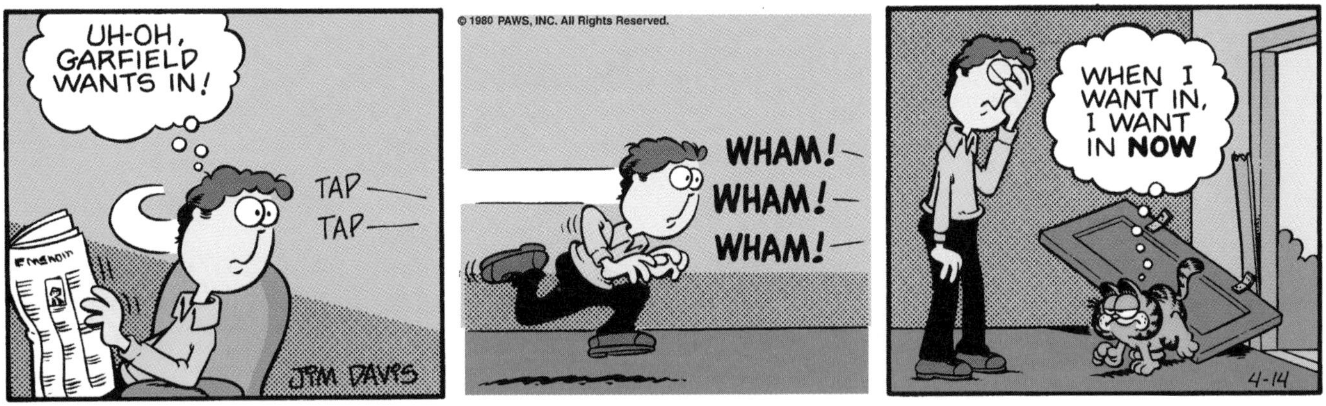
UH-OH, GARFIELD WANTS IN!
TAP
TAP
JIM DAVIS
© 1980 PAWS, INC. All Rights Reserved.
WHAM!
WHAM!
WHAM!
WHEN I WANT IN, I WANT IN **NOW**
4-14

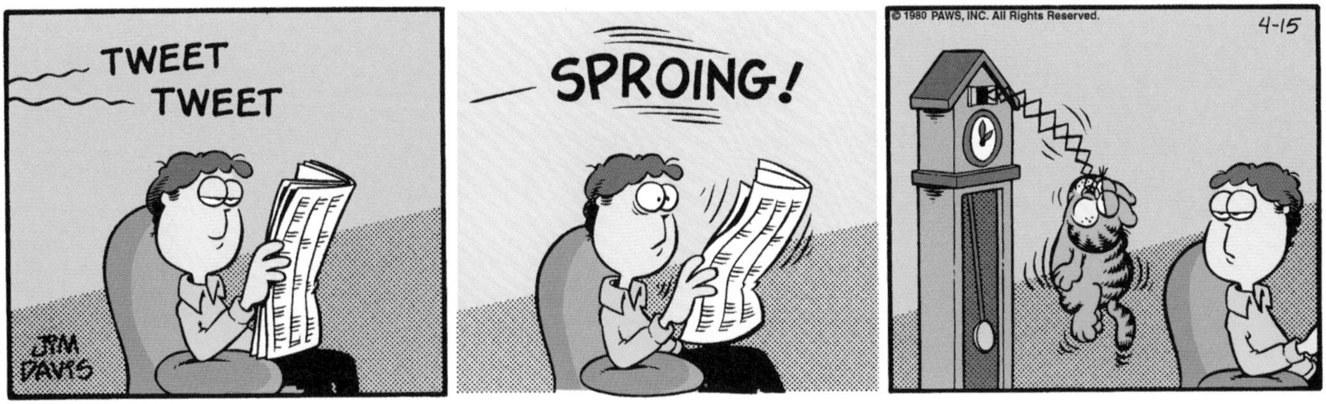
TWEET
TWEET
JIM DAVIS
SPROING!
© 1980 PAWS, INC. All Rights Reserved.
4-15

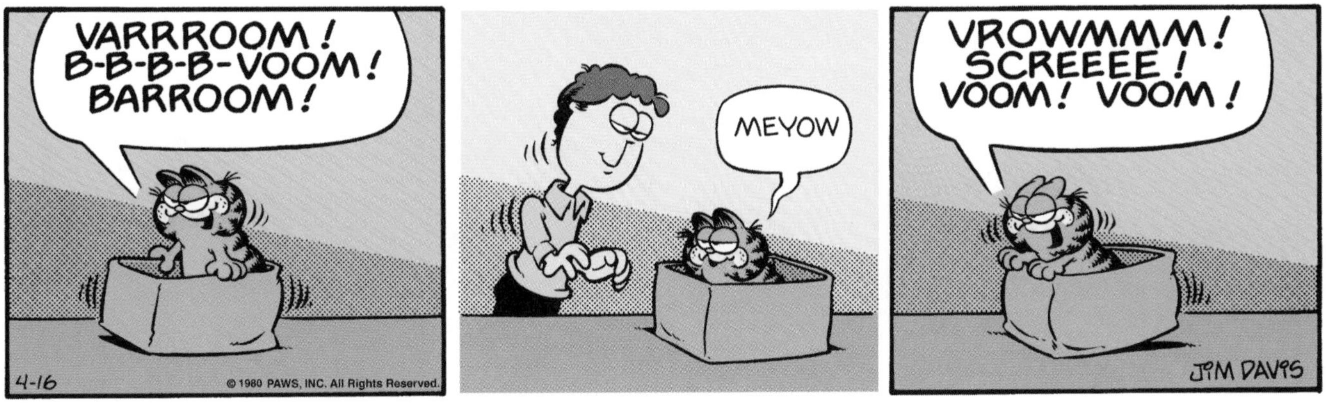
VARRROOM! B-B-B-B-VOOM! BARROOM!
4-16
© 1980 PAWS, INC. All Rights Reserved.
MEYOW
VROWMMM! SCREEEE! VOOM! VOOM!
JIM DAVIS

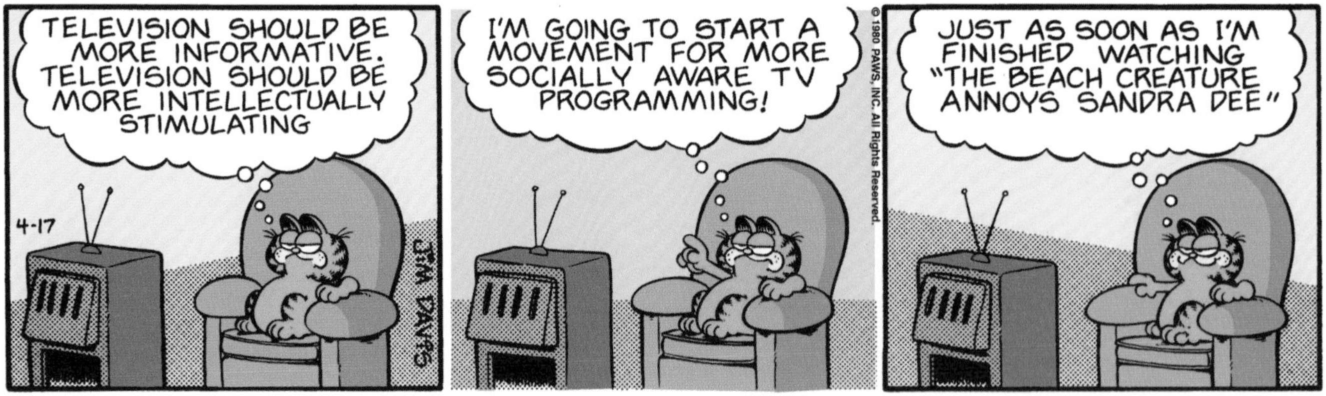
TELEVISION SHOULD BE MORE INFORMATIVE. TELEVISION SHOULD BE MORE INTELLECTUALLY STIMULATING
4-17
JIM DAVIS
I'M GOING TO START A MOVEMENT FOR MORE SOCIALLY AWARE TV PROGRAMMING!
© 1980 PAWS, INC. All Rights Reserved.
JUST AS SOON AS I'M FINISHED WATCHING "THE BEACH CREATURE ANNOYS SANDRA DEE"

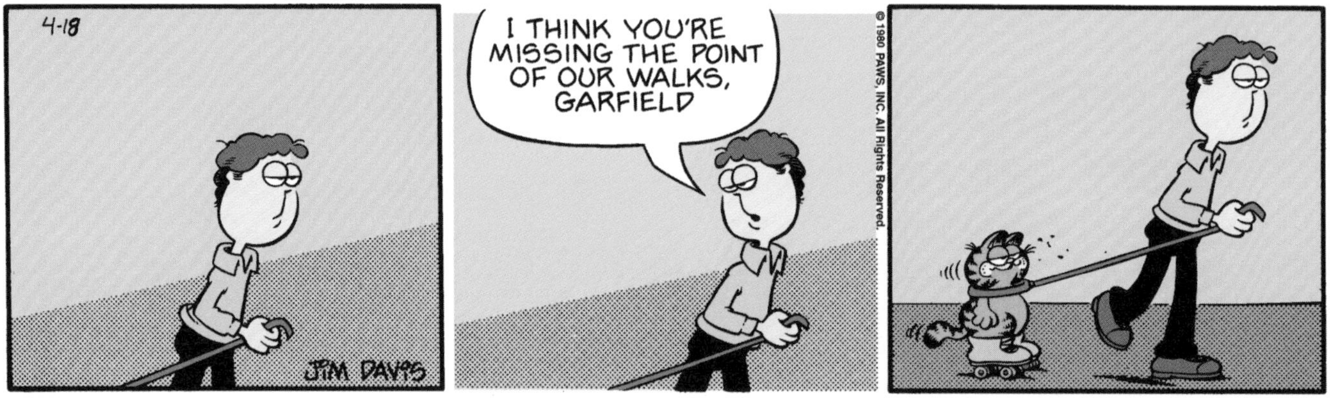
4-18
JIM DAVIS
I THINK YOU'RE MISSING THE POINT OF OUR WALKS, GARFIELD
© 1980 PAWS, INC. All Rights Reserved.

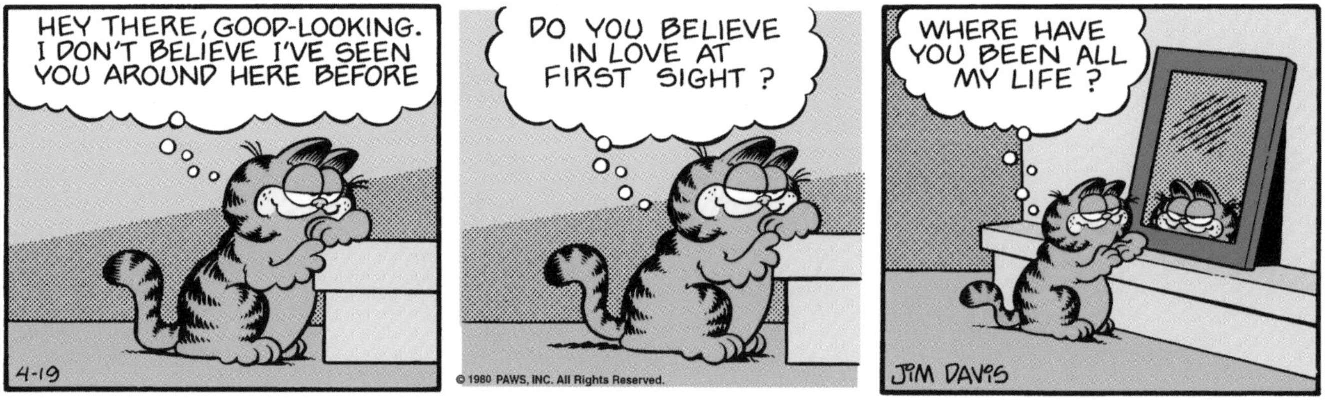
HEY THERE, GOOD-LOOKING. I DON'T BELIEVE I'VE SEEN YOU AROUND HERE BEFORE
4-19
DO YOU BELIEVE IN LOVE AT FIRST SIGHT ?
© 1980 PAWS, INC. All Rights Reserved.
WHERE HAVE YOU BEEN ALL MY LIFE ?
JIM DAVIS

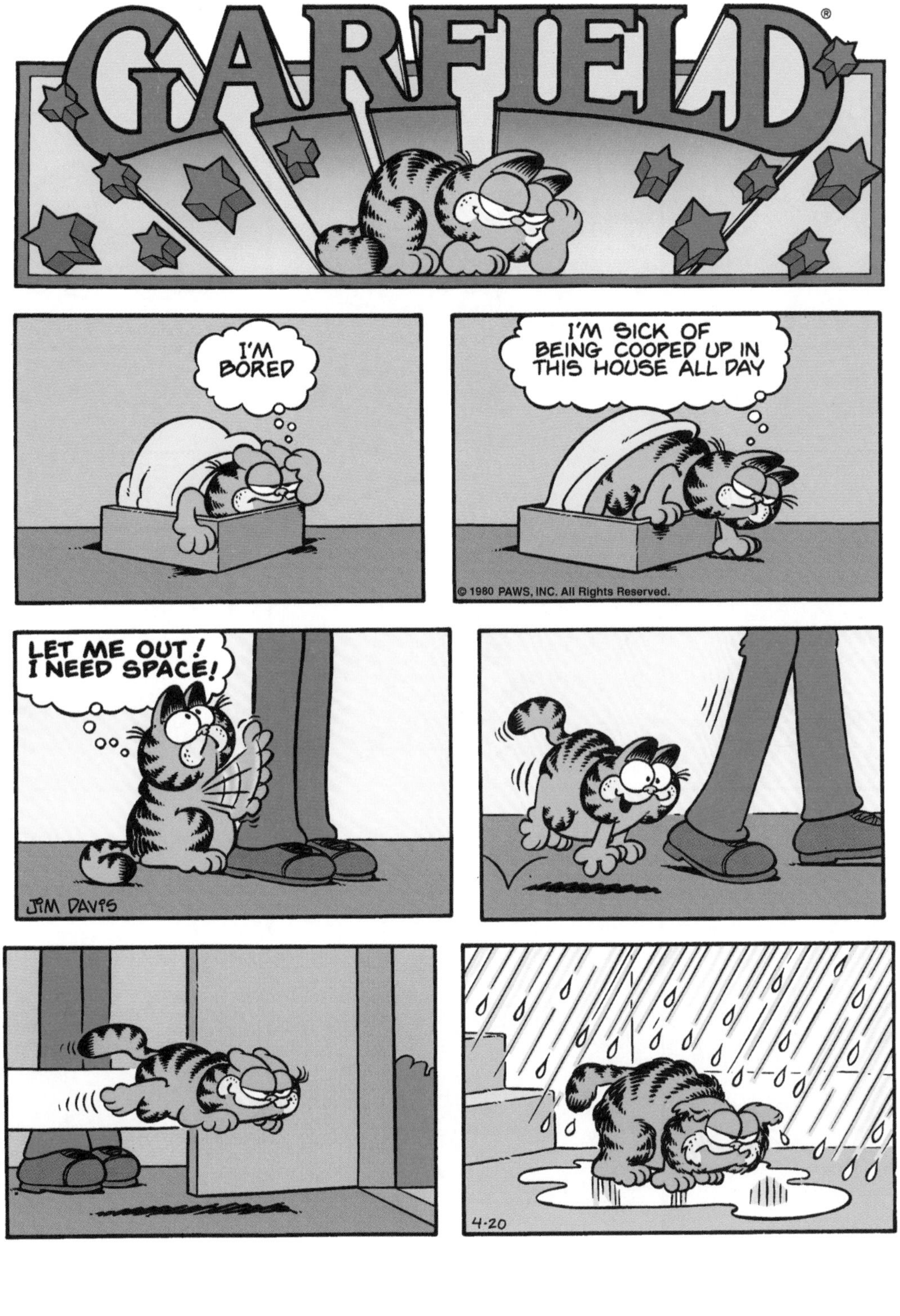
GARFIELD®
I'M BORED
I'M SICK OF BEING COOPED UP IN THIS HOUSE ALL DAY
LET ME OUT! I NEED SPACE!
JIM DAVIS
4-20

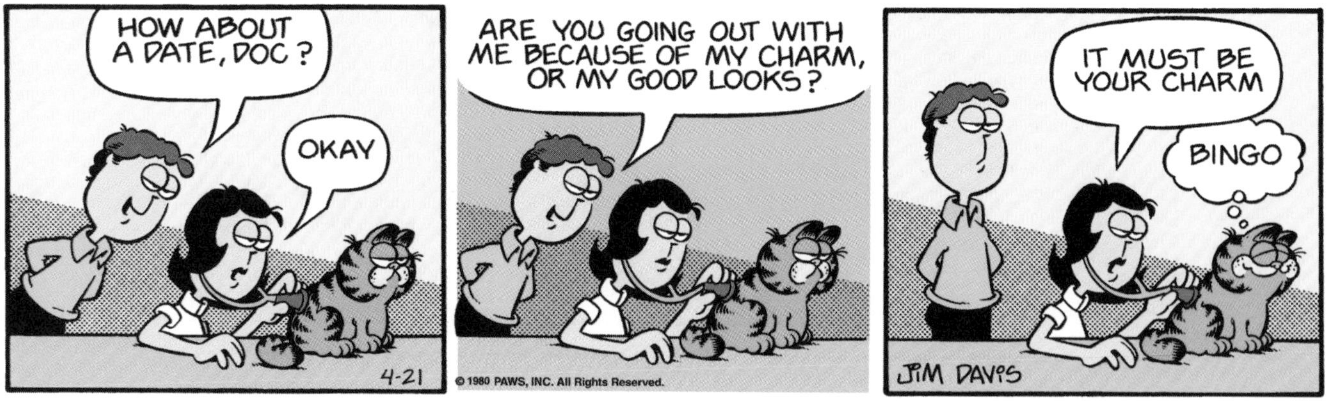
HOW ABOUT A DATE, DOC ?
OKAY
4-21
ARE YOU GOING OUT WITH ME BECAUSE OF MY CHARM, OR MY GOOD LOOKS ?
© 1980 PAWS, INC. All Rights Reserved.
IT MUST BE YOUR CHARM
BINGO
JIM DAVIS

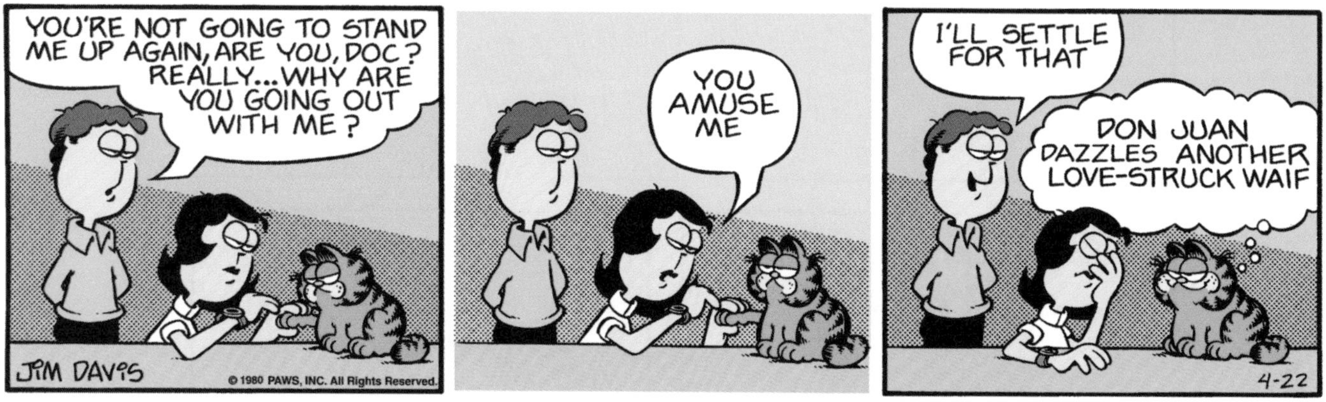
YOU'RE NOT GOING TO STAND ME UP AGAIN, ARE YOU, DOC? REALLY...WHY ARE YOU GOING OUT WITH ME ?
JIM DAVIS
© 1980 PAWS, INC. All Rights Reserved.
YOU AMUSE ME
I'LL SETTLE FOR THAT
DON JUAN DAZZLES ANOTHER LOVE-STRUCK WAIF
4-22

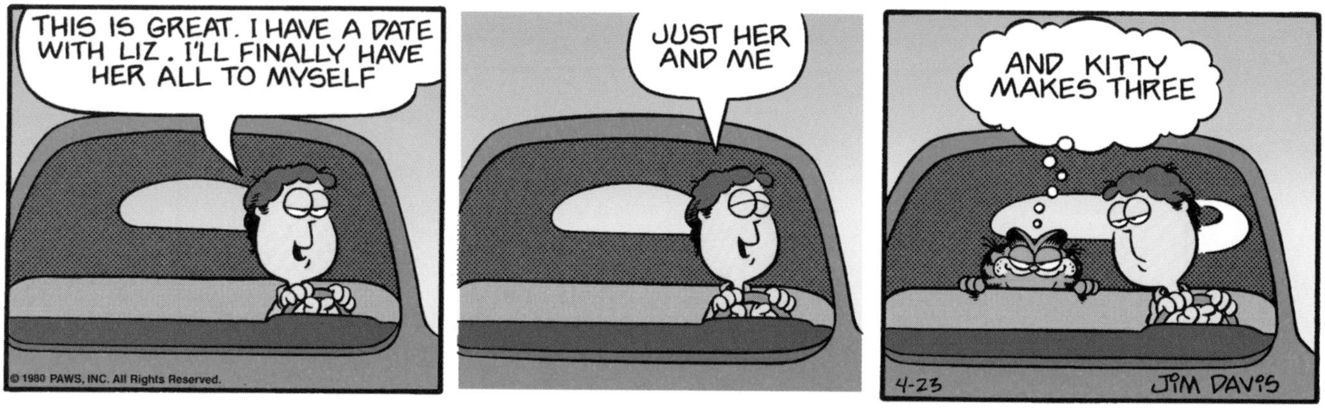
THIS IS GREAT. I HAVE A DATE WITH LIZ. I'LL FINALLY HAVE HER ALL TO MYSELF
© 1980 PAWS, INC. All Rights Reserved.
JUST HER AND ME
AND KITTY MAKES THREE
4-23
JIM DAVIS

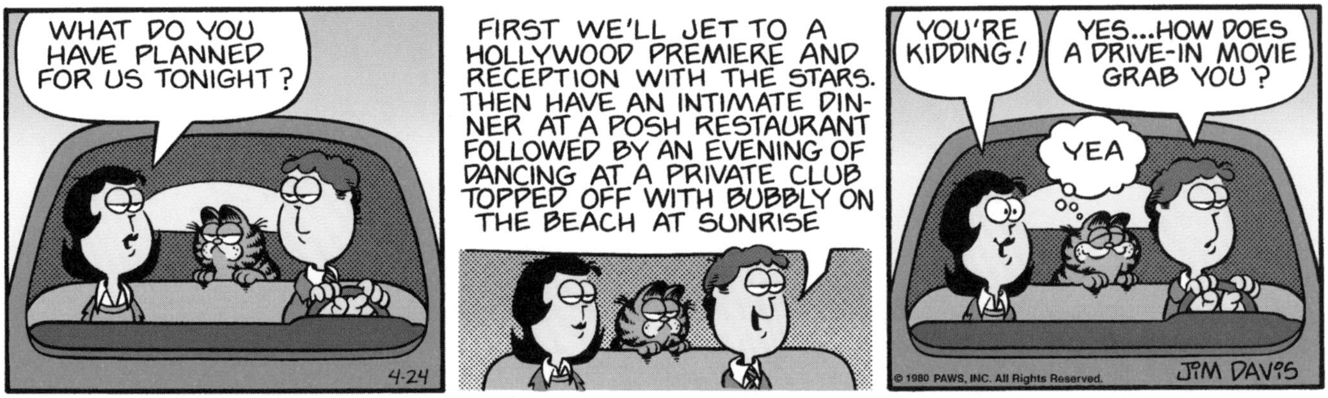
WHAT DO YOU HAVE PLANNED FOR US TONIGHT?
4-24
FIRST WE'LL JET TO A HOLLYWOOD PREMIERE AND RECEPTION WITH THE STARS. THEN HAVE AN INTIMATE DINNER AT A POSH RESTAURANT FOLLOWED BY AN EVENING OF DANCING AT A PRIVATE CLUB TOPPED OFF WITH BUBBLY ON THE BEACH AT SUNRISE
YOU'RE KIDDING!
YES...HOW DOES A DRIVE-IN MOVIE GRAB YOU?
YEA
© 1980 PAWS, INC. All Rights Reserved.
JIM DAVIS

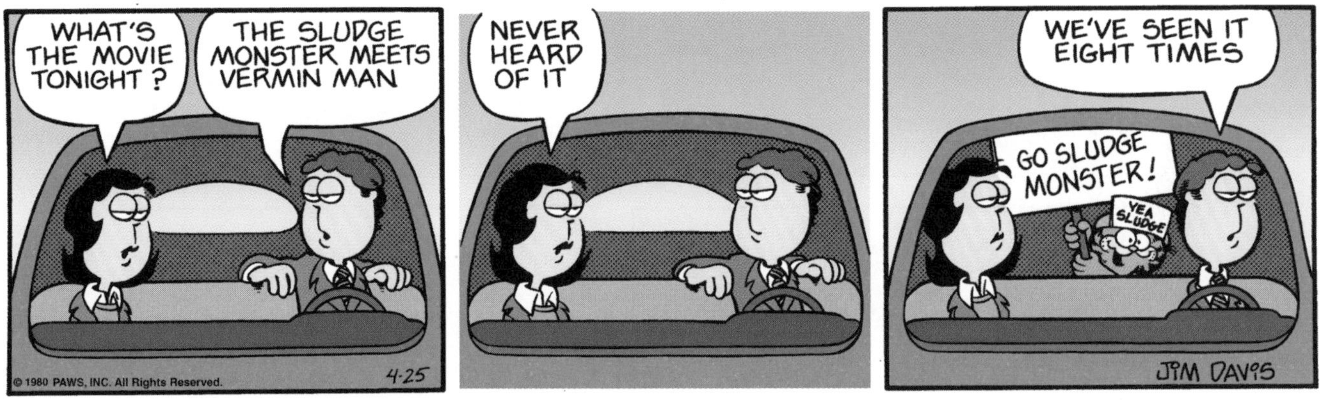
WHAT'S THE MOVIE TONIGHT?
THE SLUDGE MONSTER MEETS VERMIN MAN
© 1980 PAWS, INC. All Rights Reserved.
4-25
NEVER HEARD OF IT
WE'VE SEEN IT EIGHT TIMES
GO SLUDGE MONSTER!
YEA SLUDGE
JIM DAVIS

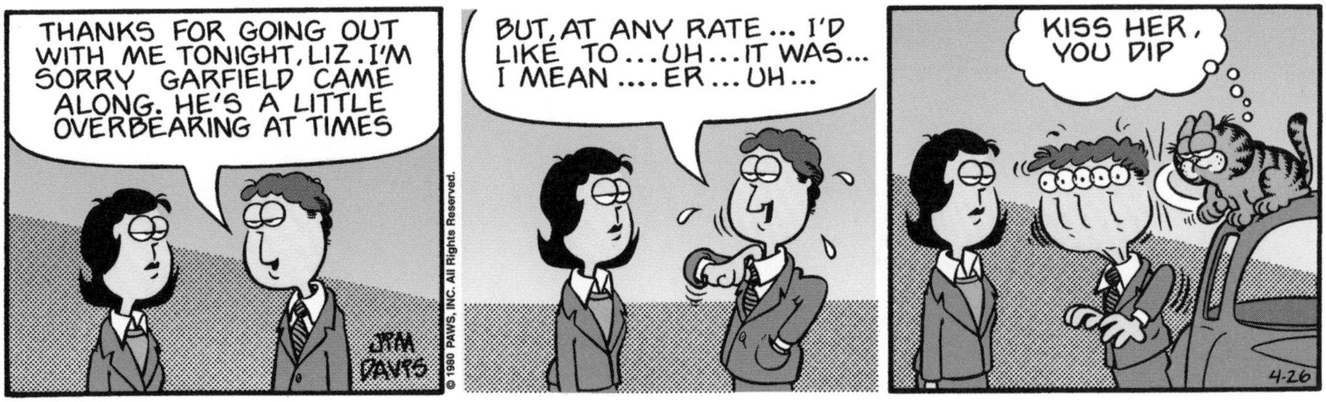
THANKS FOR GOING OUT WITH ME TONIGHT, LIZ. I'M SORRY GARFIELD CAME ALONG. HE'S A LITTLE OVERBEARING AT TIMES
JIM DAVIS
© 1980 PAWS, INC. All Rights Reserved.
BUT, AT ANY RATE ... I'D LIKE TO ... UH ... IT WAS... I MEAN .... ER ... UH...
KISS HER, YOU DIP
4-26

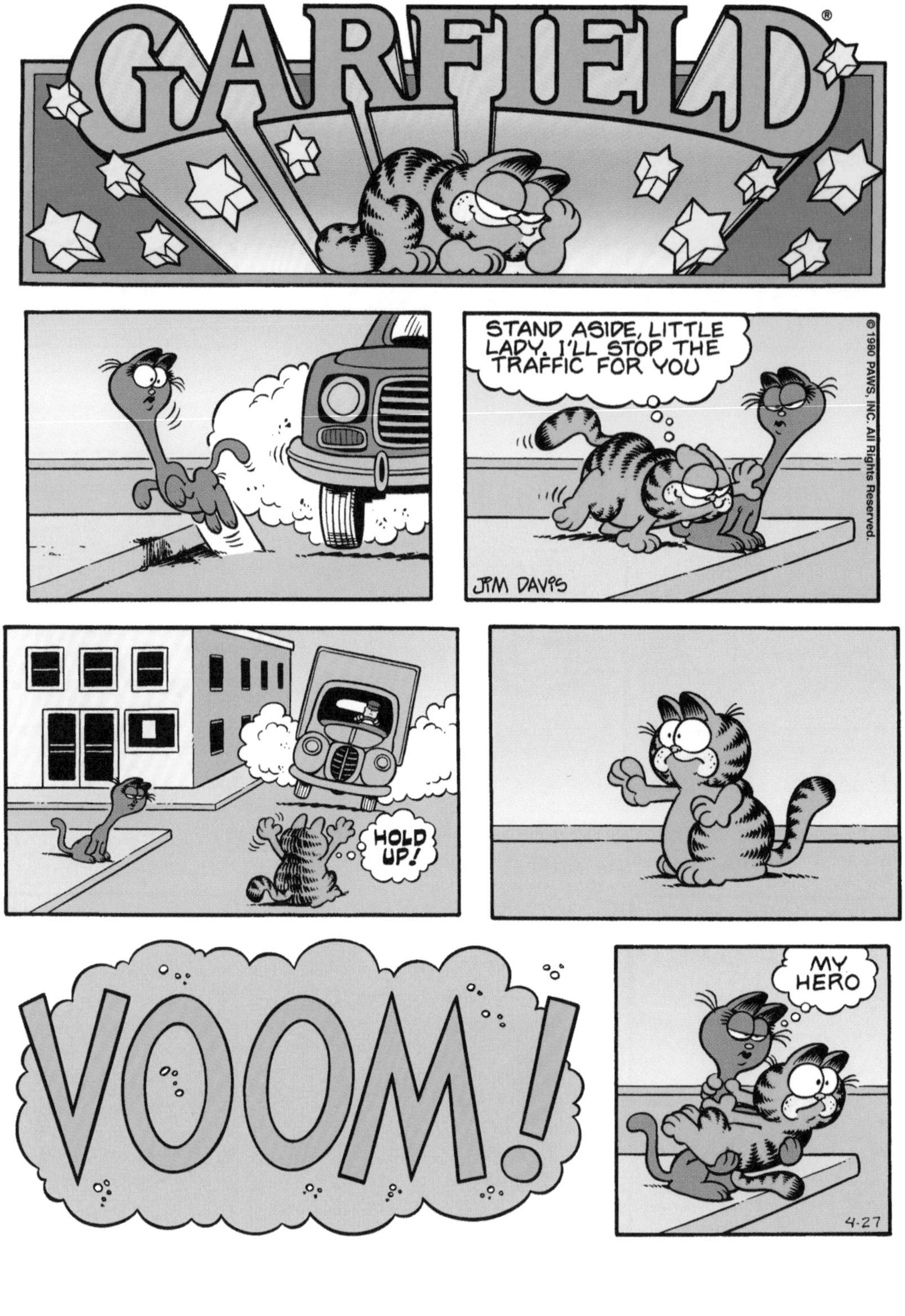
GARFIELD®
STAND ASIDE, LITTLE LADY. I'LL STOP THE TRAFFIC FOR YOU
© 1980 PAWS, INC. All Rights Reserved.
JIM DAVIS
HOLD UP!
VOOM!
MY HERO
4-27

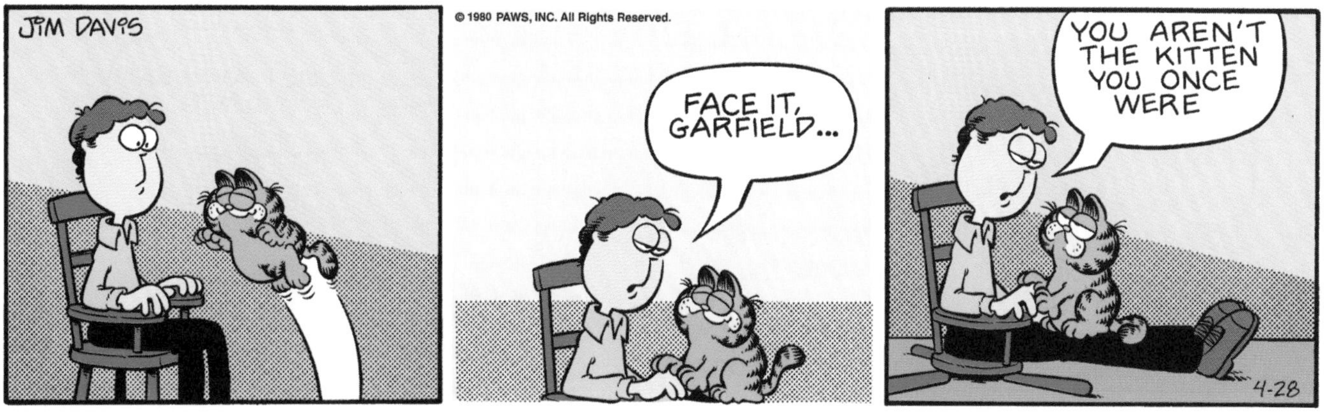
JIM DAVIS
© 1980 PAWS, INC. All Rights Reserved.
FACE IT, GARFIELD...
YOU AREN'T THE KITTEN YOU ONCE WERE
4-28

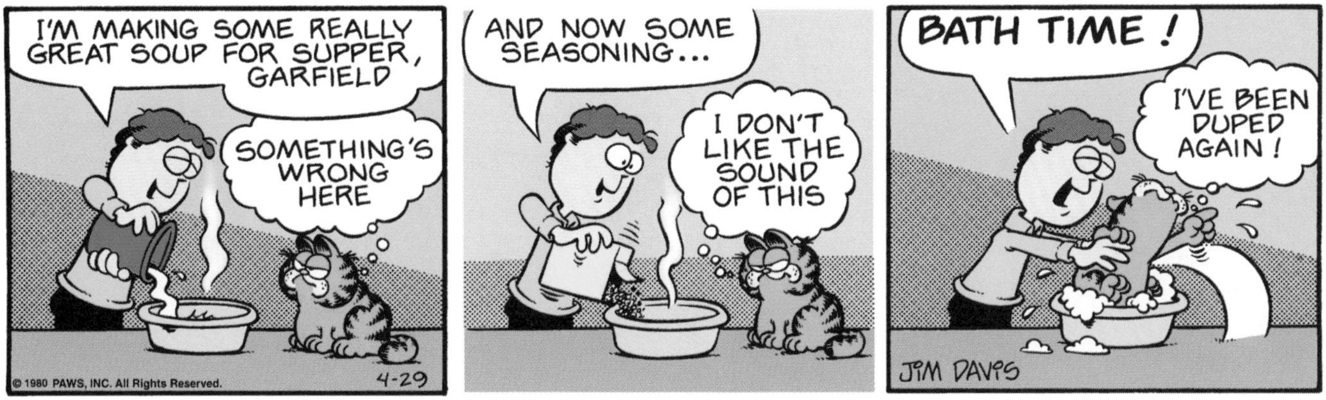
I'M MAKING SOME REALLY GREAT SOUP FOR SUPPER, GARFIELD
SOMETHING'S WRONG HERE
© 1980 PAWS, INC. All Rights Reserved.
4-29
AND NOW SOME SEASONING...
I DON'T LIKE THE SOUND OF THIS
BATH TIME!
I'VE BEEN DUPED AGAIN!
JIM DAVIS

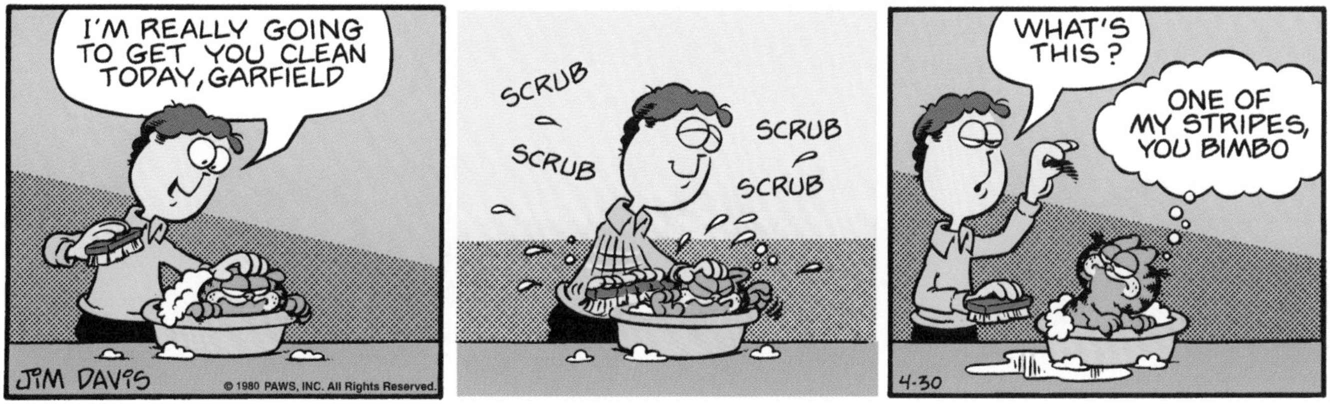
I'M REALLY GOING TO GET YOU CLEAN TODAY, GARFIELD
JIM DAVIS
© 1980 PAWS, INC. All Rights Reserved.
SCRUB
SCRUB
SCRUB
SCRUB
WHAT'S THIS?
ONE OF MY STRIPES, YOU BIMBO
4-30

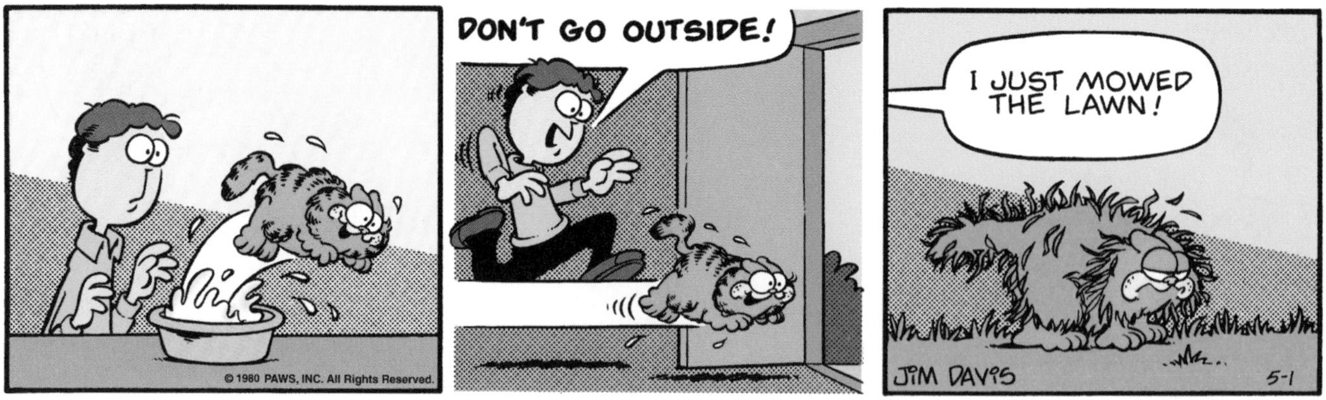
© 1980 PAWS, INC. All Rights Reserved.
DON'T GO OUTSIDE!
I JUST MOWED THE LAWN!
JIM DAVIS
5-1

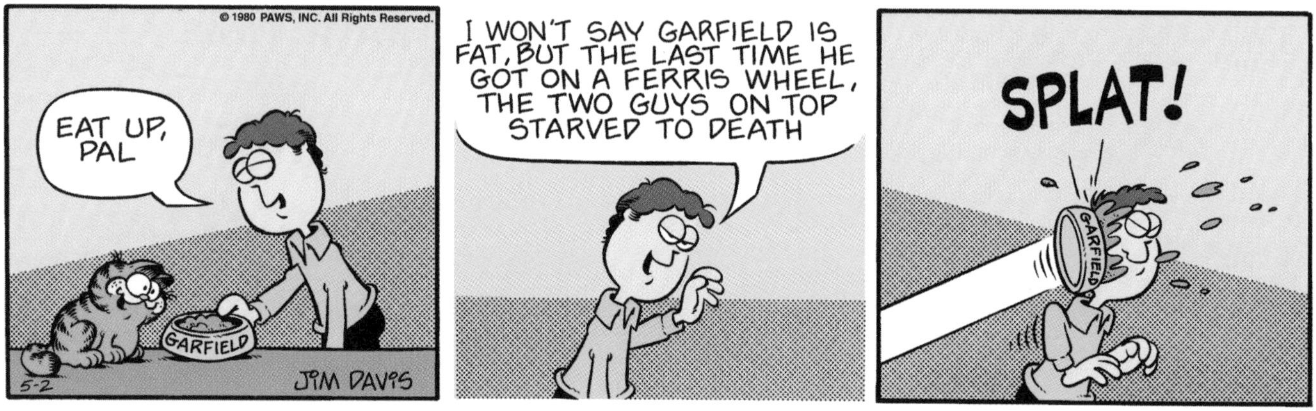
© 1980 PAWS, INC. All Rights Reserved.
EAT UP, PAL
GARFIELD
5-2
JIM DAVIS
I WON'T SAY GARFIELD IS FAT, BUT THE LAST TIME HE GOT ON A FERRIS WHEEL, THE TWO GUYS ON TOP STARVED TO DEATH
SPLAT!
GARFIELD

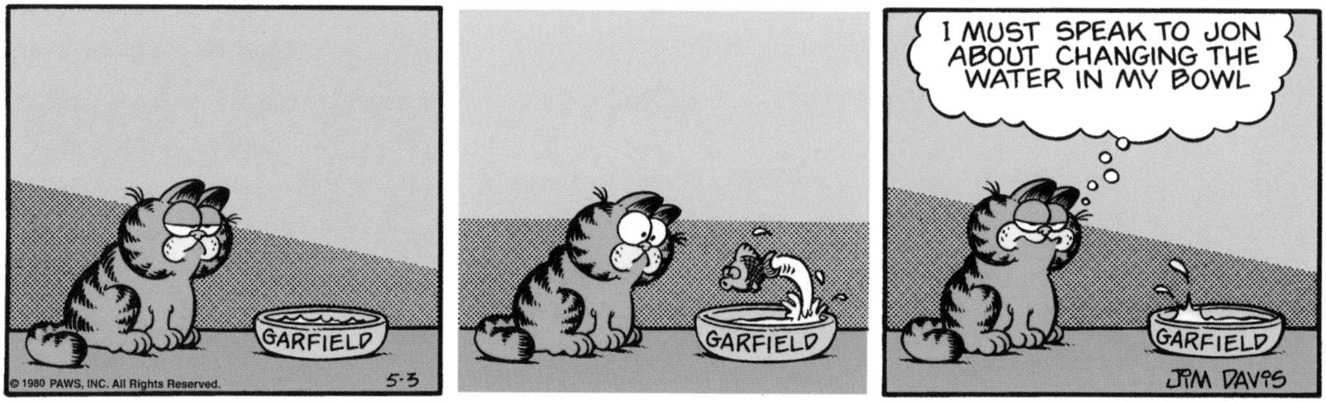
GARFIELD
© 1980 PAWS, INC. All Rights Reserved.
5-3
GARFIELD
I MUST SPEAK TO JON ABOUT CHANGING THE WATER IN MY BOWL
GARFIELD
JIM DAVIS

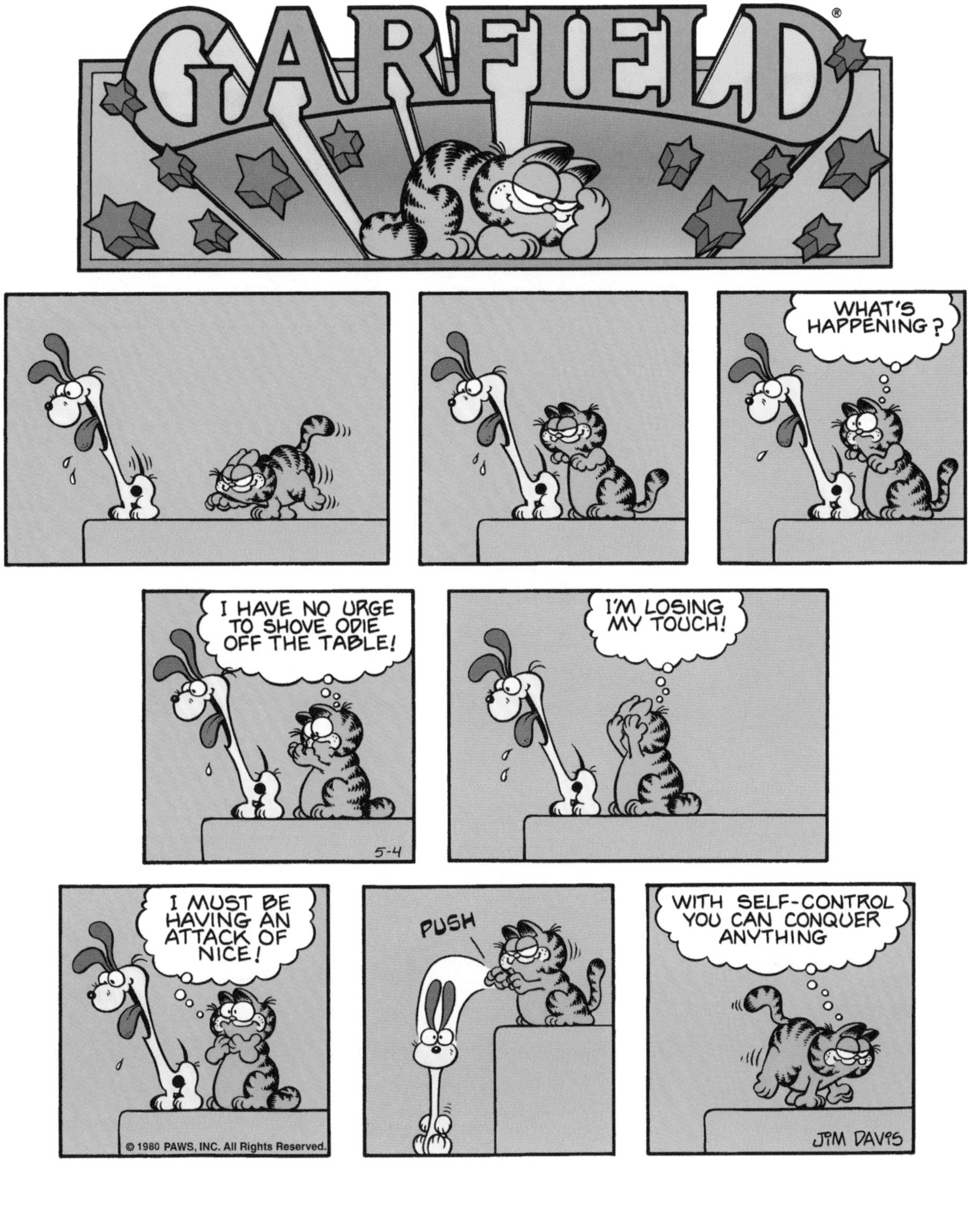

GARFIELD®
WHAT'S HAPPENING?
I HAVE NO URGE TO SHOVE ODIE OFF THE TABLE!
5-4
I'M LOSING MY TOUCH!
I MUST BE HAVING AN ATTACK OF NICE!
© 1980 PAWS, INC. All Rights Reserved.
PUSH
WITH SELF-CONTROL YOU CAN CONQUER ANYTHING
JIM DAVIS

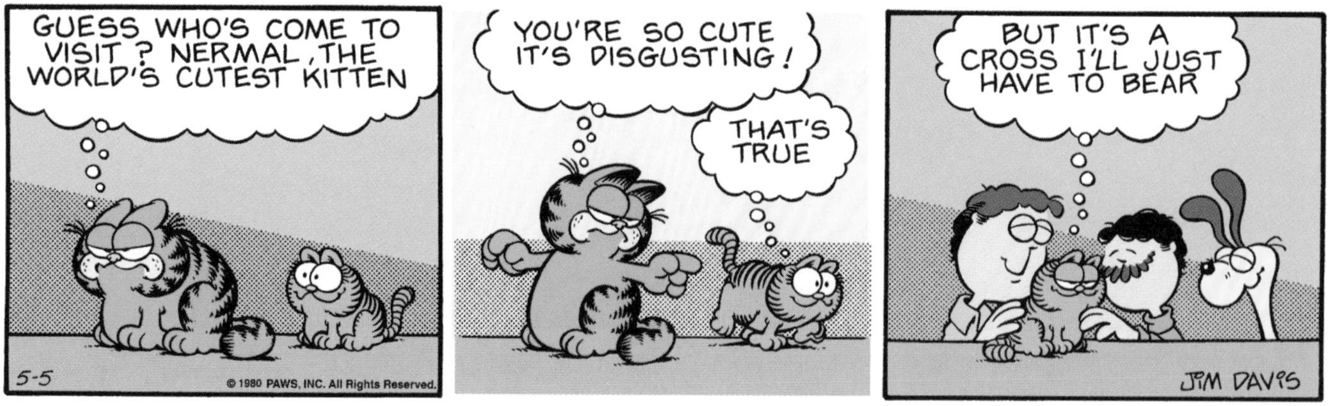
GUESS WHO'S COME TO VISIT ? NERMAL, THE WORLD'S CUTEST KITTEN
5-5
© 1980 PAWS, INC. All Rights Reserved.
YOU'RE SO CUTE IT'S DISGUSTING !
THAT'S TRUE
BUT IT'S A CROSS I'LL JUST HAVE TO BEAR
JIM DAVIS

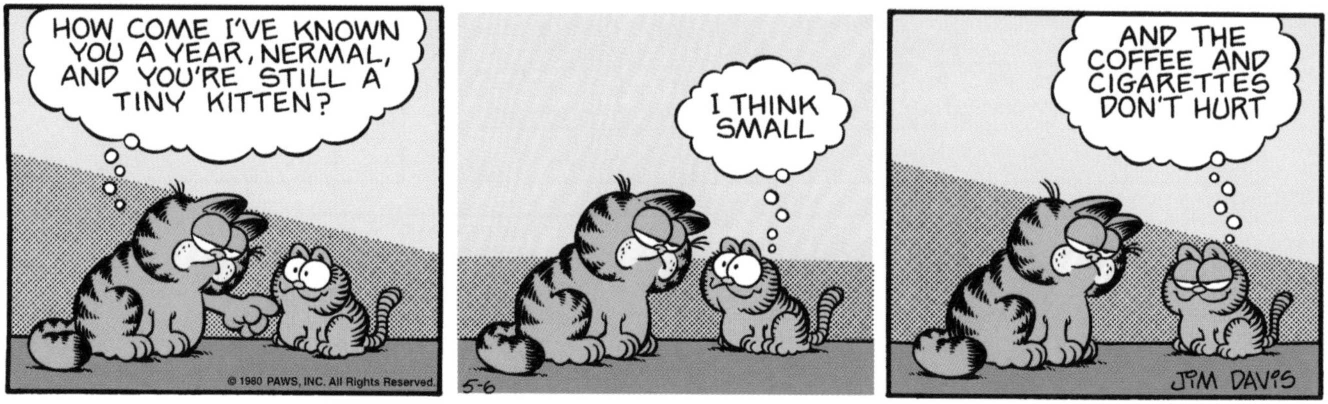
HOW COME I'VE KNOWN YOU A YEAR, NERMAL, AND YOU'RE STILL A TINY KITTEN?
© 1980 PAWS, INC. All Rights Reserved.
I THINK SMALL
5-6
AND THE COFFEE AND CIGARETTES DON'T HURT
JIM DAVIS

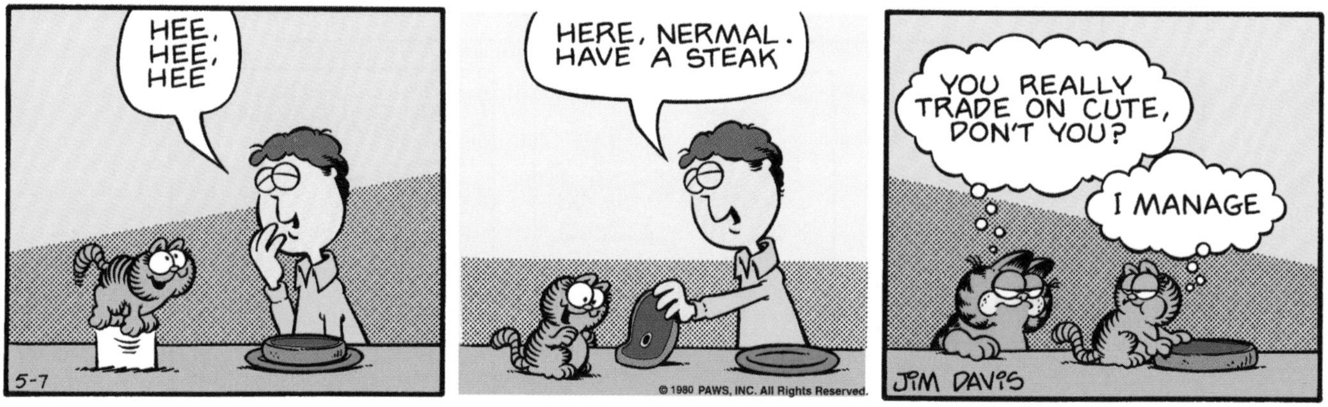
HEE, HEE, HEE
5-7
HERE, NERMAL. HAVE A STEAK
© 1980 PAWS, INC. All Rights Reserved.
YOU REALLY TRADE ON CUTE, DON'T YOU?
I MANAGE
JIM DAVIS

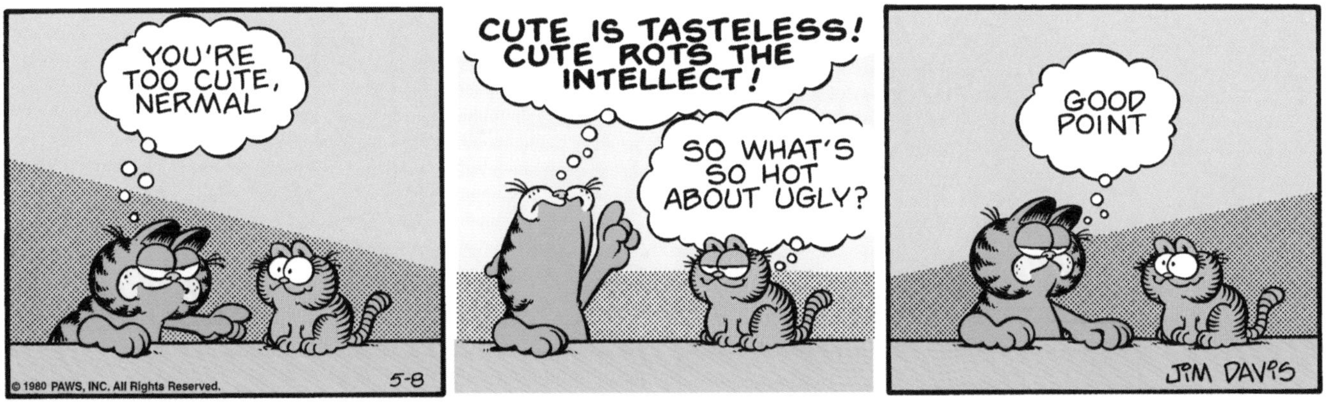
YOU'RE TOO CUTE, NERMAL
© 1980 PAWS, INC. All Rights Reserved.
5-8
CUTE IS TASTELESS! CUTE ROTS THE INTELLECT!
SO WHAT'S SO HOT ABOUT UGLY?
GOOD POINT
JIM DAVIS

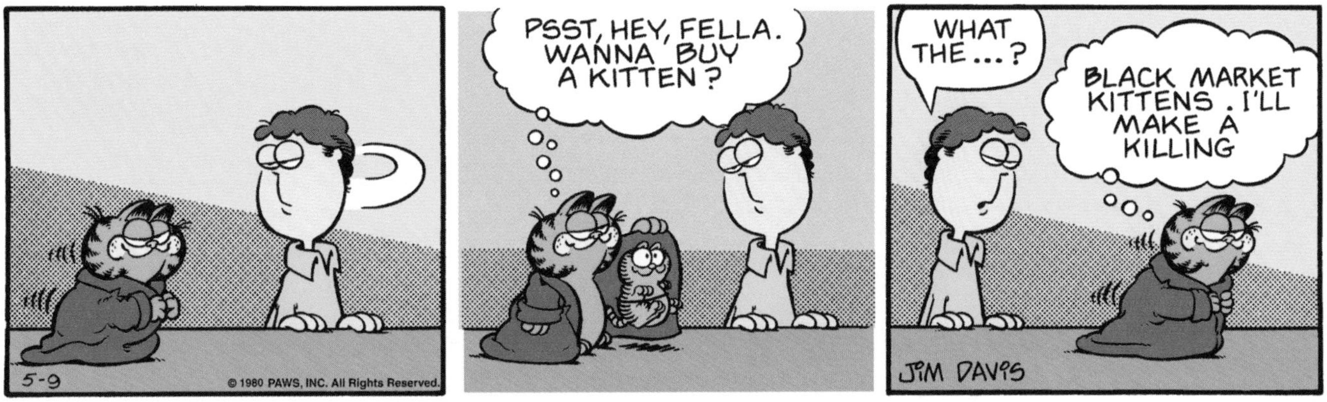
5-9
© 1980 PAWS, INC. All Rights Reserved.
PSST, HEY, FELLA. WANNA BUY A KITTEN?
WHAT THE...?
BLACK MARKET KITTENS. I'LL MAKE A KILLING
JIM DAVIS

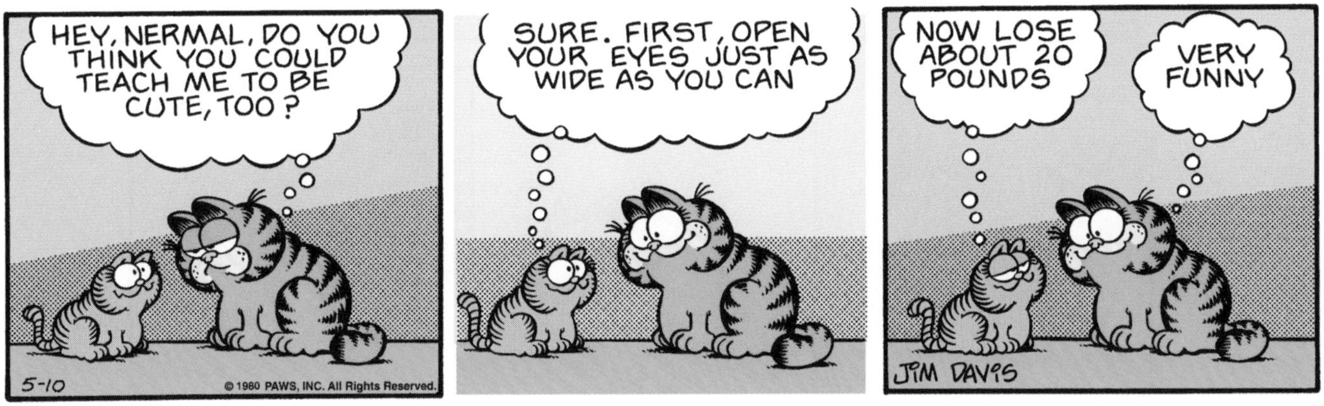
HEY, NERMAL, DO YOU THINK YOU COULD TEACH ME TO BE CUTE, TOO?
5-10
© 1980 PAWS, INC. All Rights Reserved.
SURE. FIRST, OPEN YOUR EYES JUST AS WIDE AS YOU CAN
NOW LOSE ABOUT 20 POUNDS
VERY FUNNY
JIM DAVIS

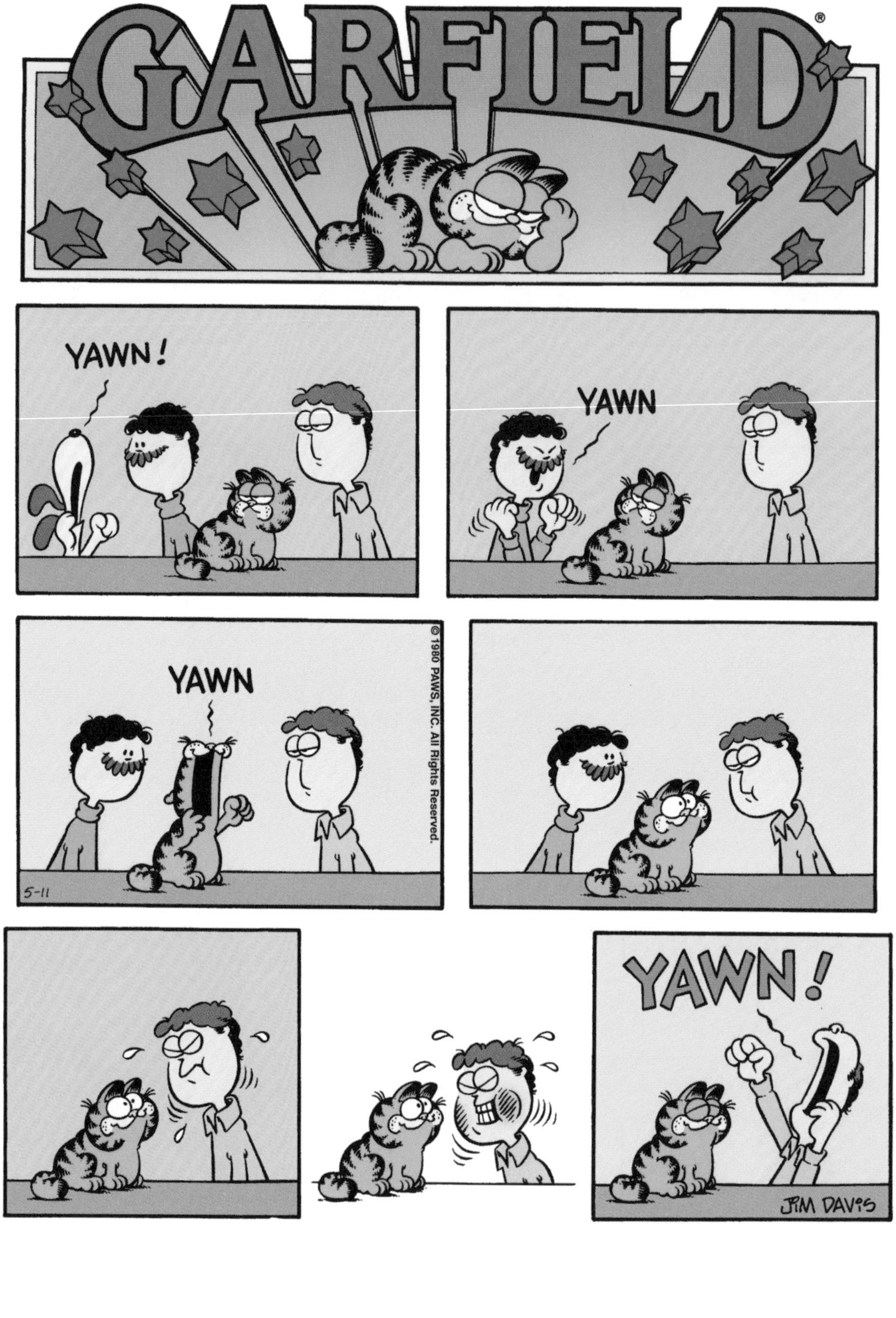
GARFIELD®
YAWN!
YAWN
YAWN
© 1980 PAWS, INC. All Rights Reserved.
5-11
YAWN!
JIM DAVIS

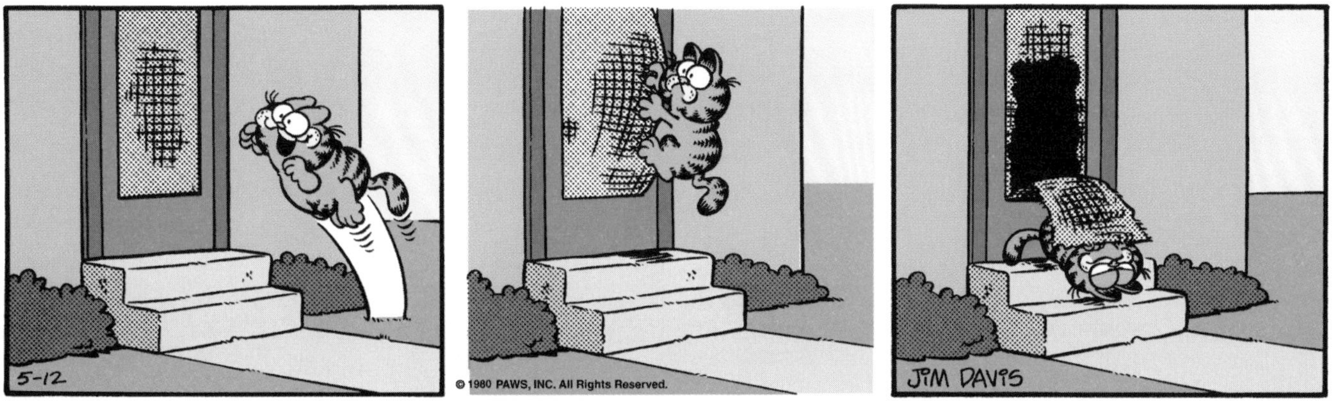
5-12
© 1980 PAWS, INC. All Rights Reserved.
JIM DAVIS

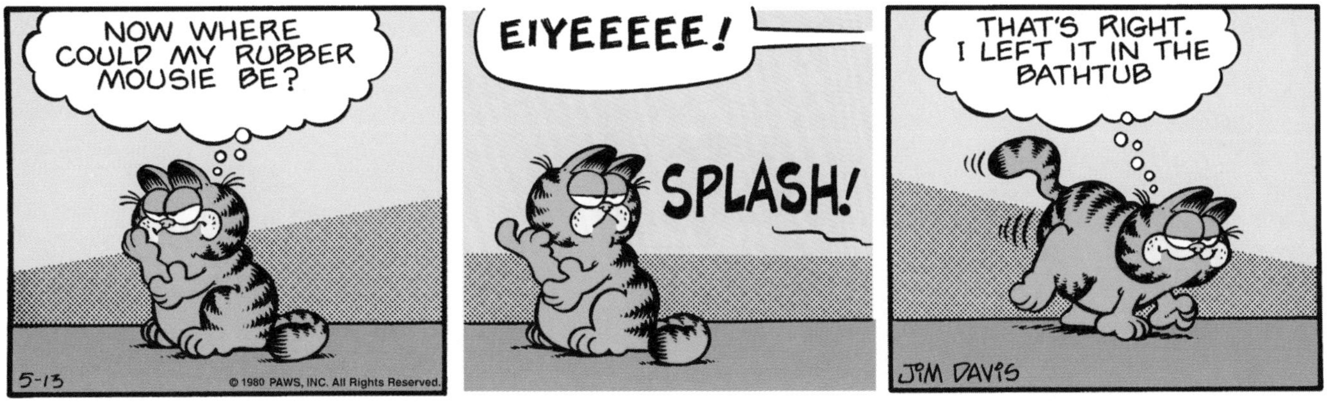
NOW WHERE COULD MY RUBBER MOUSIE BE?
5-13
© 1980 PAWS, INC. All Rights Reserved.
EIYEEEEE!
SPLASH!
THAT'S RIGHT. I LEFT IT IN THE BATHTUB
JIM DAVIS

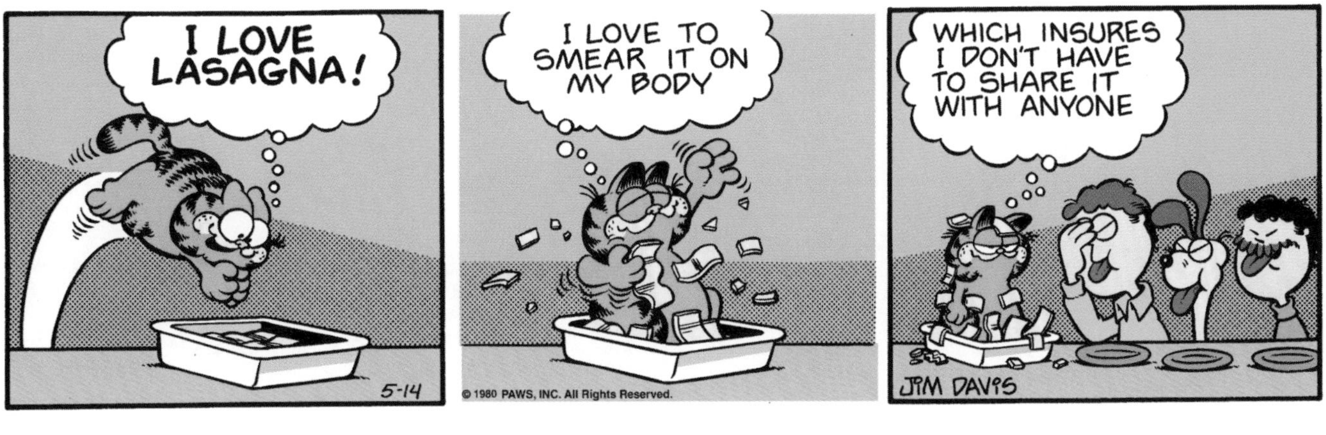
I LOVE LASAGNA!
5-14
I LOVE TO SMEAR IT ON MY BODY
© 1980 PAWS, INC. All Rights Reserved.
WHICH INSURES I DON'T HAVE TO SHARE IT WITH ANYONE
JIM DAVIS

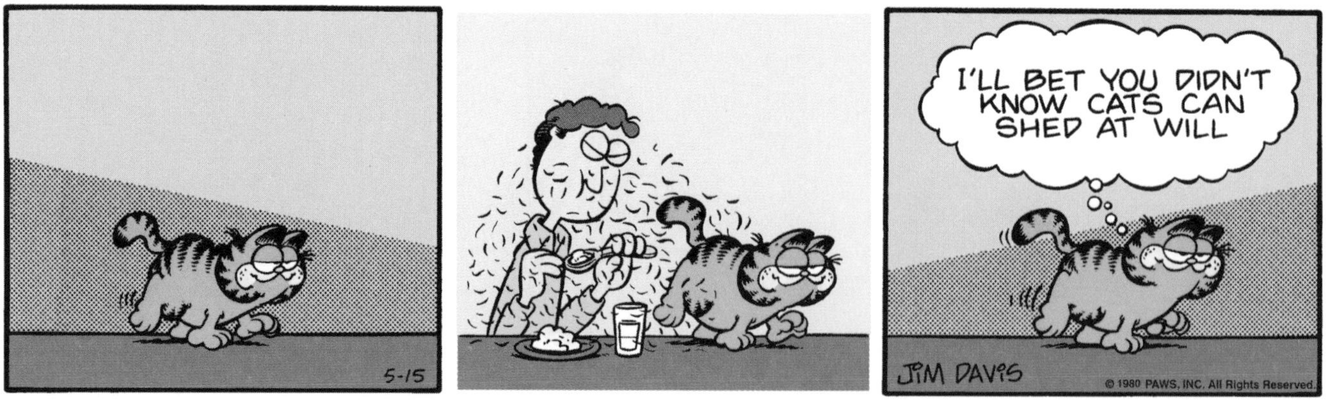
5-15
I'LL BET YOU DIDN'T KNOW CATS CAN SHED AT WILL
JIM DAVIS
© 1980 PAWS, INC. All Rights Reserved.

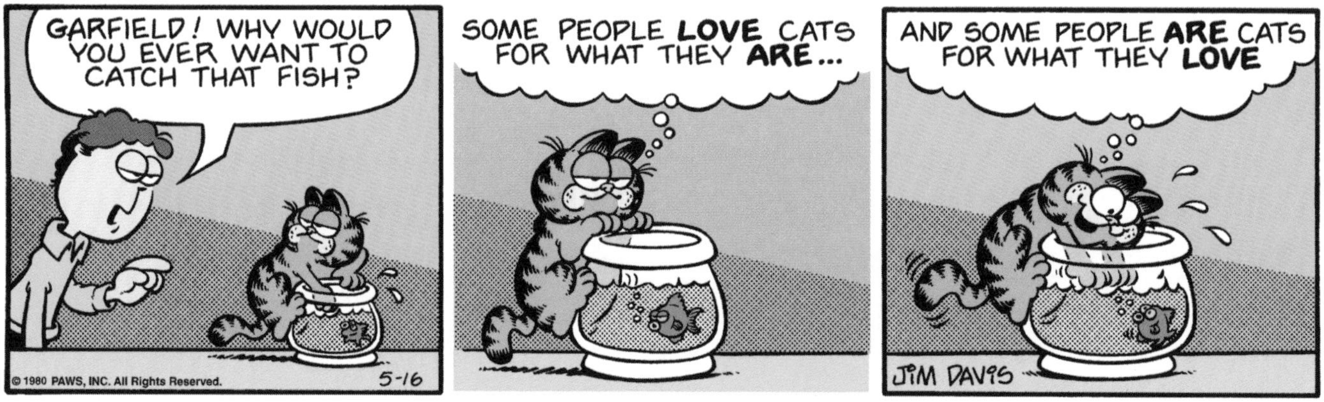
GARFIELD! WHY WOULD YOU EVER WANT TO CATCH THAT FISH?
© 1980 PAWS, INC. All Rights Reserved.
5-16
SOME PEOPLE **LOVE** CATS FOR WHAT THEY **ARE**...
AND SOME PEOPLE **ARE** CATS FOR WHAT THEY **LOVE**
JIM DAVIS

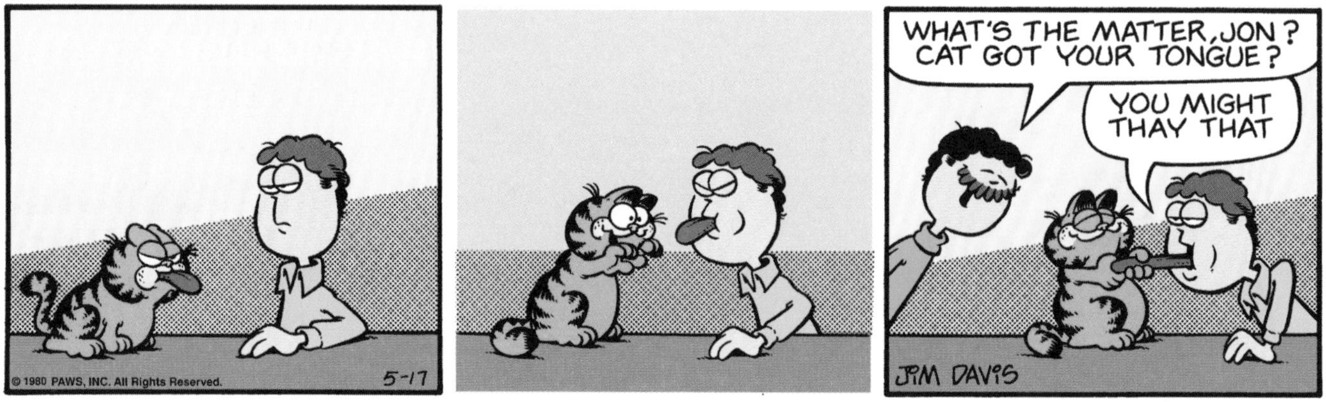
© 1980 PAWS, INC. All Rights Reserved.
5-17
WHAT'S THE MATTER, JON? CAT GOT YOUR TONGUE?
YOU MIGHT THAY THAT
JIM DAVIS

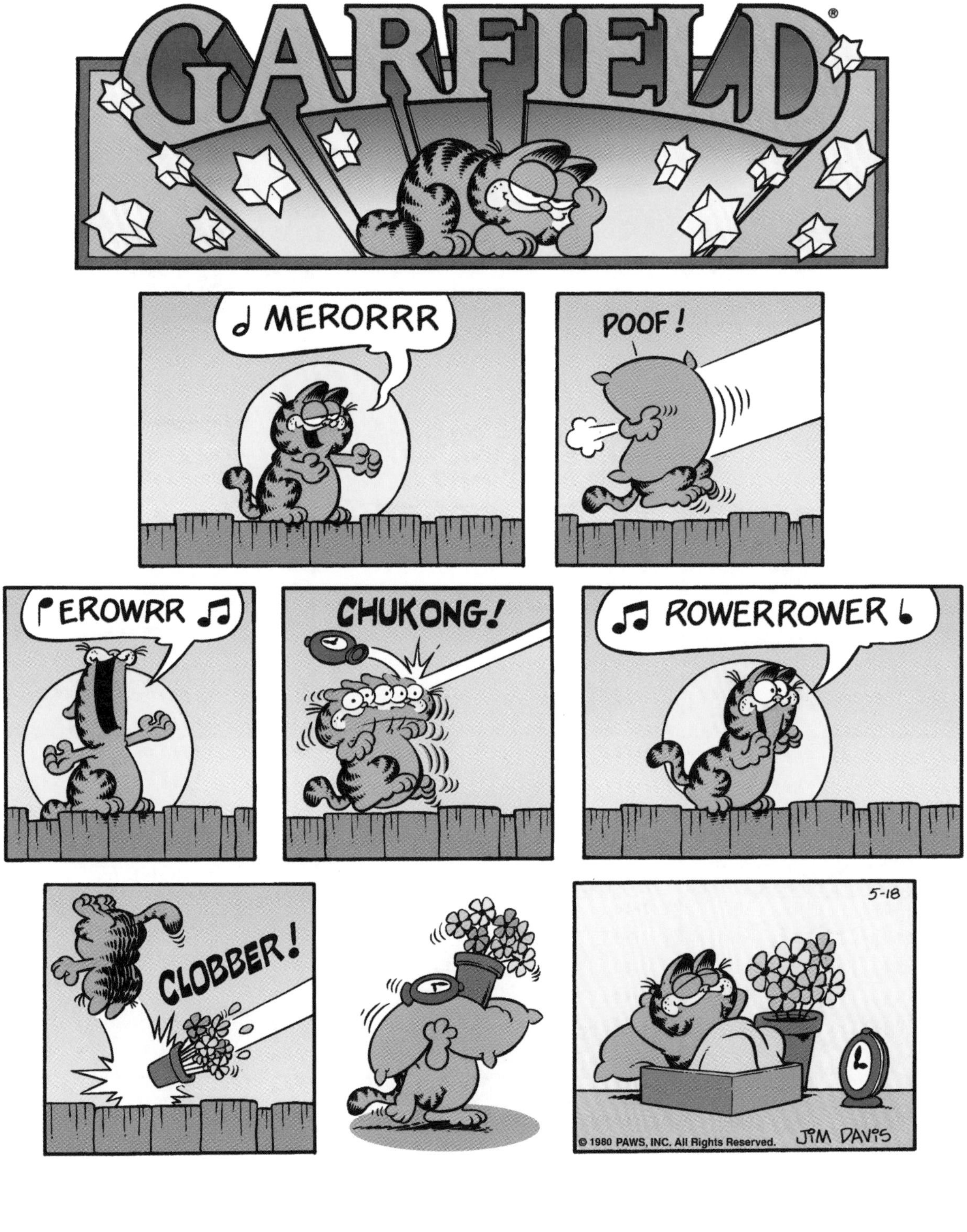
GARFIELD®
MERORRR
POOF!
EROWRR
CHUKONG!
ROWERROWER
CLOBBER!
5-18
© 1980 PAWS, INC. All Rights Reserved.
JIM DAVIS

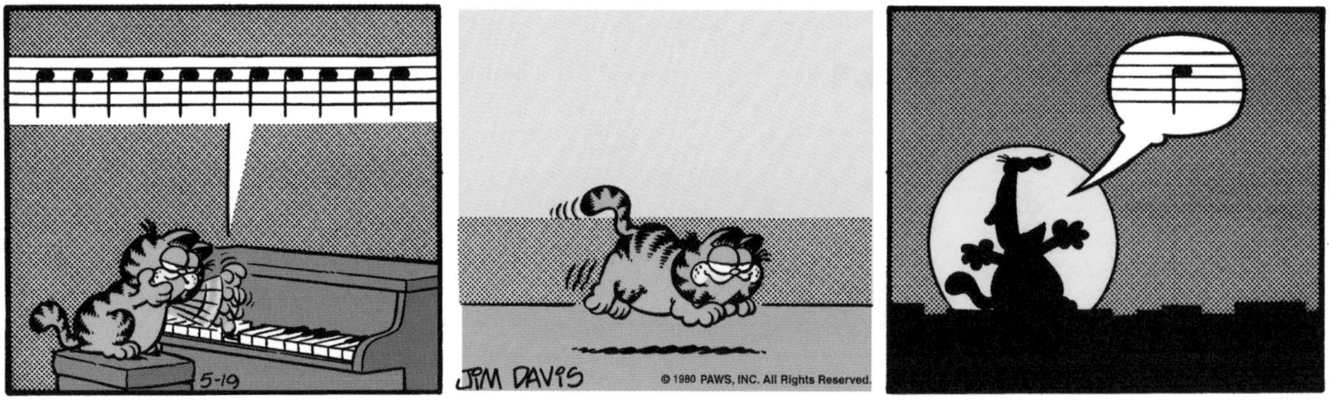
5-19
JIM DAVIS
© 1980 PAWS, INC. All Rights Reserved.

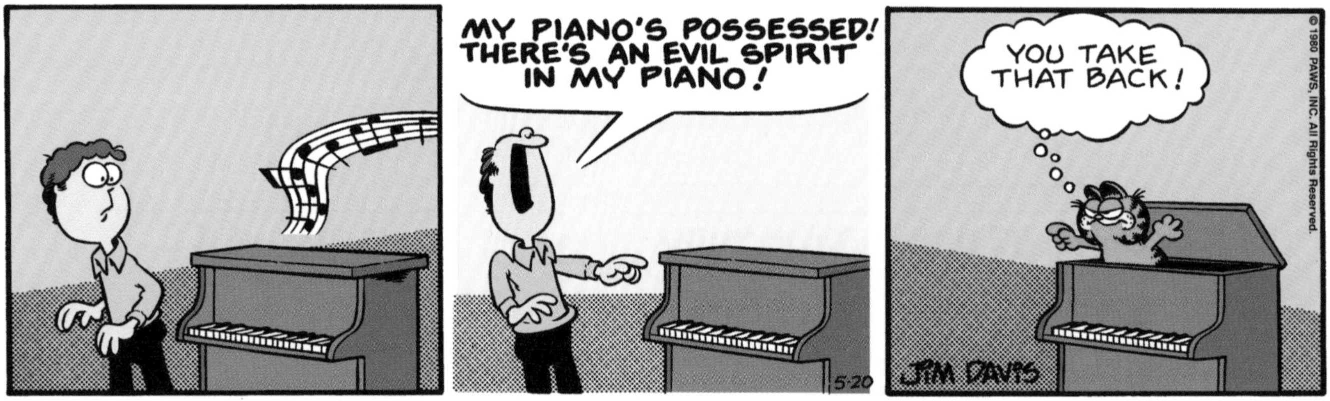
MY PIANO'S POSSESSED! THERE'S AN EVIL SPIRIT IN MY PIANO!
5-20
YOU TAKE THAT BACK!
JIM DAVIS
© 1980 PAWS, INC. All Rights Reserved.

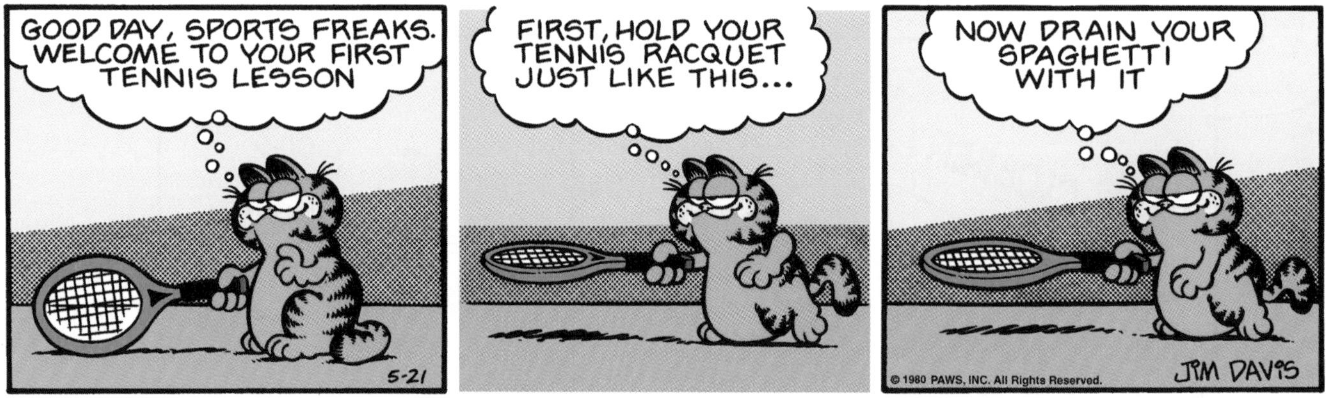
GOOD DAY, SPORTS FREAKS. WELCOME TO YOUR FIRST TENNIS LESSON
5-21
FIRST, HOLD YOUR TENNIS RACQUET JUST LIKE THIS...
NOW DRAIN YOUR SPAGHETTI WITH IT
© 1980 PAWS, INC. All Rights Reserved.
JIM DAVIS

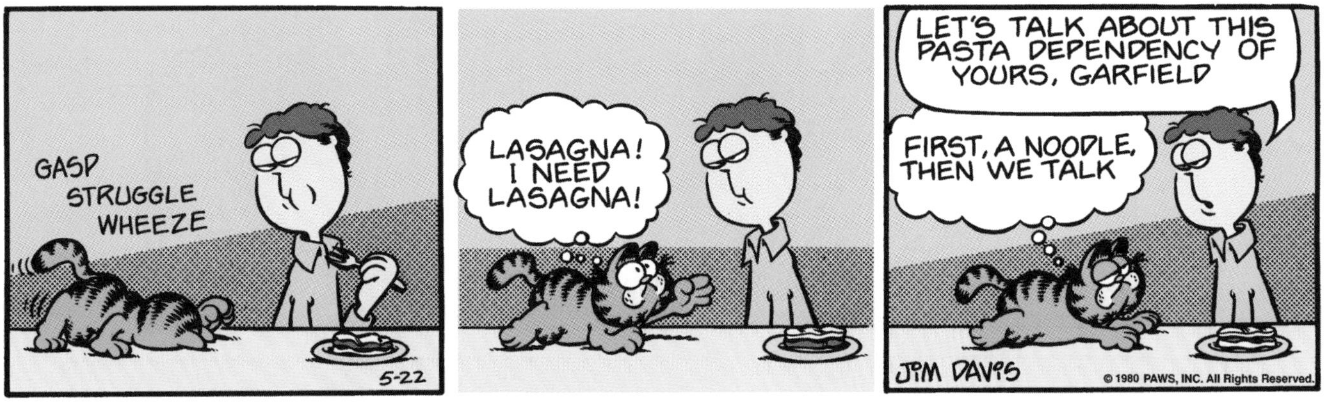
GASP
STRUGGLE
WHEEZE
5-22
LASAGNA! I NEED LASAGNA!
LET'S TALK ABOUT THIS PASTA DEPENDENCY OF YOURS, GARFIELD
FIRST, A NOODLE, THEN WE TALK
JIM DAVIS
© 1980 PAWS, INC. All Rights Reserved.

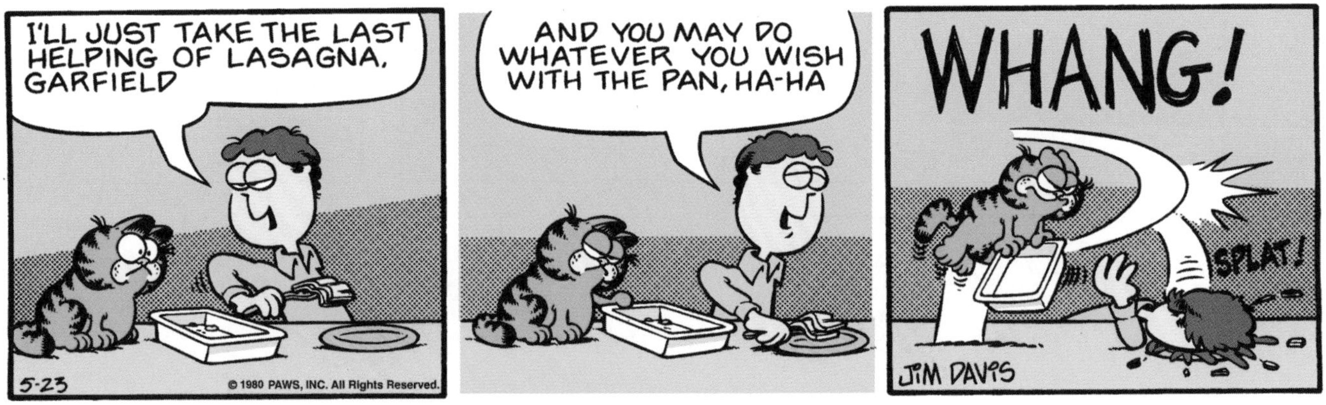
I'LL JUST TAKE THE LAST HELPING OF LASAGNA, GARFIELD
5-23
© 1980 PAWS, INC. All Rights Reserved.
AND YOU MAY DO WHATEVER YOU WISH WITH THE PAN, HA-HA
WHANG!
SPLAT!
JIM DAVIS

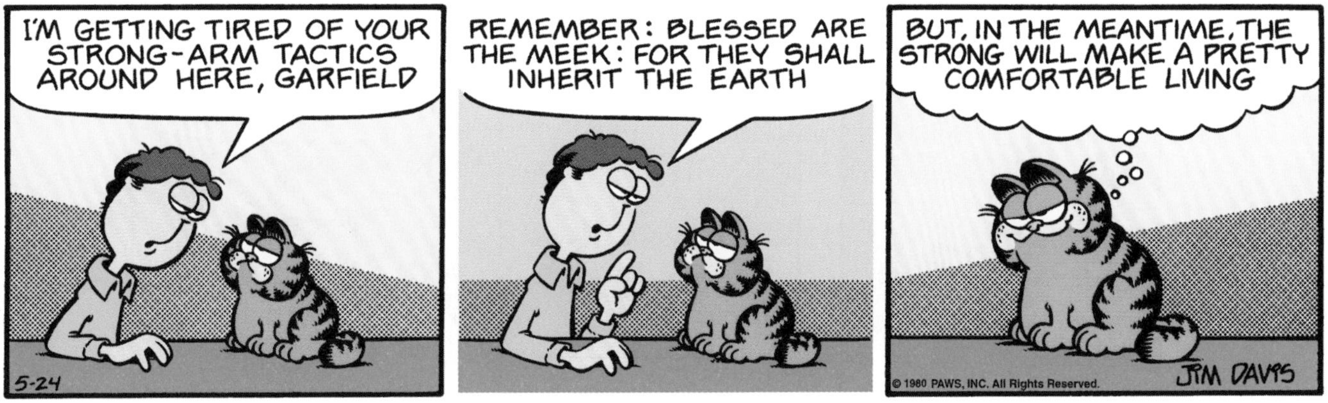
I'M GETTING TIRED OF YOUR STRONG-ARM TACTICS AROUND HERE, GARFIELD
5-24
REMEMBER: BLESSED ARE THE MEEK: FOR THEY SHALL INHERIT THE EARTH
BUT, IN THE MEANTIME, THE STRONG WILL MAKE A PRETTY COMFORTABLE LIVING
© 1980 PAWS, INC. All Rights Reserved.
JIM DAVIS

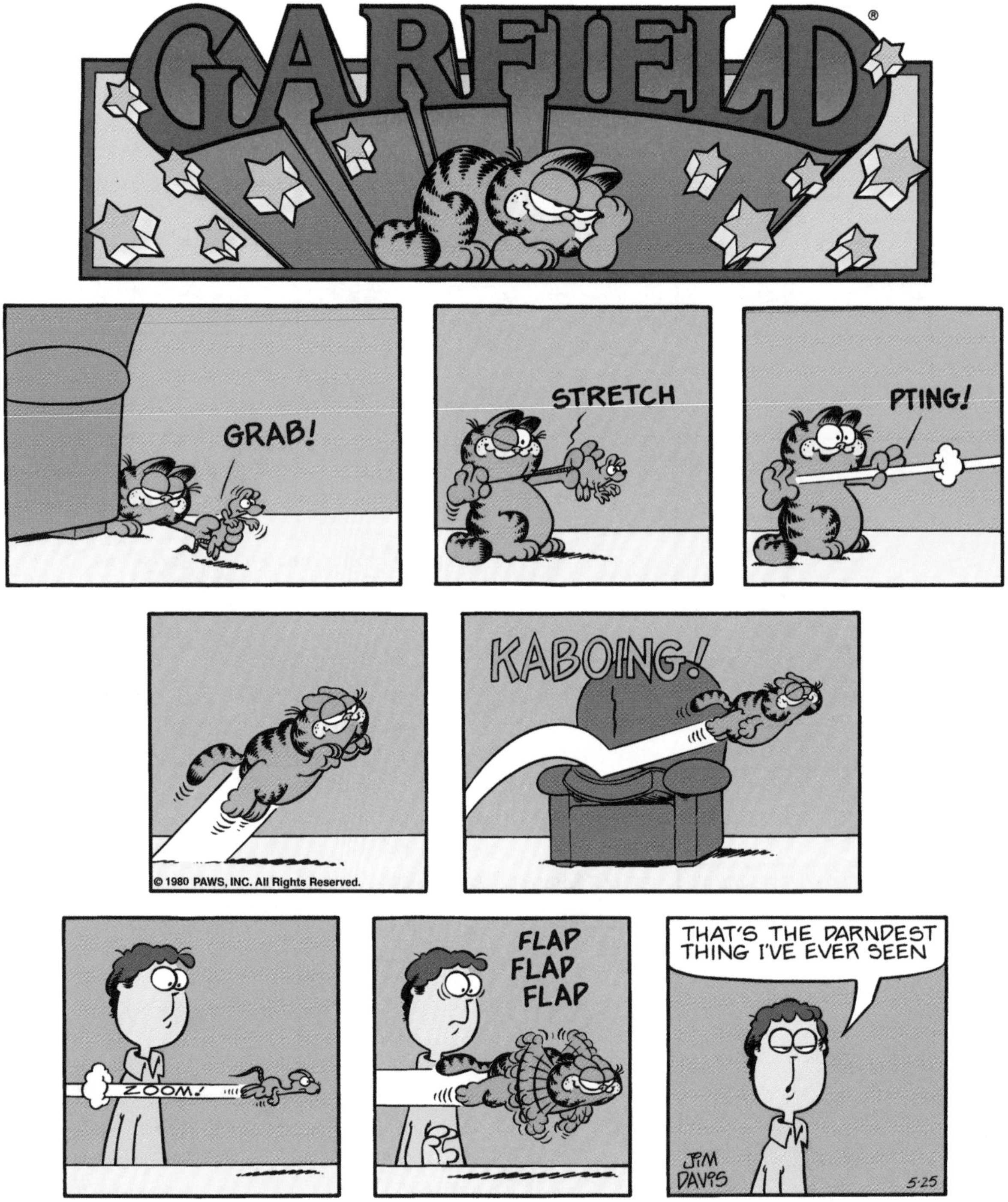
GARFIELD®
GRAB!
STRETCH
PTING!
KABOING!
© 1980 PAWS, INC. All Rights Reserved.
ZOOM!
FLAP
FLAP
FLAP
THAT'S THE DARNDEST THING I'VE EVER SEEN
JIM DAVIS
5·25

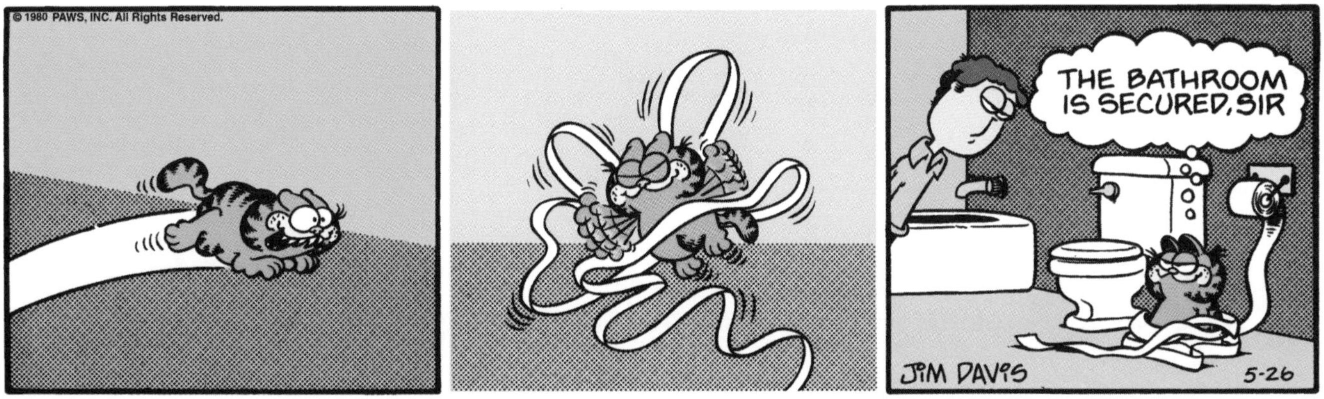
© 1980 PAWS, INC. All Rights Reserved.
THE BATHROOM IS SECURED, SIR
JIM DAVIS
5-26

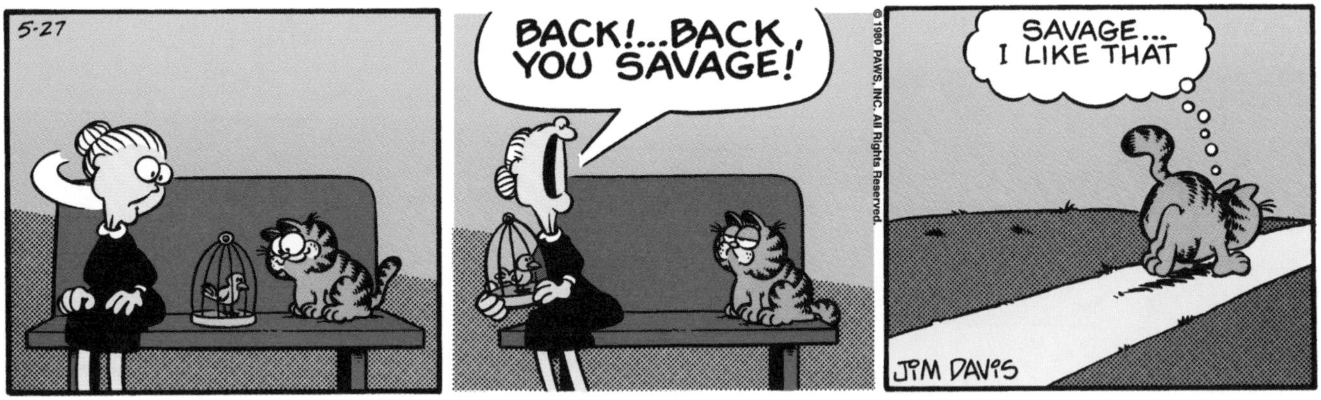
5-27
BACK!...BACK, YOU SAVAGE!
© 1980 PAWS, INC. All Rights Reserved.
SAVAGE... I LIKE THAT
JIM DAVIS

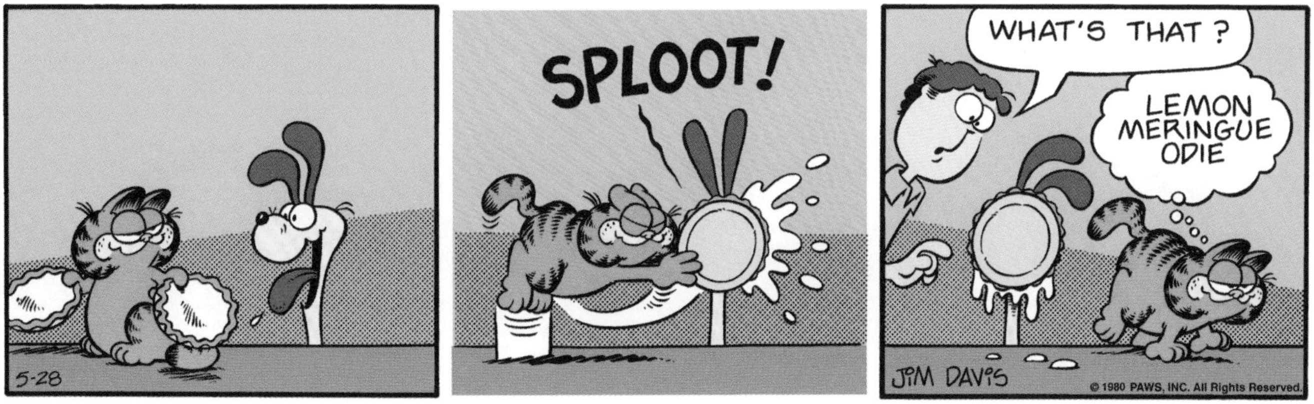
5-28
SPLOOT!
WHAT'S THAT ?
LEMON MERINGUE ODIE
JIM DAVIS
© 1980 PAWS, INC. All Rights Reserved.

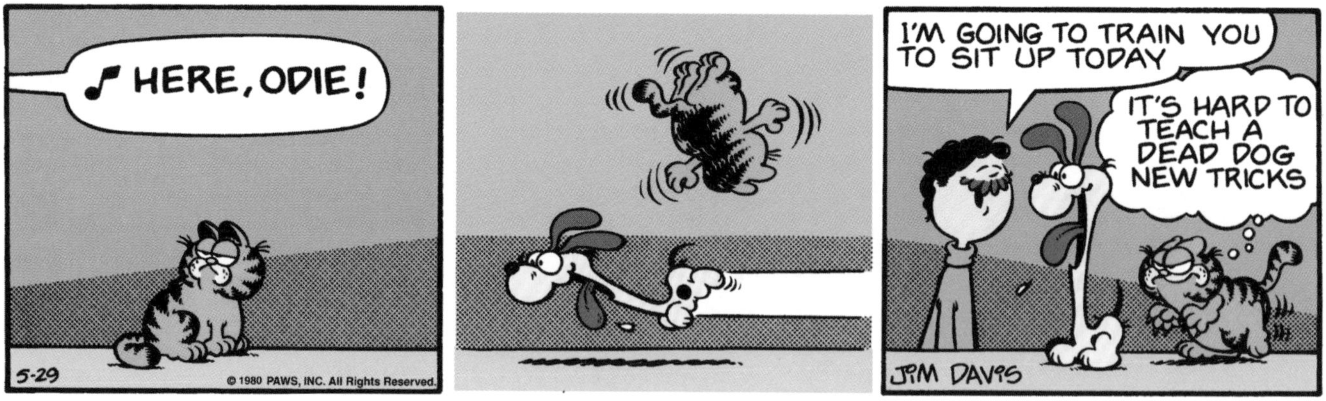

♪ HERE, ODIE!
I'M GOING TO TRAIN YOU TO SIT UP TODAY
IT'S HARD TO TEACH A DEAD DOG NEW TRICKS
5-29
© 1980 PAWS, INC. All Rights Reserved.
JIM DAVIS

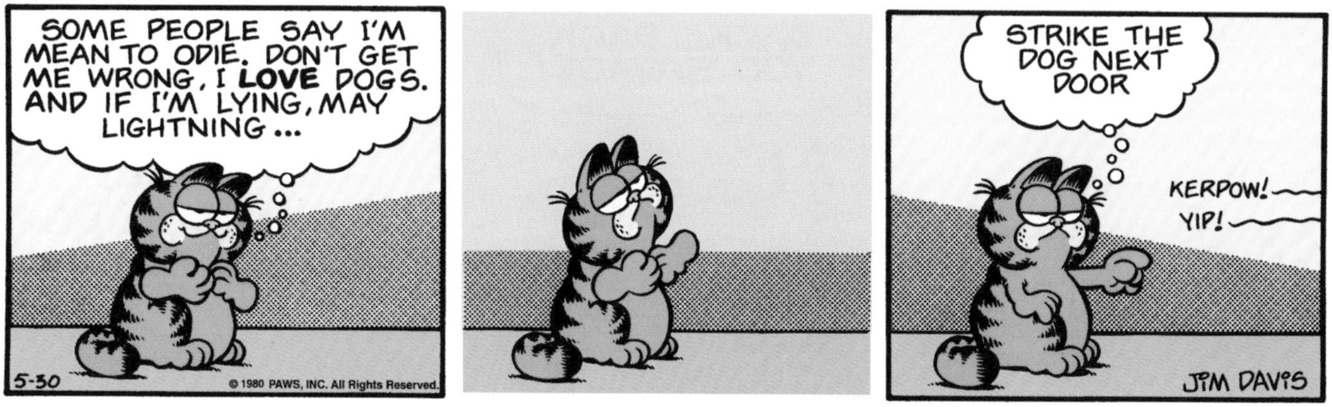

SOME PEOPLE SAY I'M MEAN TO ODIE. DON'T GET ME WRONG, I **LOVE** DOGS. AND IF I'M LYING, MAY LIGHTNING...
STRIKE THE DOG NEXT DOOR
KERPOW!
YIP!
5-30
© 1980 PAWS, INC. All Rights Reserved.
JIM DAVIS

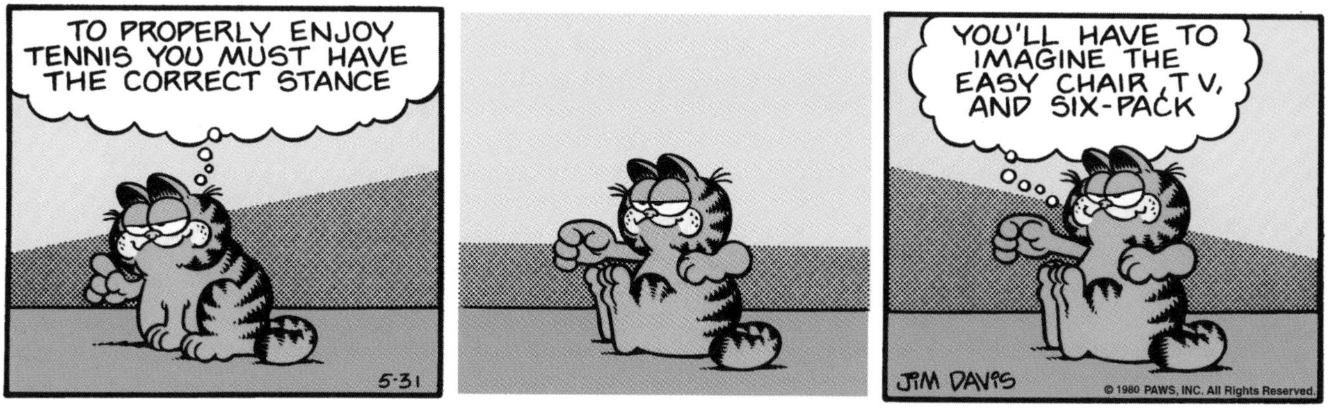

TO PROPERLY ENJOY TENNIS YOU MUST HAVE THE CORRECT STANCE
YOU'LL HAVE TO IMAGINE THE EASY CHAIR, T.V., AND SIX-PACK
5-31
JIM DAVIS
© 1980 PAWS, INC. All Rights Reserved.

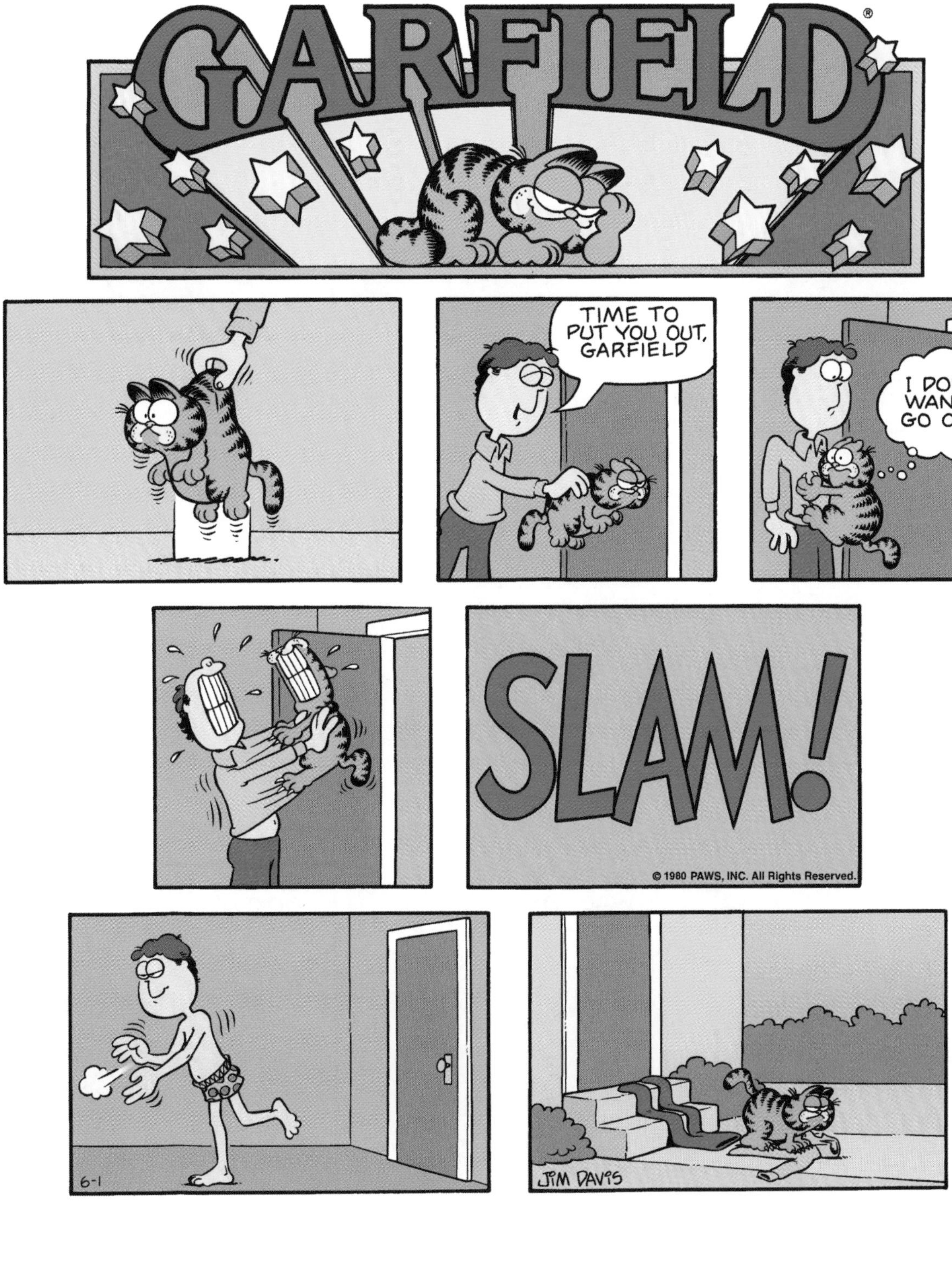
GARFIELD®
TIME TO PUT YOU OUT, GARFIELD
I DON'T WANNA GO OUT!
SLAM!
© 1980 PAWS, INC. All Rights Reserved.
6-1
JIM DAVIS

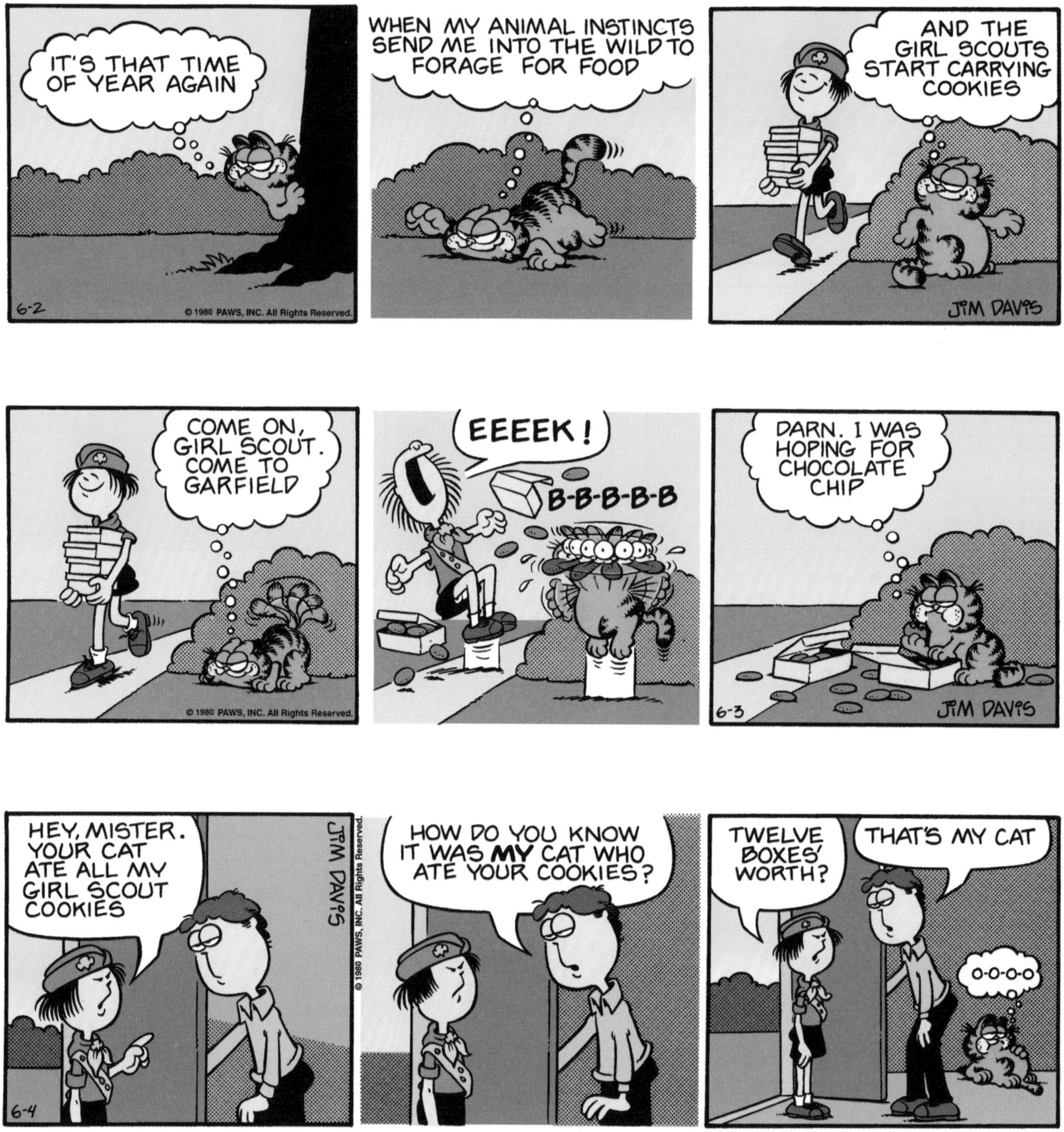
IT'S THAT TIME OF YEAR AGAIN
6-2
© 1980 PAWS, INC. All Rights Reserved.
WHEN MY ANIMAL INSTINCTS SEND ME INTO THE WILD TO FORAGE FOR FOOD
AND THE GIRL SCOUTS START CARRYING COOKIES
JIM DAVIS
COME ON, GIRL SCOUT. COME TO GARFIELD
© 1980 PAWS, INC. All Rights Reserved.
EEEEK!
B-B-B-B-B
DARN. I WAS HOPING FOR CHOCOLATE CHIP
6-3
JIM DAVIS
HEY, MISTER. YOUR CAT ATE ALL MY GIRL SCOUT COOKIES
6-4
JIM DAVIS
© 1980 PAWS, INC. All Rights Reserved.
HOW DO YOU KNOW IT WAS MY CAT WHO ATE YOUR COOKIES?
TWELVE BOXES' WORTH?
THAT'S MY CAT
O-O-O-O

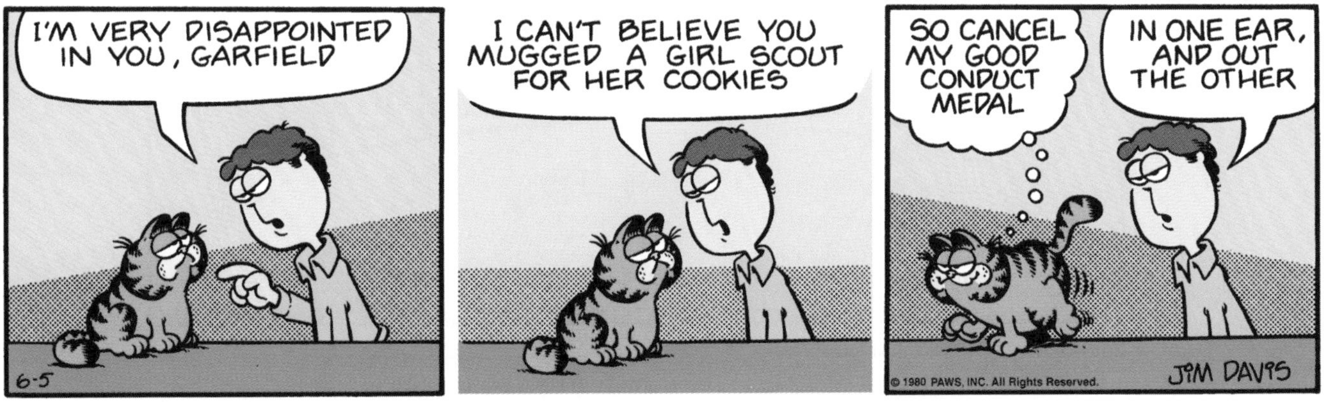
I'M VERY DISAPPOINTED IN YOU, GARFIELD
6-5
I CAN'T BELIEVE YOU MUGGED A GIRL SCOUT FOR HER COOKIES
SO CANCEL MY GOOD CONDUCT MEDAL
IN ONE EAR, AND OUT THE OTHER
© 1980 PAWS, INC. All Rights Reserved.
JIM DAVIS

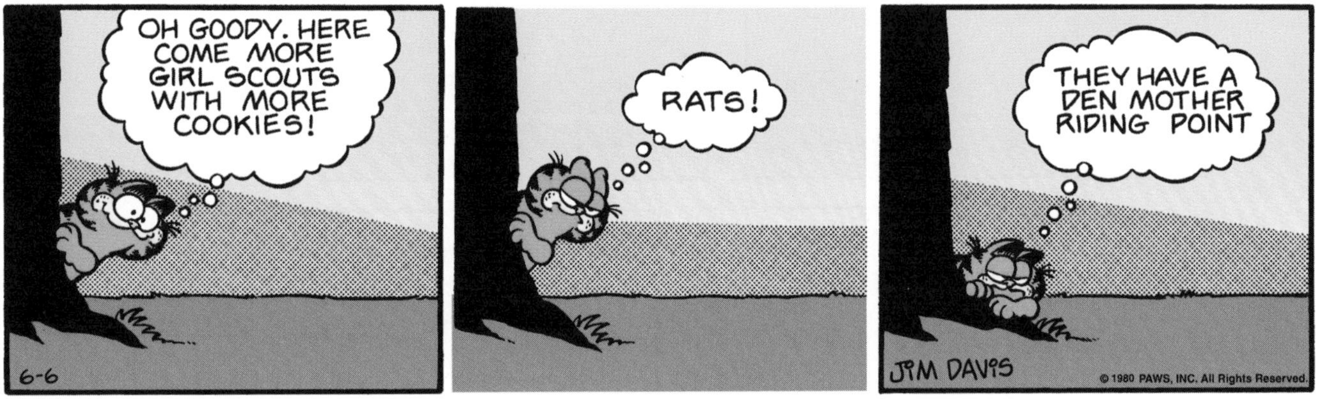
OH GOODY. HERE COME MORE GIRL SCOUTS WITH MORE COOKIES!
6-6
RATS!
THEY HAVE A DEN MOTHER RIDING POINT
JIM DAVIS
© 1980 PAWS, INC. All Rights Reserved.

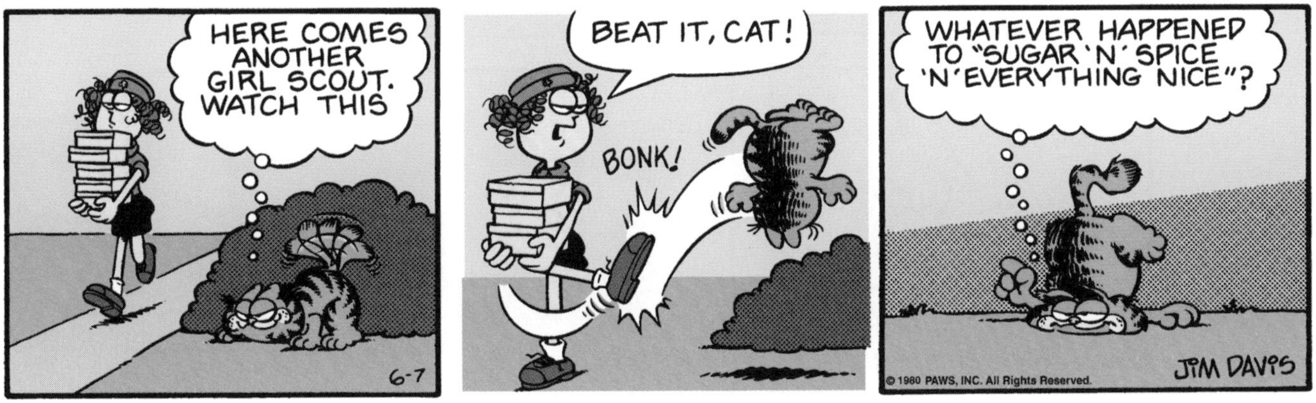
HERE COMES ANOTHER GIRL SCOUT. WATCH THIS
6-7
BEAT IT, CAT!
BONK!
WHATEVER HAPPENED TO "SUGAR 'N' SPICE 'N' EVERYTHING NICE"?
© 1980 PAWS, INC. All Rights Reserved.
JIM DAVIS

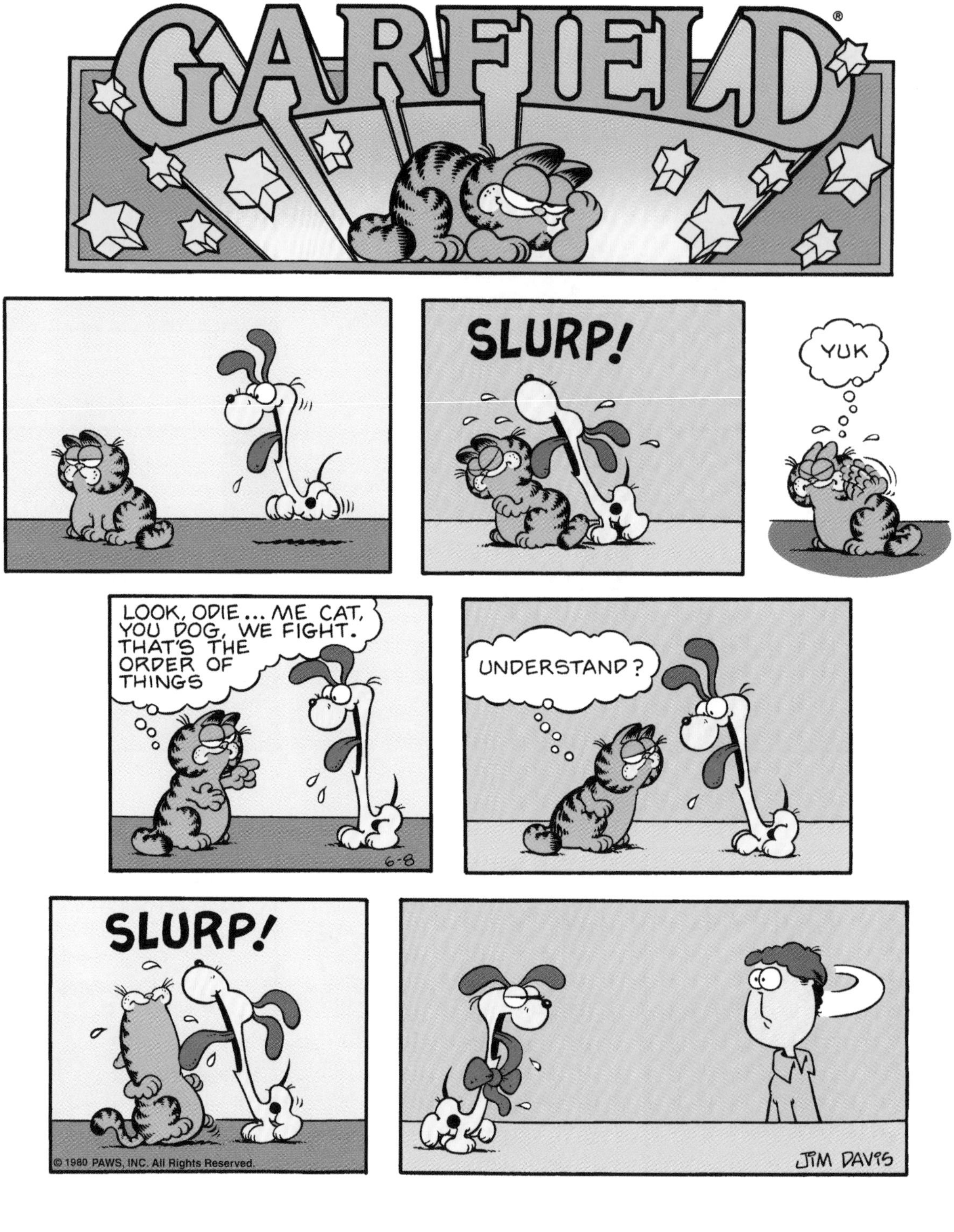
GARFIELD®
SLURP!
YUK
LOOK, ODIE... ME CAT, YOU DOG, WE FIGHT. THAT'S THE ORDER OF THINGS
6-8
UNDERSTAND?
SLURP!
© 1980 PAWS, INC. All Rights Reserved.
JIM DAVIS

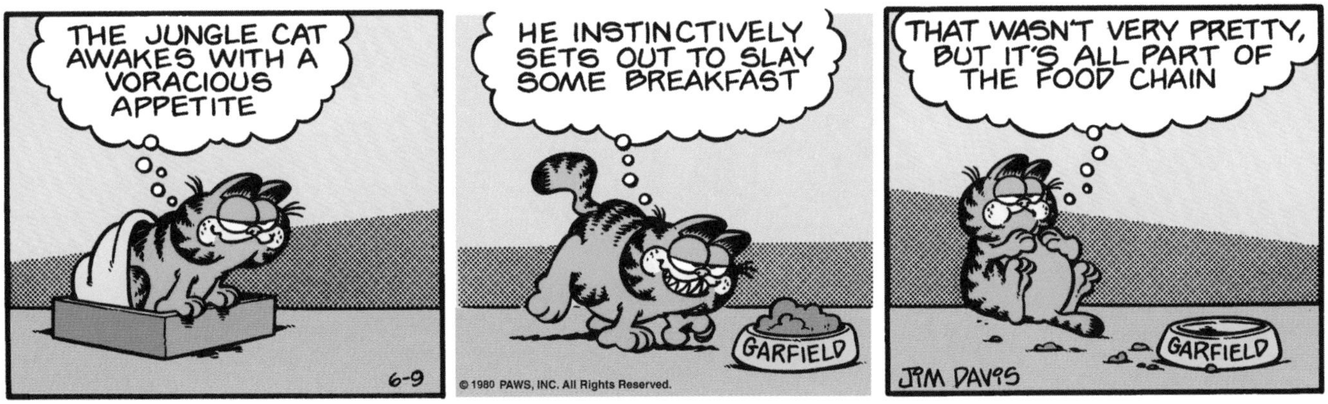
THE JUNGLE CAT AWAKES WITH A VORACIOUS APPETITE
6-9
HE INSTINCTIVELY SETS OUT TO SLAY SOME BREAKFAST
GARFIELD
© 1980 PAWS, INC. All Rights Reserved.
THAT WASN'T VERY PRETTY, BUT IT'S ALL PART OF THE FOOD CHAIN
GARFIELD
JIM DAVIS

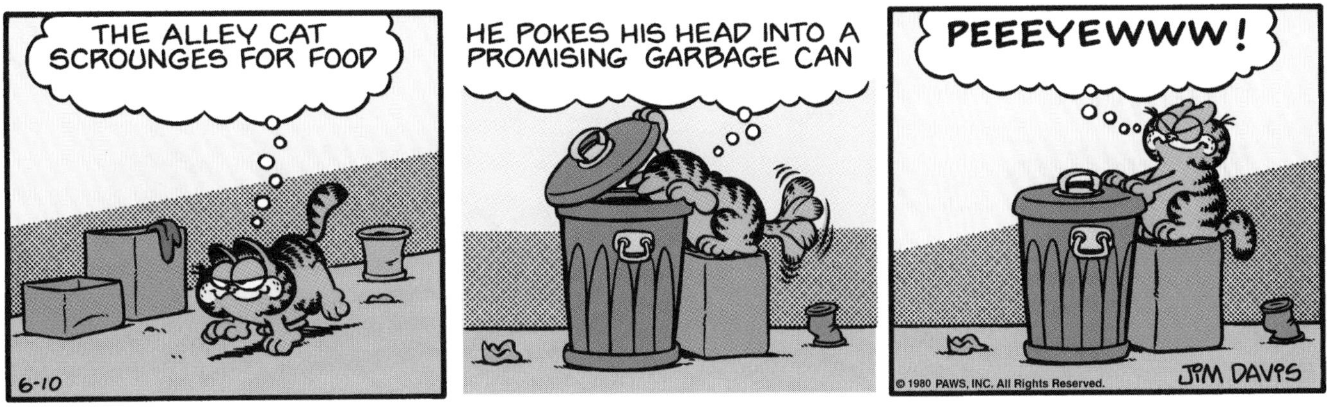
THE ALLEY CAT SCROUNGES FOR FOOD
6-10
HE POKES HIS HEAD INTO A PROMISING GARBAGE CAN
PEEEYEWWW!
© 1980 PAWS, INC. All Rights Reserved.
JIM DAVIS

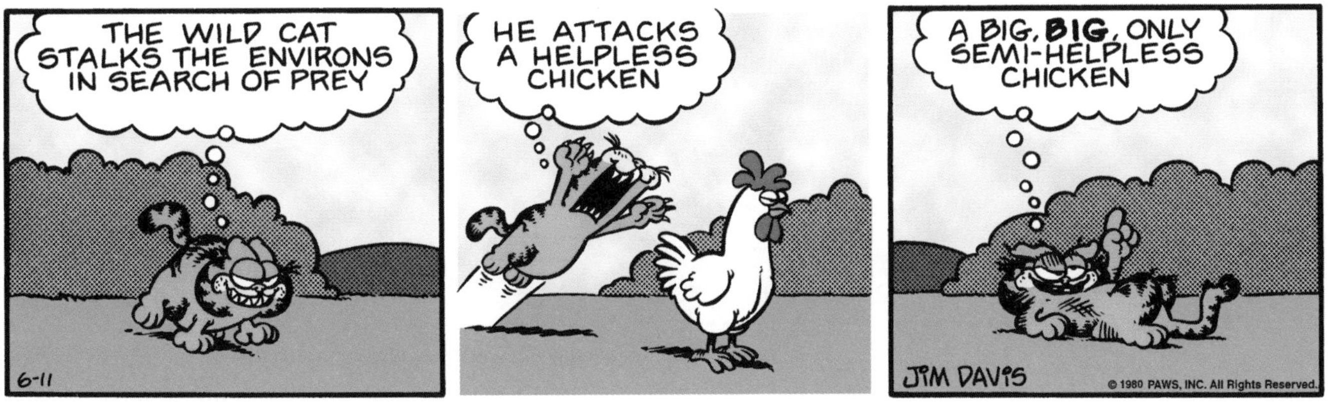
THE WILD CAT STALKS THE ENVIRONS IN SEARCH OF PREY
6-11
HE ATTACKS A HELPLESS CHICKEN
A BIG, BIG, ONLY SEMI-HELPLESS CHICKEN
JIM DAVIS
© 1980 PAWS, INC. All Rights Reserved.

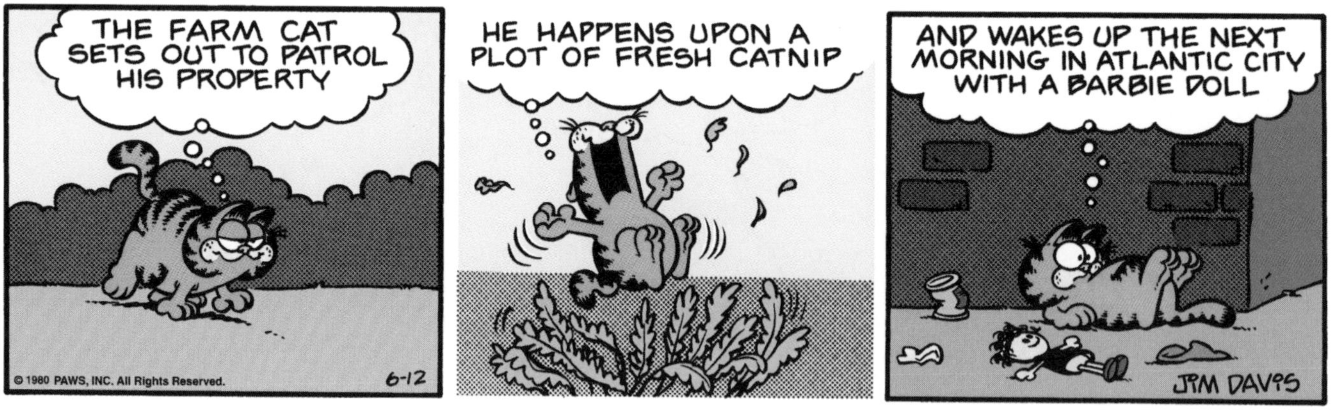
THE FARM CAT SETS OUT TO PATROL HIS PROPERTY
HE HAPPENS UPON A PLOT OF FRESH CATNIP
AND WAKES UP THE NEXT MORNING IN ATLANTIC CITY WITH A BARBIE DOLL
© 1980 PAWS, INC. All Rights Reserved.
6-12
JIM DAVIS

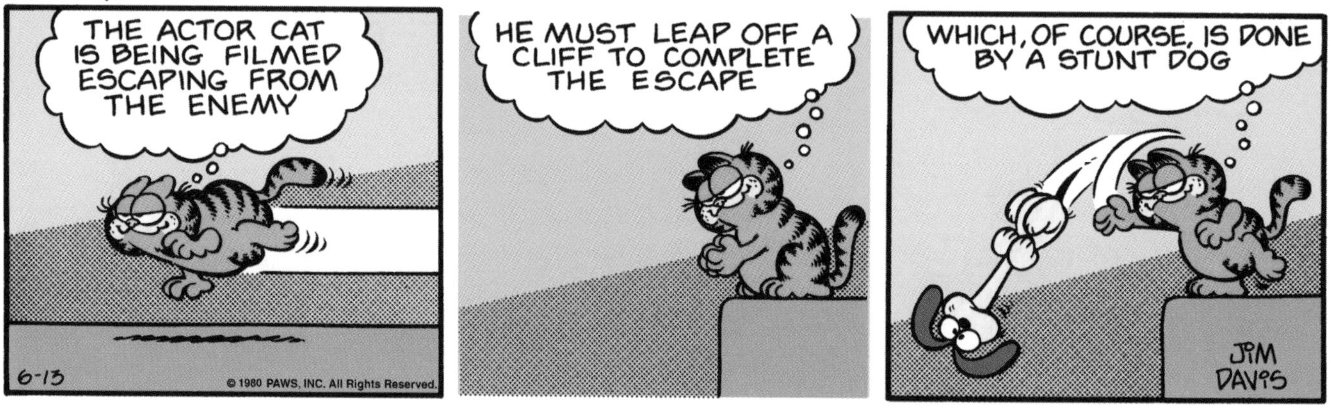
THE ACTOR CAT IS BEING FILMED ESCAPING FROM THE ENEMY
6-13
© 1980 PAWS, INC. All Rights Reserved.
HE MUST LEAP OFF A CLIFF TO COMPLETE THE ESCAPE
WHICH, OF COURSE, IS DONE BY A STUNT DOG
JIM DAVIS

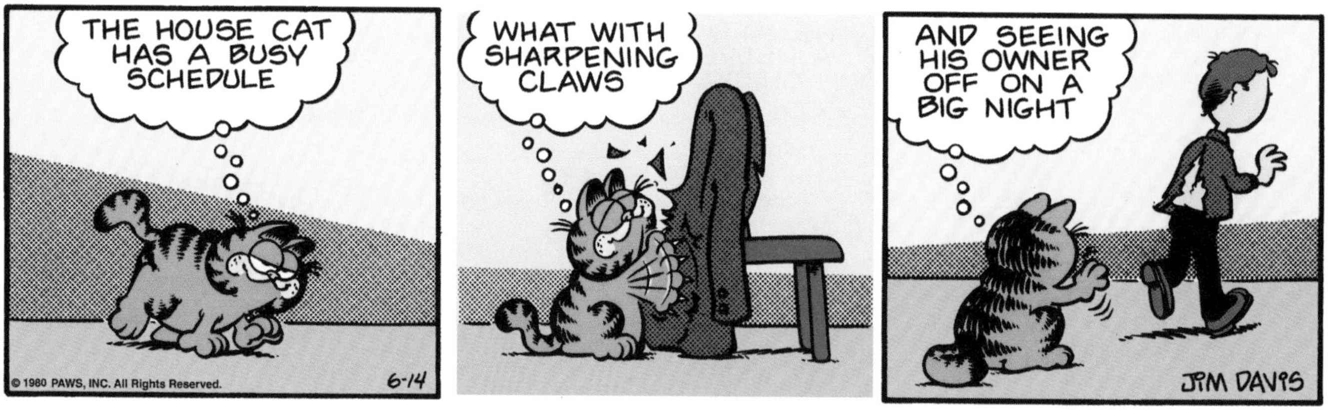
THE HOUSE CAT HAS A BUSY SCHEDULE
© 1980 PAWS, INC. All Rights Reserved.
6-14
WHAT WITH SHARPENING CLAWS
AND SEEING HIS OWNER OFF ON A BIG NIGHT
JIM DAVIS

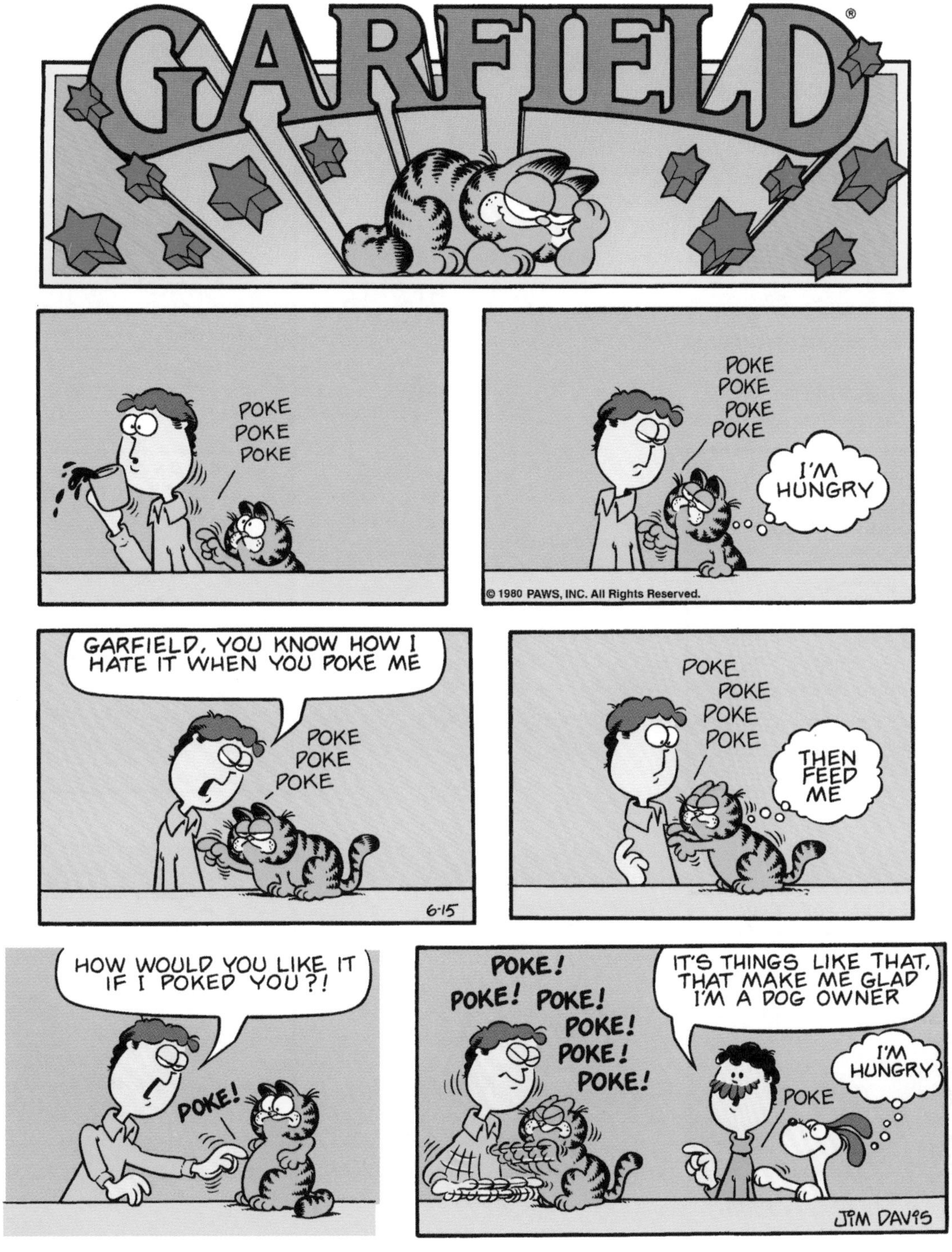
GARFIELD
POKE POKE POKE
POKE POKE POKE POKE
I'M HUNGRY
© 1980 PAWS, INC. All Rights Reserved.
GARFIELD, YOU KNOW HOW I HATE IT WHEN YOU POKE ME
POKE POKE POKE
POKE POKE POKE POKE
THEN FEED ME
6-15
HOW WOULD YOU LIKE IT IF I POKED YOU?!
POKE!
POKE! POKE! POKE! POKE! POKE! POKE!
IT'S THINGS LIKE THAT, THAT MAKE ME GLAD I'M A DOG OWNER
POKE
I'M HUNGRY
JIM DAVIS

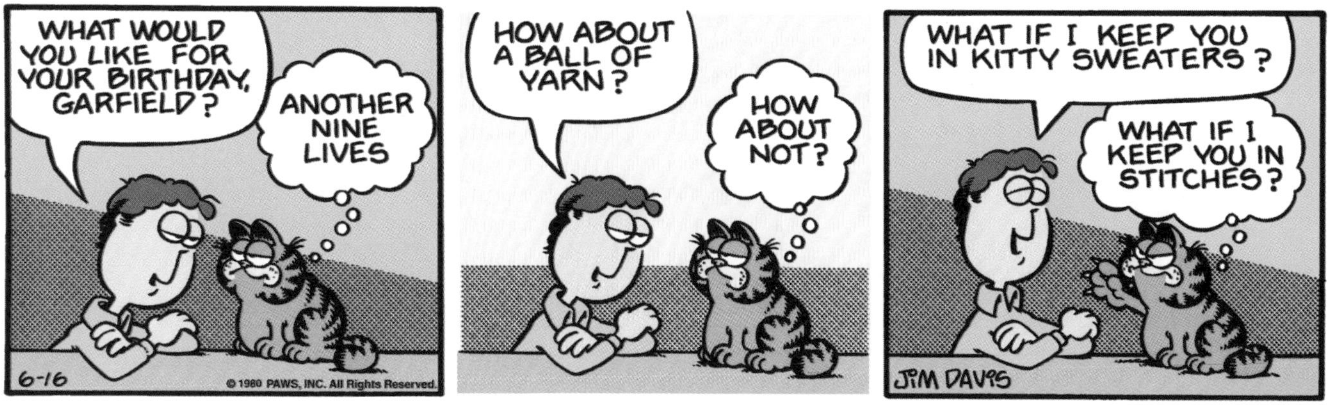
WHAT WOULD YOU LIKE FOR YOUR BIRTHDAY, GARFIELD?
ANOTHER NINE LIVES
6-16
© 1980 PAWS, INC. All Rights Reserved.
HOW ABOUT A BALL OF YARN?
HOW ABOUT NOT?
WHAT IF I KEEP YOU IN KITTY SWEATERS?
WHAT IF I KEEP YOU IN STITCHES?
JIM DAVIS

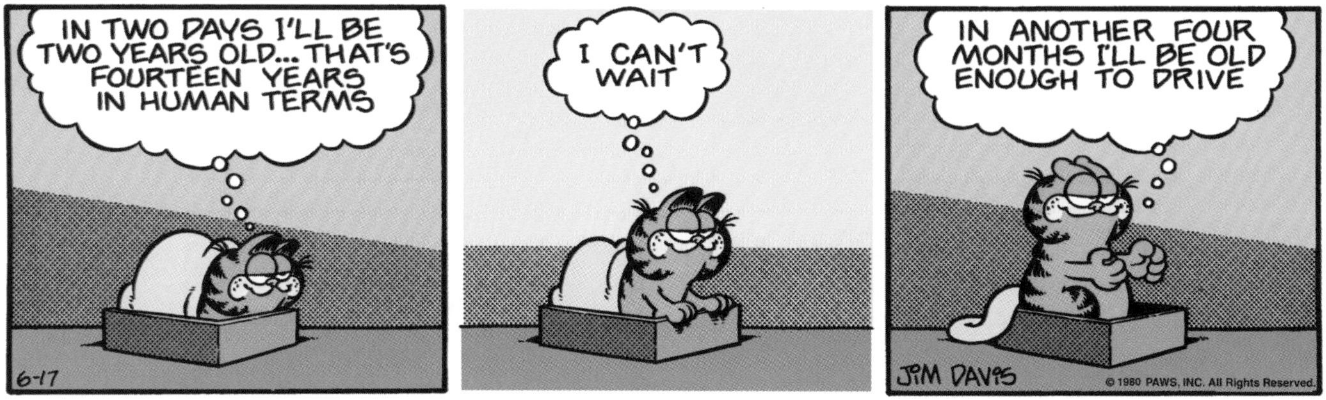
IN TWO DAYS I'LL BE TWO YEARS OLD... THAT'S FOURTEEN YEARS IN HUMAN TERMS
6-17
I CAN'T WAIT
IN ANOTHER FOUR MONTHS I'LL BE OLD ENOUGH TO DRIVE
JIM DAVIS
© 1980 PAWS, INC. All Rights Reserved.

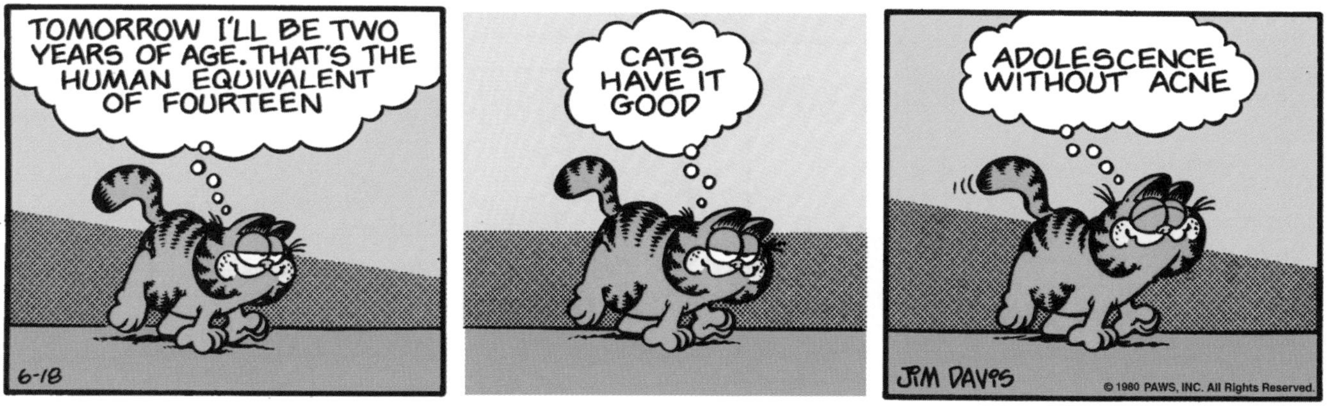
TOMORROW I'LL BE TWO YEARS OF AGE. THAT'S THE HUMAN EQUIVALENT OF FOURTEEN
6-18
CATS HAVE IT GOOD
ADOLESCENCE WITHOUT ACNE
JIM DAVIS
© 1980 PAWS, INC. All Rights Reserved.

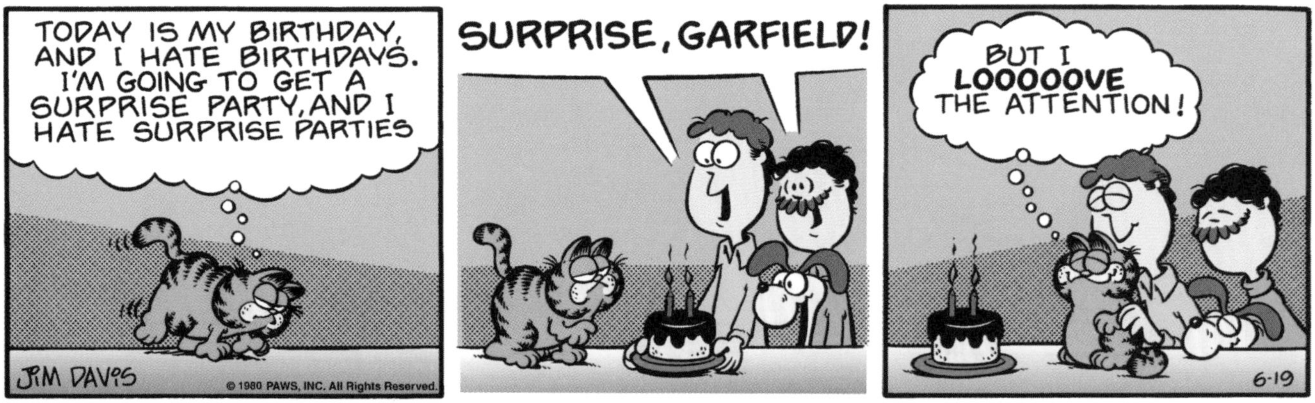
TODAY IS MY BIRTHDAY, AND I HATE BIRTHDAYS. I'M GOING TO GET A SURPRISE PARTY, AND I HATE SURPRISE PARTIES
JIM DAVIS
© 1980 PAWS, INC. All Rights Reserved.
SURPRISE, GARFIELD!
BUT I LOOOOOVE THE ATTENTION!
6-19

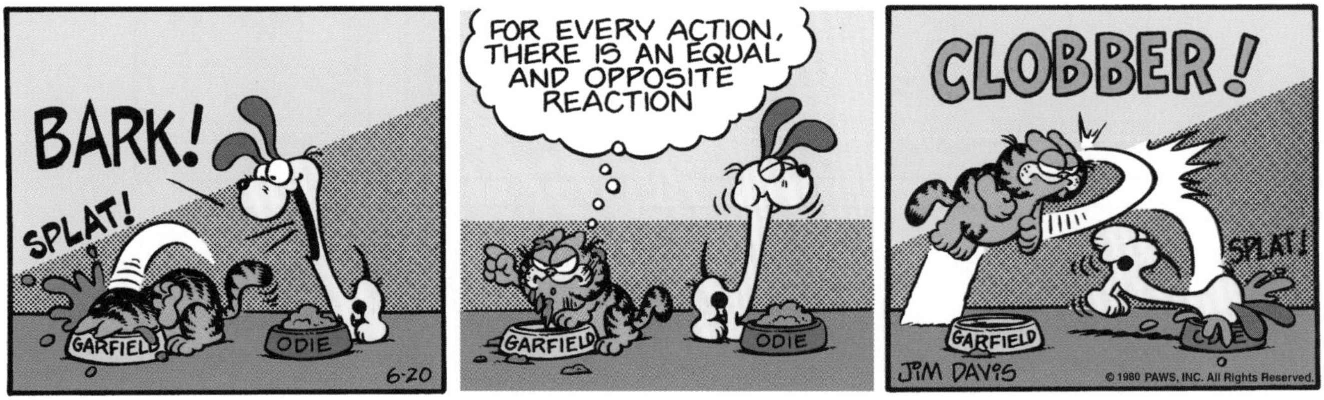
BARK!
SPLAT!
GARFIELD
ODIE
6-20
FOR EVERY ACTION, THERE IS AN EQUAL AND OPPOSITE REACTION
GARFIELD
ODIE
CLOBBER!
SPLAT!
GARFIELD
JIM DAVIS
© 1980 PAWS, INC. All Rights Reserved.

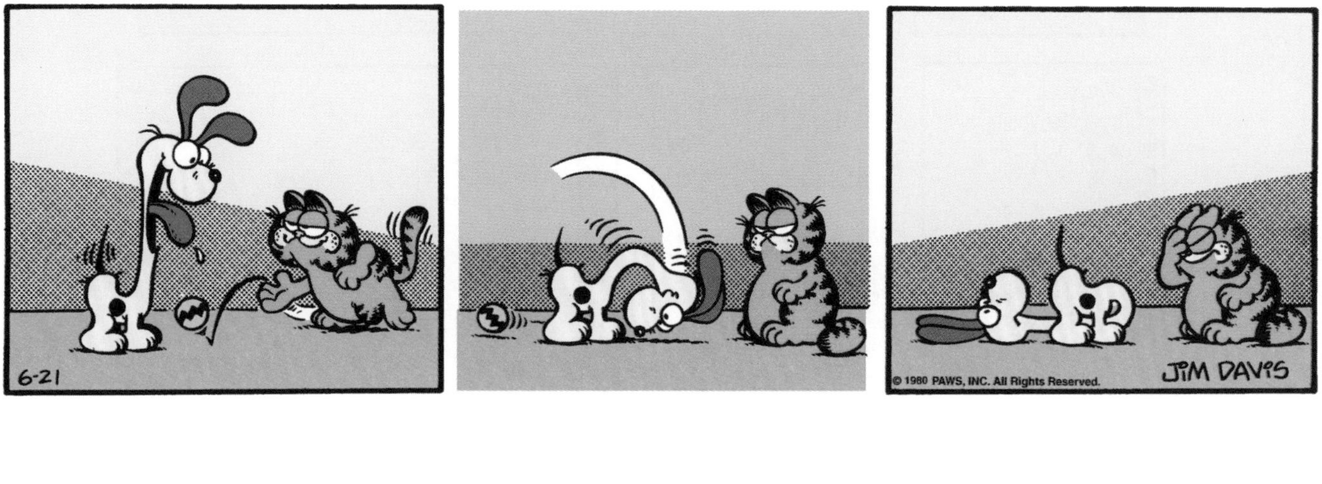
6-21
© 1980 PAWS, INC. All Rights Reserved.
JIM DAVIS

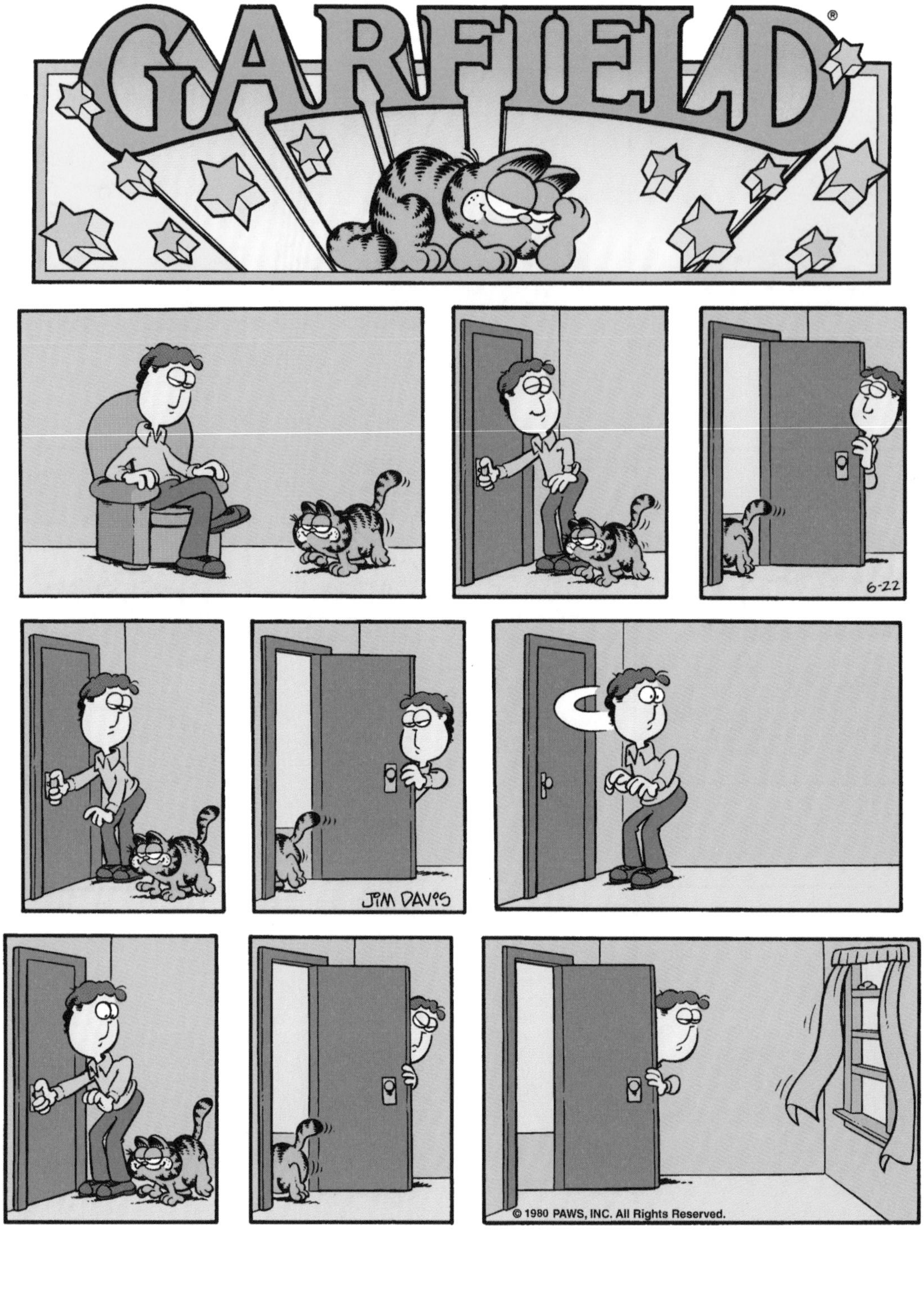
GARFIELD®
6-22
JIM DAVIS

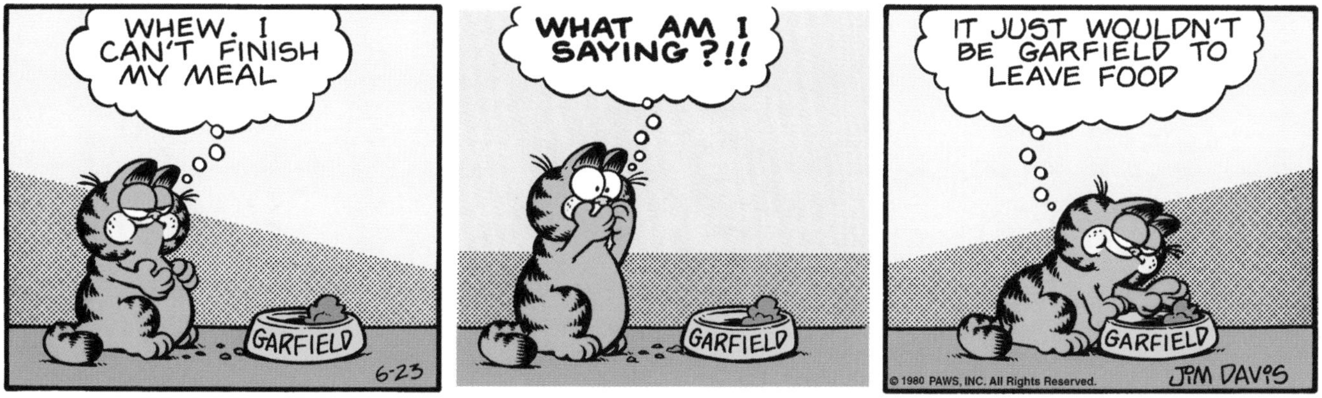
WHEW. I CAN'T FINISH MY MEAL
GARFIELD
6-23
WHAT AM I SAYING?!!
GARFIELD
IT JUST WOULDN'T BE GARFIELD TO LEAVE FOOD
GARFIELD
© 1980 PAWS, INC. All Rights Reserved.
JIM DAVIS

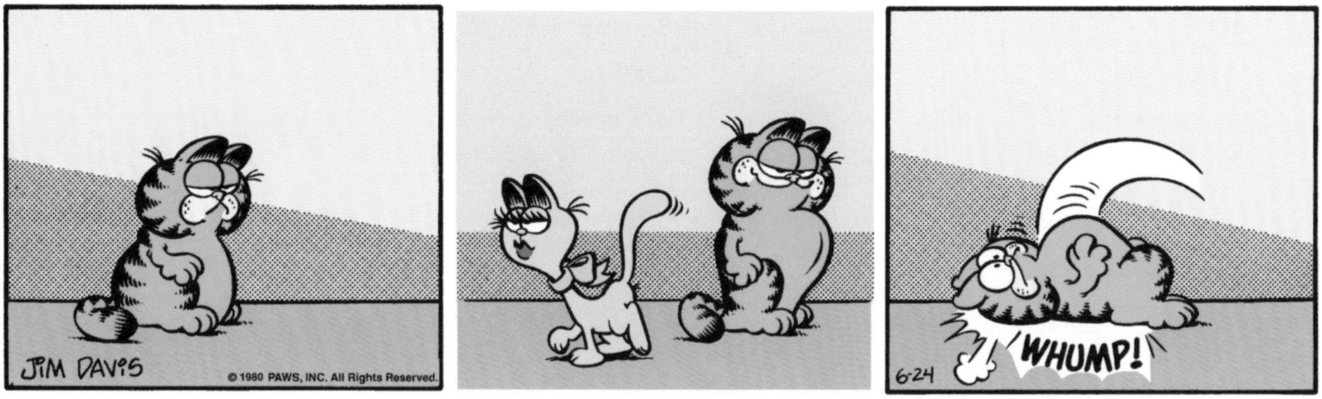
JIM DAVIS
© 1980 PAWS, INC. All Rights Reserved.
WHUMP!
6-24

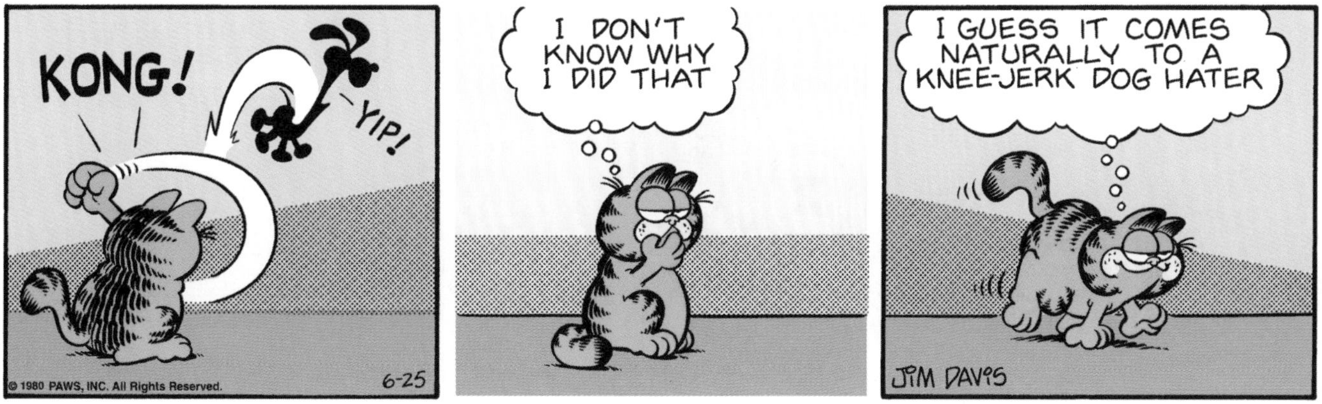
KONG!
YIP!
© 1980 PAWS, INC. All Rights Reserved.
6-25
I DON'T KNOW WHY I DID THAT
I GUESS IT COMES NATURALLY TO A KNEE-JERK DOG HATER
JIM DAVIS

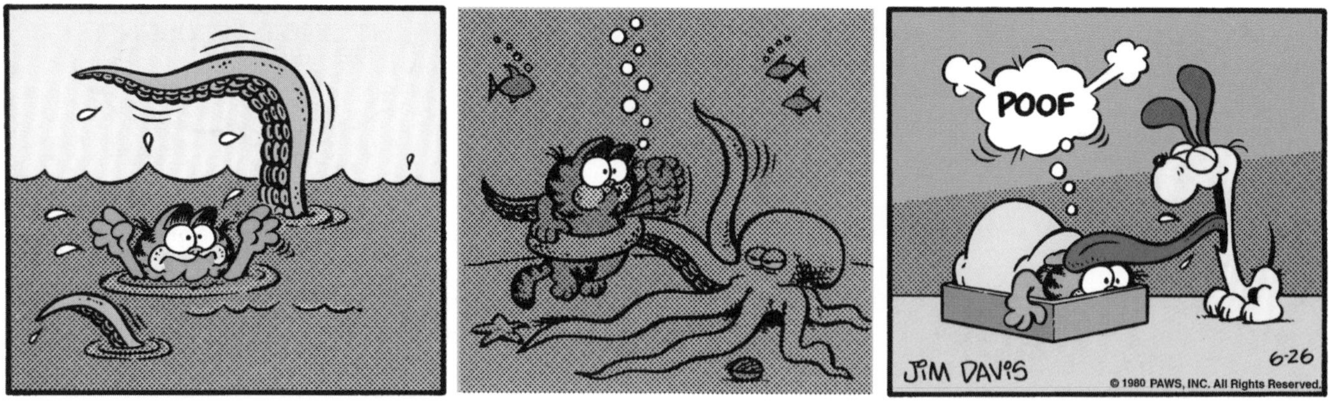
POOF
JIM DAVIS
6-26
© 1980 PAWS, INC. All Rights Reserved.

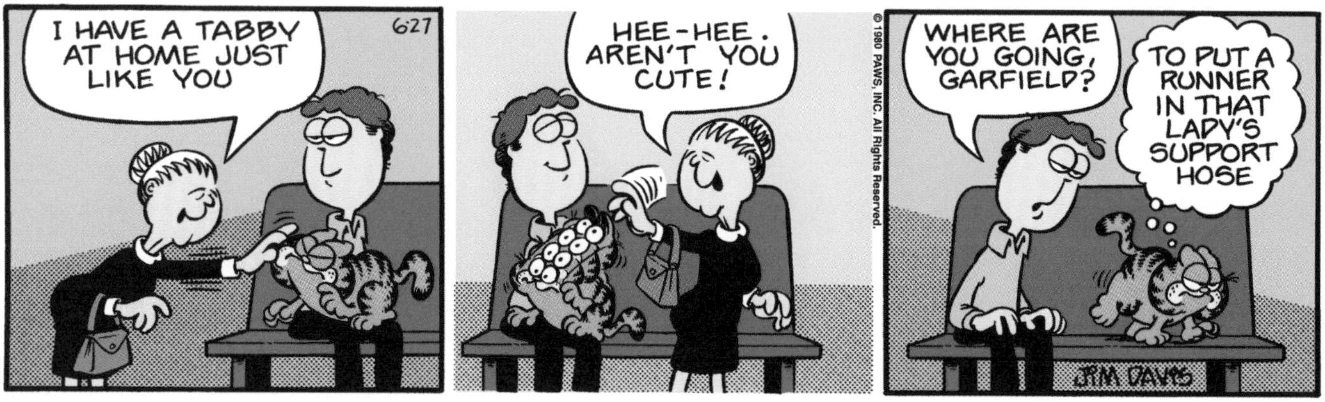
6-27
I HAVE A TABBY AT HOME JUST LIKE YOU
HEE-HEE. AREN'T YOU CUTE!
© 1980 PAWS, INC. All Rights Reserved.
WHERE ARE YOU GOING, GARFIELD?
TO PUT A RUNNER IN THAT LADY'S SUPPORT HOSE
JIM DAVIS

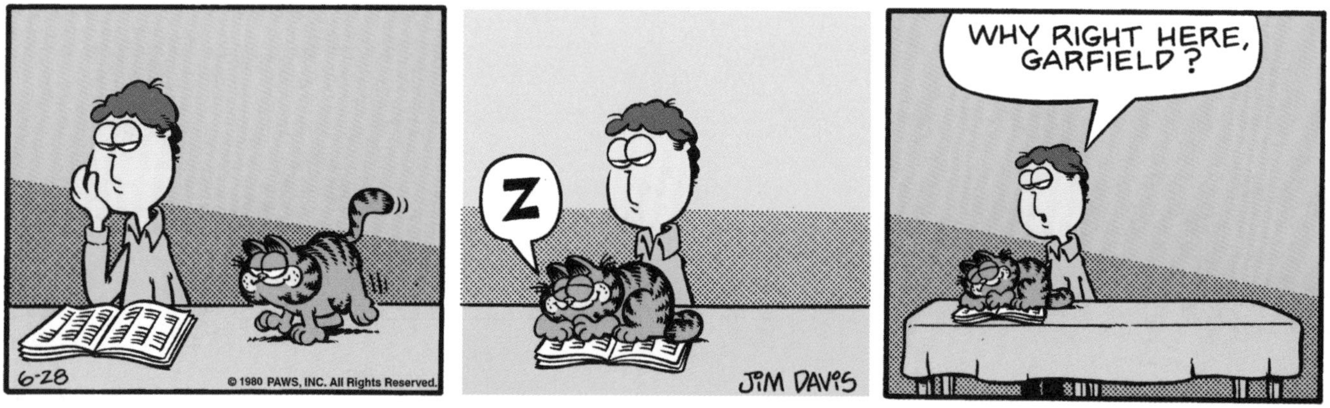
6-28
© 1980 PAWS, INC. All Rights Reserved.
Z
JIM DAVIS
WHY RIGHT HERE, GARFIELD?

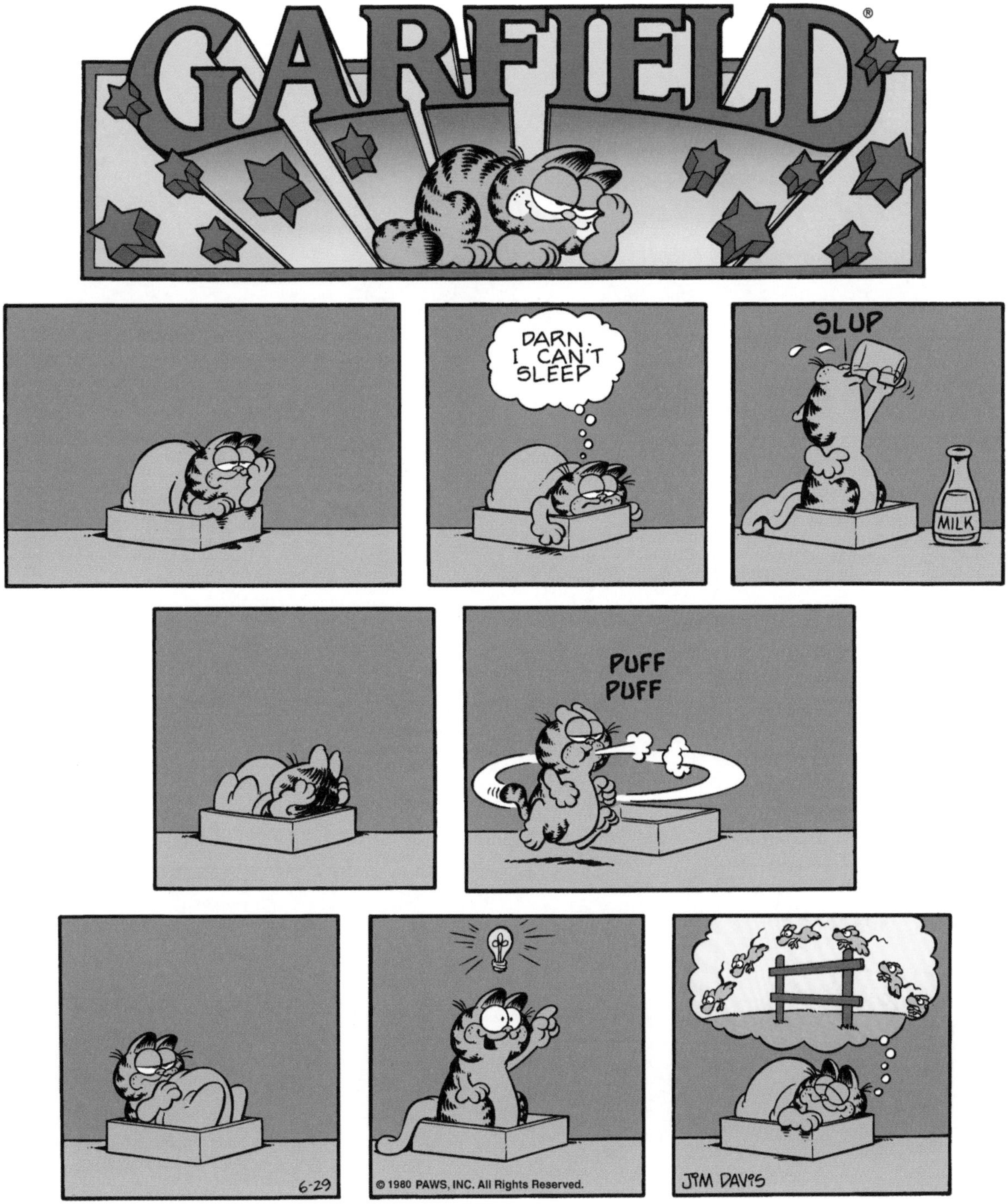
GARFIELD
DARN. I CAN'T SLEEP
SLUP
MILK
PUFF PUFF
6-29
© 1980 PAWS, INC. All Rights Reserved.
JIM DAVIS

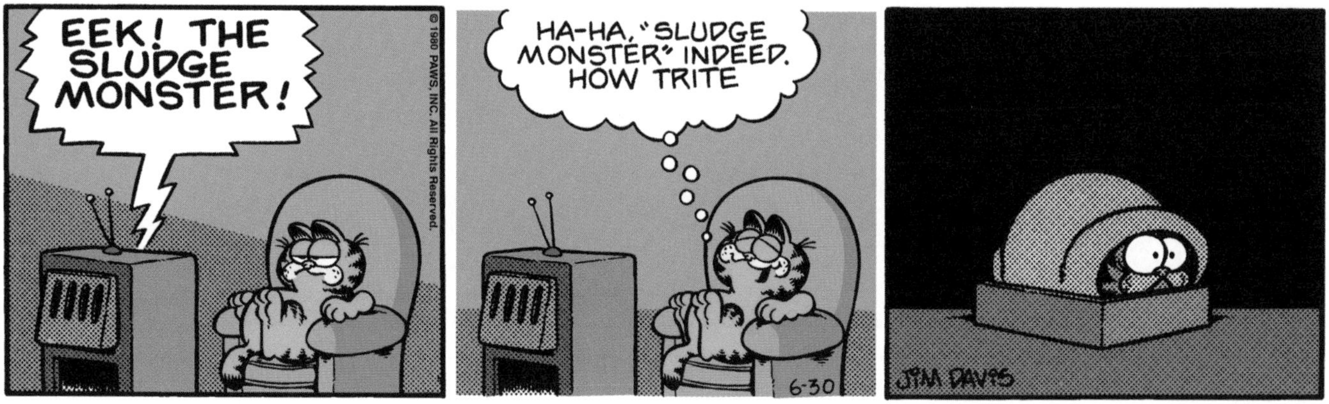
EEK! THE SLUDGE MONSTER!
© 1980 PAWS, INC. All Rights Reserved.
HA-HA, "SLUDGE MONSTER" INDEED. HOW TRITE
6-30
JIM DAVIS

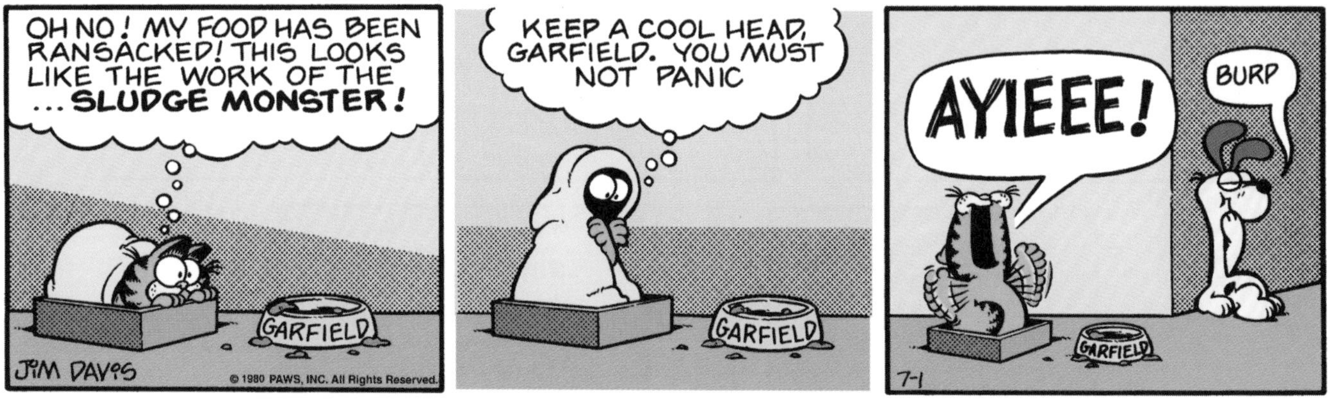
OH NO! MY FOOD HAS BEEN RANSACKED! THIS LOOKS LIKE THE WORK OF THE ... SLUDGE MONSTER!
GARFIELD
JIM DAVIS
© 1980 PAWS, INC. All Rights Reserved.
KEEP A COOL HEAD, GARFIELD. YOU MUST NOT PANIC
GARFIELD
AYIEEE!
BURP
GARFIELD
7-1

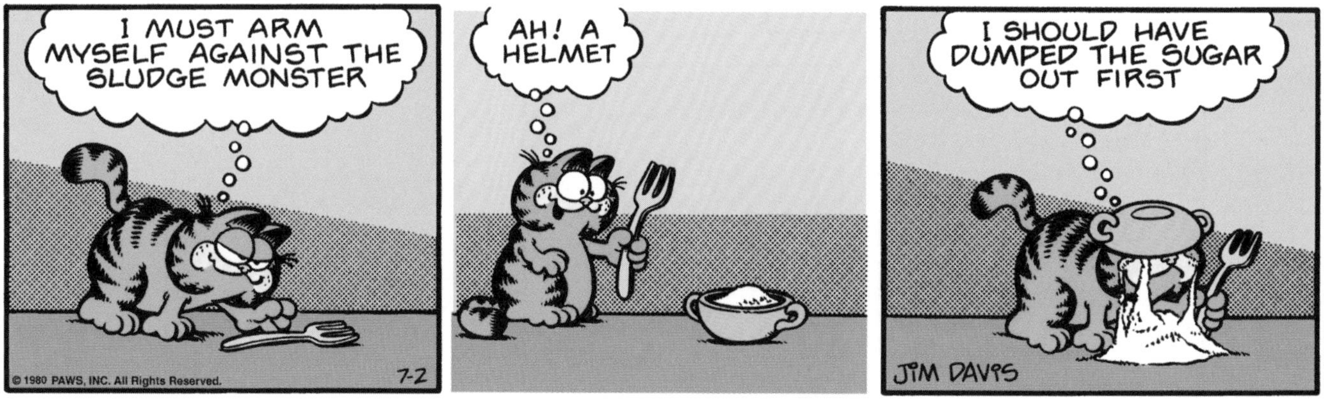
I MUST ARM MYSELF AGAINST THE SLUDGE MONSTER
© 1980 PAWS, INC. All Rights Reserved.
7-2
AH! A HELMET
I SHOULD HAVE DUMPED THE SUGAR OUT FIRST
JIM DAVIS

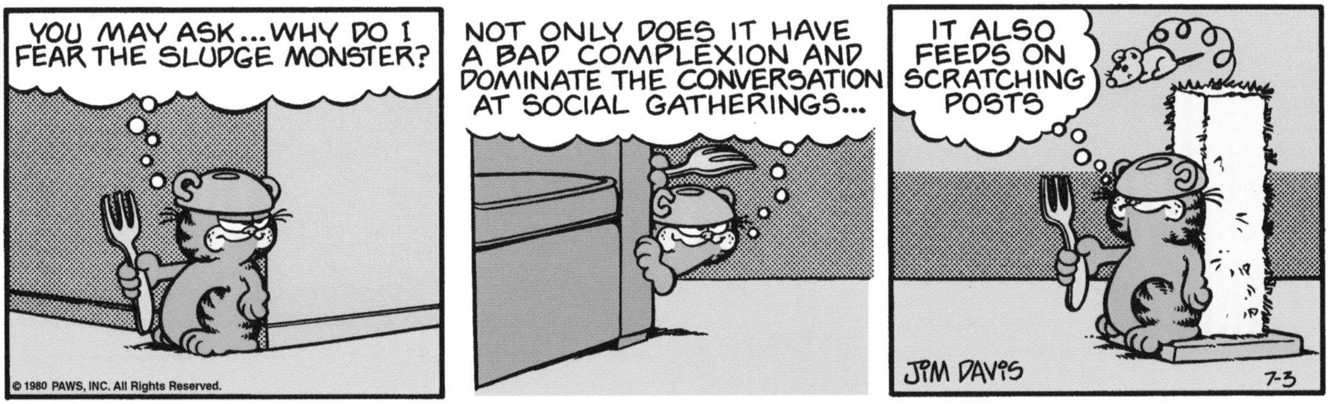
YOU MAY ASK...WHY DO I FEAR THE SLUDGE MONSTER?
© 1980 PAWS, INC. All Rights Reserved.
NOT ONLY DOES IT HAVE A BAD COMPLEXION AND DOMINATE THE CONVERSATION AT SOCIAL GATHERINGS...
IT ALSO FEEDS ON SCRATCHING POSTS
JIM DAVIS
7-3

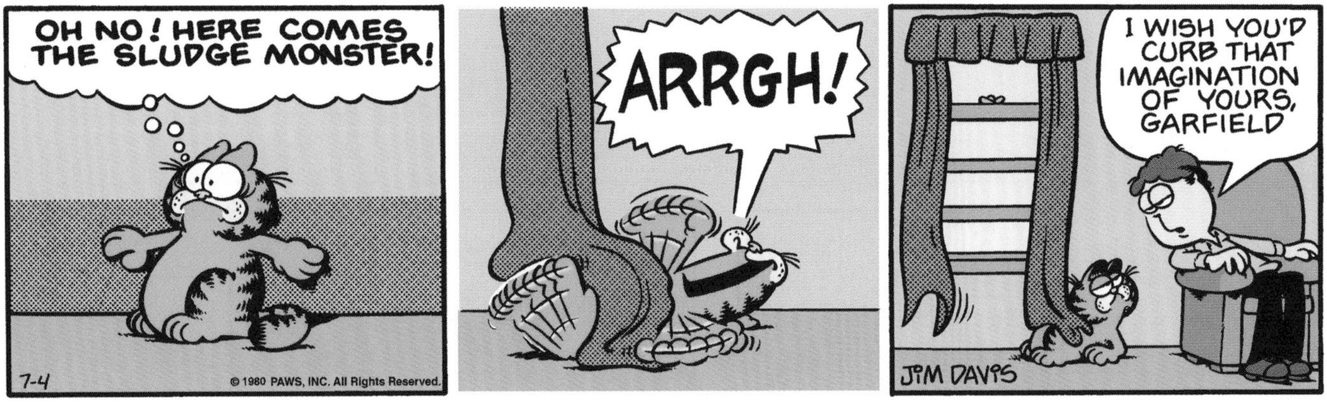
OH NO! HERE COMES THE SLUDGE MONSTER!
7-4
© 1980 PAWS, INC. All Rights Reserved.
ARRGH!
I WISH YOU'D CURB THAT IMAGINATION OF YOURS, GARFIELD
JIM DAVIS

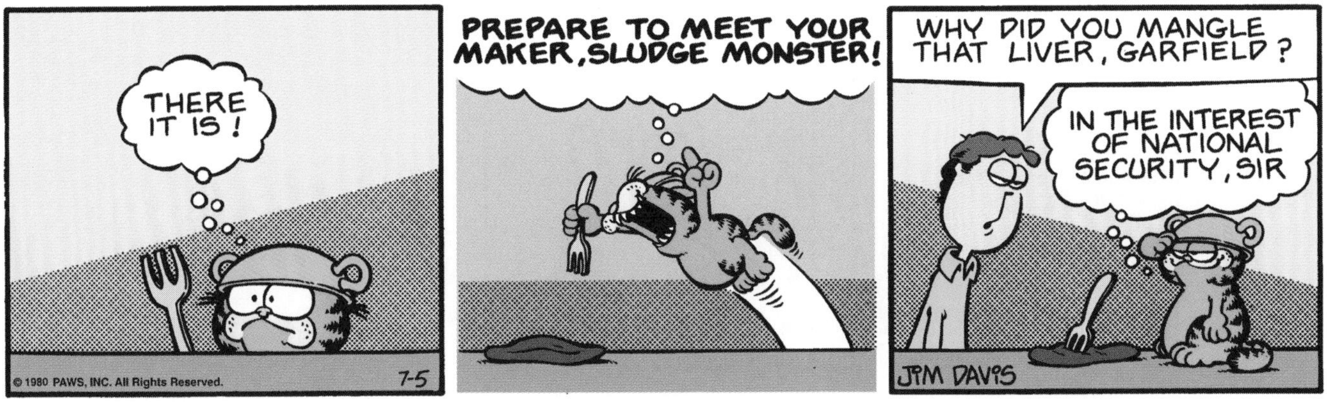
THERE IT IS!
© 1980 PAWS, INC. All Rights Reserved.
7-5
PREPARE TO MEET YOUR MAKER, SLUDGE MONSTER!
WHY DID YOU MANGLE THAT LIVER, GARFIELD?
IN THE INTEREST OF NATIONAL SECURITY, SIR
JIM DAVIS

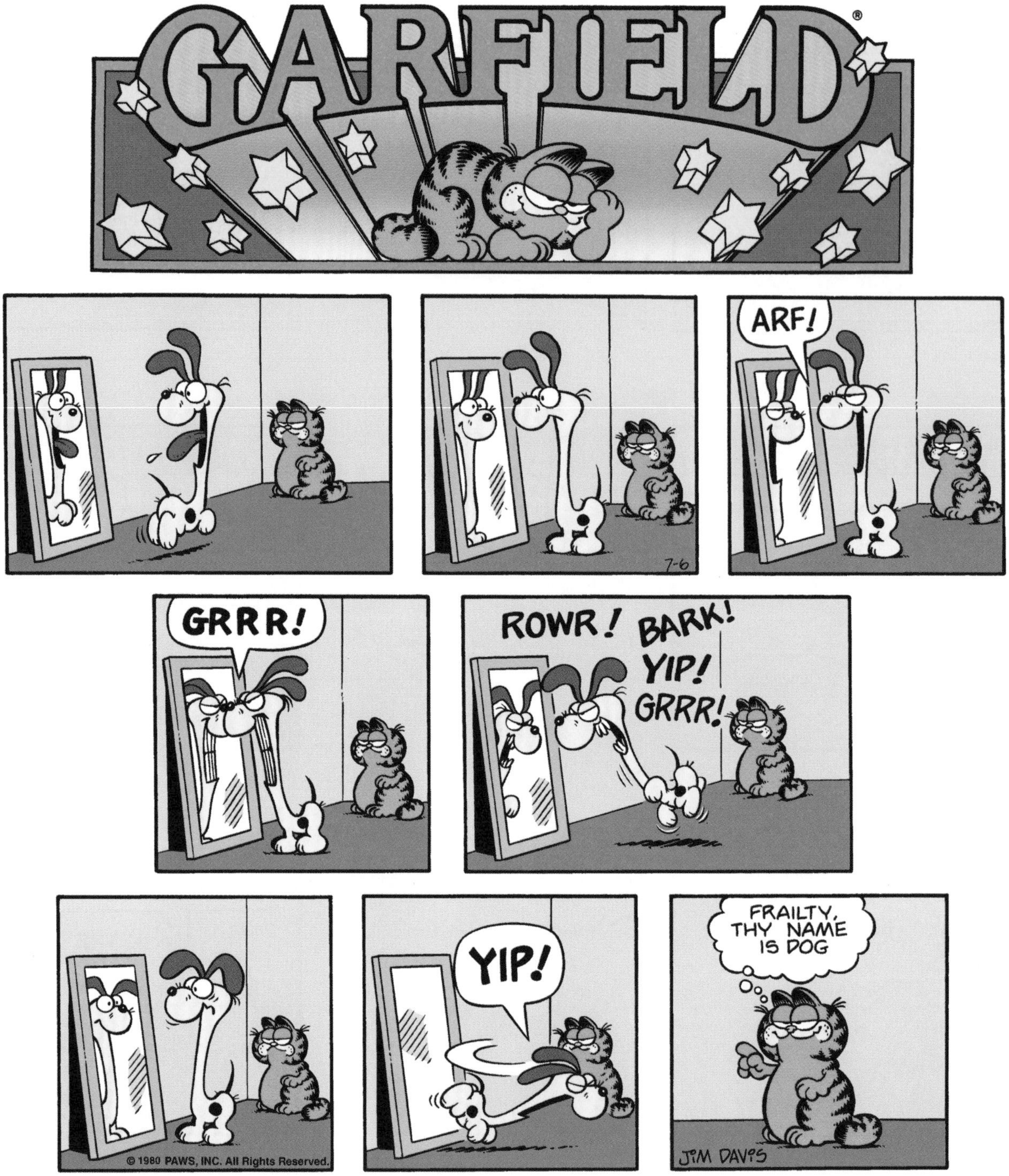
GARFIELD
7-6
ARF!
GRRR!
ROWR!
BARK!
YIP!
GRRR!
© 1980 PAWS, INC. All Rights Reserved.
YIP!
FRAILTY, THY NAME IS DOG
JIM DAVIS

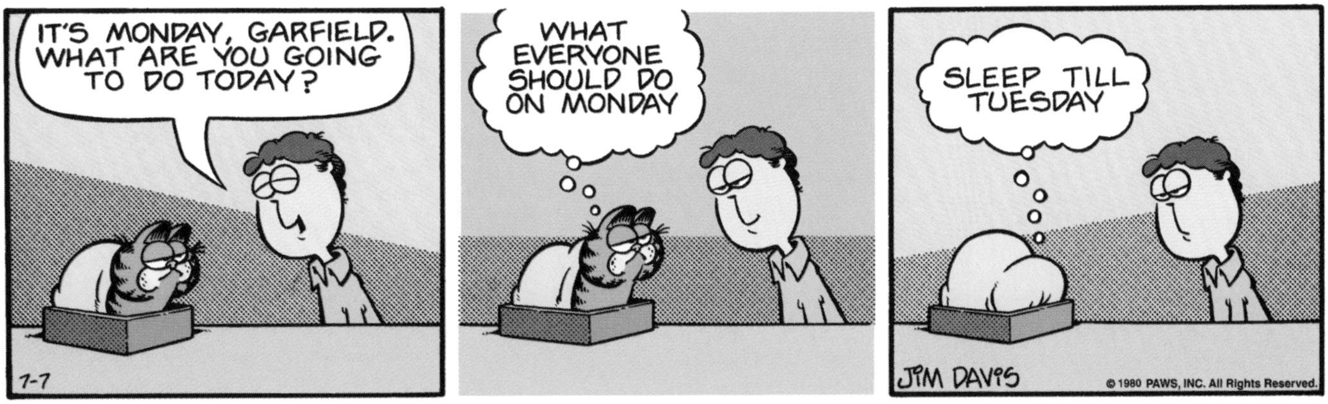
IT'S MONDAY, GARFIELD. WHAT ARE YOU GOING TO DO TODAY?
WHAT EVERYONE SHOULD DO ON MONDAY
SLEEP TILL TUESDAY
7-7
JIM DAVIS
© 1980 PAWS, INC. All Rights Reserved.

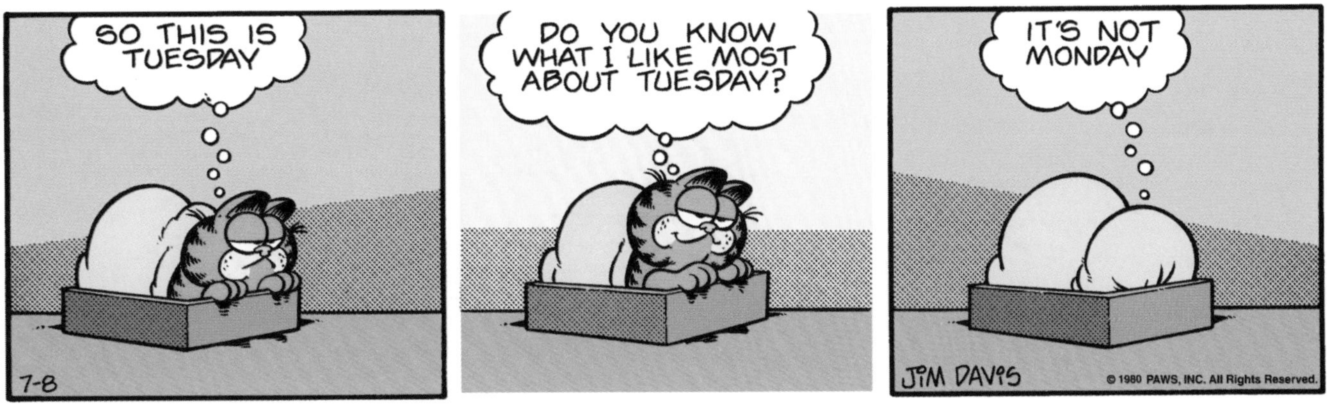
SO THIS IS TUESDAY
DO YOU KNOW WHAT I LIKE MOST ABOUT TUESDAY?
IT'S NOT MONDAY
7-8
JIM DAVIS
© 1980 PAWS, INC. All Rights Reserved.

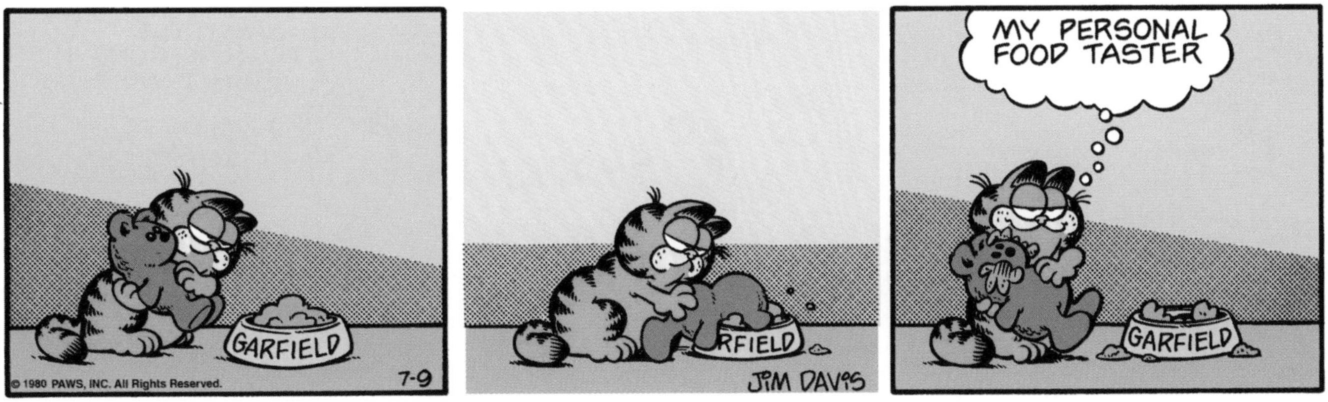
GARFIELD
© 1980 PAWS, INC. All Rights Reserved.
7-9
RFIELD
JIM DAVIS
MY PERSONAL FOOD TASTER
GARFIELD

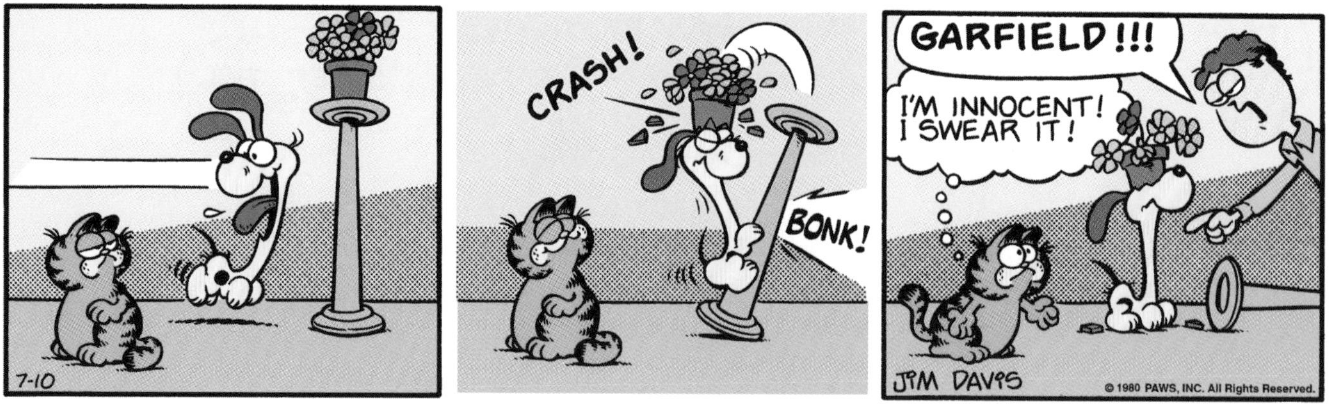
7-10
CRASH!
BONK!
GARFIELD!!!
I'M INNOCENT! I SWEAR IT!
JIM DAVIS
© 1980 PAWS, INC. All Rights Reserved.

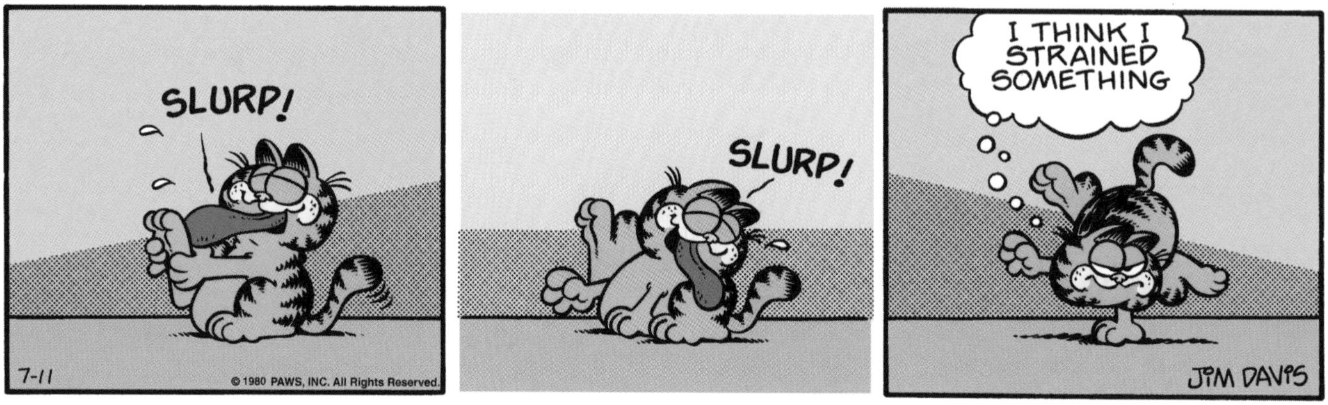
SLURP!
7-11
© 1980 PAWS, INC. All Rights Reserved.
SLURP!
I THINK I STRAINED SOMETHING
JIM DAVIS

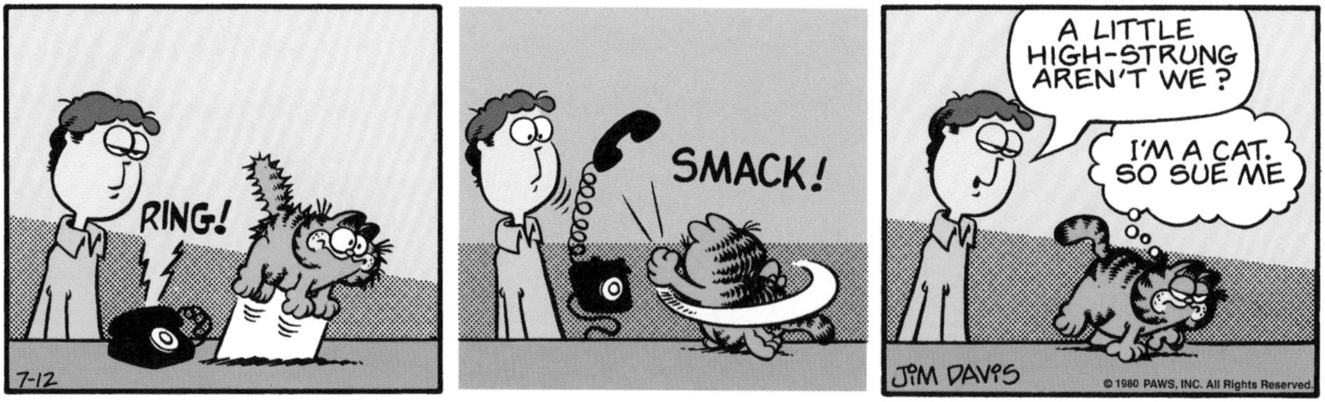
RING!
7-12
SMACK!
A LITTLE HIGH-STRUNG AREN'T WE?
I'M A CAT. SO SUE ME
JIM DAVIS
© 1980 PAWS, INC. All Rights Reserved.

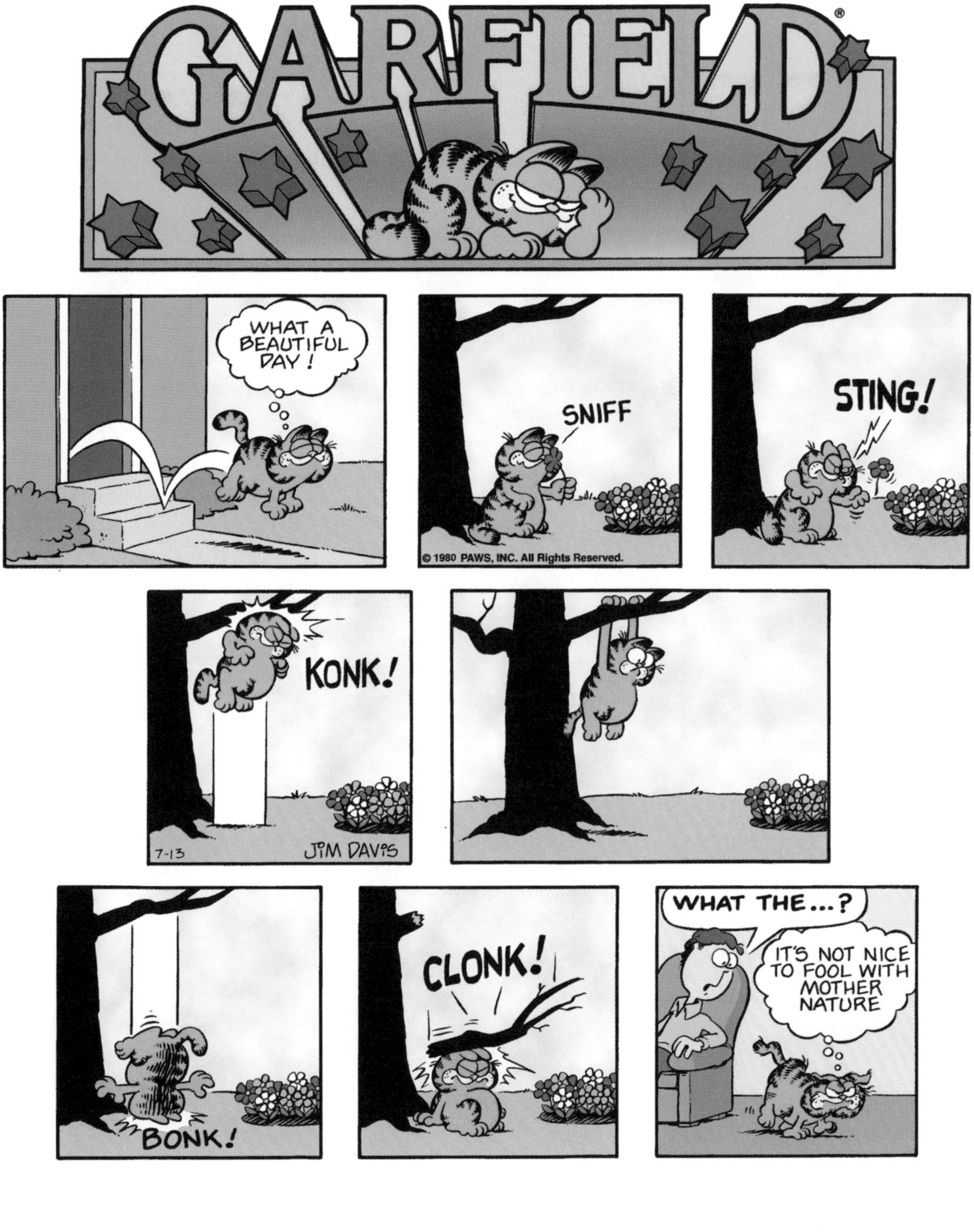
GARFIELD
WHAT A BEAUTIFUL DAY!
SNIFF
© 1980 PAWS, INC. All Rights Reserved.
STING!
KONK!
7-13
JIM DAVIS
BONK!
CLONK!
WHAT THE...?
IT'S NOT NICE TO FOOL WITH MOTHER NATURE

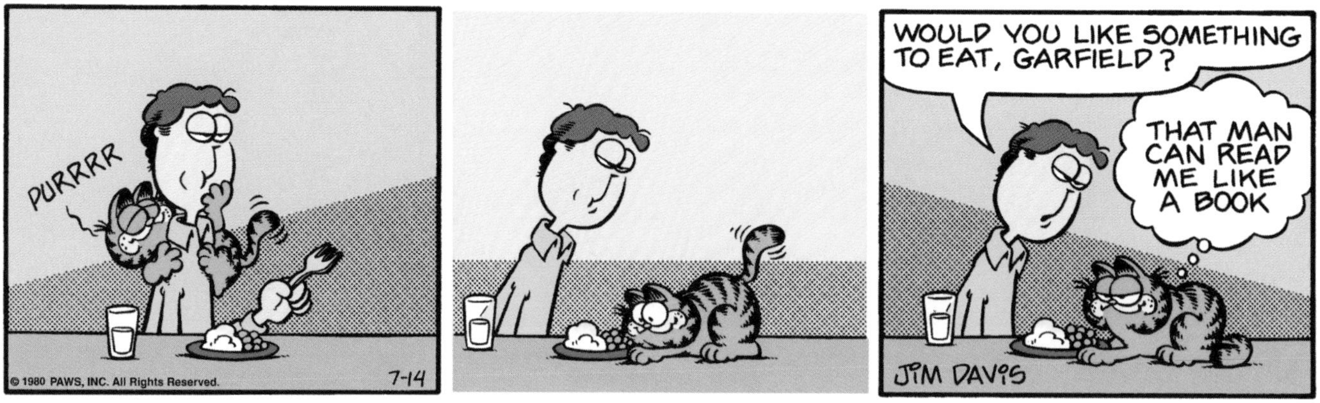
PURRRR
© 1980 PAWS, INC. All Rights Reserved.
7-14
WOULD YOU LIKE SOMETHING TO EAT, GARFIELD?
THAT MAN CAN READ ME LIKE A BOOK
JIM DAVIS

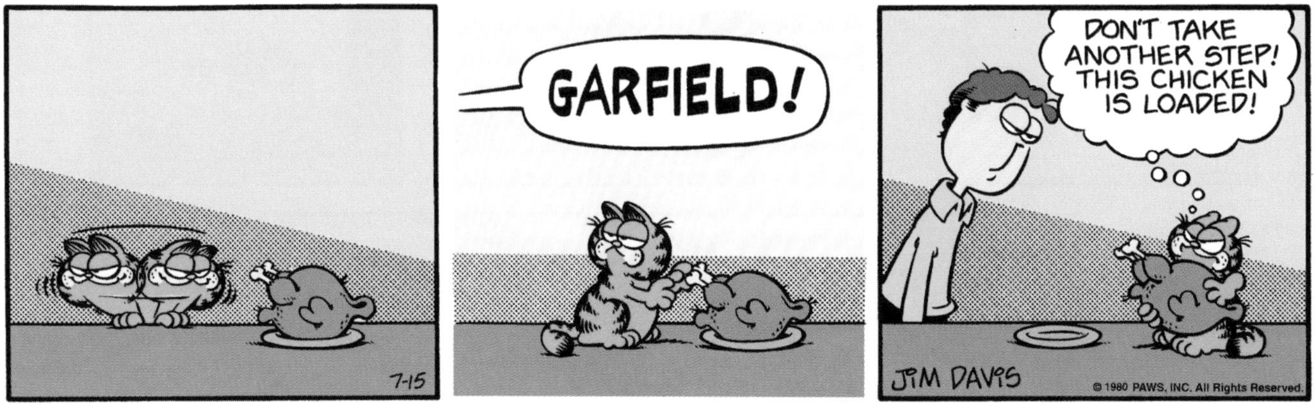
7-15
GARFIELD!
DON'T TAKE ANOTHER STEP! THIS CHICKEN IS LOADED!
JIM DAVIS
© 1980 PAWS, INC. All Rights Reserved.

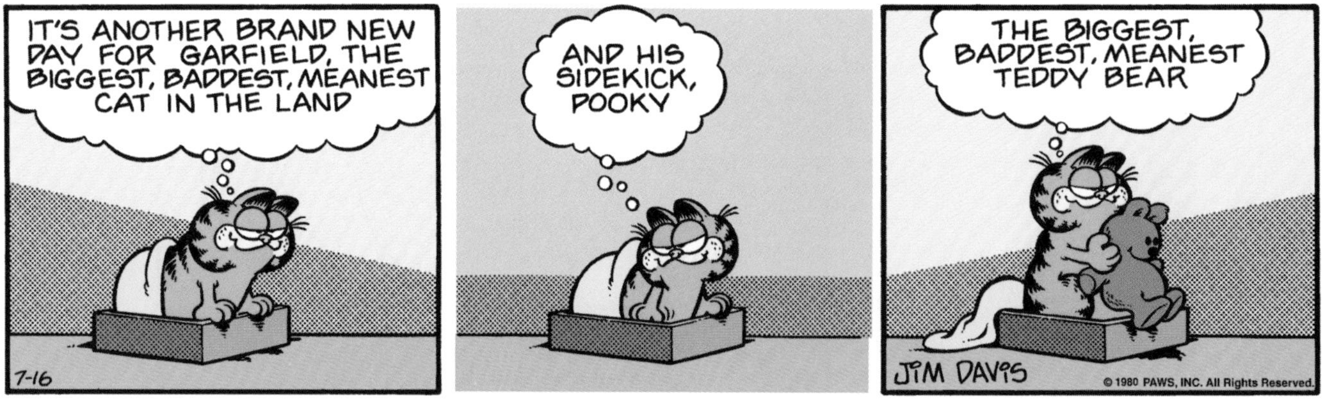
IT'S ANOTHER BRAND NEW DAY FOR GARFIELD, THE BIGGEST, BADDEST, MEANEST CAT IN THE LAND
7-16
AND HIS SIDEKICK, POOKY
THE BIGGEST, BADDEST, MEANEST TEDDY BEAR
JIM DAVIS
© 1980 PAWS, INC. All Rights Reserved.

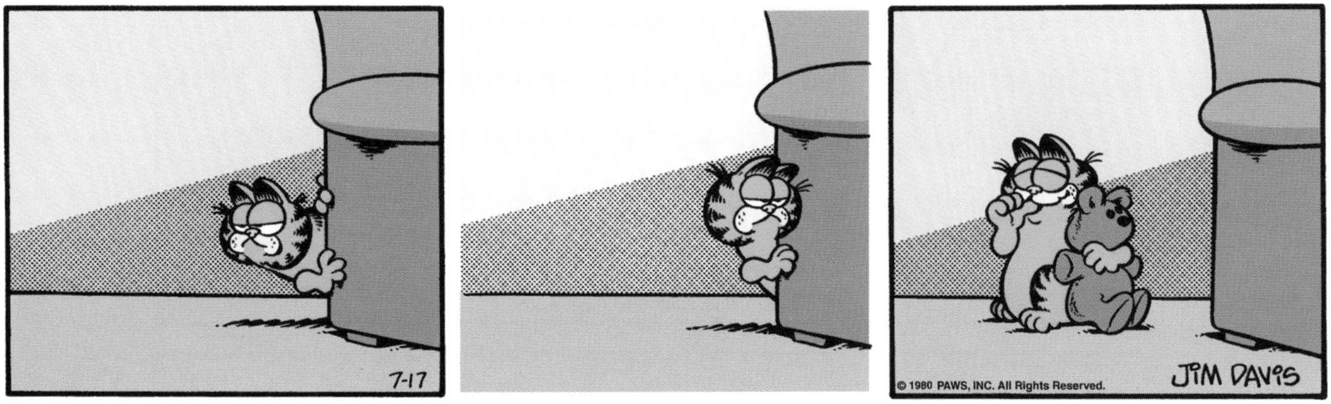
7-17
© 1980 PAWS, INC. All Rights Reserved.
JIM DAVIS

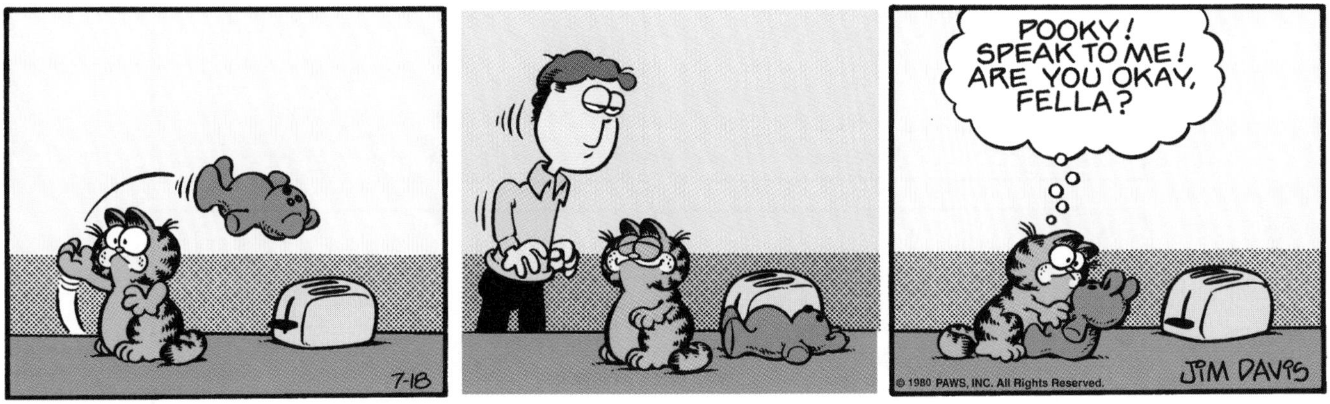
7-18
POOKY! SPEAK TO ME! ARE YOU OKAY, FELLA?
© 1980 PAWS, INC. All Rights Reserved.
JIM DAVIS

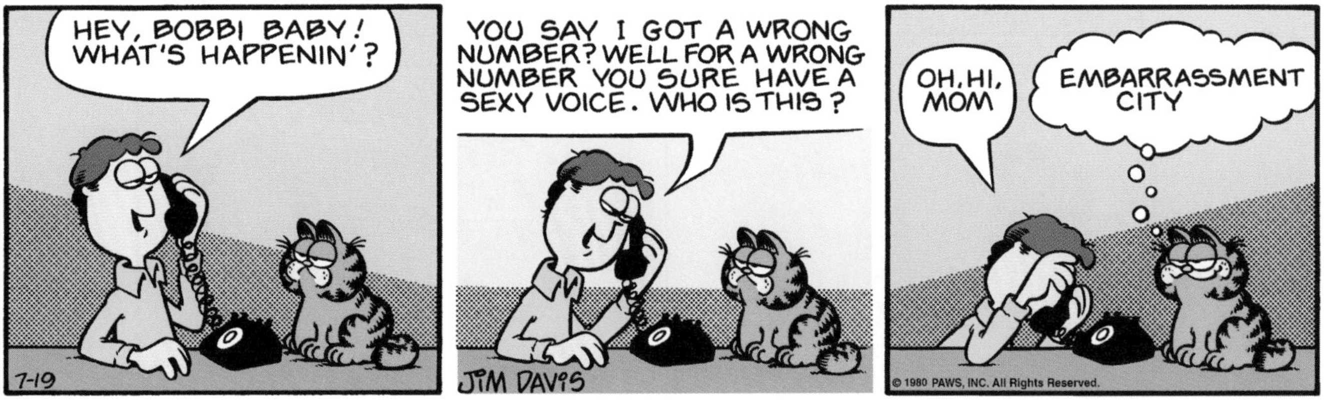
HEY, BOBBI BABY! WHAT'S HAPPENIN'?
7-19
YOU SAY I GOT A WRONG NUMBER? WELL FOR A WRONG NUMBER YOU SURE HAVE A SEXY VOICE. WHO IS THIS?
JIM DAVIS
OH, HI, MOM
EMBARRASSMENT CITY
© 1980 PAWS, INC. All Rights Reserved.

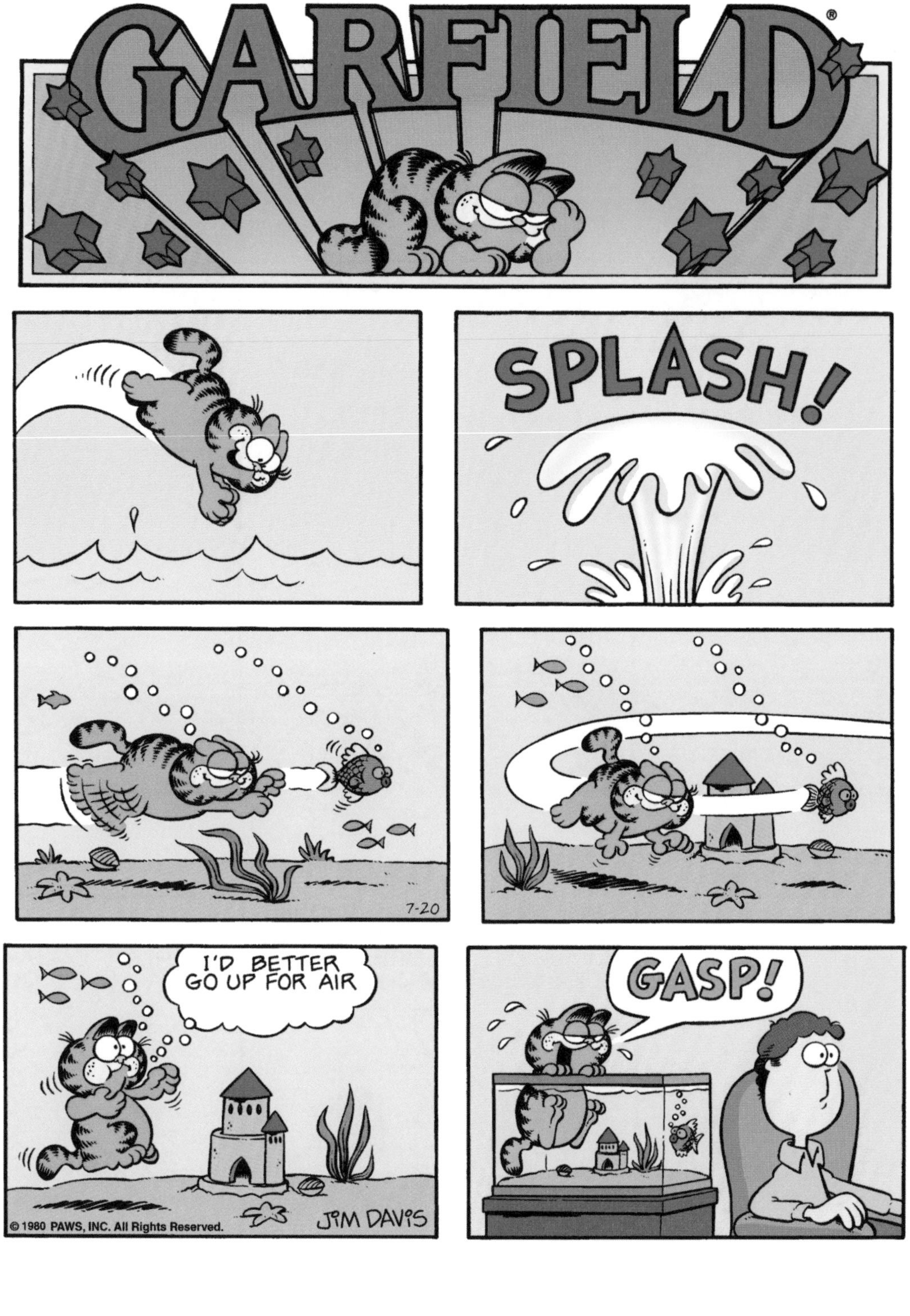
GARFIELD
SPLASH!
7-20
I'D BETTER GO UP FOR AIR
GASP!
© 1980 PAWS, INC. All Rights Reserved.
JIM DAVIS

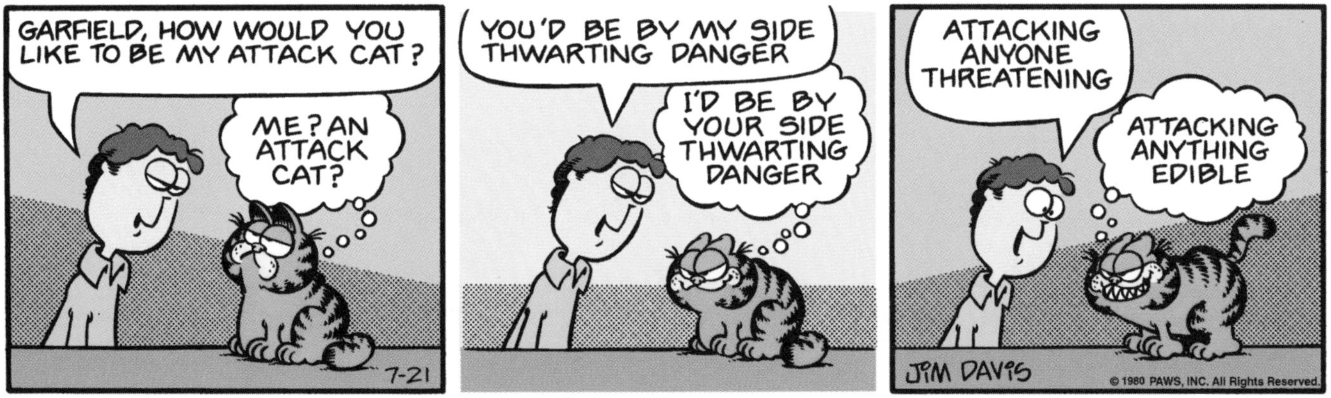
GARFIELD, HOW WOULD YOU LIKE TO BE MY ATTACK CAT?
ME? AN ATTACK CAT?
7-21
YOU'D BE BY MY SIDE THWARTING DANGER
I'D BE BY YOUR SIDE THWARTING DANGER
ATTACKING ANYONE THREATENING
ATTACKING ANYTHING EDIBLE
JIM DAVIS
© 1980 PAWS, INC. All Rights Reserved.

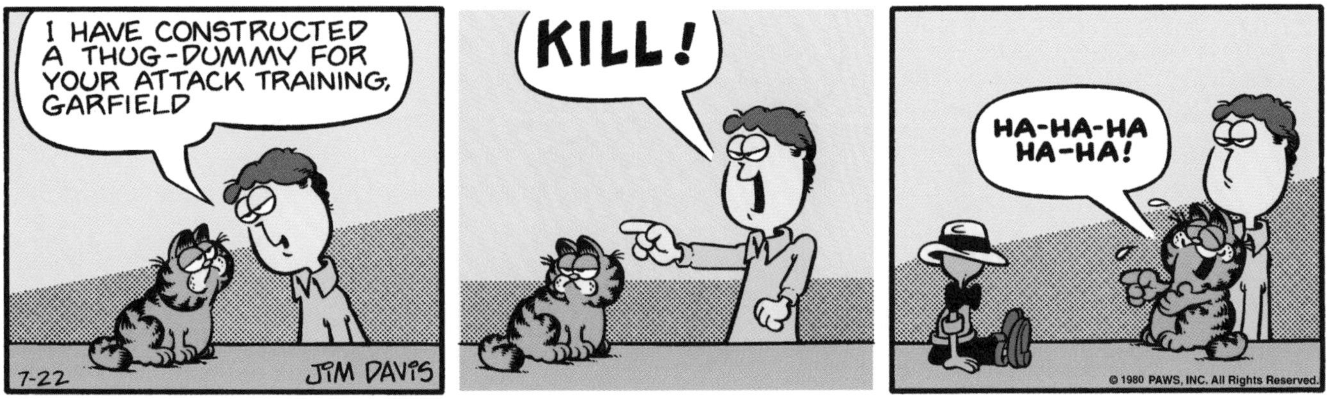
I HAVE CONSTRUCTED A THUG-DUMMY FOR YOUR ATTACK TRAINING, GARFIELD
7-22
JIM DAVIS
KILL!
HA-HA-HA HA-HA!
© 1980 PAWS, INC. All Rights Reserved.

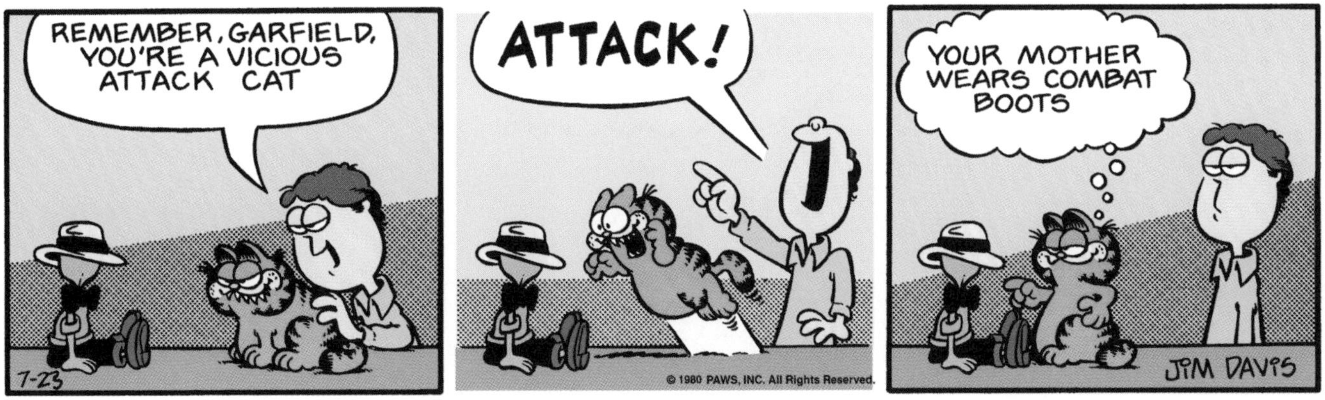
REMEMBER, GARFIELD, YOU'RE A VICIOUS ATTACK CAT
7-23
ATTACK!
© 1980 PAWS, INC. All Rights Reserved.
YOUR MOTHER WEARS COMBAT BOOTS
JIM DAVIS

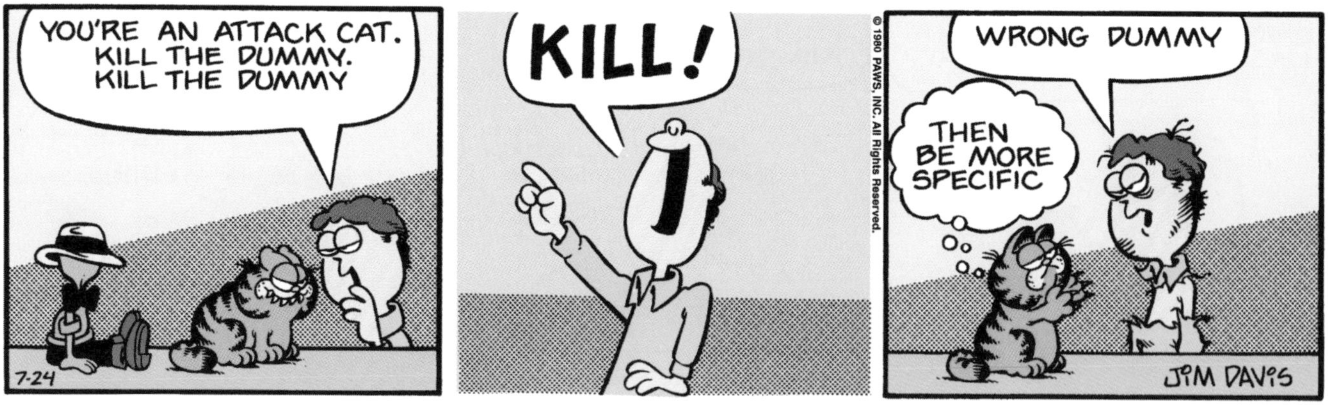
YOU'RE AN ATTACK CAT. KILL THE DUMMY. KILL THE DUMMY
7-24
KILL!
© 1980 PAWS, INC. All Rights Reserved.
WRONG DUMMY
THEN BE MORE SPECIFIC
JIM DAVIS

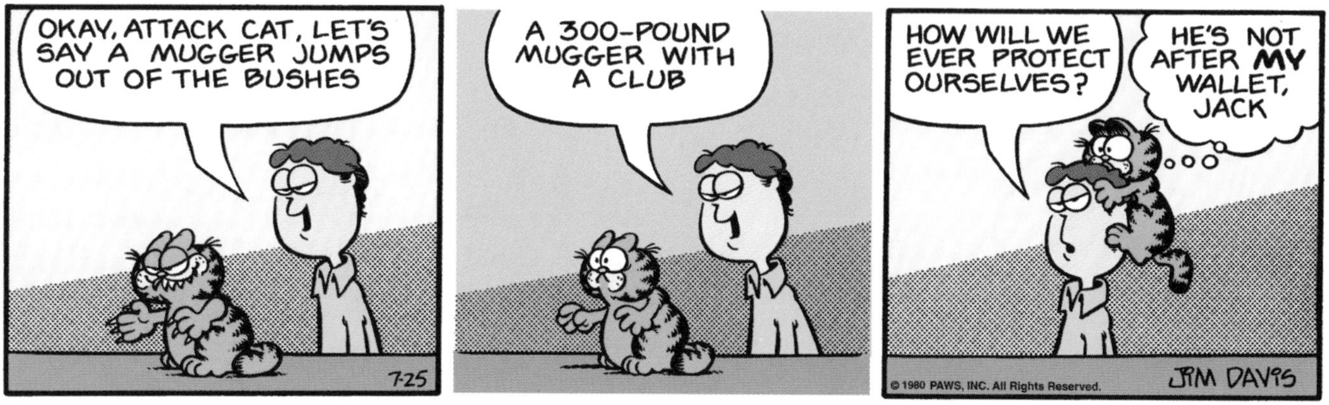
OKAY, ATTACK CAT, LET'S SAY A MUGGER JUMPS OUT OF THE BUSHES
7-25
A 300-POUND MUGGER WITH A CLUB
HOW WILL WE EVER PROTECT OURSELVES?
HE'S NOT AFTER **MY** WALLET, JACK
© 1980 PAWS, INC. All Rights Reserved.
JIM DAVIS

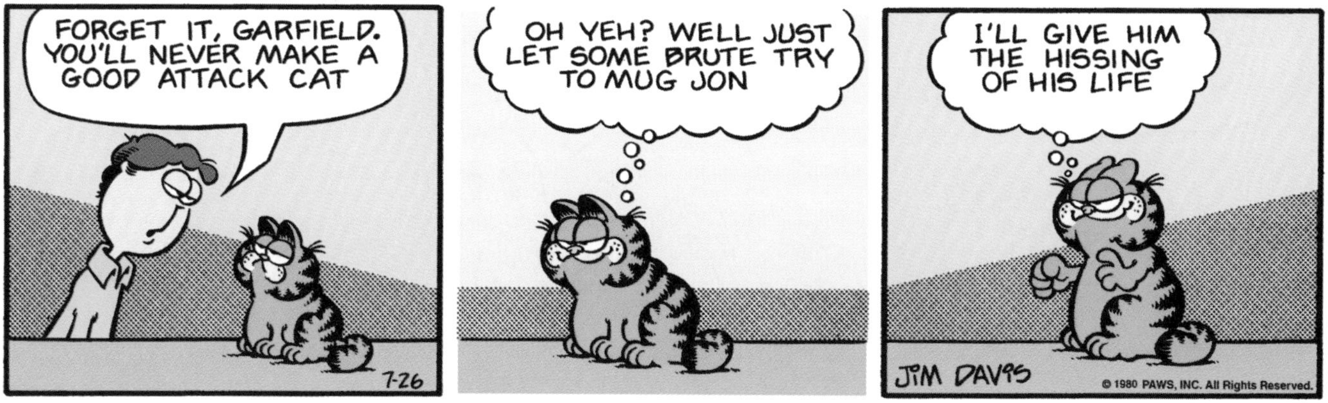
FORGET IT, GARFIELD. YOU'LL NEVER MAKE A GOOD ATTACK CAT
7-26
OH YEH? WELL JUST LET SOME BRUTE TRY TO MUG JON
I'LL GIVE HIM THE HISSING OF HIS LIFE
JIM DAVIS
© 1980 PAWS, INC. All Rights Reserved.

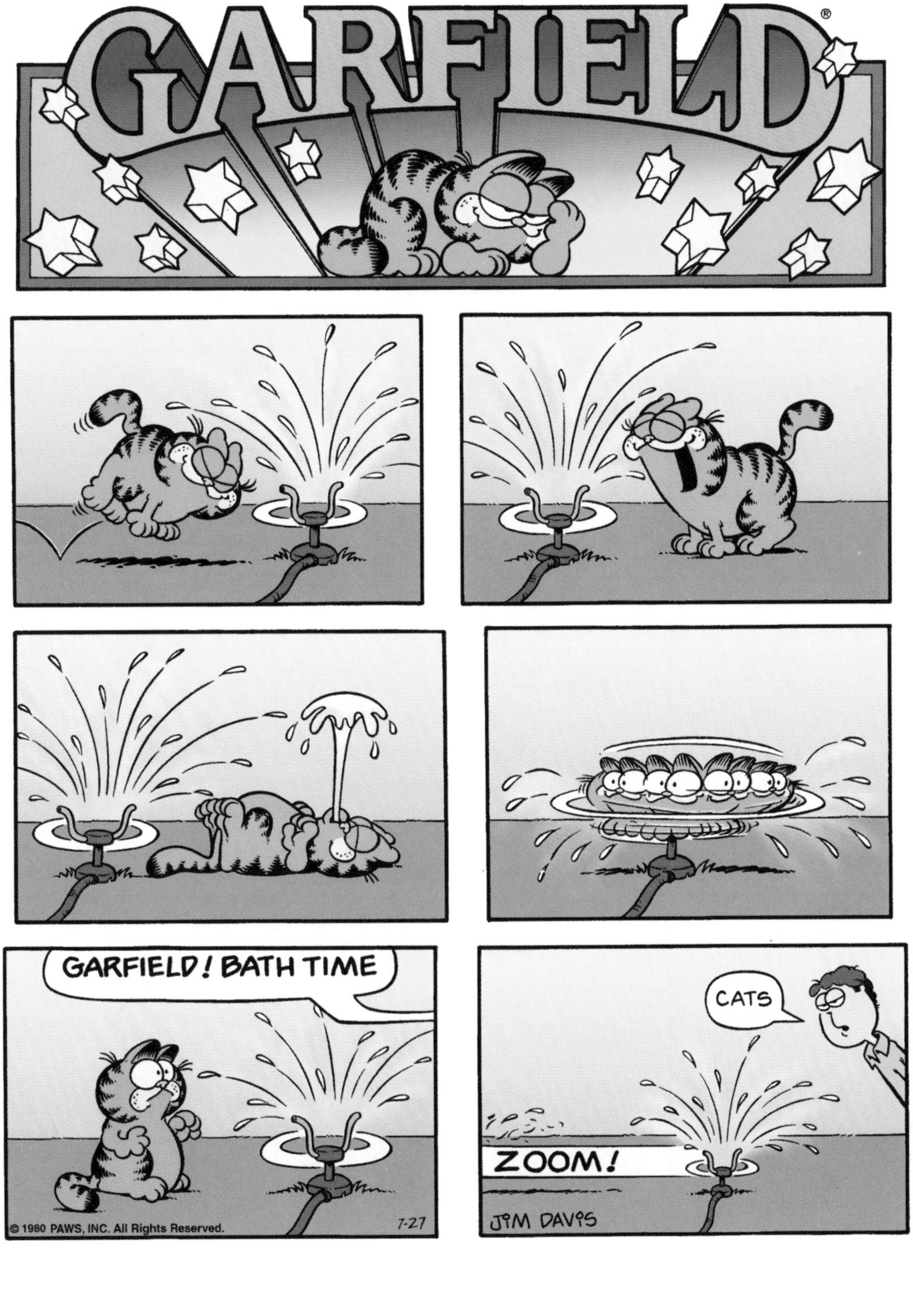
GARFIELD
GARFIELD! BATH TIME
CATS
ZOOM!
© 1980 PAWS, INC. All Rights Reserved.
7-27
JIM DAVIS

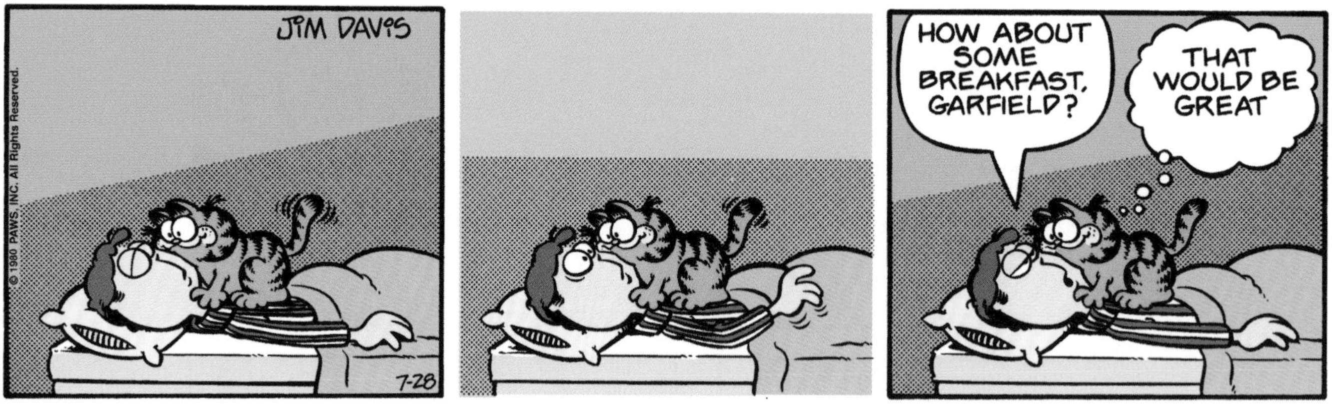
JIM DAVIS
© 1980 PAWS, INC. All Rights Reserved.
7-28
HOW ABOUT SOME BREAKFAST, GARFIELD?
THAT WOULD BE GREAT

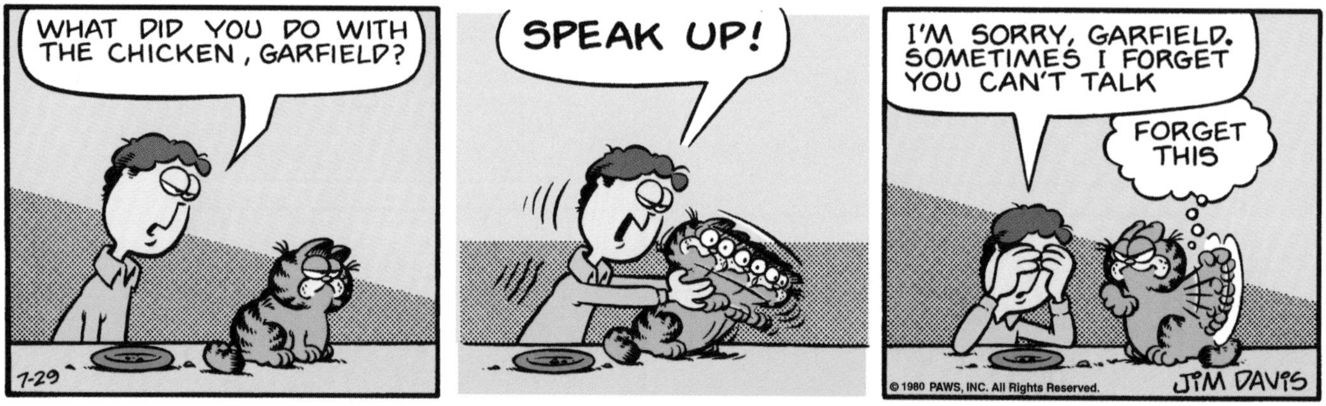
WHAT DID YOU DO WITH THE CHICKEN, GARFIELD?
7-29
SPEAK UP!
I'M SORRY, GARFIELD. SOMETIMES I FORGET YOU CAN'T TALK
FORGET THIS
© 1980 PAWS, INC. All Rights Reserved.
JIM DAVIS

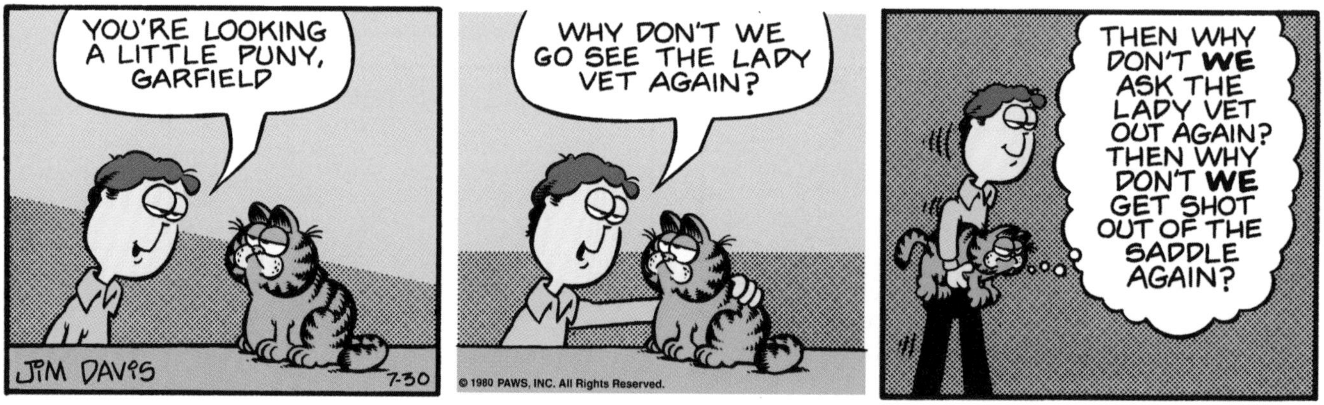
YOU'RE LOOKING A LITTLE PUNY, GARFIELD
JIM DAVIS
7-30
WHY DON'T WE GO SEE THE LADY VET AGAIN?
© 1980 PAWS, INC. All Rights Reserved.
THEN WHY DON'T **WE** ASK THE LADY VET OUT AGAIN? THEN WHY DON'T **WE** GET SHOT OUT OF THE SADDLE AGAIN?

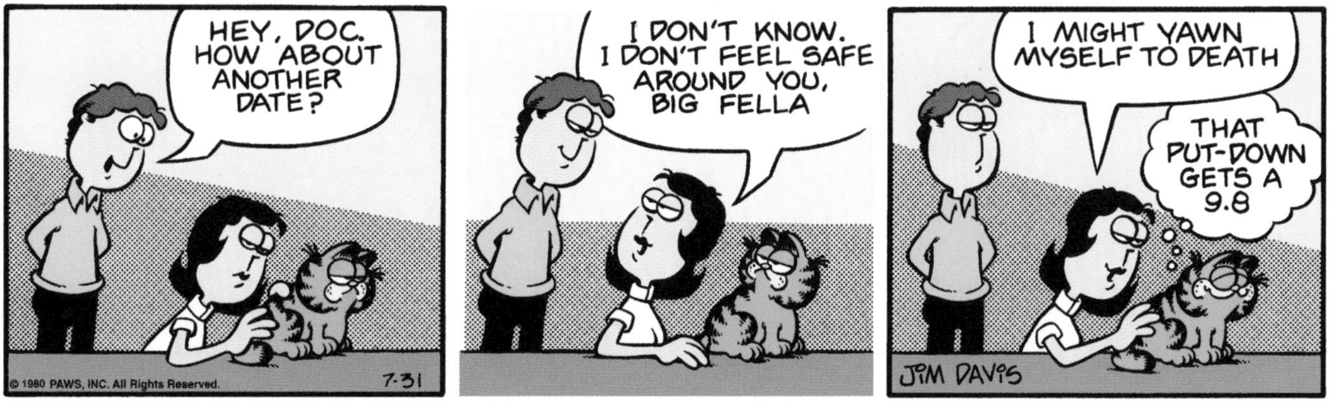
HEY, DOC. HOW ABOUT ANOTHER DATE?
I DON'T KNOW. I DON'T FEEL SAFE AROUND YOU, BIG FELLA
I MIGHT YAWN MYSELF TO DEATH
THAT PUT-DOWN GETS A 9.8
© 1980 PAWS, INC. All Rights Reserved.
7-31
JIM DAVIS

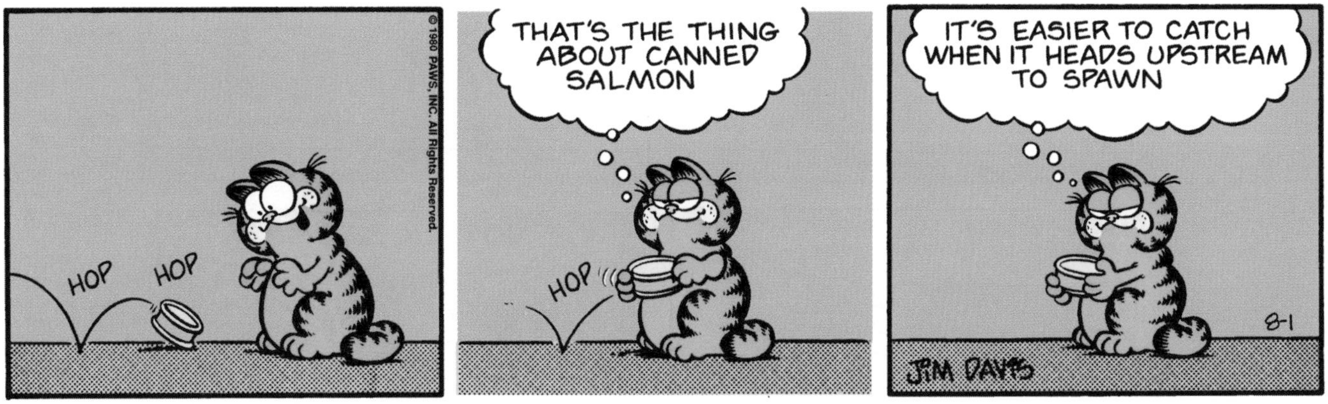
© 1980 PAWS, INC. All Rights Reserved.
HOP
HOP
HOP
THAT'S THE THING ABOUT CANNED SALMON
IT'S EASIER TO CATCH WHEN IT HEADS UPSTREAM TO SPAWN
8-1
JIM DAVIS

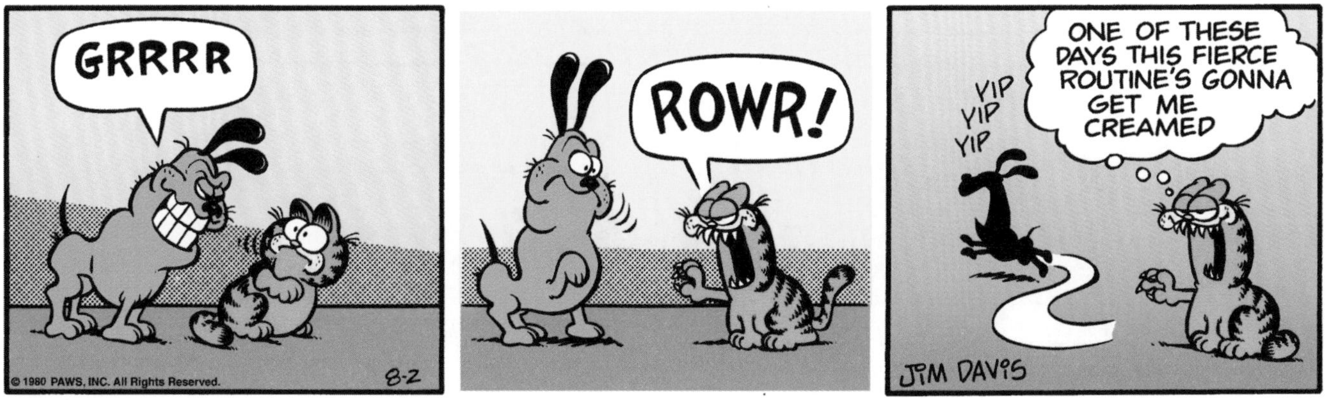
GRRRR
© 1980 PAWS, INC. All Rights Reserved.
8-2
ROWR!
YIP
YIP
YIP
ONE OF THESE DAYS THIS FIERCE ROUTINE'S GONNA GET ME CREAMED
JIM DAVIS

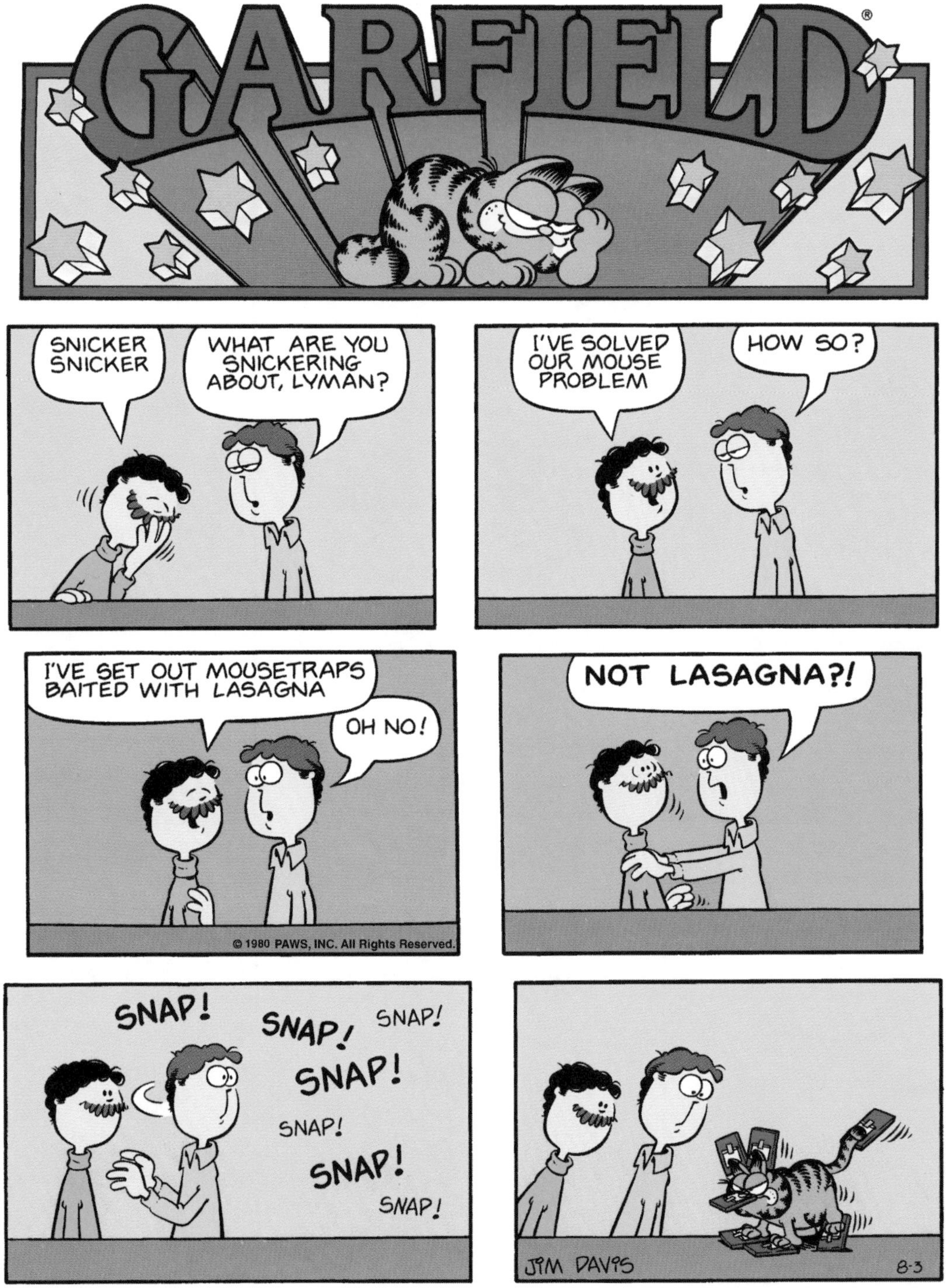
GARFIELD
SNICKER SNICKER
WHAT ARE YOU SNICKERING ABOUT, LYMAN?
I'VE SOLVED OUR MOUSE PROBLEM
HOW SO?
I'VE SET OUT MOUSETRAPS BAITED WITH LASAGNA
OH NO!
© 1980 PAWS, INC. All Rights Reserved.
NOT LASAGNA?!
SNAP! SNAP! SNAP! SNAP! SNAP! SNAP! SNAP!
JIM DAVIS
8-3

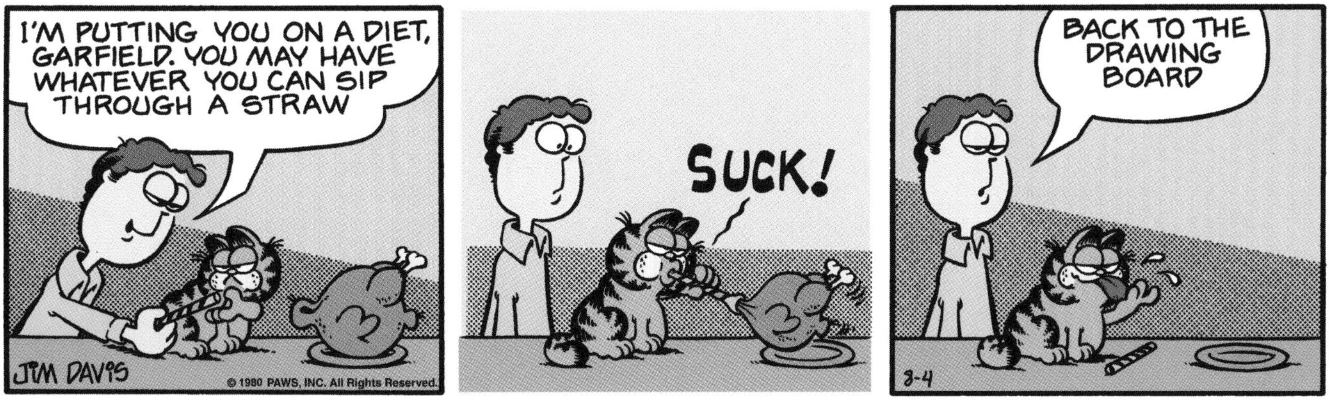
I'M PUTTING YOU ON A DIET, GARFIELD. YOU MAY HAVE WHATEVER YOU CAN SIP THROUGH A STRAW
JIM DAVIS
© 1980 PAWS, INC. All Rights Reserved.
SUCK!
BACK TO THE DRAWING BOARD
8-4

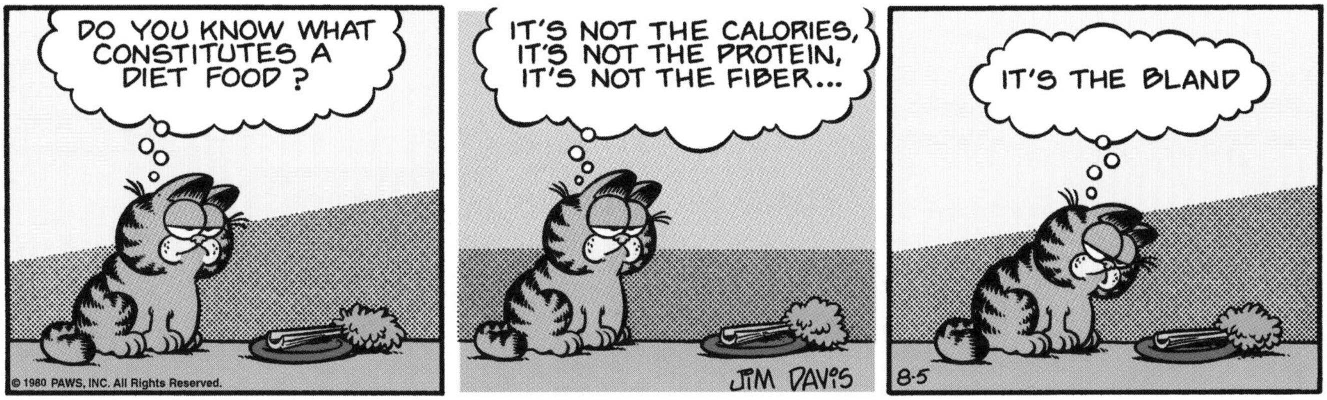
DO YOU KNOW WHAT CONSTITUTES A DIET FOOD ?
© 1980 PAWS, INC. All Rights Reserved.
IT'S NOT THE CALORIES, IT'S NOT THE PROTEIN, IT'S NOT THE FIBER...
JIM DAVIS
IT'S THE BLAND
8-5

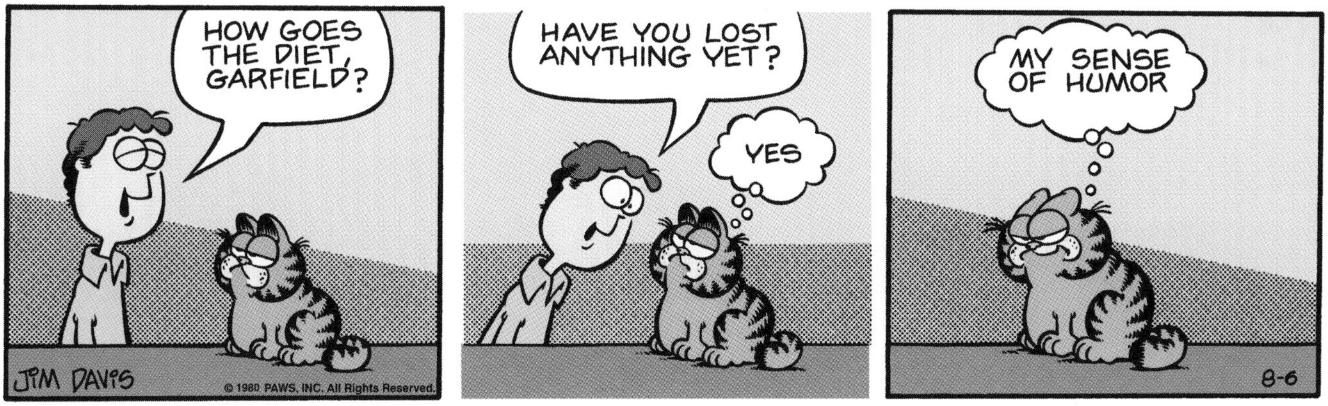
HOW GOES THE DIET, GARFIELD?
JIM DAVIS
© 1980 PAWS, INC. All Rights Reserved.
HAVE YOU LOST ANYTHING YET?
YES
MY SENSE OF HUMOR
8-6

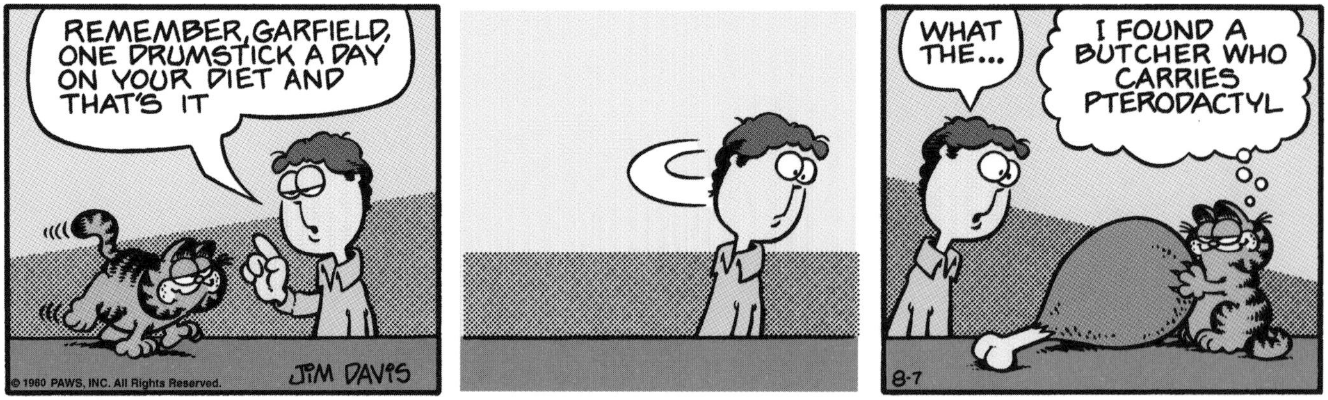
REMEMBER, GARFIELD, ONE DRUMSTICK A DAY ON YOUR DIET AND THAT'S IT
© 1980 PAWS, INC. All Rights Reserved.
JIM DAVIS
WHAT THE...
I FOUND A BUTCHER WHO CARRIES PTERODACTYL
8-7

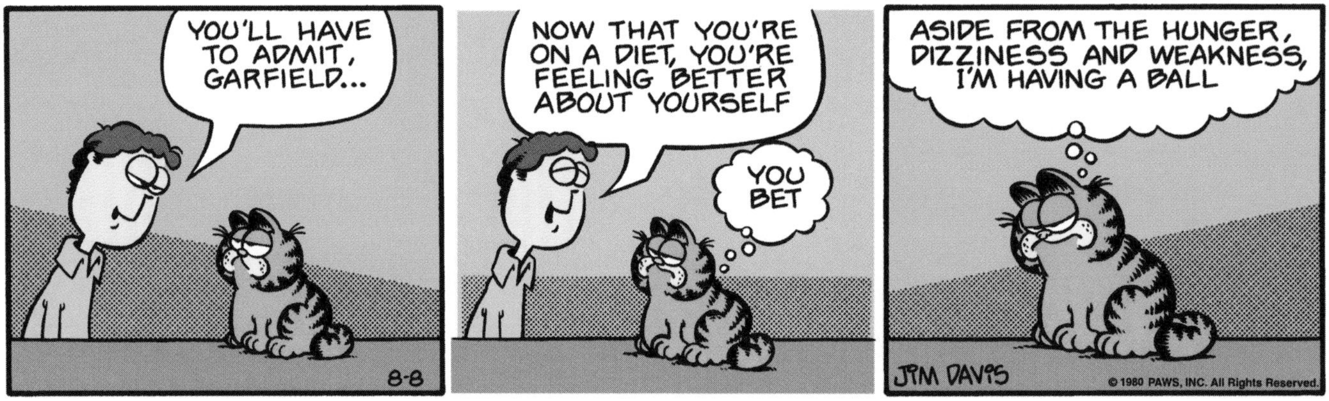
YOU'LL HAVE TO ADMIT, GARFIELD...
8-8
NOW THAT YOU'RE ON A DIET, YOU'RE FEELING BETTER ABOUT YOURSELF
YOU BET
ASIDE FROM THE HUNGER, DIZZINESS AND WEAKNESS, I'M HAVING A BALL
JIM DAVIS
© 1980 PAWS, INC. All Rights Reserved.

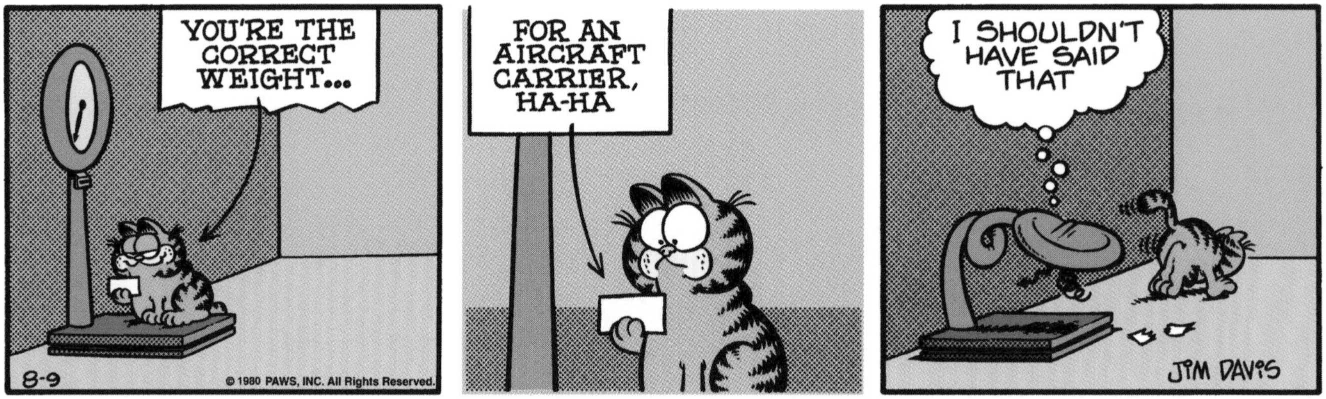
YOU'RE THE CORRECT WEIGHT...
8-9
© 1980 PAWS, INC. All Rights Reserved.
FOR AN AIRCRAFT CARRIER, HA-HA
I SHOULDN'T HAVE SAID THAT
JIM DAVIS

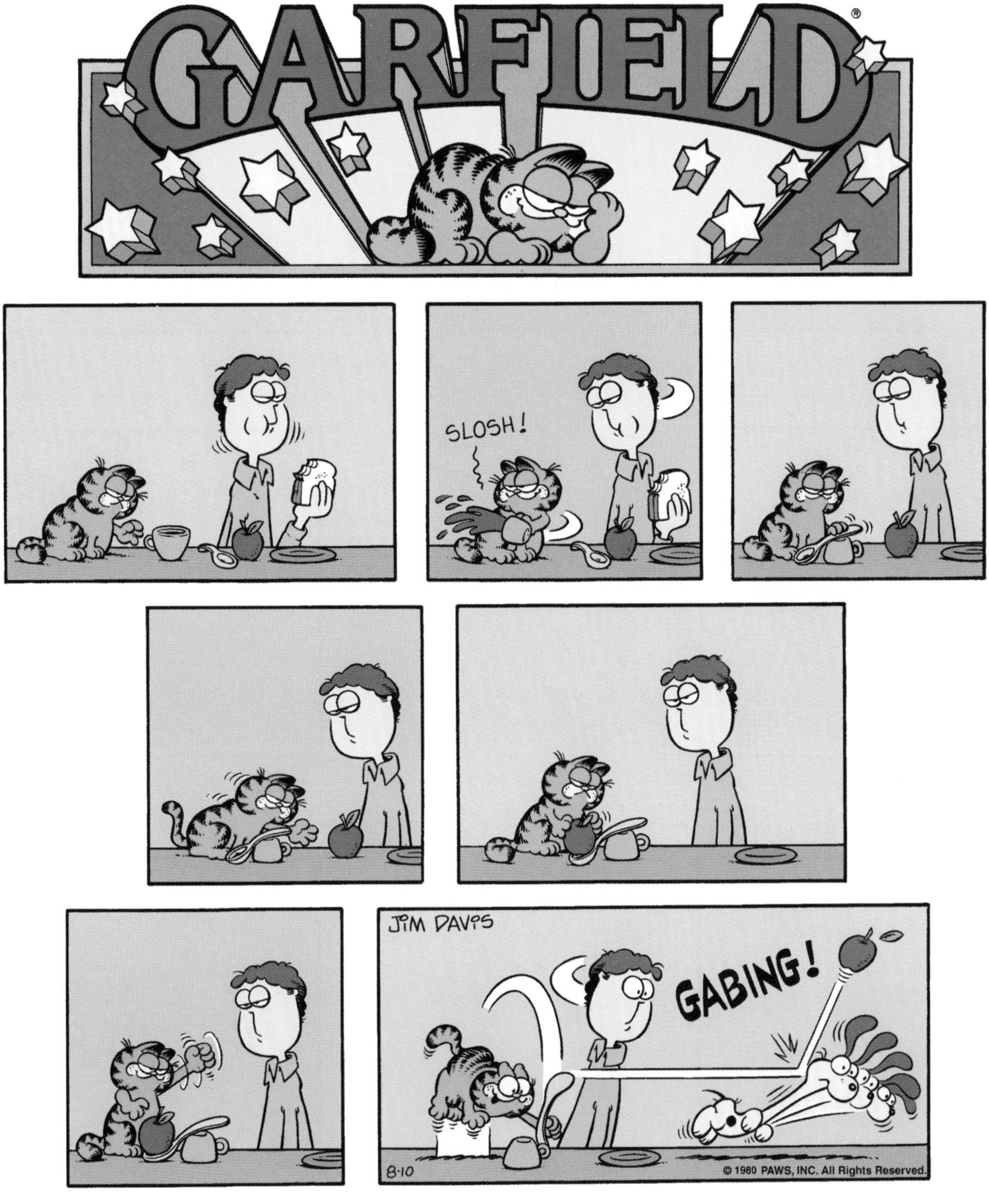
GARFIELD
SLOSH!
JIM DAVIS
GABING!
8-10
© 1980 PAWS, INC. All Rights Reserved.

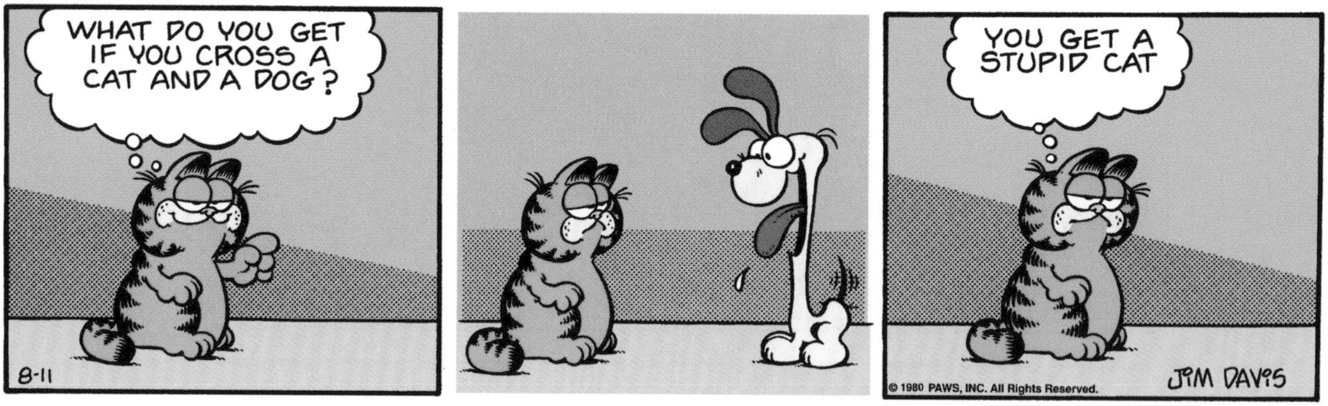
WHAT DO YOU GET IF YOU CROSS A CAT AND A DOG?
8-11
YOU GET A STUPID CAT
© 1980 PAWS, INC. All Rights Reserved.
JIM DAVIS

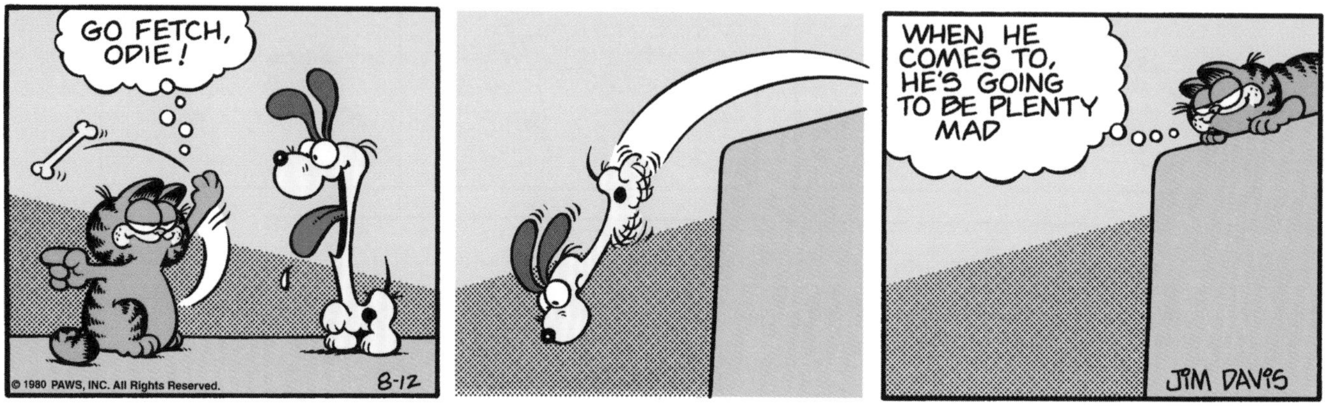
GO FETCH, ODIE!
© 1980 PAWS, INC. All Rights Reserved.
8-12
WHEN HE COMES TO, HE'S GOING TO BE PLENTY MAD
JIM DAVIS

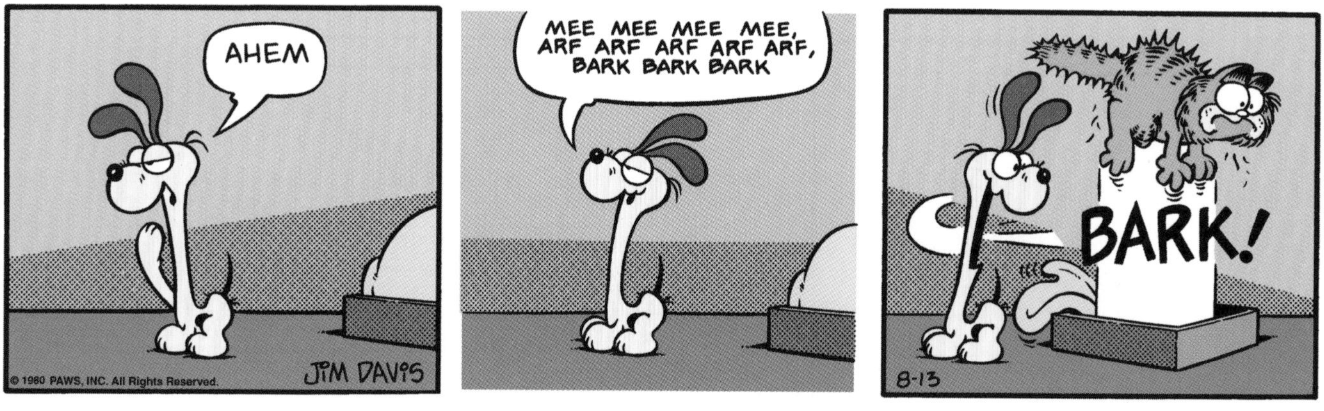
AHEM
© 1980 PAWS, INC. All Rights Reserved.
JIM DAVIS
MEE MEE MEE MEE, ARF ARF ARF ARF ARF, BARK BARK BARK
BARK!
8-13

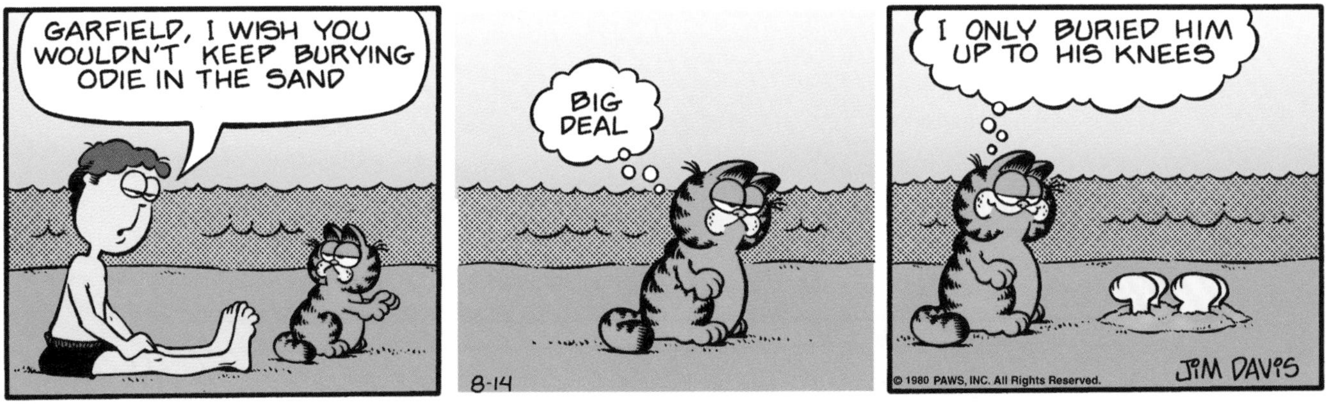
GARFIELD, I WISH YOU WOULDN'T KEEP BURYING ODIE IN THE SAND
BIG DEAL
8-14
I ONLY BURIED HIM UP TO HIS KNEES
© 1980 PAWS, INC. All Rights Reserved.
JIM DAVIS

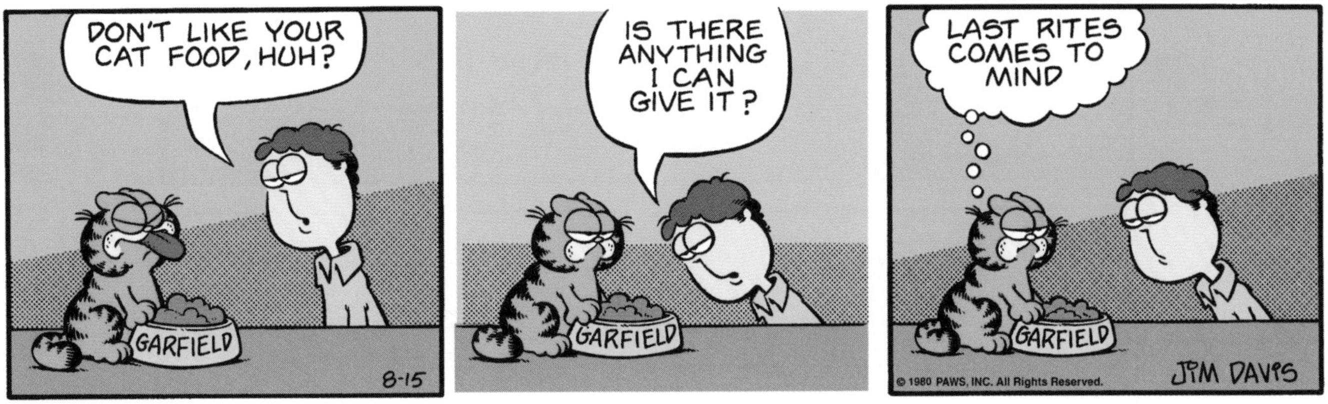
DON'T LIKE YOUR CAT FOOD, HUH?
GARFIELD
8-15
IS THERE ANYTHING I CAN GIVE IT?
GARFIELD
LAST RITES COMES TO MIND
GARFIELD
© 1980 PAWS, INC. All Rights Reserved.
JIM DAVIS

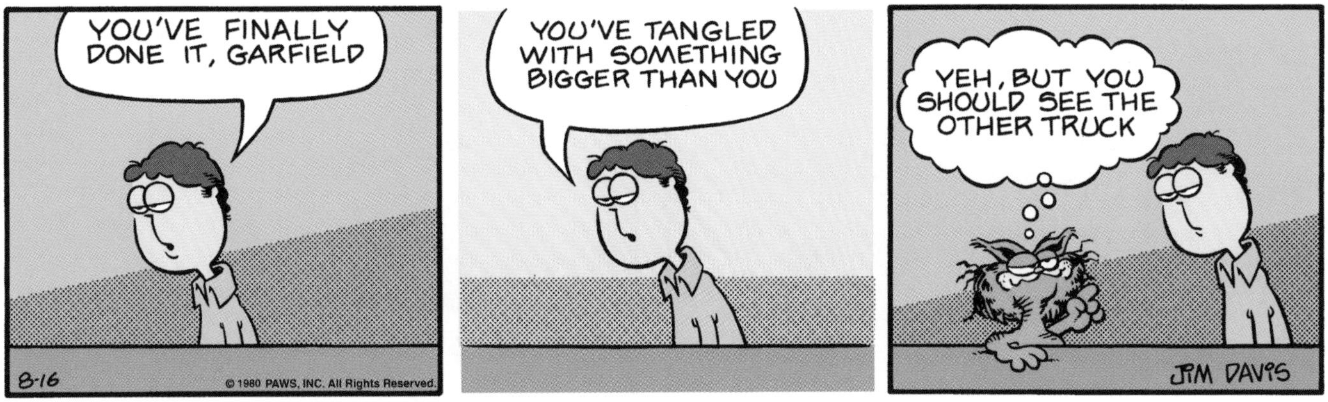
YOU'VE FINALLY DONE IT, GARFIELD
8-16
© 1980 PAWS, INC. All Rights Reserved.
YOU'VE TANGLED WITH SOMETHING BIGGER THAN YOU
YEH, BUT YOU SHOULD SEE THE OTHER TRUCK
JIM DAVIS

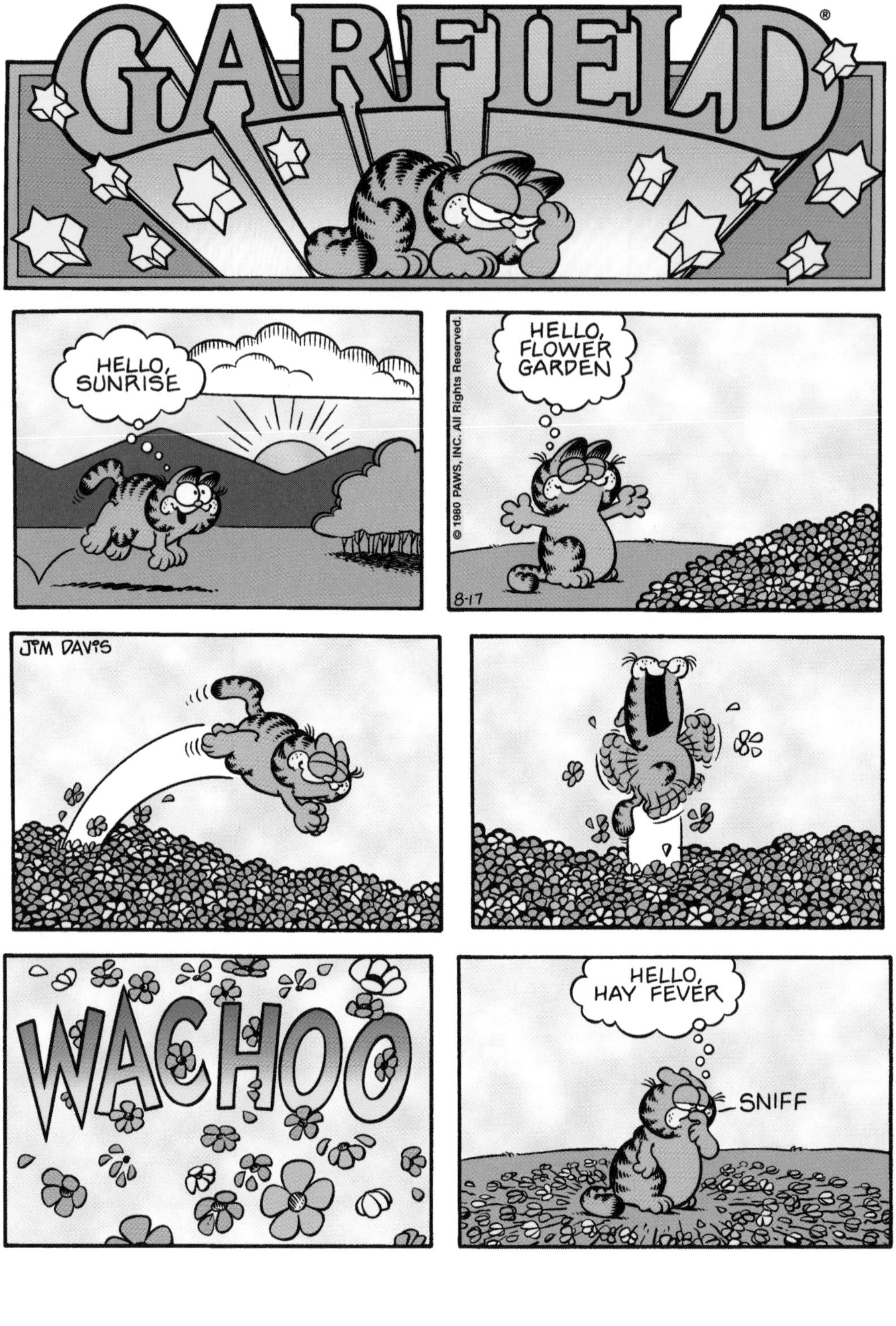
GARFIELD®
HELLO, SUNRISE
© 1980 PAWS, INC. All Rights Reserved.
HELLO, FLOWER GARDEN
8-17
JIM DAVIS
WACHOO
HELLO, HAY FEVER
SNIFF

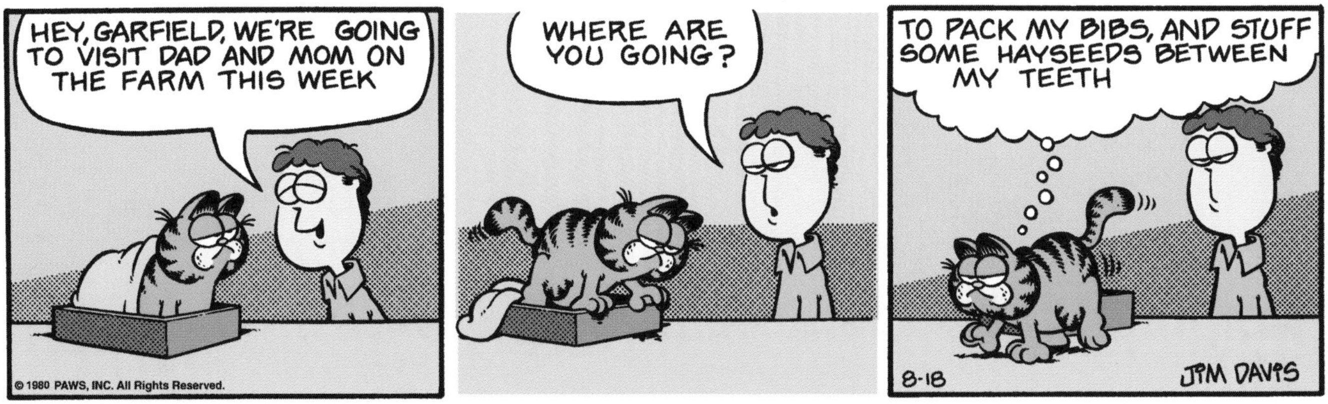
HEY, GARFIELD, WE'RE GOING TO VISIT DAD AND MOM ON THE FARM THIS WEEK
© 1980 PAWS, INC. All Rights Reserved.
WHERE ARE YOU GOING?
TO PACK MY BIBS, AND STUFF SOME HAYSEEDS BETWEEN MY TEETH
8-18
JIM DAVIS

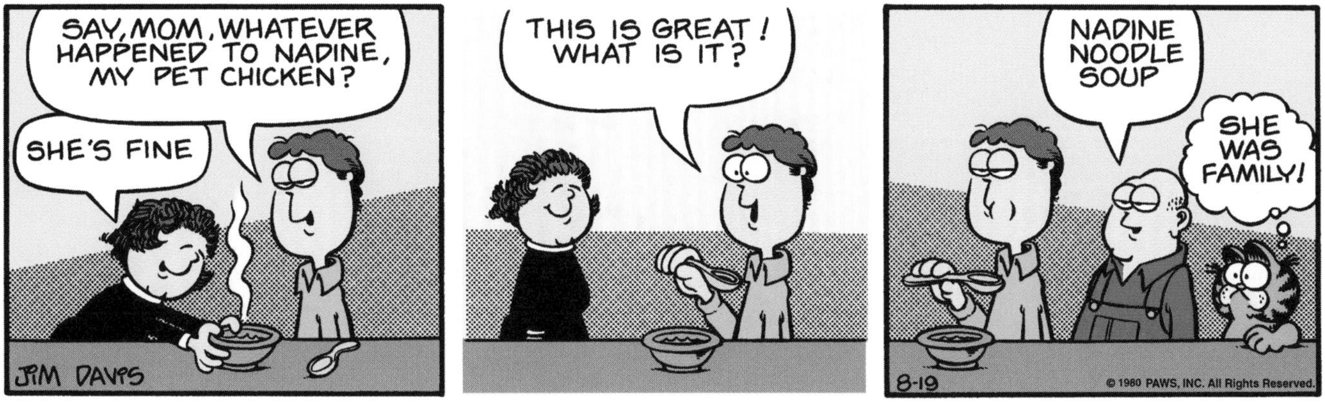
SAY, MOM, WHATEVER HAPPENED TO NADINE, MY PET CHICKEN?
SHE'S FINE
JIM DAVIS
THIS IS GREAT! WHAT IS IT?
NADINE NOODLE SOUP
SHE WAS FAMILY!
8-19
© 1980 PAWS, INC. All Rights Reserved.

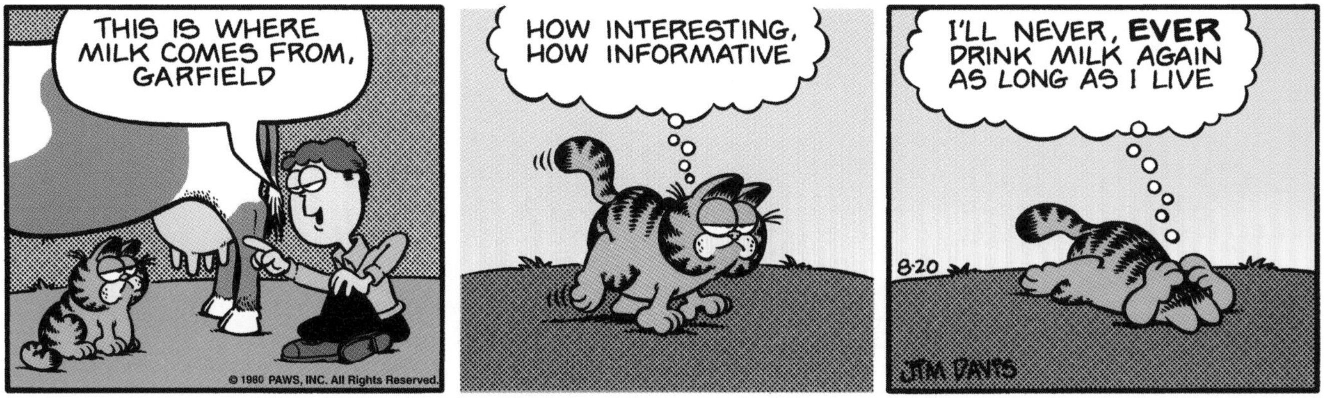
THIS IS WHERE MILK COMES FROM, GARFIELD
© 1980 PAWS, INC. All Rights Reserved.
HOW INTERESTING, HOW INFORMATIVE
I'LL NEVER, **EVER** DRINK MILK AGAIN AS LONG AS I LIVE
8-20
JIM DAVIS

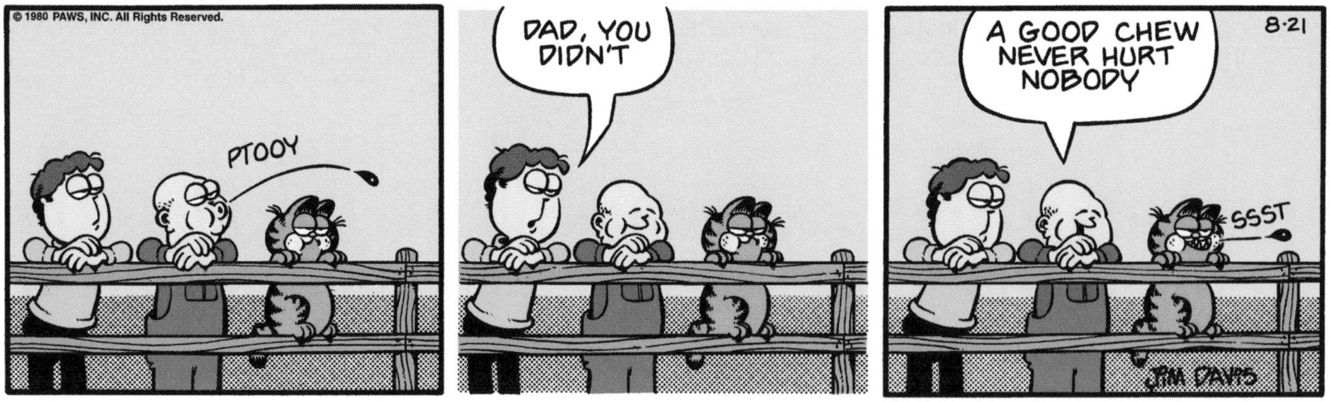
© 1980 PAWS, INC. All Rights Reserved.
PTOOY
DAD, YOU DIDN'T
8-21
A GOOD CHEW NEVER HURT NOBODY
SSST
JIM DAVIS

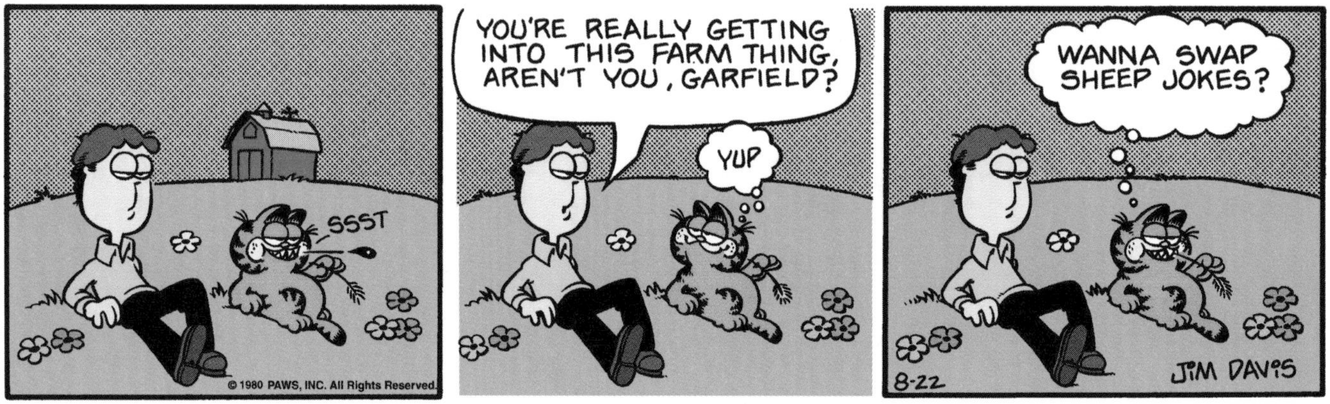
SSST
© 1980 PAWS, INC. All Rights Reserved.
YOU'RE REALLY GETTING INTO THIS FARM THING, AREN'T YOU, GARFIELD?
YUP
WANNA SWAP SHEEP JOKES?
8-22
JIM DAVIS

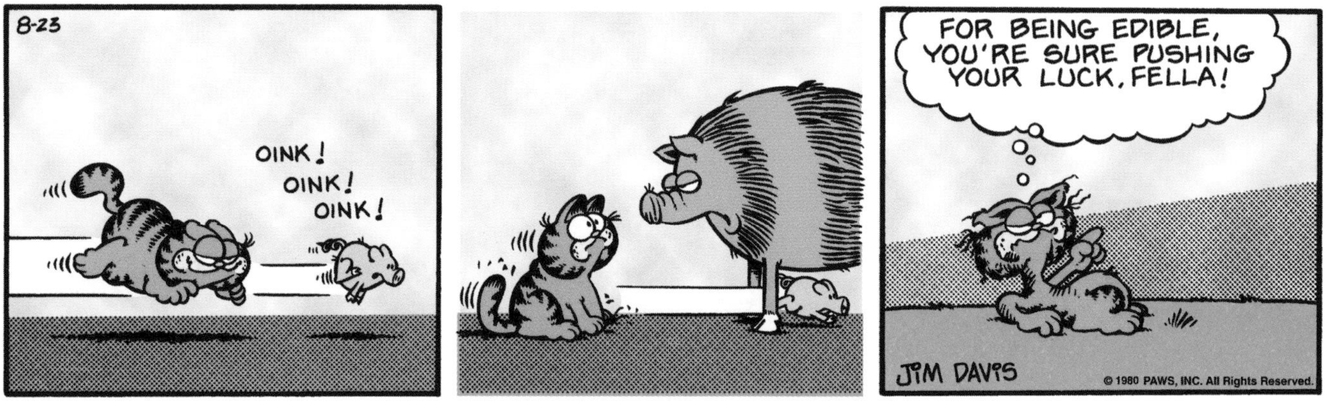
8-23
OINK!
OINK!
OINK!
FOR BEING EDIBLE, YOU'RE SURE PUSHING YOUR LUCK, FELLA!
JIM DAVIS
© 1980 PAWS, INC. All Rights Reserved.

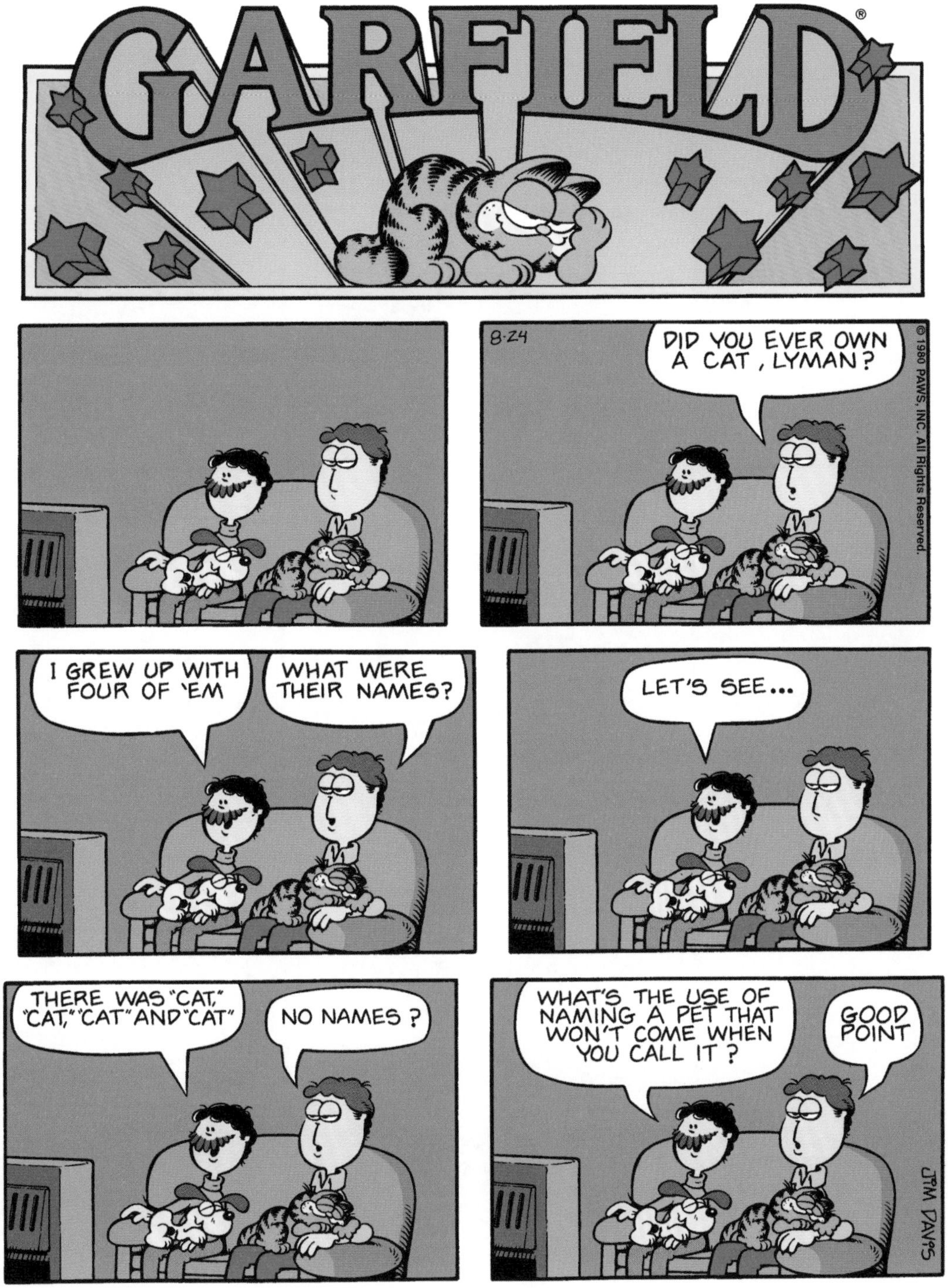
GARFIELD®
8-24
DID YOU EVER OWN A CAT, LYMAN?
© 1980 PAWS, INC. All Rights Reserved.
I GREW UP WITH FOUR OF 'EM
WHAT WERE THEIR NAMES?
LET'S SEE...
THERE WAS "CAT," "CAT," "CAT" AND "CAT"
NO NAMES?
WHAT'S THE USE OF NAMING A PET THAT WON'T COME WHEN YOU CALL IT?
GOOD POINT
JIM DAVIS

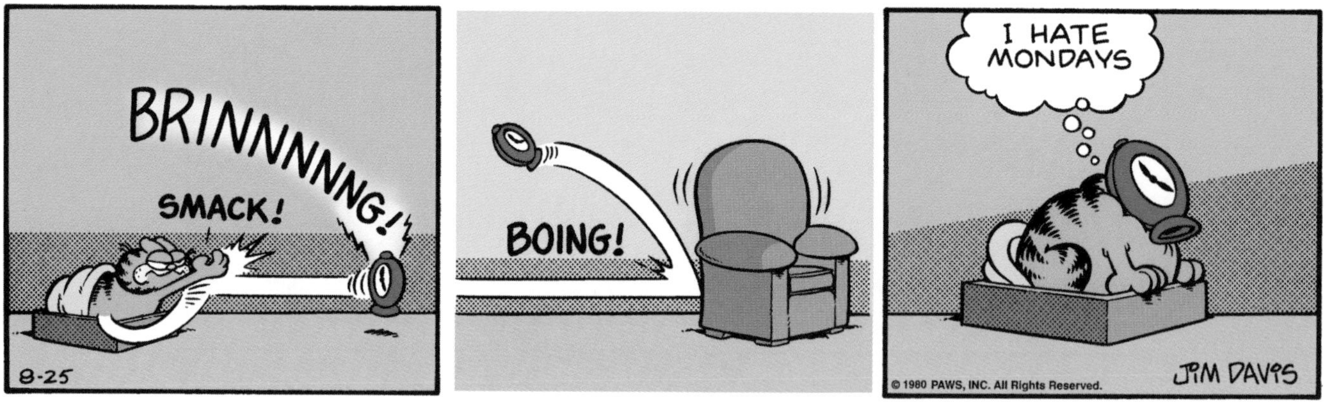
BRINNNNNNG!
SMACK!
8-25
BOING!
I HATE MONDAYS
© 1980 PAWS, INC. All Rights Reserved.
JIM DAVIS

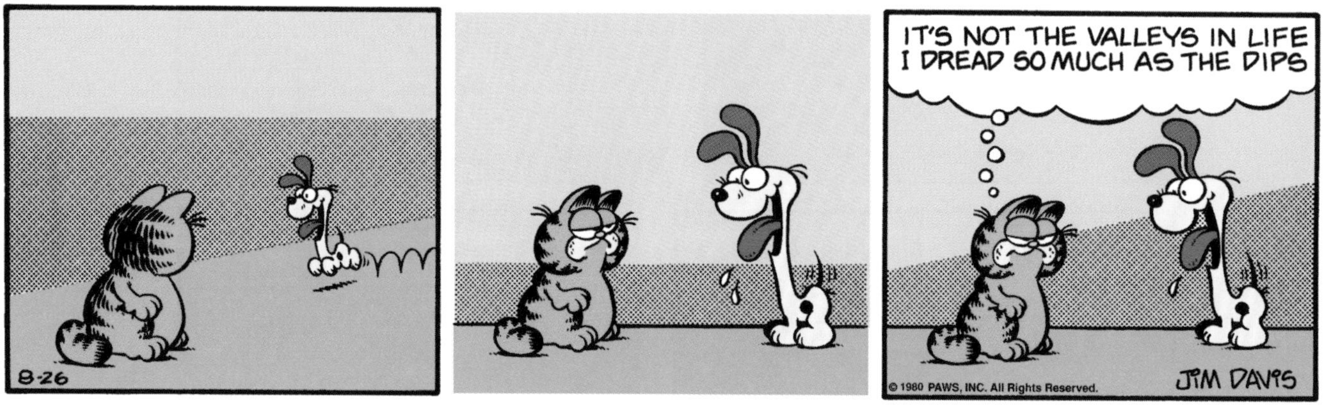
8-26
IT'S NOT THE VALLEYS IN LIFE I DREAD SO MUCH AS THE DIPS
© 1980 PAWS, INC. All Rights Reserved.
JIM DAVIS

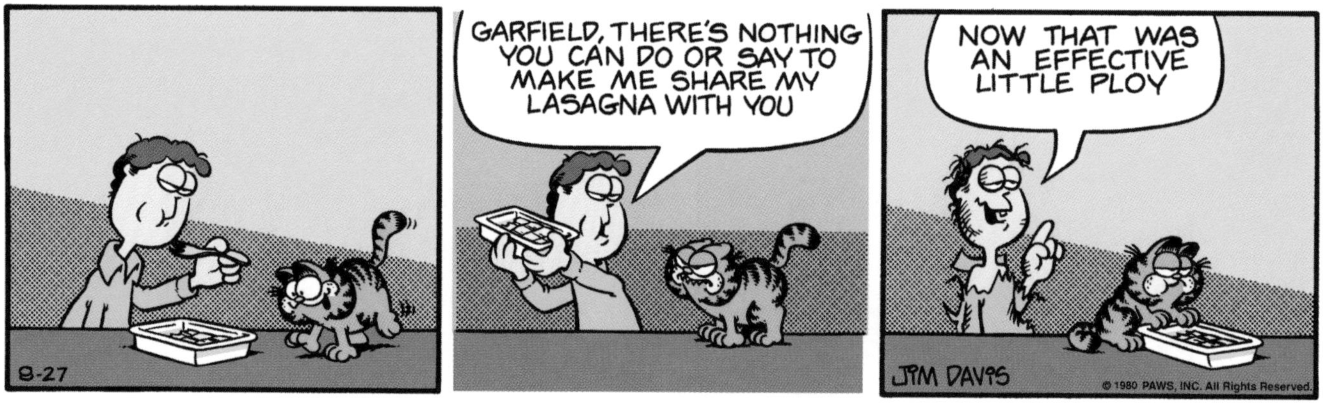
8-27
GARFIELD, THERE'S NOTHING YOU CAN DO OR SAY TO MAKE ME SHARE MY LASAGNA WITH YOU
NOW THAT WAS AN EFFECTIVE LITTLE PLOY
JIM DAVIS
© 1980 PAWS, INC. All Rights Reserved.

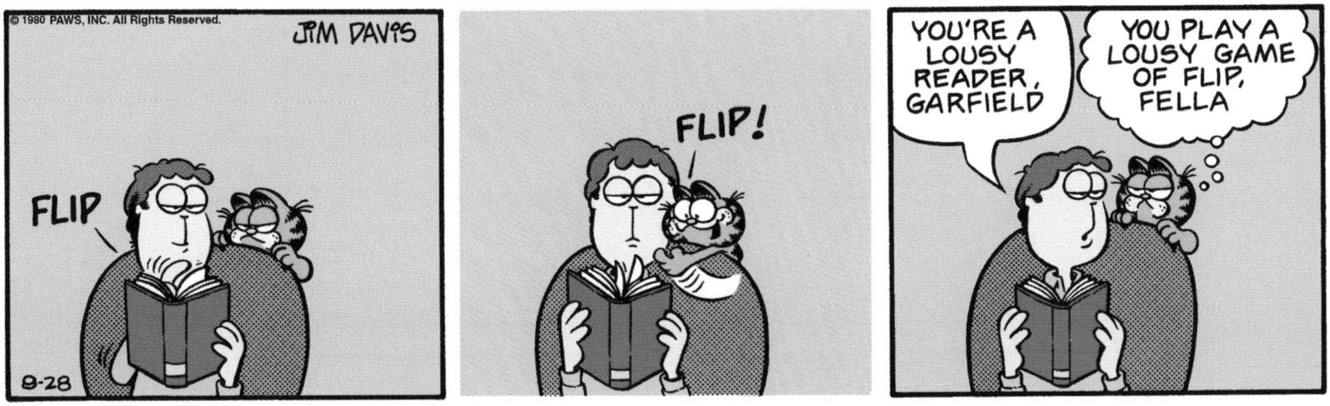
© 1980 PAWS, INC. All Rights Reserved.
JIM DAVIS
FLIP
8-28
FLIP!
YOU'RE A LOUSY READER, GARFIELD
YOU PLAY A LOUSY GAME OF FLIP, FELLA

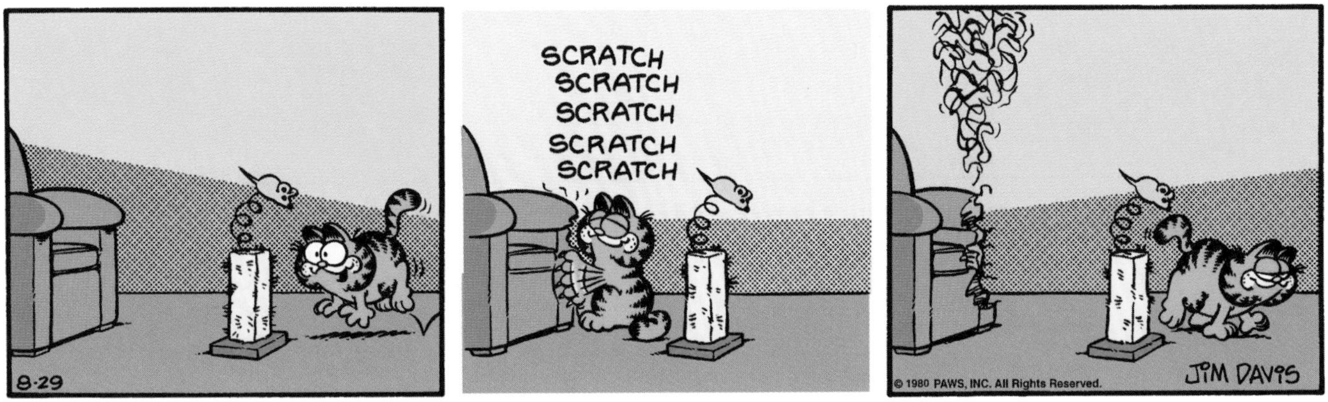
8-29
SCRATCH
SCRATCH
SCRATCH
SCRATCH
SCRATCH
© 1980 PAWS, INC. All Rights Reserved.
JIM DAVIS

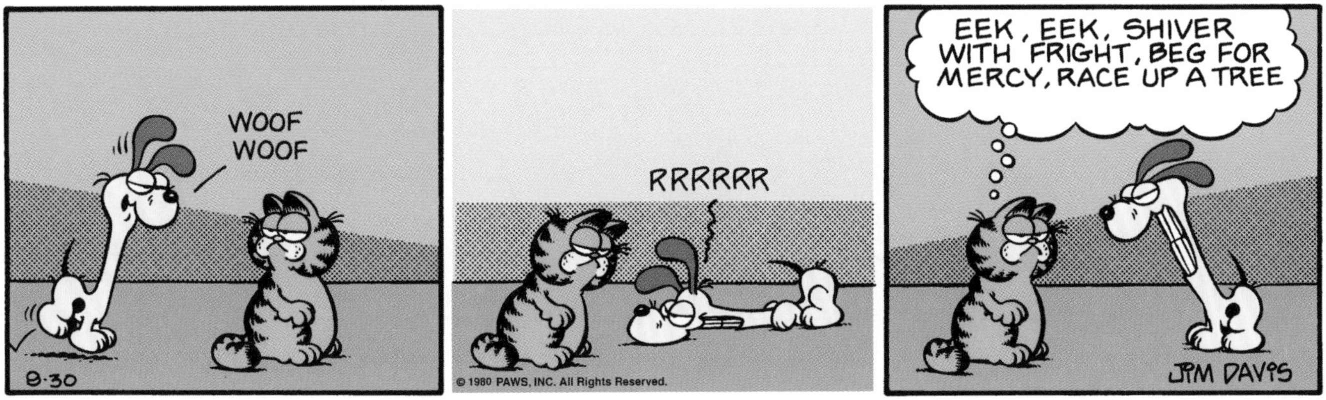
WOOF WOOF
8-30
RRRRRR
© 1980 PAWS, INC. All Rights Reserved.
EEK, EEK, SHIVER WITH FRIGHT, BEG FOR MERCY, RACE UP A TREE
JIM DAVIS

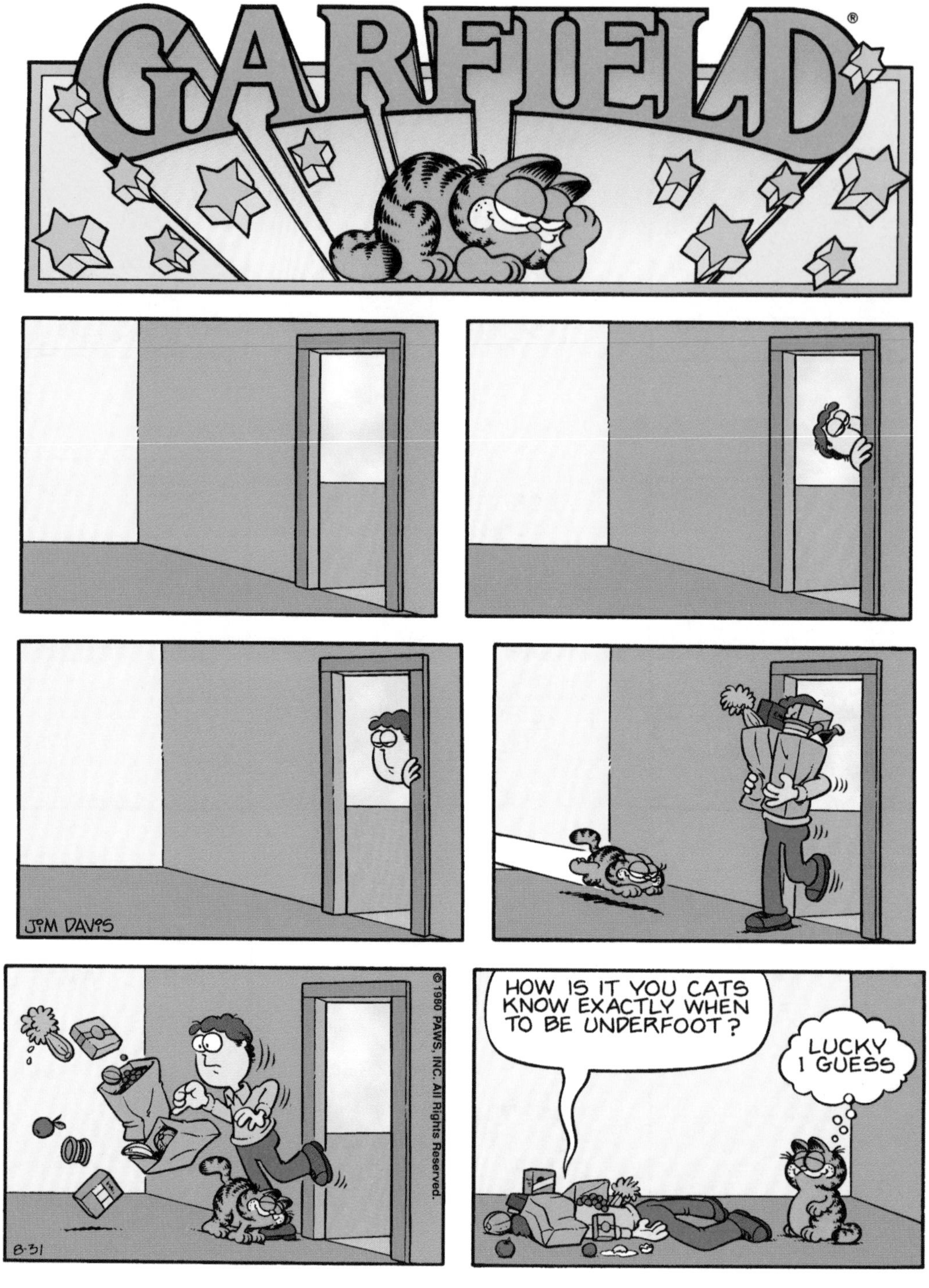
GARFIELD®
JIM DAVIS
© 1980 PAWS, INC. All Rights Reserved.
8-31
HOW IS IT YOU CATS KNOW EXACTLY WHEN TO BE UNDERFOOT?
LUCKY I GUESS

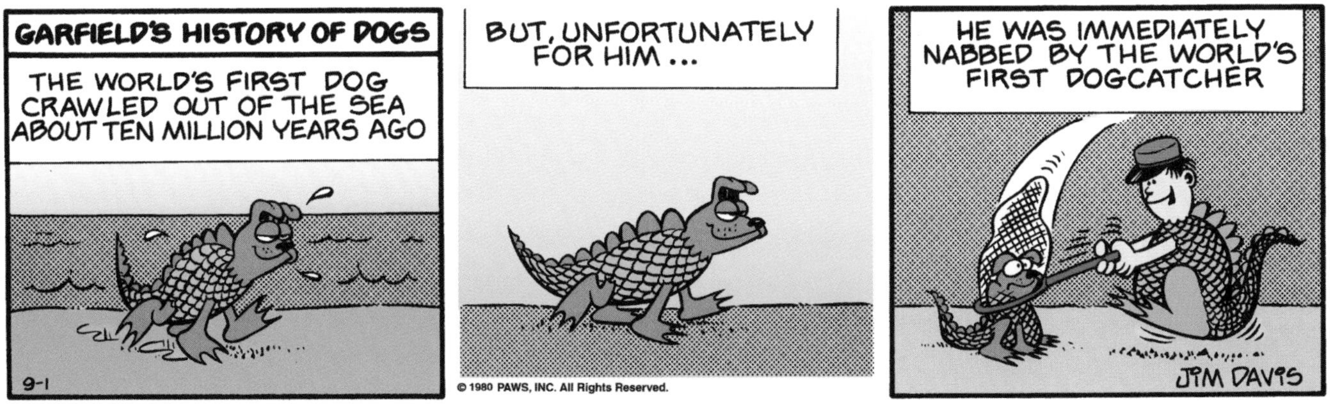
GARFIELD'S HISTORY OF DOGS
THE WORLD'S FIRST DOG CRAWLED OUT OF THE SEA ABOUT TEN MILLION YEARS AGO
9-1
BUT, UNFORTUNATELY FOR HIM ...
© 1980 PAWS, INC. All Rights Reserved.
HE WAS IMMEDIATELY NABBED BY THE WORLD'S FIRST DOGCATCHER
JIM DAVIS

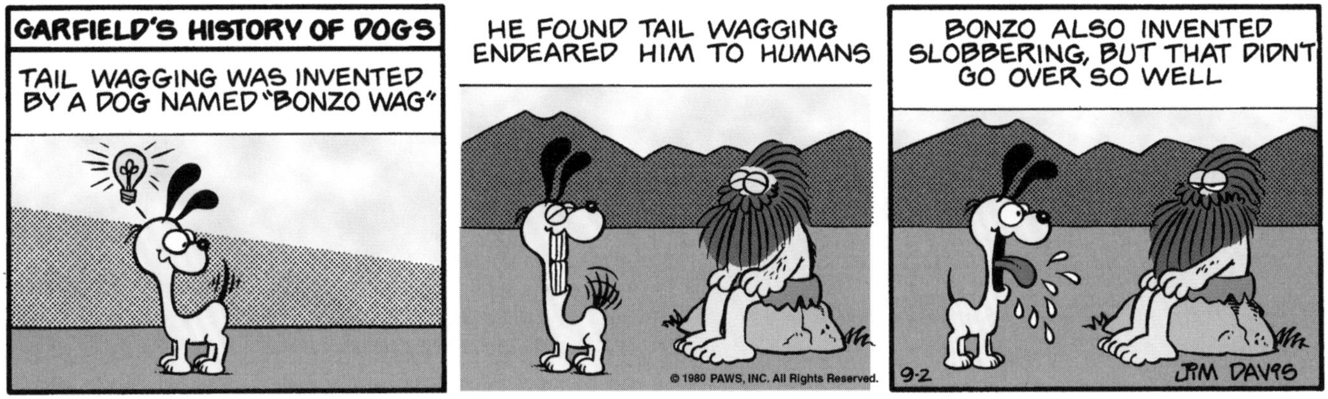
GARFIELD'S HISTORY OF DOGS
TAIL WAGGING WAS INVENTED BY A DOG NAMED "BONZO WAG"
HE FOUND TAIL WAGGING ENDEARED HIM TO HUMANS
© 1980 PAWS, INC. All Rights Reserved.
BONZO ALSO INVENTED SLOBBERING, BUT THAT DIDN'T GO OVER SO WELL
9-2
JIM DAVIS

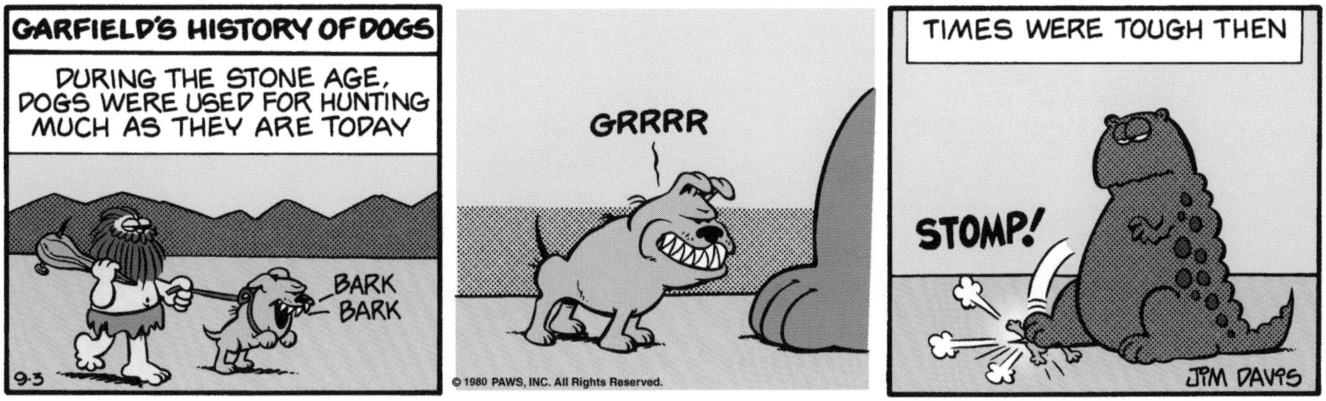
GARFIELD'S HISTORY OF DOGS
DURING THE STONE AGE, DOGS WERE USED FOR HUNTING MUCH AS THEY ARE TODAY
BARK
BARK
9-3
GRRRR
© 1980 PAWS, INC. All Rights Reserved.
TIMES WERE TOUGH THEN
STOMP!
JIM DAVIS

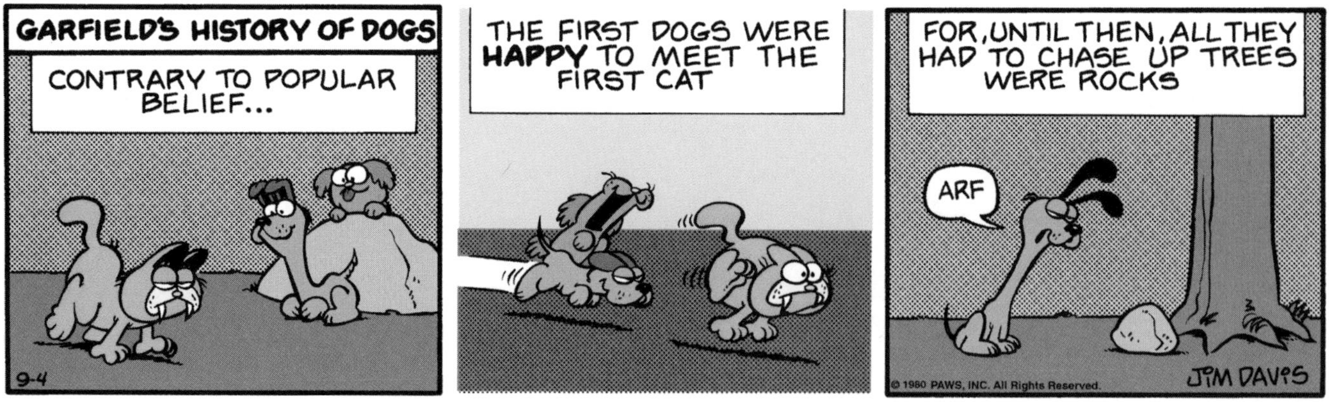
GARFIELD'S HISTORY OF DOGS
CONTRARY TO POPULAR BELIEF...
THE FIRST DOGS WERE HAPPY TO MEET THE FIRST CAT
FOR, UNTIL THEN, ALL THEY HAD TO CHASE UP TREES WERE ROCKS
ARF
9-4
© 1980 PAWS, INC. All Rights Reserved.
JIM DAVIS

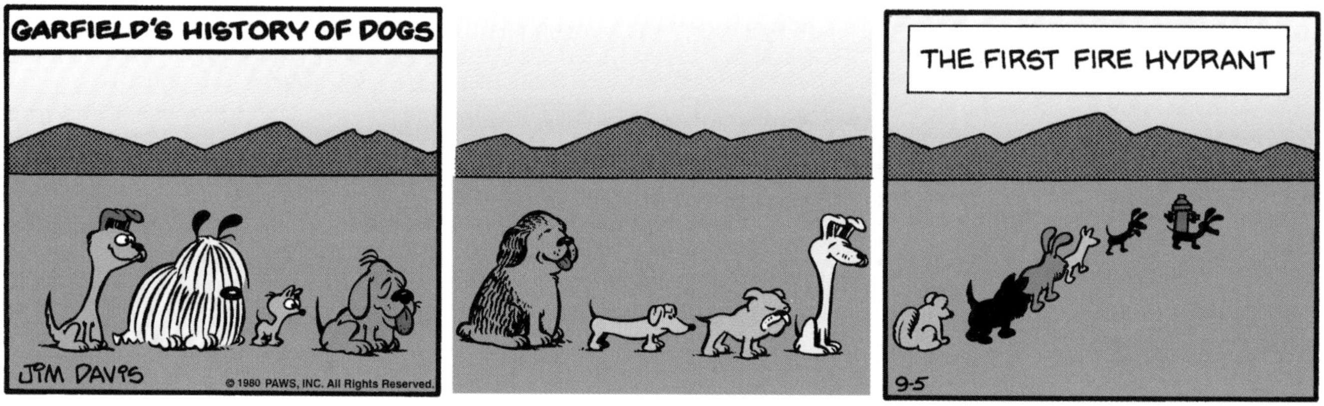
GARFIELD'S HISTORY OF DOGS
JIM DAVIS
© 1980 PAWS, INC. All Rights Reserved.
THE FIRST FIRE HYDRANT
9-5

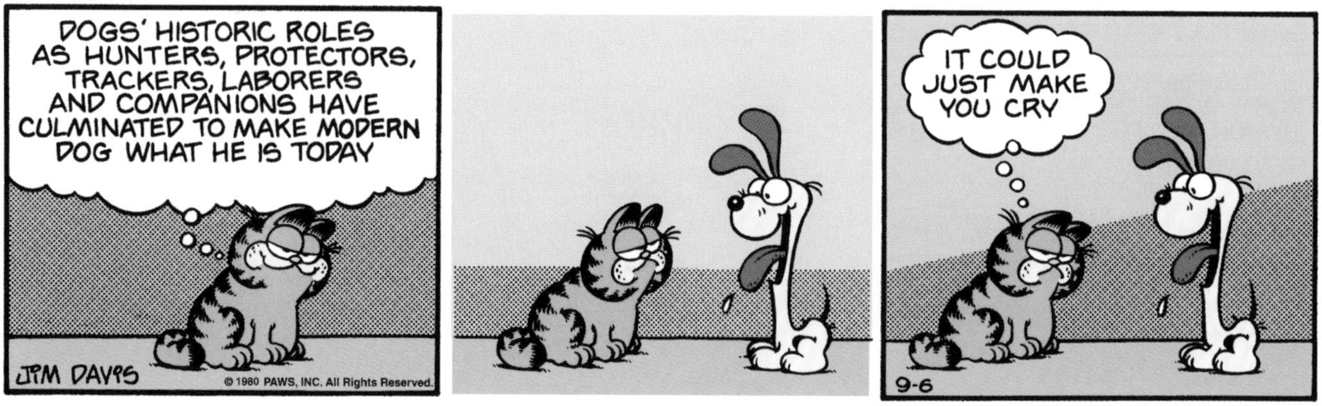
DOGS' HISTORIC ROLES AS HUNTERS, PROTECTORS, TRACKERS, LABORERS AND COMPANIONS HAVE CULMINATED TO MAKE MODERN DOG WHAT HE IS TODAY
JIM DAVIS
© 1980 PAWS, INC. All Rights Reserved.
IT COULD JUST MAKE YOU CRY
9-6

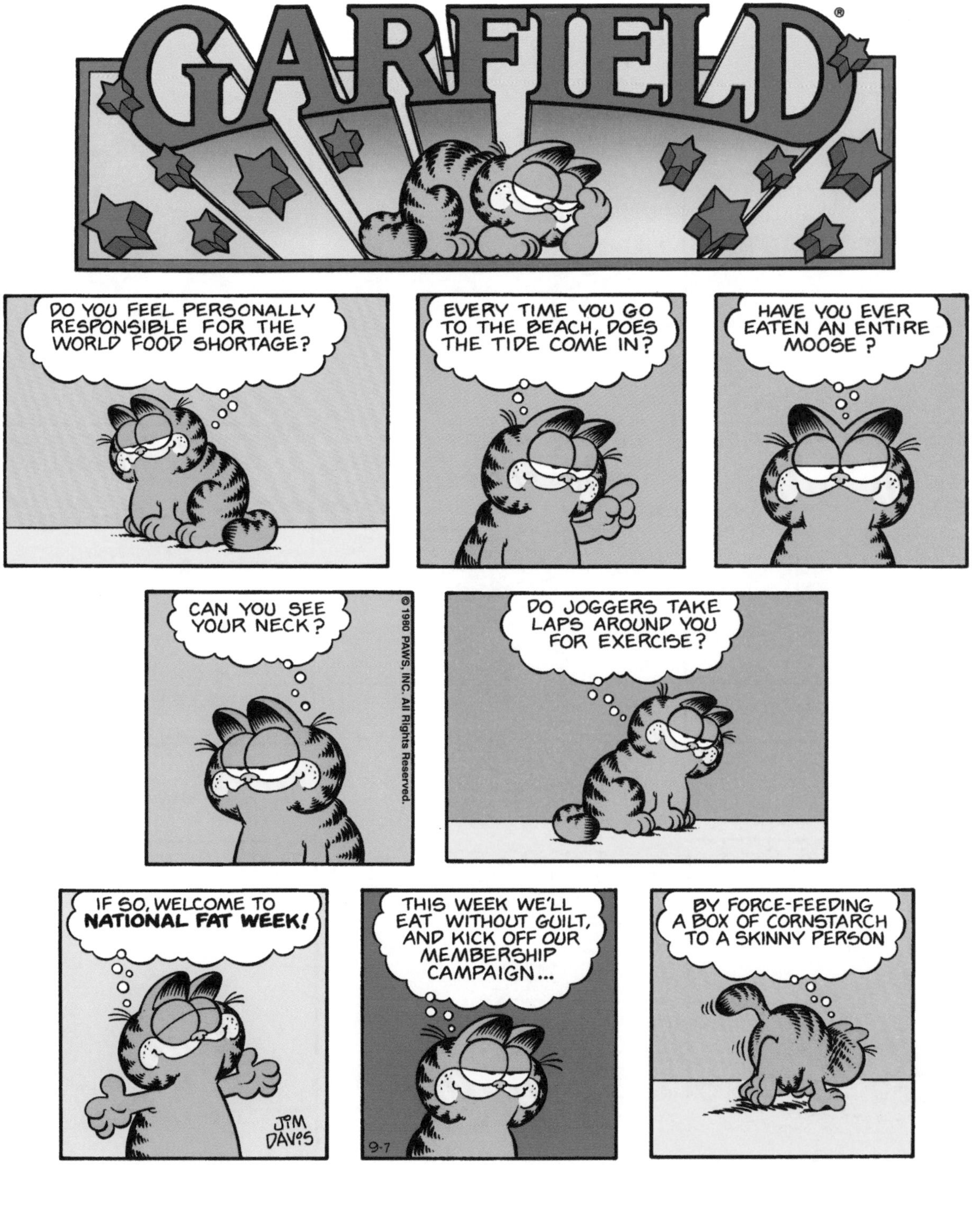
GARFIELD
DO YOU FEEL PERSONALLY RESPONSIBLE FOR THE WORLD FOOD SHORTAGE?
EVERY TIME YOU GO TO THE BEACH, DOES THE TIDE COME IN?
HAVE YOU EVER EATEN AN ENTIRE MOOSE?
CAN YOU SEE YOUR NECK?
© 1980 PAWS, INC. All Rights Reserved.
DO JOGGERS TAKE LAPS AROUND YOU FOR EXERCISE?
IF SO, WELCOME TO **NATIONAL FAT WEEK!**
JIM DAVIS
THIS WEEK WE'LL EAT WITHOUT GUILT, AND KICK OFF OUR MEMBERSHIP CAMPAIGN...
9-7
BY FORCE-FEEDING A BOX OF CORNSTARCH TO A SKINNY PERSON

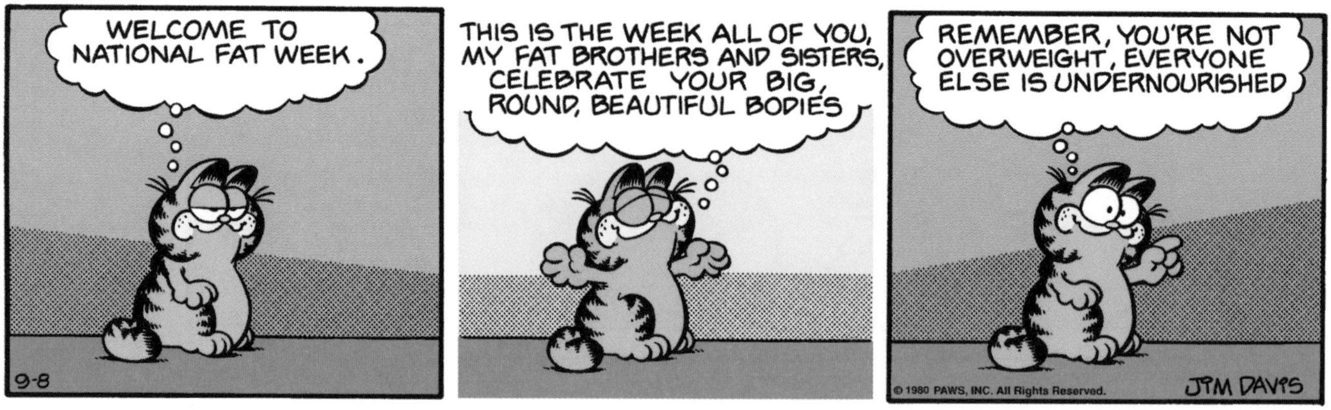
WELCOME TO NATIONAL FAT WEEK.
9-8
THIS IS THE WEEK ALL OF YOU, MY FAT BROTHERS AND SISTERS, CELEBRATE YOUR BIG, ROUND, BEAUTIFUL BODIES
REMEMBER, YOU'RE NOT OVERWEIGHT, EVERYONE ELSE IS UNDERNOURISHED
© 1980 PAWS, INC. All Rights Reserved.
JIM DAVIS

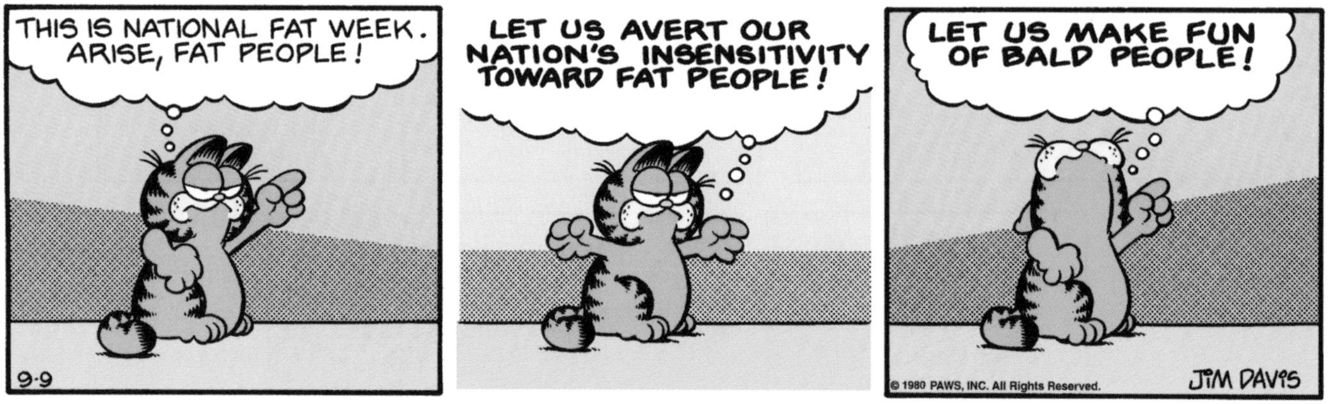
THIS IS NATIONAL FAT WEEK. ARISE, FAT PEOPLE!
9-9
LET US AVERT OUR NATION'S INSENSITIVITY TOWARD FAT PEOPLE!
LET US MAKE FUN OF BALD PEOPLE!
© 1980 PAWS, INC. All Rights Reserved.
JIM DAVIS

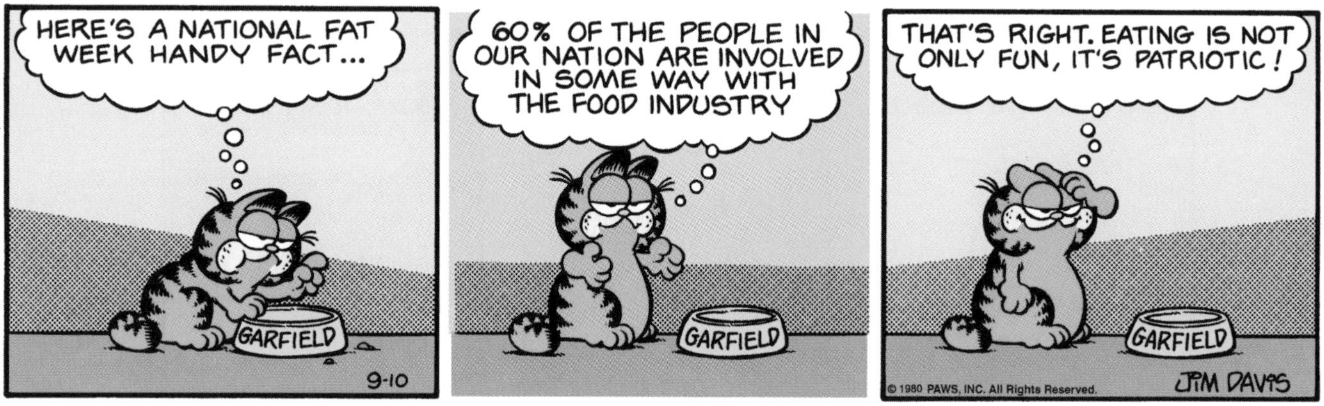
HERE'S A NATIONAL FAT WEEK HANDY FACT...
GARFIELD
9-10
60% OF THE PEOPLE IN OUR NATION ARE INVOLVED IN SOME WAY WITH THE FOOD INDUSTRY
GARFIELD
THAT'S RIGHT. EATING IS NOT ONLY FUN, IT'S PATRIOTIC!
GARFIELD
© 1980 PAWS, INC. All Rights Reserved.
JIM DAVIS

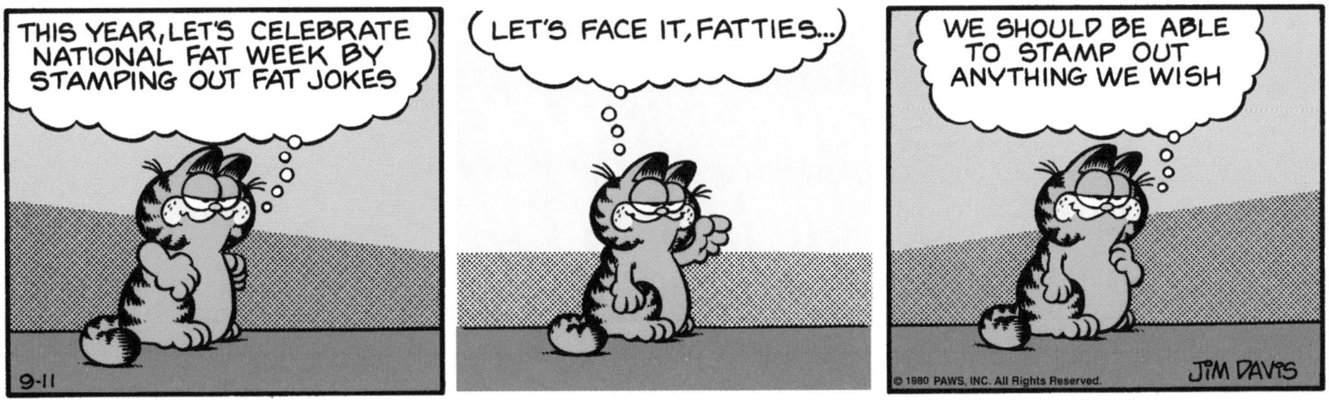
THIS YEAR, LET'S CELEBRATE NATIONAL FAT WEEK BY STAMPING OUT FAT JOKES
9-11
LET'S FACE IT, FATTIES...
WE SHOULD BE ABLE TO STAMP OUT ANYTHING WE WISH
© 1980 PAWS, INC. All Rights Reserved.
JIM DAVIS

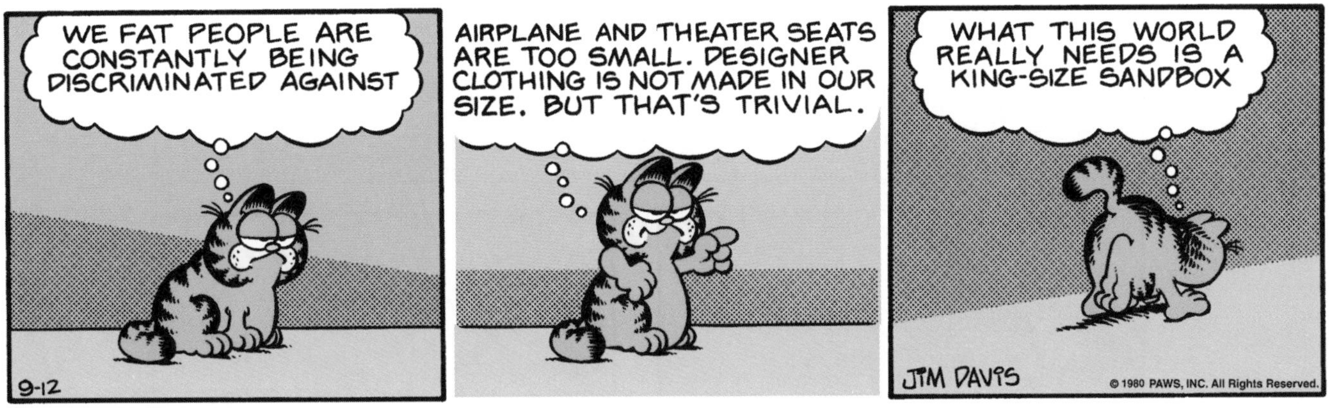
WE FAT PEOPLE ARE CONSTANTLY BEING DISCRIMINATED AGAINST
9-12
AIRPLANE AND THEATER SEATS ARE TOO SMALL. DESIGNER CLOTHING IS NOT MADE IN OUR SIZE. BUT THAT'S TRIVIAL.
WHAT THIS WORLD REALLY NEEDS IS A KING-SIZE SANDBOX
JIM DAVIS
© 1980 PAWS, INC. All Rights Reserved.

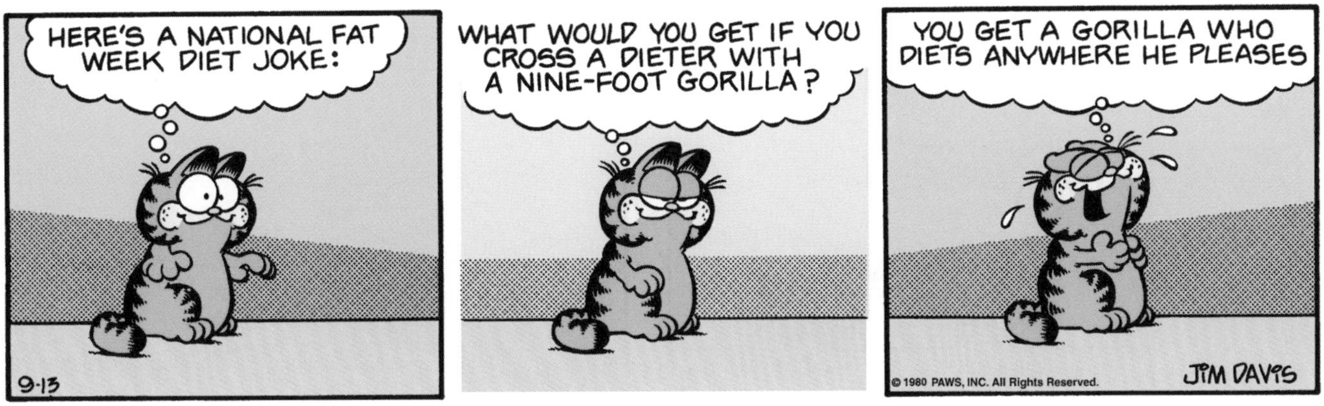
HERE'S A NATIONAL FAT WEEK DIET JOKE:
9-13
WHAT WOULD YOU GET IF YOU CROSS A DIETER WITH A NINE-FOOT GORILLA?
YOU GET A GORILLA WHO DIETS ANYWHERE HE PLEASES
© 1980 PAWS, INC. All Rights Reserved.
JIM DAVIS

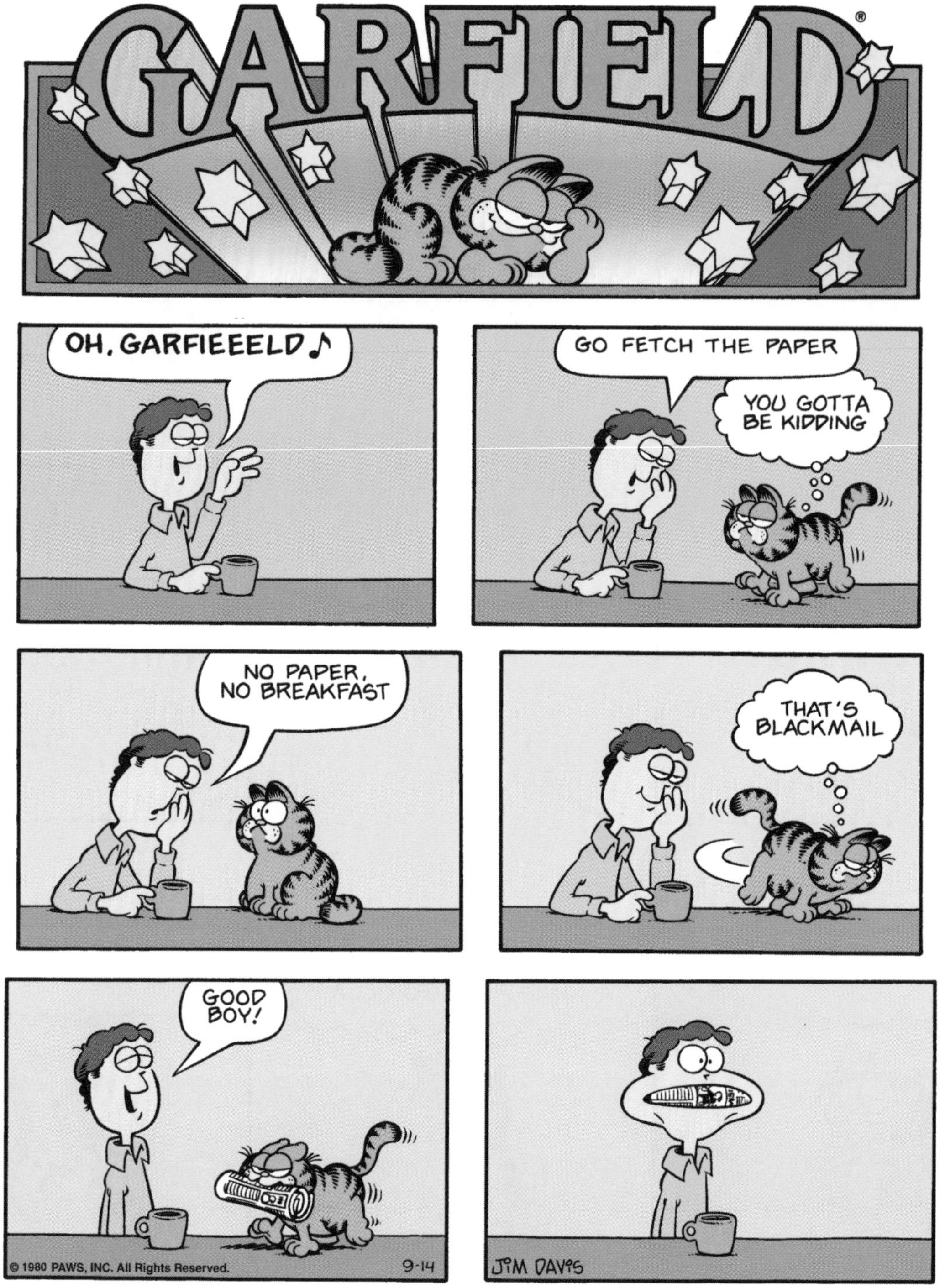

GARFIELD®
OH, GARFIEEELD♪
GO FETCH THE PAPER
YOU GOTTA BE KIDDING
NO PAPER, NO BREAKFAST
THAT'S BLACKMAIL
GOOD BOY!
© 1980 PAWS, INC. All Rights Reserved.
9-14
JIM DAVIS

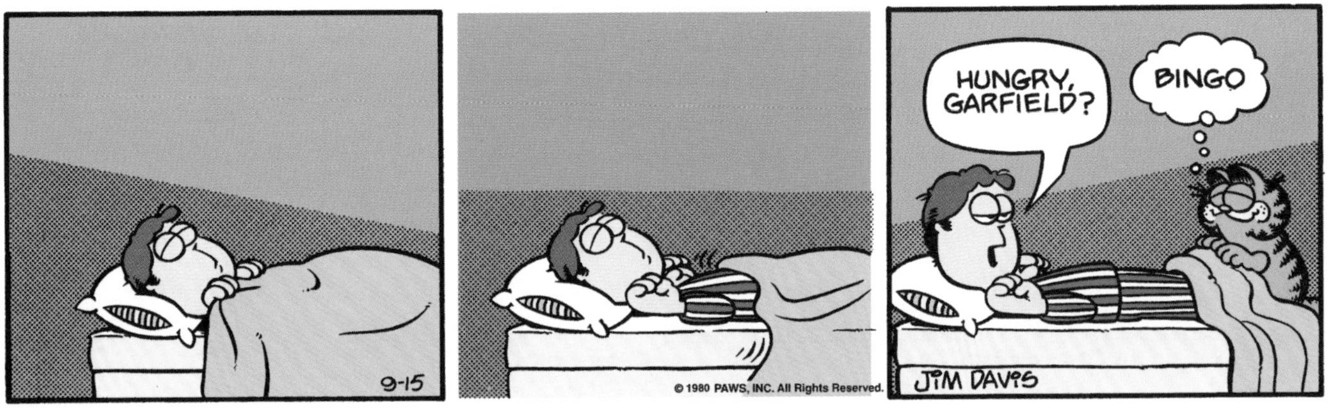
9-15
© 1980 PAWS, INC. All Rights Reserved.
HUNGRY, GARFIELD?
BINGO
JIM DAVIS

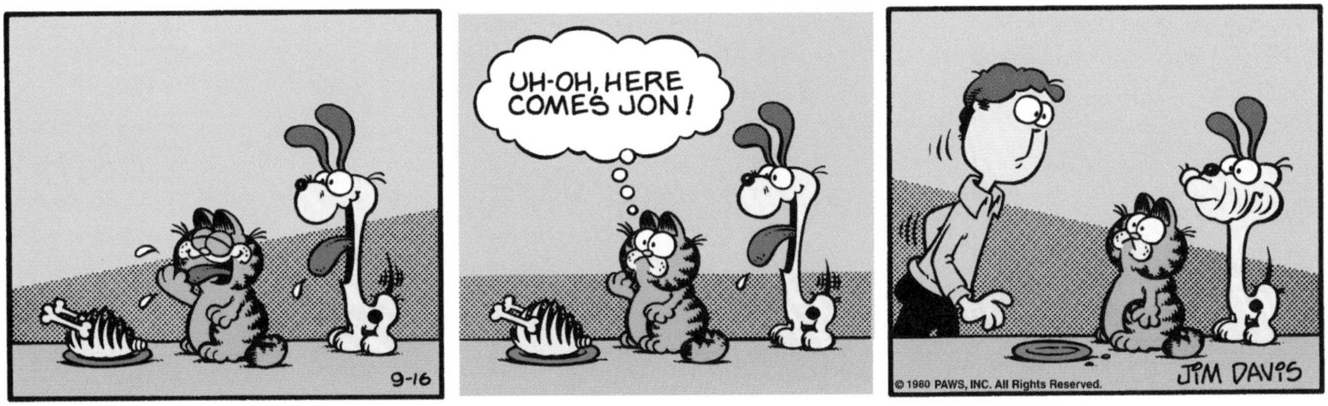
9-16
UH-OH, HERE COMES JON!
© 1980 PAWS, INC. All Rights Reserved.
JIM DAVIS

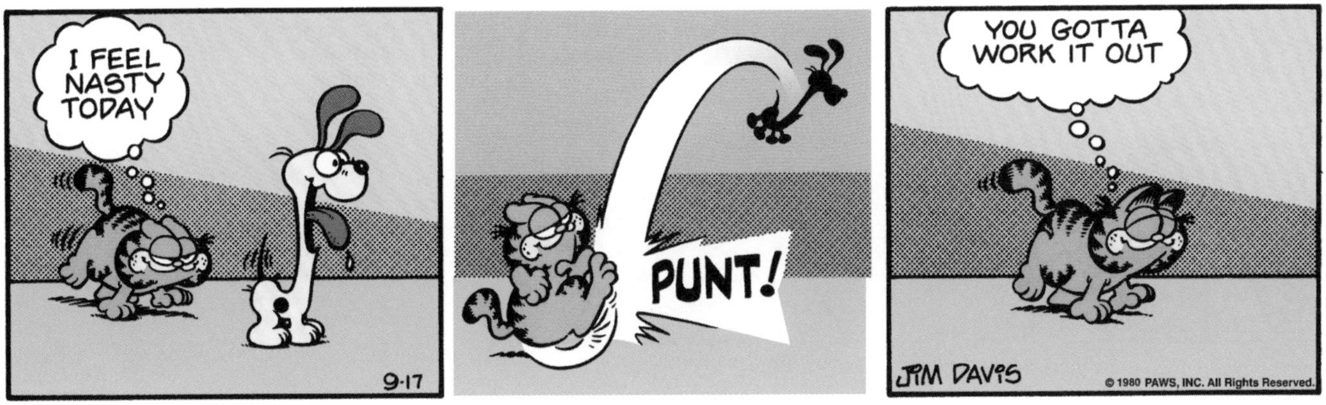
I FEEL NASTY TODAY
9-17
PUNT!
YOU GOTTA WORK IT OUT
JIM DAVIS
© 1980 PAWS, INC. All Rights Reserved.

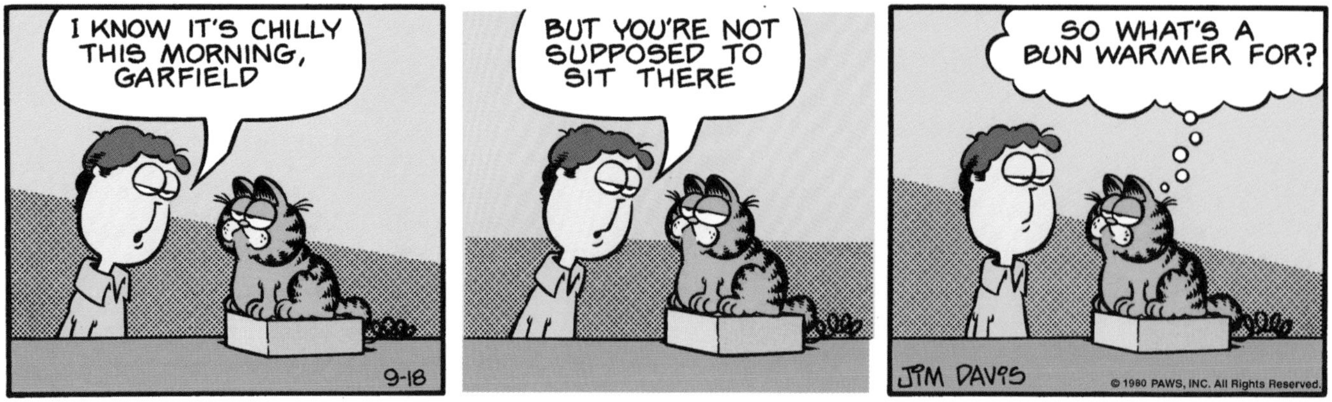
I KNOW IT'S CHILLY THIS MORNING, GARFIELD
9-18
BUT YOU'RE NOT SUPPOSED TO SIT THERE
SO WHAT'S A BUN WARMER FOR?
JIM DAVIS
© 1980 PAWS, INC. All Rights Reserved.

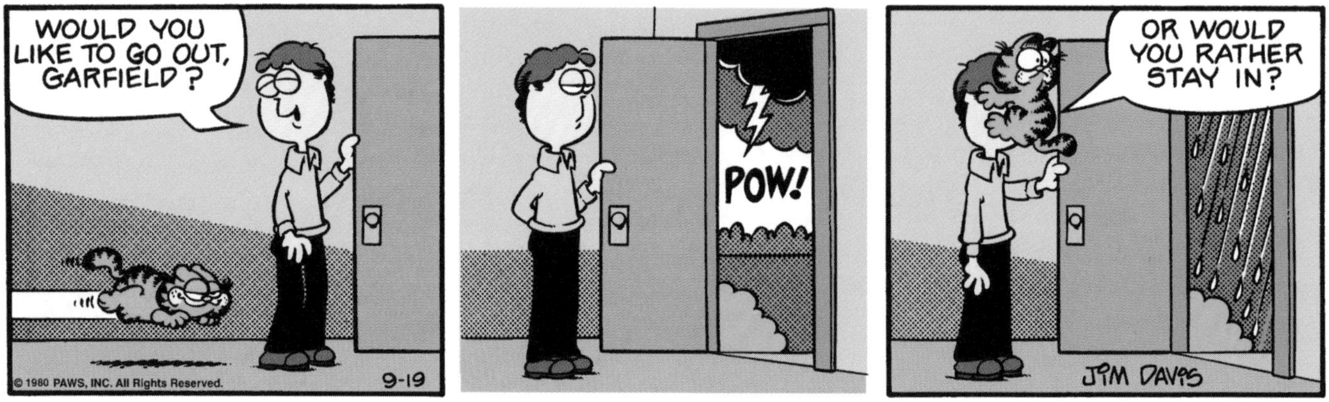
WOULD YOU LIKE TO GO OUT, GARFIELD?
© 1980 PAWS, INC. All Rights Reserved.
9-19
POW!
OR WOULD YOU RATHER STAY IN?
JIM DAVIS

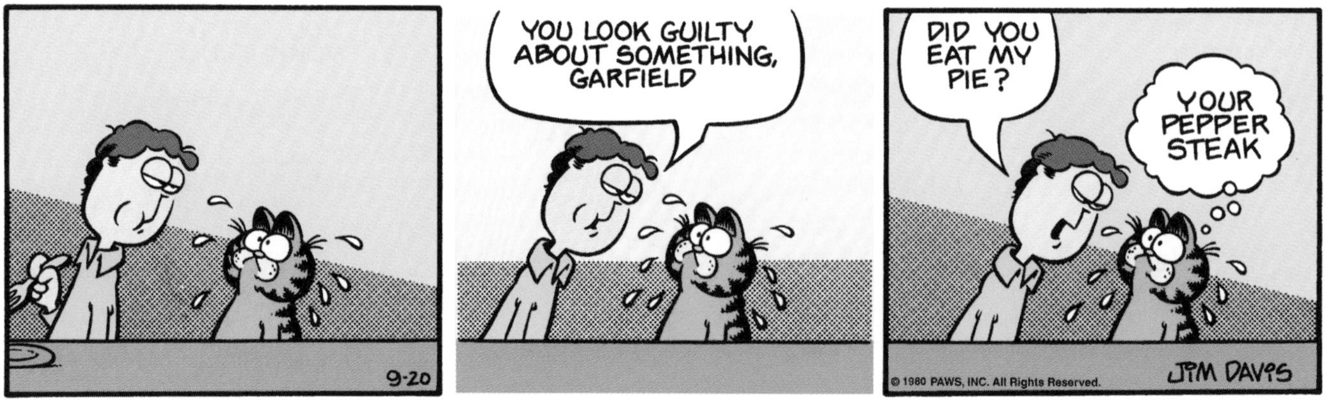
9-20
YOU LOOK GUILTY ABOUT SOMETHING, GARFIELD
DID YOU EAT MY PIE?
YOUR PEPPER STEAK
© 1980 PAWS, INC. All Rights Reserved.
JIM DAVIS

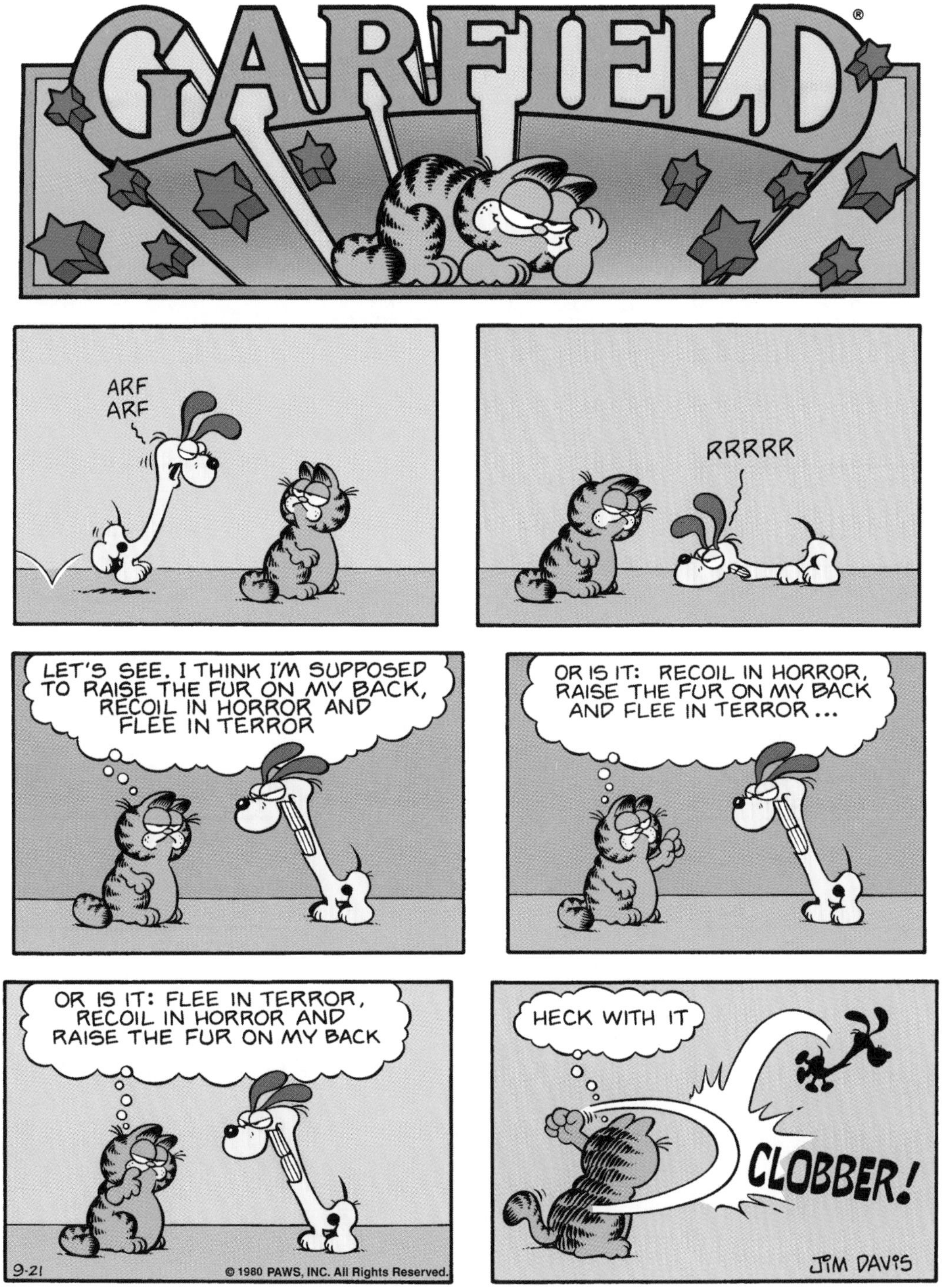
GARFIELD®
ARF ARF
RRRRR
LET'S SEE. I THINK I'M SUPPOSED TO RAISE THE FUR ON MY BACK, RECOIL IN HORROR AND FLEE IN TERROR
OR IS IT: RECOIL IN HORROR, RAISE THE FUR ON MY BACK AND FLEE IN TERROR...
OR IS IT: FLEE IN TERROR, RECOIL IN HORROR AND RAISE THE FUR ON MY BACK
9-21
© 1980 PAWS, INC. All Rights Reserved.
HECK WITH IT
CLOBBER!
JIM DAVIS

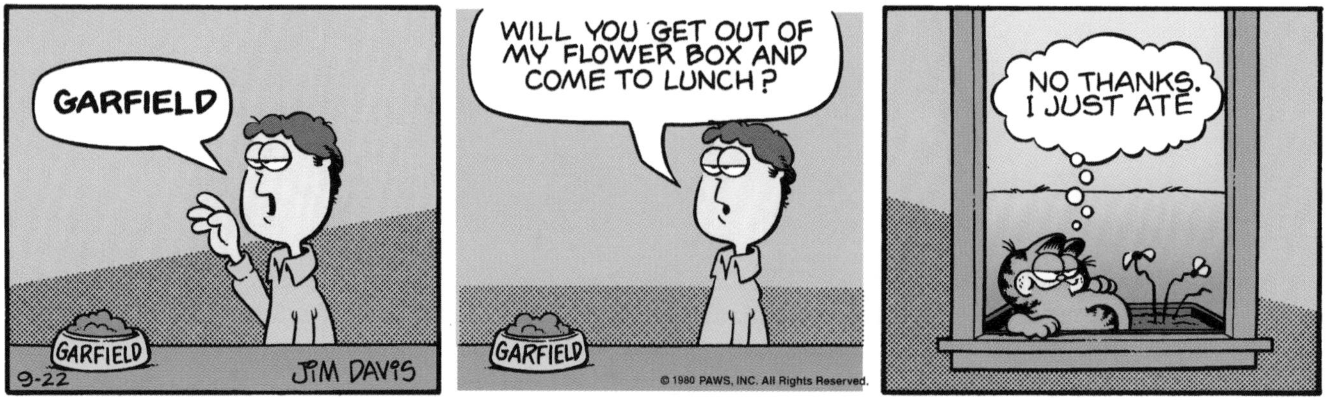
GARFIELD
GARFIELD
9-22
JIM DAVIS
WILL YOU GET OUT OF MY FLOWER BOX AND COME TO LUNCH?
GARFIELD
© 1980 PAWS, INC. All Rights Reserved.
NO THANKS. I JUST ATE

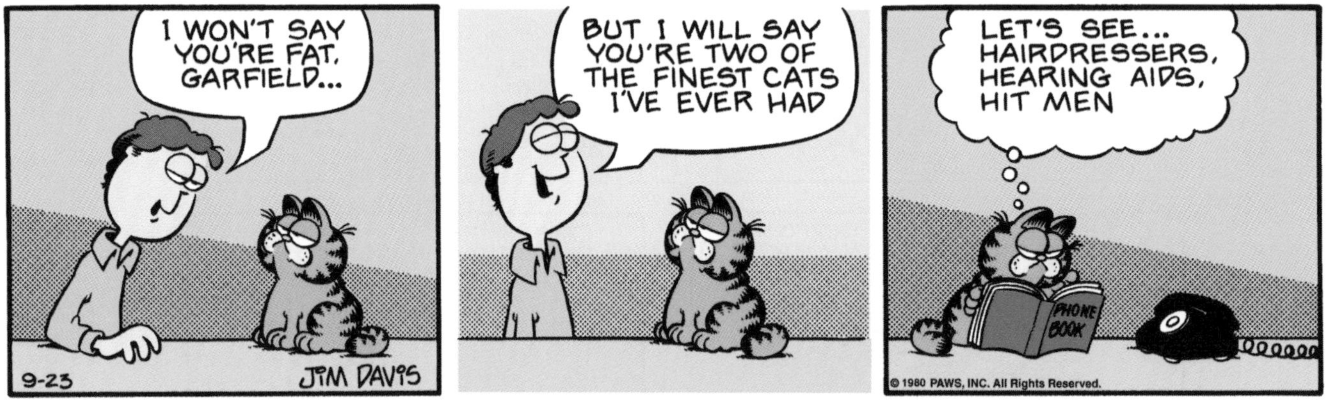
I WON'T SAY YOU'RE FAT, GARFIELD...
9-23
JIM DAVIS
BUT I WILL SAY YOU'RE TWO OF THE FINEST CATS I'VE EVER HAD
LET'S SEE... HAIRDRESSERS, HEARING AIDS, HIT MEN
PHONE BOOK
© 1980 PAWS, INC. All Rights Reserved.

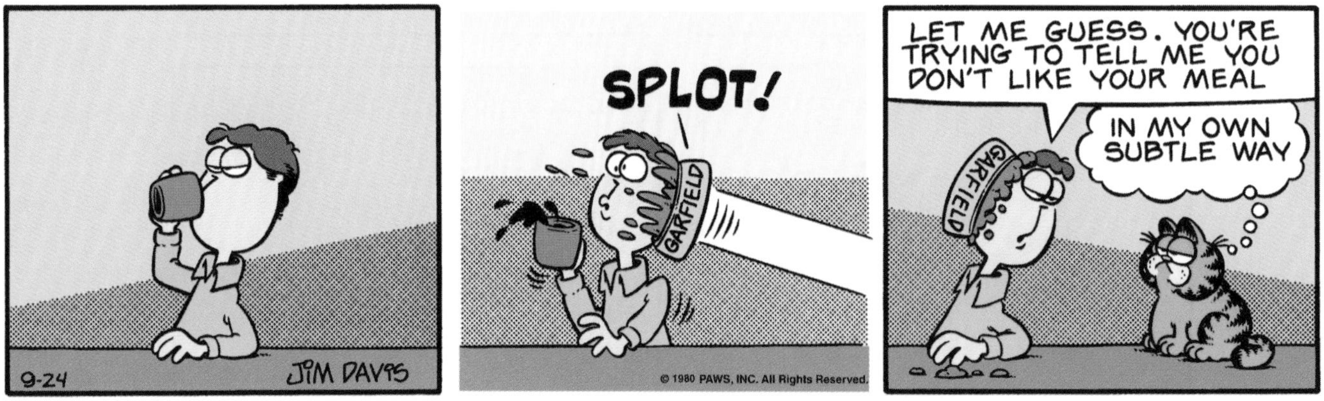
9-24
JIM DAVIS
SPLOT!
GARFIELD
© 1980 PAWS, INC. All Rights Reserved.
LET ME GUESS. YOU'RE TRYING TO TELL ME YOU DON'T LIKE YOUR MEAL
GARFIELD
IN MY OWN SUBTLE WAY

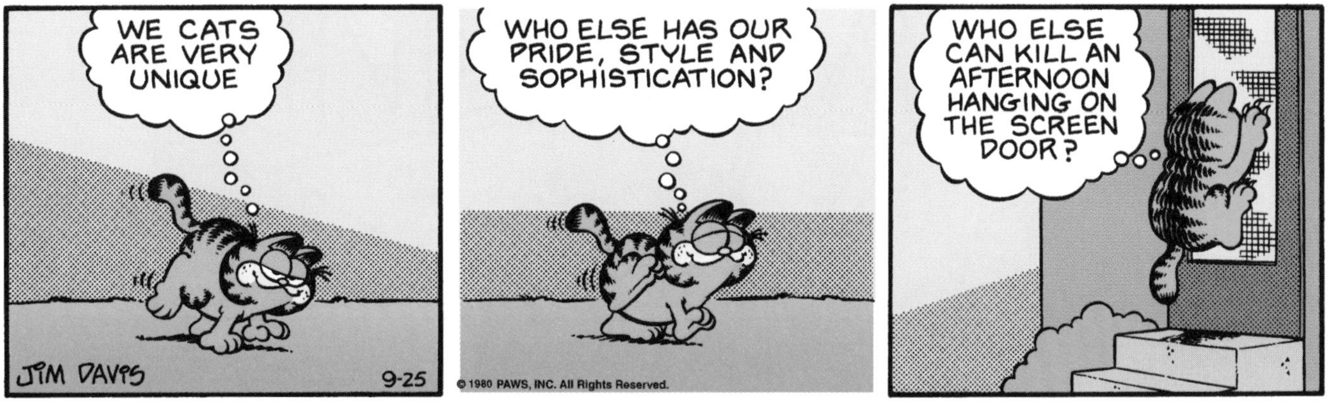
WE CATS ARE VERY UNIQUE
JIM DAVIS
9-25
WHO ELSE HAS OUR PRIDE, STYLE AND SOPHISTICATION?
© 1980 PAWS, INC. All Rights Reserved.
WHO ELSE CAN KILL AN AFTERNOON HANGING ON THE SCREEN DOOR?

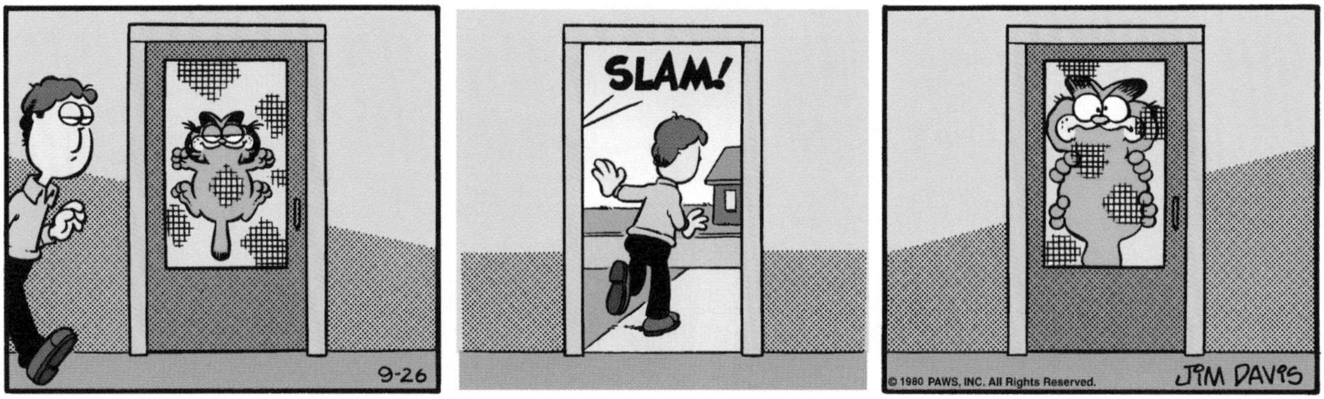
9-26
SLAM!
© 1980 PAWS, INC. All Rights Reserved.
JIM DAVIS

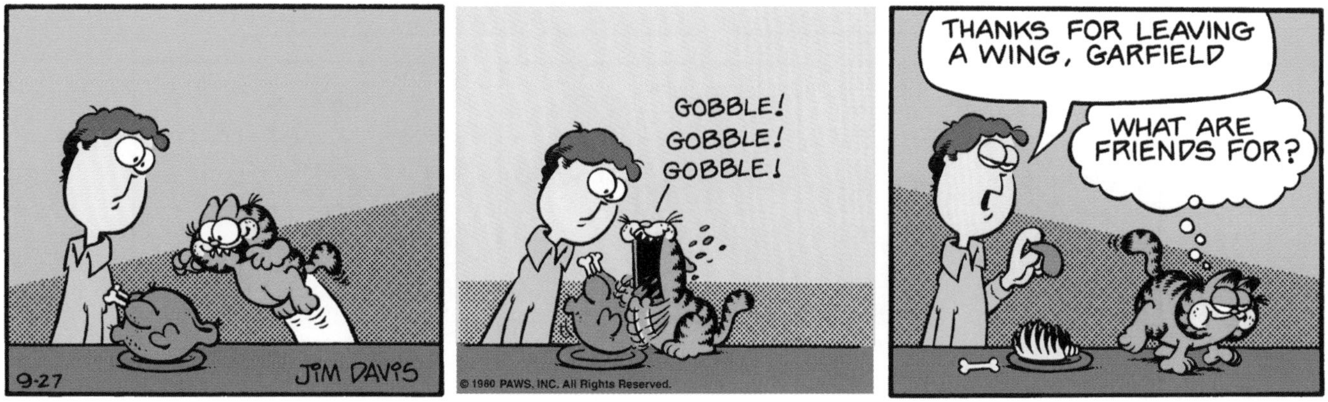
9-27
JIM DAVIS
GOBBLE! GOBBLE! GOBBLE!
© 1980 PAWS, INC. All Rights Reserved.
THANKS FOR LEAVING A WING, GARFIELD
WHAT ARE FRIENDS FOR?

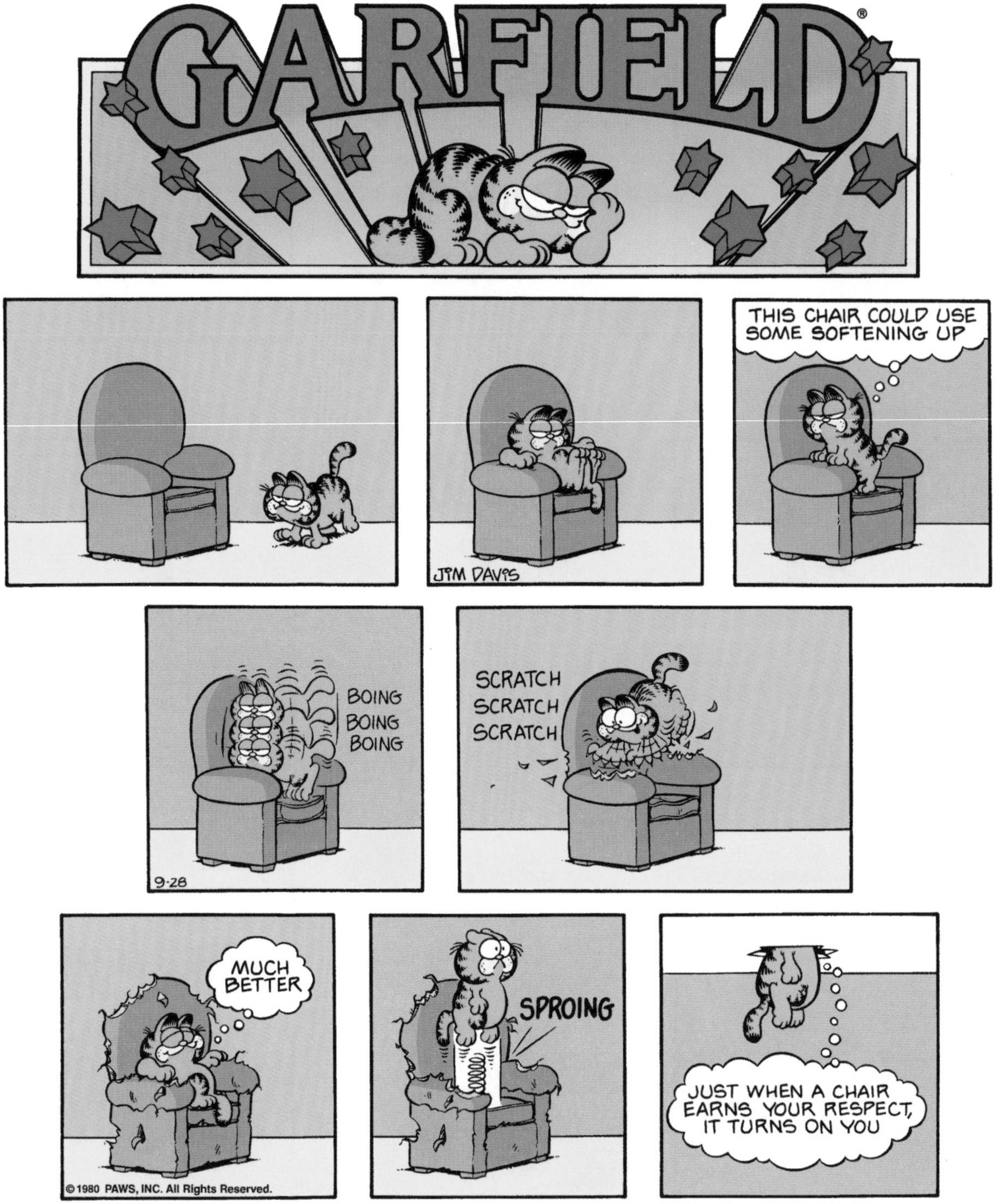

GARFIELD®
JIM DAVIS
THIS CHAIR COULD USE SOME SOFTENING UP
9-28
BOING
BOING
BOING
SCRATCH
SCRATCH
SCRATCH
MUCH BETTER
© 1980 PAWS, INC. All Rights Reserved.
SPROING
JUST WHEN A CHAIR EARNS YOUR RESPECT, IT TURNS ON YOU

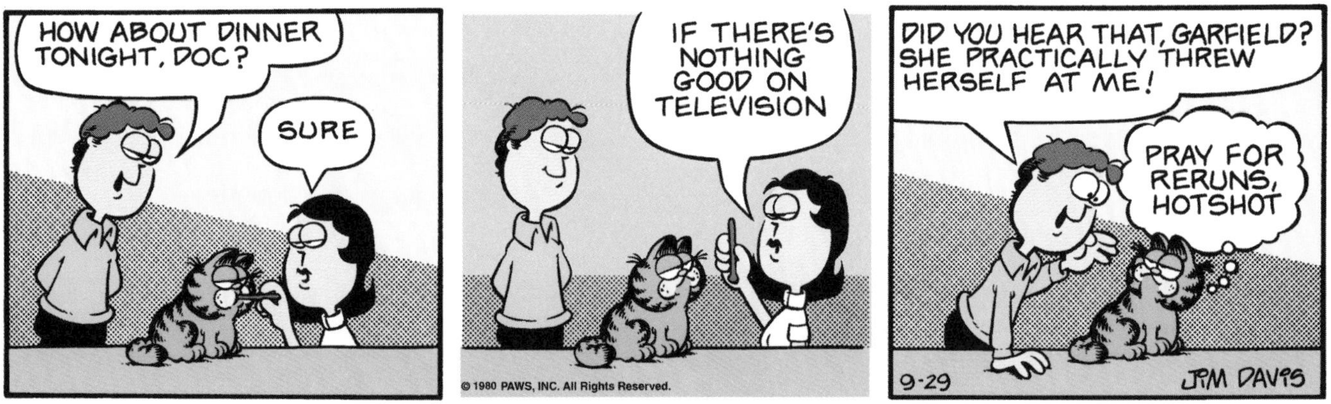
HOW ABOUT DINNER TONIGHT, DOC?
SURE
IF THERE'S NOTHING GOOD ON TELEVISION
DID YOU HEAR THAT, GARFIELD? SHE PRACTICALLY THREW HERSELF AT ME!
PRAY FOR RERUNS, HOTSHOT
© 1980 PAWS, INC. All Rights Reserved.
9-29
JIM DAVIS

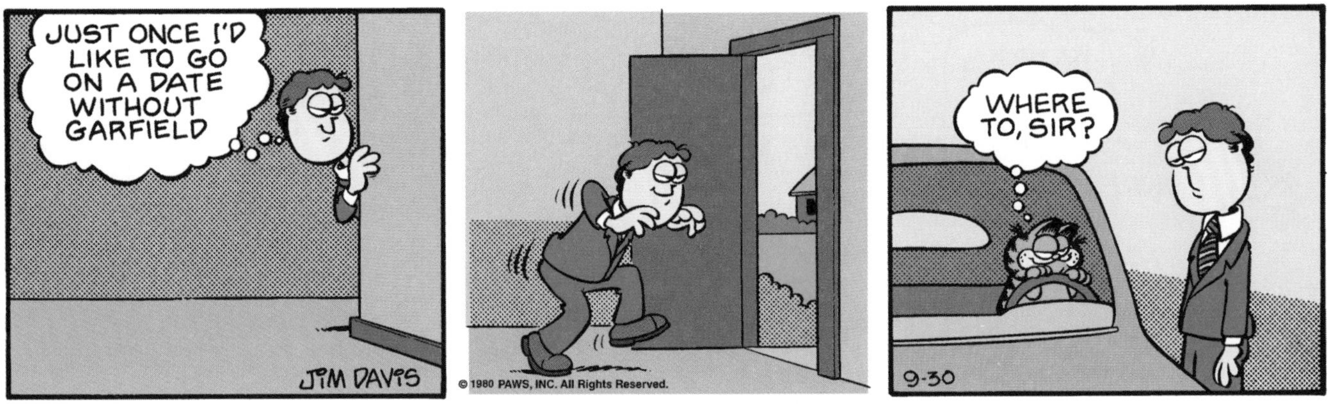
JUST ONCE I'D LIKE TO GO ON A DATE WITHOUT GARFIELD
JIM DAVIS
© 1980 PAWS, INC. All Rights Reserved.
WHERE TO, SIR?
9-30

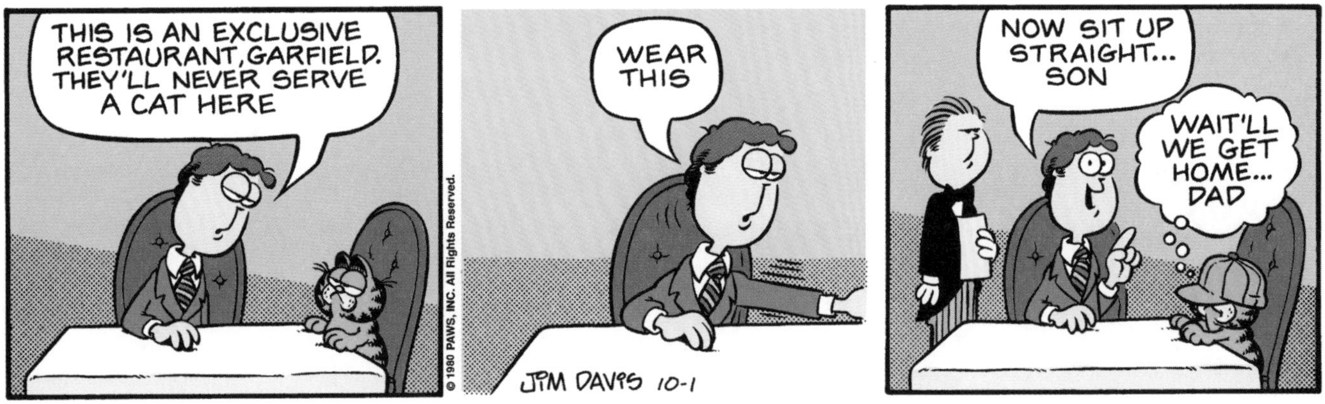
THIS IS AN EXCLUSIVE RESTAURANT, GARFIELD. THEY'LL NEVER SERVE A CAT HERE
© 1980 PAWS, INC. All Rights Reserved.
WEAR THIS
JIM DAVIS 10-1
NOW SIT UP STRAIGHT... SON
WAIT'LL WE GET HOME... DAD

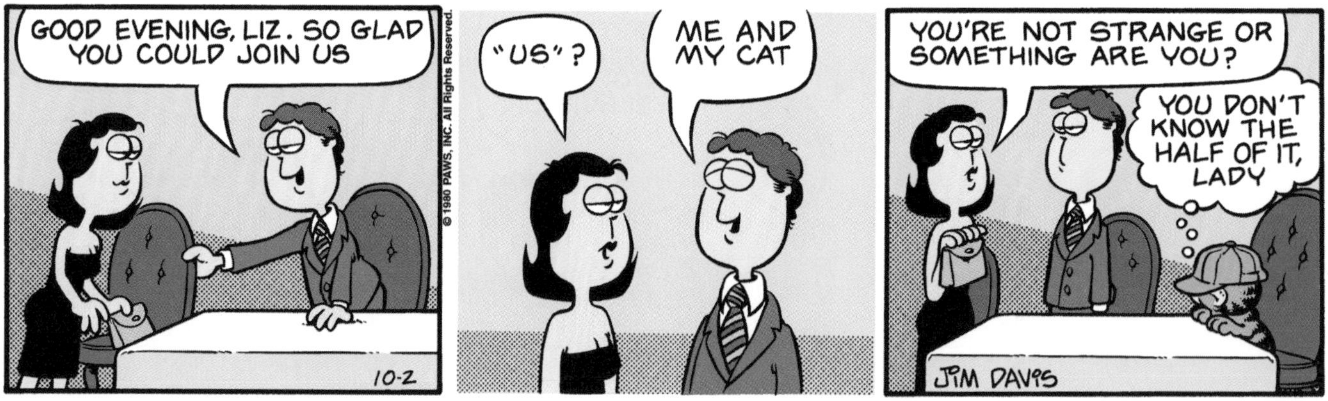
GOOD EVENING, LIZ. SO GLAD YOU COULD JOIN US
© 1980 PAWS, INC. All Rights Reserved.
10-2
"US"?
ME AND MY CAT
YOU'RE NOT STRANGE OR SOMETHING ARE YOU?
YOU DON'T KNOW THE HALF OF IT, LADY
JIM DAVIS

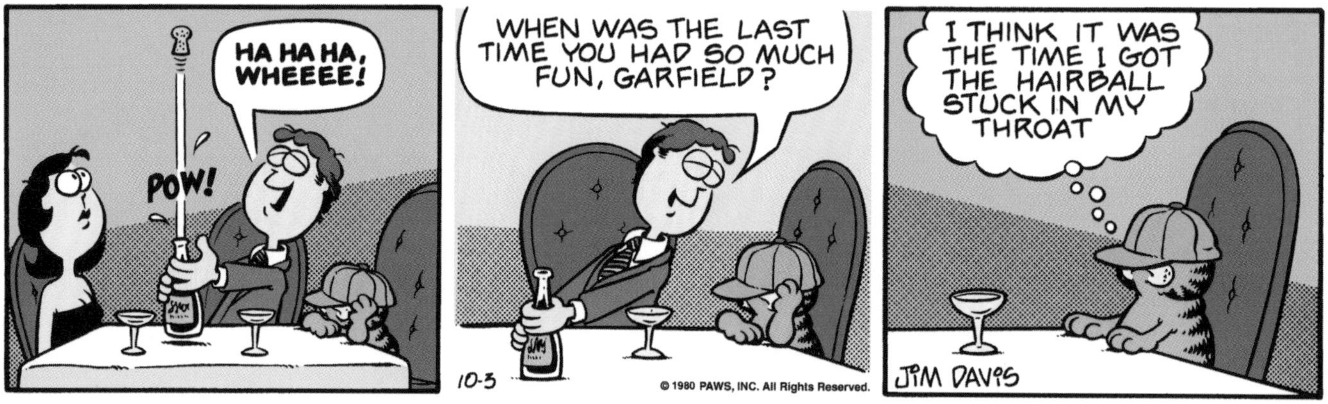
HA HA HA, WHEEEE!
POW!
WHEN WAS THE LAST TIME YOU HAD SO MUCH FUN, GARFIELD?
10-3
© 1980 PAWS, INC. All Rights Reserved.
I THINK IT WAS THE TIME I GOT THE HAIRBALL STUCK IN MY THROAT
JIM DAVIS

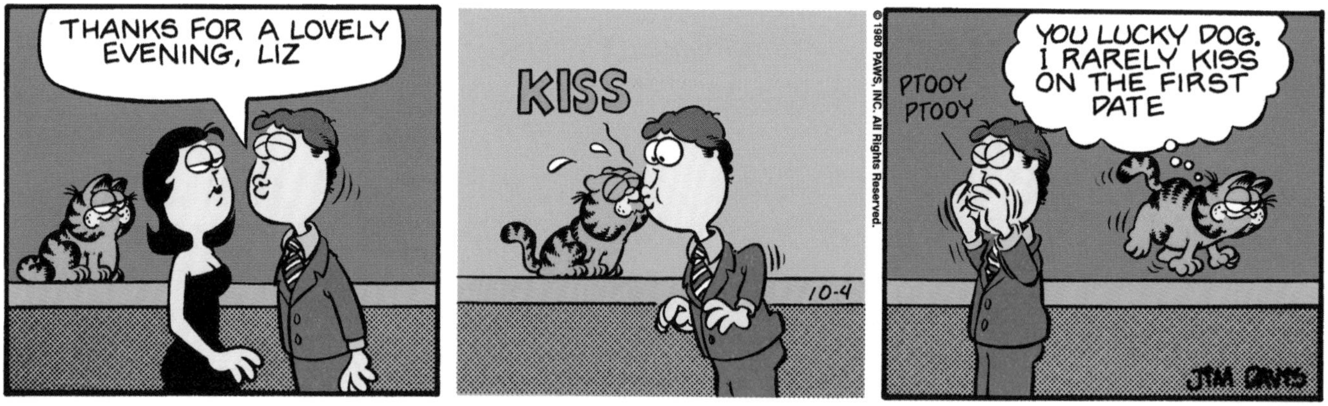
THANKS FOR A LOVELY EVENING, LIZ
KISS
10-4
© 1980 PAWS, INC. All Rights Reserved.
PTOOY PTOOY
YOU LUCKY DOG. I RARELY KISS ON THE FIRST DATE
JIM DAVIS

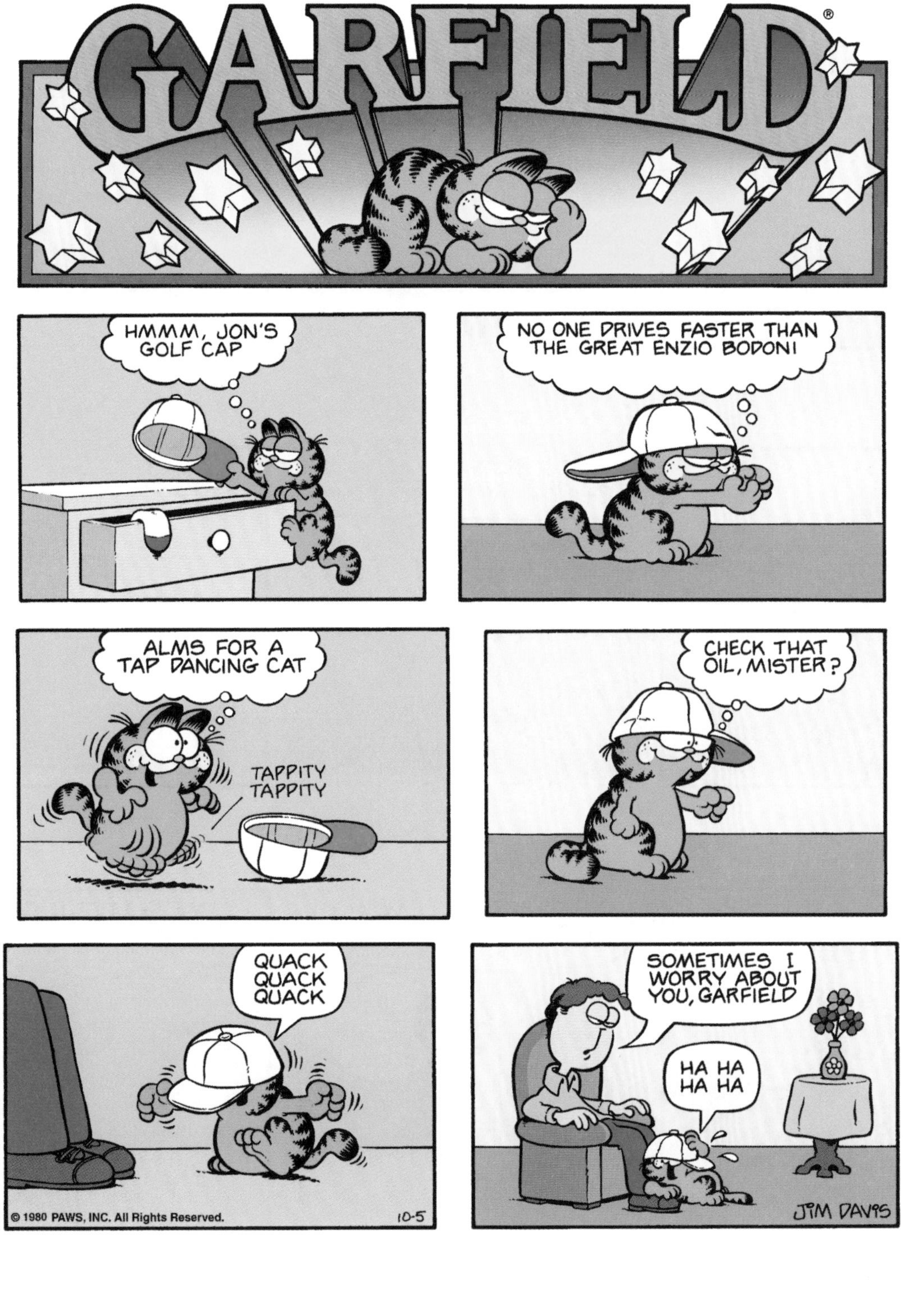
GARFIELD
HMMM, JON'S GOLF CAP
NO ONE DRIVES FASTER THAN THE GREAT ENZIO BODONI
ALMS FOR A TAP DANCING CAT
TAPPITY TAPPITY
CHECK THAT OIL, MISTER?
QUACK QUACK QUACK
SOMETIMES I WORRY ABOUT YOU, GARFIELD
HA HA HA HA
© 1980 PAWS, INC. All Rights Reserved.
10-5
JIM DAVIS

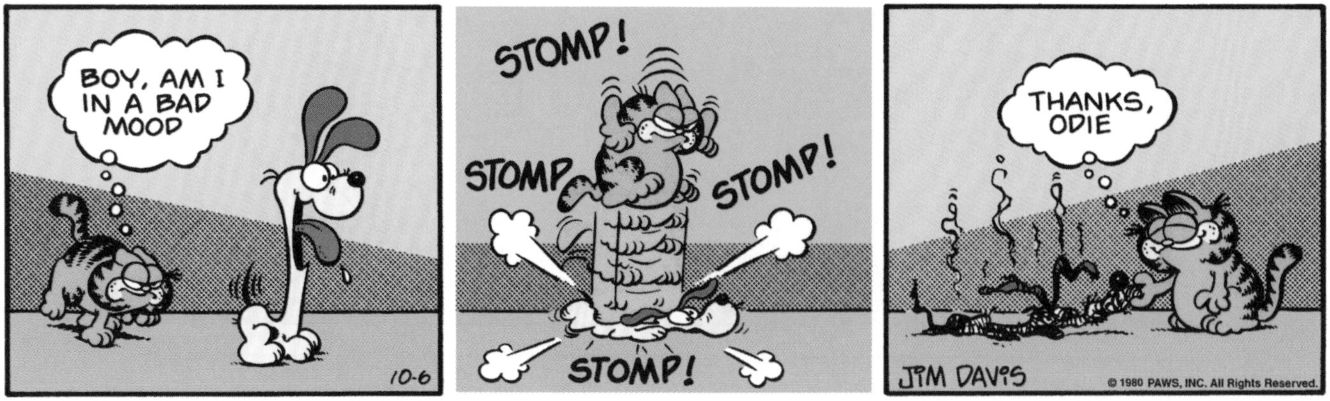
BOY, AM I IN A BAD MOOD
10-6
STOMP!
STOMP
STOMP!
STOMP!
THANKS, ODIE
JIM DAVIS
© 1980 PAWS, INC. All Rights Reserved.

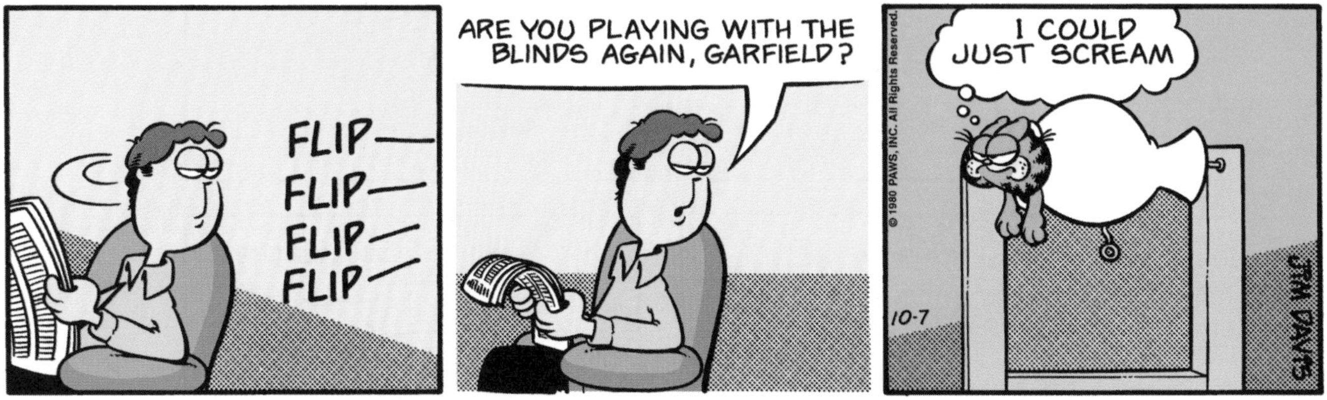
FLIP
FLIP
FLIP
FLIP
ARE YOU PLAYING WITH THE BLINDS AGAIN, GARFIELD?
© 1980 PAWS, INC. All Rights Reserved.
I COULD JUST SCREAM
10-7
JIM DAVIS

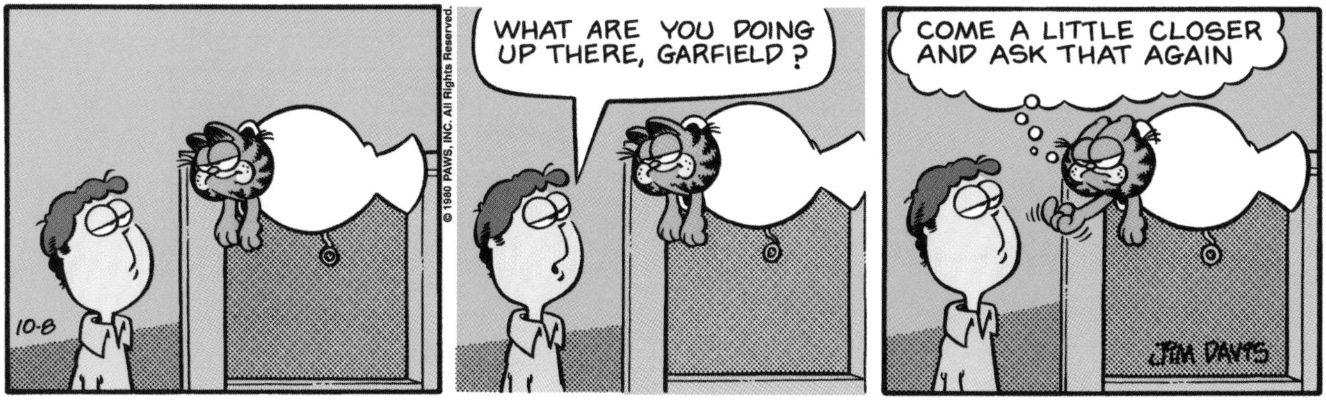
10-8
© 1980 PAWS, INC. All Rights Reserved.
WHAT ARE YOU DOING UP THERE, GARFIELD?
COME A LITTLE CLOSER AND ASK THAT AGAIN
JIM DAVIS

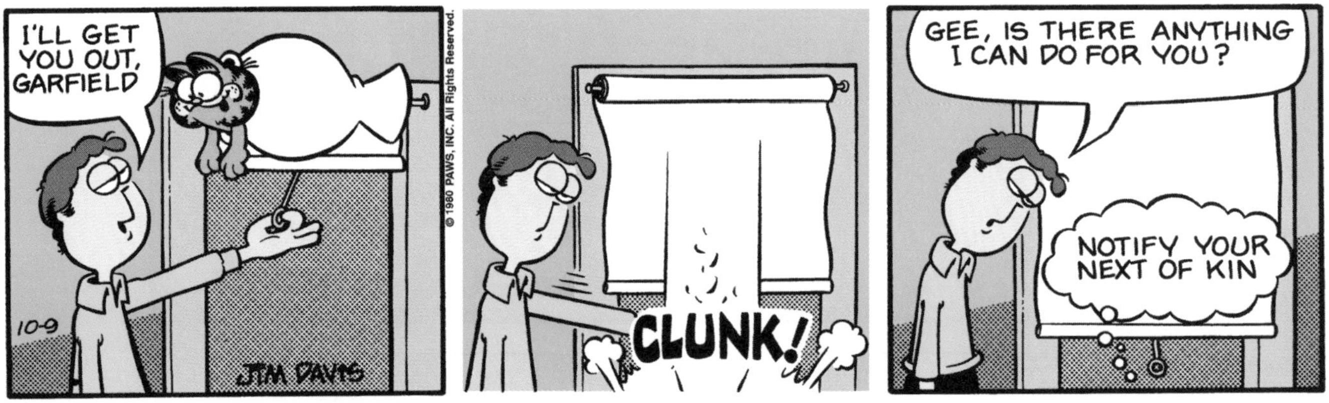
I'LL GET YOU OUT, GARFIELD
10-9
JIM DAVIS
© 1980 PAWS, INC. All Rights Reserved.
CLUNK!
GEE, IS THERE ANYTHING I CAN DO FOR YOU?
NOTIFY YOUR NEXT OF KIN

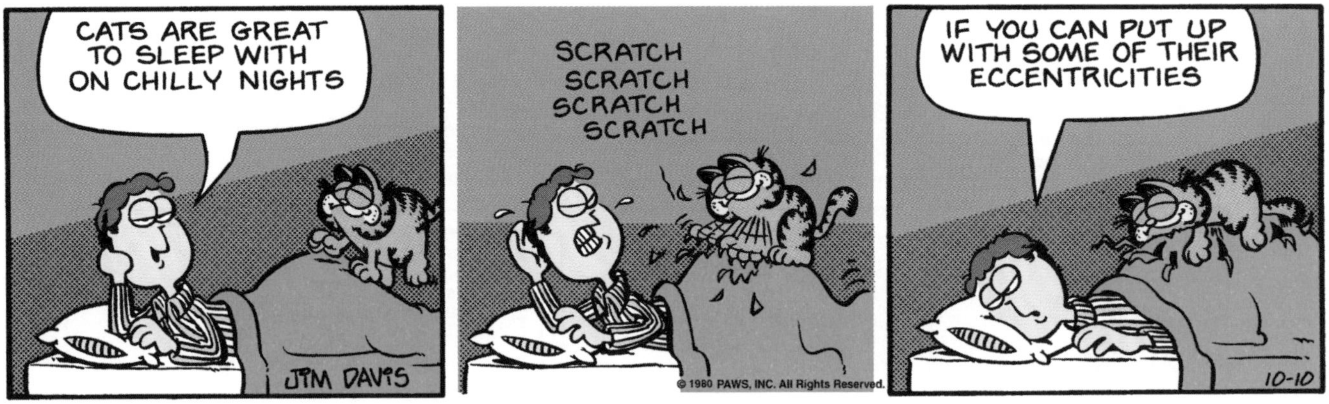
CATS ARE GREAT TO SLEEP WITH ON CHILLY NIGHTS
JIM DAVIS
SCRATCH SCRATCH SCRATCH SCRATCH
© 1980 PAWS, INC. All Rights Reserved.
IF YOU CAN PUT UP WITH SOME OF THEIR ECCENTRICITIES
10-10

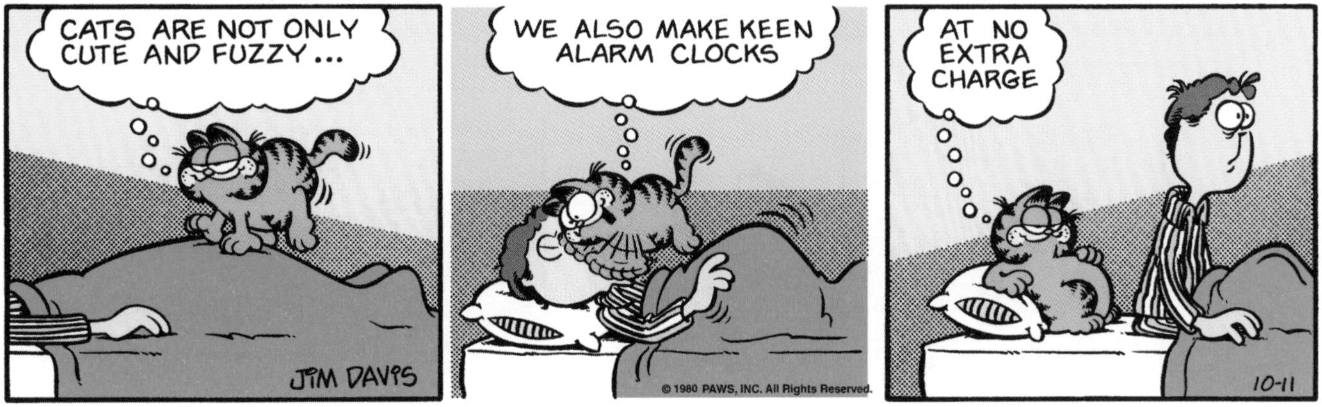
CATS ARE NOT ONLY CUTE AND FUZZY...
JIM DAVIS
WE ALSO MAKE KEEN ALARM CLOCKS
© 1980 PAWS, INC. All Rights Reserved.
AT NO EXTRA CHARGE
10-11

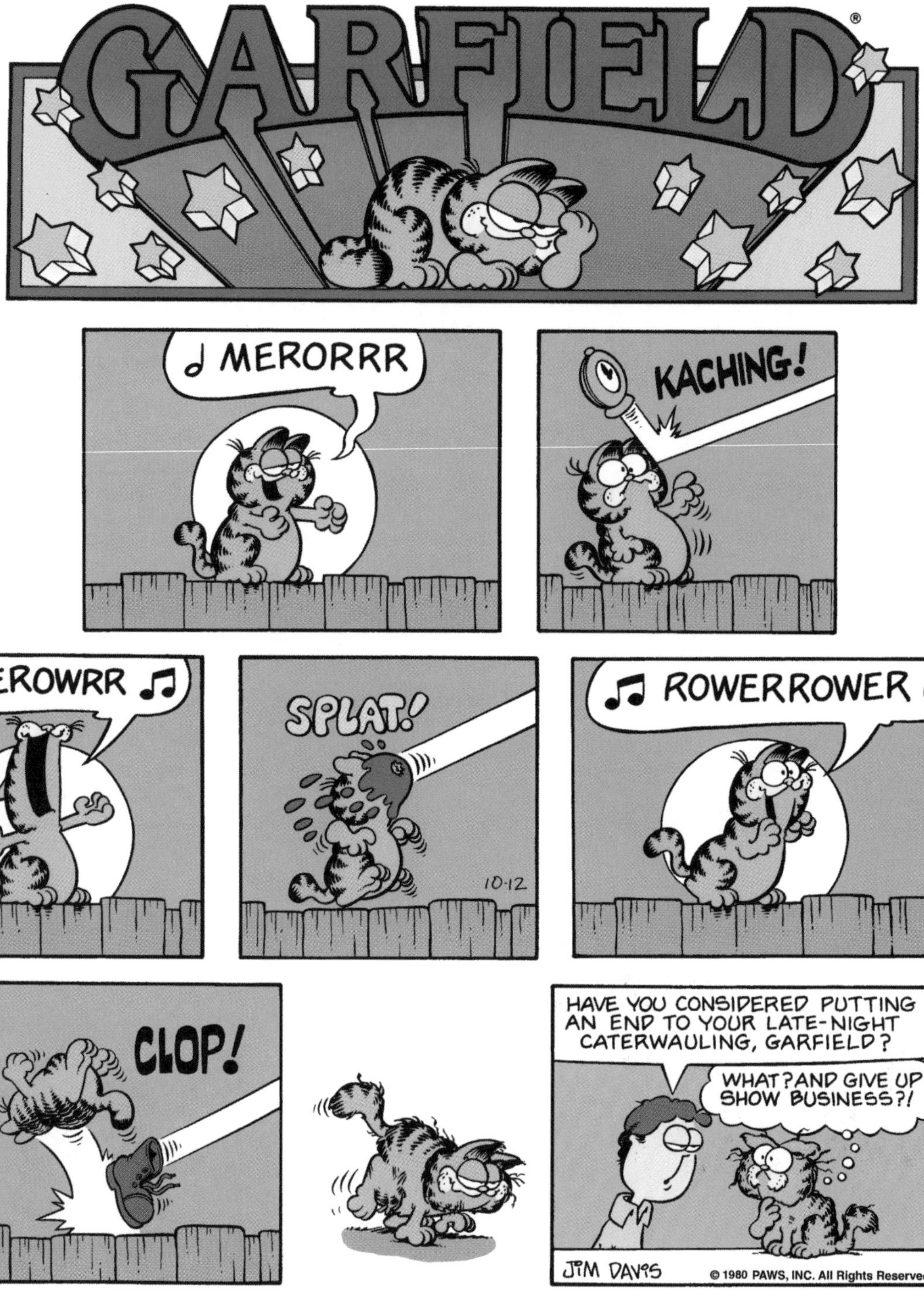
GARFIELD®
♩ MERORRR
KACHING!
♪ EROWRR ♫
SPLAT!
10-12
♫ ROWERROWER ♪
CLOP!
HAVE YOU CONSIDERED PUTTING AN END TO YOUR LATE-NIGHT CATERWAULING, GARFIELD?
WHAT? AND GIVE UP SHOW BUSINESS?!
JIM DAVIS
© 1980 PAWS, INC. All Rights Reserved.

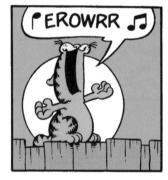

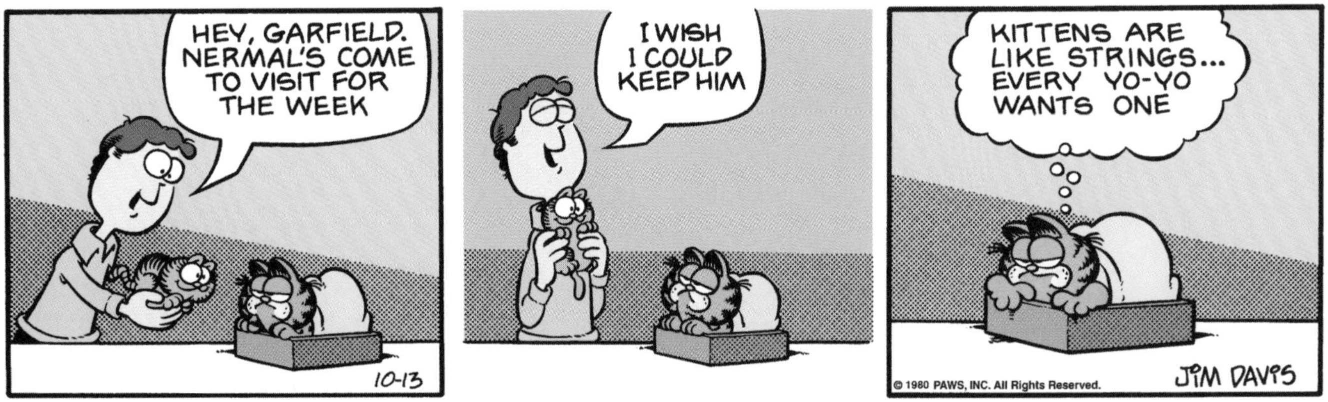
HEY, GARFIELD. NERMAL'S COME TO VISIT FOR THE WEEK
10-13
I WISH I COULD KEEP HIM
KITTENS ARE LIKE STRINGS... EVERY YO-YO WANTS ONE
© 1980 PAWS, INC. All Rights Reserved.
JIM DAVIS

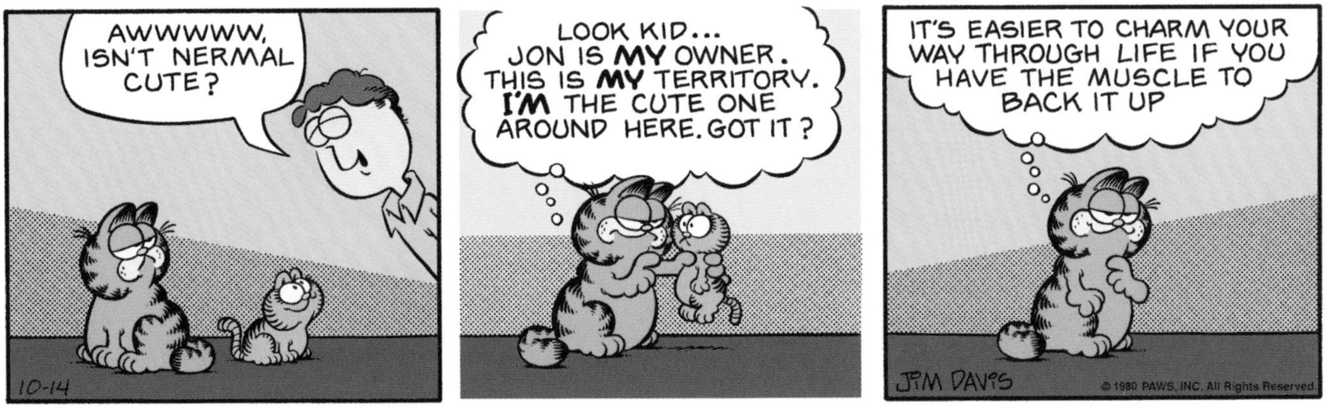
AWWWWW, ISN'T NERMAL CUTE?
10-14
LOOK KID... JON IS MY OWNER. THIS IS MY TERRITORY. I'M THE CUTE ONE AROUND HERE. GOT IT?
IT'S EASIER TO CHARM YOUR WAY THROUGH LIFE IF YOU HAVE THE MUSCLE TO BACK IT UP
JIM DAVIS
© 1980 PAWS, INC. All Rights Reserved.

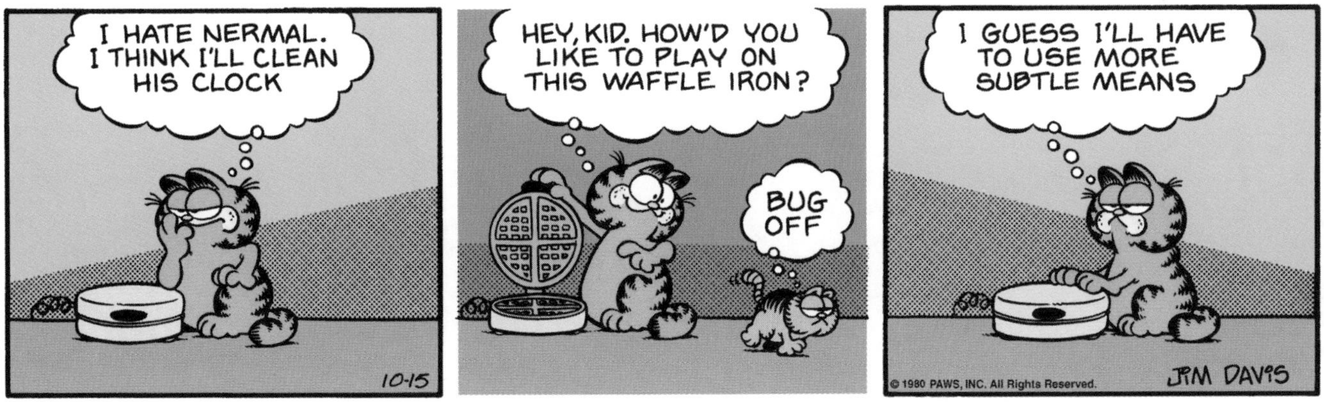
I HATE NERMAL. I THINK I'LL CLEAN HIS CLOCK
10-15
HEY, KID. HOW'D YOU LIKE TO PLAY ON THIS WAFFLE IRON?
BUG OFF
I GUESS I'LL HAVE TO USE MORE SUBTLE MEANS
© 1980 PAWS, INC. All Rights Reserved.
JIM DAVIS

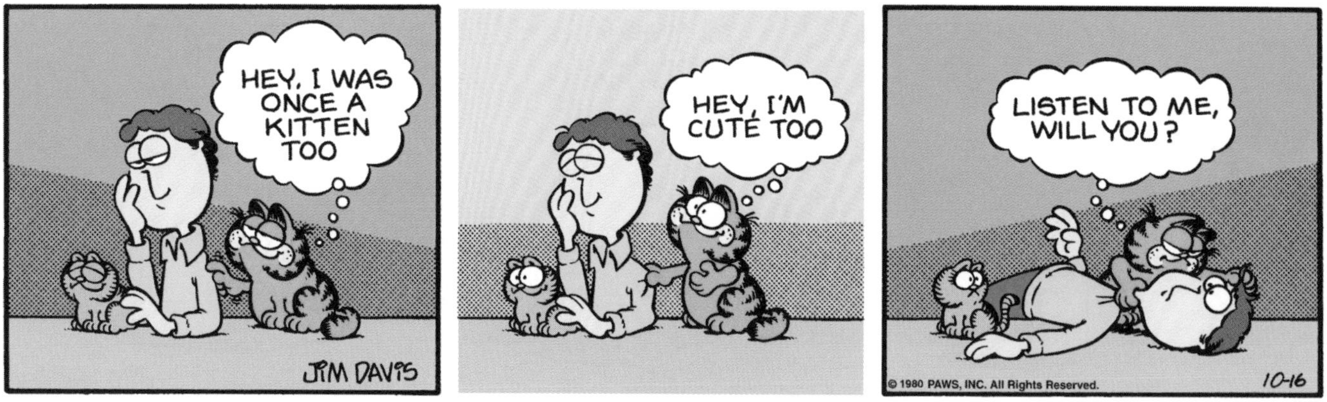
HEY, I WAS ONCE A KITTEN TOO
JIM DAVIS
HEY, I'M CUTE TOO
LISTEN TO ME, WILL YOU?
© 1980 PAWS, INC. All Rights Reserved.
10-16

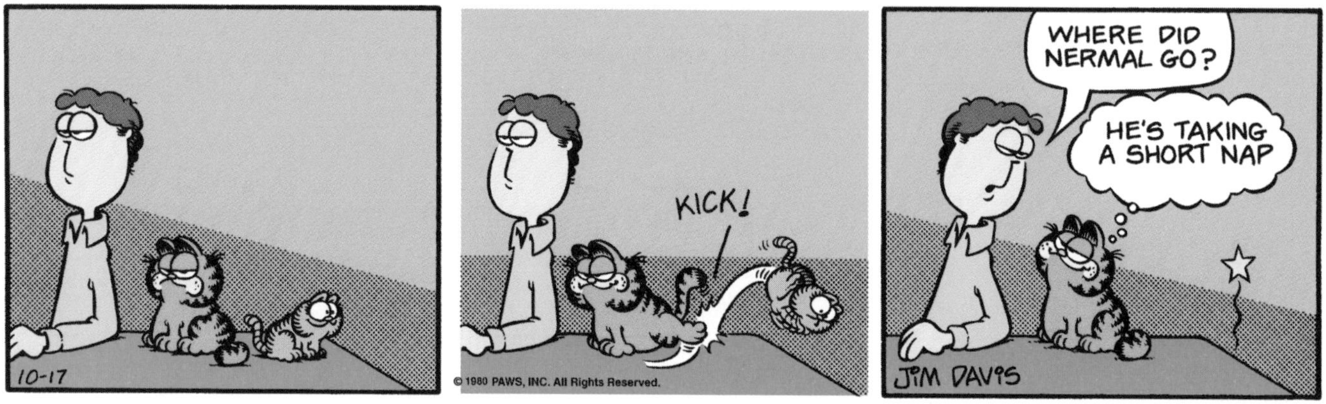
10-17
KICK!
© 1980 PAWS, INC. All Rights Reserved.
WHERE DID NERMAL GO?
HE'S TAKING A SHORT NAP
JIM DAVIS

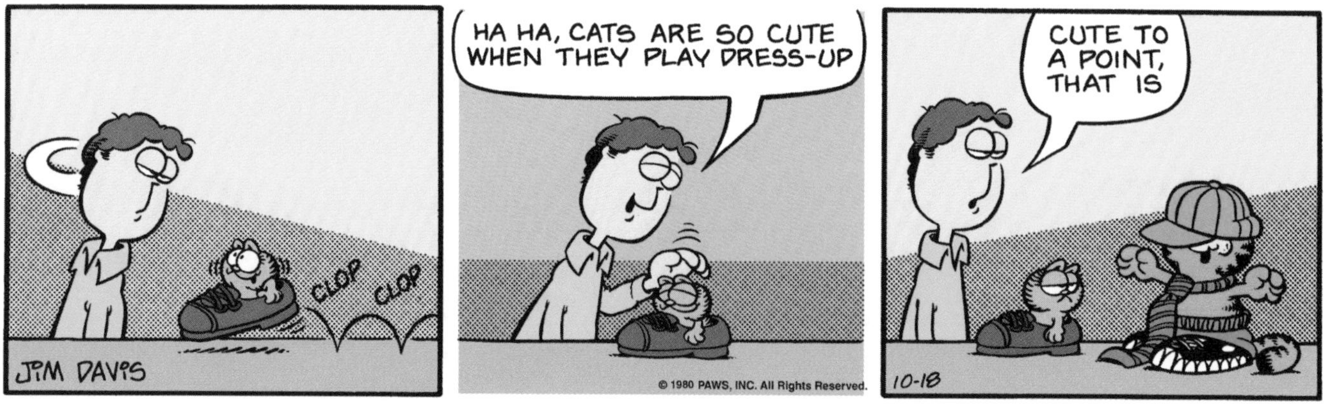
CLOP
CLOP
JIM DAVIS
HA HA, CATS ARE SO CUTE WHEN THEY PLAY DRESS-UP
© 1980 PAWS, INC. All Rights Reserved.
CUTE TO A POINT, THAT IS
10-18

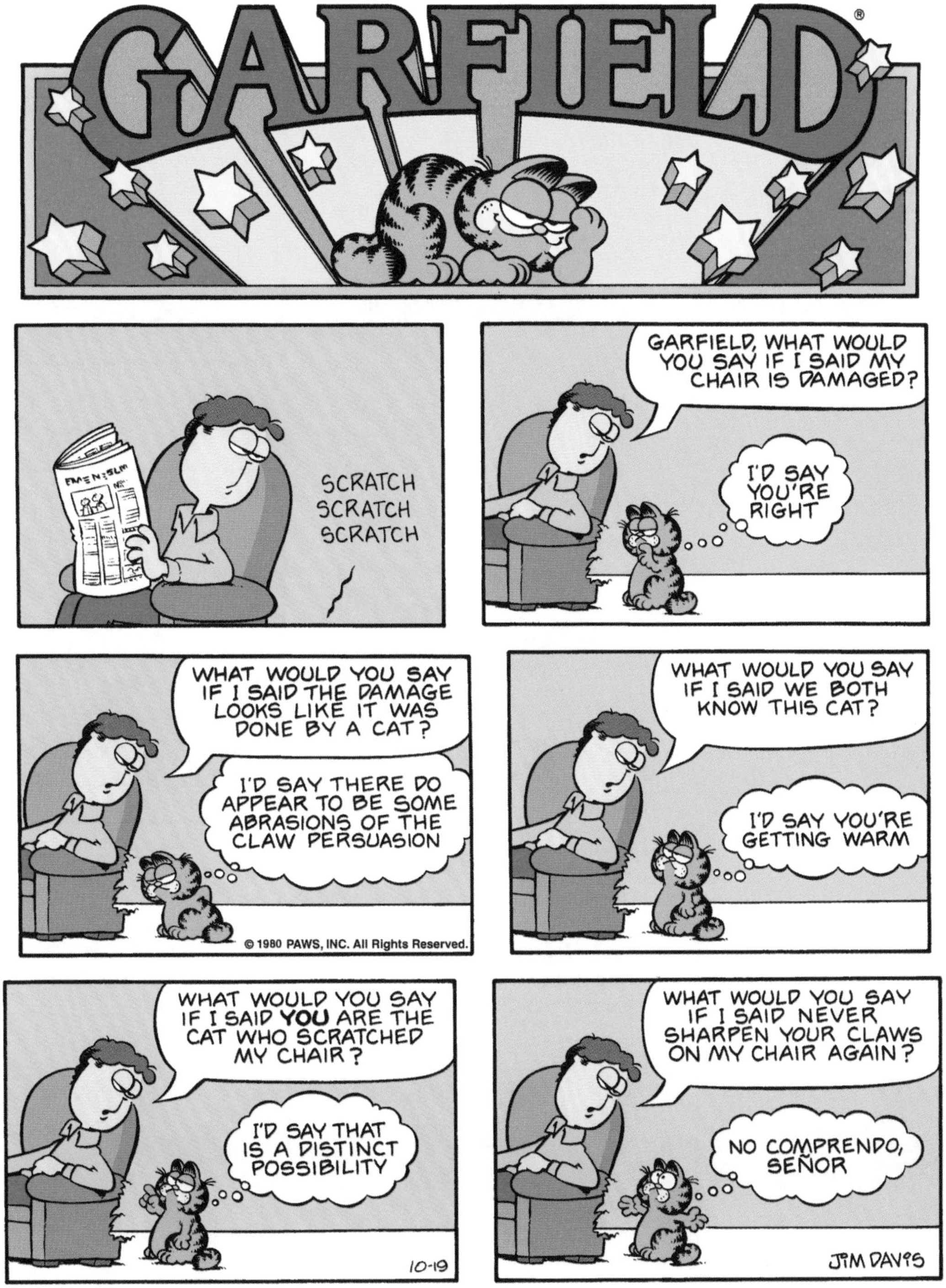
GARFIELD®
SCRATCH SCRATCH SCRATCH
GARFIELD, WHAT WOULD YOU SAY IF I SAID MY CHAIR IS DAMAGED?
I'D SAY YOU'RE RIGHT
WHAT WOULD YOU SAY IF I SAID THE DAMAGE LOOKS LIKE IT WAS DONE BY A CAT?
I'D SAY THERE DO APPEAR TO BE SOME ABRASIONS OF THE CLAW PERSUASION
© 1980 PAWS, INC. All Rights Reserved.
WHAT WOULD YOU SAY IF I SAID WE BOTH KNOW THIS CAT?
I'D SAY YOU'RE GETTING WARM
WHAT WOULD YOU SAY IF I SAID **YOU** ARE THE CAT WHO SCRATCHED MY CHAIR?
I'D SAY THAT IS A DISTINCT POSSIBILITY
10-19
WHAT WOULD YOU SAY IF I SAID NEVER SHARPEN YOUR CLAWS ON MY CHAIR AGAIN?
NO COMPRENDO, SEÑOR
JIM DAVIS

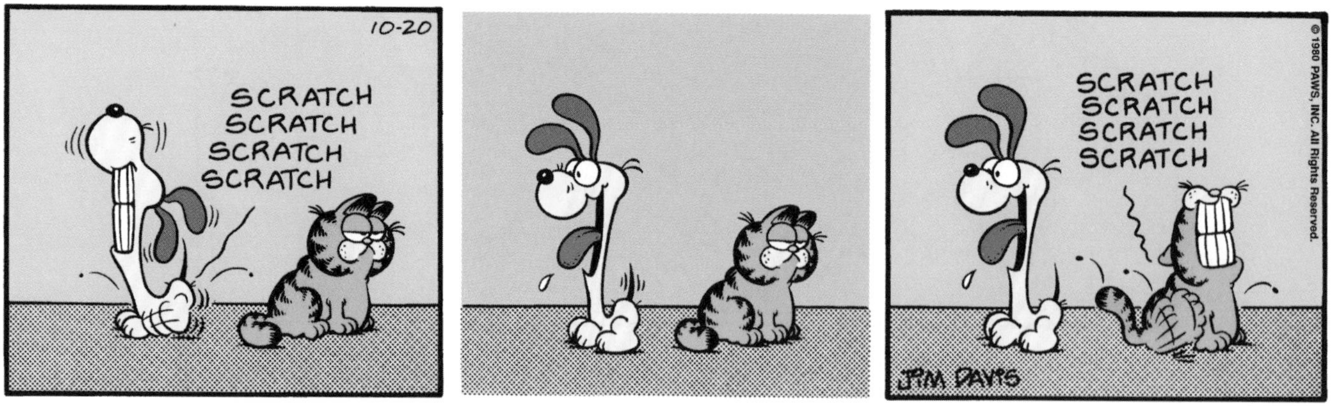
10-20
SCRATCH SCRATCH SCRATCH SCRATCH
SCRATCH SCRATCH SCRATCH SCRATCH
© 1980 PAWS, INC. All Rights Reserved.
JIM DAVIS

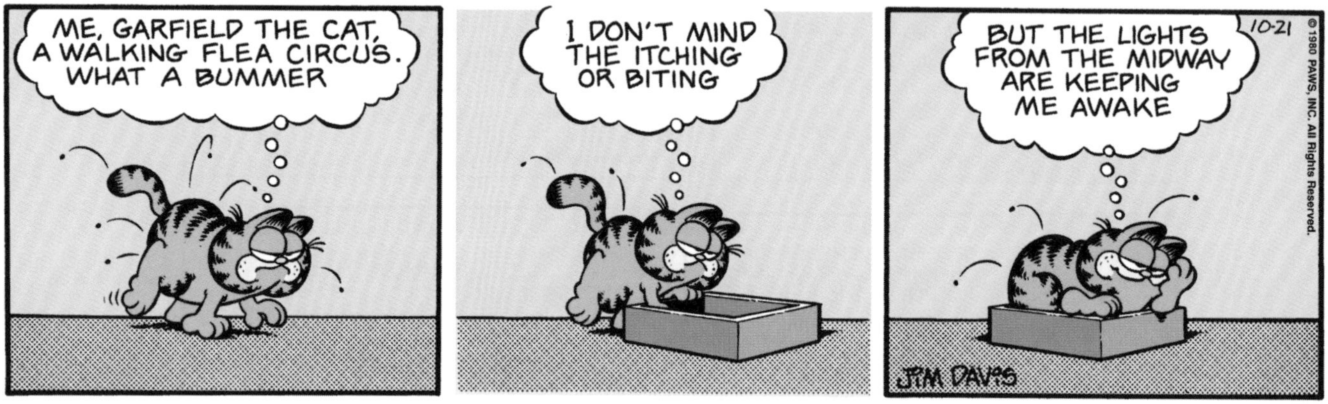
ME, GARFIELD THE CAT, A WALKING FLEA CIRCUS. WHAT A BUMMER
I DON'T MIND THE ITCHING OR BITING
BUT THE LIGHTS FROM THE MIDWAY ARE KEEPING ME AWAKE
10-21
© 1980 PAWS, INC. All Rights Reserved.
JIM DAVIS

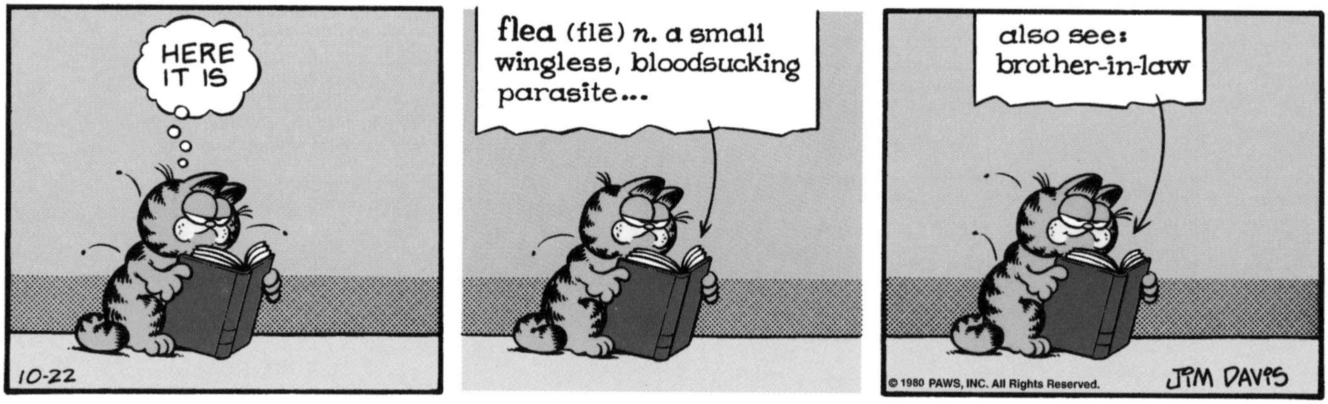
HERE IT IS
10-22
flea (flē) n. a small wingless, bloodsucking parasite...
also see: brother-in-law
© 1980 PAWS, INC. All Rights Reserved.
JIM DAVIS

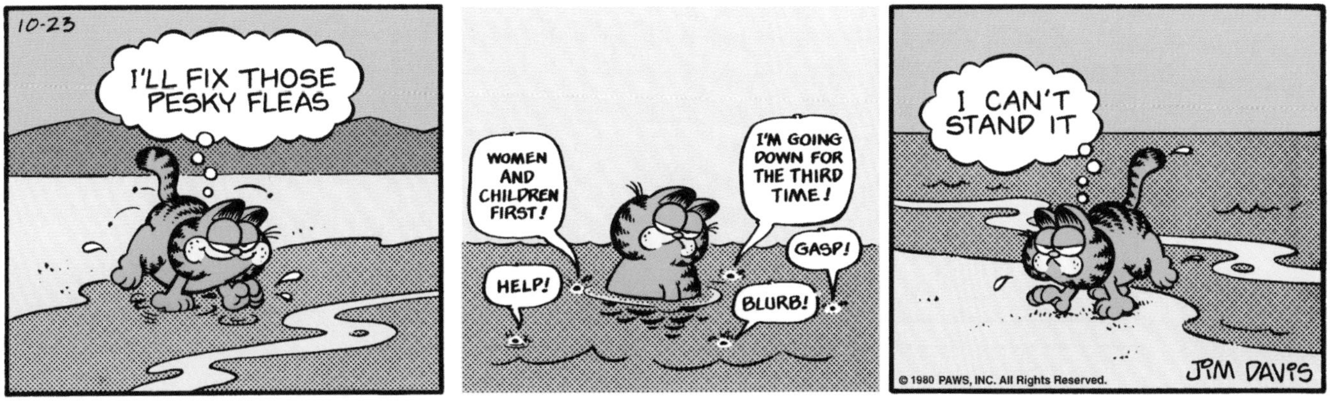
10-23
I'LL FIX THOSE PESKY FLEAS
WOMEN AND CHILDREN FIRST!
HELP!
I'M GOING DOWN FOR THE THIRD TIME!
GASP!
BLURB!
I CAN'T STAND IT
© 1980 PAWS, INC. All Rights Reserved.
JIM DAVIS

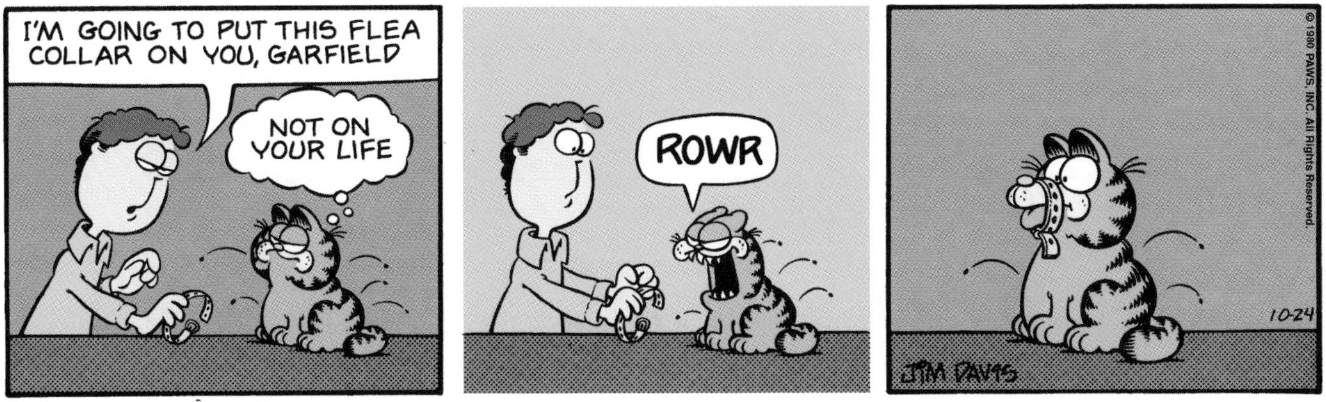
I'M GOING TO PUT THIS FLEA COLLAR ON YOU, GARFIELD
NOT ON YOUR LIFE
ROWR
© 1980 PAWS, INC. All Rights Reserved.
10-24
JIM DAVIS

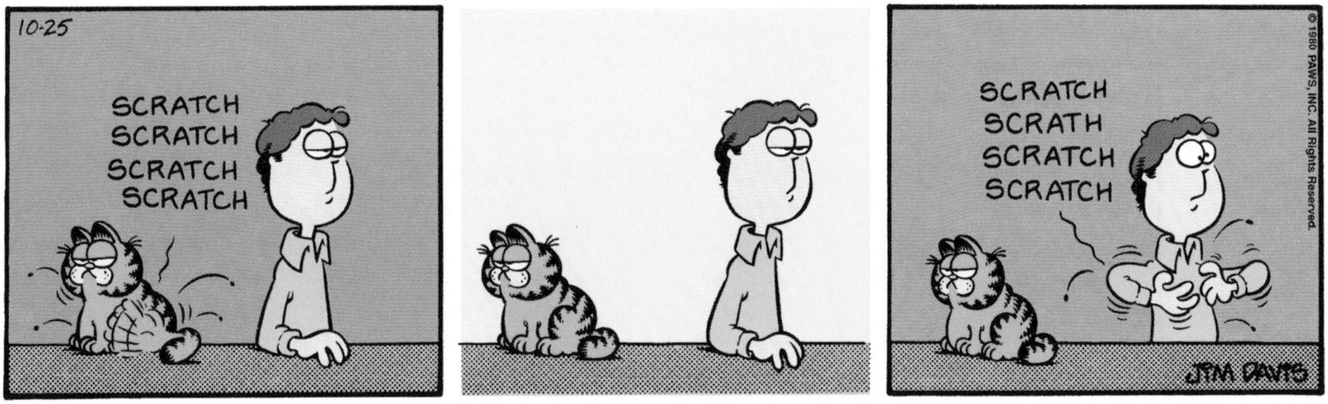
10-25
SCRATCH
SCRATCH
SCRATCH
SCRATCH
SCRATCH
SCRATH
SCRATCH
SCRATCH
© 1980 PAWS, INC. All Rights Reserved.
JIM DAVIS

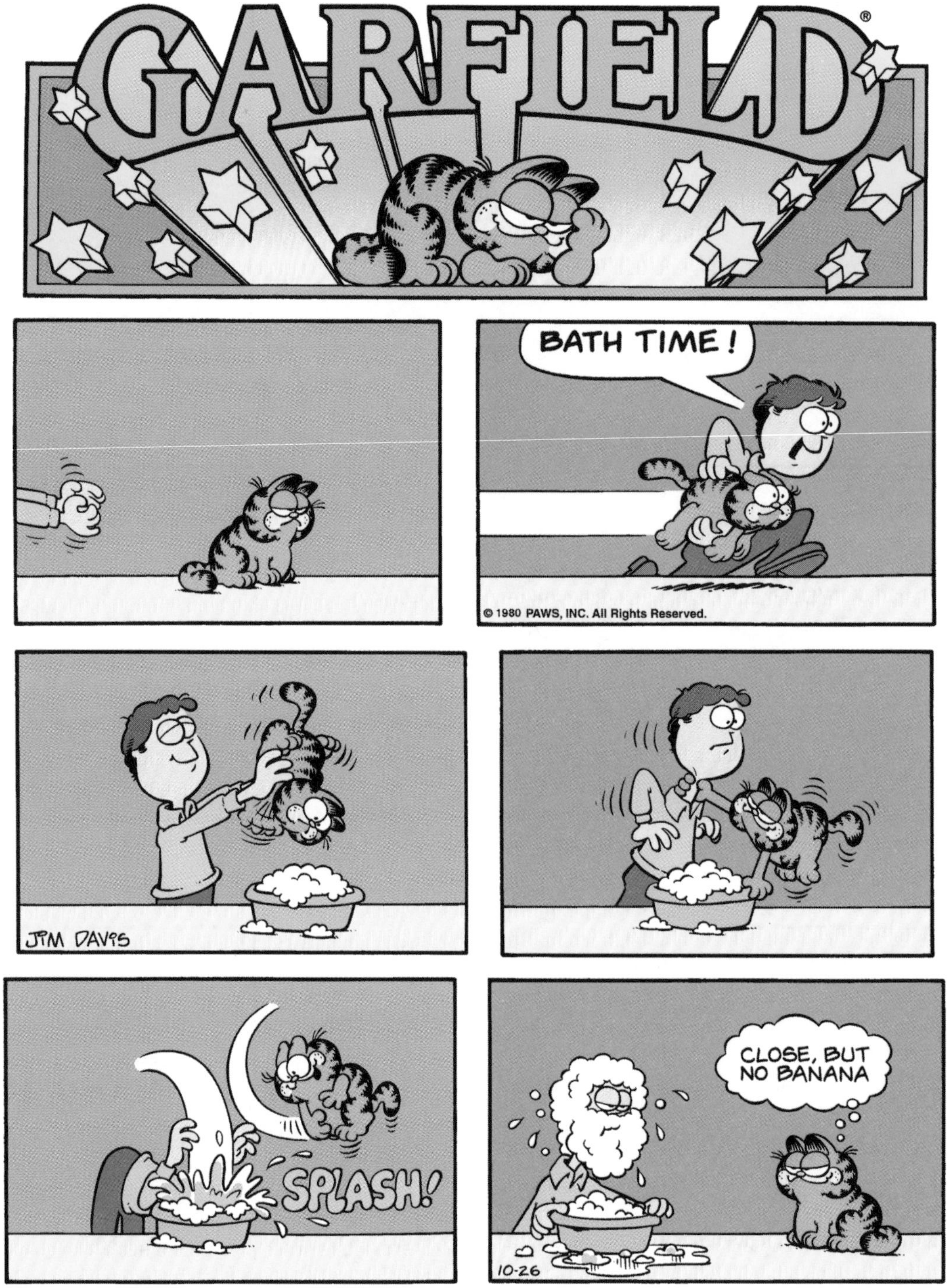
GARFIELD®
BATH TIME!
© 1980 PAWS, INC. All Rights Reserved.
JIM DAVIS
SPLASH!
CLOSE, BUT NO BANANA
10-26

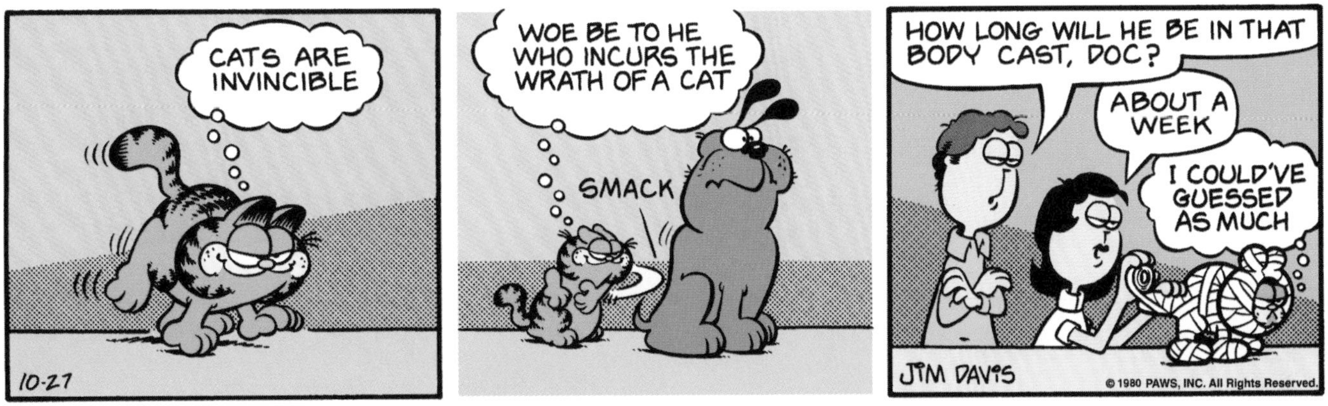
CATS ARE INVINCIBLE
10-27
WOE BE TO HE WHO INCURS THE WRATH OF A CAT
SMACK
HOW LONG WILL HE BE IN THAT BODY CAST, DOC?
ABOUT A WEEK
I COULD'VE GUESSED AS MUCH
JIM DAVIS
© 1980 PAWS, INC. All Rights Reserved.

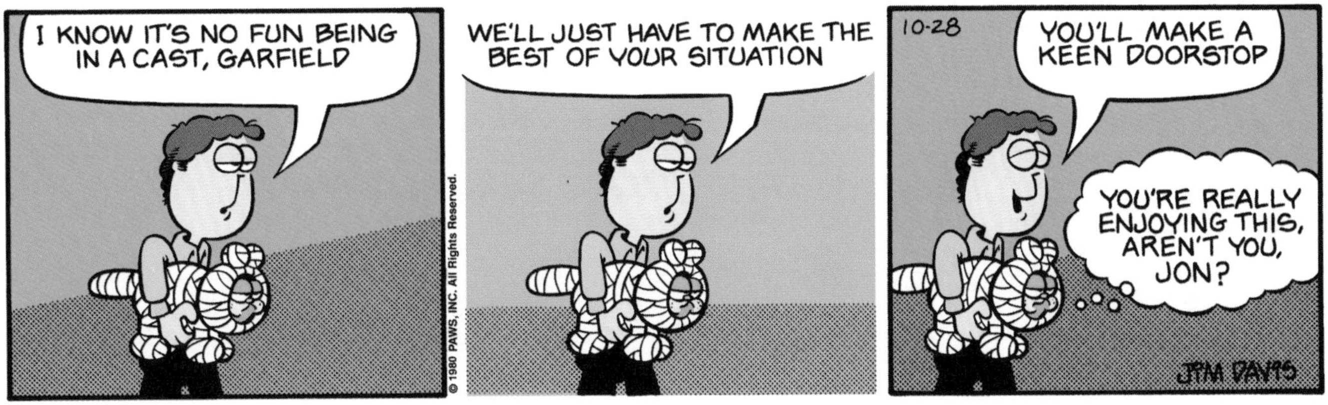
I KNOW IT'S NO FUN BEING IN A CAST, GARFIELD
© 1980 PAWS, INC. All Rights Reserved.
WE'LL JUST HAVE TO MAKE THE BEST OF YOUR SITUATION
10-28
YOU'LL MAKE A KEEN DOORSTOP
YOU'RE REALLY ENJOYING THIS, AREN'T YOU, JON?
JIM DAVIS

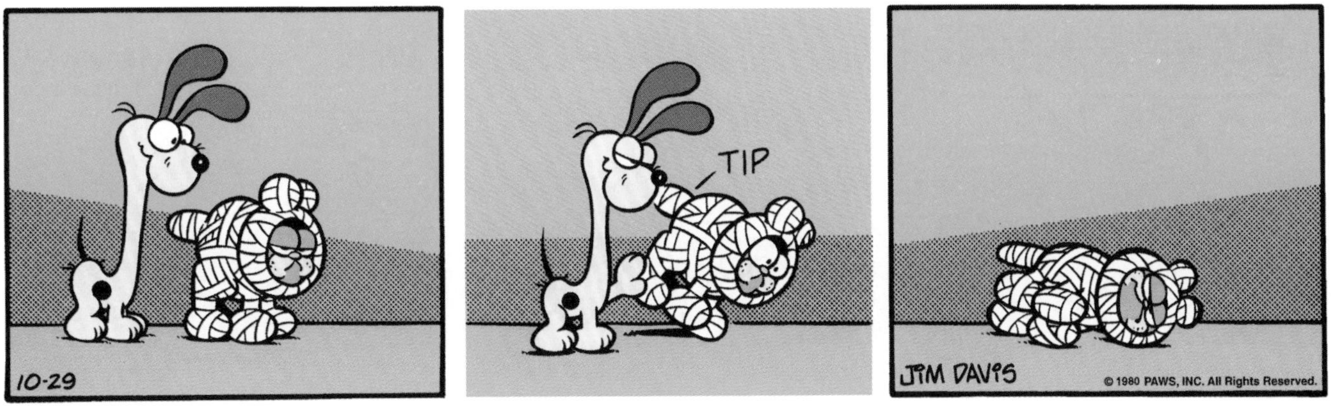
10-29
TIP
JIM DAVIS
© 1980 PAWS, INC. All Rights Reserved.

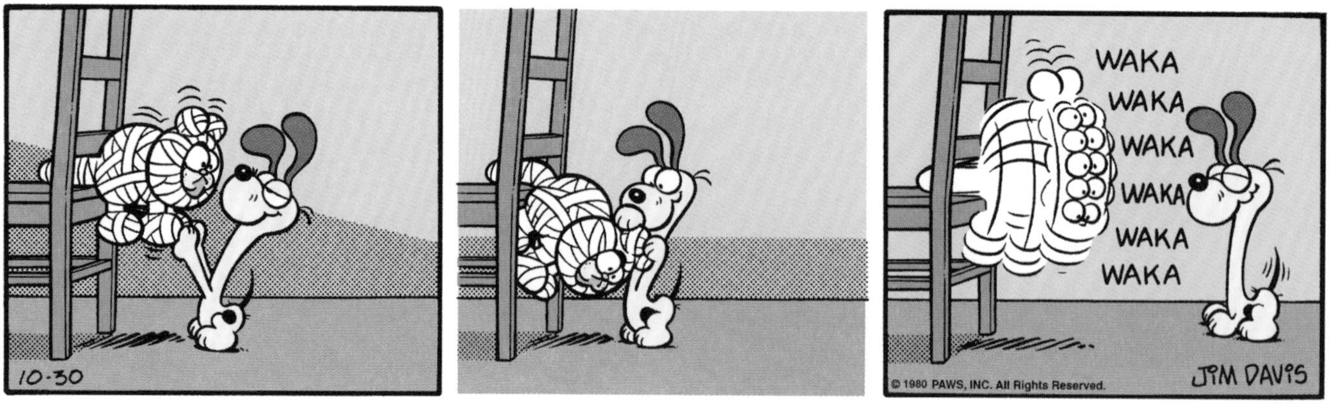
WAKA
WAKA
WAKA
WAKA
WAKA
WAKA
10-30
© 1980 PAWS, INC. All Rights Reserved.
JIM DAVIS

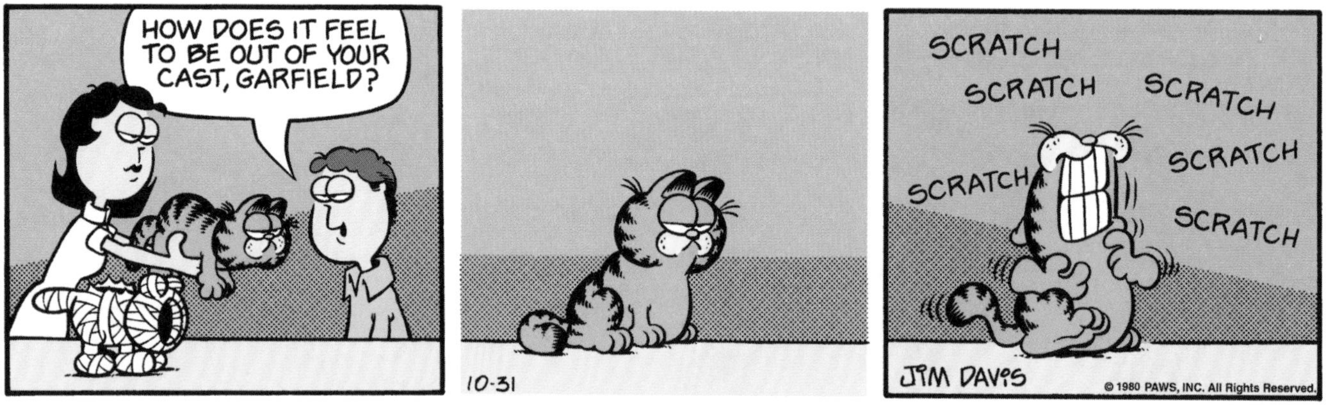
HOW DOES IT FEEL TO BE OUT OF YOUR CAST, GARFIELD?
10-31
SCRATCH
SCRATCH
SCRATCH
SCRATCH
SCRATCH
SCRATCH
JIM DAVIS
© 1980 PAWS, INC. All Rights Reserved.

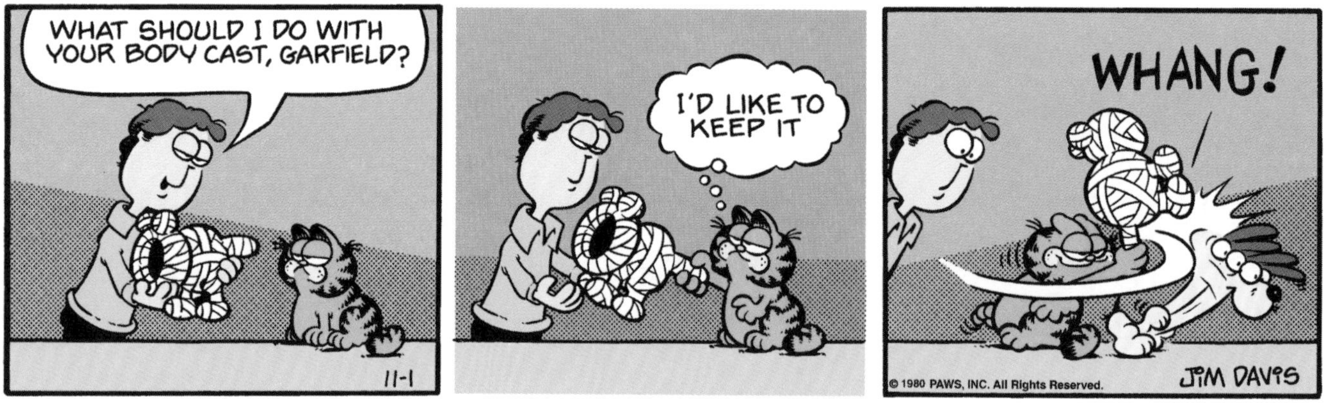
WHAT SHOULD I DO WITH YOUR BODY CAST, GARFIELD?
11-1
I'D LIKE TO KEEP IT
WHANG!
© 1980 PAWS, INC. All Rights Reserved.
JIM DAVIS

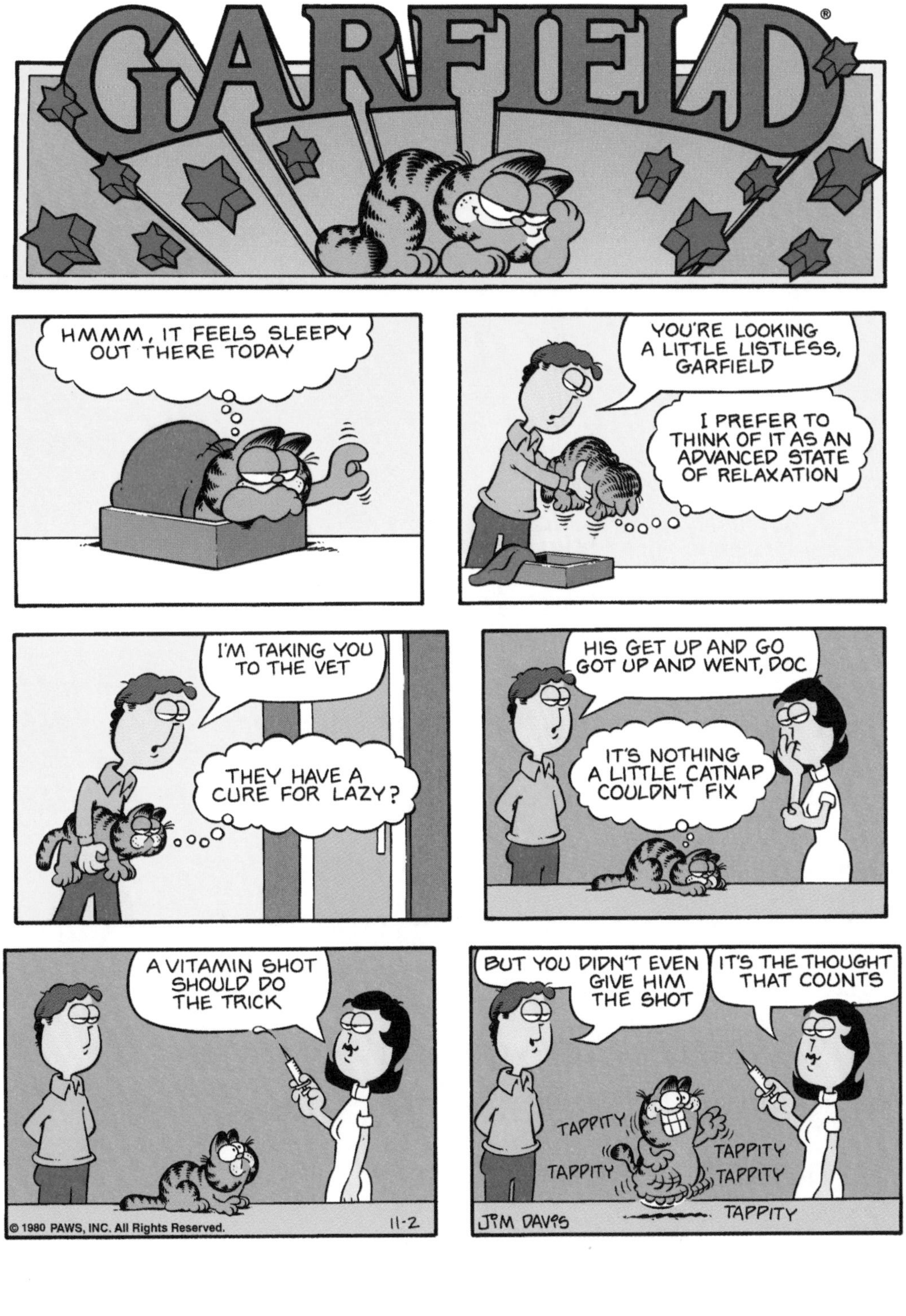
GARFIELD®
HMMM, IT FEELS SLEEPY OUT THERE TODAY
YOU'RE LOOKING A LITTLE LISTLESS, GARFIELD
I PREFER TO THINK OF IT AS AN ADVANCED STATE OF RELAXATION
I'M TAKING YOU TO THE VET
THEY HAVE A CURE FOR LAZY?
HIS GET UP AND GO GOT UP AND WENT, DOC
IT'S NOTHING A LITTLE CATNAP COULDN'T FIX
A VITAMIN SHOT SHOULD DO THE TRICK
© 1980 PAWS, INC. All Rights Reserved.
11-2
BUT YOU DIDN'T EVEN GIVE HIM THE SHOT
IT'S THE THOUGHT THAT COUNTS
TAPPITY TAPPITY TAPPITY TAPPITY TAPPITY TAPPITY
JIM DAVIS

GARFIELD EATING TIPS

1. Never eat anything that's on fire.
2. Never leave your food dish under a bird cage.
3. Only play in your food if you've already eaten your toys.
4. Eat every meal as though it were your last.
5. Only snack between meals.
6. Chew your food at least once.
7. Never put off till tomorrow what you can eat today.
8. Always dress up your leftovers: one clever way is with top hats and canes.
9. A handy breakfast tip: always check your Grape-Nuts for squirrels.
10. Don't save your dessert for last. Eat it first.

Garfield
takes the cake

BY JIM DAVIS

Ballantine Books • New York

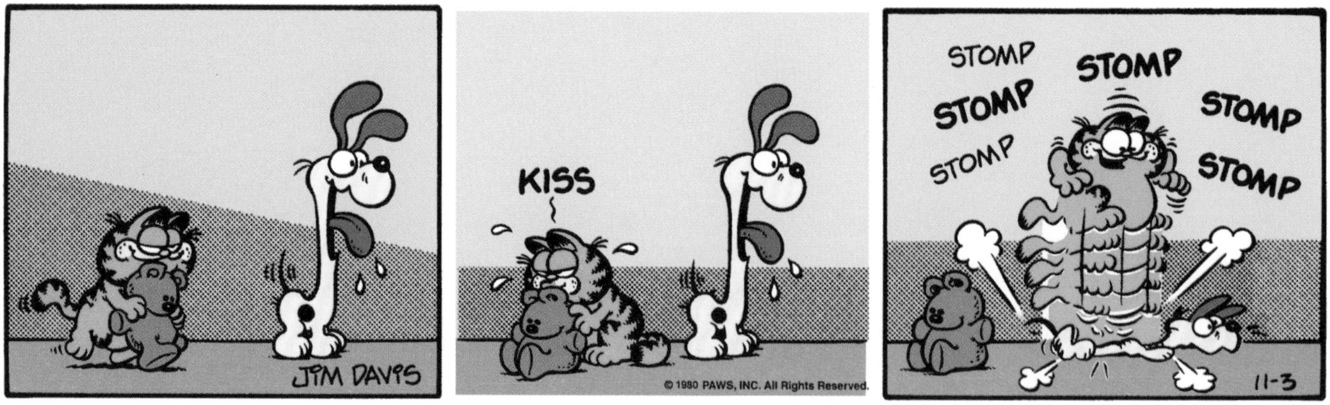
JIM DAVIS
KISS
© 1980 PAWS, INC. All Rights Reserved.
STOMP
STOMP
STOMP
STOMP
STOMP
STOMP
11-3

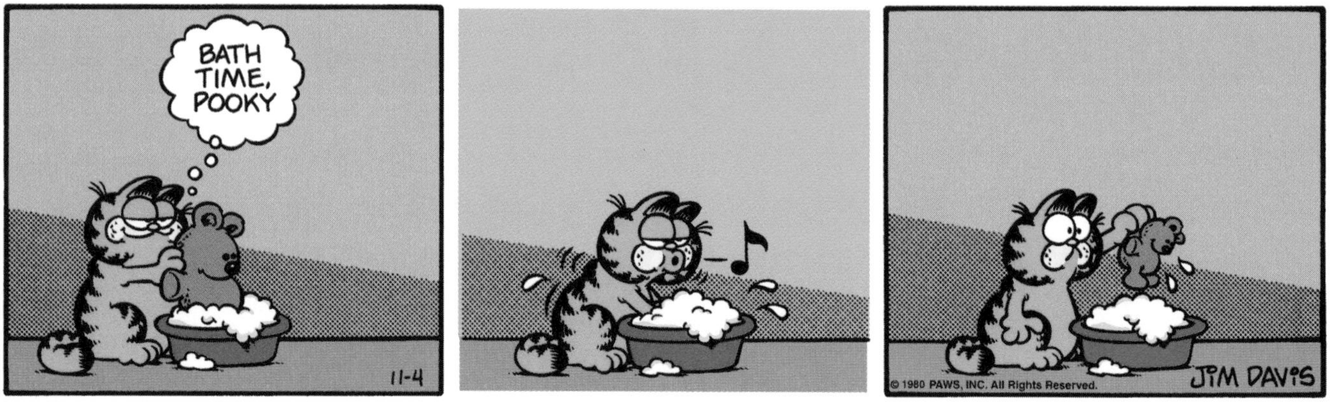
BATH TIME, POOKY
11-4
© 1980 PAWS, INC. All Rights Reserved.
JIM DAVIS

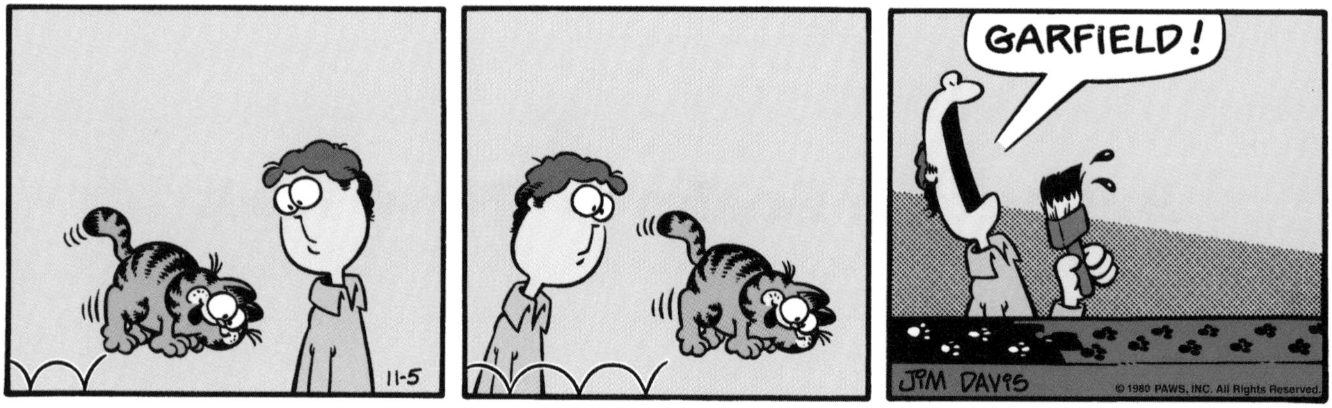
11-5
GARFIELD!
JIM DAVIS
© 1980 PAWS, INC. All Rights Reserved.

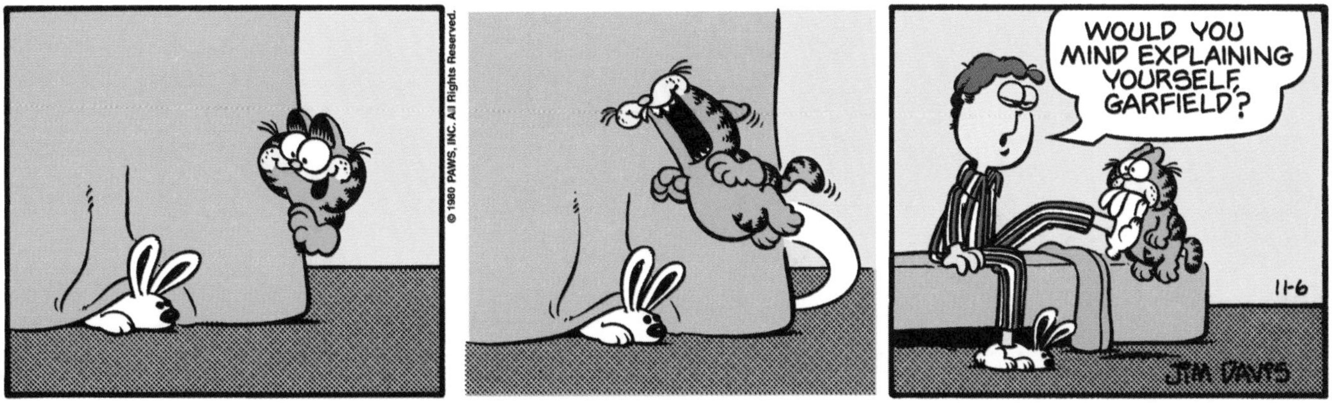
© 1980 PAWS, INC. All Rights Reserved.
WOULD YOU MIND EXPLAINING YOURSELF, GARFIELD?
11-6
JIM DAVIS

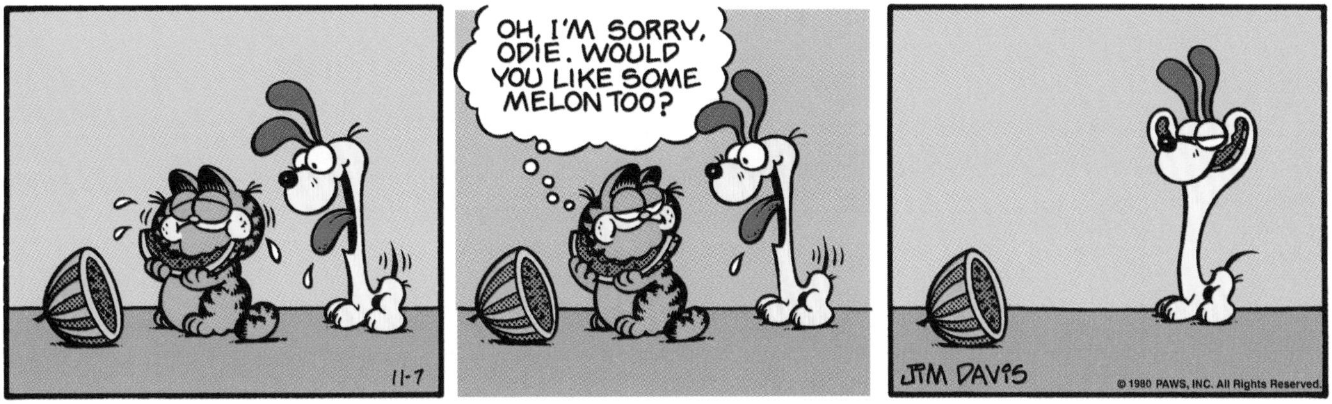
11-7
OH, I'M SORRY, ODIE. WOULD YOU LIKE SOME MELON TOO?
JIM DAVIS
© 1980 PAWS, INC. All Rights Reserved.

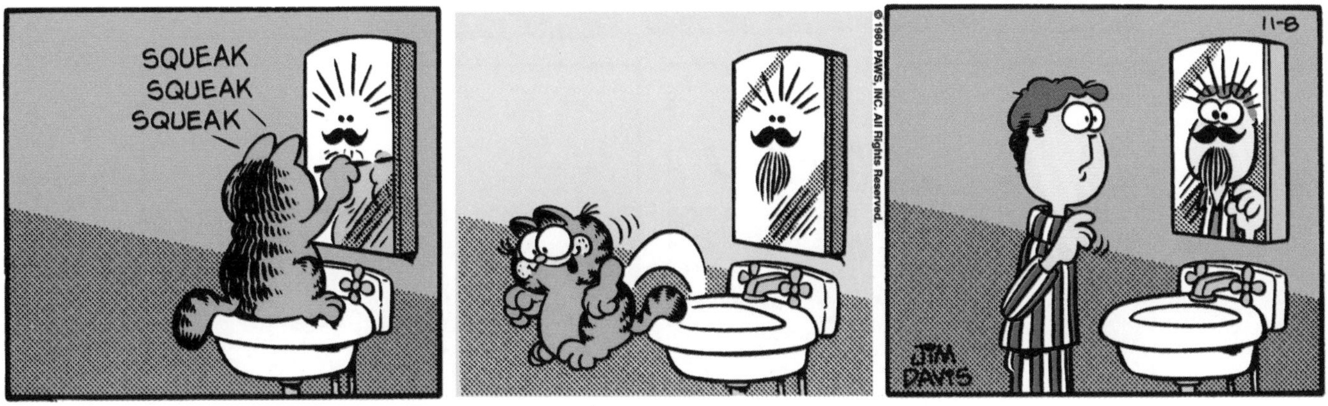
SQUEAK
SQUEAK
SQUEAK
© 1980 PAWS, INC. All Rights Reserved.
11-8
JIM DAVIS

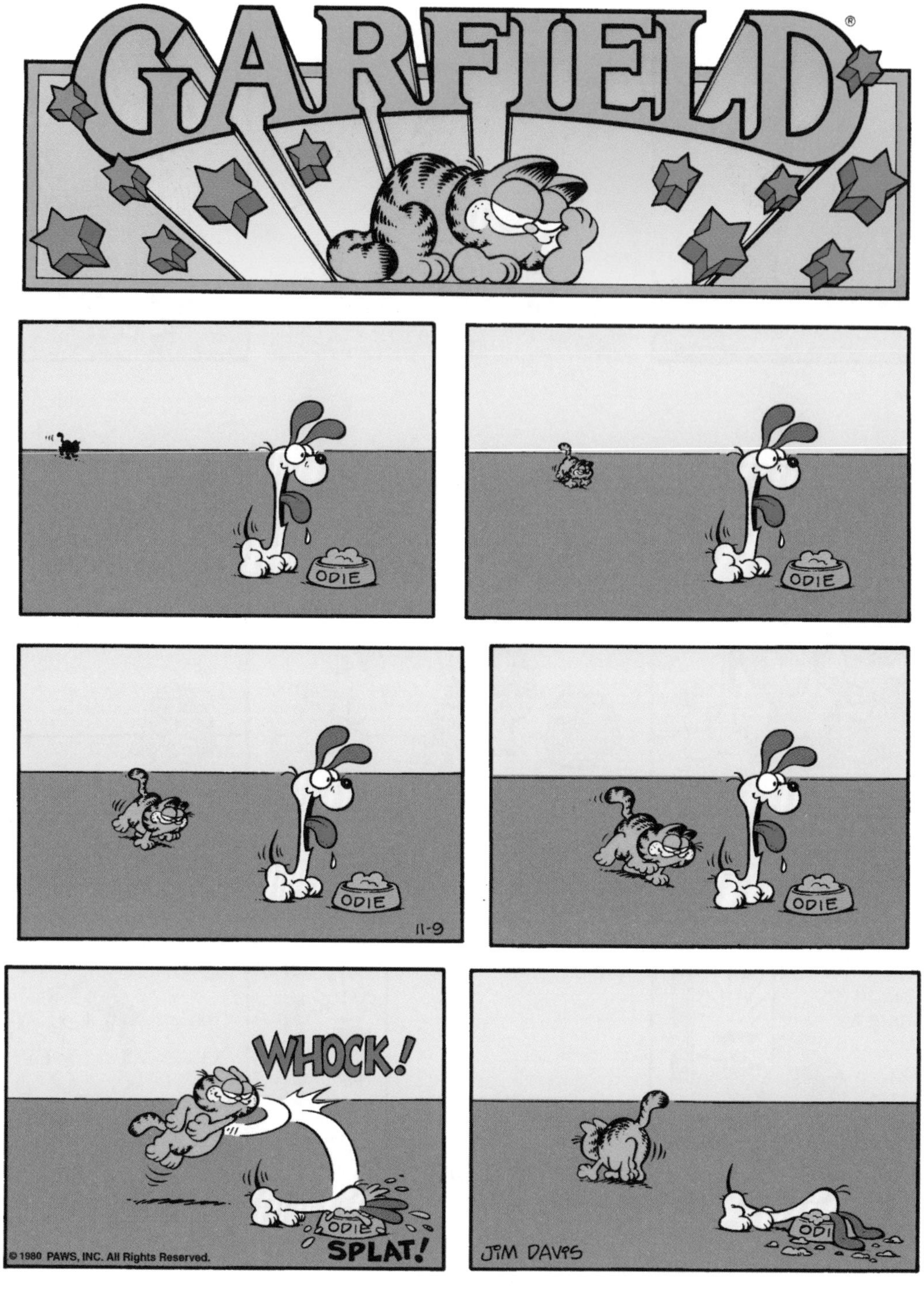
GARFIELD®
ODIE
ODIE
ODIE
11-9
ODIE
WHOCK!
ODIE
SPLAT!
© 1980 PAWS, INC. All Rights Reserved.
JIM DAVIS
ODI

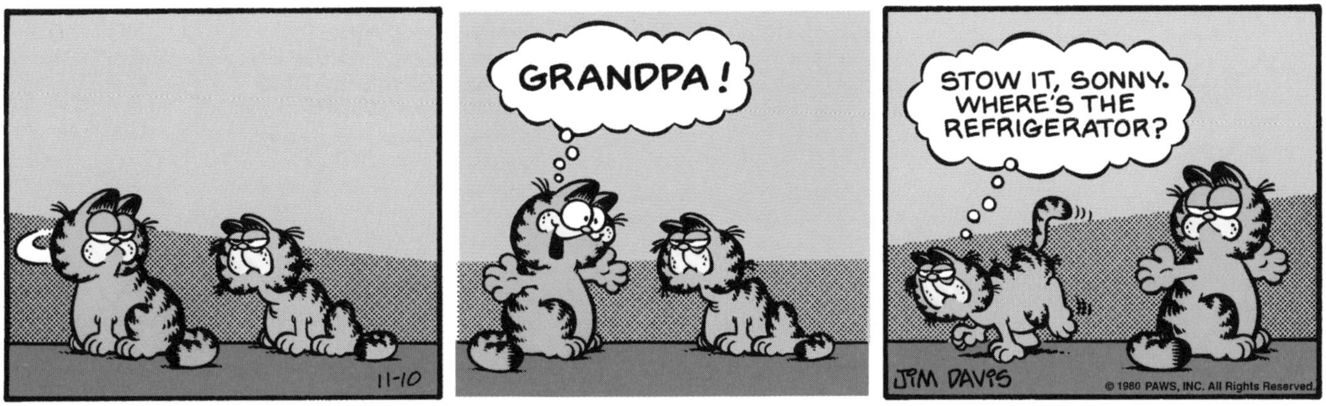
11-10
GRANDPA!
STOW IT, SONNY. WHERE'S THE REFRIGERATOR?
JIM DAVIS
© 1980 PAWS, INC. All Rights Reserved.

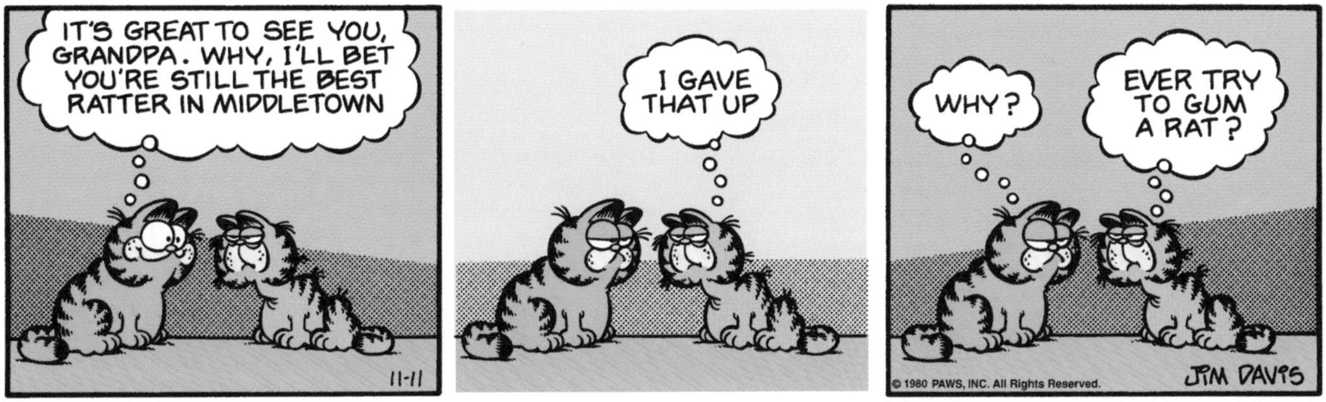
IT'S GREAT TO SEE YOU, GRANDPA. WHY, I'LL BET YOU'RE STILL THE BEST RATTER IN MIDDLETOWN
11-11
I GAVE THAT UP
WHY?
EVER TRY TO GUM A RAT?
© 1980 PAWS, INC. All Rights Reserved.
JIM DAVIS

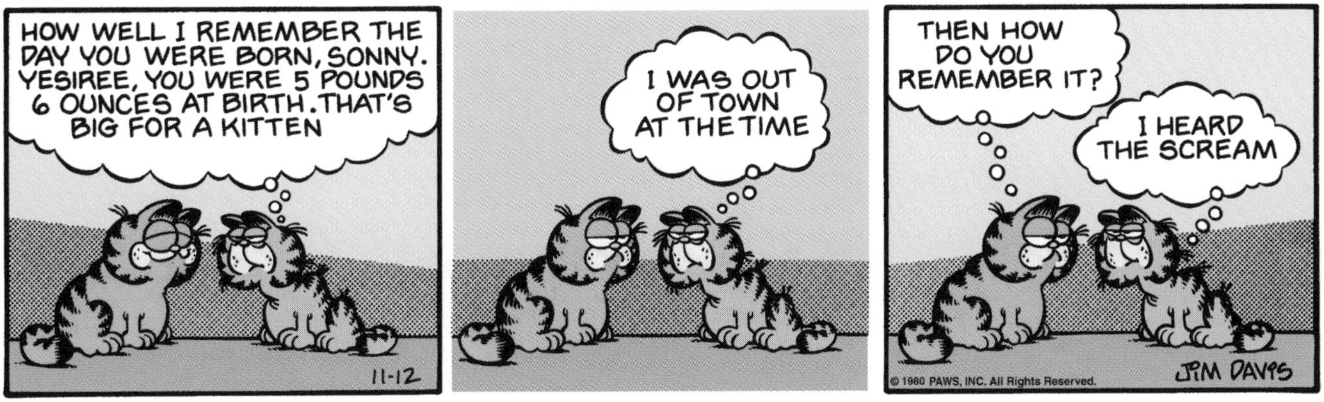
HOW WELL I REMEMBER THE DAY YOU WERE BORN, SONNY. YESIREE, YOU WERE 5 POUNDS 6 OUNCES AT BIRTH. THAT'S BIG FOR A KITTEN
11-12
I WAS OUT OF TOWN AT THE TIME
THEN HOW DO YOU REMEMBER IT?
I HEARD THE SCREAM
© 1980 PAWS, INC. All Rights Reserved.
JIM DAVIS

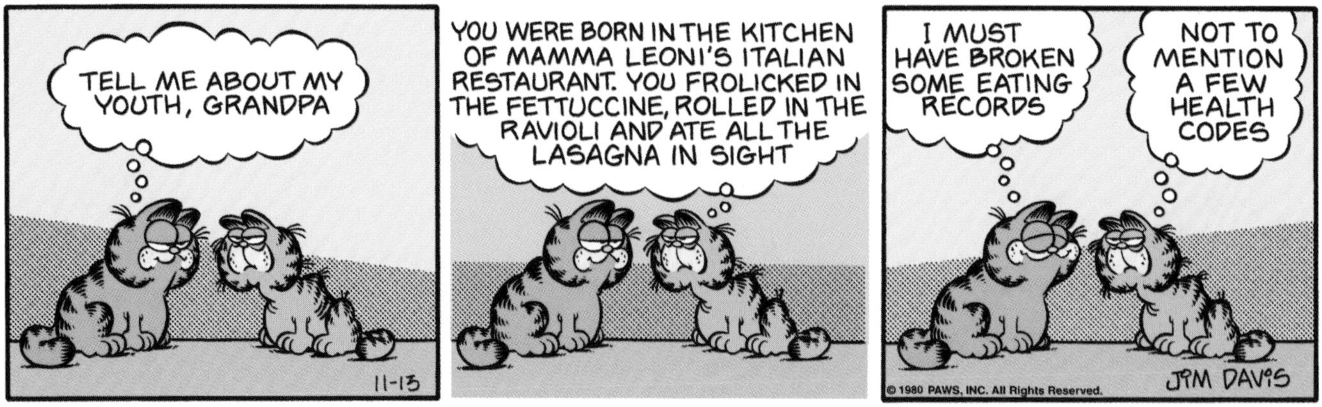
TELL ME ABOUT MY YOUTH, GRANDPA
11-13
YOU WERE BORN IN THE KITCHEN OF MAMMA LEONI'S ITALIAN RESTAURANT. YOU FROLICKED IN THE FETTUCCINE, ROLLED IN THE RAVIOLI AND ATE ALL THE LASAGNA IN SIGHT
I MUST HAVE BROKEN SOME EATING RECORDS
NOT TO MENTION A FEW HEALTH CODES
© 1980 PAWS, INC. All Rights Reserved.
JIM DAVIS

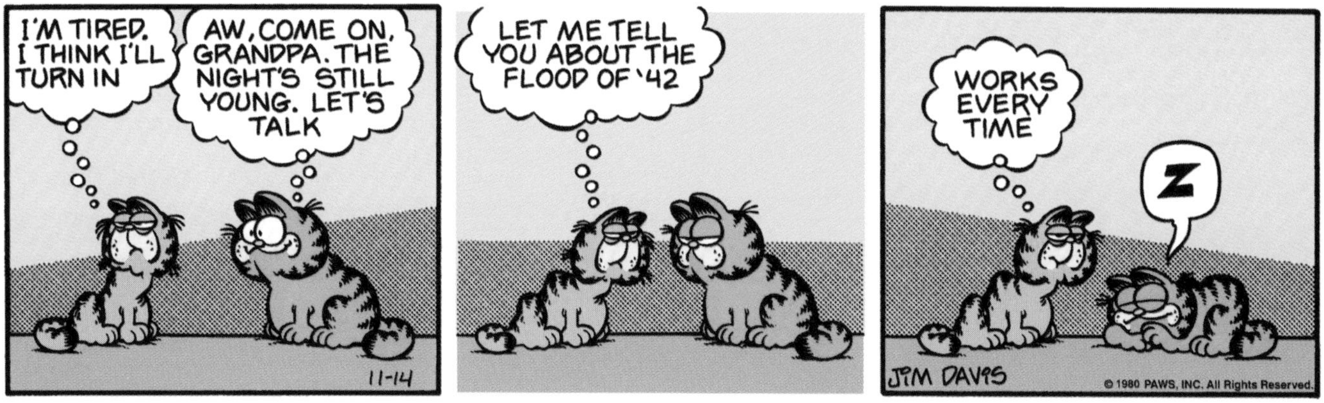
I'M TIRED. I THINK I'LL TURN IN
AW, COME ON, GRANDPA. THE NIGHT'S STILL YOUNG. LET'S TALK
11-14
LET ME TELL YOU ABOUT THE FLOOD OF '42
WORKS EVERY TIME
Z
JIM DAVIS
© 1980 PAWS, INC. All Rights Reserved.

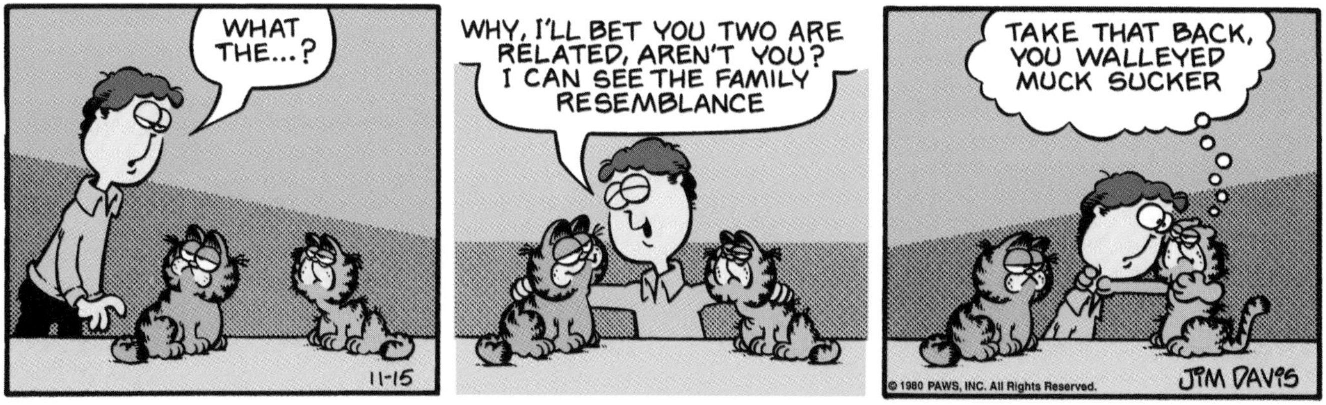
WHAT THE...?
11-15
WHY, I'LL BET YOU TWO ARE RELATED, AREN'T YOU? I CAN SEE THE FAMILY RESEMBLANCE
TAKE THAT BACK, YOU WALLEYED MUCK SUCKER
© 1980 PAWS, INC. All Rights Reserved.
JIM DAVIS

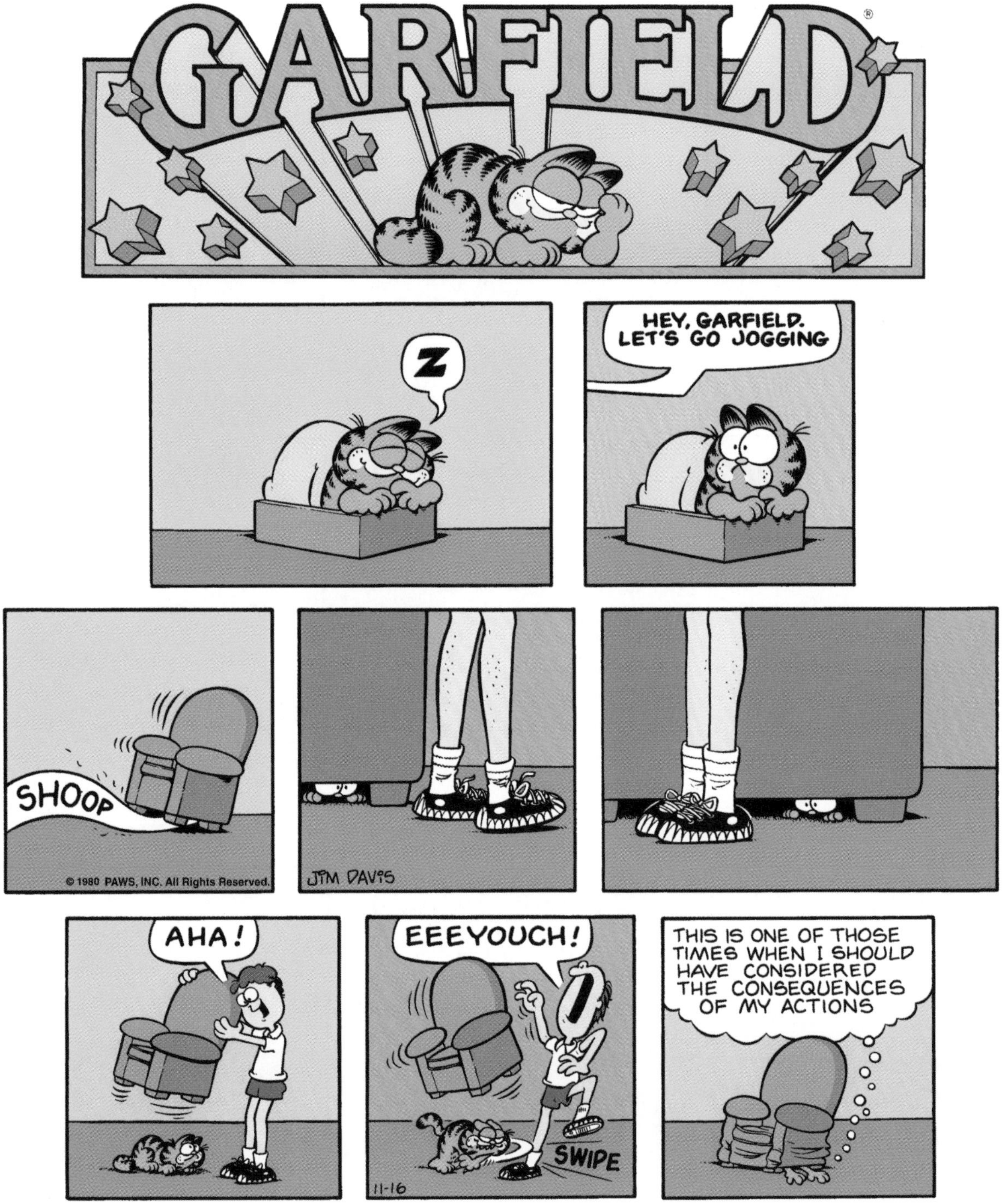
GARFIELD
Z
HEY, GARFIELD. LET'S GO JOGGING
SHOOP
© 1980 PAWS, INC. All Rights Reserved.
JIM DAVIS
AHA!
EEEYOUCH!
SWIPE
11-16
THIS IS ONE OF THOSE TIMES WHEN I SHOULD HAVE CONSIDERED THE CONSEQUENCES OF MY ACTIONS

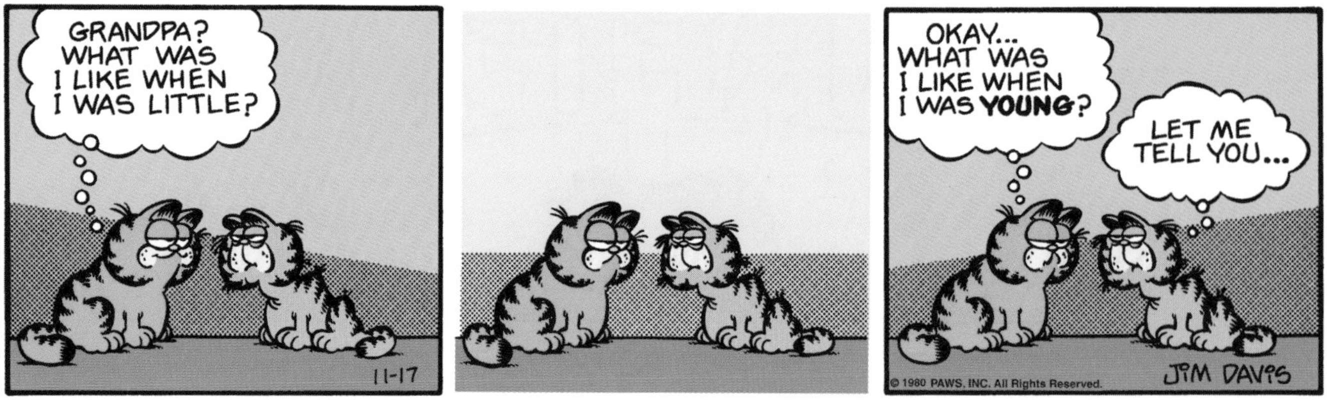
GRANDPA? WHAT WAS I LIKE WHEN I WAS LITTLE?
11-17
OKAY... WHAT WAS I LIKE WHEN I WAS **YOUNG**?
LET ME TELL YOU...
© 1980 PAWS, INC. All Rights Reserved.
JIM DAVIS

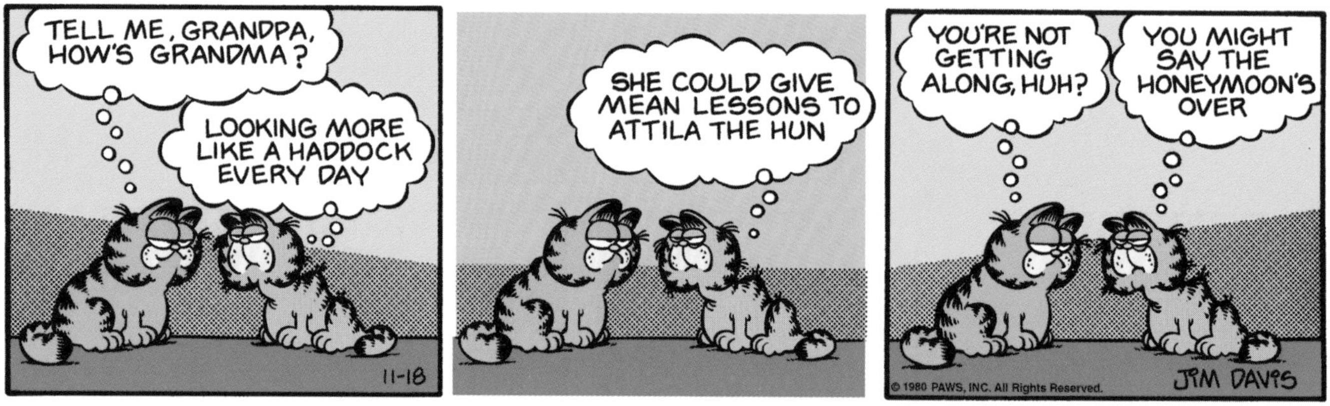
TELL ME, GRANDPA, HOW'S GRANDMA?
LOOKING MORE LIKE A HADDOCK EVERY DAY
11-18
SHE COULD GIVE MEAN LESSONS TO ATTILA THE HUN
YOU'RE NOT GETTING ALONG, HUH?
YOU MIGHT SAY THE HONEYMOON'S OVER
© 1980 PAWS, INC. All Rights Reserved.
JIM DAVIS

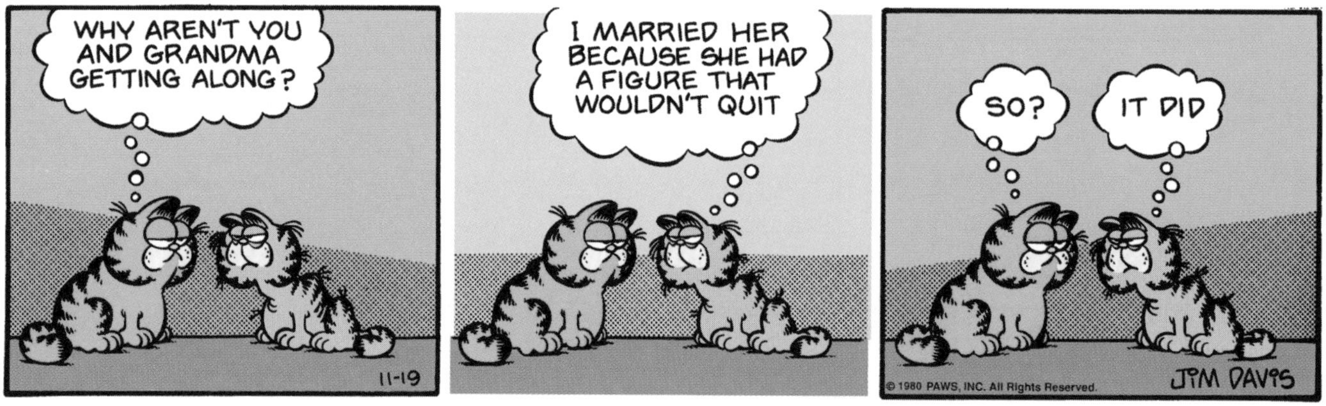
WHY AREN'T YOU AND GRANDMA GETTING ALONG?
11-19
I MARRIED HER BECAUSE SHE HAD A FIGURE THAT WOULDN'T QUIT
SO?
IT DID
© 1980 PAWS, INC. All Rights Reserved.
JIM DAVIS

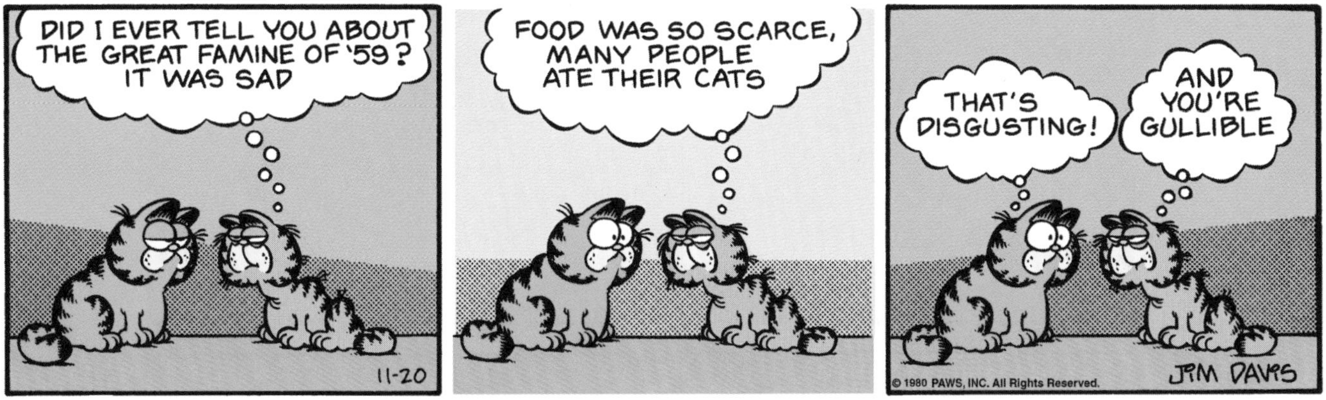
DID I EVER TELL YOU ABOUT THE GREAT FAMINE OF '59? IT WAS SAD
11-20
FOOD WAS SO SCARCE, MANY PEOPLE ATE THEIR CATS
THAT'S DISGUSTING!
AND YOU'RE GULLIBLE
© 1980 PAWS, INC. All Rights Reserved.
JIM DAVIS

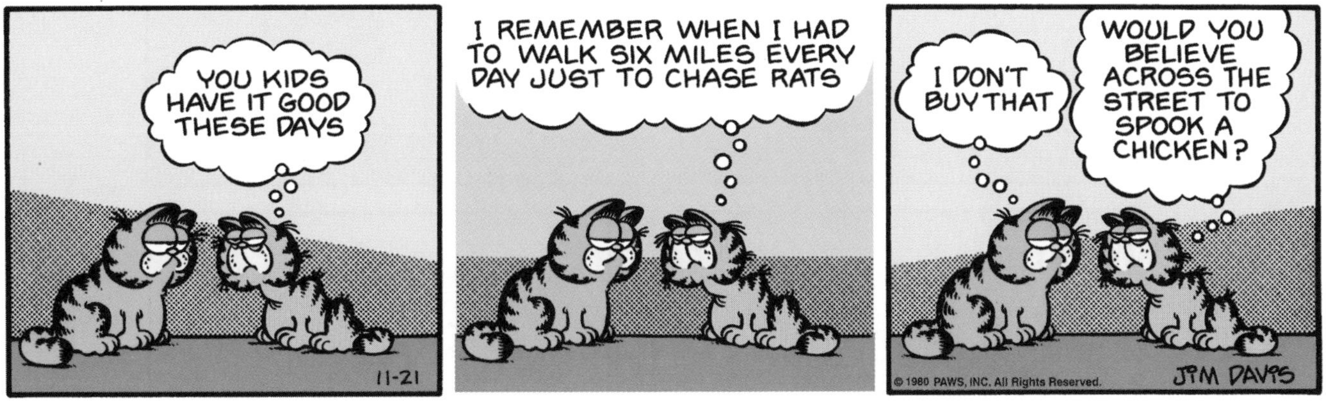
YOU KIDS HAVE IT GOOD THESE DAYS
11-21
I REMEMBER WHEN I HAD TO WALK SIX MILES EVERY DAY JUST TO CHASE RATS
I DON'T BUY THAT
WOULD YOU BELIEVE ACROSS THE STREET TO SPOOK A CHICKEN?
© 1980 PAWS, INC. All Rights Reserved.
JIM DAVIS

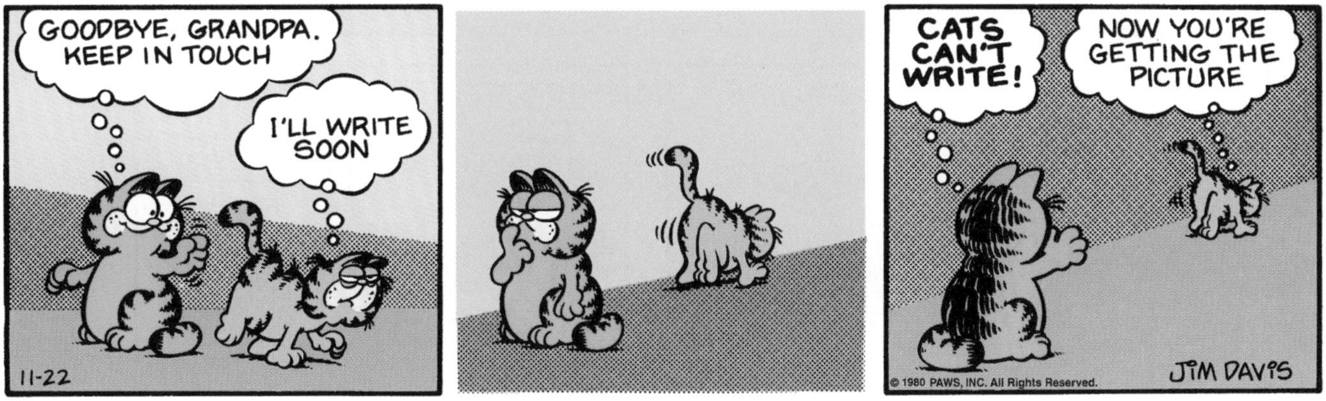
GOODBYE, GRANDPA. KEEP IN TOUCH
I'LL WRITE SOON
11-22
CATS CAN'T WRITE!
NOW YOU'RE GETTING THE PICTURE
© 1980 PAWS, INC. All Rights Reserved.
JIM DAVIS

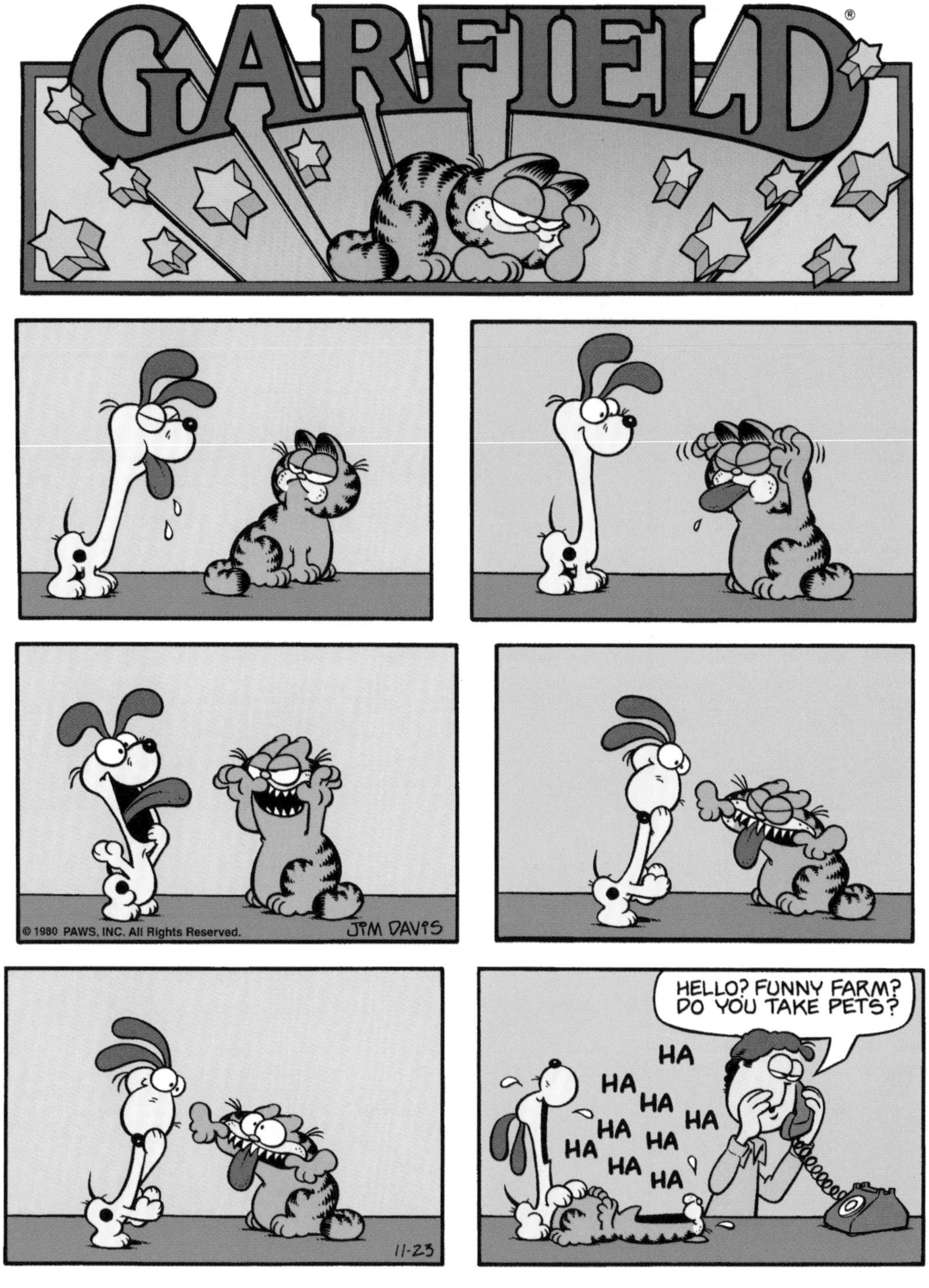
GARFIELD®
© 1980 PAWS, INC. All Rights Reserved.
JIM DAVIS
11-23
HA
HA
HA
HA
HA
HA
HA
HA
HA
HA
HELLO? FUNNY FARM? DO YOU TAKE PETS?

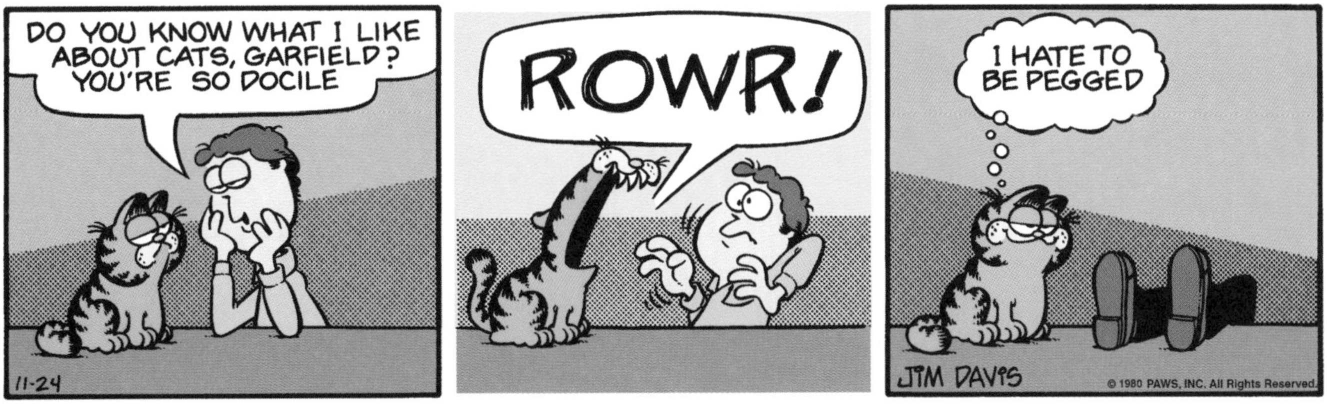
DO YOU KNOW WHAT I LIKE ABOUT CATS, GARFIELD? YOU'RE SO DOCILE
ROWR!
I HATE TO BE PEGGED
11-24
JIM DAVIS
© 1980 PAWS, INC. All Rights Reserved.

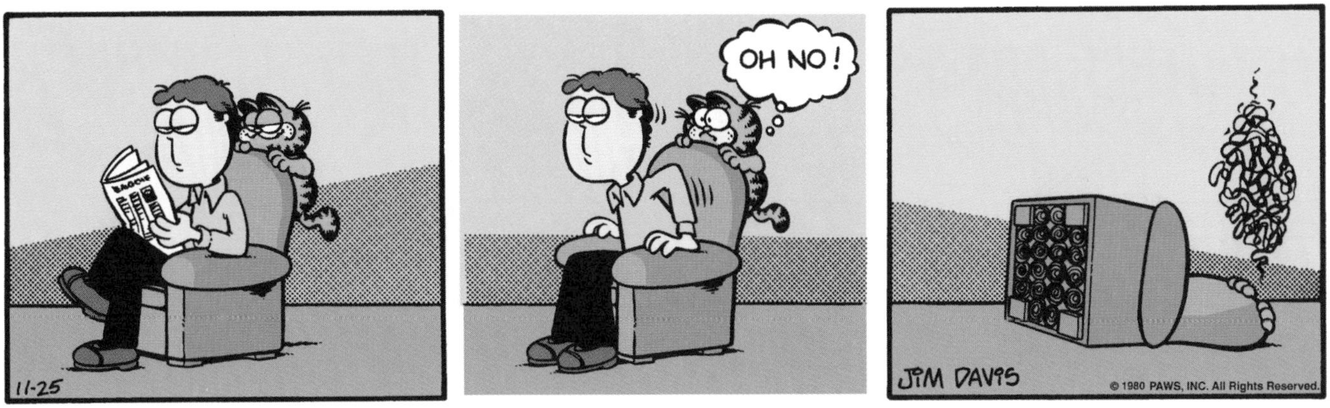
OH NO!
11-25
JIM DAVIS
© 1980 PAWS, INC. All Rights Reserved.

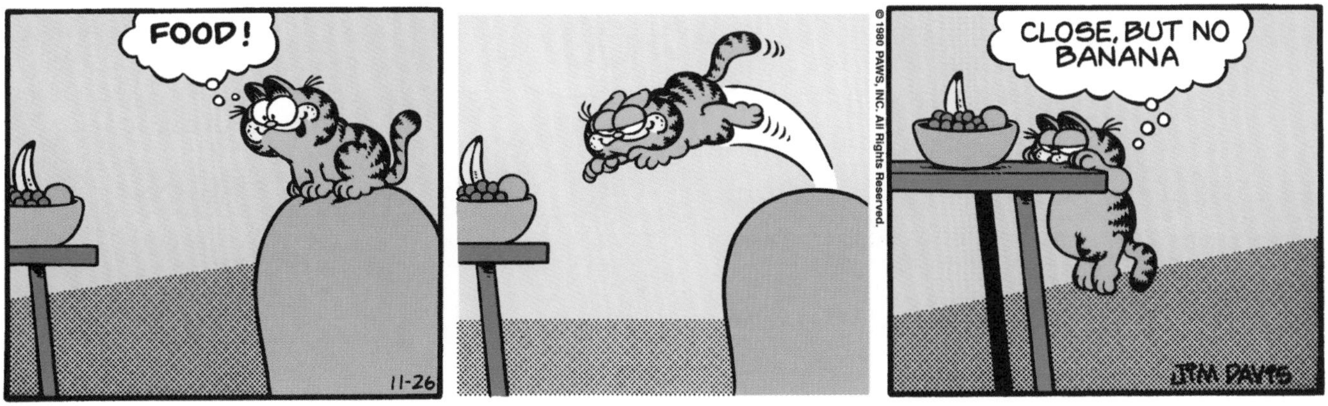
FOOD!
© 1980 PAWS, INC. All Rights Reserved.
CLOSE, BUT NO BANANA
11-26
JIM DAVIS

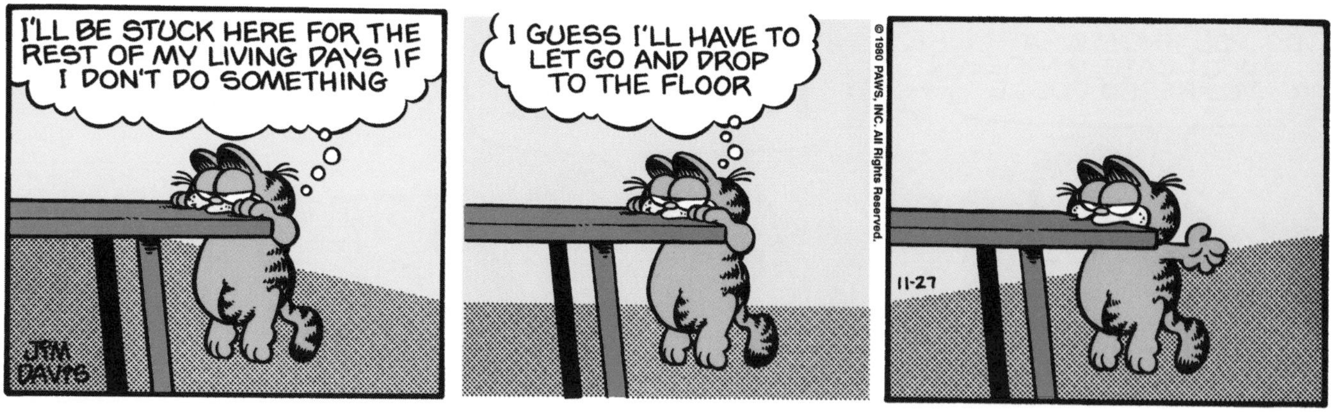
I'LL BE STUCK HERE FOR THE REST OF MY LIVING DAYS IF I DON'T DO SOMETHING
I GUESS I'LL HAVE TO LET GO AND DROP TO THE FLOOR
JIM DAVIS
11-27
© 1980 PAWS, INC. All Rights Reserved.

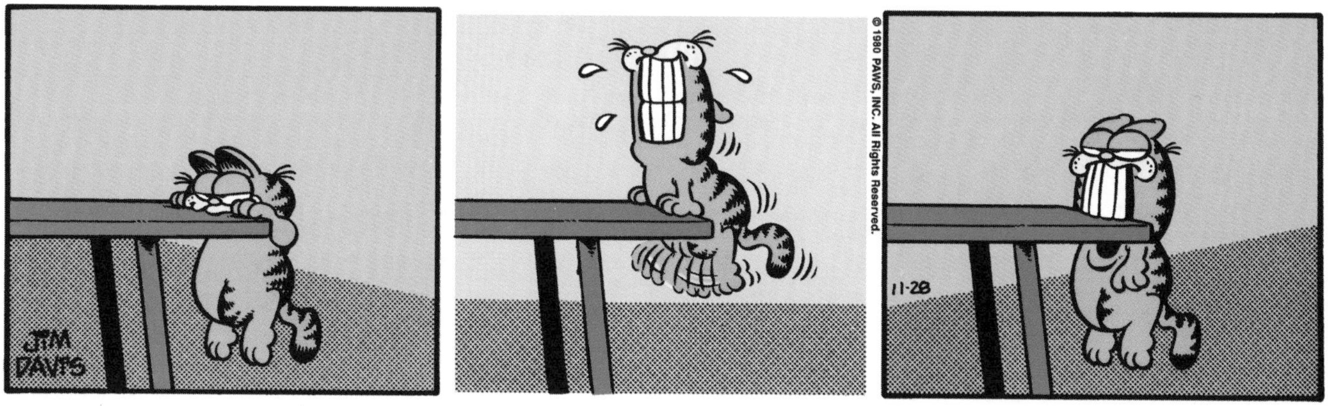
JIM DAVIS
11-28
© 1980 PAWS, INC. All Rights Reserved.

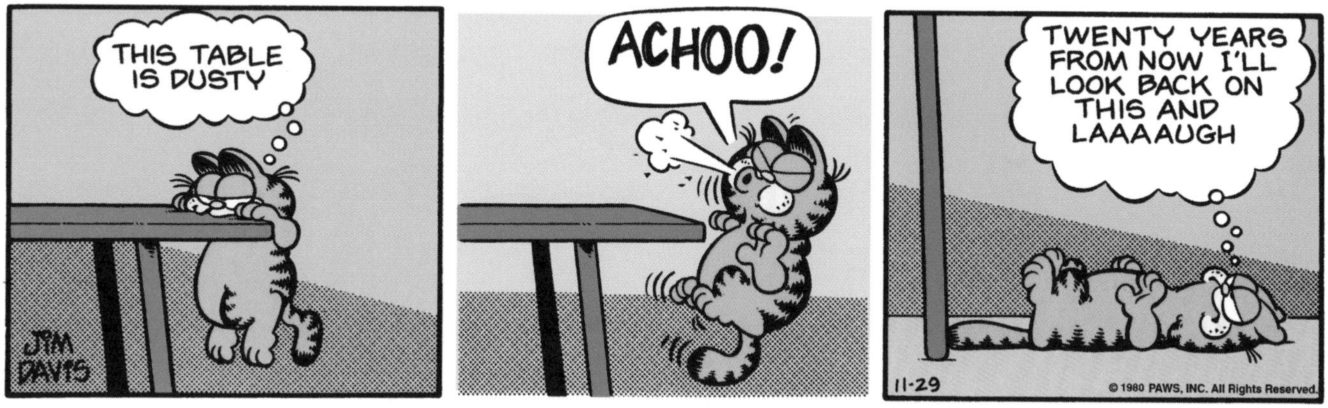
THIS TABLE IS DUSTY
ACHOO!
TWENTY YEARS FROM NOW I'LL LOOK BACK ON THIS AND LAAAAUGH
JIM DAVIS
11-29
© 1980 PAWS, INC. All Rights Reserved.

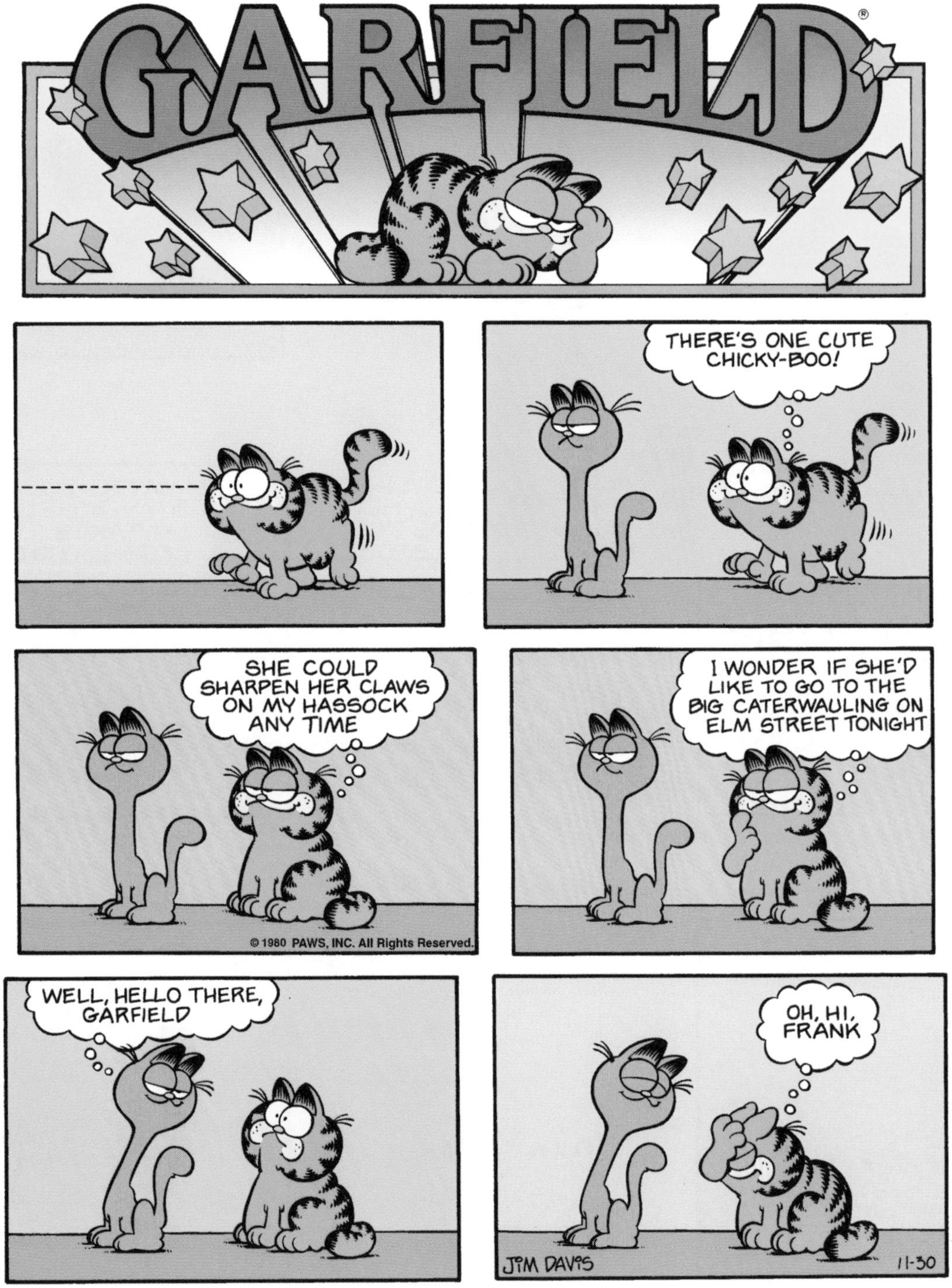
GARFIELD
THERE'S ONE CUTE CHICKY-BOO!
SHE COULD SHARPEN HER CLAWS ON MY HASSOCK ANY TIME
I WONDER IF SHE'D LIKE TO GO TO THE BIG CATERWAULING ON ELM STREET TONIGHT
© 1980 PAWS, INC. All Rights Reserved.
WELL, HELLO THERE, GARFIELD
OH, HI, FRANK
JIM DAVIS
11-30

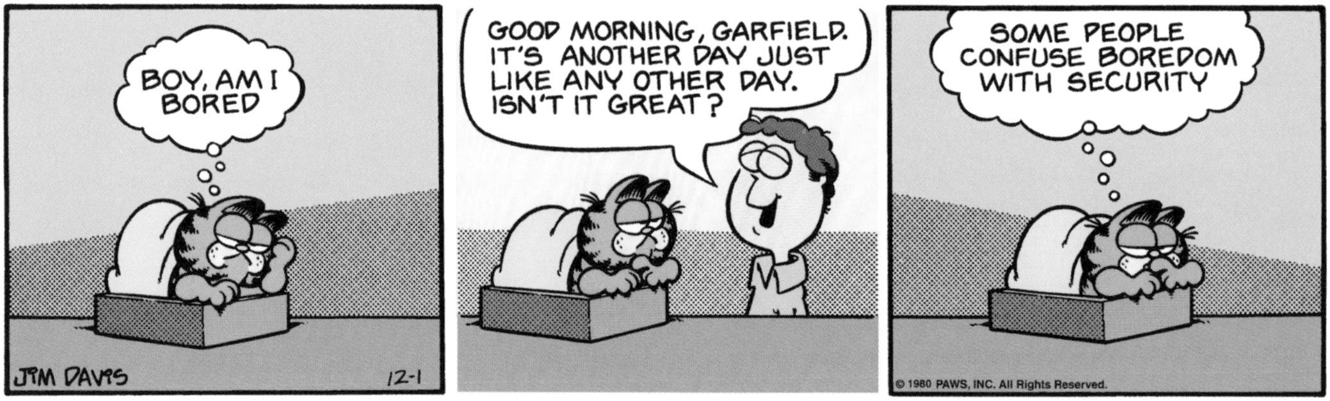
BOY, AM I BORED
GOOD MORNING, GARFIELD. IT'S ANOTHER DAY JUST LIKE ANY OTHER DAY. ISN'T IT GREAT?
SOME PEOPLE CONFUSE BOREDOM WITH SECURITY
JIM DAVIS
12-1
© 1980 PAWS, INC. All Rights Reserved.

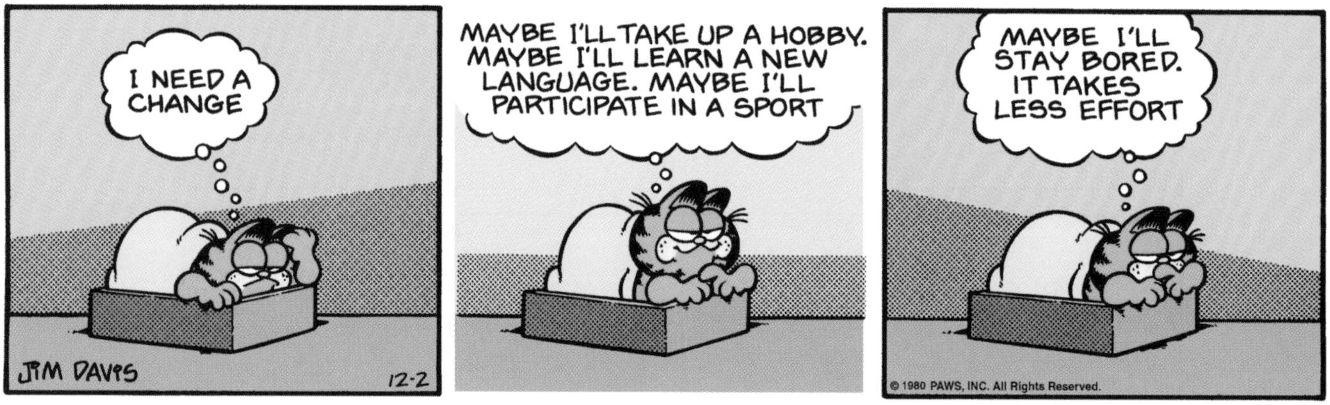
I NEED A CHANGE
MAYBE I'LL TAKE UP A HOBBY. MAYBE I'LL LEARN A NEW LANGUAGE. MAYBE I'LL PARTICIPATE IN A SPORT
MAYBE I'LL STAY BORED. IT TAKES LESS EFFORT
JIM DAVIS
12-2
© 1980 PAWS, INC. All Rights Reserved.

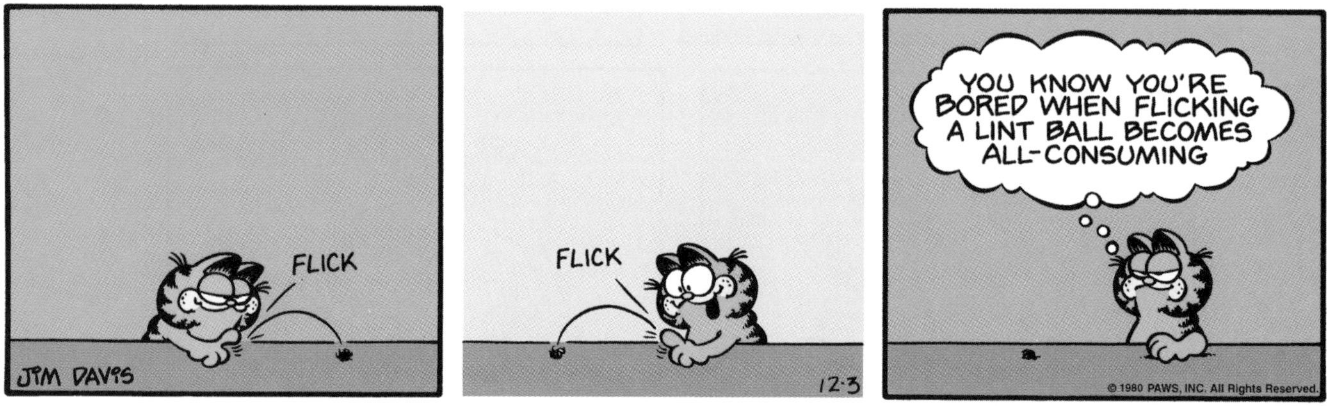
FLICK
FLICK
YOU KNOW YOU'RE BORED WHEN FLICKING A LINT BALL BECOMES ALL-CONSUMING
JIM DAVIS
12-3
© 1980 PAWS, INC. All Rights Reserved.

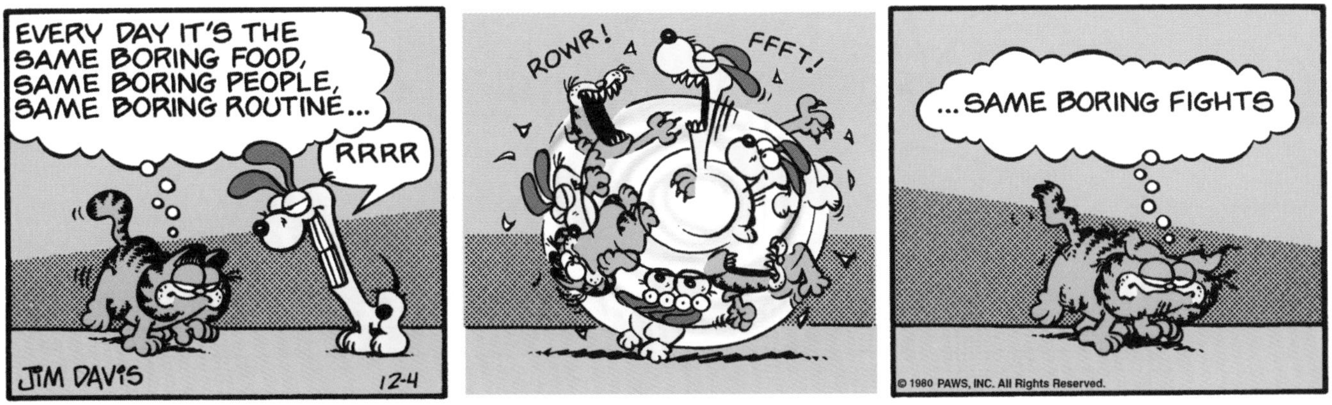
EVERY DAY IT'S THE SAME BORING FOOD, SAME BORING PEOPLE, SAME BORING ROUTINE...
RRRR
JIM DAVIS
12-4
ROWR!
FFFT!
...SAME BORING FIGHTS
© 1980 PAWS, INC. All Rights Reserved.

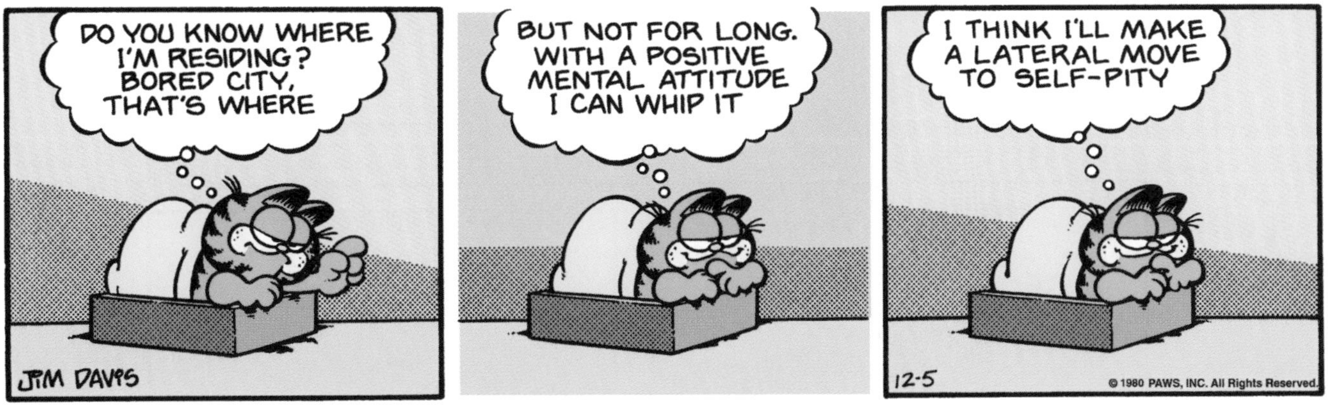
DO YOU KNOW WHERE I'M RESIDING? BORED CITY, THAT'S WHERE
JIM DAVIS
BUT NOT FOR LONG. WITH A POSITIVE MENTAL ATTITUDE I CAN WHIP IT
I THINK I'LL MAKE A LATERAL MOVE TO SELF-PITY
12-5
© 1980 PAWS, INC. All Rights Reserved.

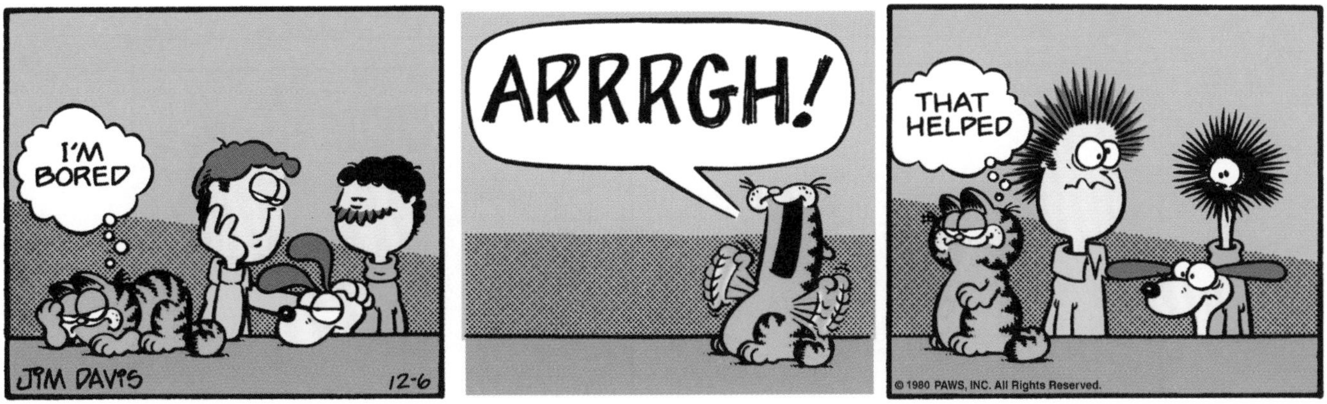
I'M BORED
JIM DAVIS
12-6
ARRRGH!
THAT HELPED
© 1980 PAWS, INC. All Rights Reserved.

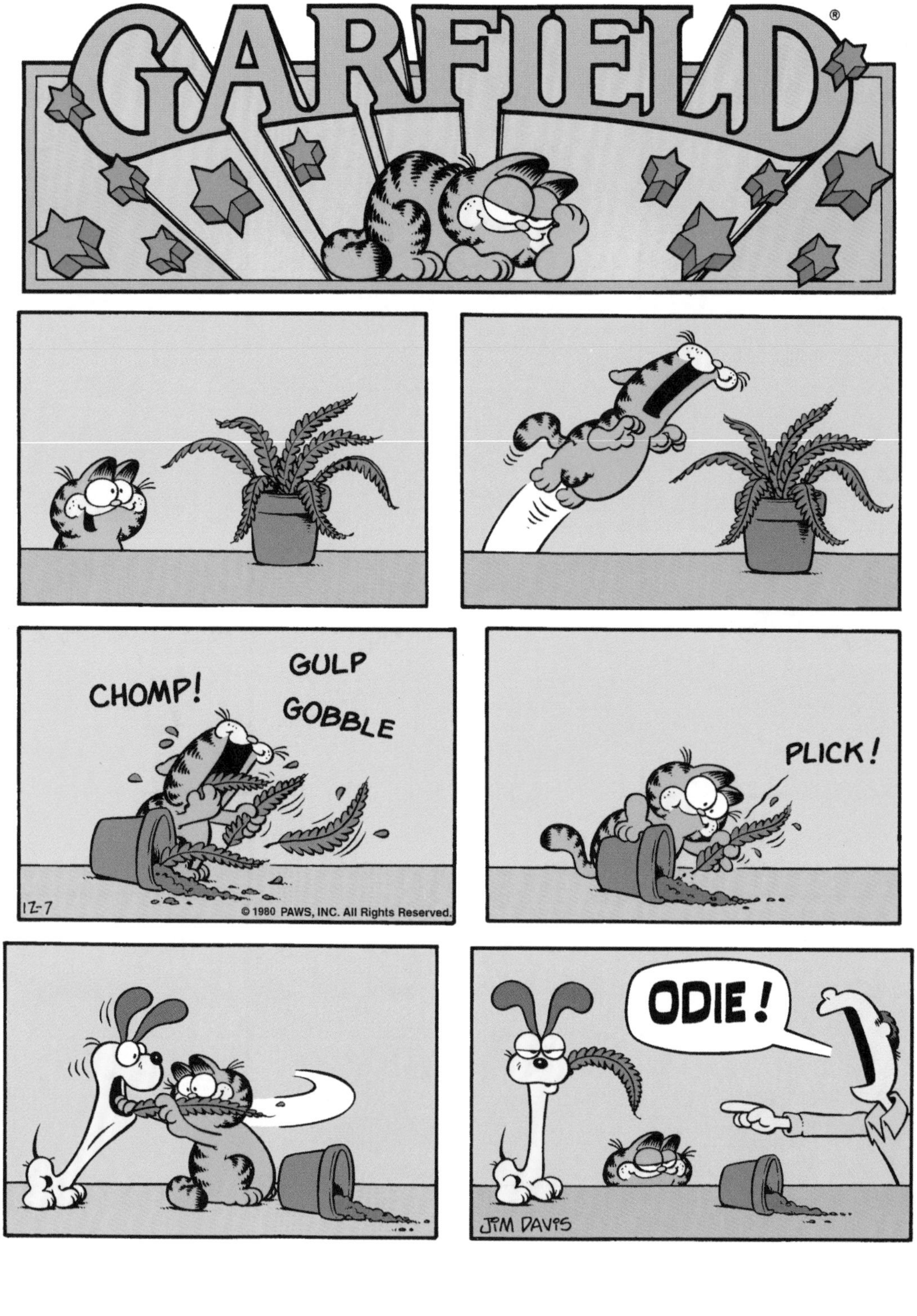
GARFIELD®
CHOMP!
GULP
GOBBLE
12-7
© 1980 PAWS, INC. All Rights Reserved.
PLICK!
ODIE!
JIM DAVIS

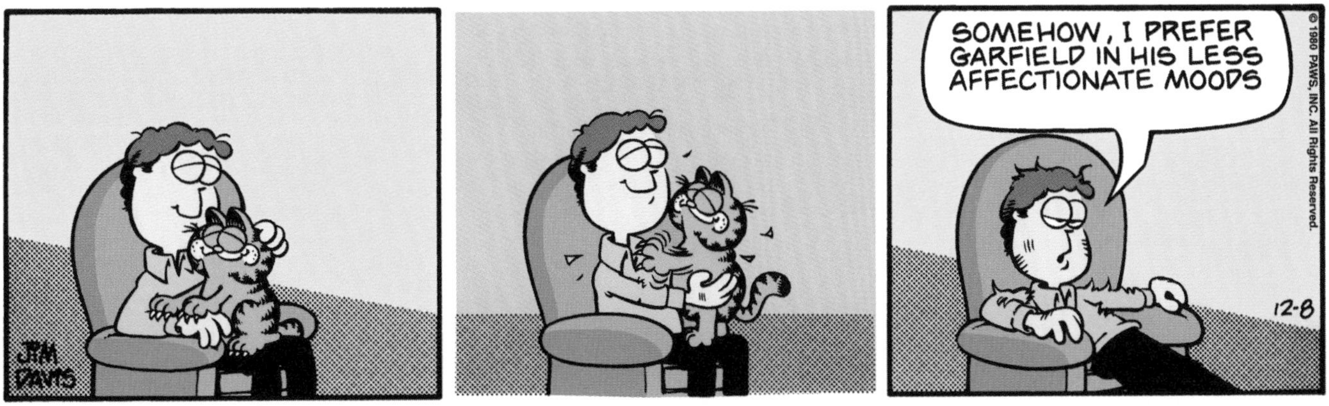
SOMEHOW, I PREFER GARFIELD IN HIS LESS AFFECTIONATE MOODS
JIM DAVIS
© 1980 PAWS, INC. All Rights Reserved.
12-8

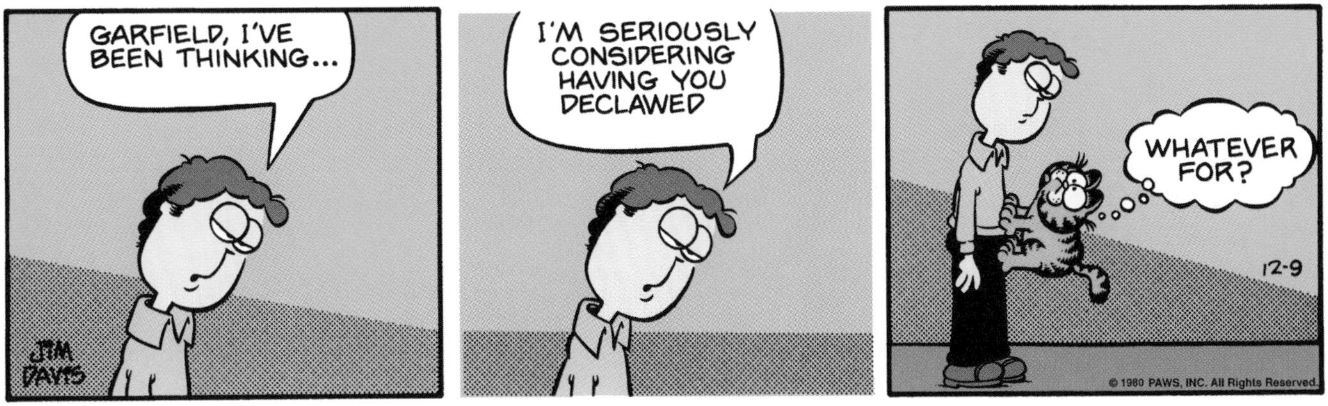
GARFIELD, I'VE BEEN THINKING...
I'M SERIOUSLY CONSIDERING HAVING YOU DECLAWED
WHATEVER FOR?
JIM DAVIS
12-9
© 1980 PAWS, INC. All Rights Reserved.

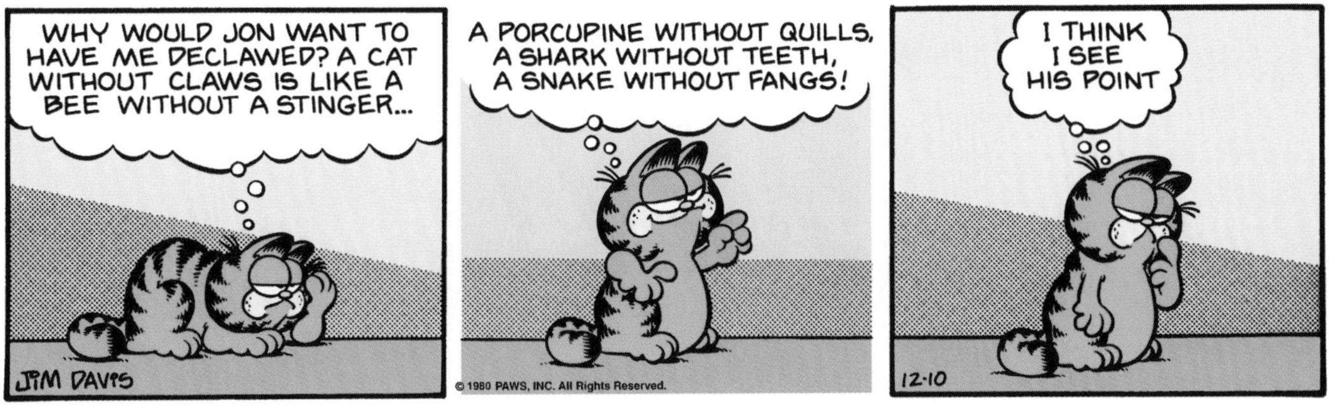
WHY WOULD JON WANT TO HAVE ME DECLAWED? A CAT WITHOUT CLAWS IS LIKE A BEE WITHOUT A STINGER...
A PORCUPINE WITHOUT QUILLS, A SHARK WITHOUT TEETH, A SNAKE WITHOUT FANGS!
I THINK I SEE HIS POINT
JIM DAVIS
© 1980 PAWS, INC. All Rights Reserved.
12-10

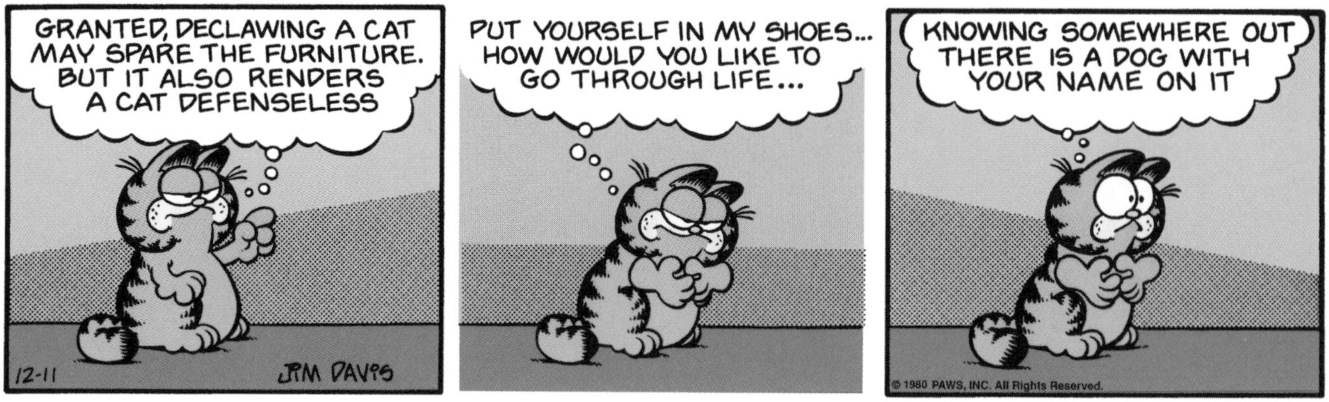
GRANTED, DECLAWING A CAT MAY SPARE THE FURNITURE. BUT IT ALSO RENDERS A CAT DEFENSELESS
12-11
JIM DAVIS
PUT YOURSELF IN MY SHOES... HOW WOULD YOU LIKE TO GO THROUGH LIFE...
KNOWING SOMEWHERE OUT THERE IS A DOG WITH YOUR NAME ON IT
© 1980 PAWS, INC. All Rights Reserved.

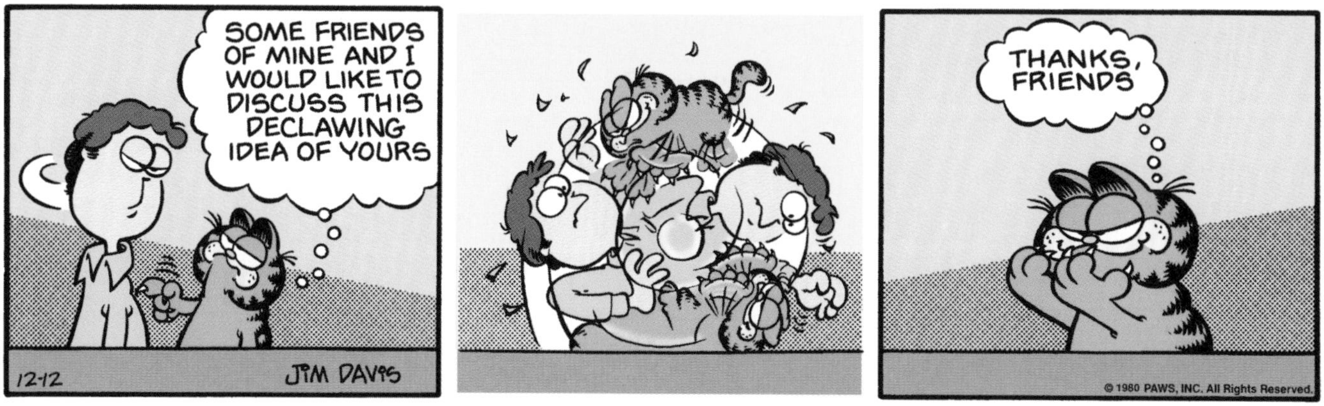
SOME FRIENDS OF MINE AND I WOULD LIKE TO DISCUSS THIS DECLAWING IDEA OF YOURS
12-12
JIM DAVIS
THANKS, FRIENDS
© 1980 PAWS, INC. All Rights Reserved.

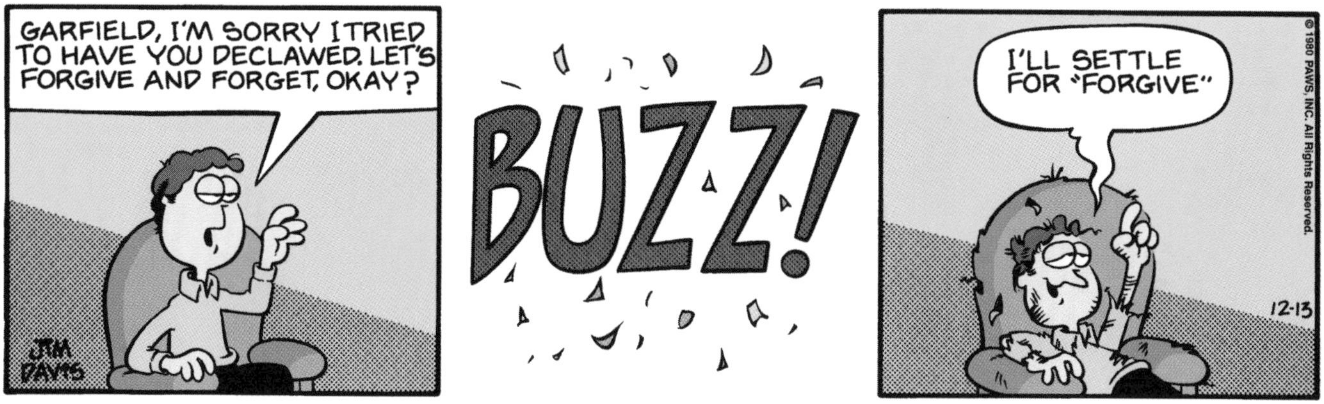
GARFIELD, I'M SORRY I TRIED TO HAVE YOU DECLAWED. LET'S FORGIVE AND FORGET, OKAY?
JIM DAVIS
BUZZ!
I'LL SETTLE FOR "FORGIVE"
12-13
© 1980 PAWS, INC. All Rights Reserved.

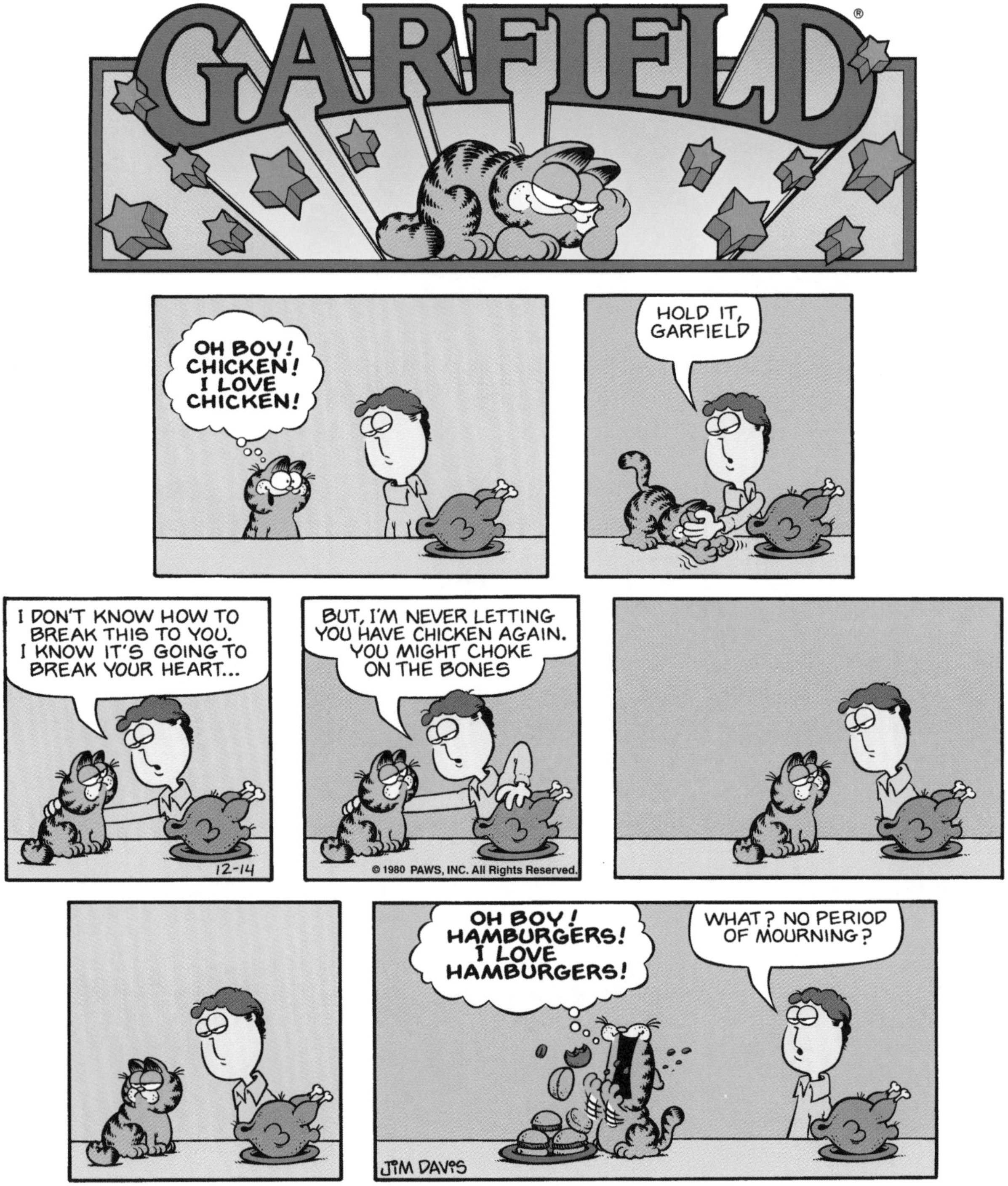
GARFIELD®
OH BOY! CHICKEN! I LOVE CHICKEN!
HOLD IT, GARFIELD
I DON'T KNOW HOW TO BREAK THIS TO YOU. I KNOW IT'S GOING TO BREAK YOUR HEART...
12-14
BUT, I'M NEVER LETTING YOU HAVE CHICKEN AGAIN. YOU MIGHT CHOKE ON THE BONES
© 1980 PAWS, INC. All Rights Reserved.
OH BOY! HAMBURGERS! I LOVE HAMBURGERS!
WHAT? NO PERIOD OF MOURNING?
JIM DAVIS

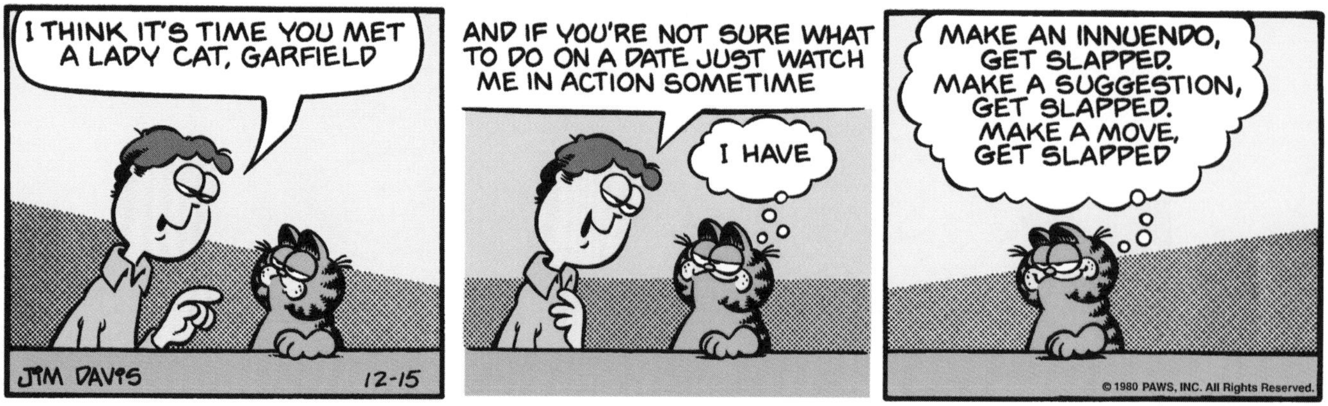
I THINK IT'S TIME YOU MET A LADY CAT, GARFIELD
JIM DAVIS
12-15
AND IF YOU'RE NOT SURE WHAT TO DO ON A DATE JUST WATCH ME IN ACTION SOMETIME
I HAVE
MAKE AN INNUENDO, GET SLAPPED. MAKE A SUGGESTION, GET SLAPPED. MAKE A MOVE, GET SLAPPED
© 1980 PAWS, INC. All Rights Reserved.

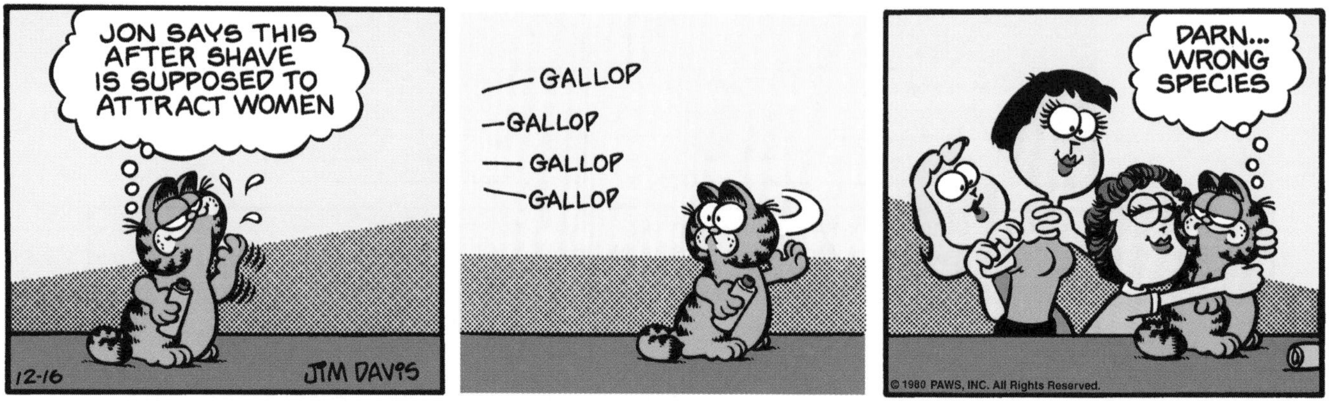
JON SAYS THIS AFTER SHAVE IS SUPPOSED TO ATTRACT WOMEN
12-16
JIM DAVIS
GALLOP
GALLOP
GALLOP
GALLOP
DARN... WRONG SPECIES
© 1980 PAWS, INC. All Rights Reserved.

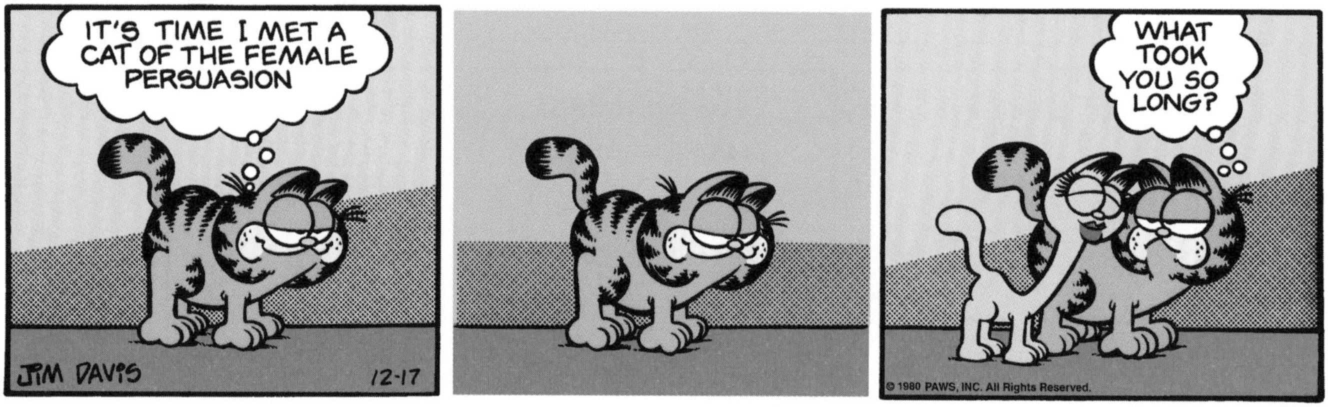
IT'S TIME I MET A CAT OF THE FEMALE PERSUASION
JIM DAVIS
12-17
WHAT TOOK YOU SO LONG?
© 1980 PAWS, INC. All Rights Reserved.

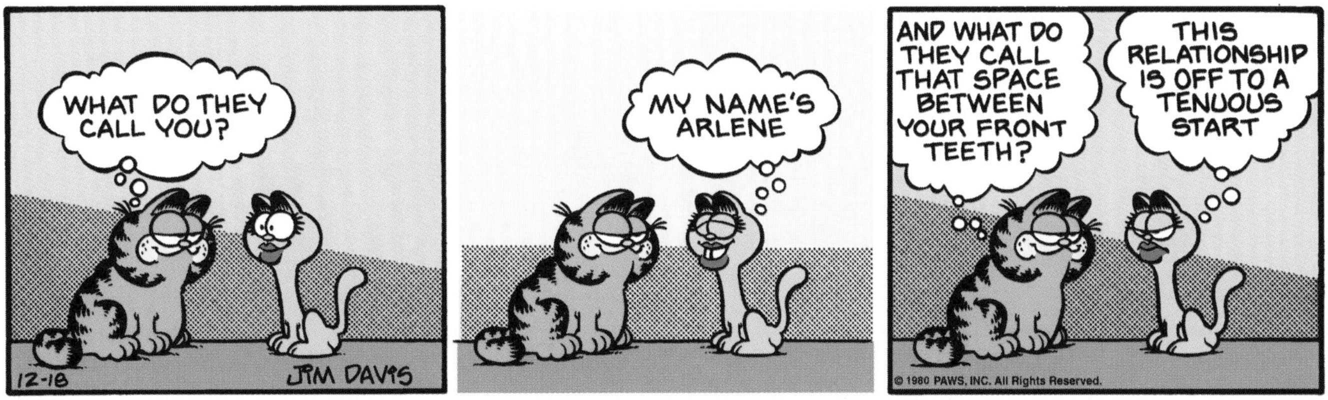
WHAT DO THEY CALL YOU?
12-18
JIM DAVIS
MY NAME'S ARLENE
AND WHAT DO THEY CALL THAT SPACE BETWEEN YOUR FRONT TEETH?
THIS RELATIONSHIP IS OFF TO A TENUOUS START
© 1980 PAWS, INC. All Rights Reserved.

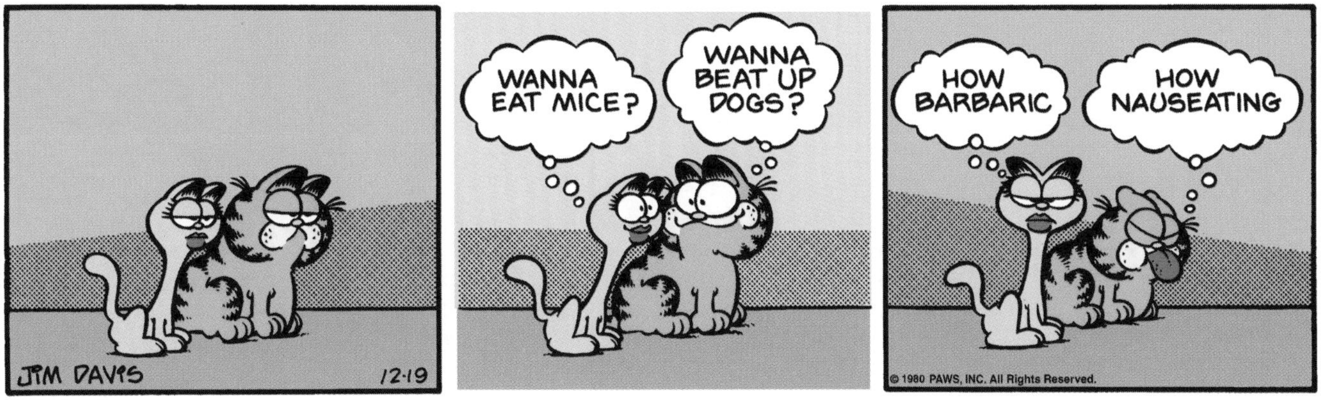
JIM DAVIS
12-19
WANNA EAT MICE?
WANNA BEAT UP DOGS?
HOW BARBARIC
HOW NAUSEATING
© 1980 PAWS, INC. All Rights Reserved.

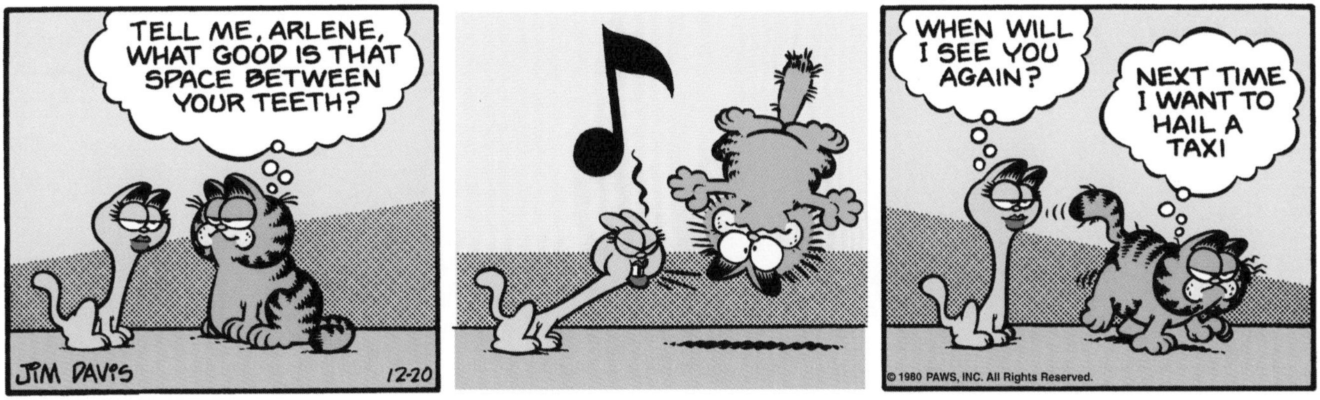
TELL ME, ARLENE, WHAT GOOD IS THAT SPACE BETWEEN YOUR TEETH?
JIM DAVIS
12-20
WHEN WILL I SEE YOU AGAIN?
NEXT TIME I WANT TO HAIL A TAXI
© 1980 PAWS, INC. All Rights Reserved.

CATS CAN BE BROKEN TO THE LEASH IF YOU JUST HANG IN THERE

© 1980 PAWS, INC. All Rights Reserved.

JIM DAVIS   12-21

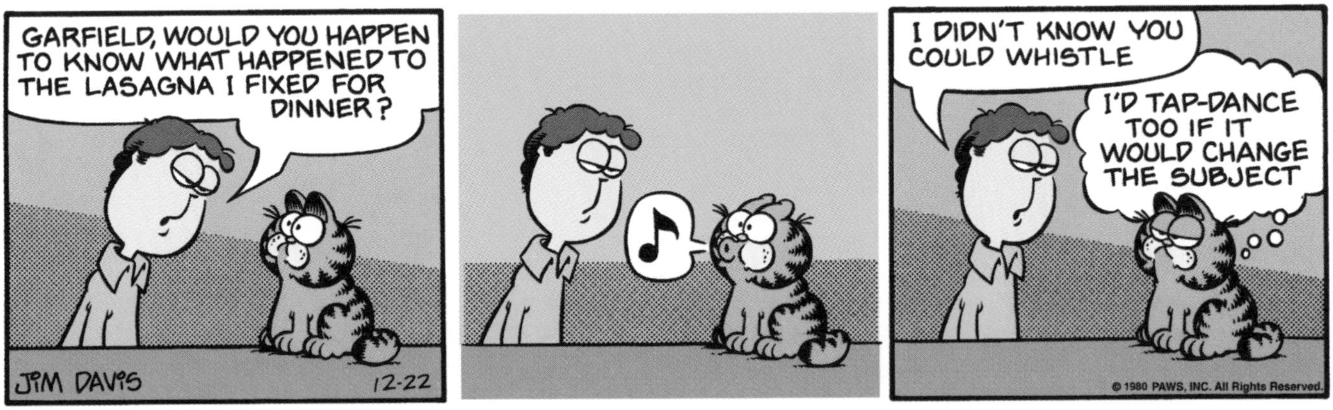
GARFIELD, WOULD YOU HAPPEN TO KNOW WHAT HAPPENED TO THE LASAGNA I FIXED FOR DINNER?
JIM DAVIS
12-22
I DIDN'T KNOW YOU COULD WHISTLE
I'D TAP-DANCE TOO IF IT WOULD CHANGE THE SUBJECT
© 1980 PAWS, INC. All Rights Reserved.

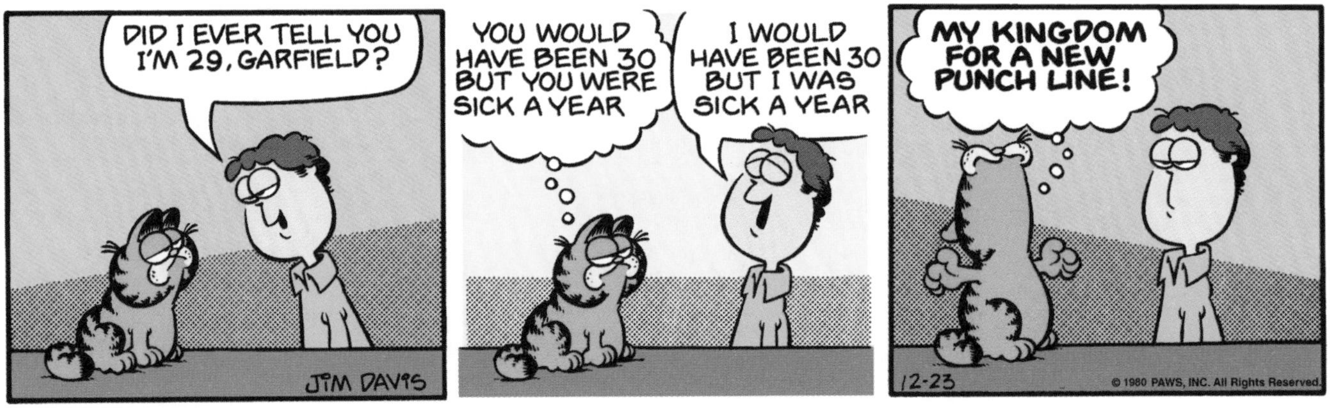
DID I EVER TELL YOU I'M 29, GARFIELD?
JIM DAVIS
YOU WOULD HAVE BEEN 30 BUT YOU WERE SICK A YEAR
I WOULD HAVE BEEN 30 BUT I WAS SICK A YEAR
MY KINGDOM FOR A NEW PUNCH LINE!
12-23
© 1980 PAWS, INC. All Rights Reserved.

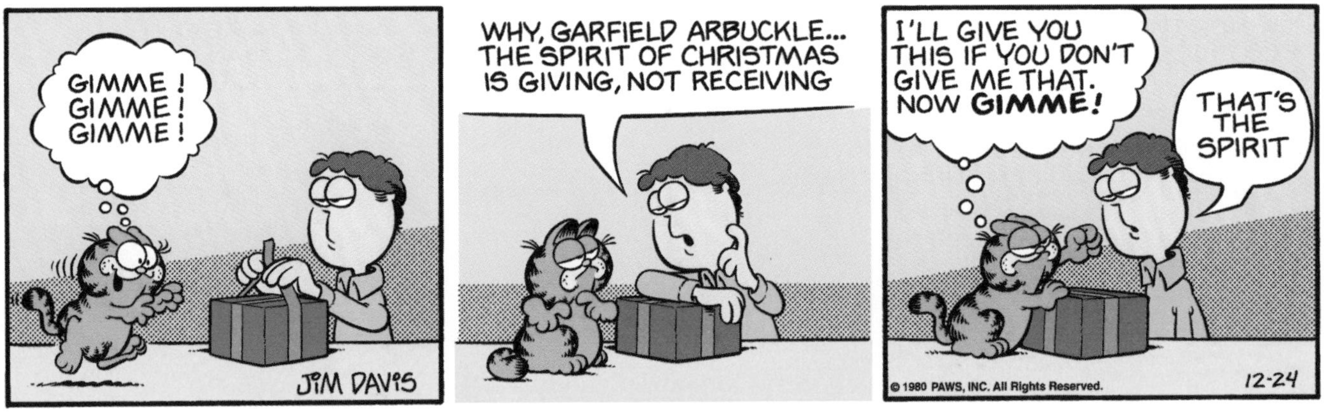
GIMME! GIMME! GIMME!
JIM DAVIS
WHY, GARFIELD ARBUCKLE... THE SPIRIT OF CHRISTMAS IS GIVING, NOT RECEIVING
I'LL GIVE YOU THIS IF YOU DON'T GIVE ME THAT. NOW GIMME!
THAT'S THE SPIRIT
© 1980 PAWS, INC. All Rights Reserved.
12-24

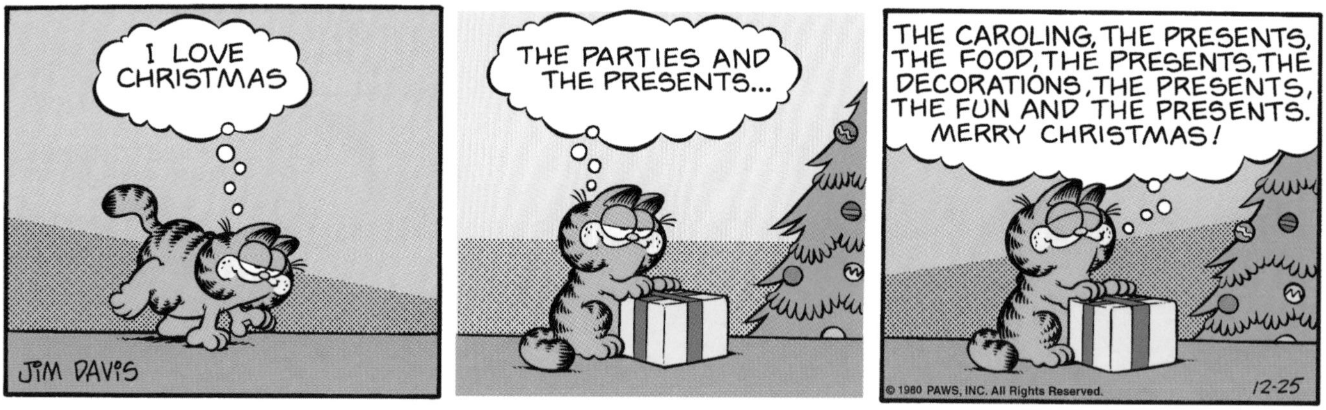
I LOVE CHRISTMAS
JIM DAVIS
THE PARTIES AND THE PRESENTS...
THE CAROLING, THE PRESENTS, THE FOOD, THE PRESENTS, THE DECORATIONS, THE PRESENTS, THE FUN AND THE PRESENTS. MERRY CHRISTMAS!
© 1980 PAWS, INC. All Rights Reserved.
12-25

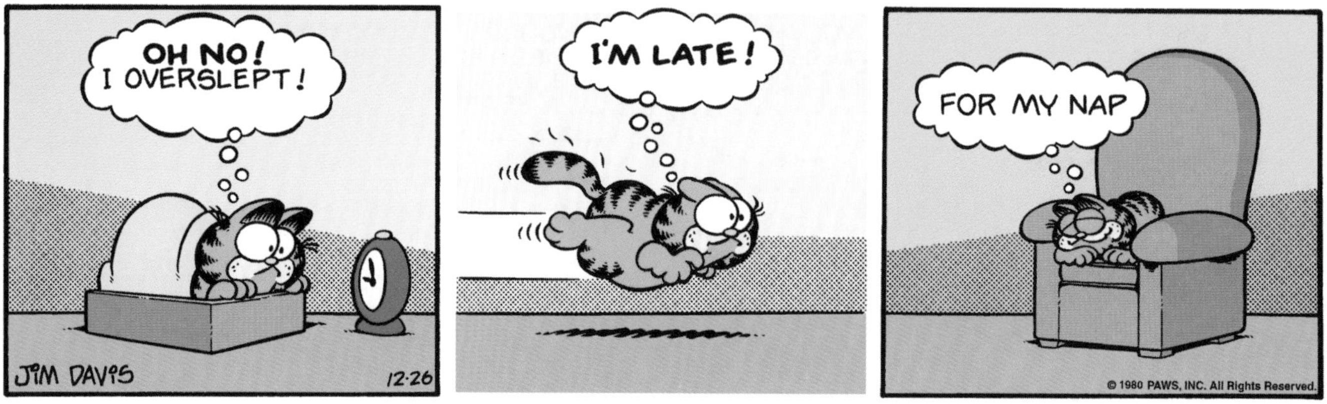
OH NO! I OVERSLEPT!
JIM DAVIS
12-26
I'M LATE!
FOR MY NAP
© 1980 PAWS, INC. All Rights Reserved.

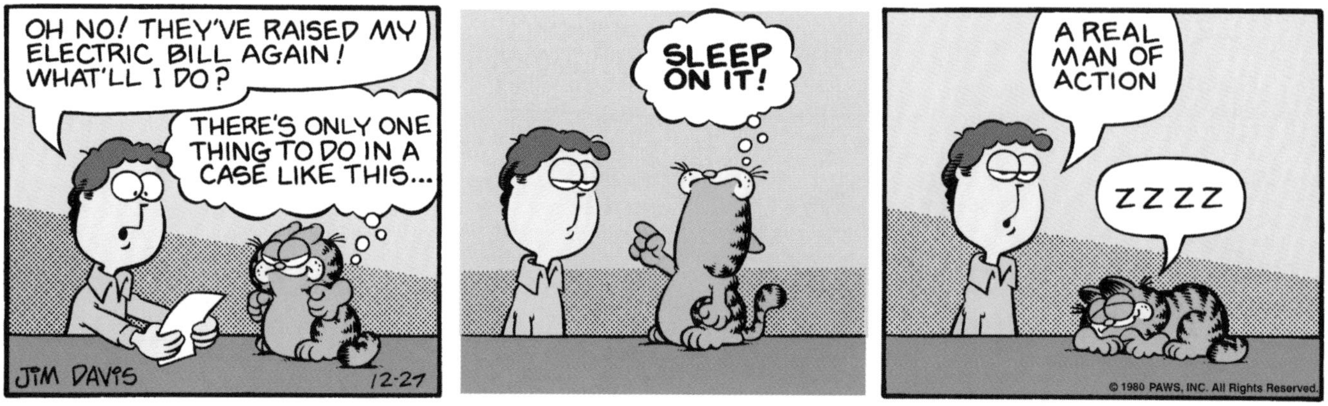
OH NO! THEY'VE RAISED MY ELECTRIC BILL AGAIN! WHAT'LL I DO?
THERE'S ONLY ONE THING TO DO IN A CASE LIKE THIS...
JIM DAVIS
12-27
SLEEP ON IT!
A REAL MAN OF ACTION
Z Z Z Z
© 1980 PAWS, INC. All Rights Reserved.

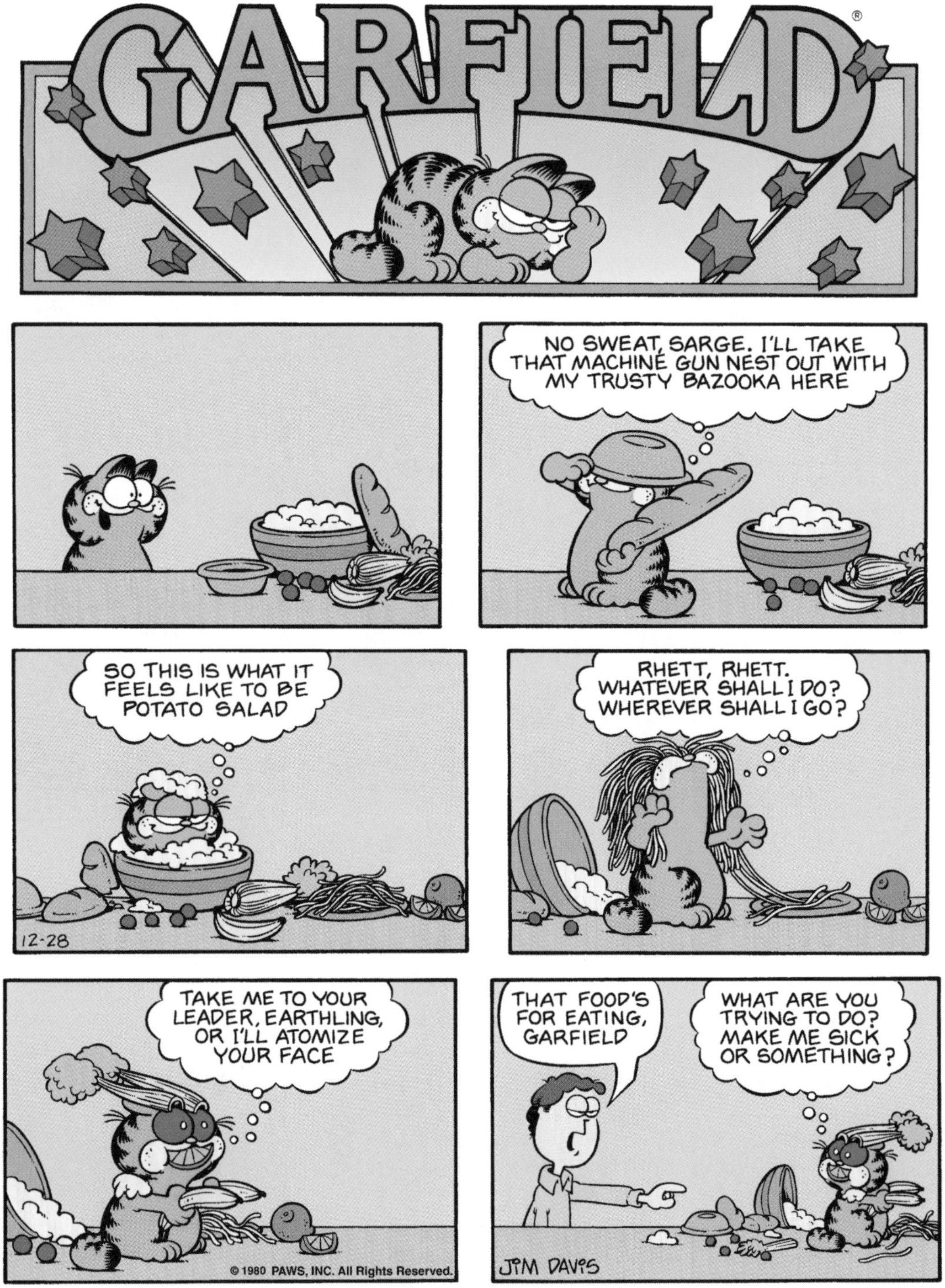
GARFIELD®
NO SWEAT, SARGE. I'LL TAKE THAT MACHINE GUN NEST OUT WITH MY TRUSTY BAZOOKA HERE
SO THIS IS WHAT IT FEELS LIKE TO BE POTATO SALAD
12-28
RHETT, RHETT. WHATEVER SHALL I DO? WHEREVER SHALL I GO?
TAKE ME TO YOUR LEADER, EARTHLING, OR I'LL ATOMIZE YOUR FACE
© 1980 PAWS, INC. All Rights Reserved.
THAT FOOD'S FOR EATING, GARFIELD
WHAT ARE YOU TRYING TO DO? MAKE ME SICK OR SOMETHING?
JIM DAVIS

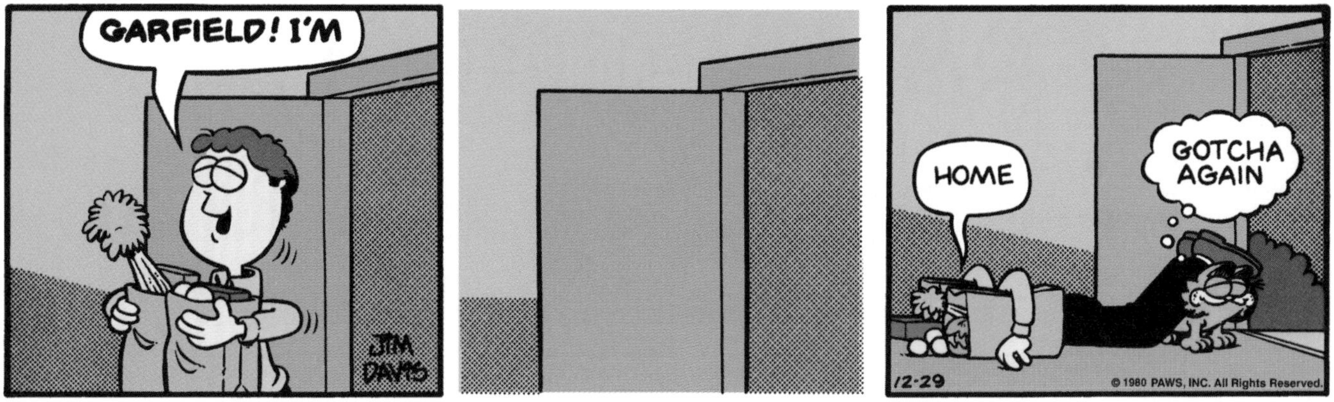
GARFIELD! I'M
HOME
GOTCHA AGAIN
JIM DAVIS
12-29
© 1980 PAWS, INC. All Rights Reserved.

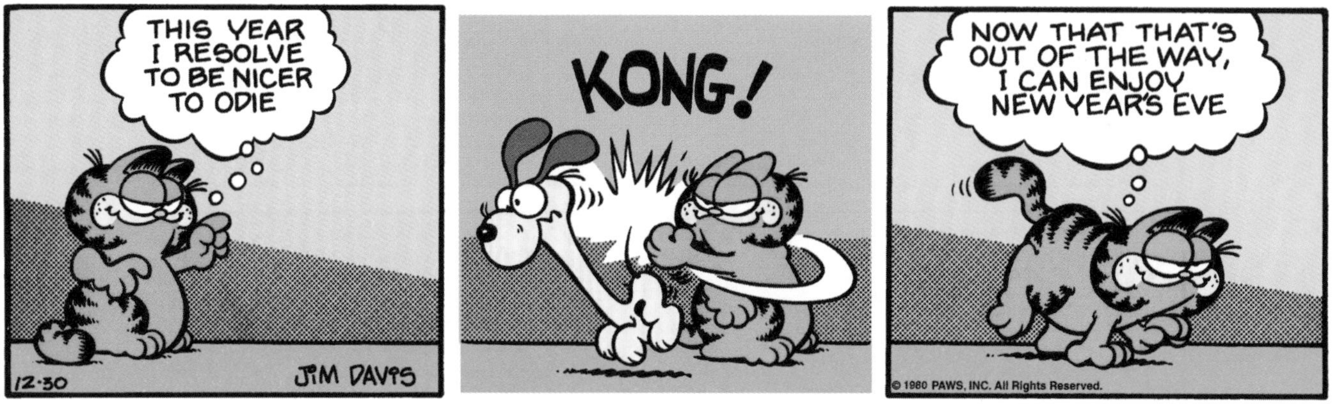
THIS YEAR I RESOLVE TO BE NICER TO ODIE
KONG!
NOW THAT THAT'S OUT OF THE WAY, I CAN ENJOY NEW YEAR'S EVE
12-30
JIM DAVIS
© 1980 PAWS, INC. All Rights Reserved.

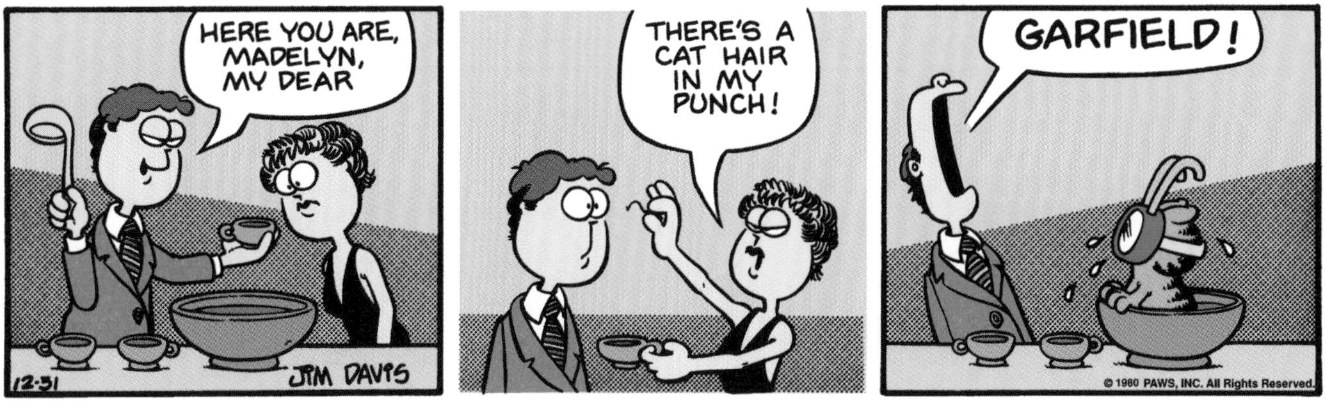
HERE YOU ARE, MADELYN, MY DEAR
THERE'S A CAT HAIR IN MY PUNCH!
GARFIELD!
12-31
JIM DAVIS
© 1980 PAWS, INC. All Rights Reserved.

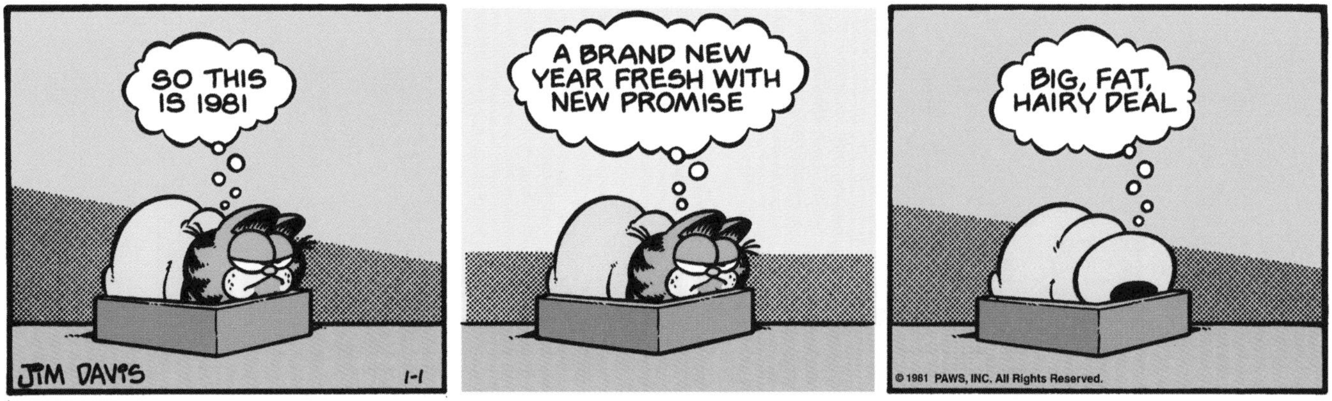
SO THIS IS 1981
JIM DAVIS
1-1
A BRAND NEW YEAR FRESH WITH NEW PROMISE
BIG, FAT, HAIRY DEAL
© 1981 PAWS, INC. All Rights Reserved.

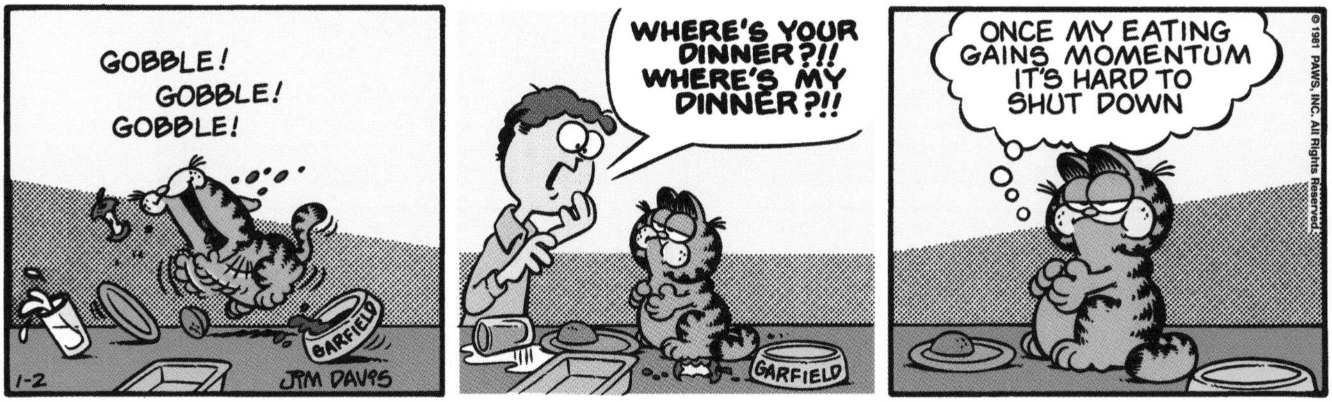
GOBBLE! GOBBLE! GOBBLE!
GARFIELD
1-2
JIM DAVIS
WHERE'S YOUR DINNER?!! WHERE'S MY DINNER?!!
GARFIELD
ONCE MY EATING GAINS MOMENTUM IT'S HARD TO SHUT DOWN
© 1981 PAWS, INC. All Rights Reserved.

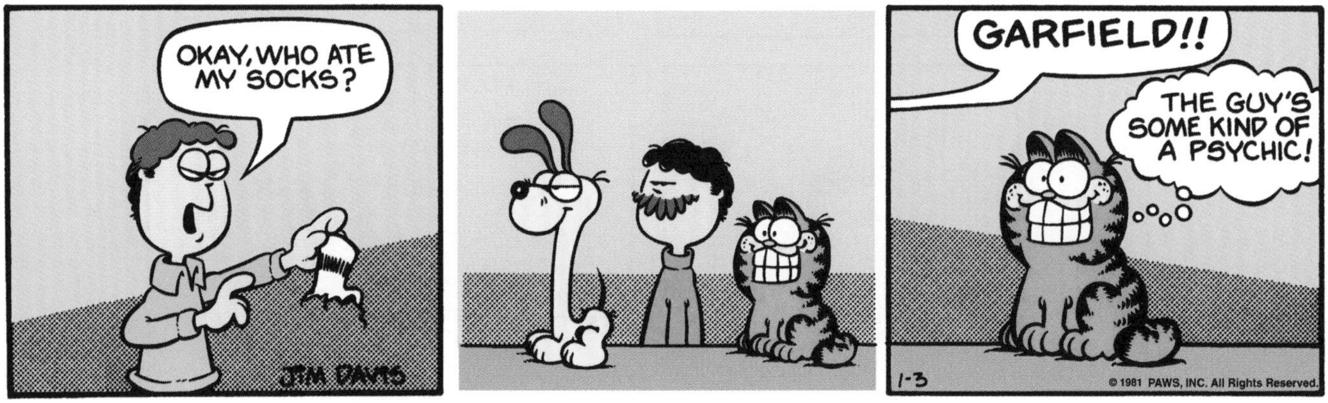
OKAY, WHO ATE MY SOCKS?
JIM DAVIS
GARFIELD!!
THE GUY'S SOME KIND OF A PSYCHIC!
1-3
© 1981 PAWS, INC. All Rights Reserved.

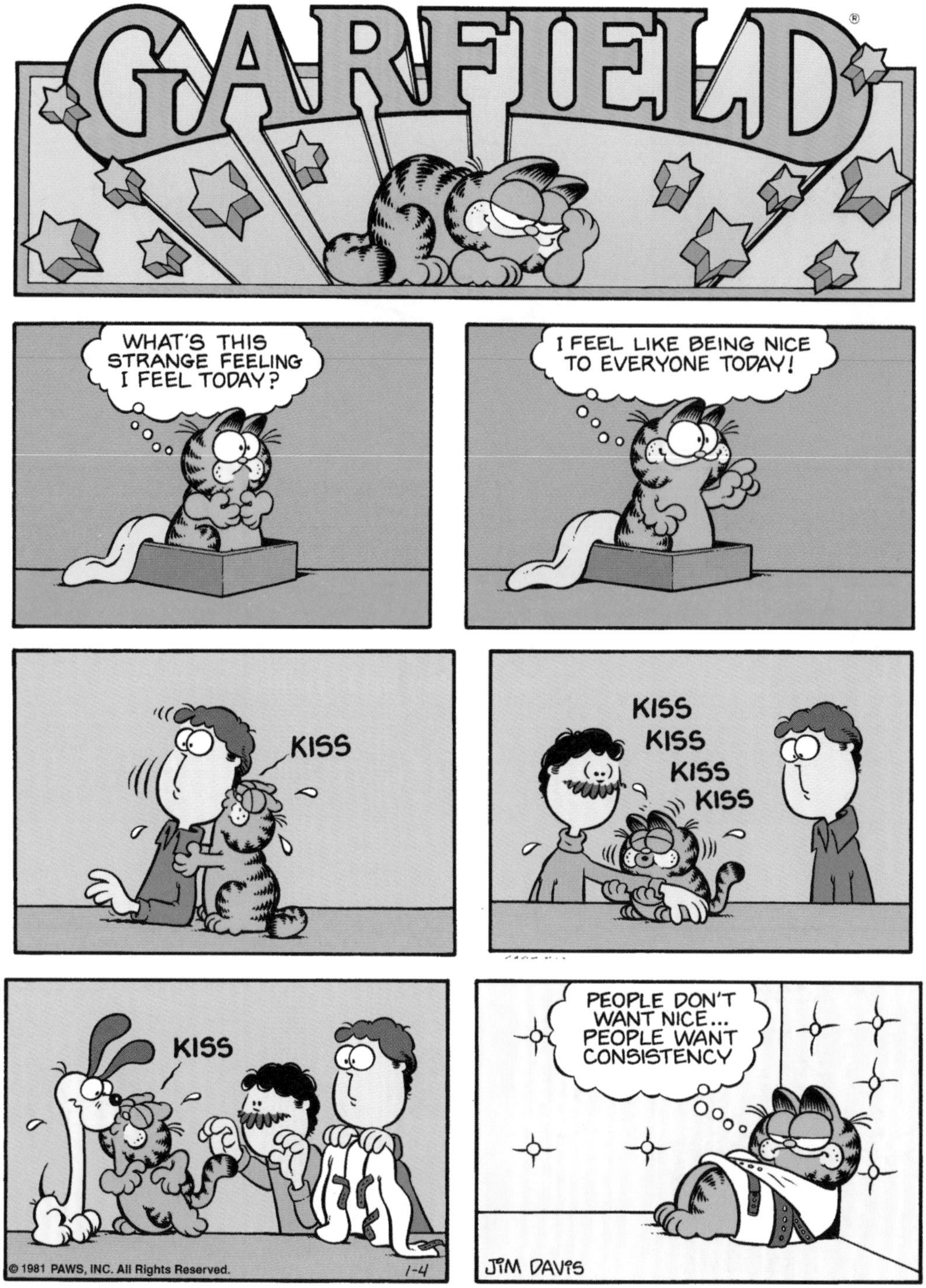
GARFIELD
WHAT'S THIS STRANGE FEELING I FEEL TODAY?
I FEEL LIKE BEING NICE TO EVERYONE TODAY!
KISS
KISS
KISS
KISS
KISS
KISS
PEOPLE DON'T WANT NICE... PEOPLE WANT CONSISTENCY
© 1981 PAWS, INC. All Rights Reserved.
1-4
JIM DAVIS

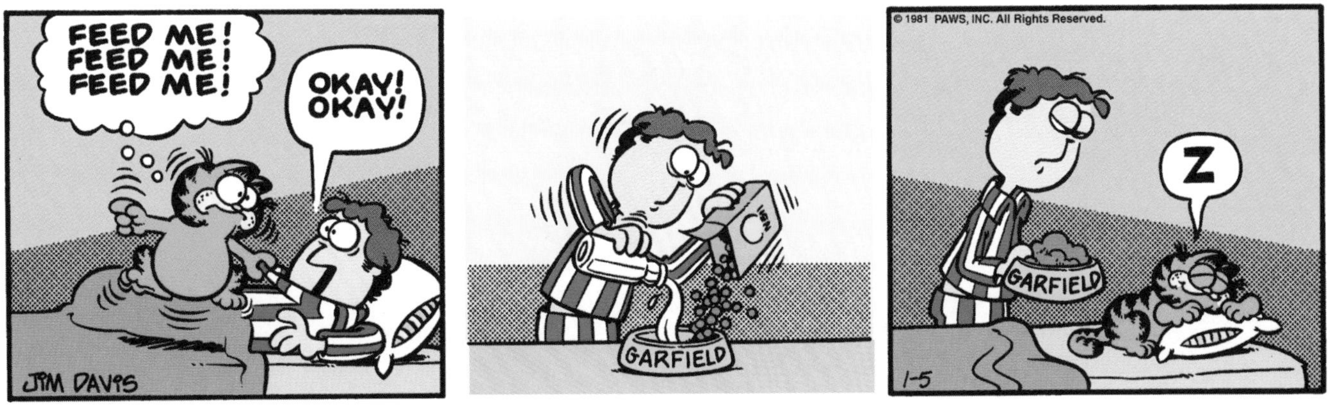
FEED ME! FEED ME! FEED ME!
OKAY! OKAY!
GARFIELD
© 1981 PAWS, INC. All Rights Reserved.
Z
GARFIELD
JIM DAVIS
1-5

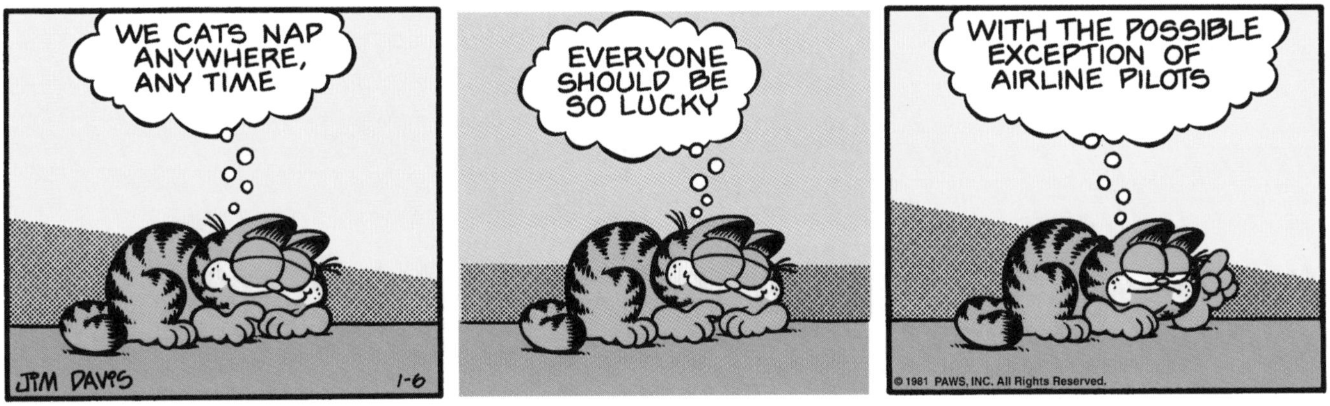
WE CATS NAP ANYWHERE, ANY TIME
EVERYONE SHOULD BE SO LUCKY
WITH THE POSSIBLE EXCEPTION OF AIRLINE PILOTS
JIM DAVIS
1-6
© 1981 PAWS, INC. All Rights Reserved.

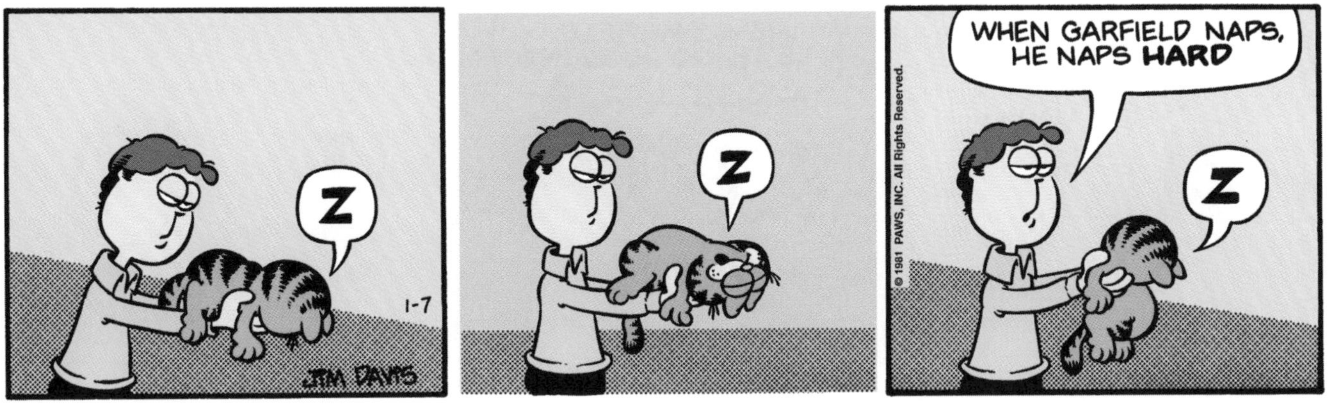
Z
Z
WHEN GARFIELD NAPS, HE NAPS **HARD**
Z
1-7
JIM DAVIS
© 1981 PAWS, INC. All Rights Reserved.

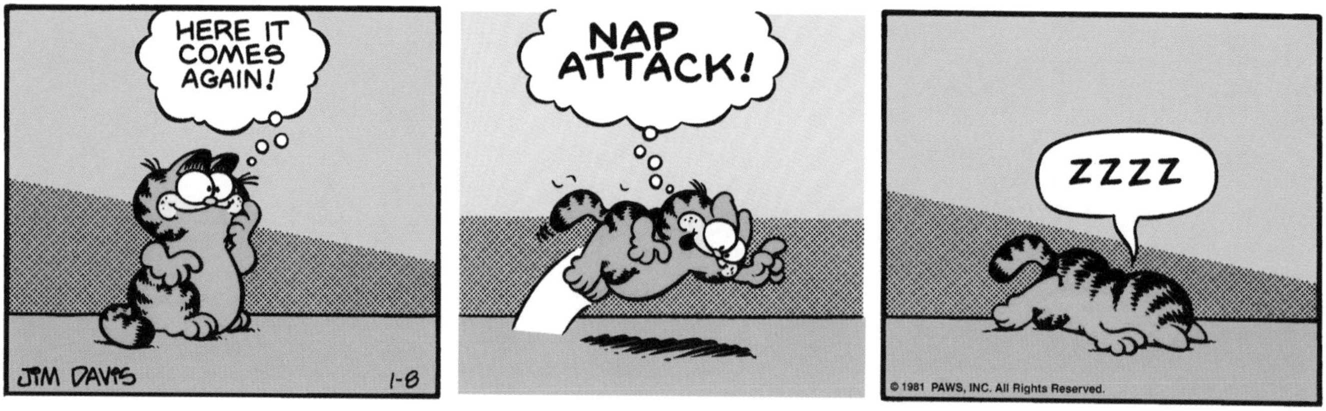
HERE IT COMES AGAIN!
JIM DAVIS
1-8
NAP ATTACK!
ZZZZ
© 1981 PAWS, INC. All Rights Reserved.

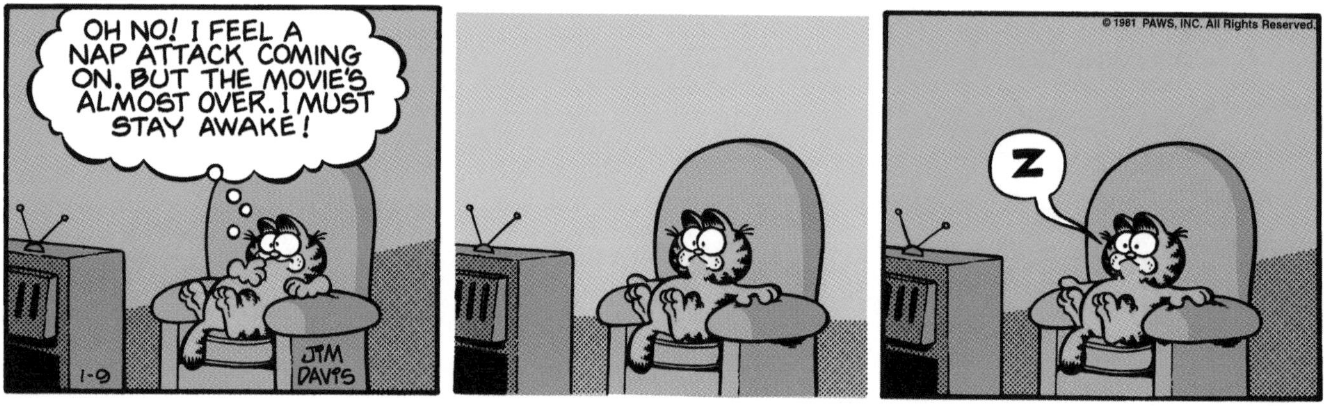
OH NO! I FEEL A NAP ATTACK COMING ON. BUT THE MOVIE'S ALMOST OVER. I MUST STAY AWAKE!
1-9
JIM DAVIS
© 1981 PAWS, INC. All Rights Reserved.
Z

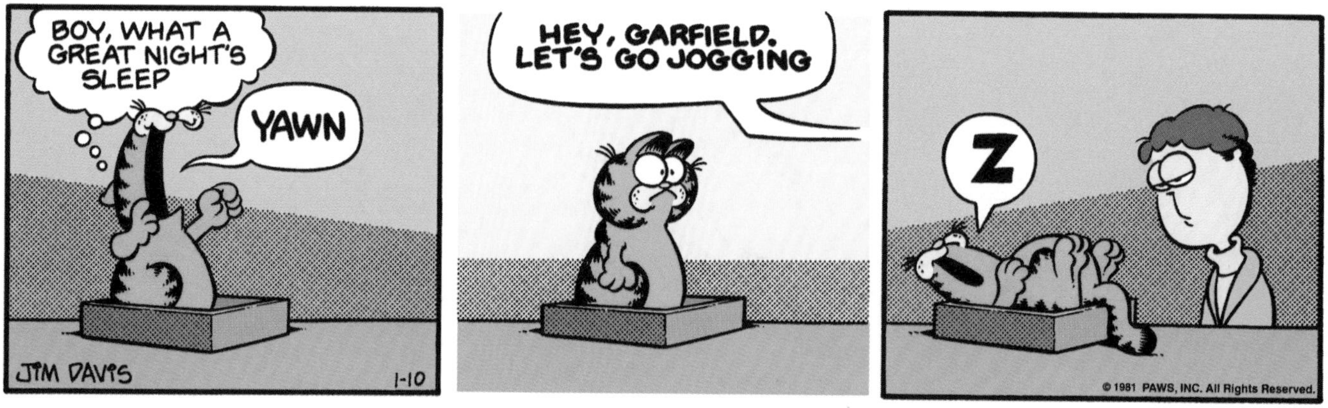
BOY, WHAT A GREAT NIGHT'S SLEEP
YAWN
JIM DAVIS
1-10
HEY, GARFIELD. LET'S GO JOGGING
Z
© 1981 PAWS, INC. All Rights Reserved.

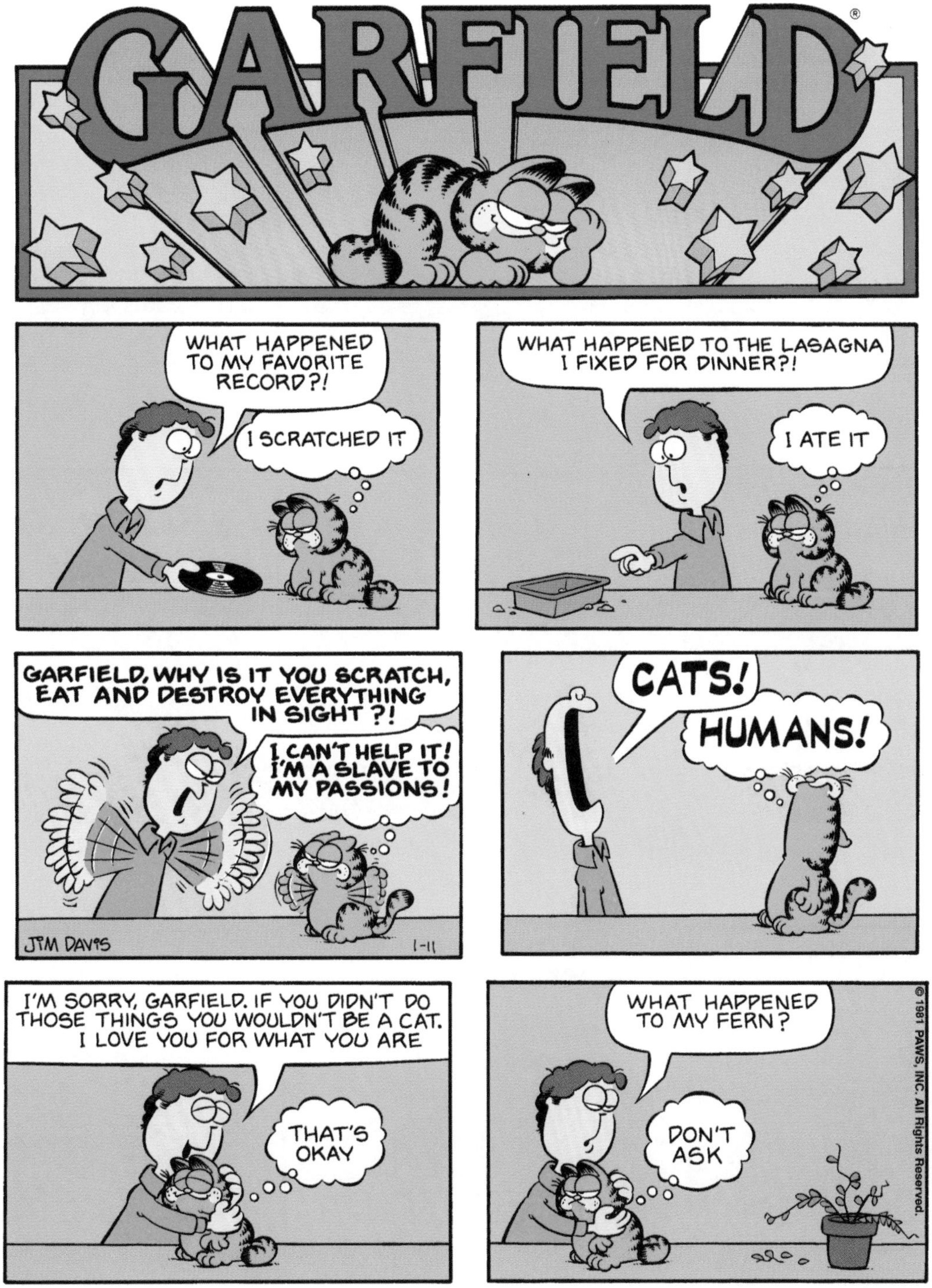
GARFIELD®
WHAT HAPPENED TO MY FAVORITE RECORD?!
I SCRATCHED IT
WHAT HAPPENED TO THE LASAGNA I FIXED FOR DINNER?!
I ATE IT
GARFIELD, WHY IS IT YOU SCRATCH, EAT AND DESTROY EVERYTHING IN SIGHT ?!
I CAN'T HELP IT! I'M A SLAVE TO MY PASSIONS!
JIM DAVIS
1-11
CATS!
HUMANS!
I'M SORRY, GARFIELD. IF YOU DIDN'T DO THOSE THINGS YOU WOULDN'T BE A CAT. I LOVE YOU FOR WHAT YOU ARE
THAT'S OKAY
WHAT HAPPENED TO MY FERN?
DON'T ASK
© 1981 PAWS, INC. All Rights Reserved.

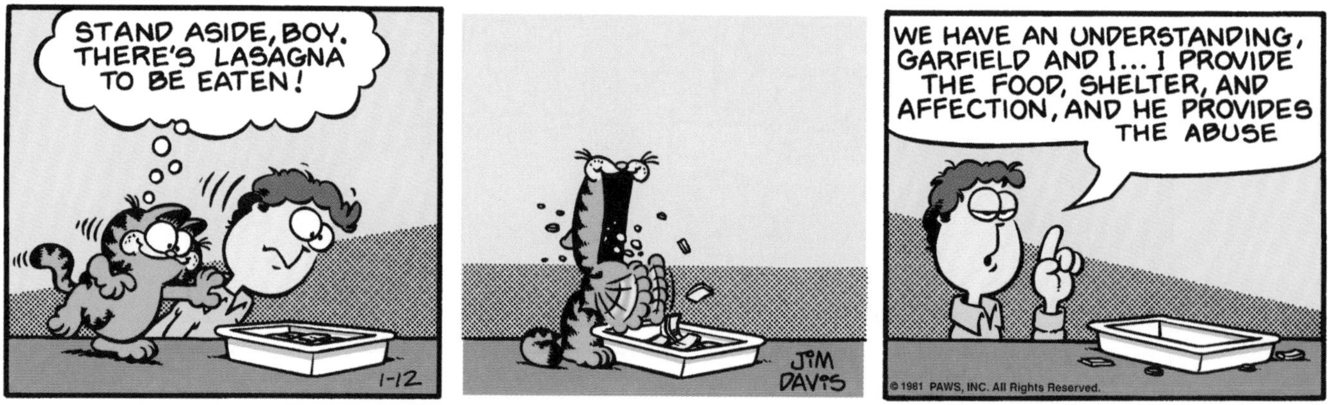
STAND ASIDE, BOY. THERE'S LASAGNA TO BE EATEN!
1-12
JIM DAVIS
WE HAVE AN UNDERSTANDING, GARFIELD AND I... I PROVIDE THE FOOD, SHELTER, AND AFFECTION, AND HE PROVIDES THE ABUSE
© 1981 PAWS, INC. All Rights Reserved.

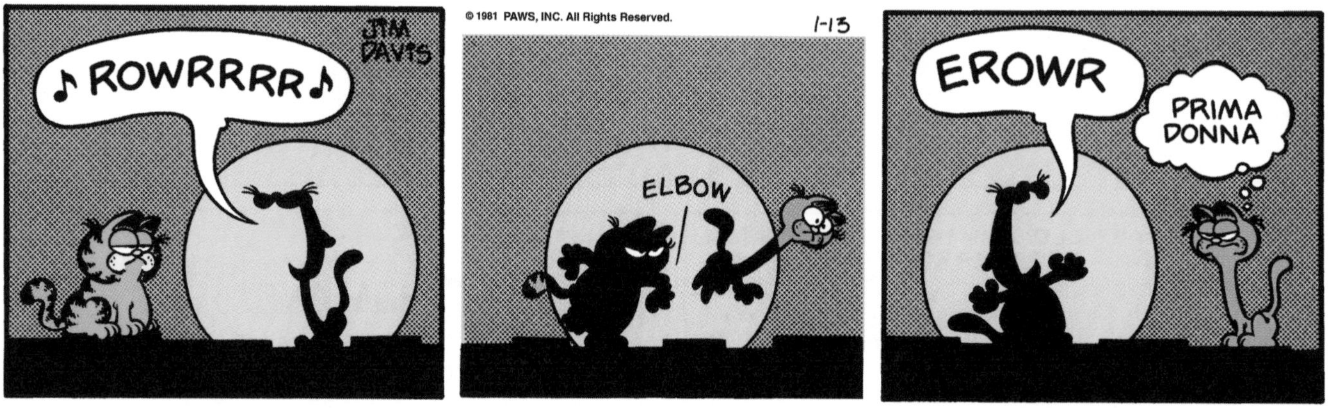
JIM DAVIS
♪ ROWRRRR ♪
© 1981 PAWS, INC. All Rights Reserved.
1-13
ELBOW
EROWR
PRIMA DONNA

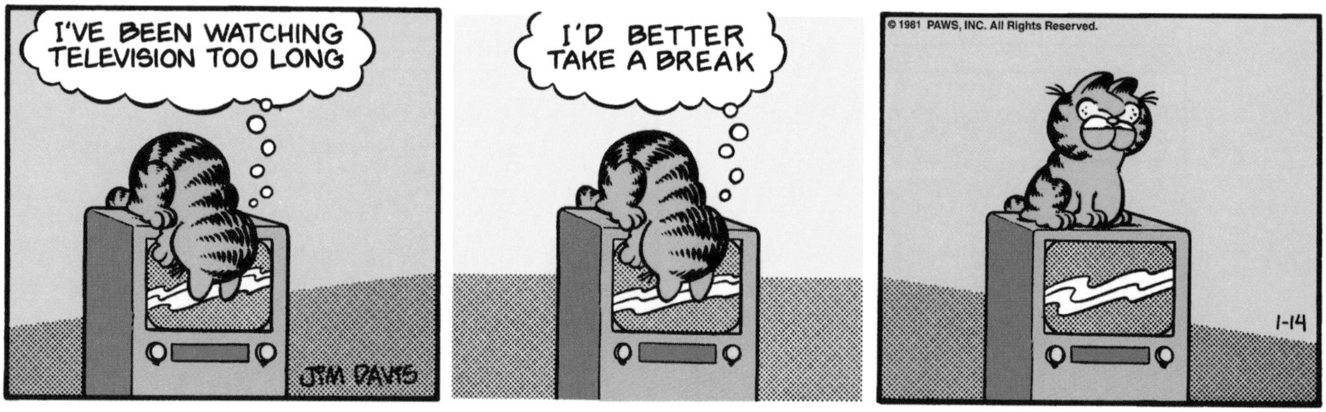
I'VE BEEN WATCHING TELEVISION TOO LONG
JIM DAVIS
I'D BETTER TAKE A BREAK
© 1981 PAWS, INC. All Rights Reserved.
1-14

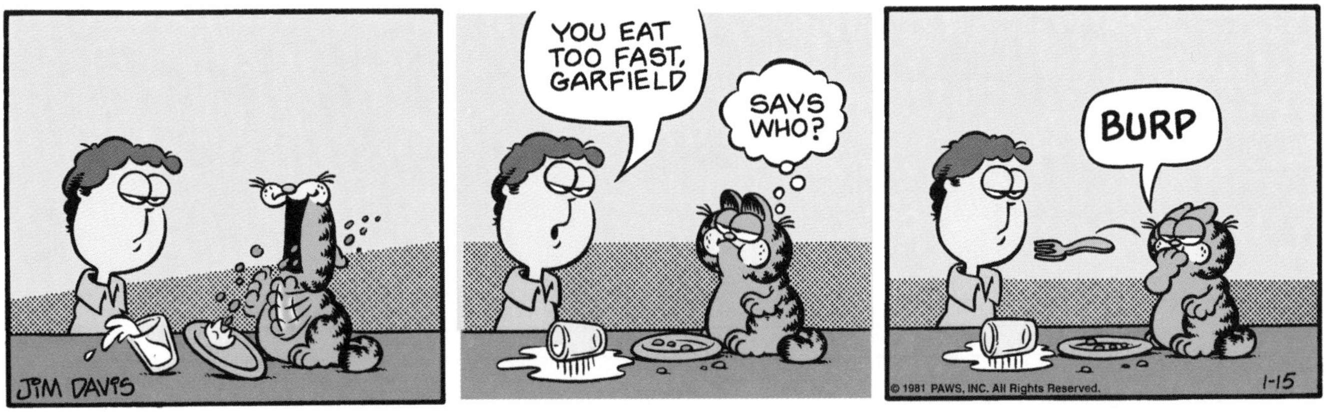
JIM DAVIS
YOU EAT TOO FAST, GARFIELD
SAYS WHO?
BURP
© 1981 PAWS, INC. All Rights Reserved.
1-15

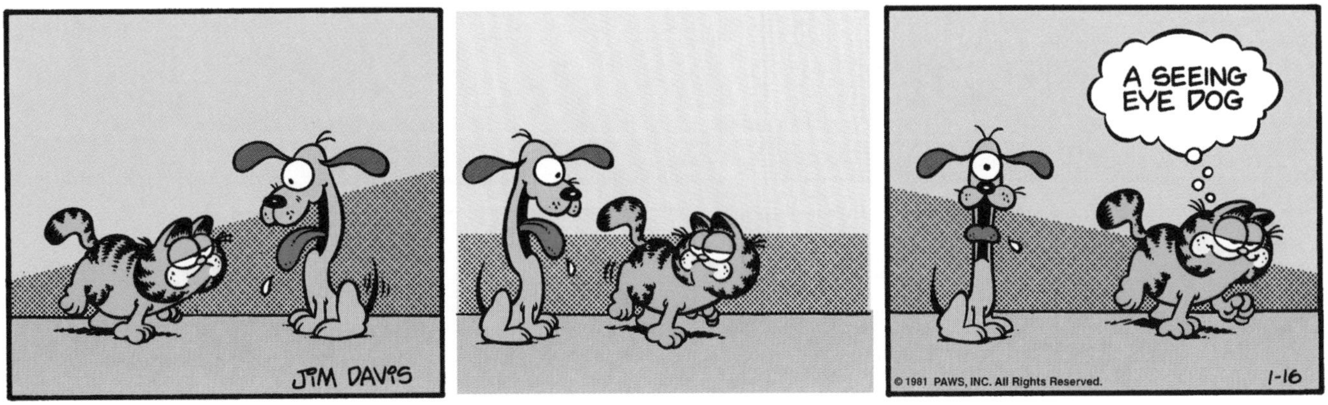
JIM DAVIS
A SEEING EYE DOG
© 1981 PAWS, INC. All Rights Reserved.
1-16

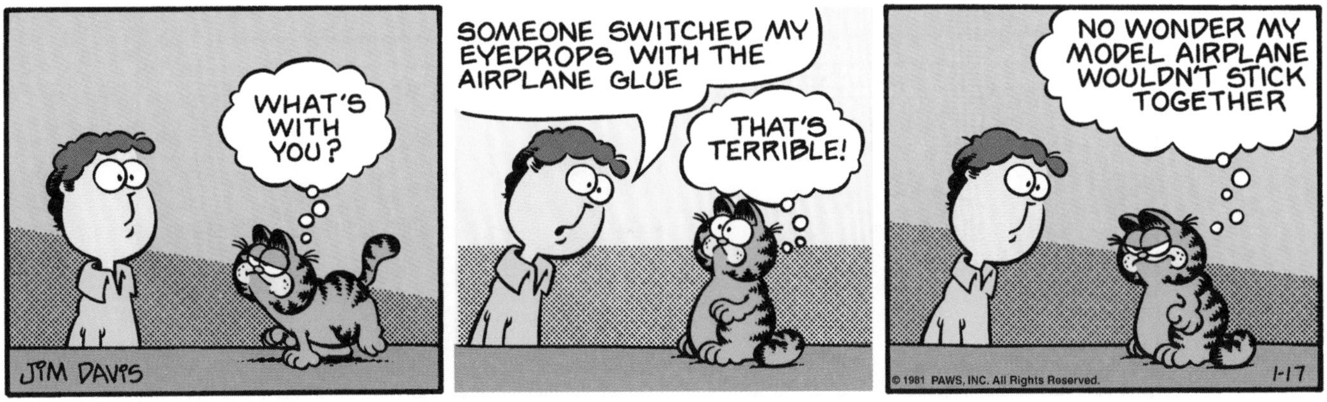
JIM DAVIS
WHAT'S WITH YOU?
SOMEONE SWITCHED MY EYEDROPS WITH THE AIRPLANE GLUE
THAT'S TERRIBLE!
NO WONDER MY MODEL AIRPLANE WOULDN'T STICK TOGETHER
© 1981 PAWS, INC. All Rights Reserved.
1-17

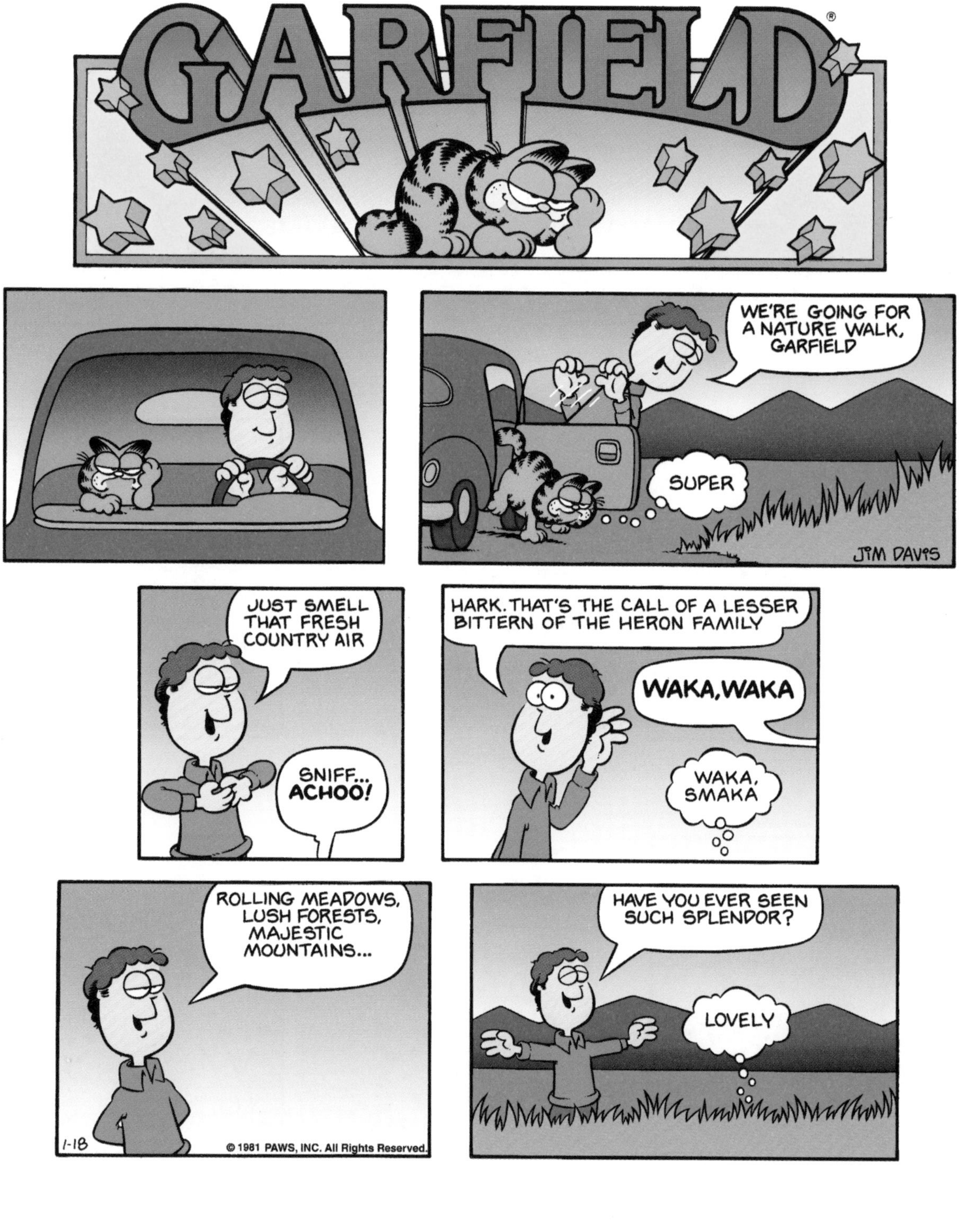
GARFIELD
WE'RE GOING FOR A NATURE WALK, GARFIELD
SUPER
JIM DAVIS
JUST SMELL THAT FRESH COUNTRY AIR
SNIFF... ACHOO!
HARK. THAT'S THE CALL OF A LESSER BITTERN OF THE HERON FAMILY
WAKA, WAKA
WAKA, SMAKA
ROLLING MEADOWS, LUSH FORESTS, MAJESTIC MOUNTAINS...
1-18
© 1981 PAWS, INC. All Rights Reserved.
HAVE YOU EVER SEEN SUCH SPLENDOR?
LOVELY

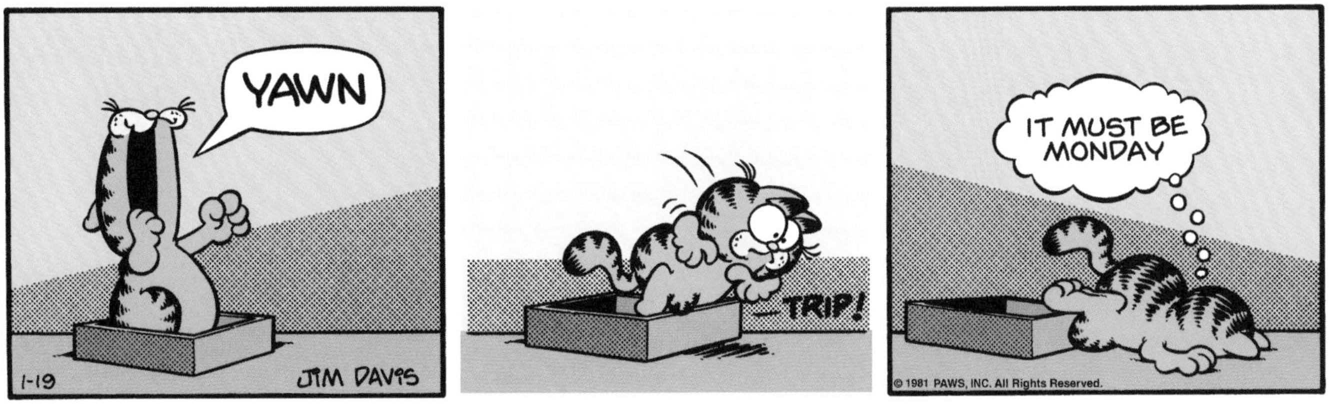
YAWN
1-19
JIM DAVIS
TRIP!
IT MUST BE MONDAY
© 1981 PAWS, INC. All Rights Reserved.

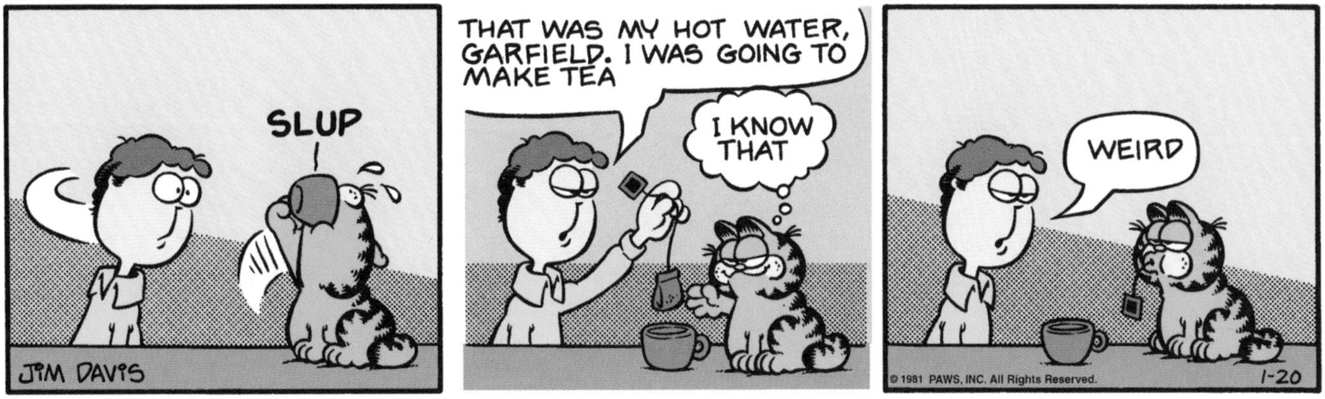
SLUP
JIM DAVIS
THAT WAS MY HOT WATER, GARFIELD. I WAS GOING TO MAKE TEA
I KNOW THAT
WEIRD
© 1981 PAWS, INC. All Rights Reserved.
1-20

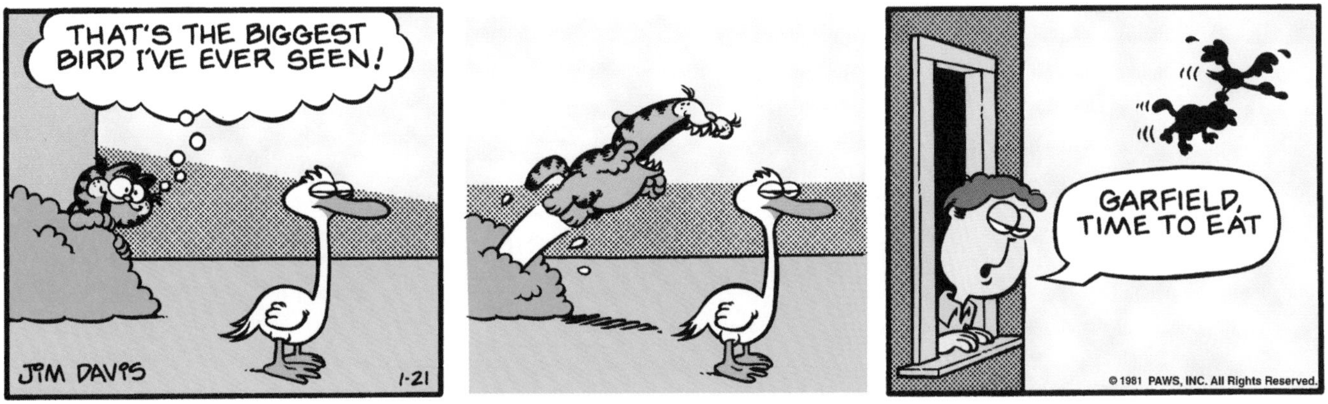
THAT'S THE BIGGEST BIRD I'VE EVER SEEN!
JIM DAVIS
1-21
GARFIELD, TIME TO EAT
© 1981 PAWS, INC. All Rights Reserved.

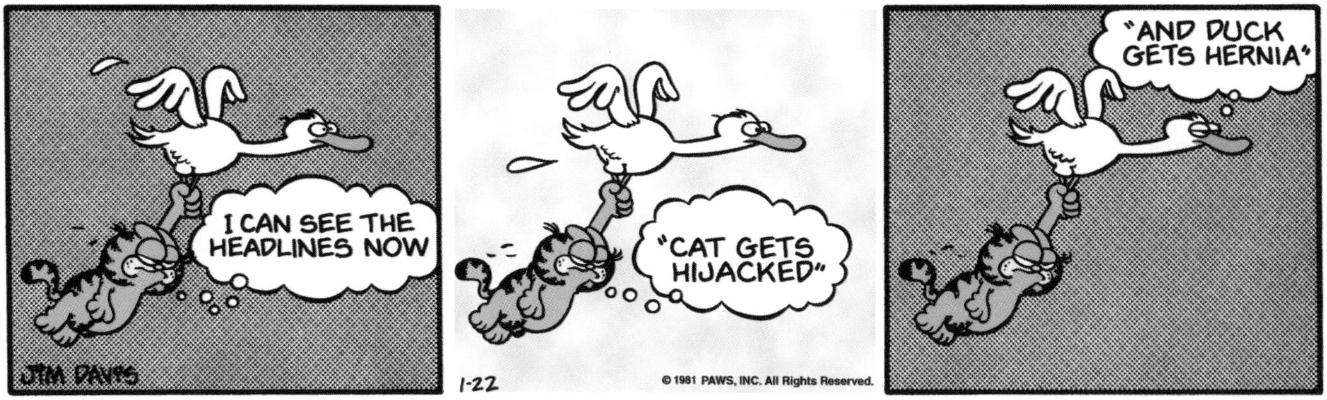
I CAN SEE THE HEADLINES NOW
"CAT GETS HIJACKED"
"AND DUCK GETS HERNIA"
JIM DAVIS
1-22
© 1981 PAWS, INC. All Rights Reserved.

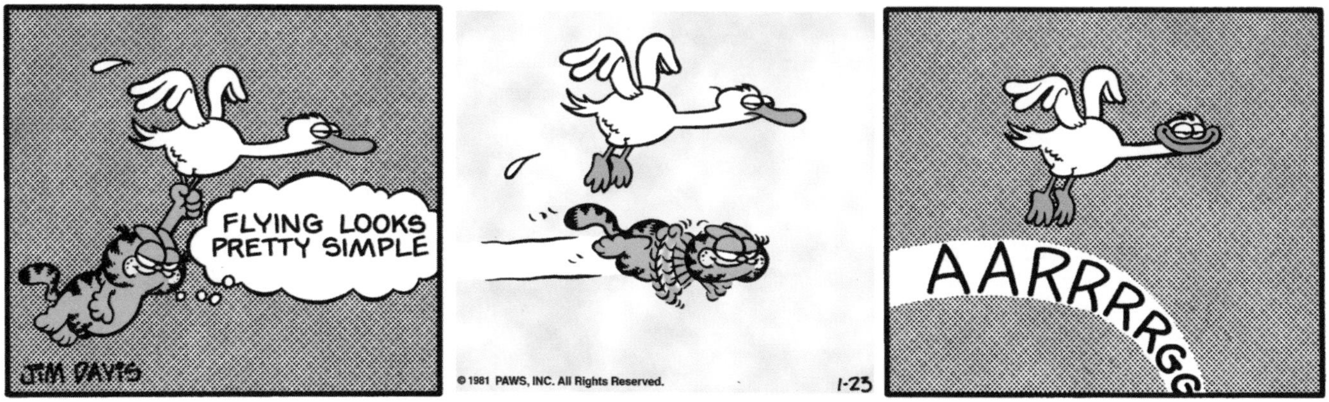
FLYING LOOKS PRETTY SIMPLE
AARRRRRGG
JIM DAVIS
1-23
© 1981 PAWS, INC. All Rights Reserved.

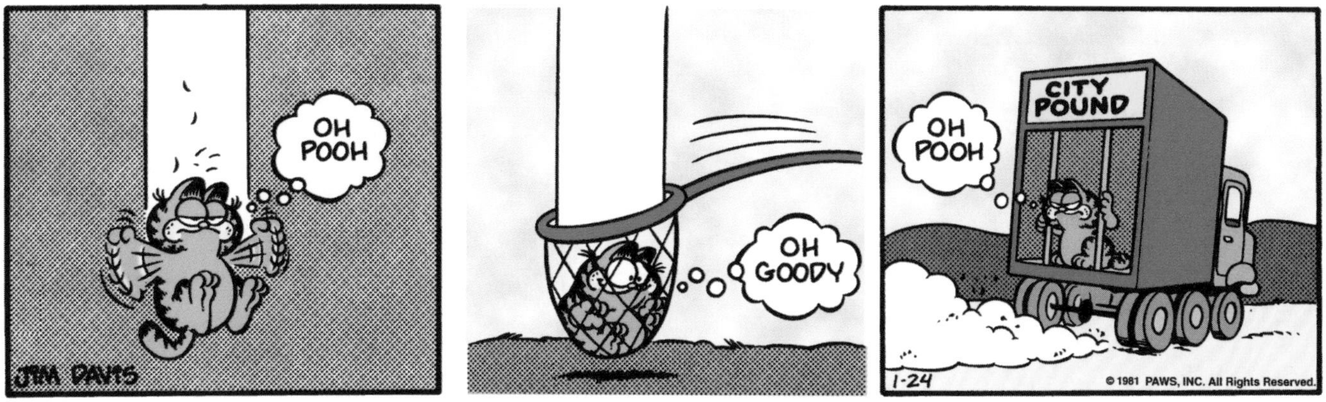
OH POOH
OH GOODY
CITY POUND
OH POOH
JIM DAVIS
1-24
© 1981 PAWS, INC. All Rights Reserved.

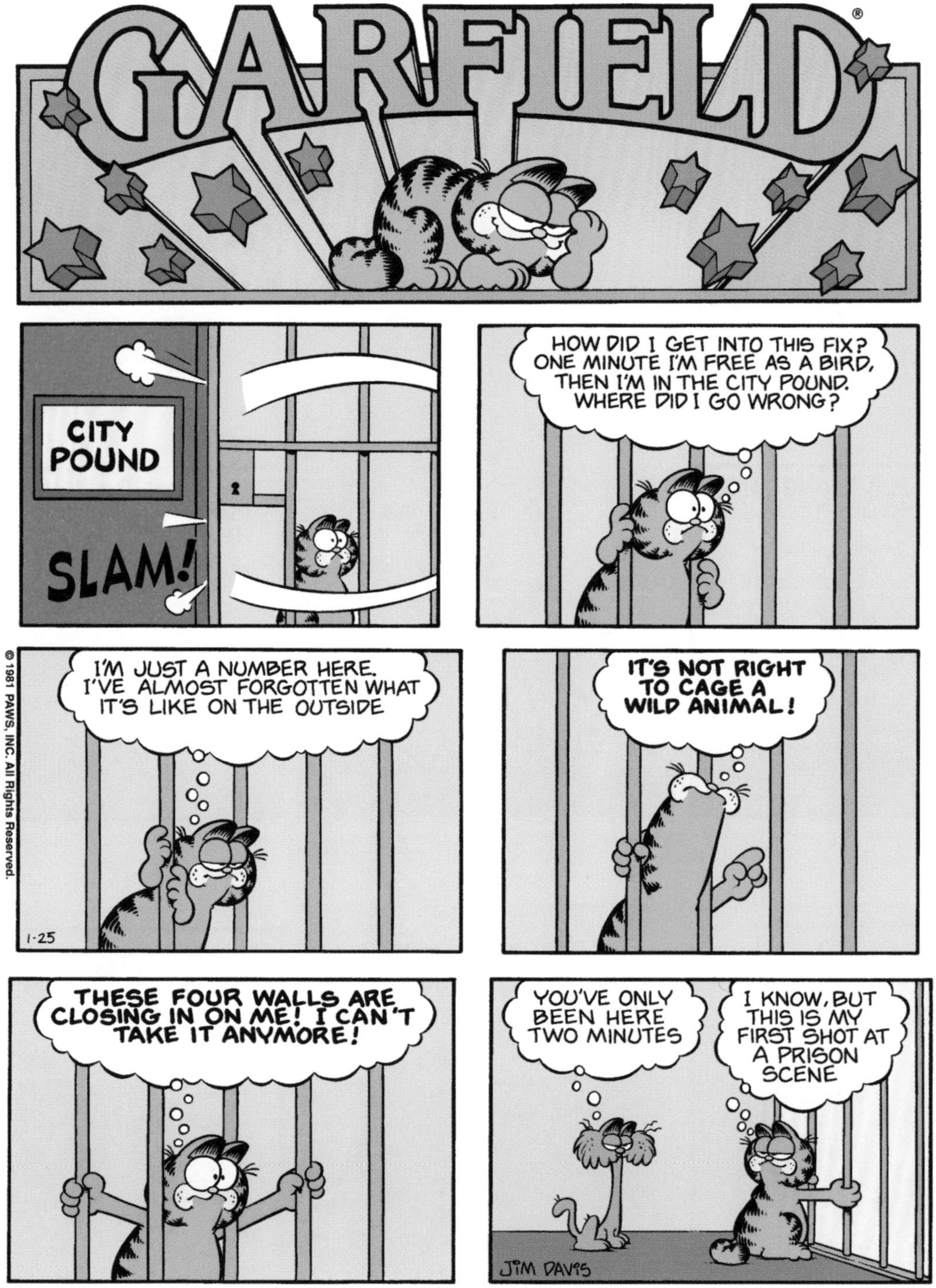
GARFIELD
CITY POUND
SLAM!
HOW DID I GET INTO THIS FIX? ONE MINUTE I'M FREE AS A BIRD, THEN I'M IN THE CITY POUND. WHERE DID I GO WRONG?
I'M JUST A NUMBER HERE. I'VE ALMOST FORGOTTEN WHAT IT'S LIKE ON THE OUTSIDE
IT'S NOT RIGHT TO CAGE A WILD ANIMAL!
THESE FOUR WALLS ARE CLOSING IN ON ME! I CAN'T TAKE IT ANYMORE!
YOU'VE ONLY BEEN HERE TWO MINUTES
I KNOW, BUT THIS IS MY FIRST SHOT AT A PRISON SCENE
JIM DAVIS
1-25

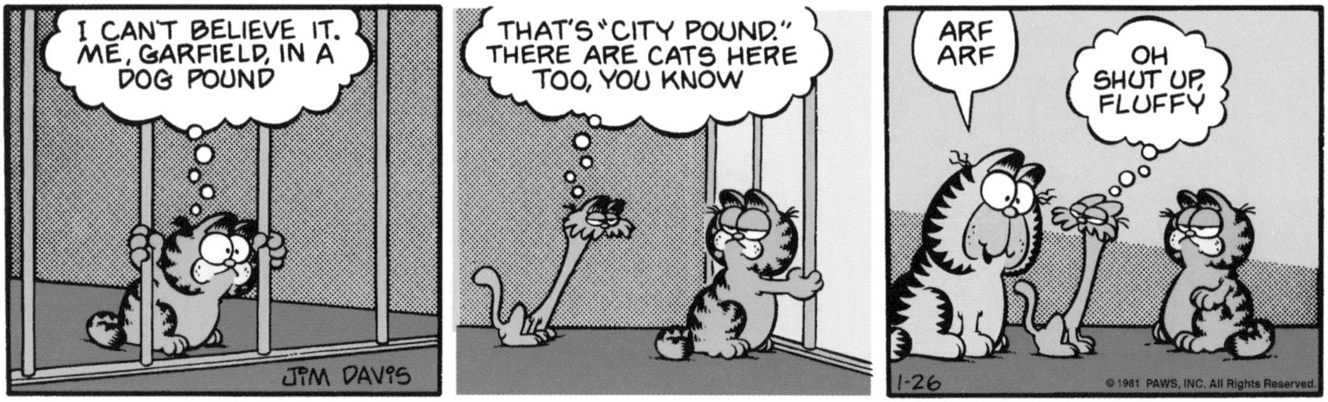
I CAN'T BELIEVE IT. ME, GARFIELD, IN A DOG POUND
JIM DAVIS
THAT'S "CITY POUND." THERE ARE CATS HERE TOO, YOU KNOW
ARF ARF
OH SHUT UP, FLUFFY
1-26
© 1981 PAWS, INC. All Rights Reserved.

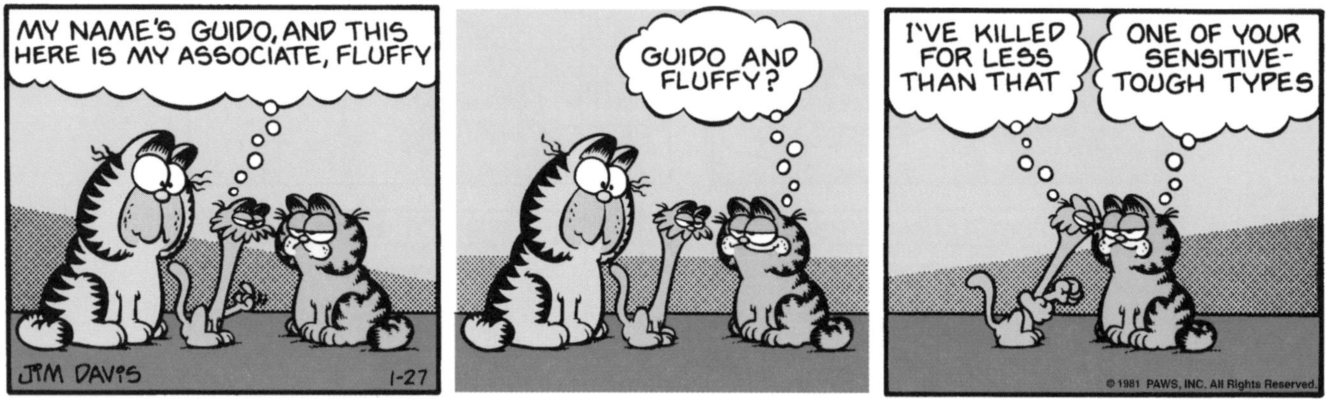
MY NAME'S GUIDO, AND THIS HERE IS MY ASSOCIATE, FLUFFY
JIM DAVIS
1-27
GUIDO AND FLUFFY?
I'VE KILLED FOR LESS THAN THAT
ONE OF YOUR SENSITIVE-TOUGH TYPES
© 1981 PAWS, INC. All Rights Reserved.

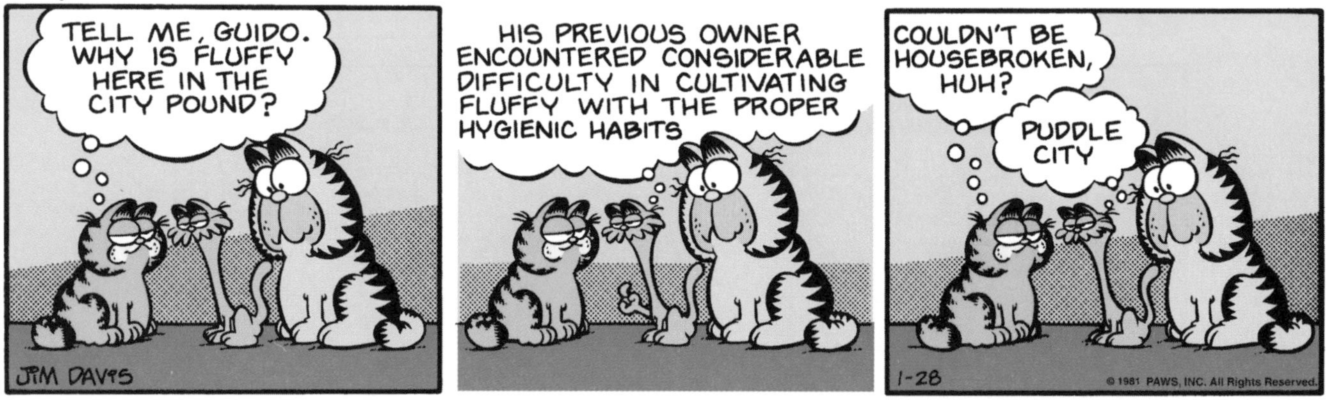
TELL ME, GUIDO. WHY IS FLUFFY HERE IN THE CITY POUND?
JIM DAVIS
HIS PREVIOUS OWNER ENCOUNTERED CONSIDERABLE DIFFICULTY IN CULTIVATING FLUFFY WITH THE PROPER HYGIENIC HABITS
COULDN'T BE HOUSEBROKEN, HUH?
PUDDLE CITY
1-28
© 1981 PAWS, INC. All Rights Reserved.

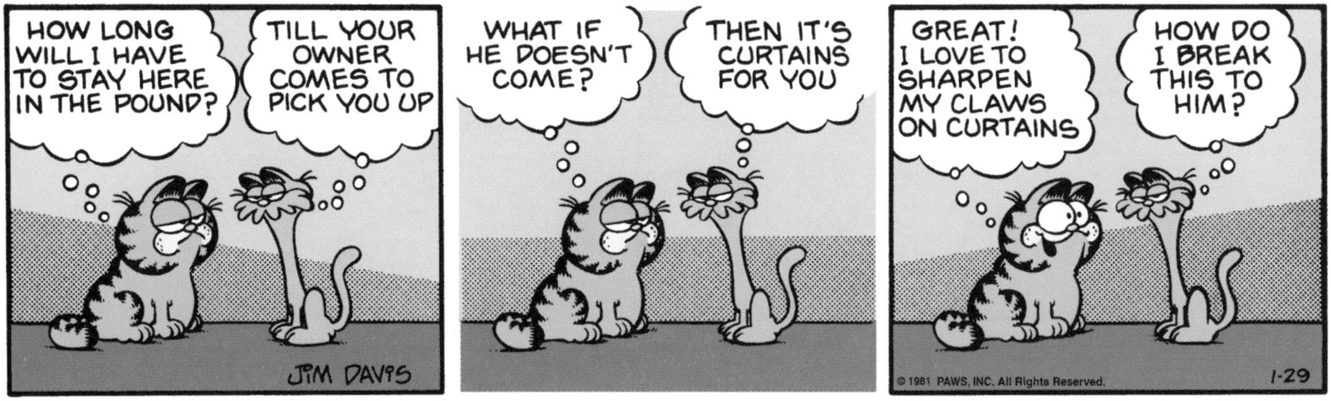
HOW LONG WILL I HAVE TO STAY HERE IN THE POUND?
TILL YOUR OWNER COMES TO PICK YOU UP
JIM DAVIS
WHAT IF HE DOESN'T COME?
THEN IT'S CURTAINS FOR YOU
GREAT! I LOVE TO SHARPEN MY CLAWS ON CURTAINS
HOW DO I BREAK THIS TO HIM?
© 1981 PAWS, INC. All Rights Reserved.
1-29

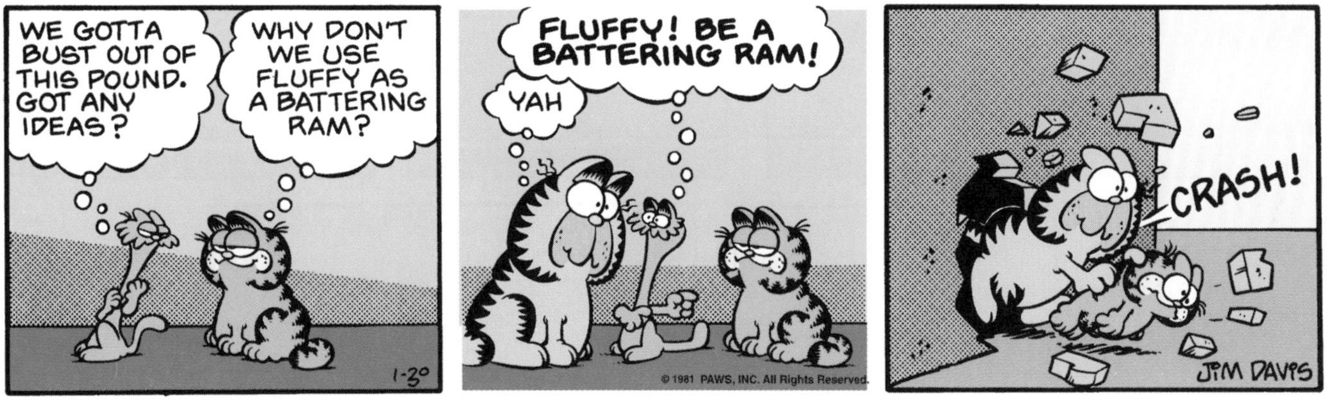
WE GOTTA BUST OUT OF THIS POUND. GOT ANY IDEAS?
WHY DON'T WE USE FLUFFY AS A BATTERING RAM?
1-30
FLUFFY! BE A BATTERING RAM!
YAH
© 1981 PAWS, INC. All Rights Reserved.
CRASH!
JIM DAVIS

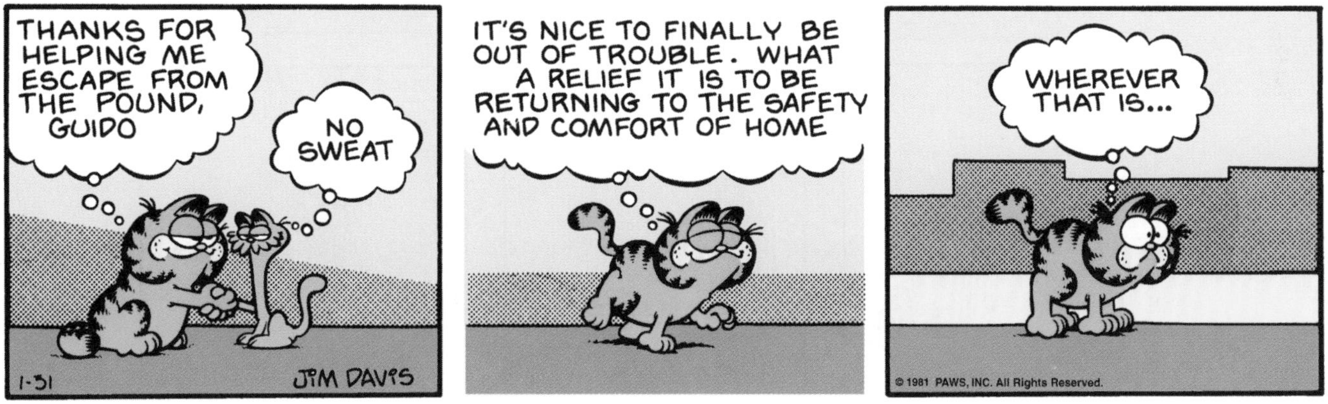
THANKS FOR HELPING ME ESCAPE FROM THE POUND, GUIDO
NO SWEAT
1-31
JIM DAVIS
IT'S NICE TO FINALLY BE OUT OF TROUBLE. WHAT A RELIEF IT IS TO BE RETURNING TO THE SAFETY AND COMFORT OF HOME
WHEREVER THAT IS...
© 1981 PAWS, INC. All Rights Reserved.

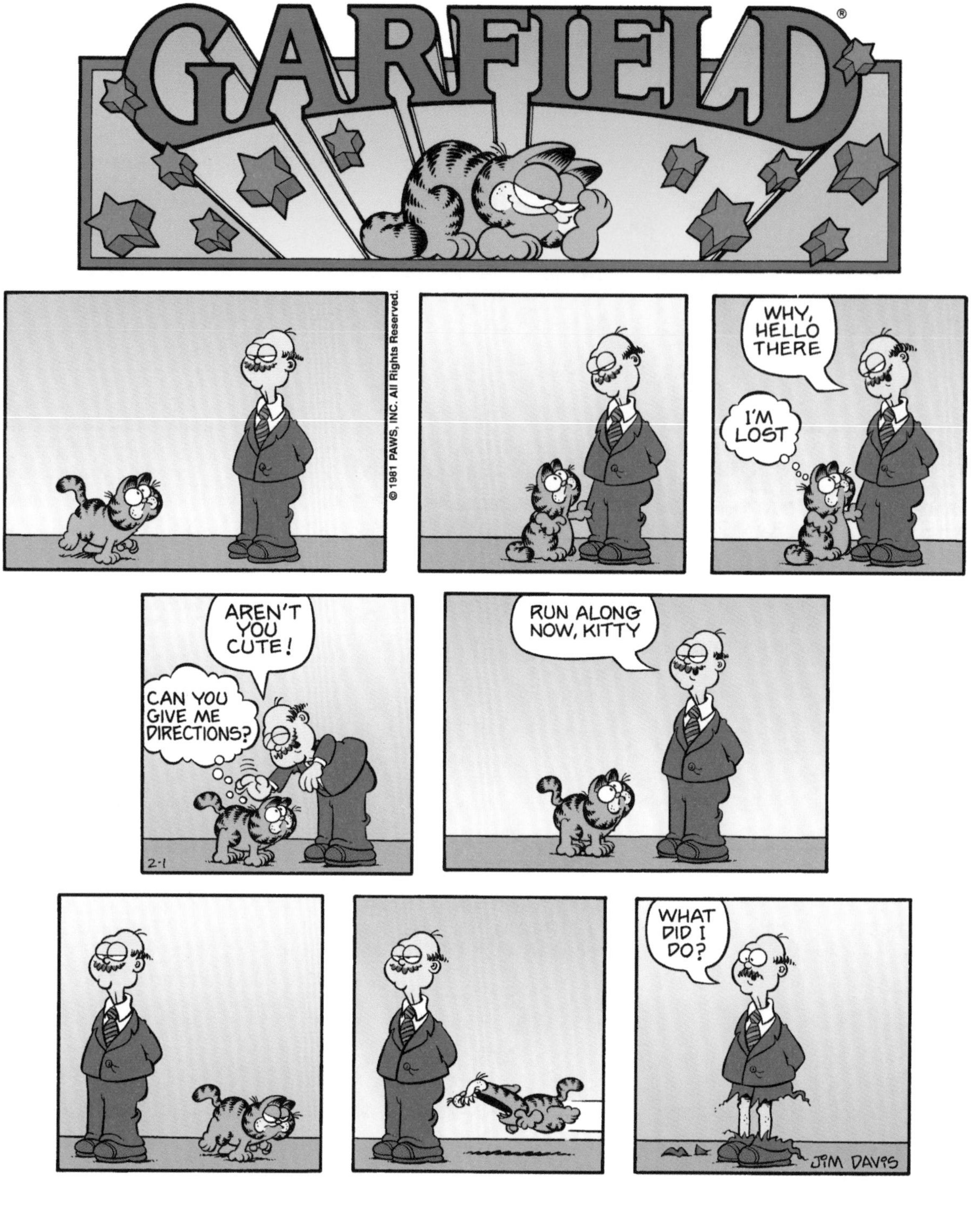
GARFIELD
© 1981 PAWS, INC. All Rights Reserved.
WHY, HELLO THERE
I'M LOST
AREN'T YOU CUTE!
CAN YOU GIVE ME DIRECTIONS?
2-1
RUN ALONG NOW, KITTY
WHAT DID I DO?
JIM DAVIS

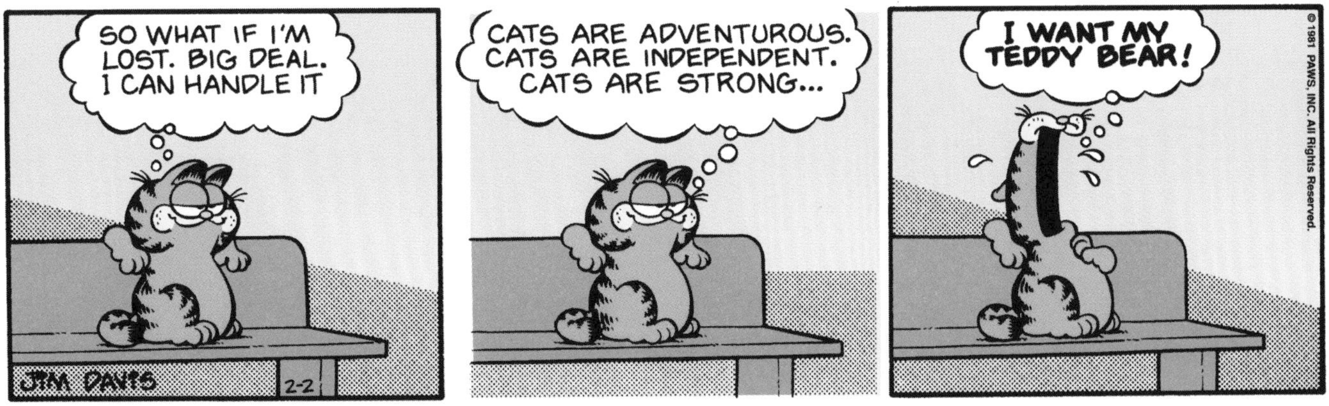
SO WHAT IF I'M LOST. BIG DEAL. I CAN HANDLE IT
JIM DAVIS
2-2
CATS ARE ADVENTUROUS. CATS ARE INDEPENDENT. CATS ARE STRONG...
I WANT MY TEDDY BEAR!
© 1981 PAWS, INC. All Rights Reserved.

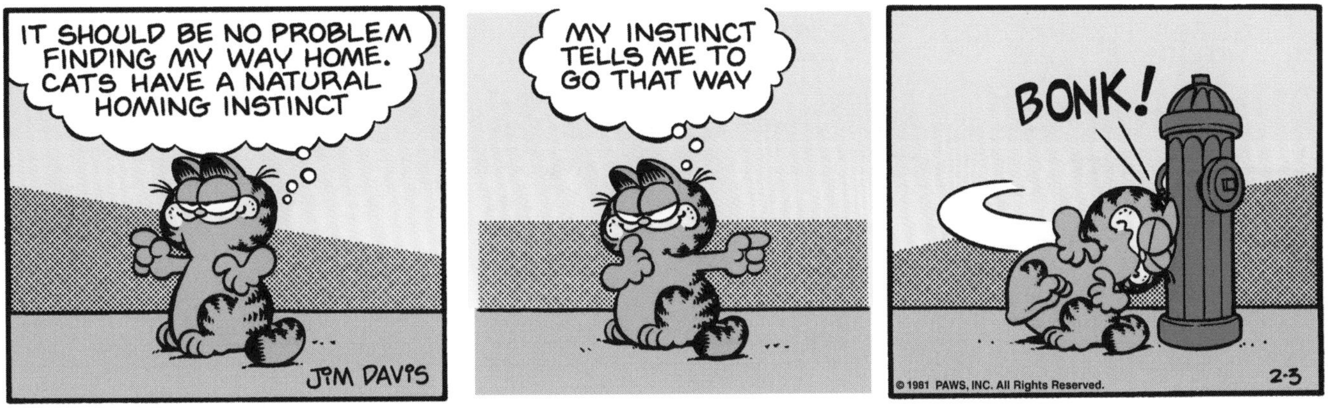
IT SHOULD BE NO PROBLEM FINDING MY WAY HOME. CATS HAVE A NATURAL HOMING INSTINCT
JIM DAVIS
MY INSTINCT TELLS ME TO GO THAT WAY
BONK!
© 1981 PAWS, INC. All Rights Reserved.
2-3

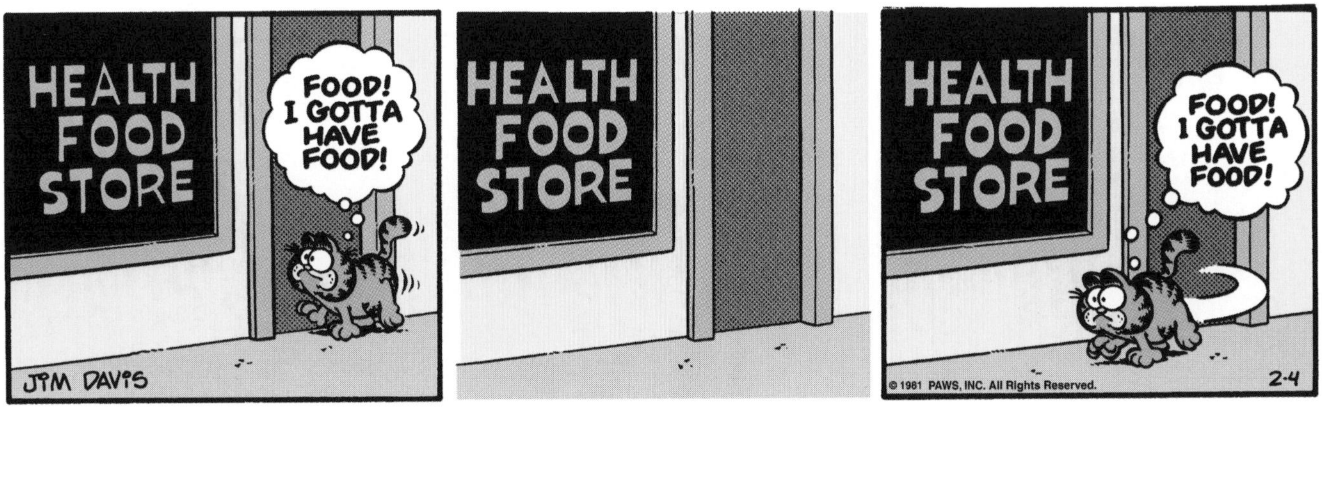
HEALTH FOOD STORE
FOOD! I GOTTA HAVE FOOD!
JIM DAVIS
HEALTH FOOD STORE
HEALTH FOOD STORE
FOOD! I GOTTA HAVE FOOD!
© 1981 PAWS, INC. All Rights Reserved.
2-4

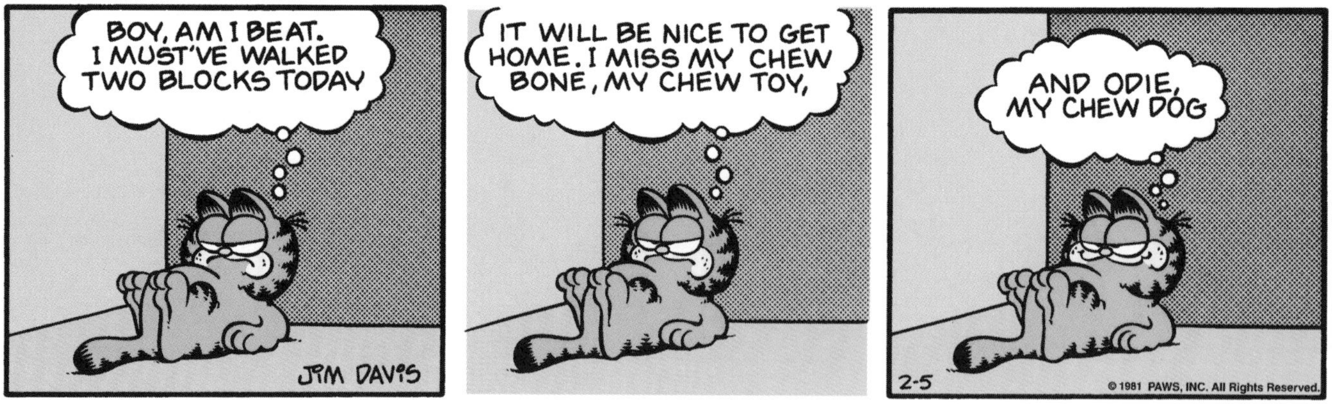
BOY, AM I BEAT. I MUST'VE WALKED TWO BLOCKS TODAY
JIM DAVIS
IT WILL BE NICE TO GET HOME. I MISS MY CHEW BONE, MY CHEW TOY,
AND ODIE, MY CHEW DOG
2-5
© 1981 PAWS, INC. All Rights Reserved.

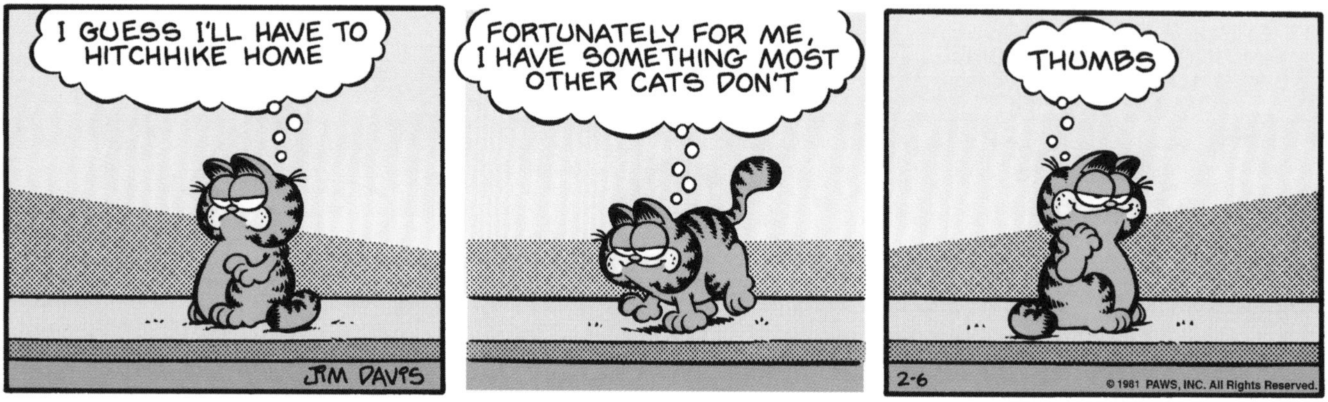
I GUESS I'LL HAVE TO HITCHHIKE HOME
JIM DAVIS
FORTUNATELY FOR ME, I HAVE SOMETHING MOST OTHER CATS DON'T
THUMBS
2-6
© 1981 PAWS, INC. All Rights Reserved.

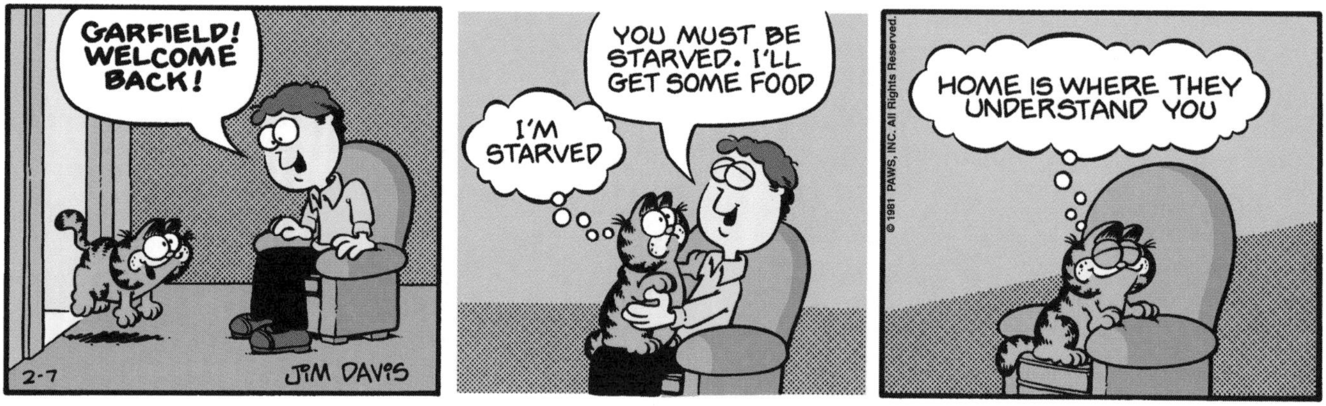
GARFIELD! WELCOME BACK!
2-7
JIM DAVIS
YOU MUST BE STARVED. I'LL GET SOME FOOD
I'M STARVED
© 1981 PAWS, INC. All Rights Reserved.
HOME IS WHERE THEY UNDERSTAND YOU

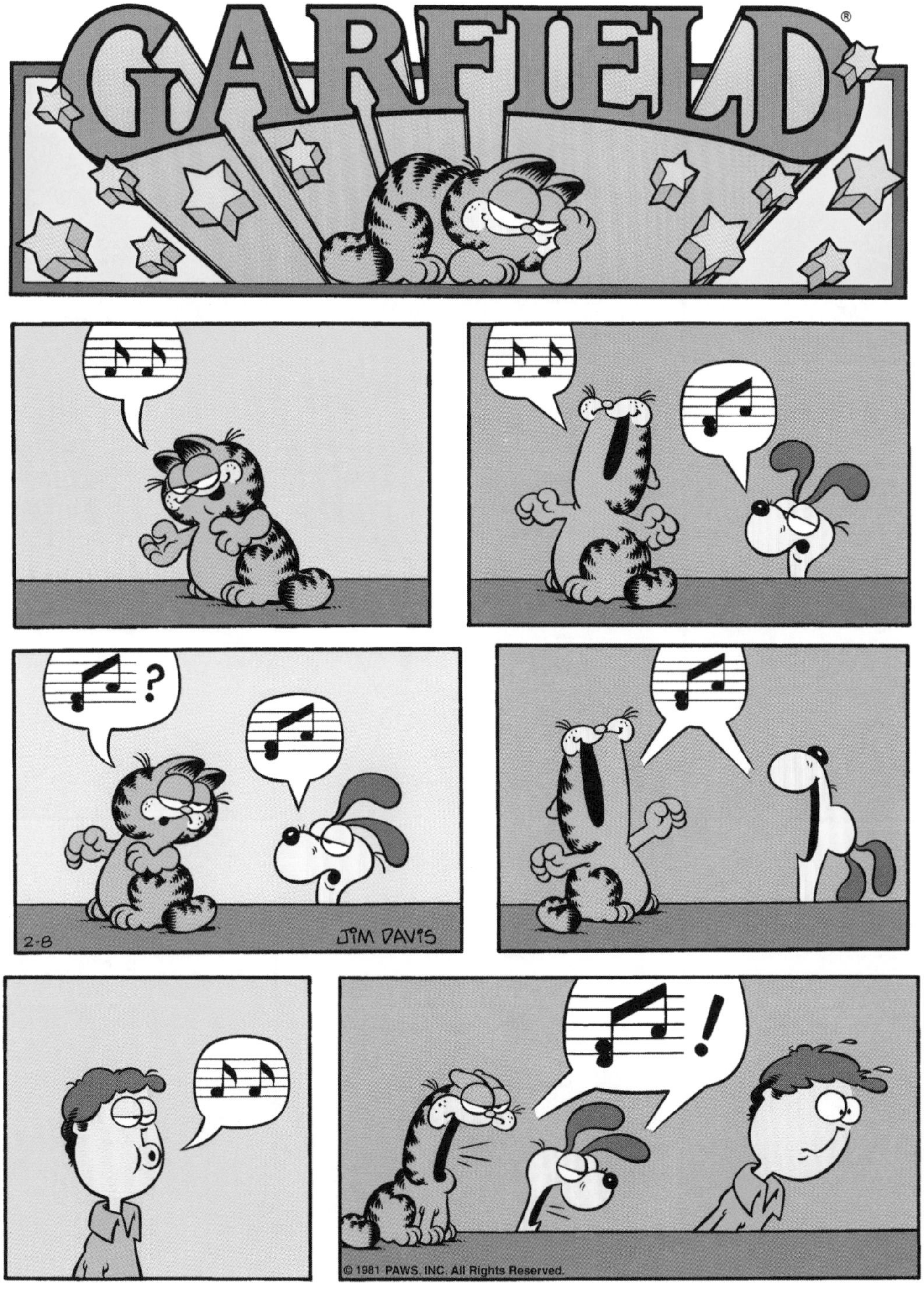
GARFIELD
?
2-8
JIM DAVIS
!
© 1981 PAWS, INC. All Rights Reserved.

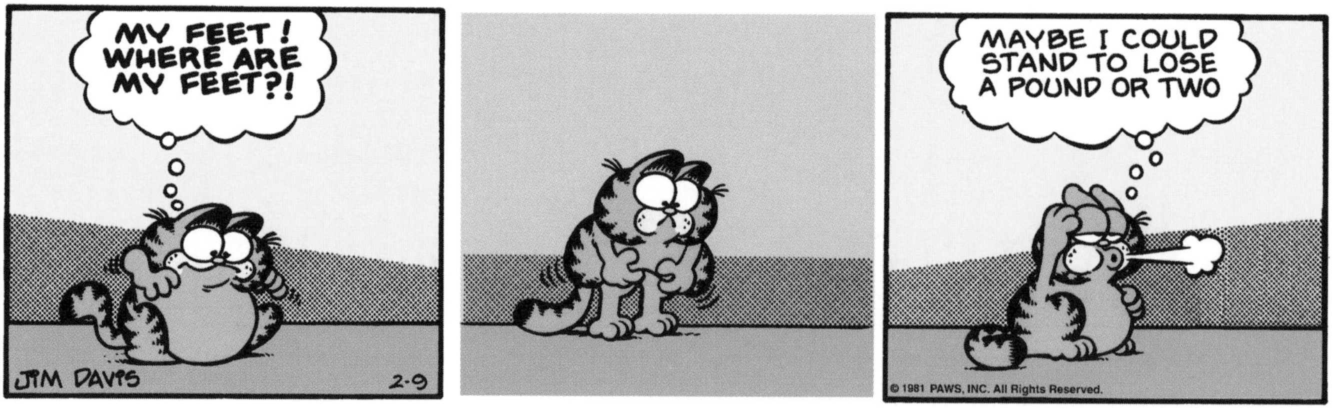
MY FEET! WHERE ARE MY FEET?!
JIM DAVIS
2-9
MAYBE I COULD STAND TO LOSE A POUND OR TWO
© 1981 PAWS, INC. All Rights Reserved.

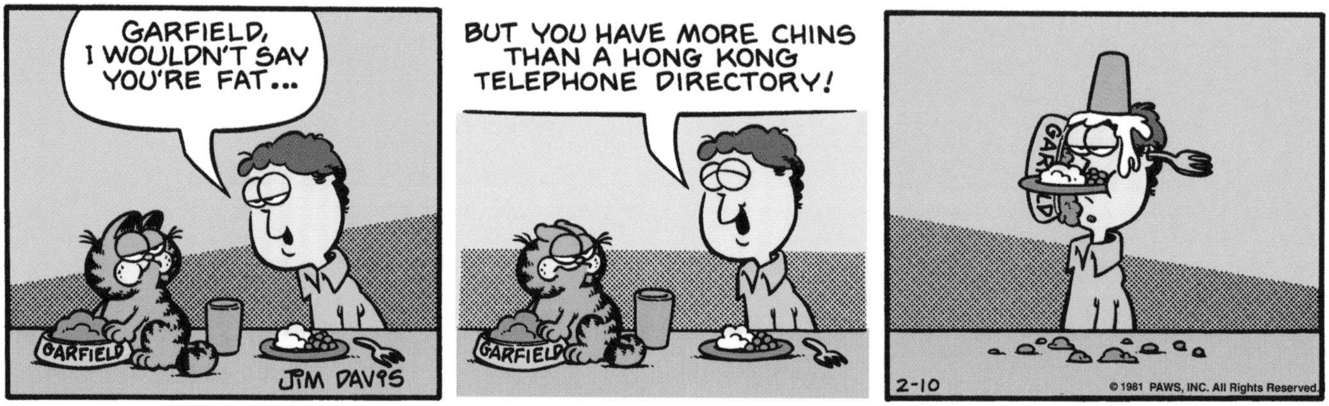
GARFIELD, I WOULDN'T SAY YOU'RE FAT...
GARFIELD
JIM DAVIS
BUT YOU HAVE MORE CHINS THAN A HONG KONG TELEPHONE DIRECTORY!
GARFIELD
2-10
© 1981 PAWS, INC. All Rights Reserved.

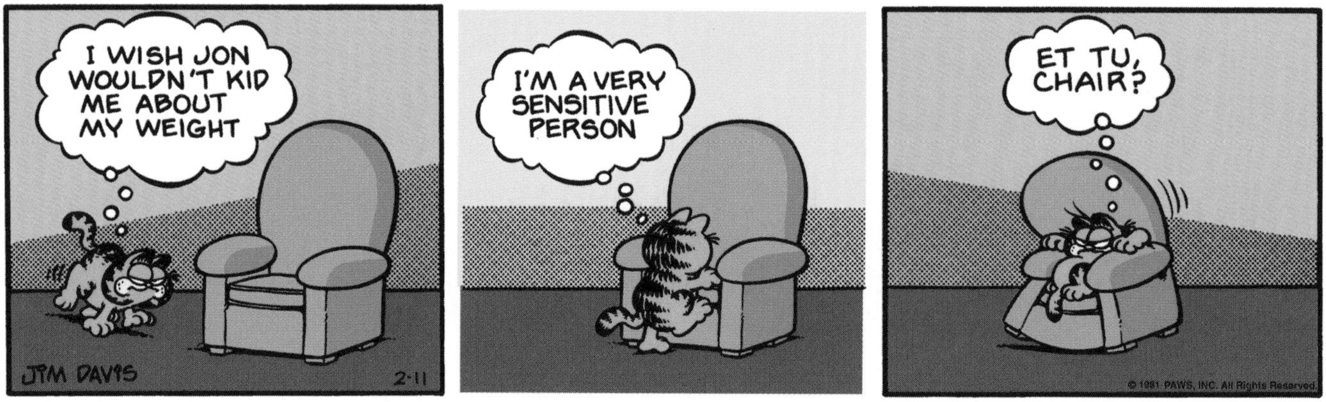
I WISH JON WOULDN'T KID ME ABOUT MY WEIGHT
JIM DAVIS
2-11
I'M A VERY SENSITIVE PERSON
ET TU, CHAIR?
© 1981 PAWS, INC. All Rights Reserved.

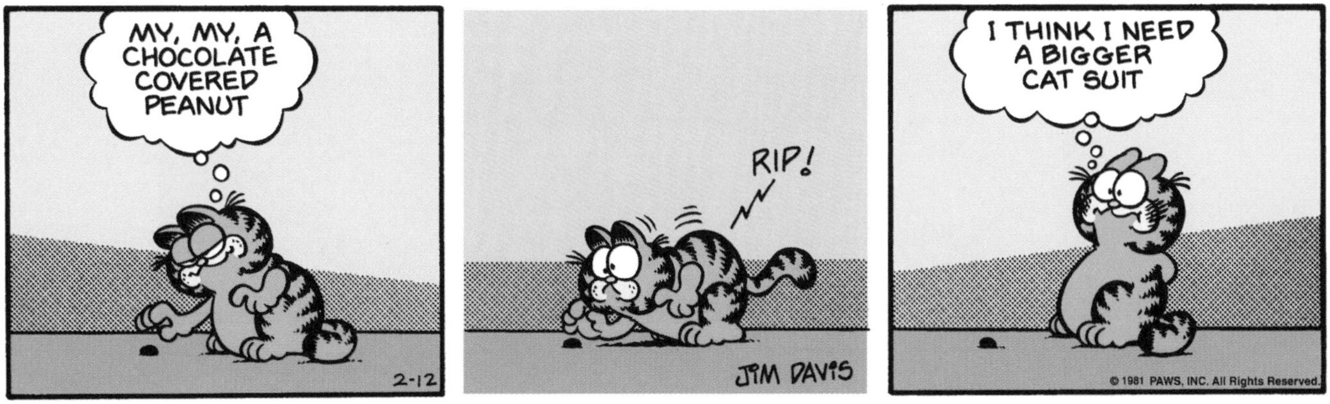
MY, MY, A CHOCOLATE COVERED PEANUT
2-12
RIP!
JIM DAVIS
I THINK I NEED A BIGGER CAT SUIT
© 1981 PAWS, INC. All Rights Reserved.

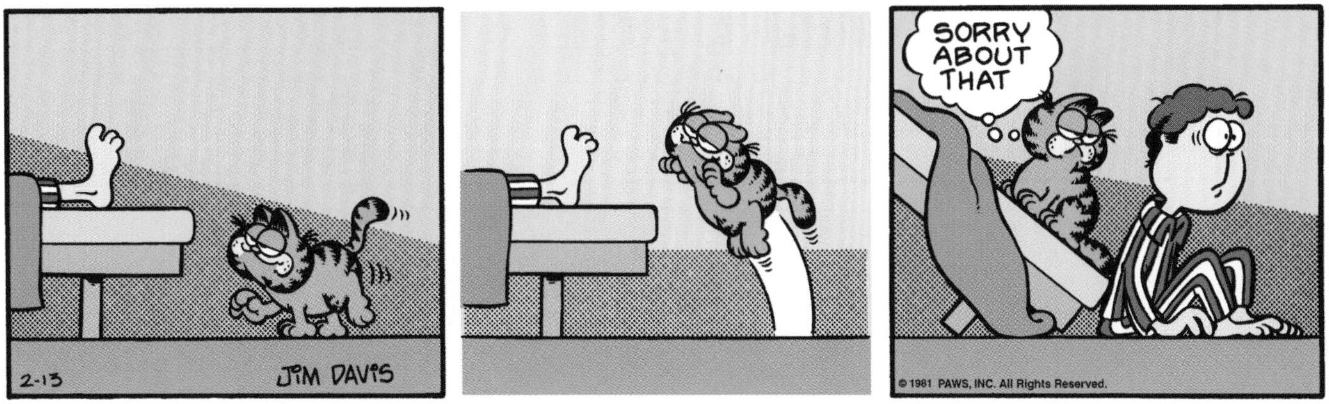
2-13
JIM DAVIS
SORRY ABOUT THAT
© 1981 PAWS, INC. All Rights Reserved.

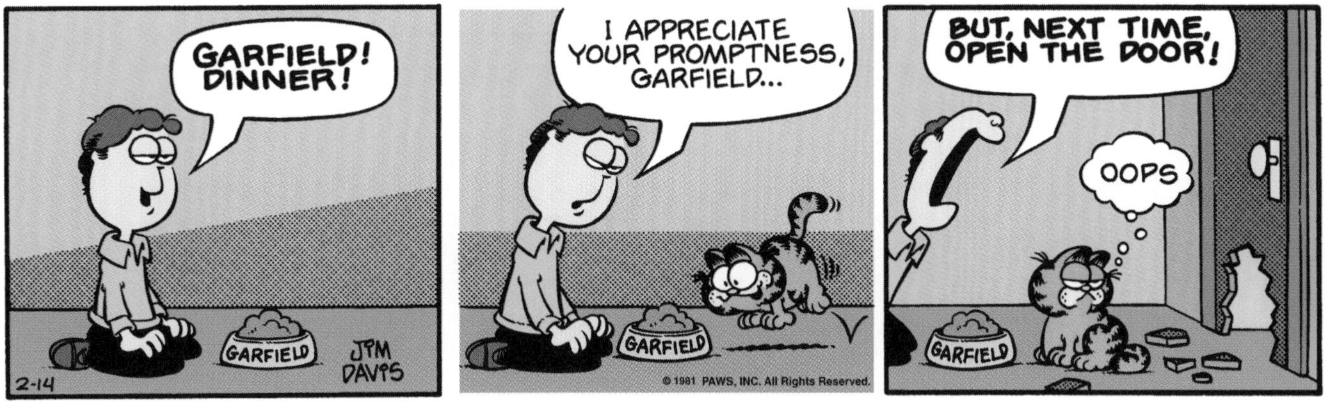
GARFIELD! DINNER!
GARFIELD
JIM DAVIS
2-14
I APPRECIATE YOUR PROMPTNESS, GARFIELD...
GARFIELD
© 1981 PAWS, INC. All Rights Reserved.
BUT, NEXT TIME, OPEN THE DOOR!
OOPS
GARFIELD

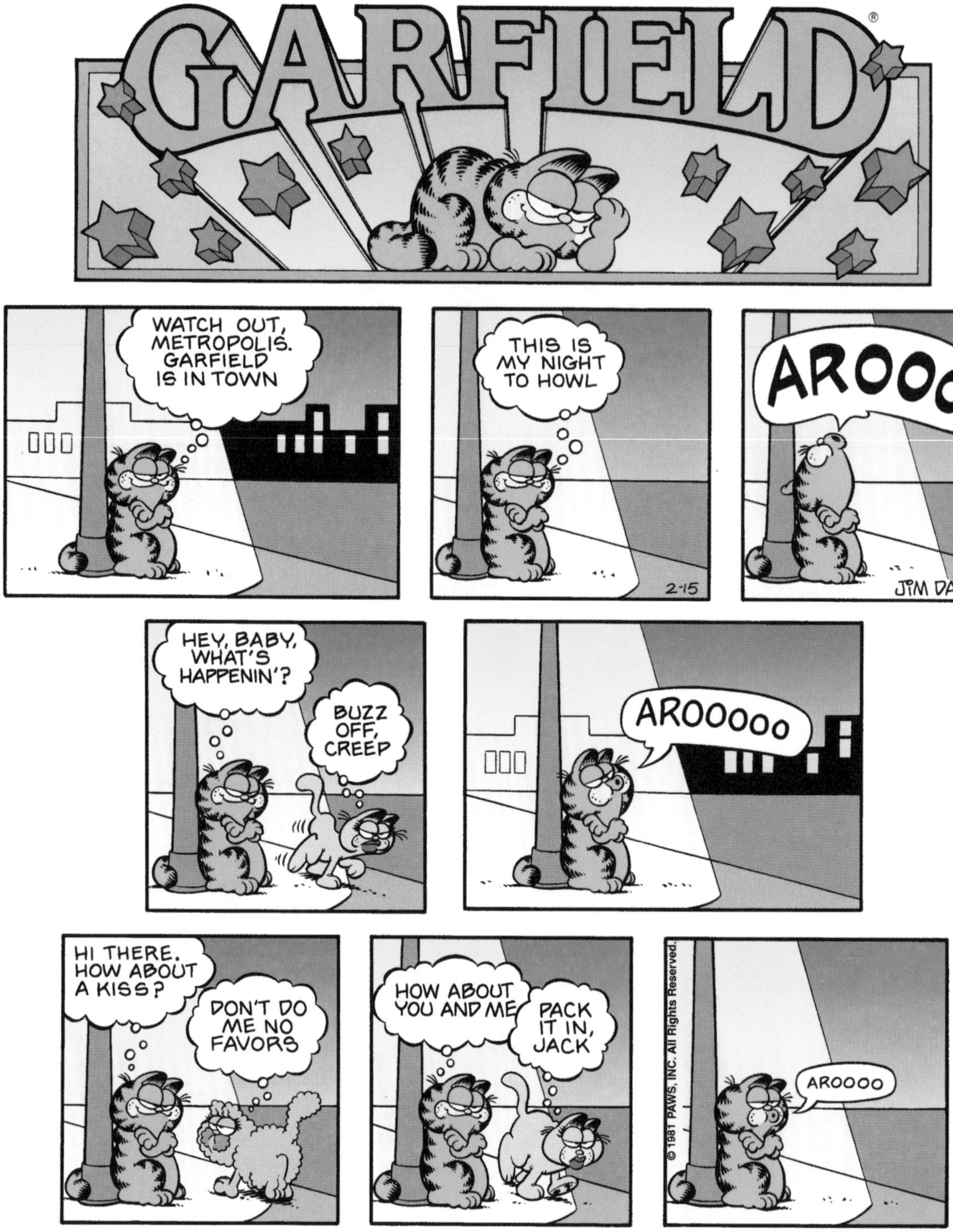
GARFIELD
WATCH OUT, METROPOLIS. GARFIELD IS IN TOWN
THIS IS MY NIGHT TO HOWL
AROOO
2-15
JIM DAVIS
HEY, BABY, WHAT'S HAPPENIN'?
BUZZ OFF, CREEP
AROOOOO
HI THERE. HOW ABOUT A KISS?
DON'T DO ME NO FAVORS
HOW ABOUT YOU AND ME
PACK IT IN, JACK
© 1981 PAWS, INC. All Rights Reserved.
AROOOO

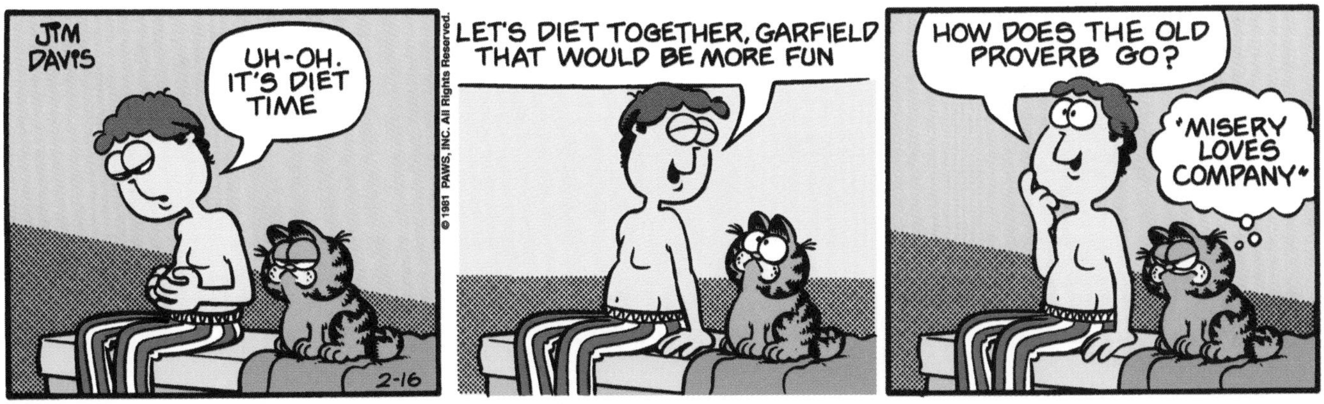
JIM DAVIS
UH-OH. IT'S DIET TIME
2-16
© 1981 PAWS, INC. All Rights Reserved.
LET'S DIET TOGETHER, GARFIELD THAT WOULD BE MORE FUN
HOW DOES THE OLD PROVERB GO?
"MISERY LOVES COMPANY"

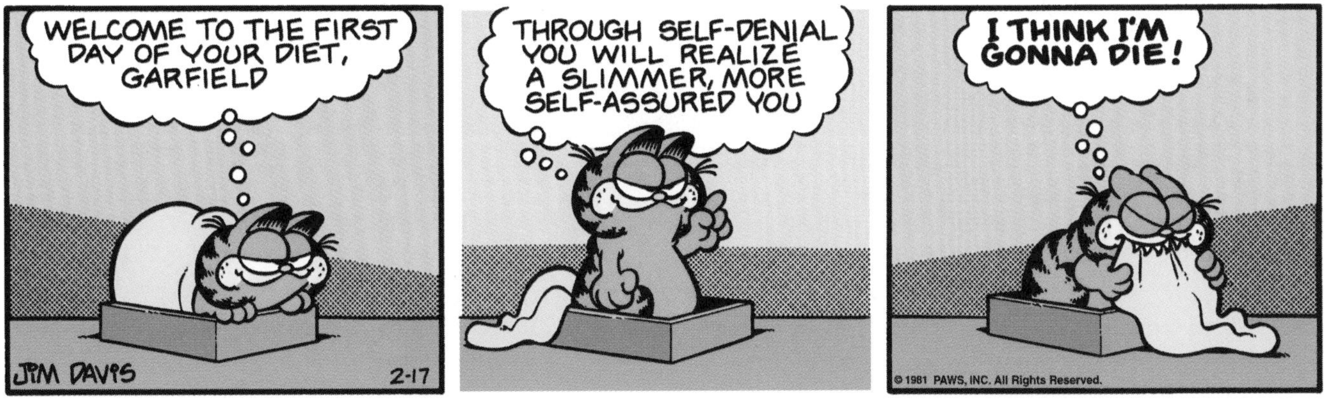
WELCOME TO THE FIRST DAY OF YOUR DIET, GARFIELD
JIM DAVIS
2-17
THROUGH SELF-DENIAL YOU WILL REALIZE A SLIMMER, MORE SELF-ASSURED YOU
I THINK I'M GONNA DIE!
© 1981 PAWS, INC. All Rights Reserved.

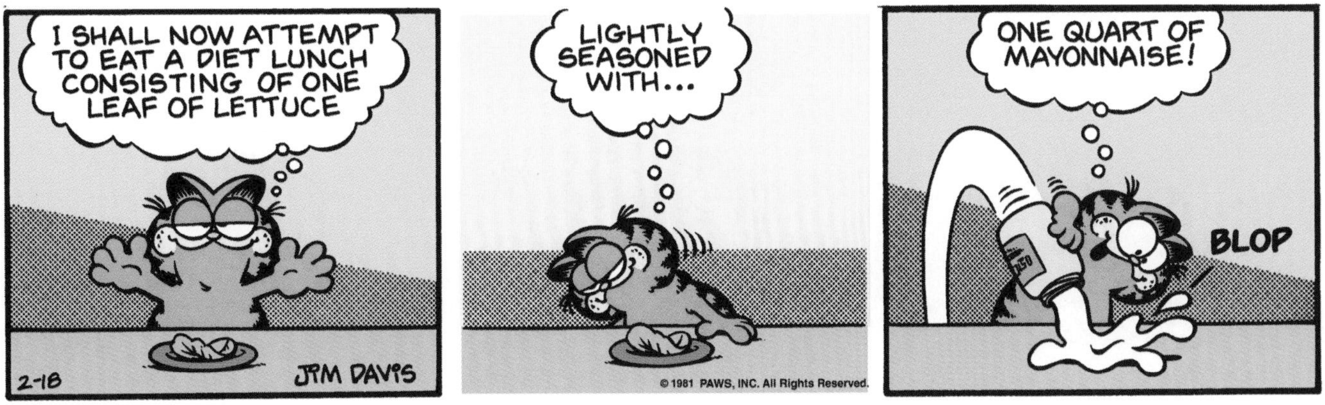
I SHALL NOW ATTEMPT TO EAT A DIET LUNCH CONSISTING OF ONE LEAF OF LETTUCE
2-18
JIM DAVIS
LIGHTLY SEASONED WITH...
© 1981 PAWS, INC. All Rights Reserved.
ONE QUART OF MAYONNAISE!
BLOP

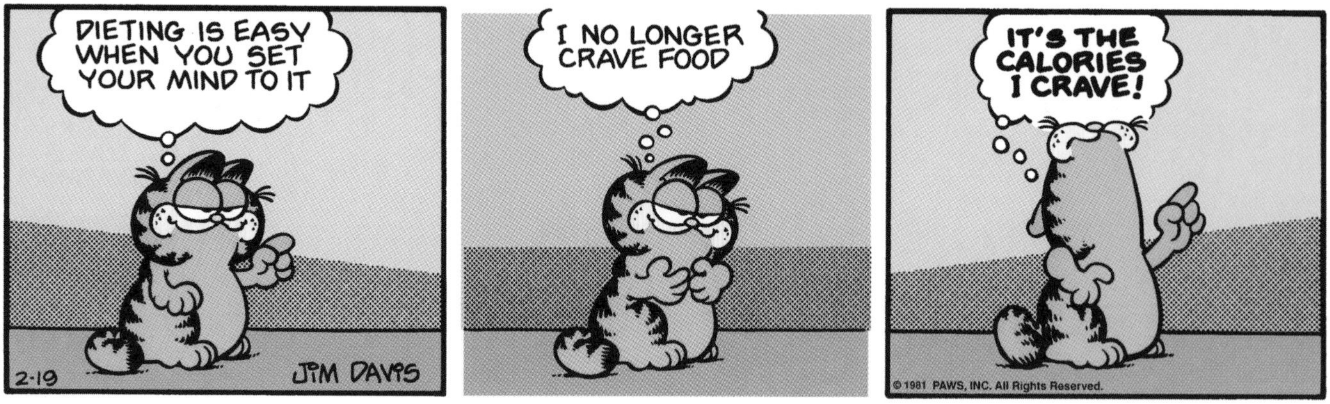
DIETING IS EASY WHEN YOU SET YOUR MIND TO IT
2-19
JIM DAVIS
I NO LONGER CRAVE FOOD
IT'S THE CALORIES I CRAVE!
© 1981 PAWS, INC. All Rights Reserved.

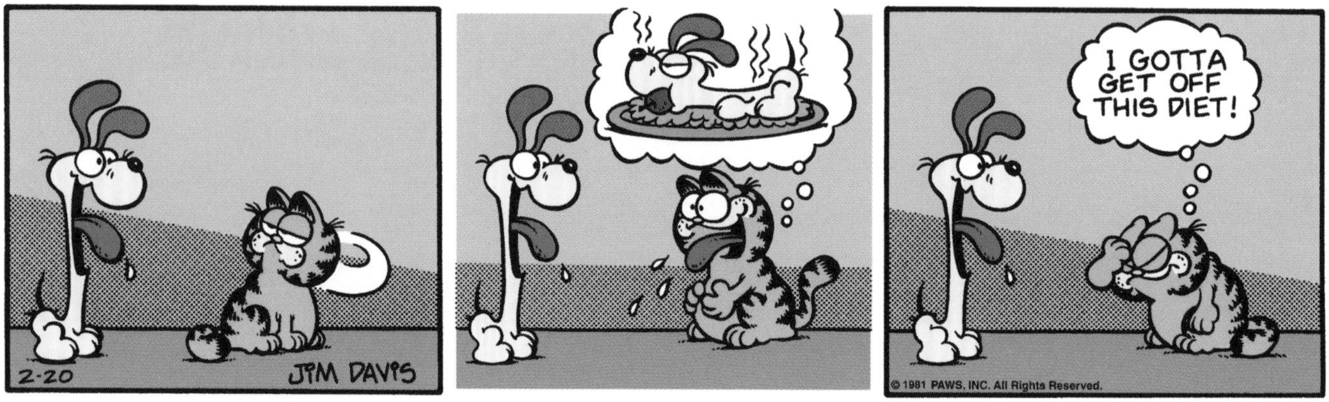
2-20
JIM DAVIS
I GOTTA GET OFF THIS DIET!
© 1981 PAWS, INC. All Rights Reserved.

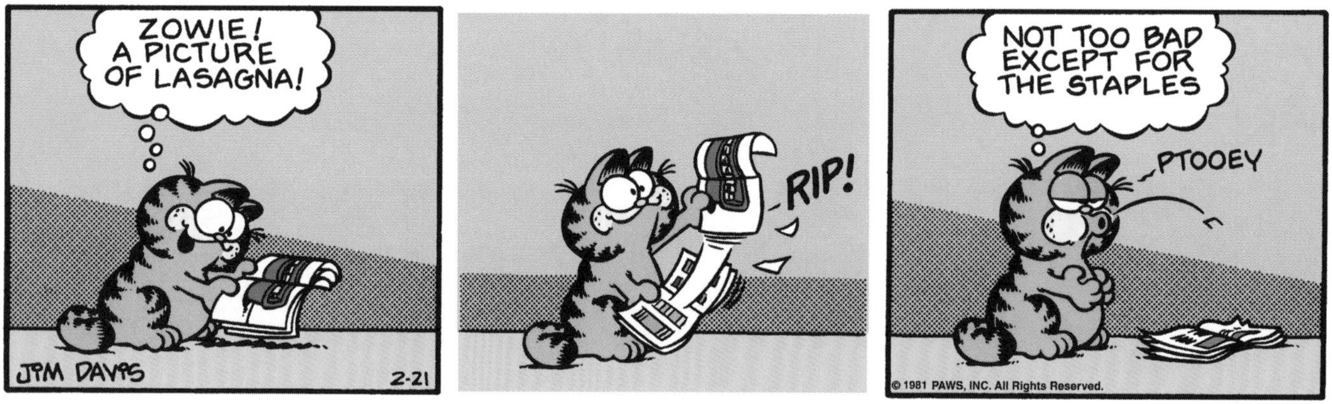
ZOWIE! A PICTURE OF LASAGNA!
JIM DAVIS
2-21
RIP!
NOT TOO BAD EXCEPT FOR THE STAPLES
PTOOEY
© 1981 PAWS, INC. All Rights Reserved.

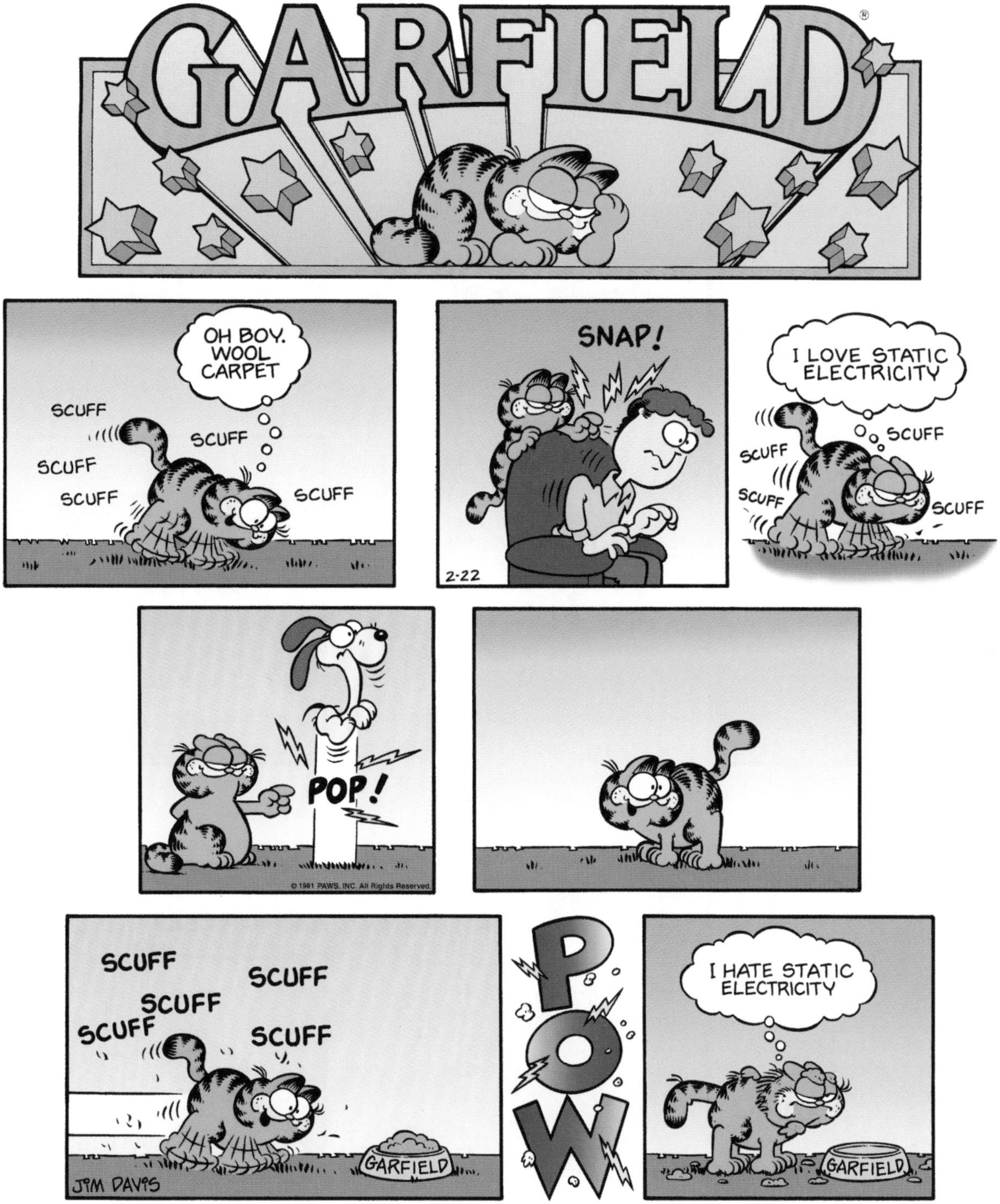
GARFIELD
OH BOY. WOOL CARPET
SCUFF
SCUFF
SCUFF
SCUFF
SCUFF
SNAP!
2-22
I LOVE STATIC ELECTRICITY
SCUFF
SCUFF
SCUFF
SCUFF
POP!
© 1981 PAWS, INC. All Rights Reserved.
SCUFF
SCUFF
SCUFF
SCUFF
SCUFF
GARFIELD
JIM DAVIS
POW
I HATE STATIC ELECTRICITY
GARFIELD

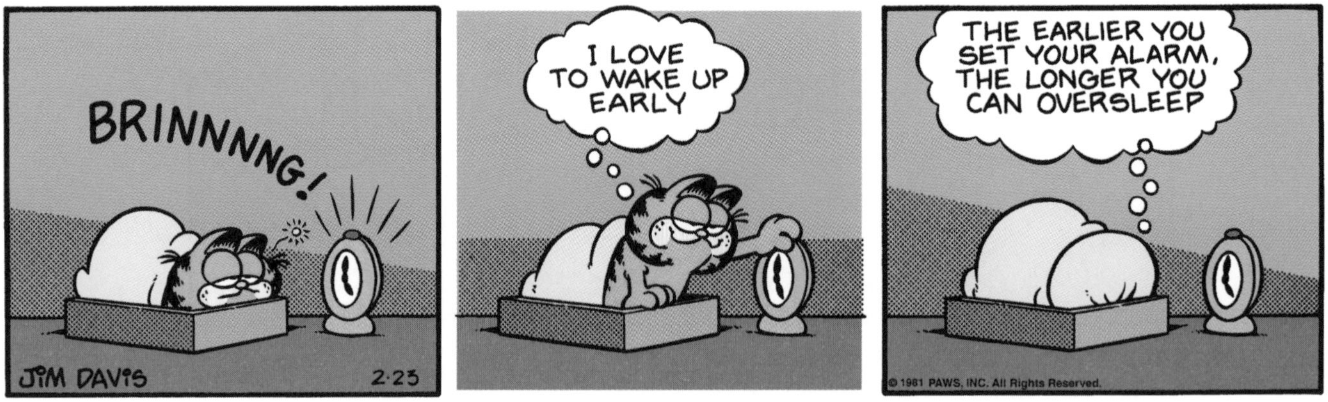
BRINNNNG!
I LOVE TO WAKE UP EARLY
THE EARLIER YOU SET YOUR ALARM, THE LONGER YOU CAN OVERSLEEP
JIM DAVIS 2·23
© 1981 PAWS, INC. All Rights Reserved.

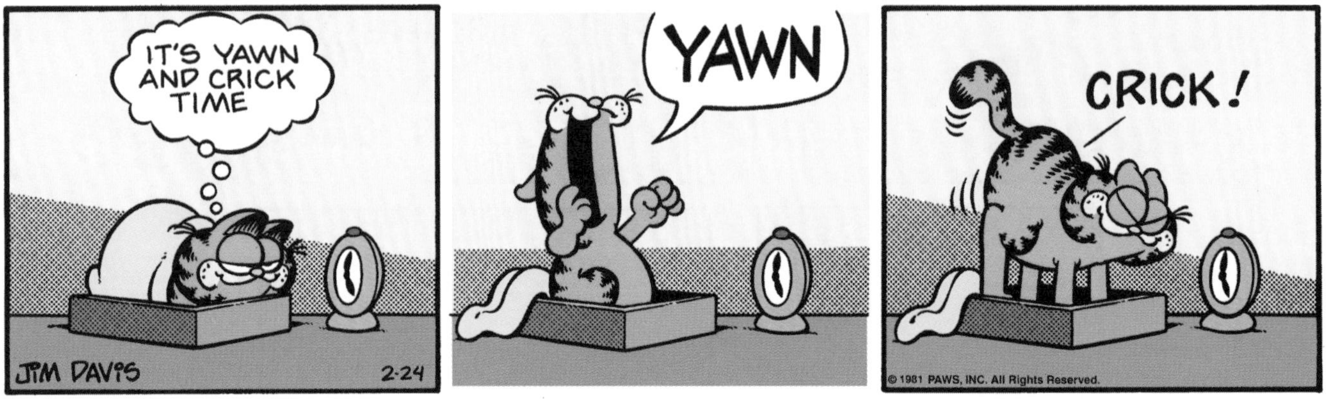
IT'S YAWN AND CRICK TIME
YAWN
CRICK!
JIM DAVIS 2·24
© 1981 PAWS, INC. All Rights Reserved.

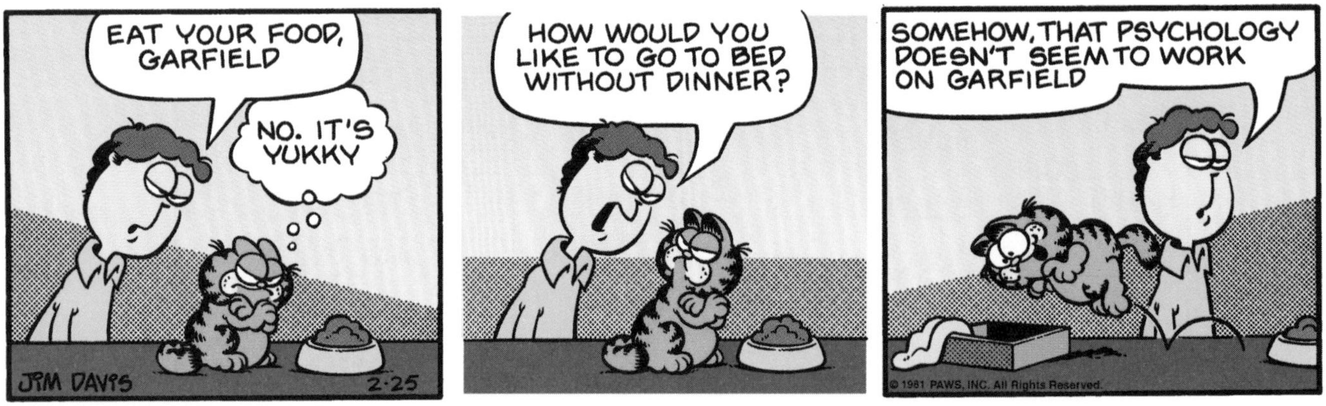
EAT YOUR FOOD, GARFIELD
NO. IT'S YUKKY
HOW WOULD YOU LIKE TO GO TO BED WITHOUT DINNER?
SOMEHOW, THAT PSYCHOLOGY DOESN'T SEEM TO WORK ON GARFIELD
JIM DAVIS 2·25
© 1981 PAWS, INC. All Rights Reserved.

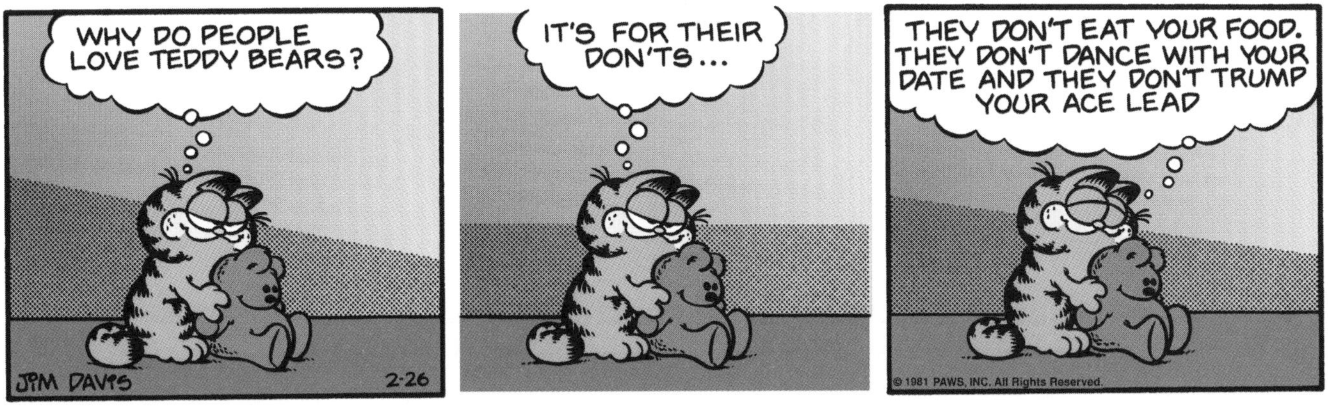
WHY DO PEOPLE LOVE TEDDY BEARS?
JIM DAVIS
2-26
IT'S FOR THEIR DON'TS...
THEY DON'T EAT YOUR FOOD. THEY DON'T DANCE WITH YOUR DATE AND THEY DON'T TRUMP YOUR ACE LEAD
© 1981 PAWS, INC. All Rights Reserved.

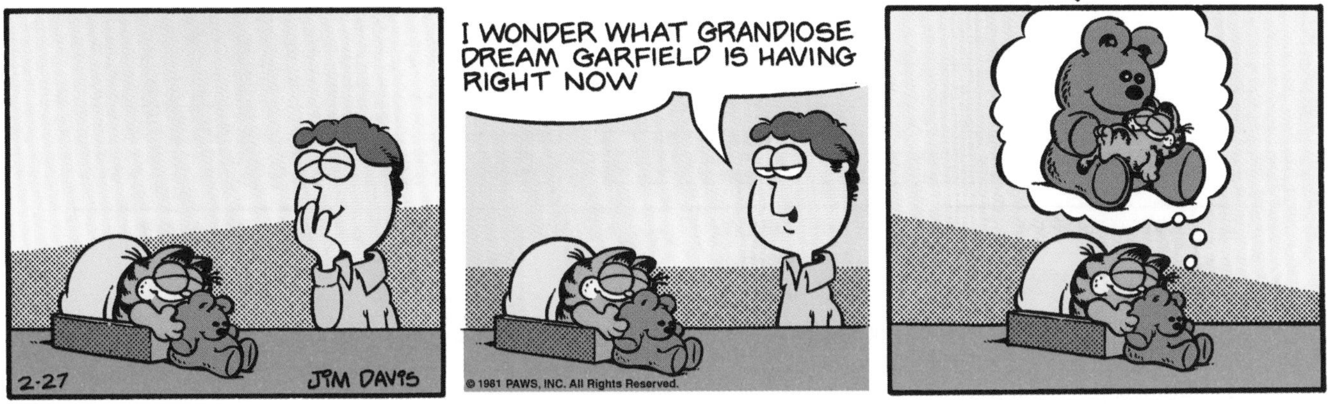
2-27
JIM DAVIS
I WONDER WHAT GRANDIOSE DREAM GARFIELD IS HAVING RIGHT NOW
© 1981 PAWS, INC. All Rights Reserved.

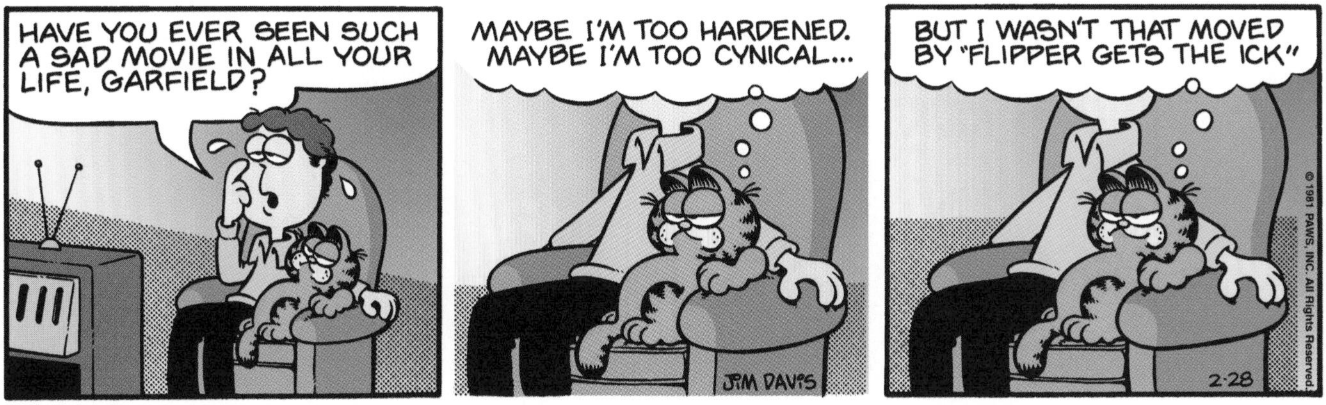
HAVE YOU EVER SEEN SUCH A SAD MOVIE IN ALL YOUR LIFE, GARFIELD?
MAYBE I'M TOO HARDENED. MAYBE I'M TOO CYNICAL...
JIM DAVIS
BUT I WASN'T THAT MOVED BY "FLIPPER GETS THE ICK"
2-28
© 1981 PAWS, INC. All Rights Reserved.

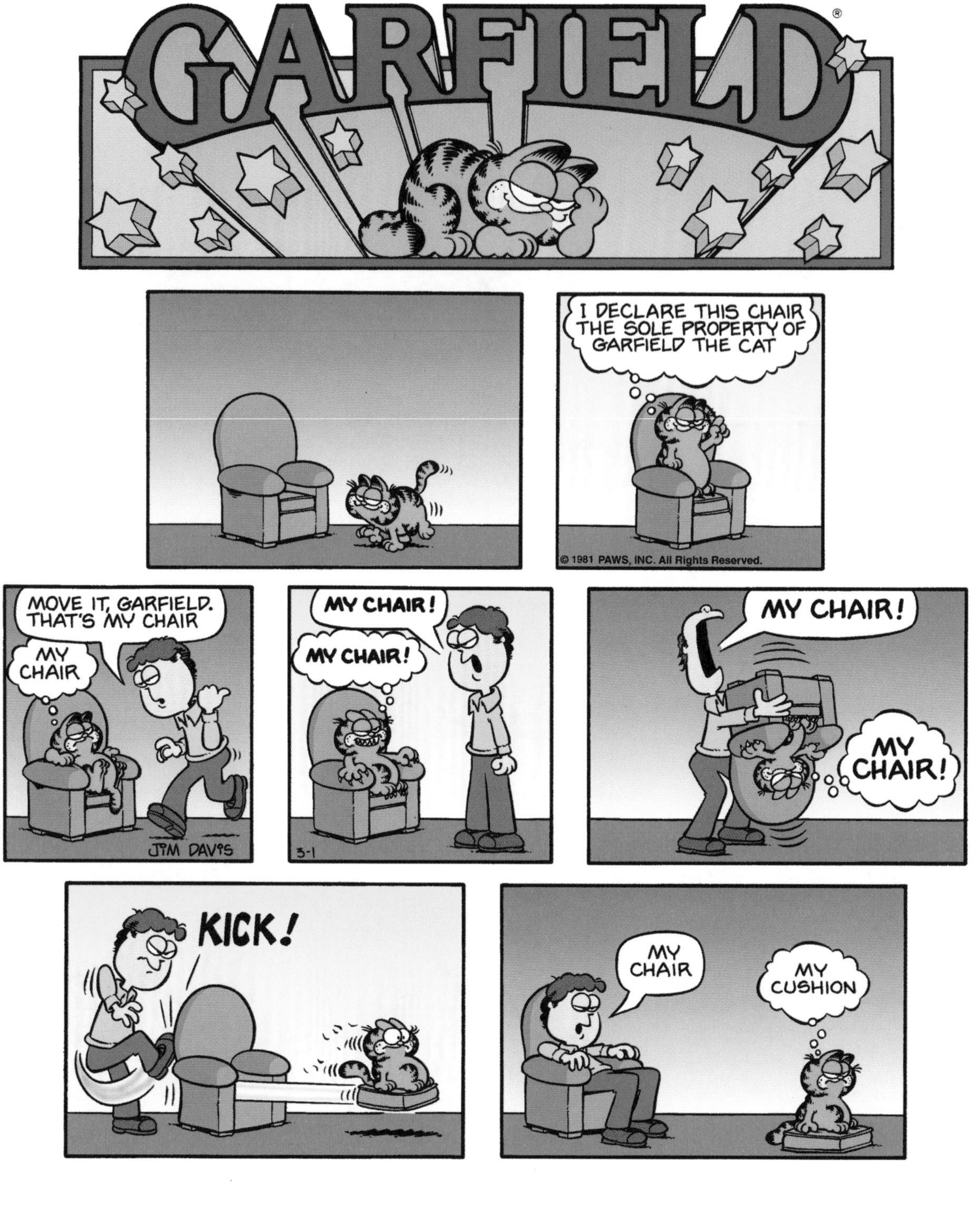
GARFIELD
I DECLARE THIS CHAIR THE SOLE PROPERTY OF GARFIELD THE CAT
© 1981 PAWS, INC. All Rights Reserved.
MOVE IT, GARFIELD. THAT'S MY CHAIR
MY CHAIR
JIM DAVIS
MY CHAIR!
MY CHAIR!
3-1
MY CHAIR!
MY CHAIR!
KICK!
MY CHAIR
MY CUSHION

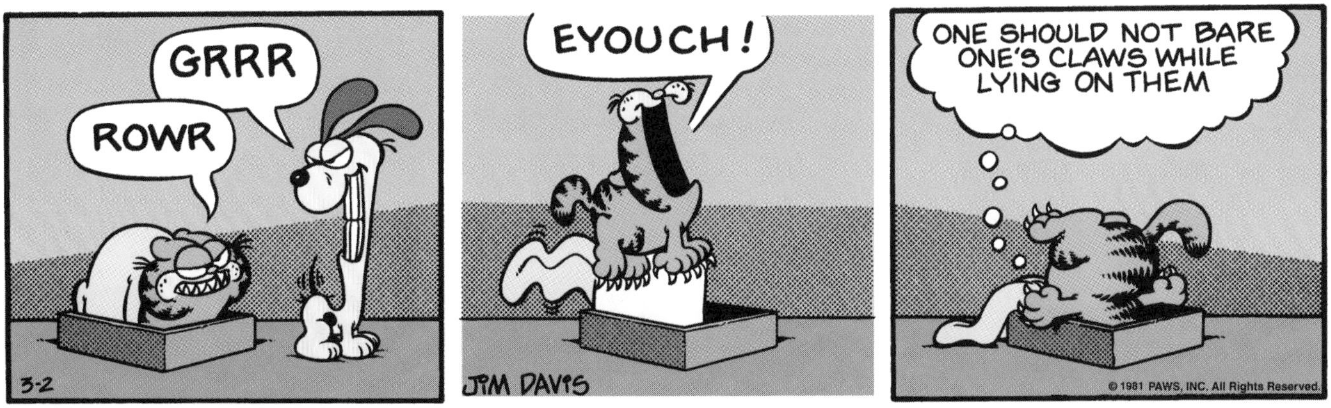
ROWR
GRRR
3-2
EYOUCH!
JIM DAVIS
ONE SHOULD NOT BARE ONE'S CLAWS WHILE LYING ON THEM
© 1981 PAWS, INC. All Rights Reserved.

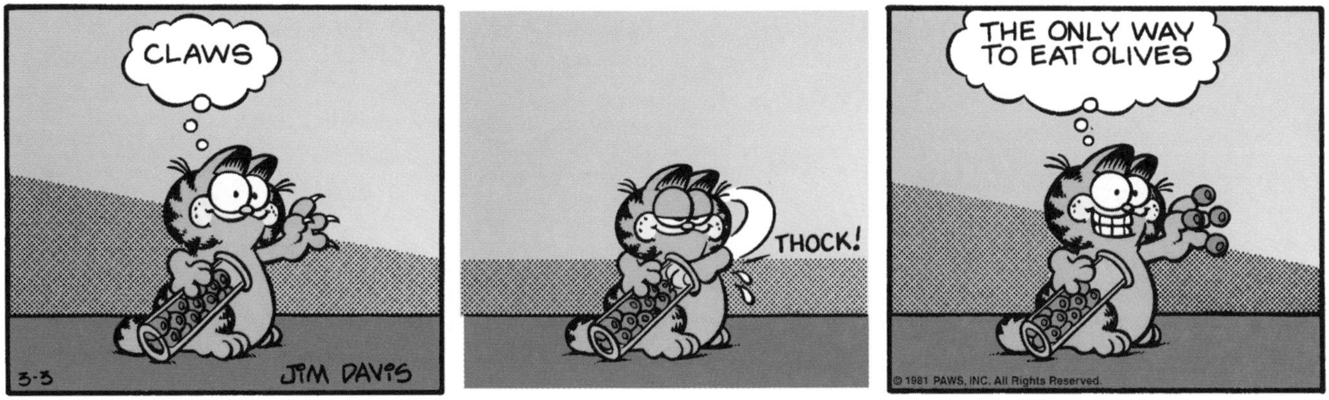
CLAWS
3-3
JIM DAVIS
THOCK!
THE ONLY WAY TO EAT OLIVES
© 1981 PAWS, INC. All Rights Reserved.

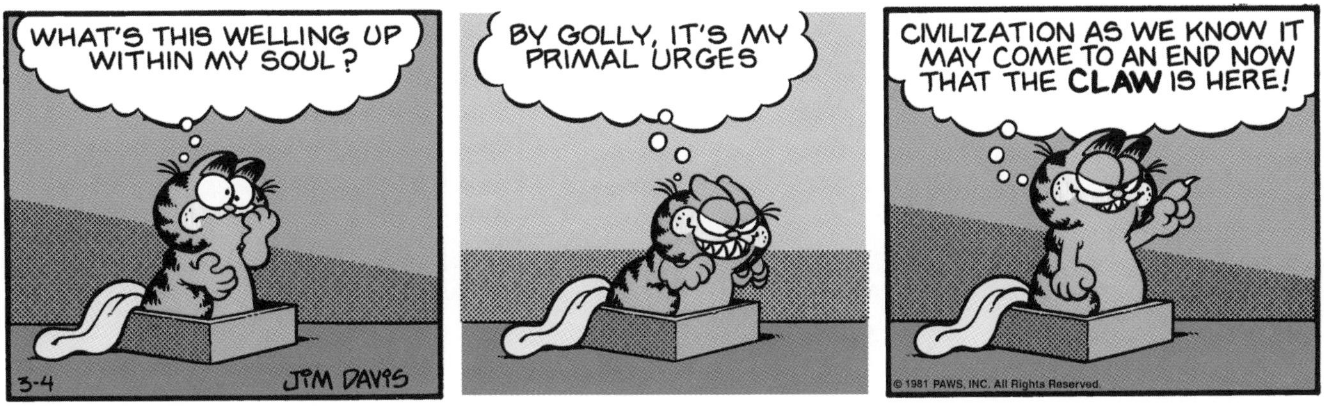
WHAT'S THIS WELLING UP WITHIN MY SOUL?
3-4
JIM DAVIS
BY GOLLY, IT'S MY PRIMAL URGES
CIVILIZATION AS WE KNOW IT MAY COME TO AN END NOW THAT THE **CLAW** IS HERE!
© 1981 PAWS, INC. All Rights Reserved.

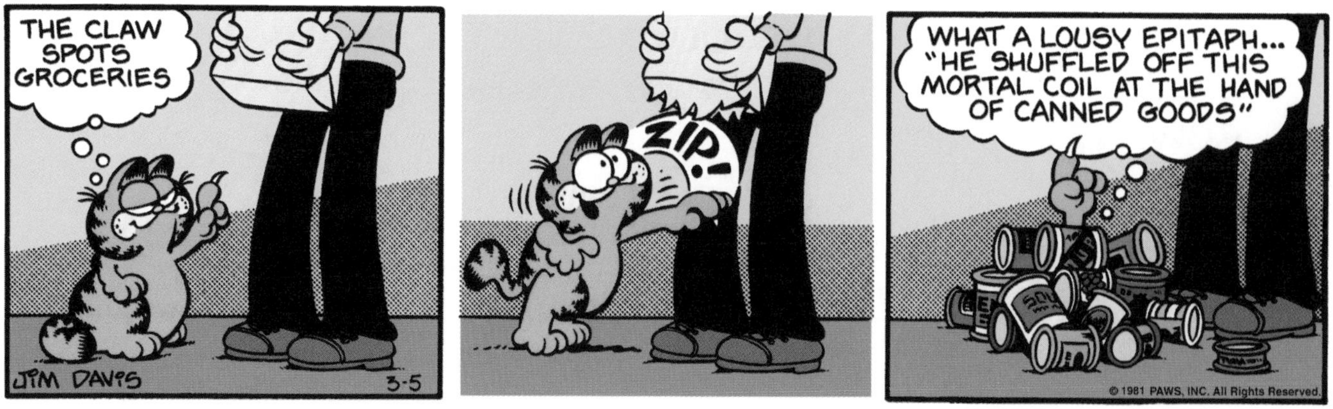
THE CLAW SPOTS GROCERIES
JIM DAVIS
3-5
ZIP!
WHAT A LOUSY EPITAPH... "HE SHUFFLED OFF THIS MORTAL COIL AT THE HAND OF CANNED GOODS"
© 1981 PAWS, INC. All Rights Reserved.

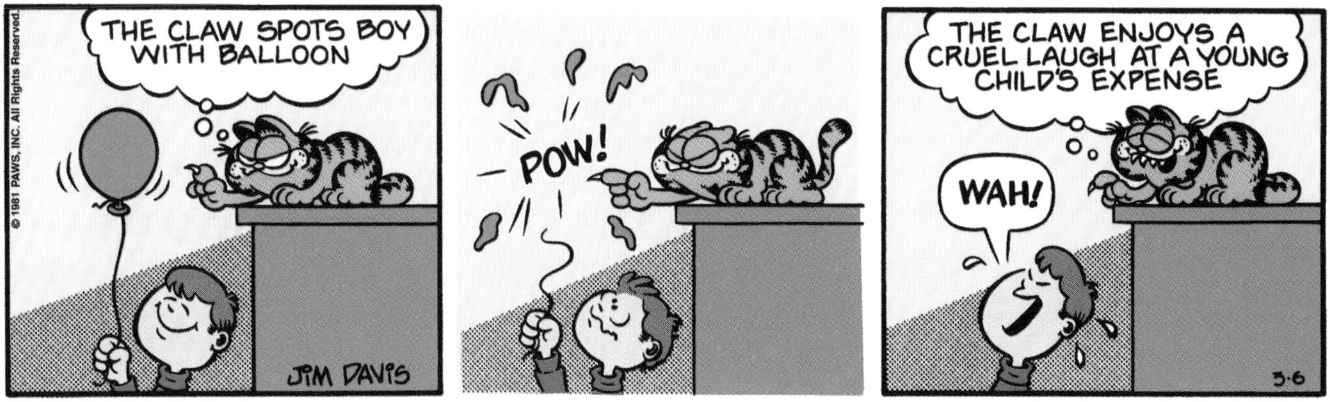
THE CLAW SPOTS BOY WITH BALLOON
© 1981 PAWS, INC. All Rights Reserved.
JIM DAVIS
POW!
THE CLAW ENJOYS A CRUEL LAUGH AT A YOUNG CHILD'S EXPENSE
WAH!
3-6

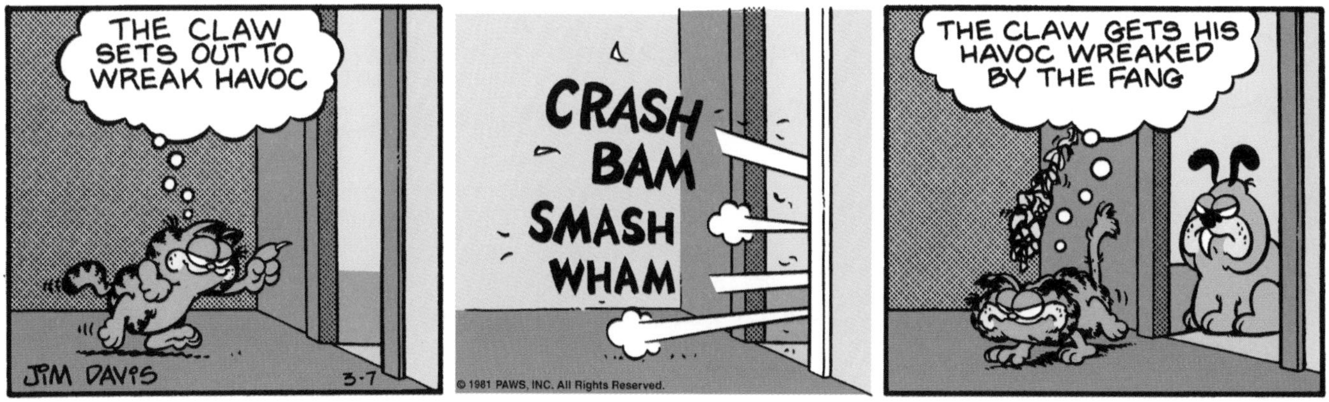
THE CLAW SETS OUT TO WREAK HAVOC
JIM DAVIS
3-7
CRASH
BAM
SMASH
WHAM
© 1981 PAWS, INC. All Rights Reserved.
THE CLAW GETS HIS HAVOC WREAKED BY THE FANG

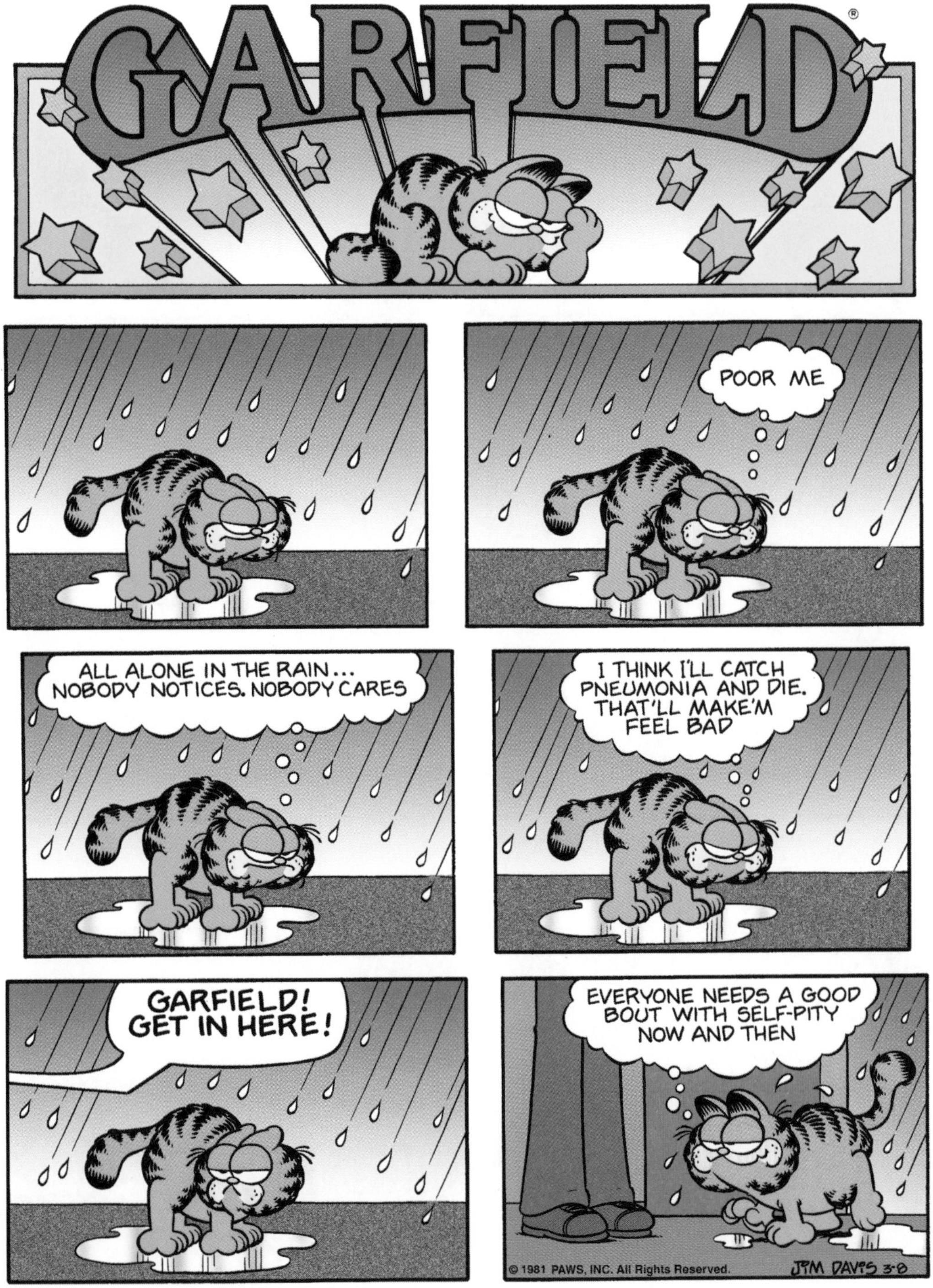
GARFIELD
POOR ME
ALL ALONE IN THE RAIN... NOBODY NOTICES. NOBODY CARES
I THINK I'LL CATCH PNEUMONIA AND DIE. THAT'LL MAKE'M FEEL BAD
GARFIELD! GET IN HERE!
EVERYONE NEEDS A GOOD BOUT WITH SELF-PITY NOW AND THEN
© 1981 PAWS, INC. All Rights Reserved.
JIM DAVIS 3-8

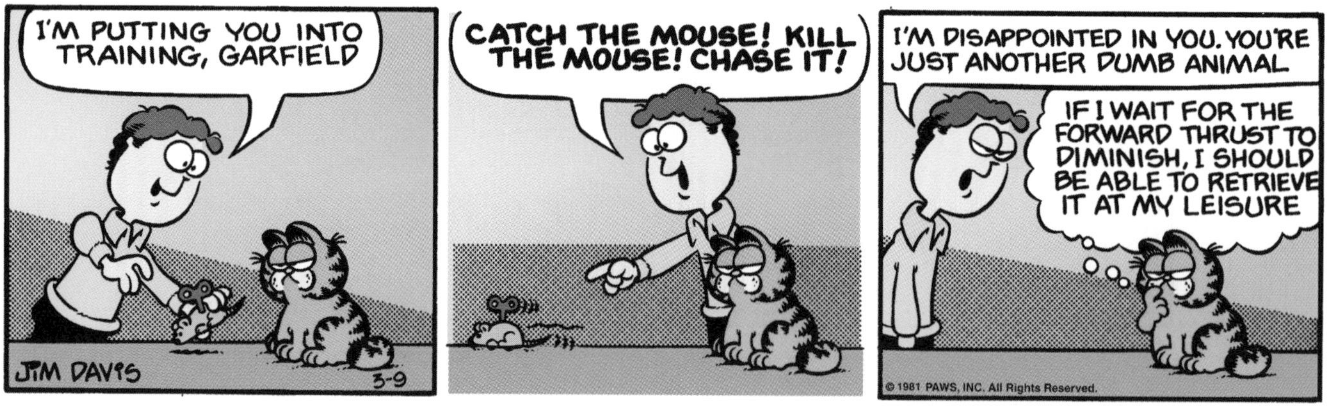
I'M PUTTING YOU INTO TRAINING, GARFIELD
JIM DAVIS
3-9
CATCH THE MOUSE! KILL THE MOUSE! CHASE IT!
I'M DISAPPOINTED IN YOU. YOU'RE JUST ANOTHER DUMB ANIMAL
IF I WAIT FOR THE FORWARD THRUST TO DIMINISH, I SHOULD BE ABLE TO RETRIEVE IT AT MY LEISURE
© 1981 PAWS, INC. All Rights Reserved.

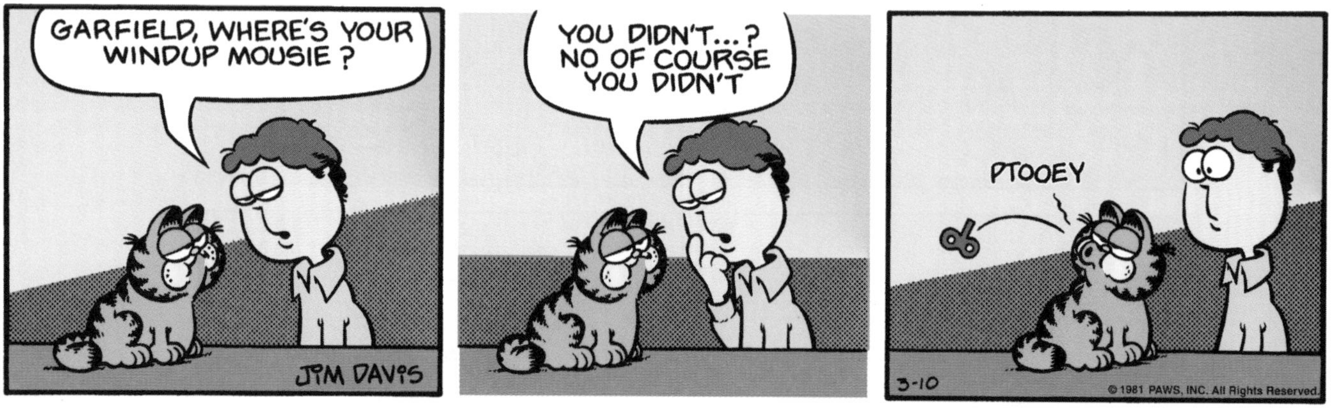
GARFIELD, WHERE'S YOUR WINDUP MOUSIE ?
JIM DAVIS
YOU DIDN'T...? NO OF COURSE YOU DIDN'T
PTOOEY
3-10
© 1981 PAWS, INC. All Rights Reserved.

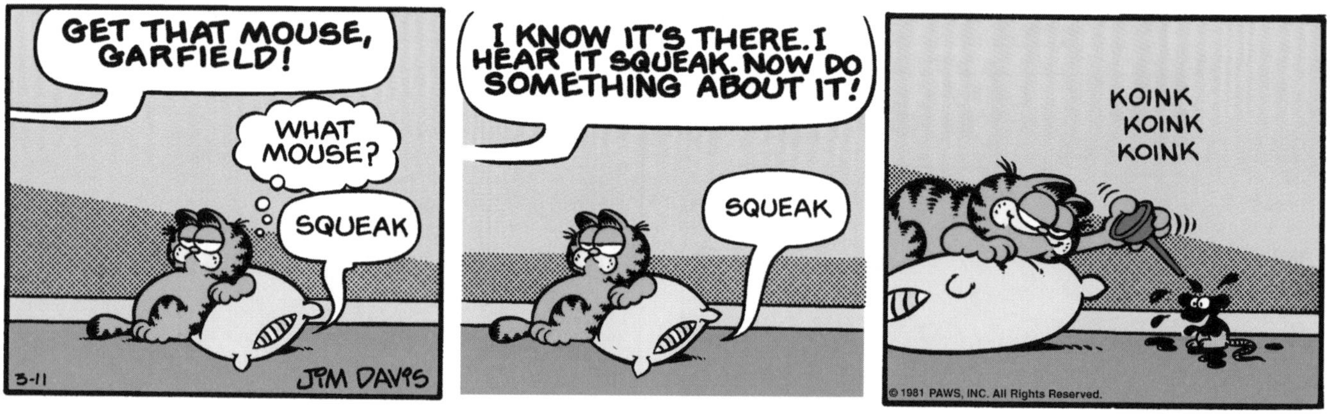
GET THAT MOUSE, GARFIELD!
WHAT MOUSE?
SQUEAK
3-11
JIM DAVIS
I KNOW IT'S THERE. I HEAR IT SQUEAK. NOW DO SOMETHING ABOUT IT!
SQUEAK
KOINK
KOINK
KOINK
© 1981 PAWS, INC. All Rights Reserved.

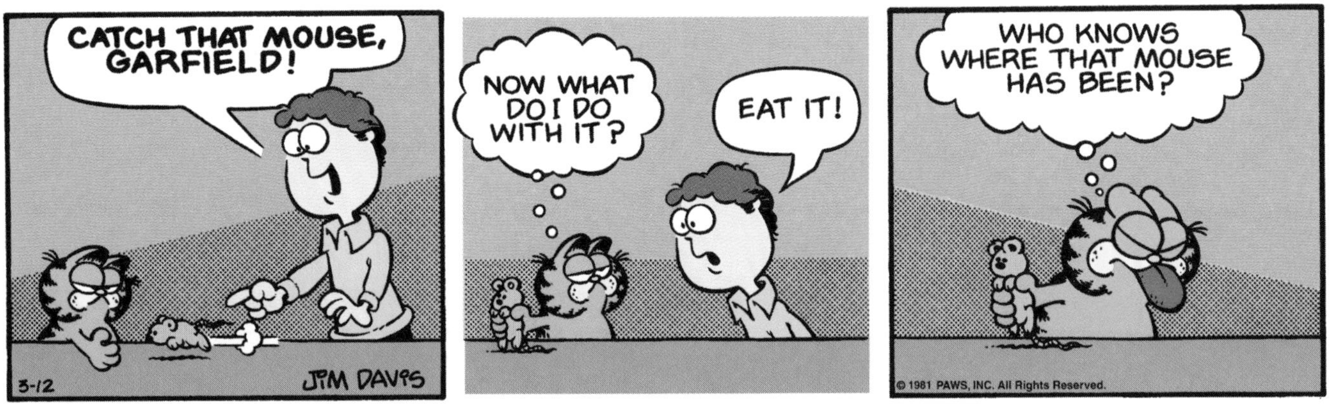
CATCH THAT MOUSE, GARFIELD!
3-12
JIM DAVIS
NOW WHAT DO I DO WITH IT?
EAT IT!
WHO KNOWS WHERE THAT MOUSE HAS BEEN?
© 1981 PAWS, INC. All Rights Reserved.

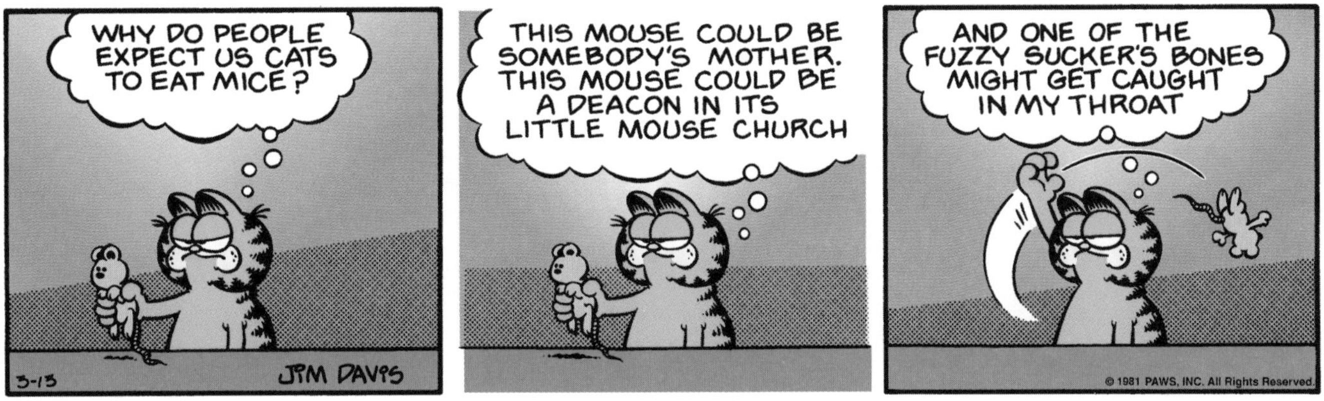
WHY DO PEOPLE EXPECT US CATS TO EAT MICE?
3-13
JIM DAVIS
THIS MOUSE COULD BE SOMEBODY'S MOTHER. THIS MOUSE COULD BE A DEACON IN ITS LITTLE MOUSE CHURCH
AND ONE OF THE FUZZY SUCKER'S BONES MIGHT GET CAUGHT IN MY THROAT
© 1981 PAWS, INC. All Rights Reserved.

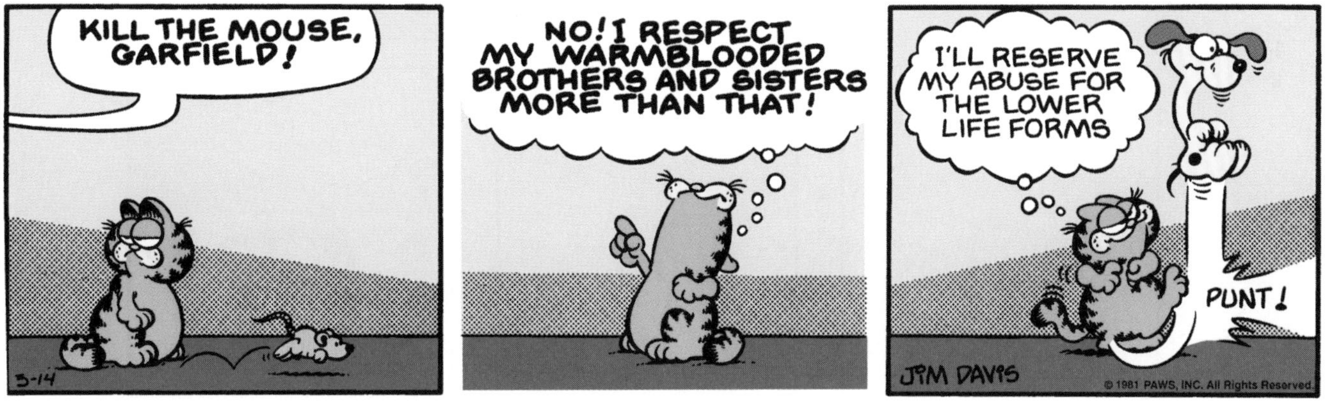
KILL THE MOUSE, GARFIELD!
3-14
NO! I RESPECT MY WARMBLOODED BROTHERS AND SISTERS MORE THAN THAT!
I'LL RESERVE MY ABUSE FOR THE LOWER LIFE FORMS
PUNT!
JIM DAVIS
© 1981 PAWS, INC. All Rights Reserved.

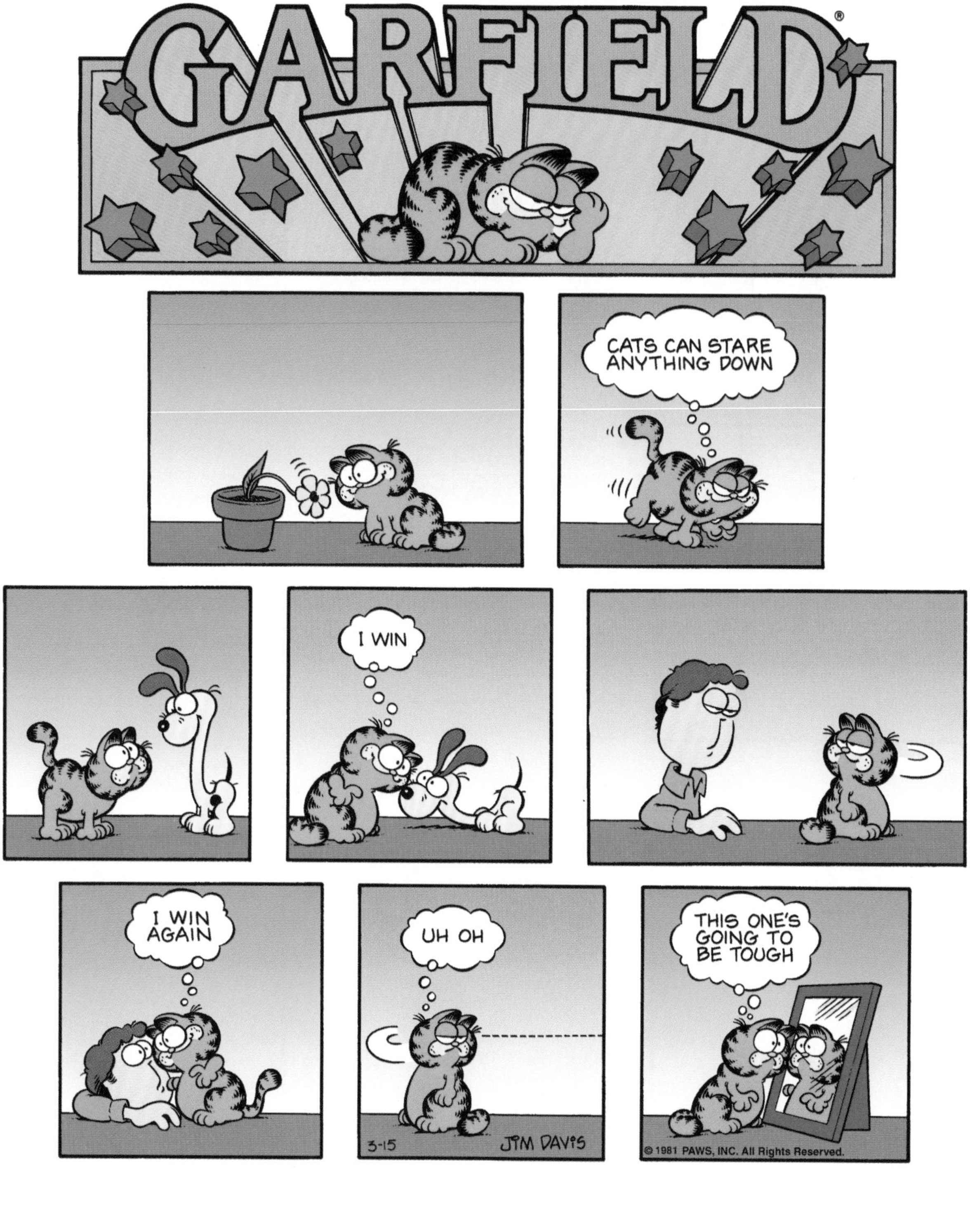
GARFIELD
CATS CAN STARE ANYTHING DOWN
I WIN
I WIN AGAIN
UH OH
THIS ONE'S GOING TO BE TOUGH
3-15
JIM DAVIS
© 1981 PAWS, INC. All Rights Reserved.

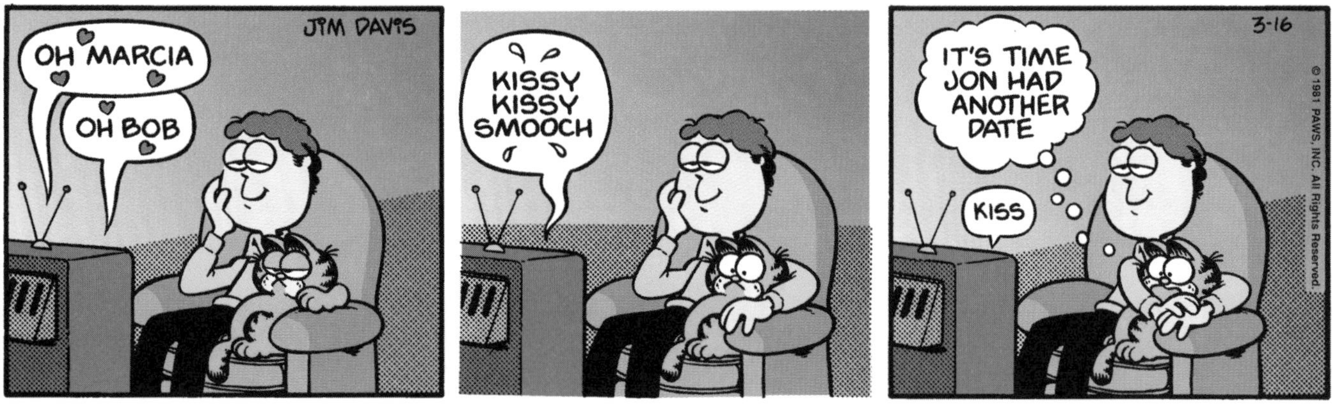
JIM DAVIS
OH MARCIA
OH BOB
KISSY KISSY SMOOCH
3-16
IT'S TIME JON HAD ANOTHER DATE
KISS
© 1981 PAWS, INC. All Rights Reserved.

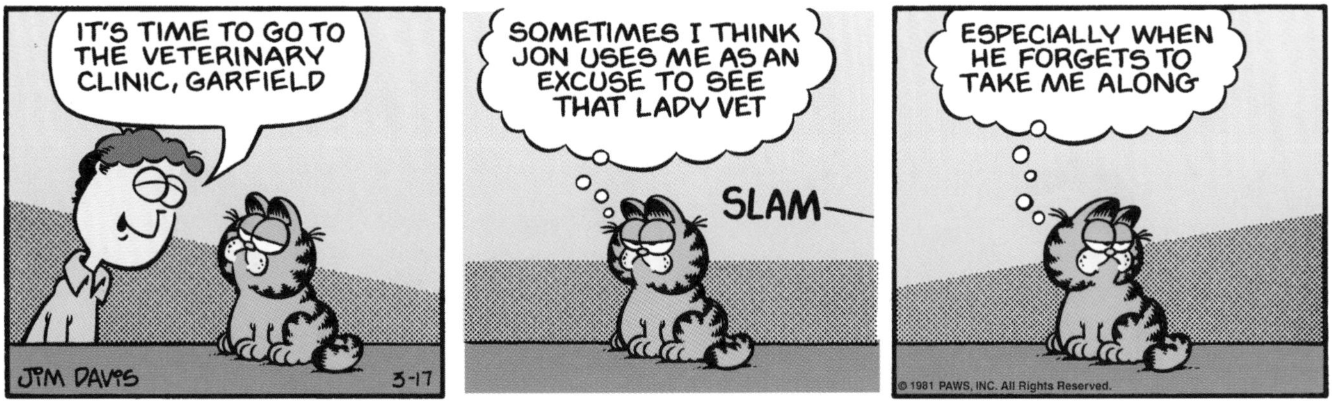
IT'S TIME TO GO TO THE VETERINARY CLINIC, GARFIELD
JIM DAVIS
3-17
SOMETIMES I THINK JON USES ME AS AN EXCUSE TO SEE THAT LADY VET
SLAM
ESPECIALLY WHEN HE FORGETS TO TAKE ME ALONG
© 1981 PAWS, INC. All Rights Reserved.

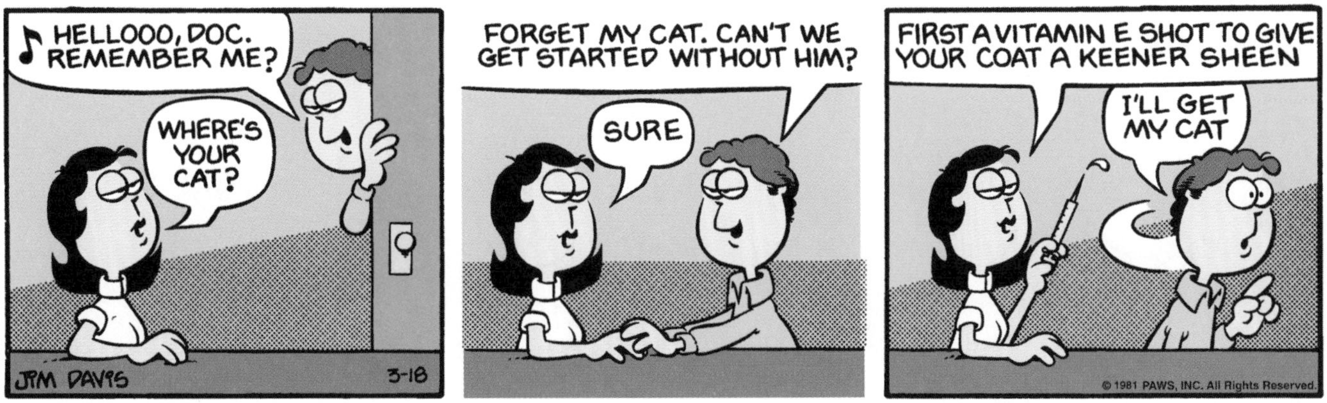
♪ HELLOOO, DOC. REMEMBER ME?
WHERE'S YOUR CAT?
JIM DAVIS
3-18
FORGET MY CAT. CAN'T WE GET STARTED WITHOUT HIM?
SURE
FIRST A VITAMIN E SHOT TO GIVE YOUR COAT A KEENER SHEEN
I'LL GET MY CAT
© 1981 PAWS, INC. All Rights Reserved.

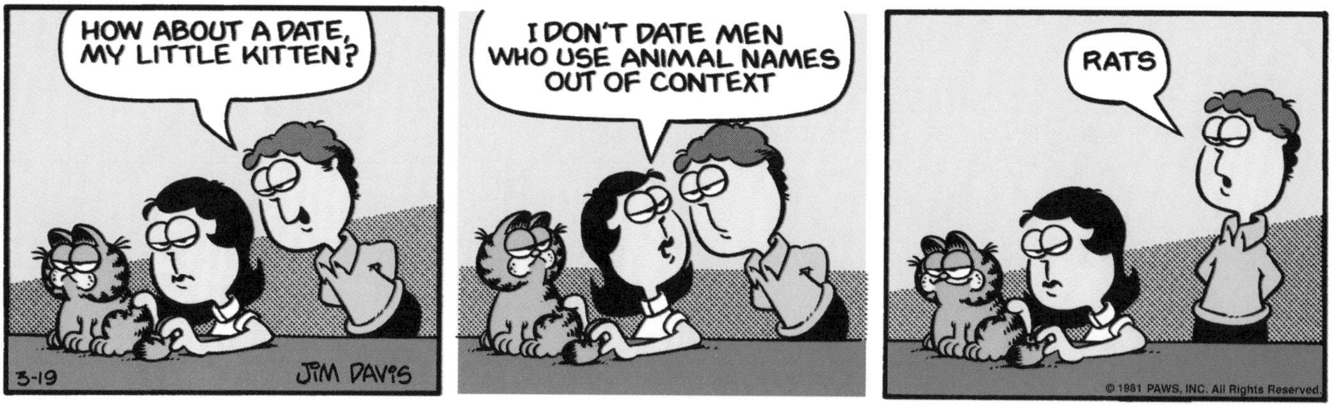
HOW ABOUT A DATE, MY LITTLE KITTEN?
3-19
JIM DAVIS
I DON'T DATE MEN WHO USE ANIMAL NAMES OUT OF CONTEXT
RATS
© 1981 PAWS, INC. All Rights Reserved.

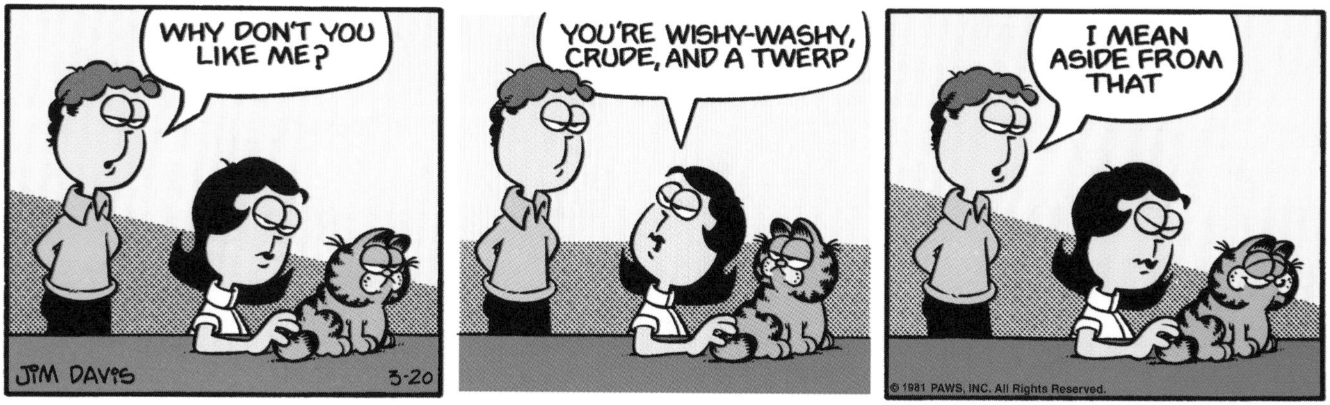
WHY DON'T YOU LIKE ME?
JIM DAVIS
3-20
YOU'RE WISHY-WASHY, CRUDE, AND A TWERP
I MEAN ASIDE FROM THAT
© 1981 PAWS, INC. All Rights Reserved.

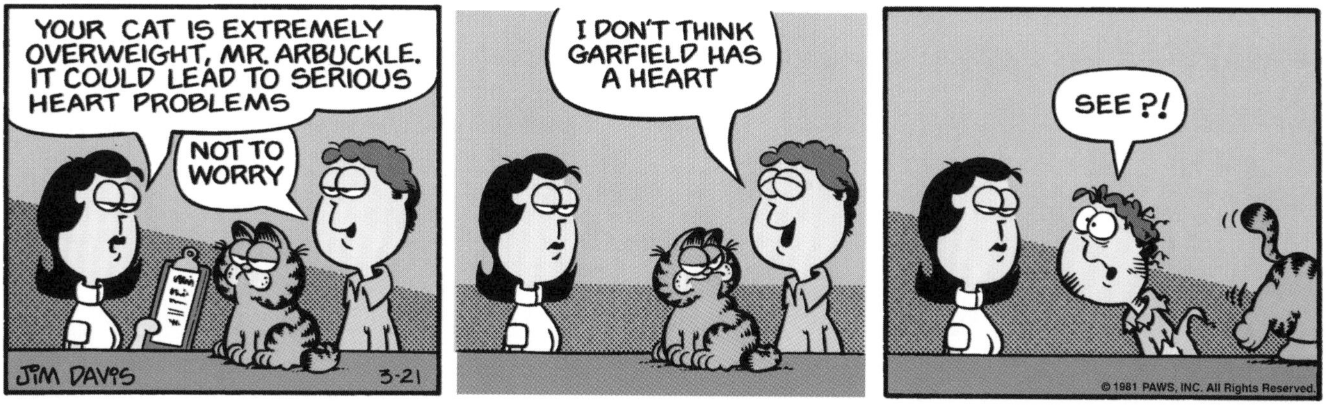
YOUR CAT IS EXTREMELY OVERWEIGHT, MR. ARBUCKLE. IT COULD LEAD TO SERIOUS HEART PROBLEMS
NOT TO WORRY
JIM DAVIS
3-21
I DON'T THINK GARFIELD HAS A HEART
SEE ?!
© 1981 PAWS, INC. All Rights Reserved.

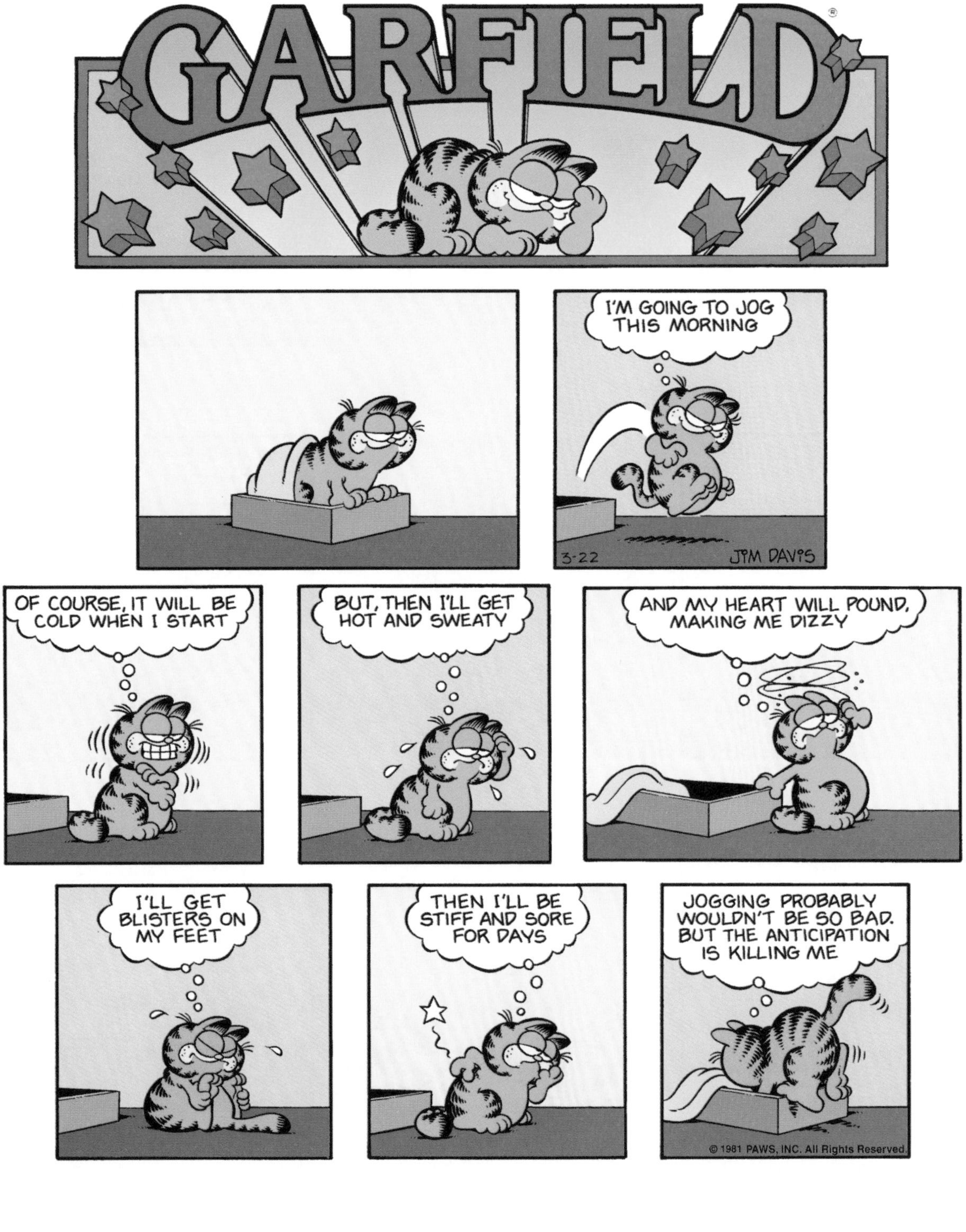
GARFIELD
I'M GOING TO JOG THIS MORNING
3-22
JIM DAVIS
OF COURSE, IT WILL BE COLD WHEN I START
BUT, THEN I'LL GET HOT AND SWEATY
AND MY HEART WILL POUND, MAKING ME DIZZY
I'LL GET BLISTERS ON MY FEET
THEN I'LL BE STIFF AND SORE FOR DAYS
JOGGING PROBABLY WOULDN'T BE SO BAD. BUT THE ANTICIPATION IS KILLING ME
© 1981 PAWS, INC. All Rights Reserved.

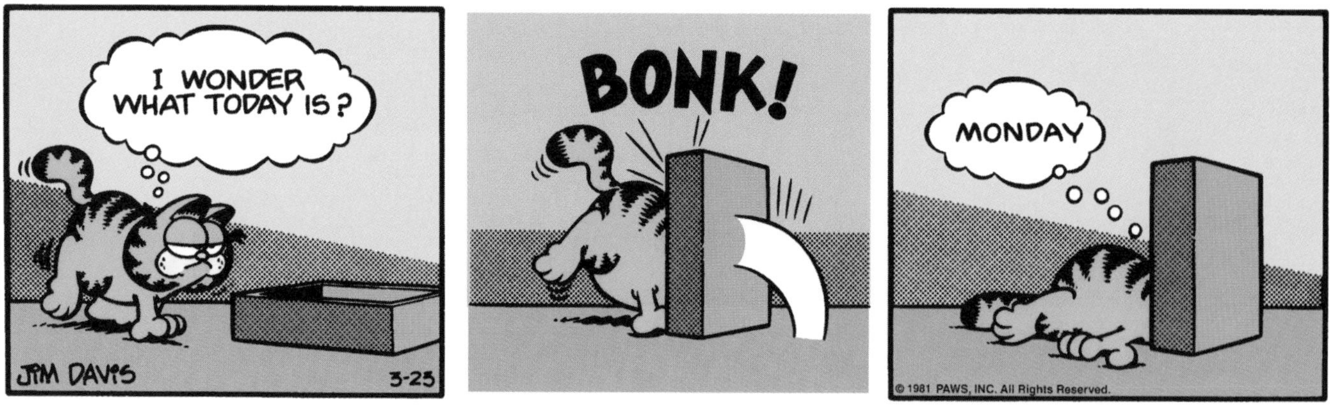
I WONDER WHAT TODAY IS?
JIM DAVIS
3-23
BONK!
MONDAY
© 1981 PAWS, INC. All Rights Reserved.

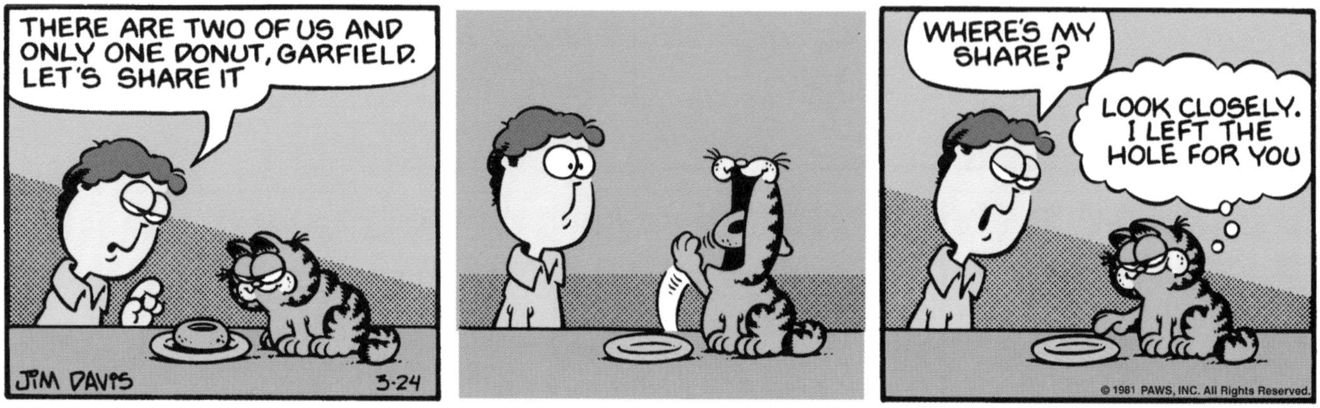
THERE ARE TWO OF US AND ONLY ONE DONUT, GARFIELD. LET'S SHARE IT
JIM DAVIS
3-24
WHERE'S MY SHARE?
LOOK CLOSELY. I LEFT THE HOLE FOR YOU
© 1981 PAWS, INC. All Rights Reserved.

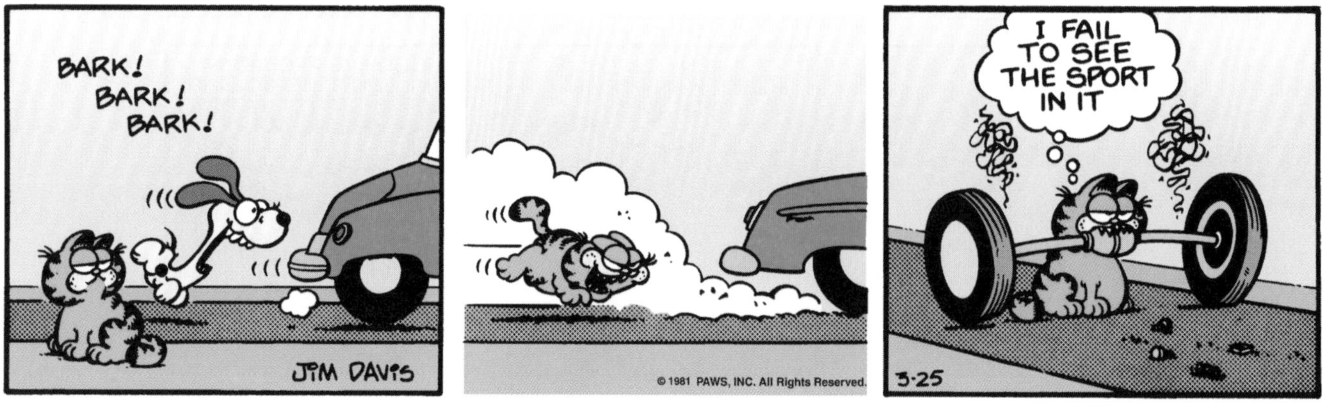
BARK! BARK! BARK!
JIM DAVIS
© 1981 PAWS, INC. All Rights Reserved.
I FAIL TO SEE THE SPORT IN IT
3-25

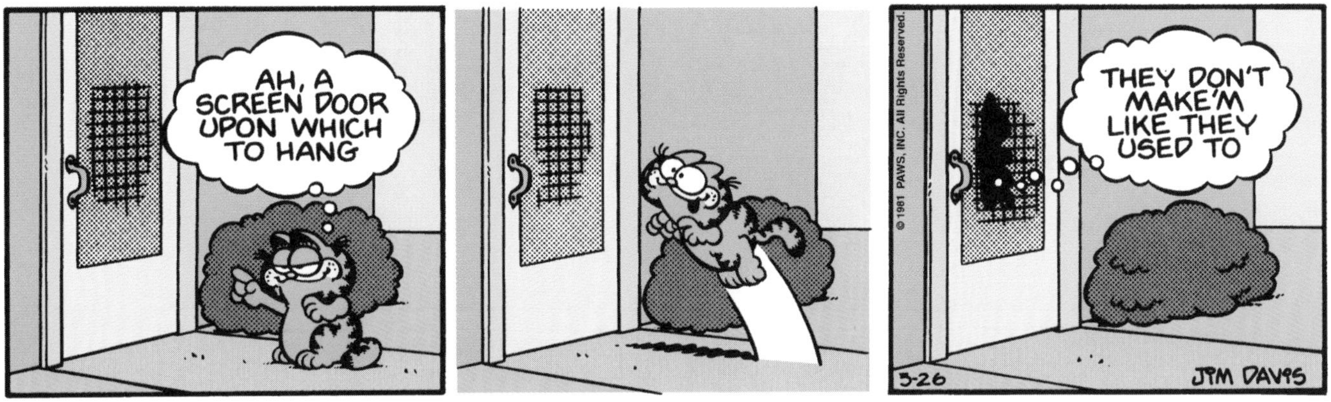
AH, A SCREEN DOOR UPON WHICH TO HANG
THEY DON'T MAKE'M LIKE THEY USED TO
© 1981 PAWS, INC. All Rights Reserved.
3-26
JIM DAVIS

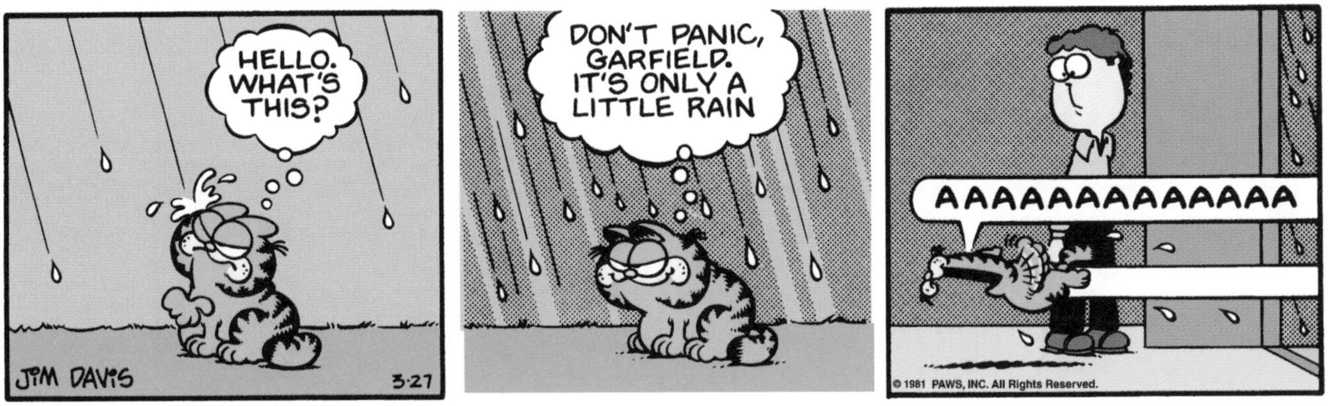
HELLO. WHAT'S THIS?
JIM DAVIS
3-27
DON'T PANIC, GARFIELD. IT'S ONLY A LITTLE RAIN
AAAAAAAAAAAAA
© 1981 PAWS, INC. All Rights Reserved.

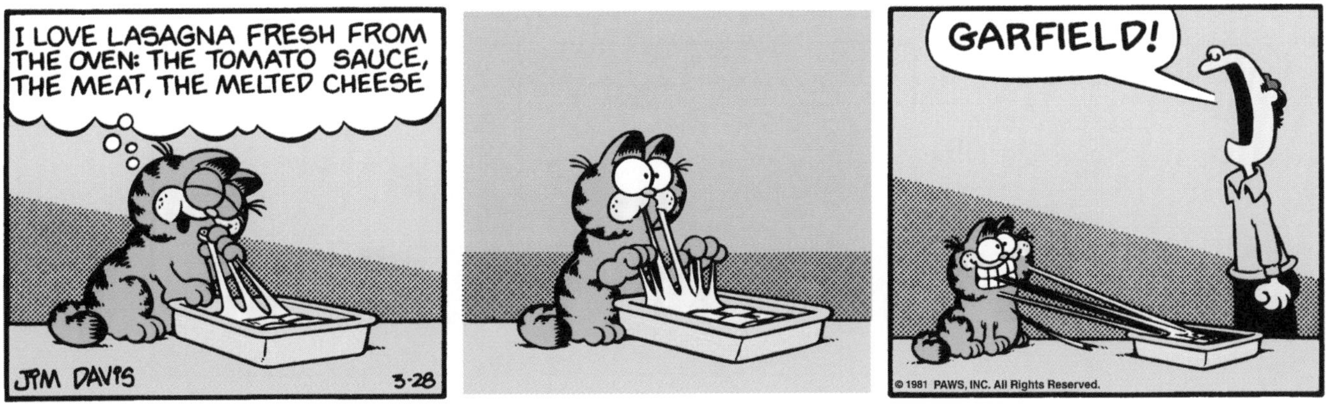
I LOVE LASAGNA FRESH FROM THE OVEN: THE TOMATO SAUCE, THE MEAT, THE MELTED CHEESE
JIM DAVIS
3-28
GARFIELD!
© 1981 PAWS, INC. All Rights Reserved.

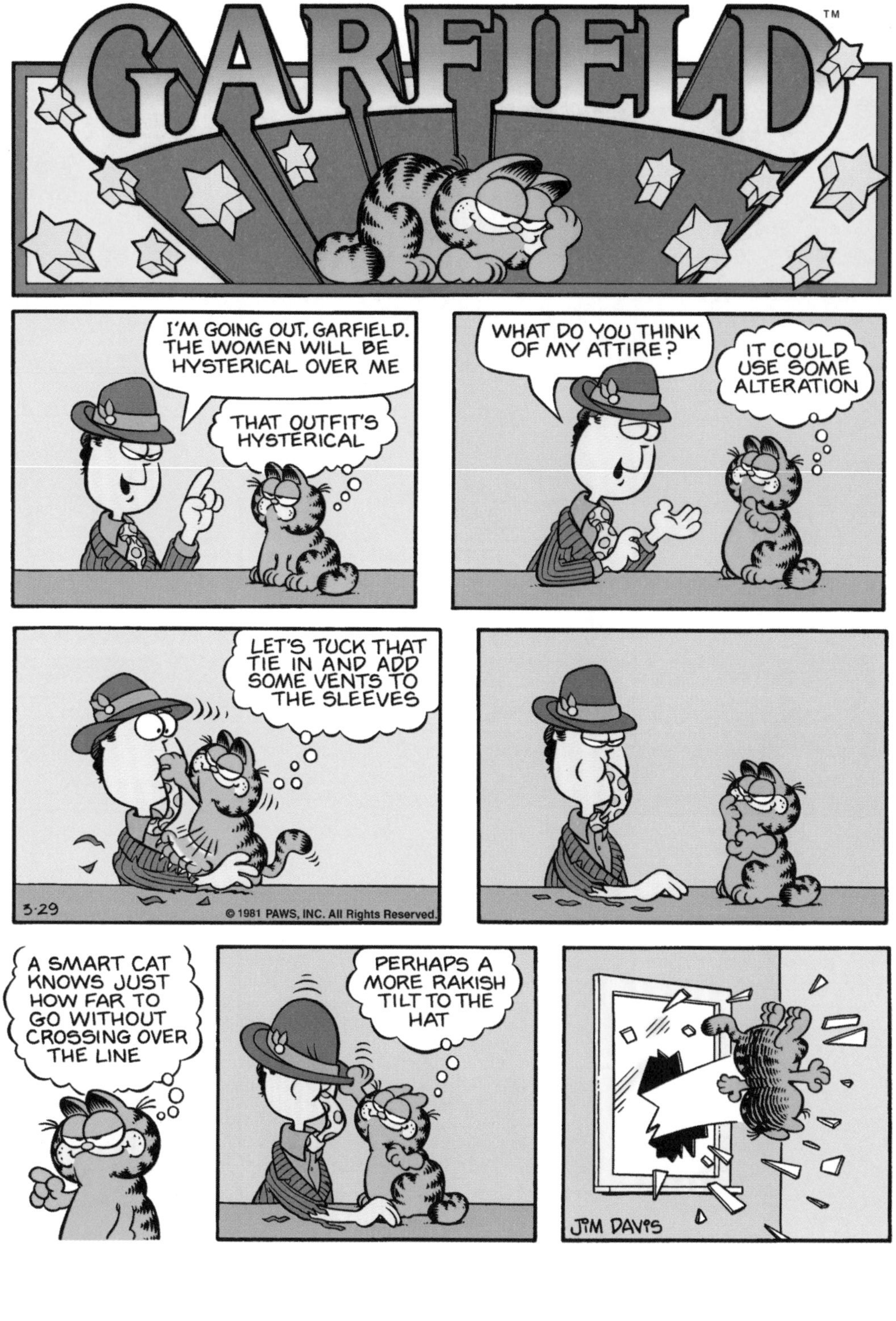
GARFIELD
I'M GOING OUT, GARFIELD. THE WOMEN WILL BE HYSTERICAL OVER ME
THAT OUTFIT'S HYSTERICAL
WHAT DO YOU THINK OF MY ATTIRE?
IT COULD USE SOME ALTERATION
LET'S TUCK THAT TIE IN AND ADD SOME VENTS TO THE SLEEVES
3-29
© 1981 PAWS, INC. All Rights Reserved.
A SMART CAT KNOWS JUST HOW FAR TO GO WITHOUT CROSSING OVER THE LINE
PERHAPS A MORE RAKISH TILT TO THE HAT
JIM DAVIS

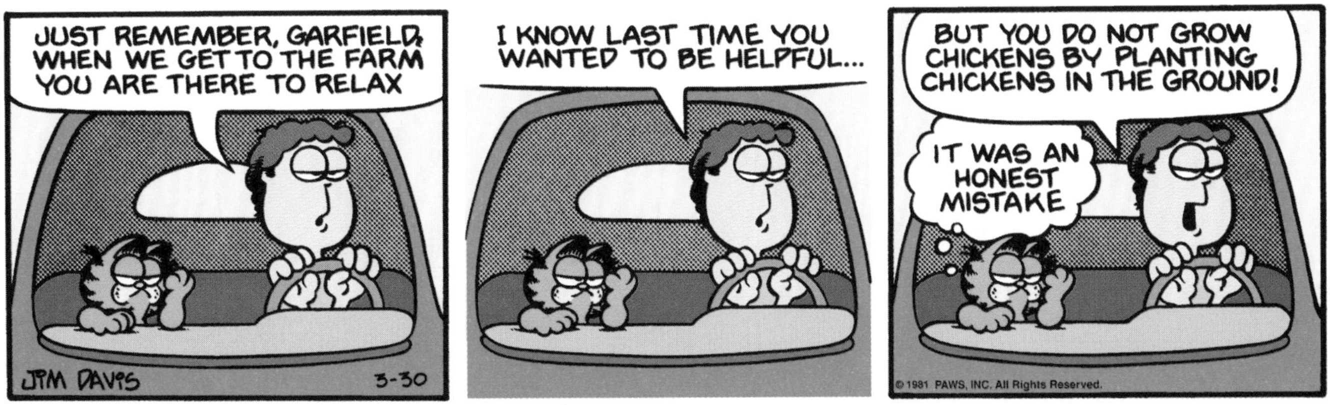
JUST REMEMBER, GARFIELD, WHEN WE GET TO THE FARM YOU ARE THERE TO RELAX
JIM DAVIS
3-30
I KNOW LAST TIME YOU WANTED TO BE HELPFUL...
BUT YOU DO NOT GROW CHICKENS BY PLANTING CHICKENS IN THE GROUND!
IT WAS AN HONEST MISTAKE
© 1981 PAWS, INC. All Rights Reserved.

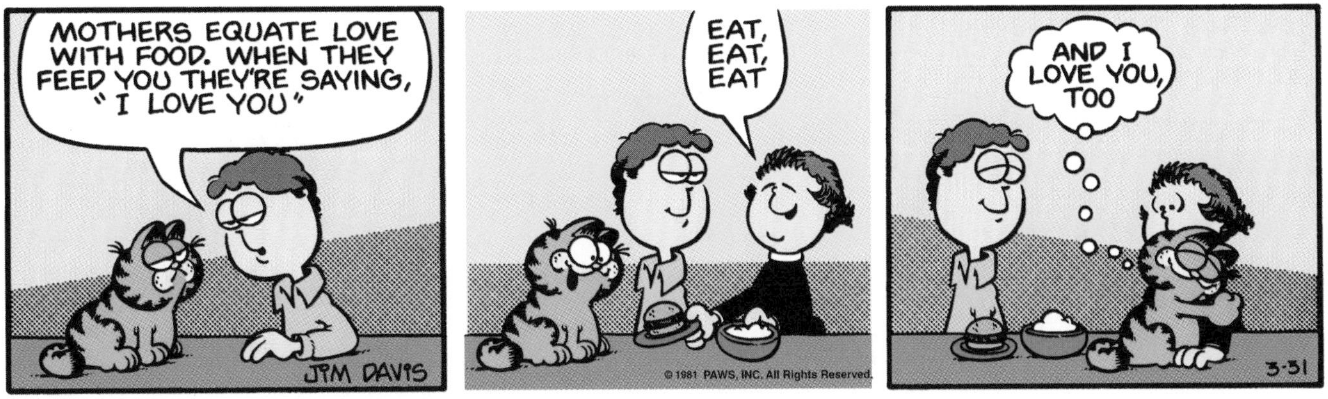
MOTHERS EQUATE LOVE WITH FOOD. WHEN THEY FEED YOU THEY'RE SAYING, "I LOVE YOU"
JIM DAVIS
EAT, EAT, EAT
© 1981 PAWS, INC. All Rights Reserved.
AND I LOVE YOU, TOO
3-31

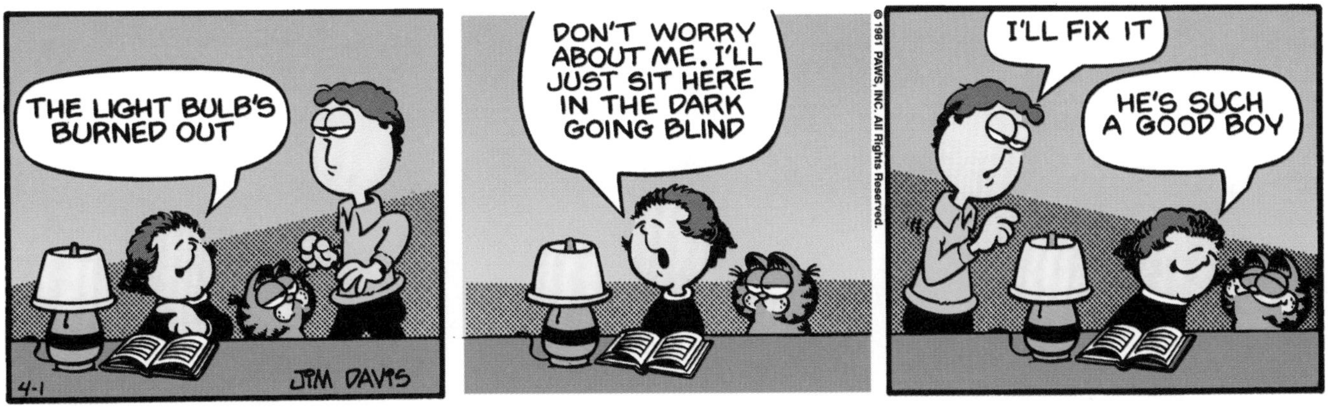
THE LIGHT BULB'S BURNED OUT
4-1
JIM DAVIS
DON'T WORRY ABOUT ME. I'LL JUST SIT HERE IN THE DARK GOING BLIND
© 1981 PAWS, INC. All Rights Reserved.
I'LL FIX IT
HE'S SUCH A GOOD BOY

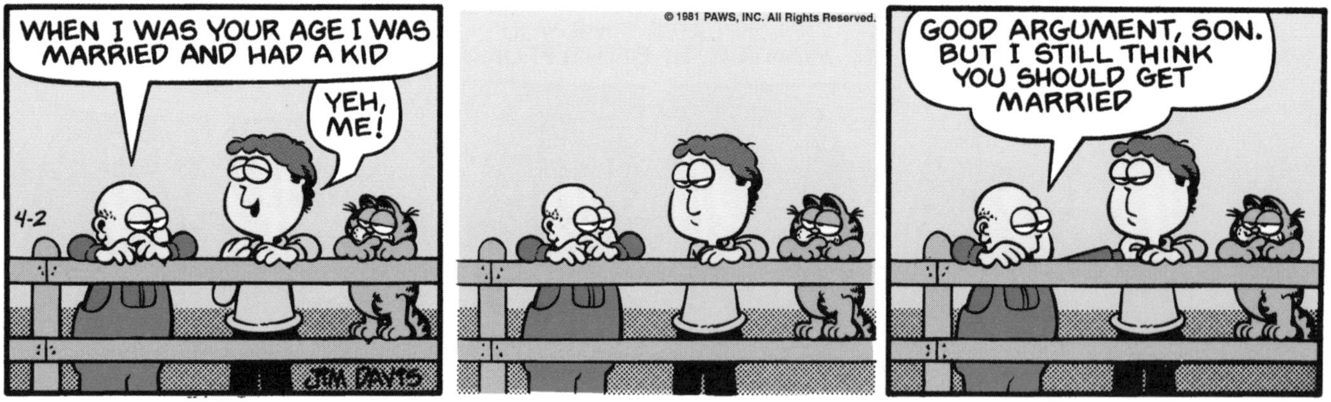
WHEN I WAS YOUR AGE I WAS MARRIED AND HAD A KID
YEH, ME!
4-2
JIM DAVIS
© 1981 PAWS, INC. All Rights Reserved.
GOOD ARGUMENT, SON. BUT I STILL THINK YOU SHOULD GET MARRIED

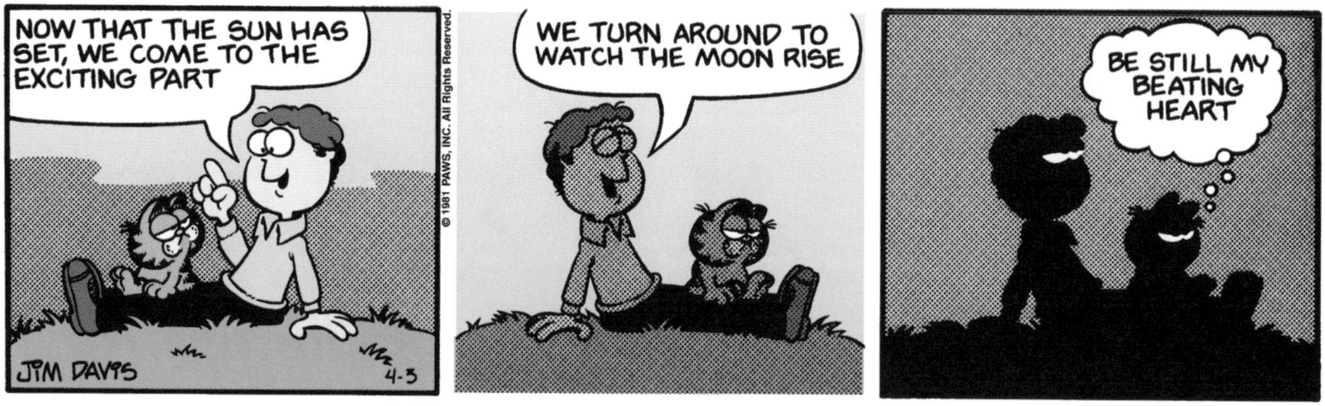
NOW THAT THE SUN HAS SET, WE COME TO THE EXCITING PART
JIM DAVIS
4-3
© 1981 PAWS, INC. All Rights Reserved.
WE TURN AROUND TO WATCH THE MOON RISE
BE STILL MY BEATING HEART

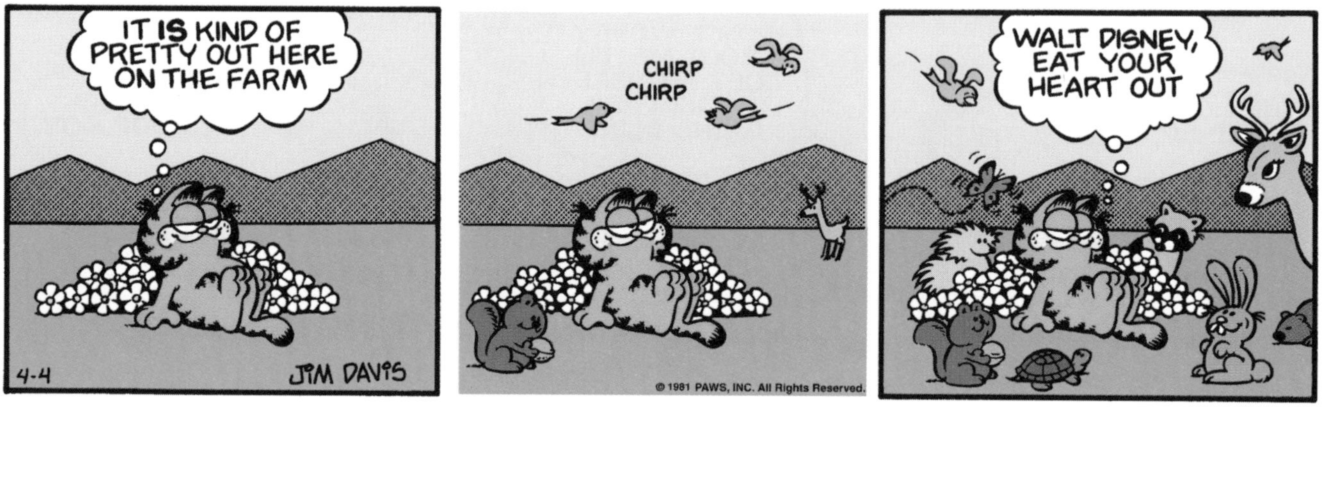
IT IS KIND OF PRETTY OUT HERE ON THE FARM
4-4
JIM DAVIS
CHIRP
CHIRP
© 1981 PAWS, INC. All Rights Reserved.
WALT DISNEY, EAT YOUR HEART OUT

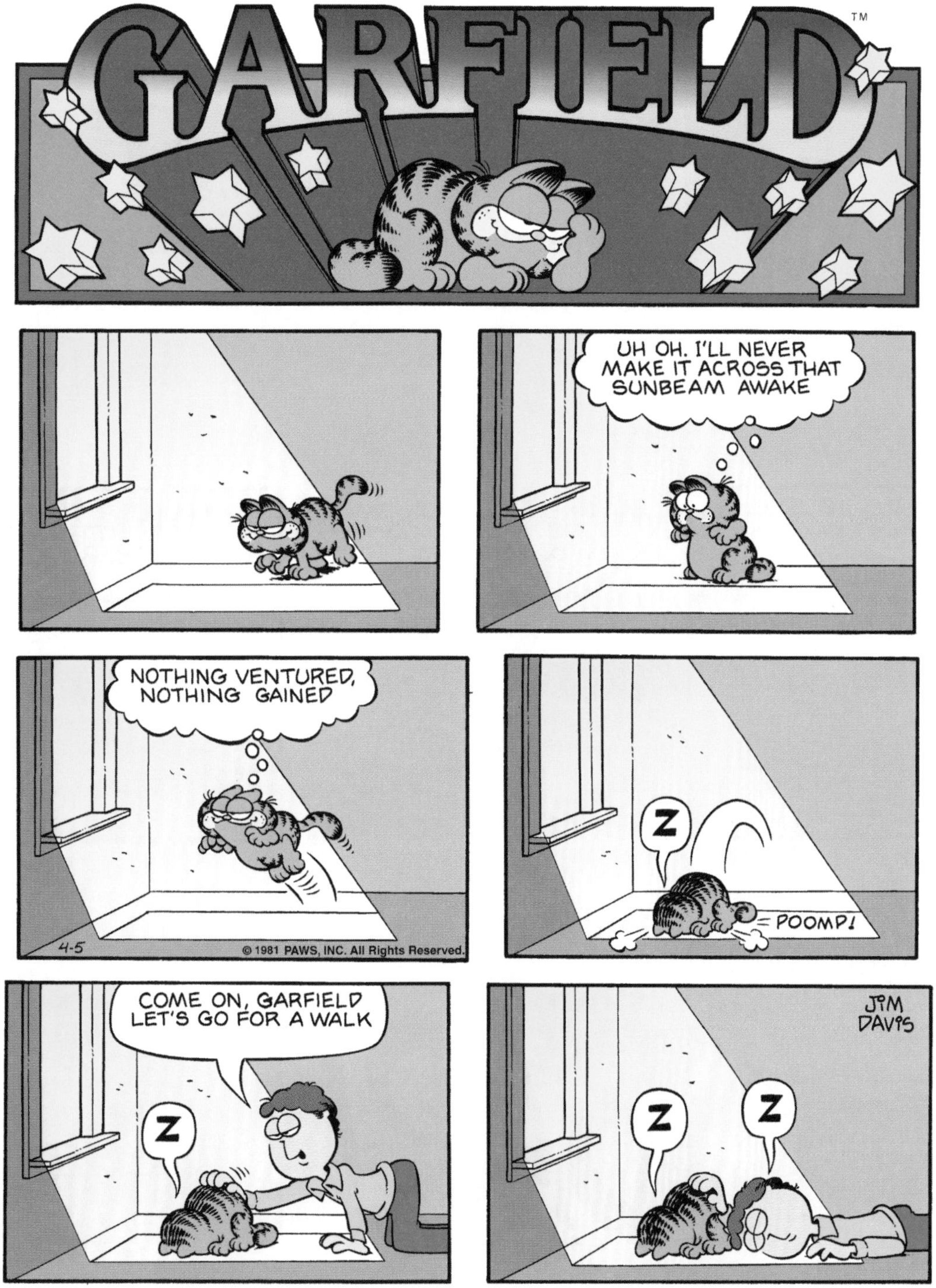
GARFIELD™
UH OH. I'LL NEVER MAKE IT ACROSS THAT SUNBEAM AWAKE
NOTHING VENTURED, NOTHING GAINED
4-5
© 1981 PAWS, INC. All Rights Reserved.
Z
POOMP!
COME ON, GARFIELD LET'S GO FOR A WALK
Z
JIM DAVIS
Z
Z

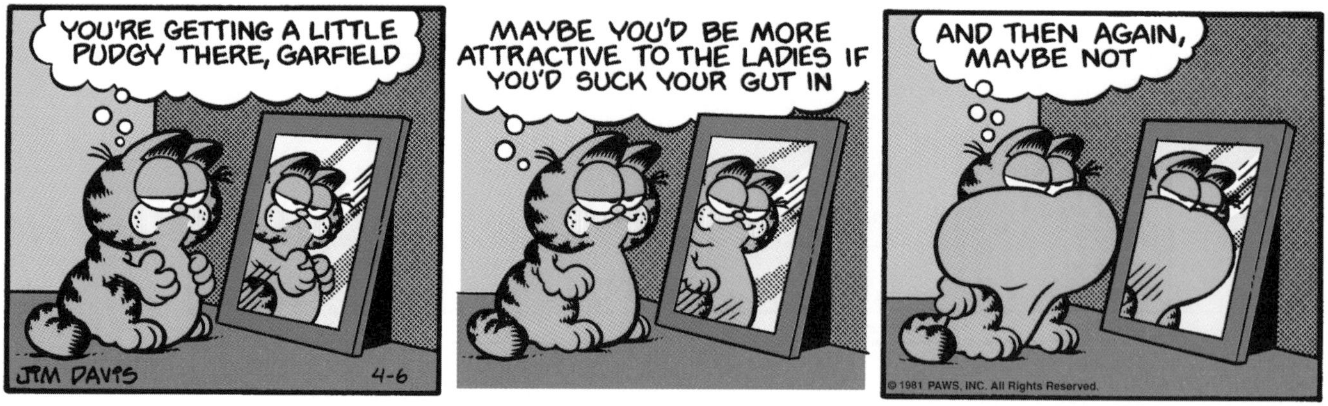
YOU'RE GETTING A LITTLE PUDGY THERE, GARFIELD
JIM DAVIS
4-6
MAYBE YOU'D BE MORE ATTRACTIVE TO THE LADIES IF YOU'D SUCK YOUR GUT IN
AND THEN AGAIN, MAYBE NOT
© 1981 PAWS, INC. All Rights Reserved.

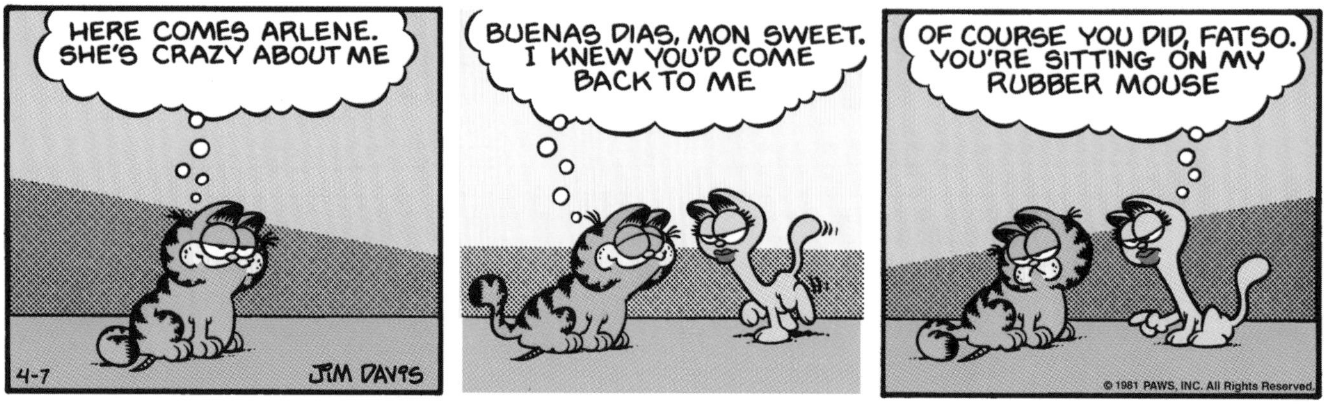
HERE COMES ARLENE. SHE'S CRAZY ABOUT ME
4-7
JIM DAVIS
BUENAS DIAS, MON SWEET. I KNEW YOU'D COME BACK TO ME
OF COURSE YOU DID, FATSO. YOU'RE SITTING ON MY RUBBER MOUSE
© 1981 PAWS, INC. All Rights Reserved.

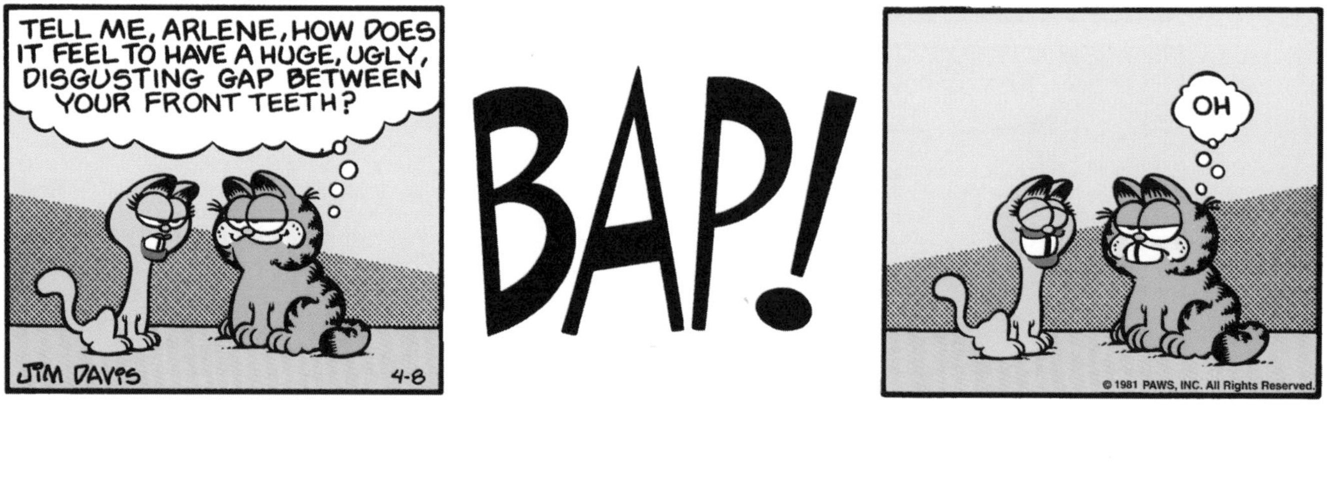
TELL ME, ARLENE, HOW DOES IT FEEL TO HAVE A HUGE, UGLY, DISGUSTING GAP BETWEEN YOUR FRONT TEETH?
JIM DAVIS
4-8
BAP!
OH
© 1981 PAWS, INC. All Rights Reserved.

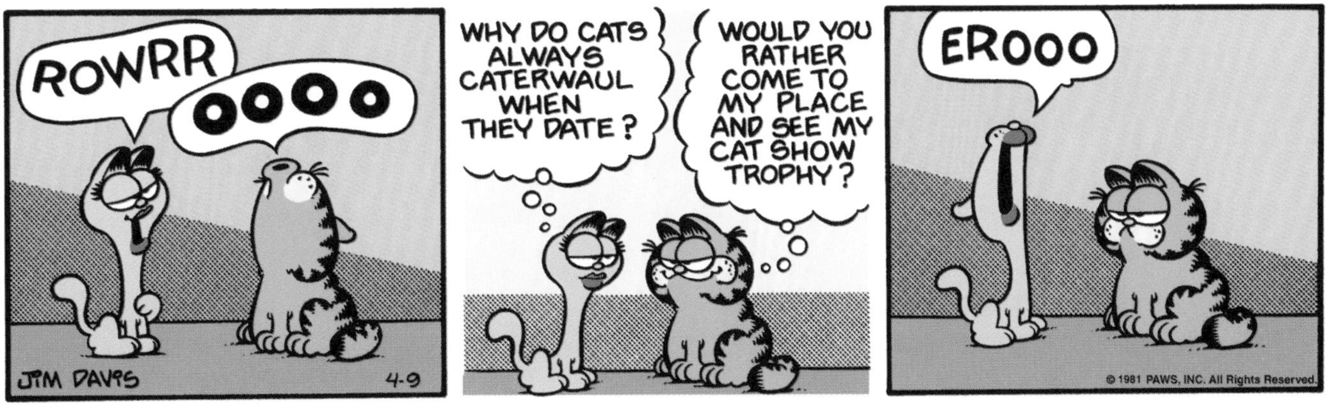
ROWRR
OOOO
JIM DAVIS
4-9
WHY DO CATS ALWAYS CATERWAUL WHEN THEY DATE?
WOULD YOU RATHER COME TO MY PLACE AND SEE MY CAT SHOW TROPHY?
EROOO
© 1981 PAWS, INC. All Rights Reserved.

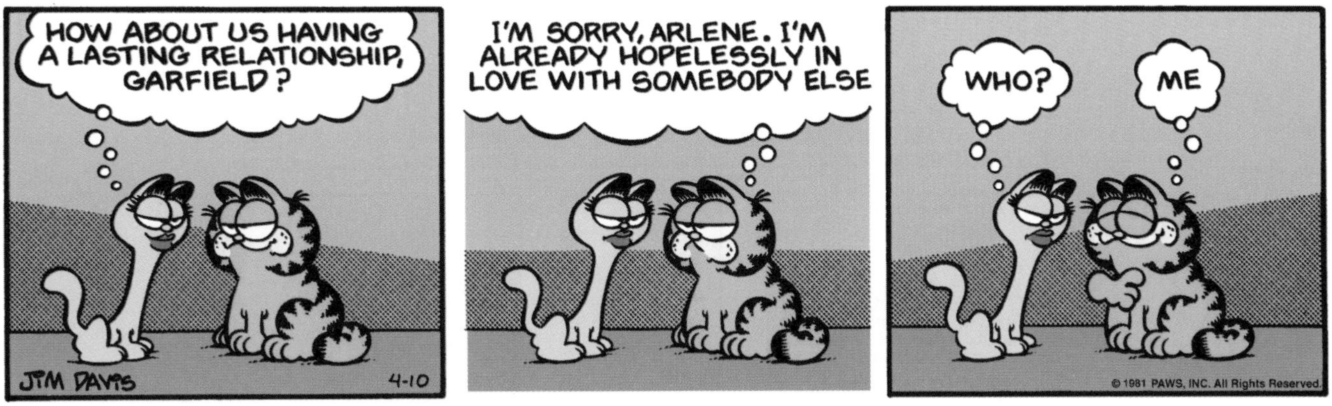
HOW ABOUT US HAVING A LASTING RELATIONSHIP, GARFIELD?
JIM DAVIS
4-10
I'M SORRY, ARLENE. I'M ALREADY HOPELESSLY IN LOVE WITH SOMEBODY ELSE
WHO?
ME
© 1981 PAWS, INC. All Rights Reserved.

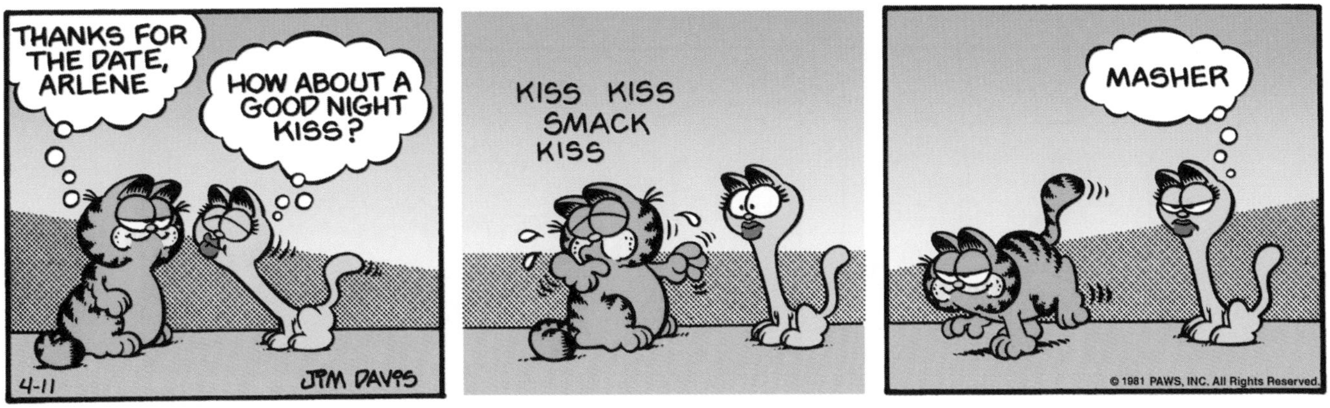
THANKS FOR THE DATE, ARLENE
HOW ABOUT A GOOD NIGHT KISS?
4-11
JIM DAVIS
KISS KISS
SMACK
KISS
MASHER
© 1981 PAWS, INC. All Rights Reserved.

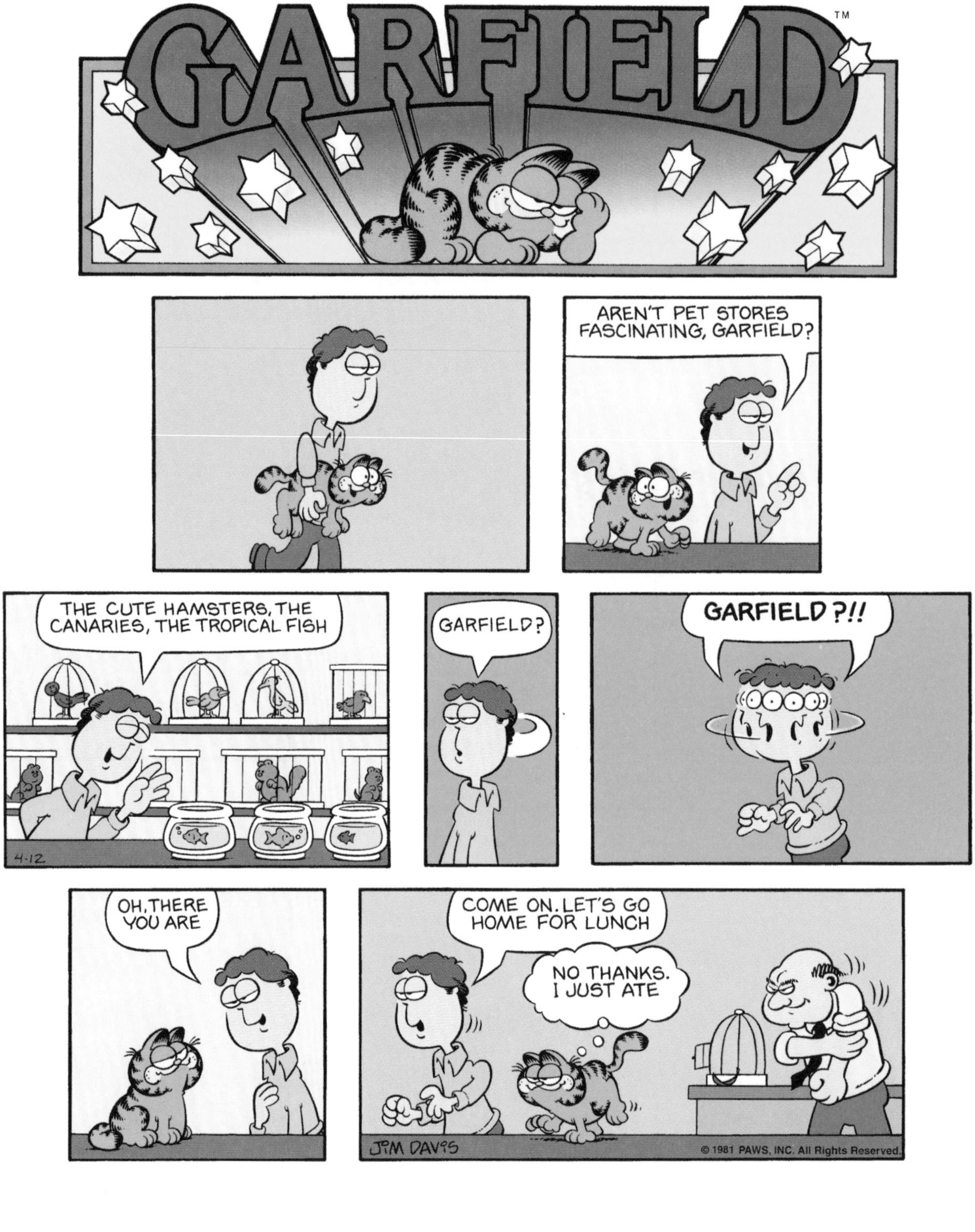
GARFIELD™
AREN'T PET STORES FASCINATING, GARFIELD?
THE CUTE HAMSTERS, THE CANARIES, THE TROPICAL FISH
4-12
GARFIELD?
GARFIELD?!!
OH, THERE YOU ARE
COME ON. LET'S GO HOME FOR LUNCH
NO THANKS. I JUST ATE
JIM DAVIS
© 1981 PAWS, INC. All Rights Reserved.

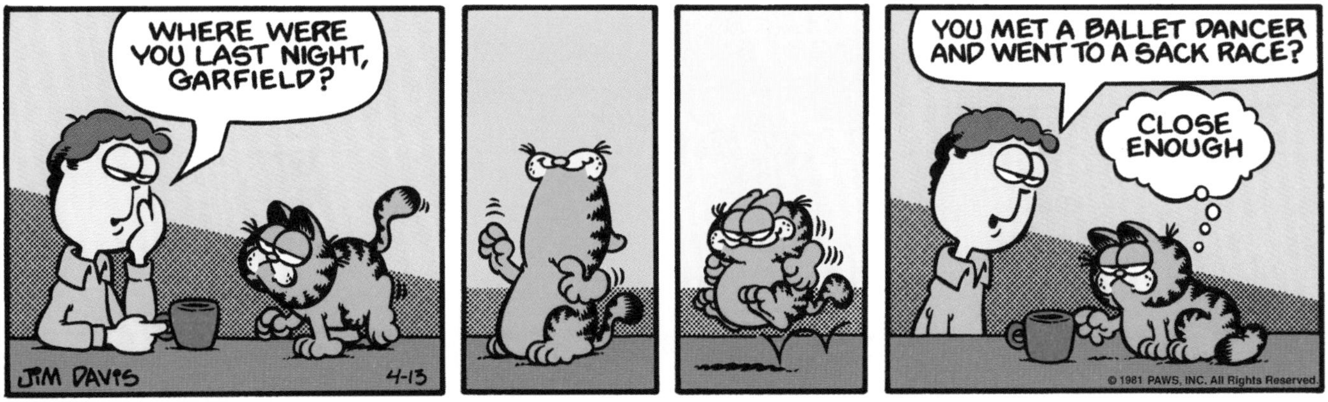
WHERE WERE YOU LAST NIGHT, GARFIELD?
JIM DAVIS
4-13
YOU MET A BALLET DANCER AND WENT TO A SACK RACE?
CLOSE ENOUGH
© 1981 PAWS, INC. All Rights Reserved.

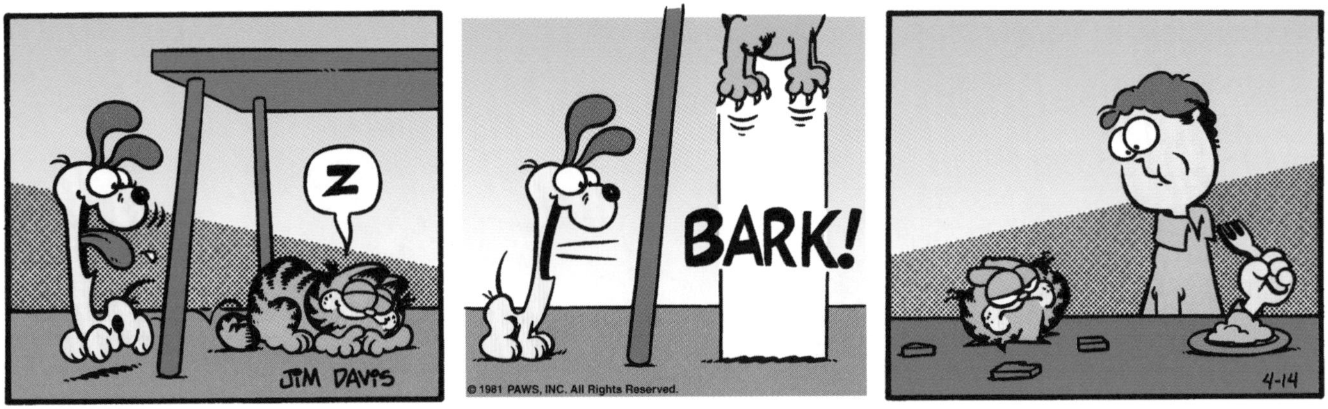
Z
JIM DAVIS
BARK!
© 1981 PAWS, INC. All Rights Reserved.
4-14

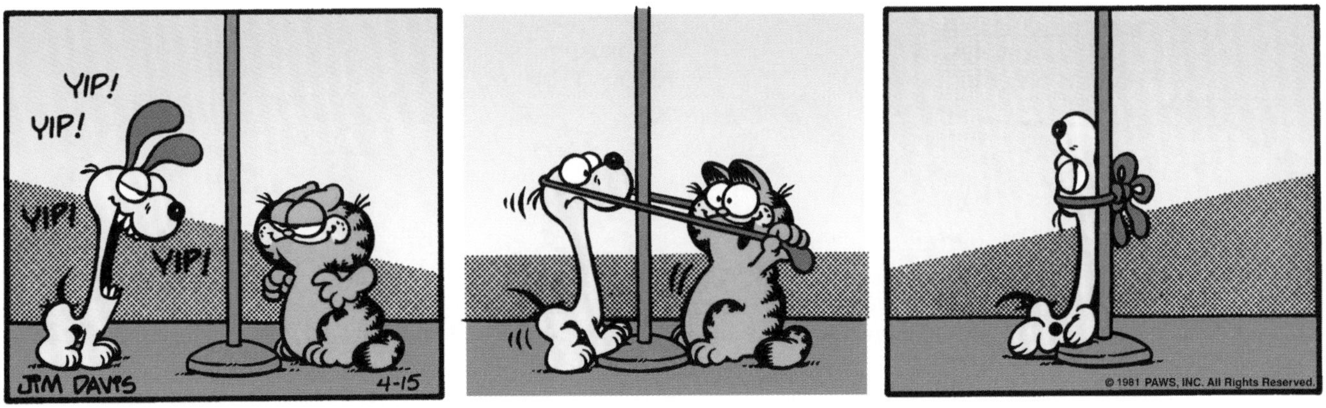
YIP!
YIP!
YIP!
YIP!
JIM DAVIS
4-15
© 1981 PAWS, INC. All Rights Reserved.

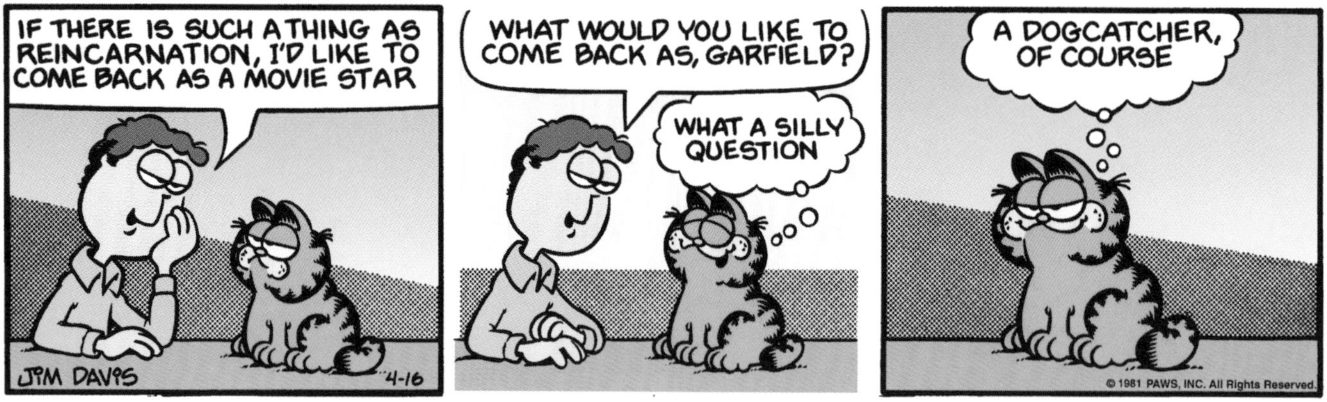
IF THERE IS SUCH A THING AS REINCARNATION, I'D LIKE TO COME BACK AS A MOVIE STAR
JIM DAVIS
4-16
WHAT WOULD YOU LIKE TO COME BACK AS, GARFIELD?
WHAT A SILLY QUESTION
A DOGCATCHER, OF COURSE
© 1981 PAWS, INC. All Rights Reserved.

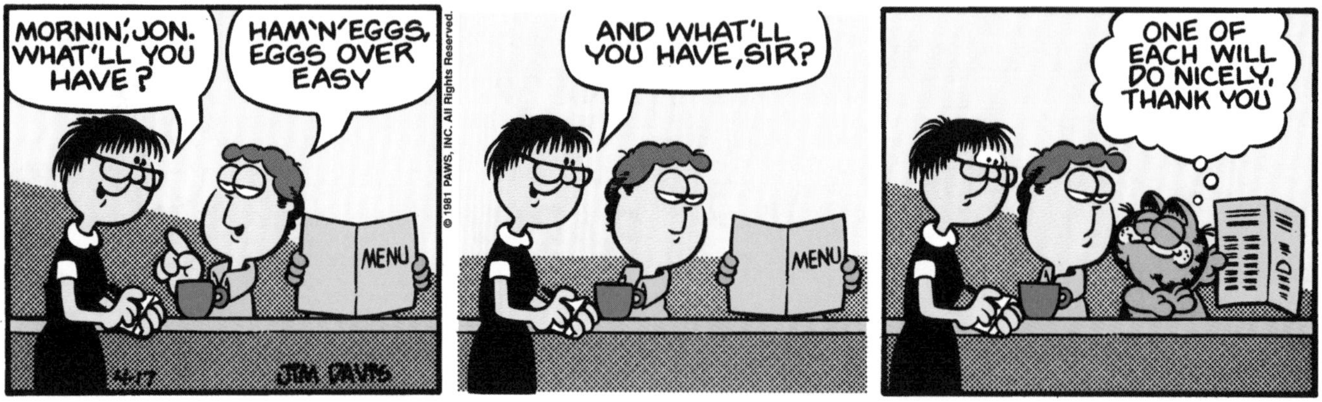
MORNIN', JON. WHAT'LL YOU HAVE?
HAM 'N' EGGS, EGGS OVER EASY
MENU
4-17
JIM DAVIS
© 1981 PAWS, INC. All Rights Reserved.
AND WHAT'LL YOU HAVE, SIR?
MENU
ONE OF EACH WILL DO NICELY, THANK YOU

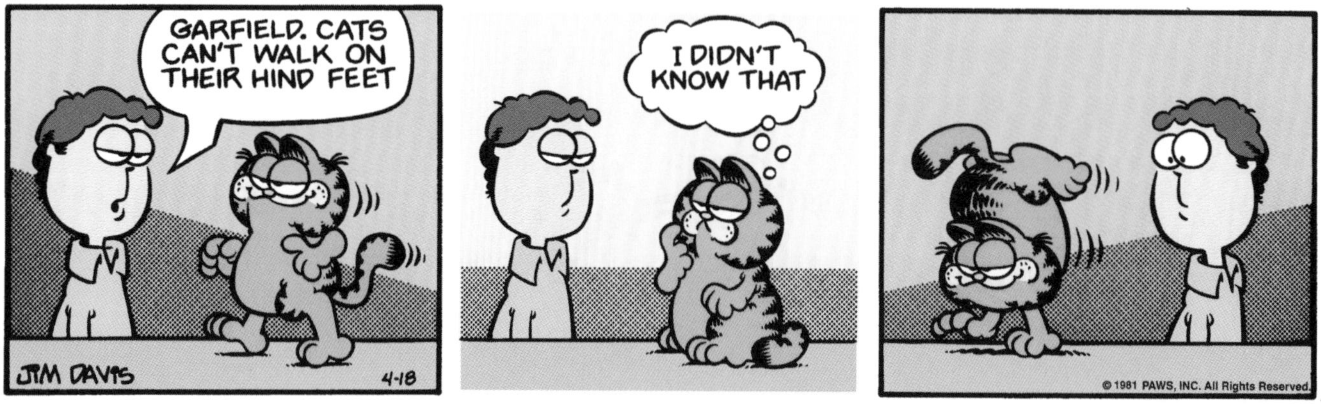
GARFIELD. CATS CAN'T WALK ON THEIR HIND FEET
JIM DAVIS
4-18
I DIDN'T KNOW THAT
© 1981 PAWS, INC. All Rights Reserved.

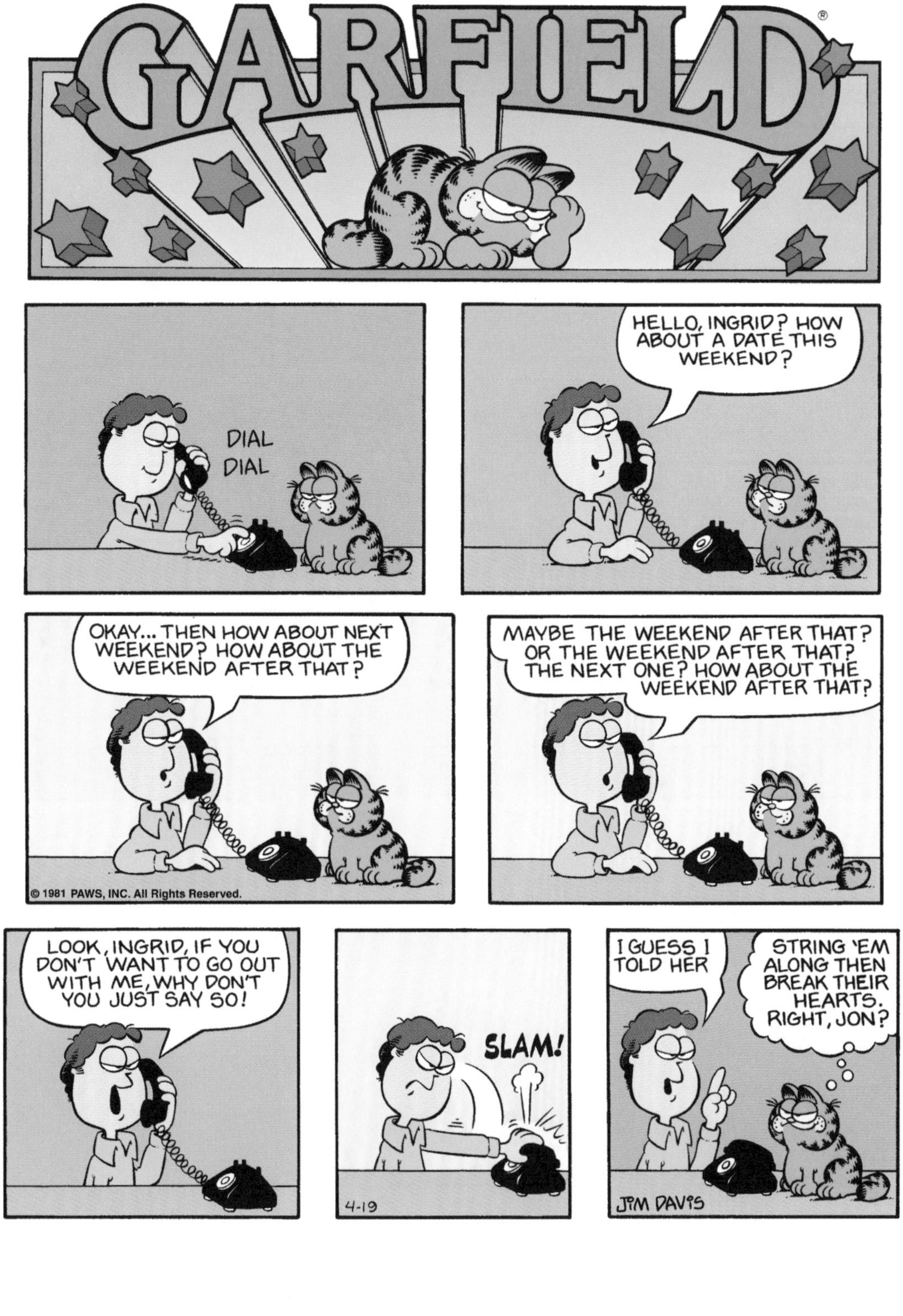
GARFIELD®
DIAL
DIAL
HELLO, INGRID? HOW ABOUT A DATE THIS WEEKEND?
OKAY... THEN HOW ABOUT NEXT WEEKEND? HOW ABOUT THE WEEKEND AFTER THAT?
MAYBE THE WEEKEND AFTER THAT? OR THE WEEKEND AFTER THAT? THE NEXT ONE? HOW ABOUT THE WEEKEND AFTER THAT?
© 1981 PAWS, INC. All Rights Reserved.
LOOK, INGRID, IF YOU DON'T WANT TO GO OUT WITH ME, WHY DON'T YOU JUST SAY SO!
SLAM!
4-19
I GUESS I TOLD HER
STRING 'EM ALONG THEN BREAK THEIR HEARTS. RIGHT, JON?
JIM DAVIS

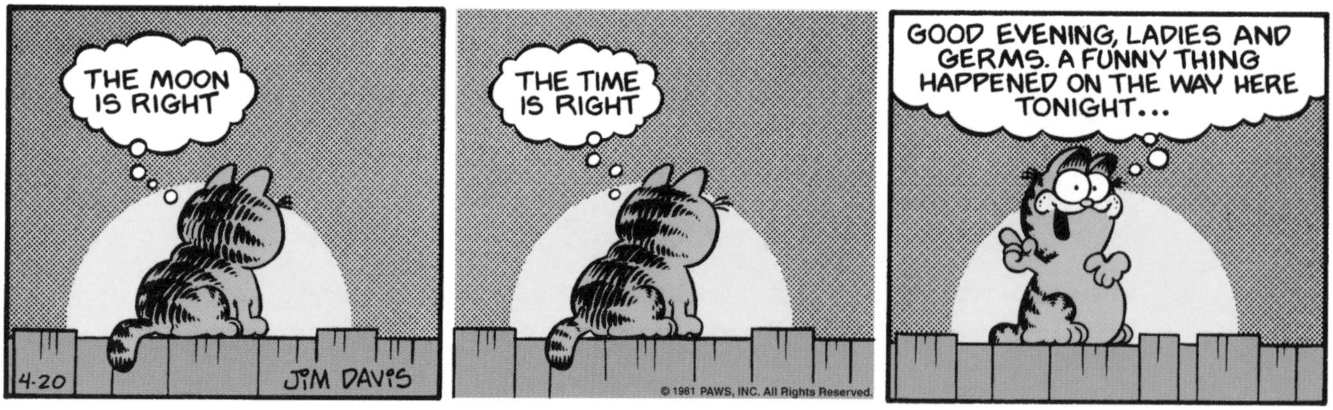
THE MOON IS RIGHT
4-20
JIM DAVIS
THE TIME IS RIGHT
© 1981 PAWS, INC. All Rights Reserved.
GOOD EVENING, LADIES AND GERMS. A FUNNY THING HAPPENED ON THE WAY HERE TONIGHT...

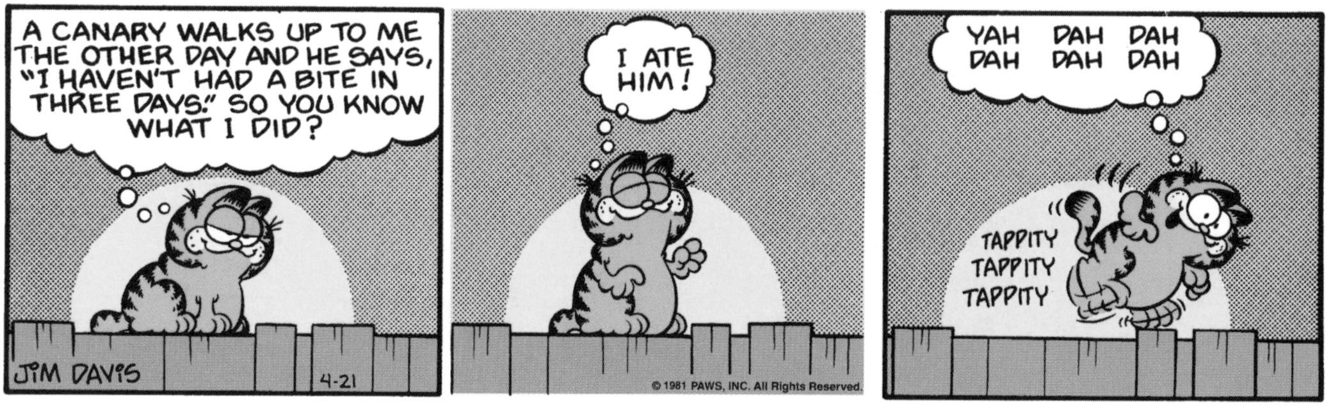
A CANARY WALKS UP TO ME THE OTHER DAY AND HE SAYS, "I HAVEN'T HAD A BITE IN THREE DAYS." SO YOU KNOW WHAT I DID?
JIM DAVIS
4-21
I ATE HIM!
© 1981 PAWS, INC. All Rights Reserved.
YAH DAH DAH DAH DAH DAH
TAPPITY TAPPITY TAPPITY

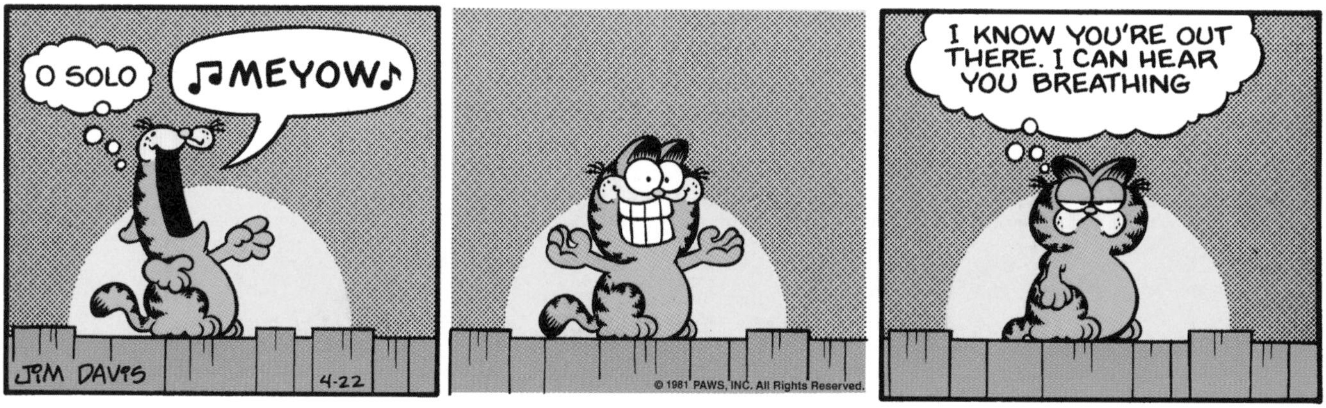
O SOLO
♫MEYOW♪
JIM DAVIS
4-22
© 1981 PAWS, INC. All Rights Reserved.
I KNOW YOU'RE OUT THERE. I CAN HEAR YOU BREATHING

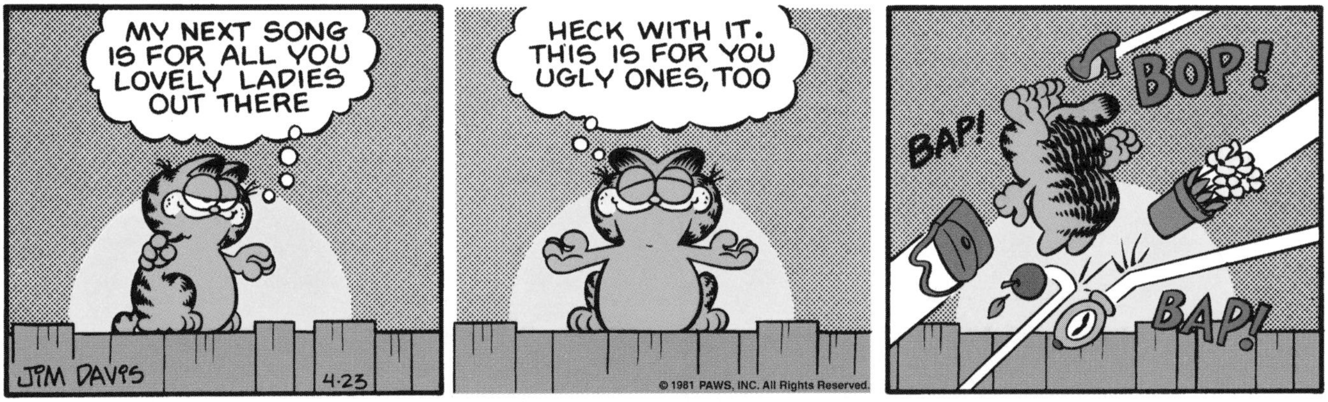
MY NEXT SONG IS FOR ALL YOU LOVELY LADIES OUT THERE
JIM DAVIS
4-23
HECK WITH IT. THIS IS FOR YOU UGLY ONES, TOO
© 1981 PAWS, INC. All Rights Reserved.
BAP!
BOP!
BAP!

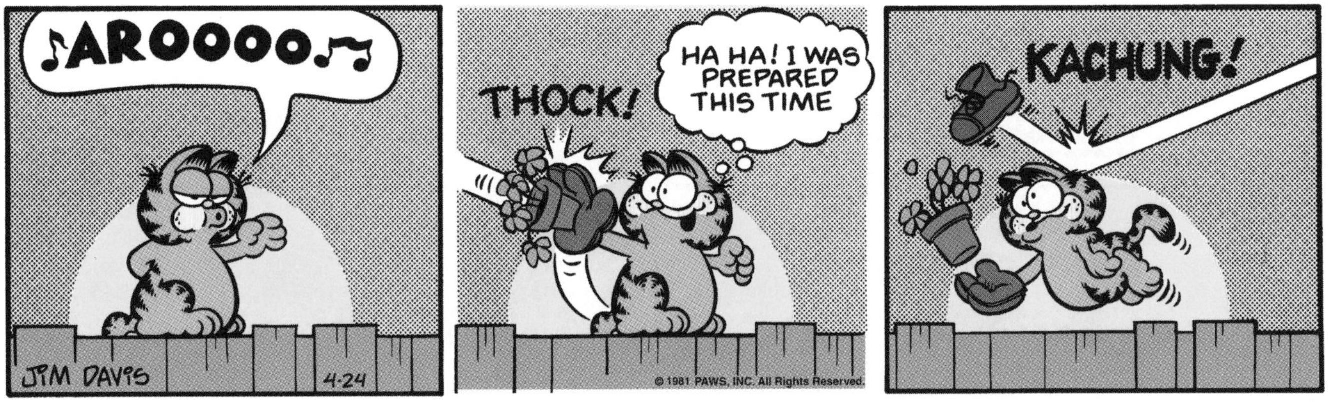
♪AROOOO.♫
JIM DAVIS
4-24
THOCK!
HA HA! I WAS PREPARED THIS TIME
© 1981 PAWS, INC. All Rights Reserved.
KACHUNG!

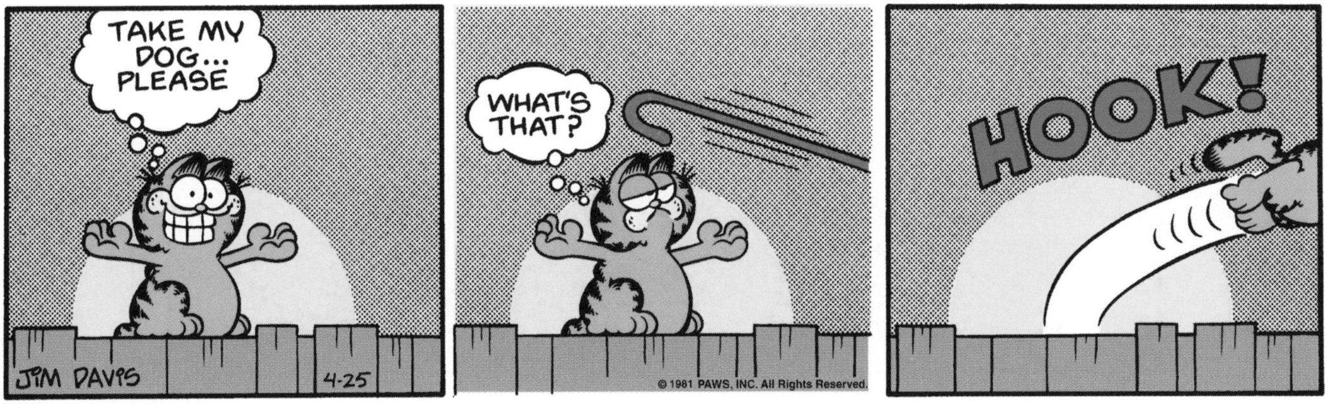
TAKE MY DOG... PLEASE
JIM DAVIS
4-25
WHAT'S THAT?
© 1981 PAWS, INC. All Rights Reserved.
HOOK!

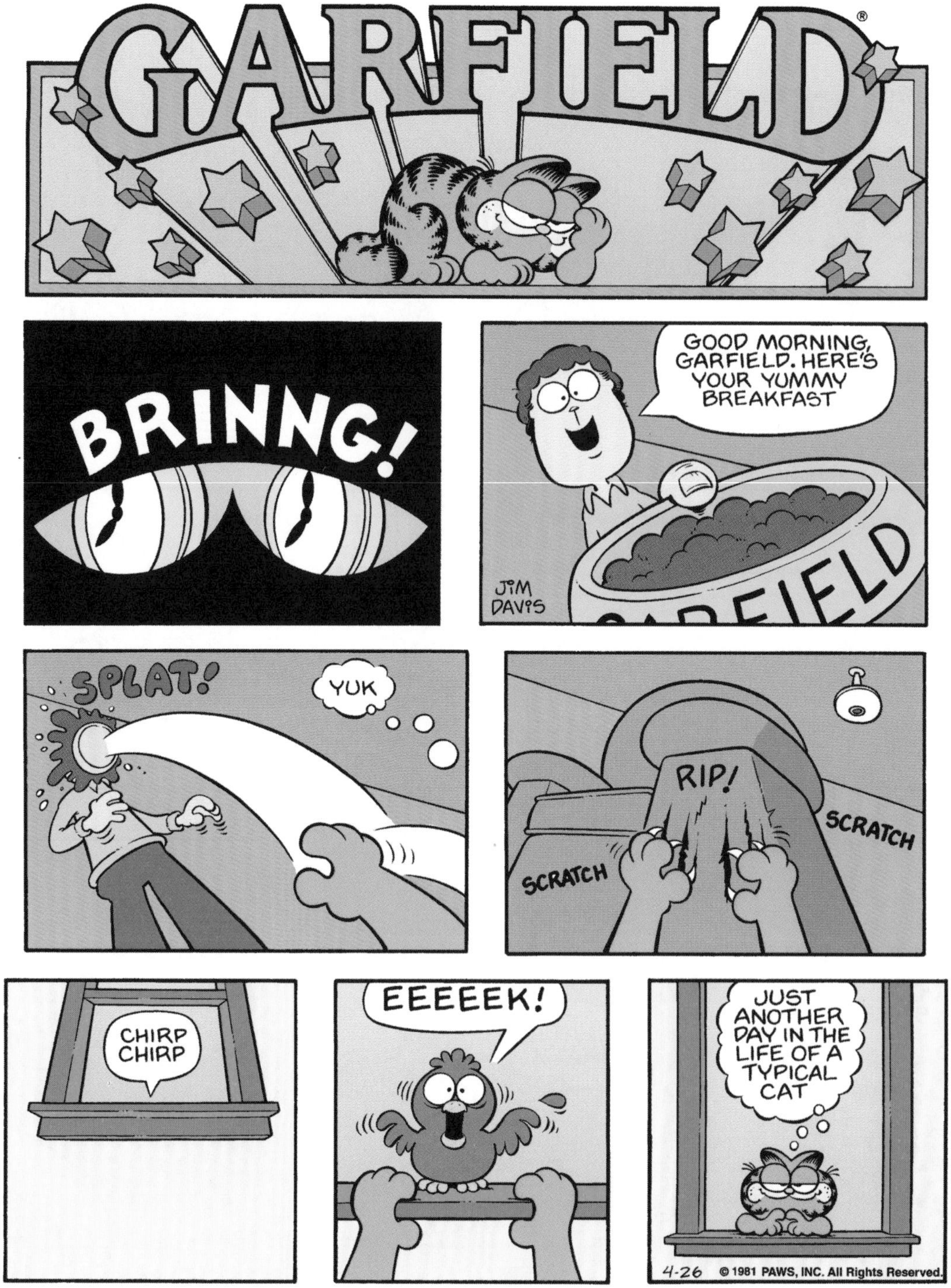
GARFIELD
BRINNG!
GOOD MORNING, GARFIELD. HERE'S YOUR YUMMY BREAKFAST
JIM DAVIS
GARFIELD
SPLAT!
YUK
RIP!
SCRATCH
SCRATCH
CHIRP CHIRP
EEEEEK!
JUST ANOTHER DAY IN THE LIFE OF A TYPICAL CAT
4-26
© 1981 PAWS, INC. All Rights Reserved.

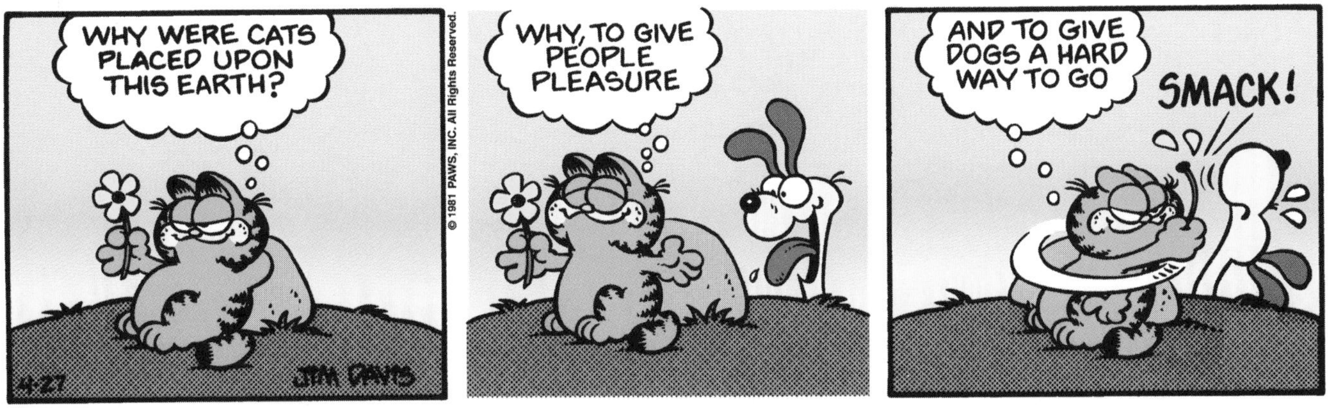
WHY WERE CATS PLACED UPON THIS EARTH?
4-27
JIM DAVIS
© 1981 PAWS, INC. All Rights Reserved.
WHY, TO GIVE PEOPLE PLEASURE
AND TO GIVE DOGS A HARD WAY TO GO
SMACK!

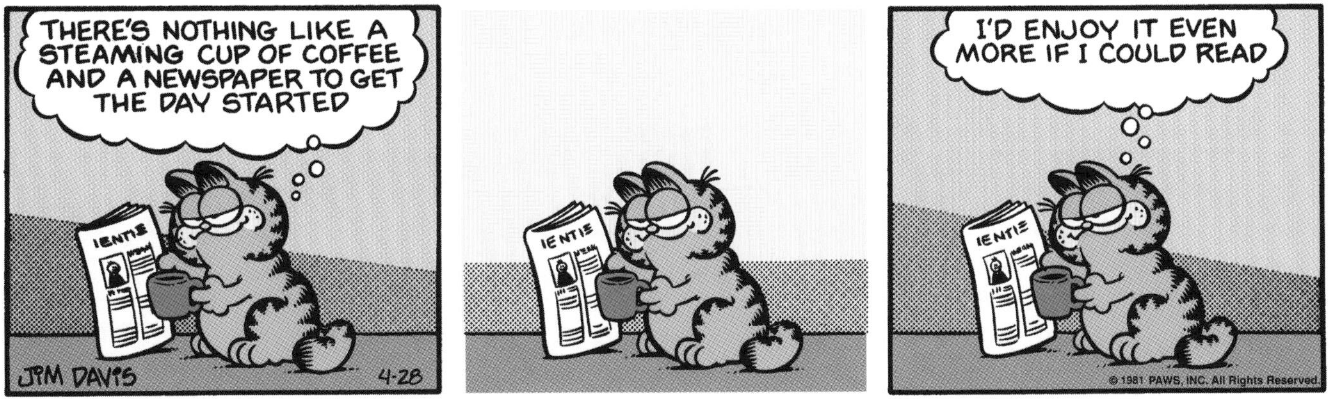
THERE'S NOTHING LIKE A STEAMING CUP OF COFFEE AND A NEWSPAPER TO GET THE DAY STARTED
JIM DAVIS
4-28
I'D ENJOY IT EVEN MORE IF I COULD READ
© 1981 PAWS, INC. All Rights Reserved.

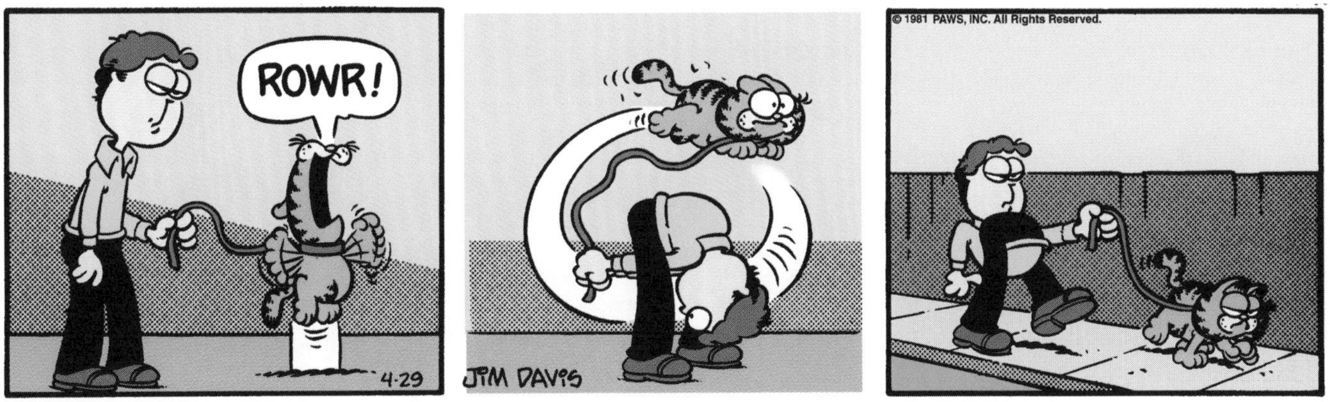
ROWR!
4-29
JIM DAVIS
© 1981 PAWS, INC. All Rights Reserved.

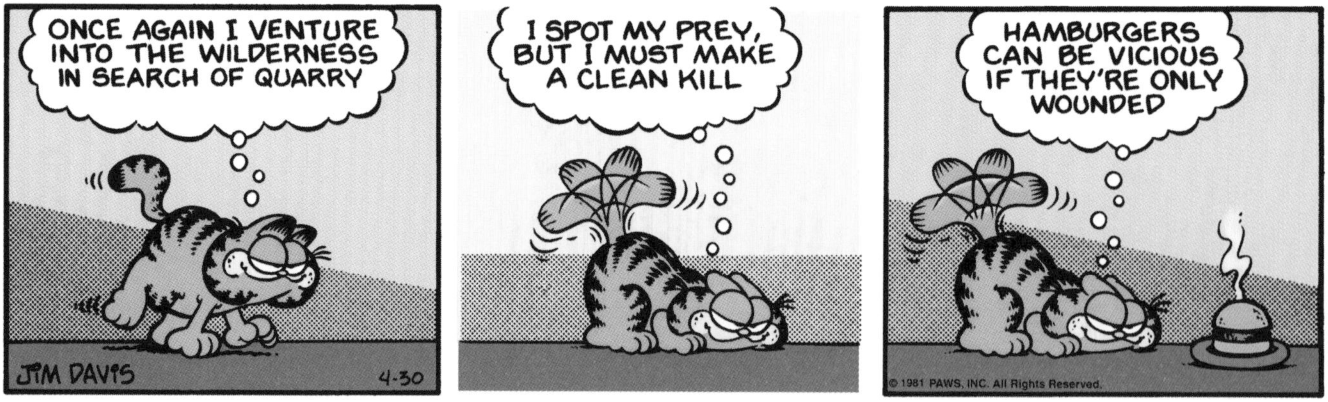
ONCE AGAIN I VENTURE INTO THE WILDERNESS IN SEARCH OF QUARRY
JIM DAVIS
4-30
I SPOT MY PREY, BUT I MUST MAKE A CLEAN KILL
HAMBURGERS CAN BE VICIOUS IF THEY'RE ONLY WOUNDED
© 1981 PAWS, INC. All Rights Reserved.

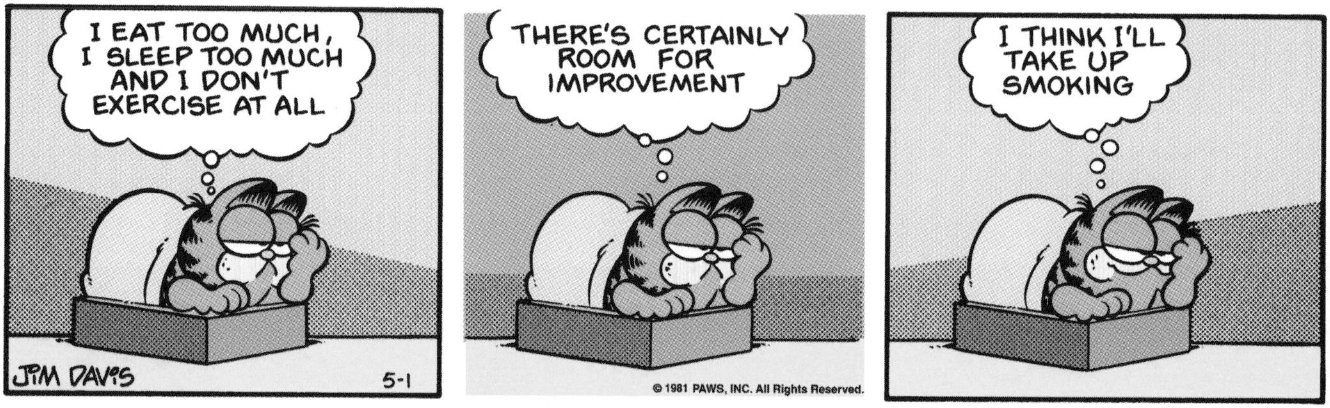
I EAT TOO MUCH, I SLEEP TOO MUCH AND I DON'T EXERCISE AT ALL
JIM DAVIS
5-1
THERE'S CERTAINLY ROOM FOR IMPROVEMENT
© 1981 PAWS, INC. All Rights Reserved.
I THINK I'LL TAKE UP SMOKING

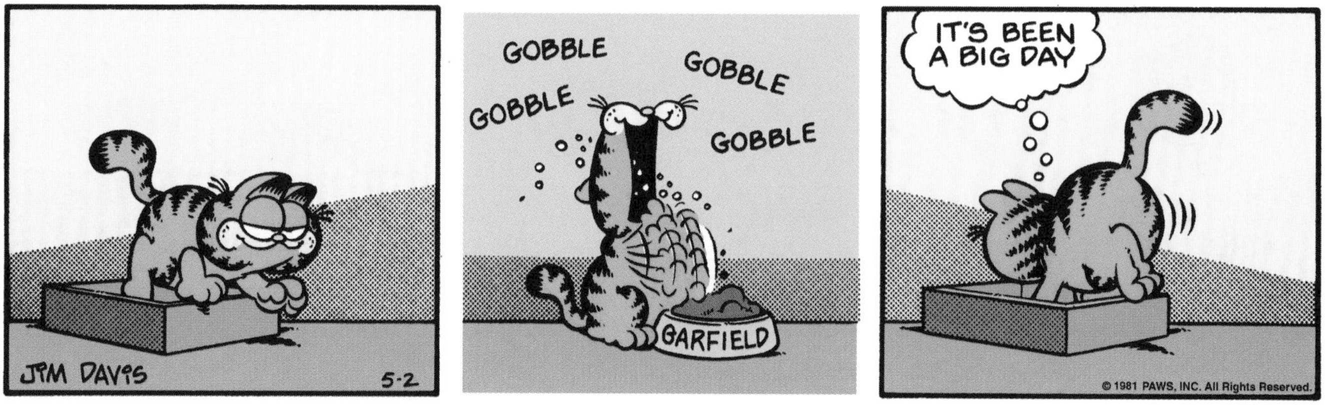
JIM DAVIS
5-2
GOBBLE
GOBBLE
GOBBLE
GOBBLE
GARFIELD
IT'S BEEN A BIG DAY
© 1981 PAWS, INC. All Rights Reserved.

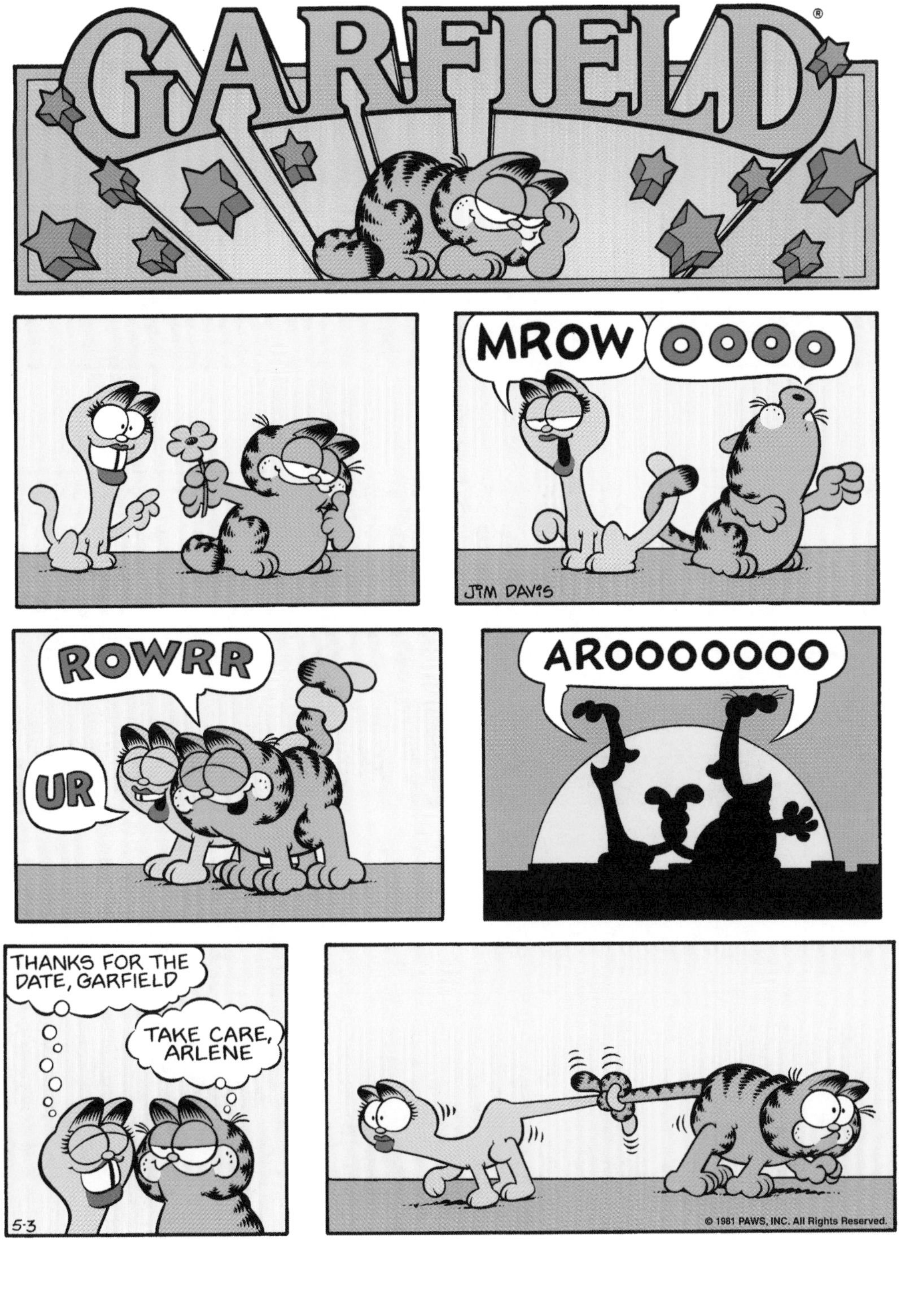
GARFIELD
MROW
OOOO
JIM DAVIS
ROWRR
UR
AROOOOOOO
THANKS FOR THE DATE, GARFIELD
TAKE CARE, ARLENE
5-3
© 1981 PAWS, INC. All Rights Reserved.

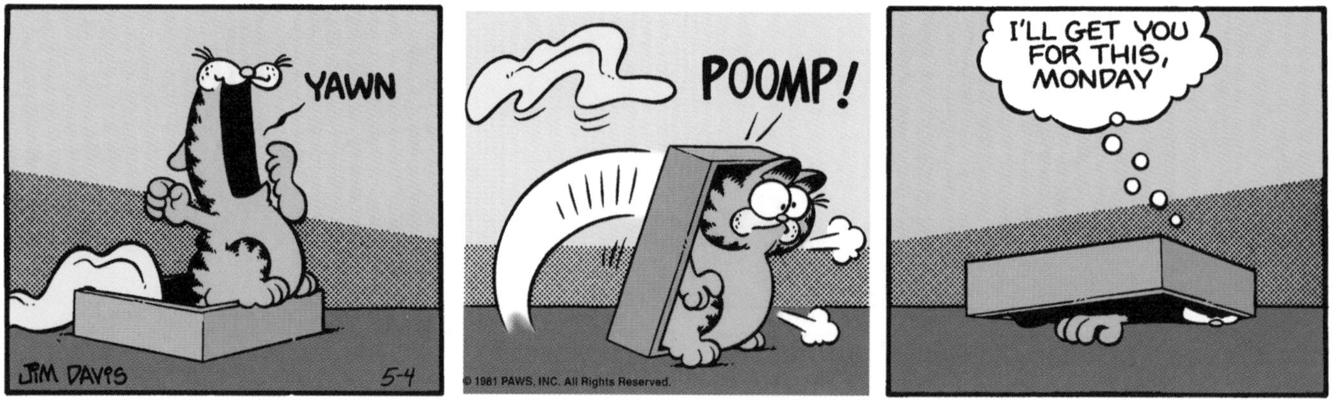
YAWN
JIM DAVIS
5-4
POOMP!
© 1981 PAWS, INC. All Rights Reserved.
I'LL GET YOU FOR THIS, MONDAY

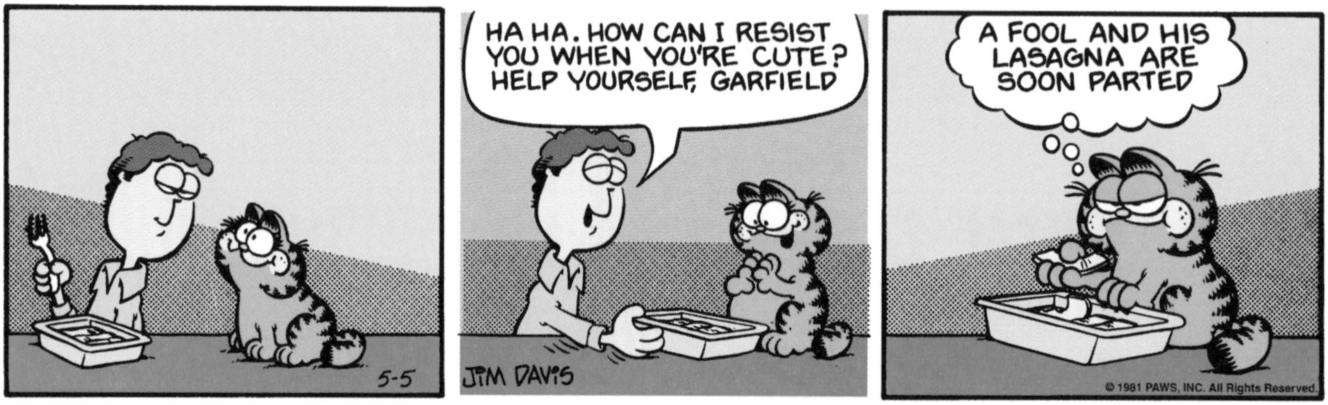
5-5
HA HA. HOW CAN I RESIST YOU WHEN YOU'RE CUTE? HELP YOURSELF, GARFIELD
JIM DAVIS
A FOOL AND HIS LASAGNA ARE SOON PARTED
© 1981 PAWS, INC. All Rights Reserved.

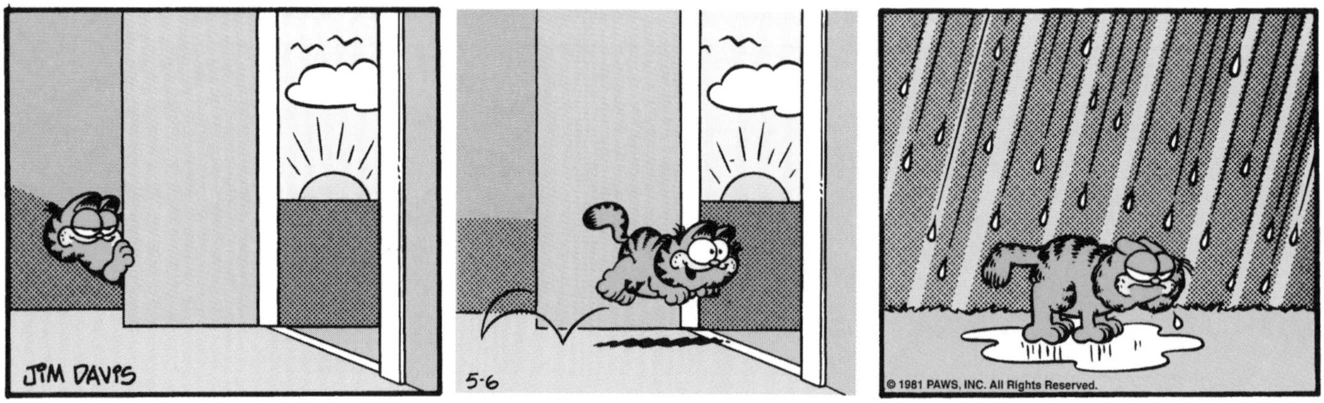
JIM DAVIS
5-6
© 1981 PAWS, INC. All Rights Reserved.

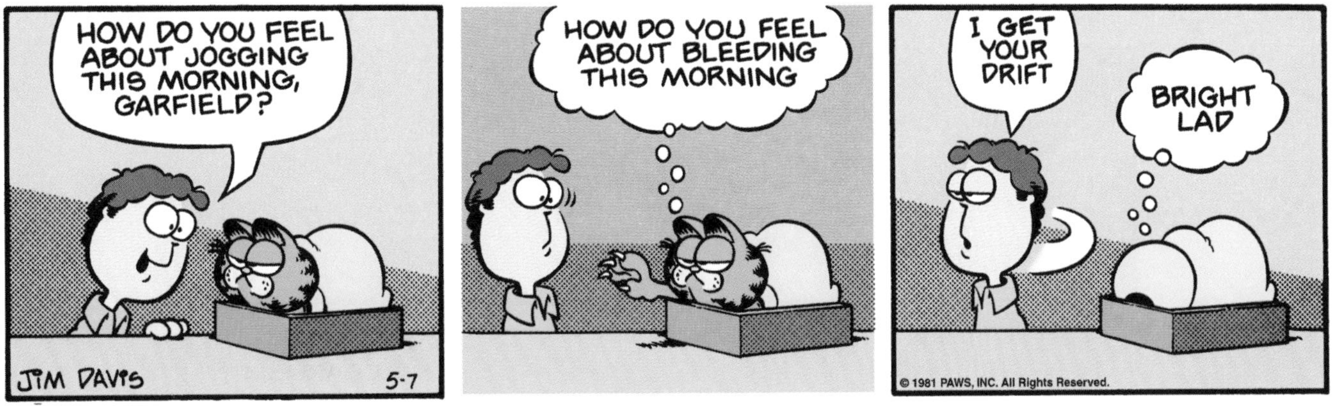
HOW DO YOU FEEL ABOUT JOGGING THIS MORNING, GARFIELD?
JIM DAVIS
5-7
HOW DO YOU FEEL ABOUT BLEEDING THIS MORNING
I GET YOUR DRIFT
BRIGHT LAD
© 1981 PAWS, INC. All Rights Reserved.

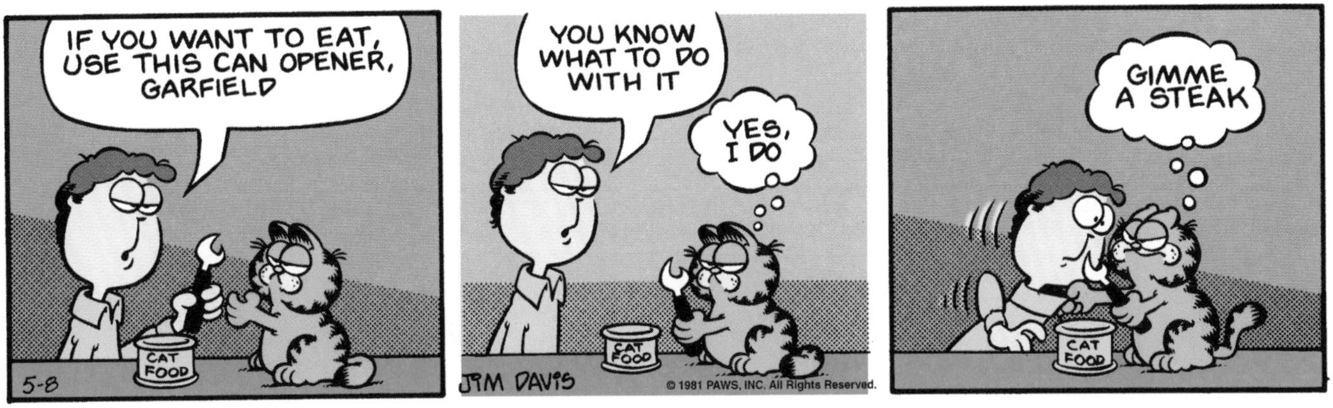
IF YOU WANT TO EAT, USE THIS CAN OPENER, GARFIELD
CAT FOOD
5-8
YOU KNOW WHAT TO DO WITH IT
YES, I DO
CAT FOOD
JIM DAVIS
© 1981 PAWS, INC. All Rights Reserved.
GIMME A STEAK
CAT FOOD

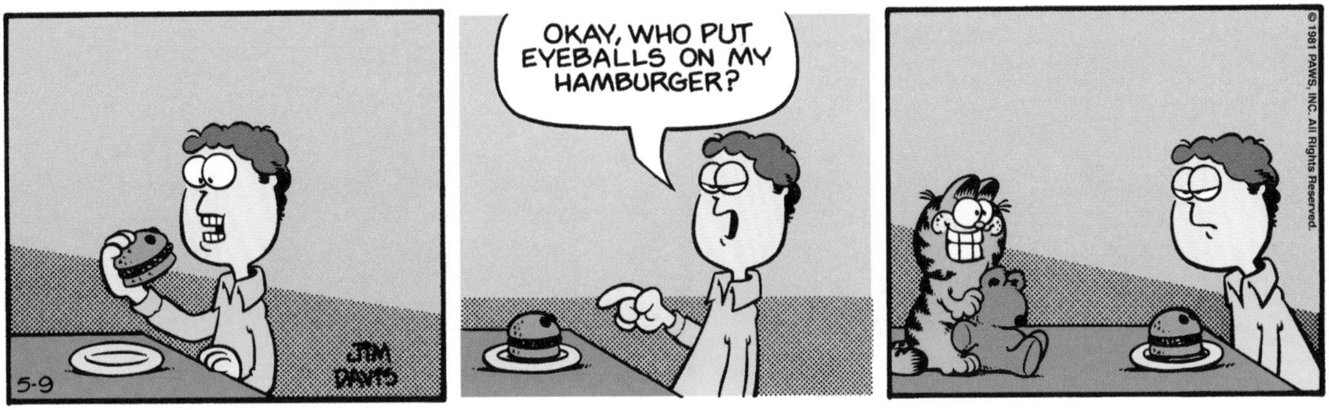
JIM DAVIS
5-9
OKAY, WHO PUT EYEBALLS ON MY HAMBURGER?
© 1981 PAWS, INC. All Rights Reserved.

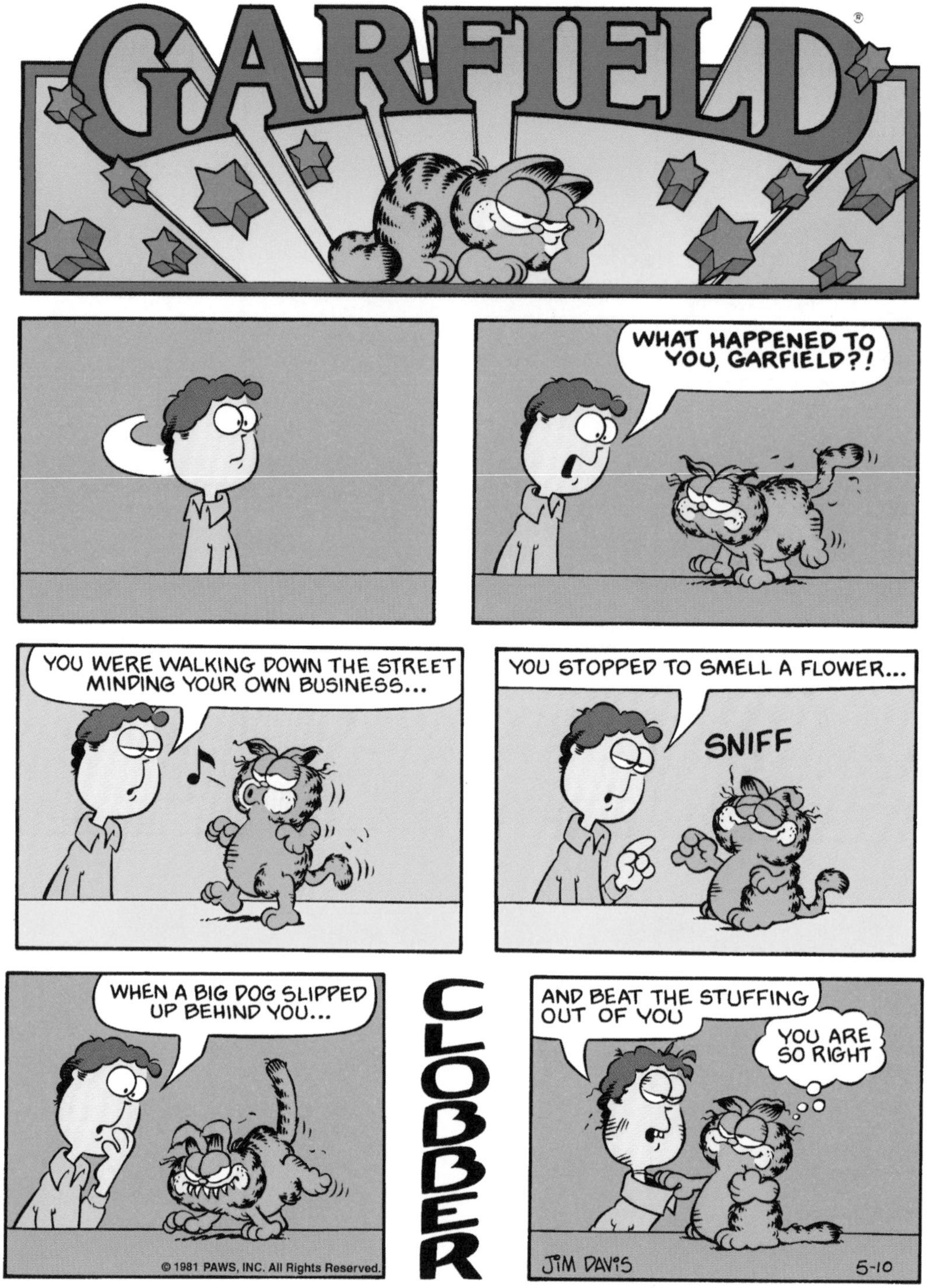
GARFIELD®
WHAT HAPPENED TO YOU, GARFIELD?!
YOU WERE WALKING DOWN THE STREET MINDING YOUR OWN BUSINESS...
YOU STOPPED TO SMELL A FLOWER...
SNIFF
WHEN A BIG DOG SLIPPED UP BEHIND YOU...
CLOBBER
AND BEAT THE STUFFING OUT OF YOU
YOU ARE SO RIGHT
© 1981 PAWS, INC. All Rights Reserved.
JIM DAVIS
5-10

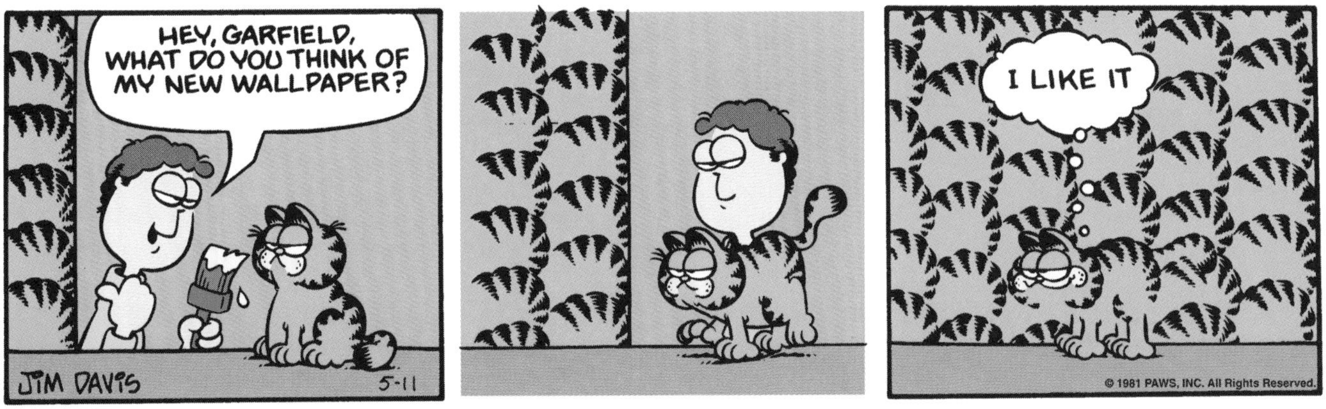
HEY, GARFIELD, WHAT DO YOU THINK OF MY NEW WALLPAPER?
JIM DAVIS
5-11
I LIKE IT
© 1981 PAWS, INC. All Rights Reserved.

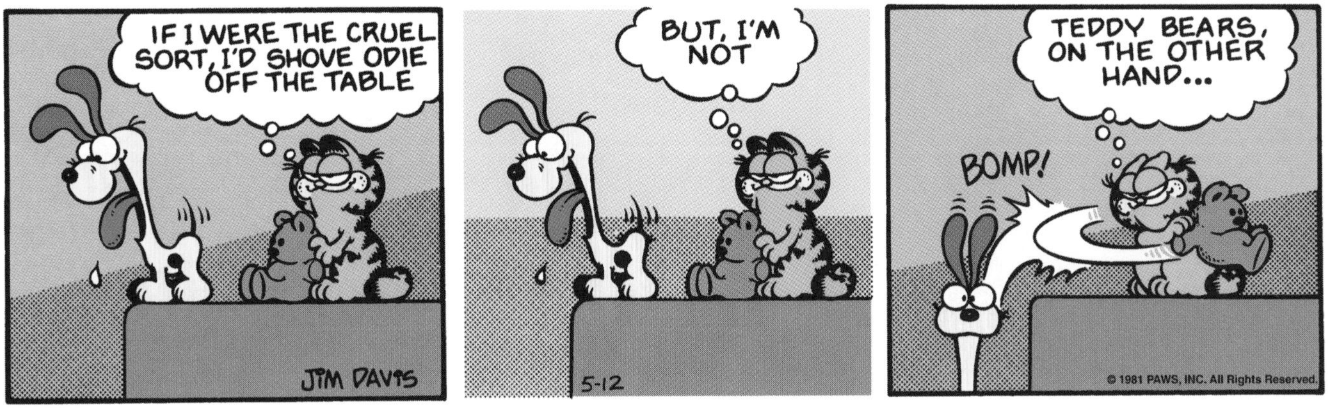
IF I WERE THE CRUEL SORT, I'D SHOVE ODIE OFF THE TABLE
JIM DAVIS
BUT, I'M NOT
5-12
TEDDY BEARS, ON THE OTHER HAND...
BOMP!
© 1981 PAWS, INC. All Rights Reserved.

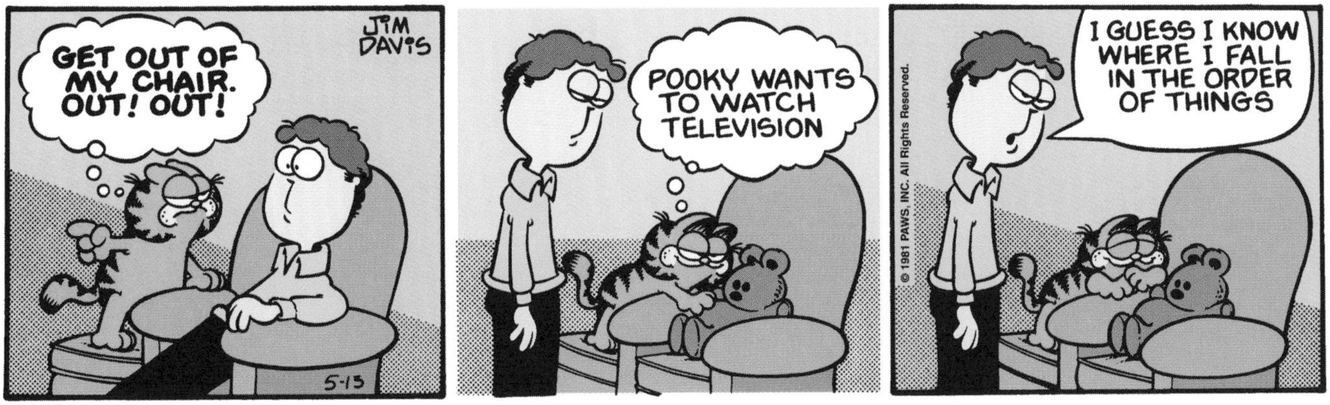
JIM DAVIS
GET OUT OF MY CHAIR. OUT! OUT!
5-13
POOKY WANTS TO WATCH TELEVISION
© 1981 PAWS, INC. All Rights Reserved.
I GUESS I KNOW WHERE I FALL IN THE ORDER OF THINGS

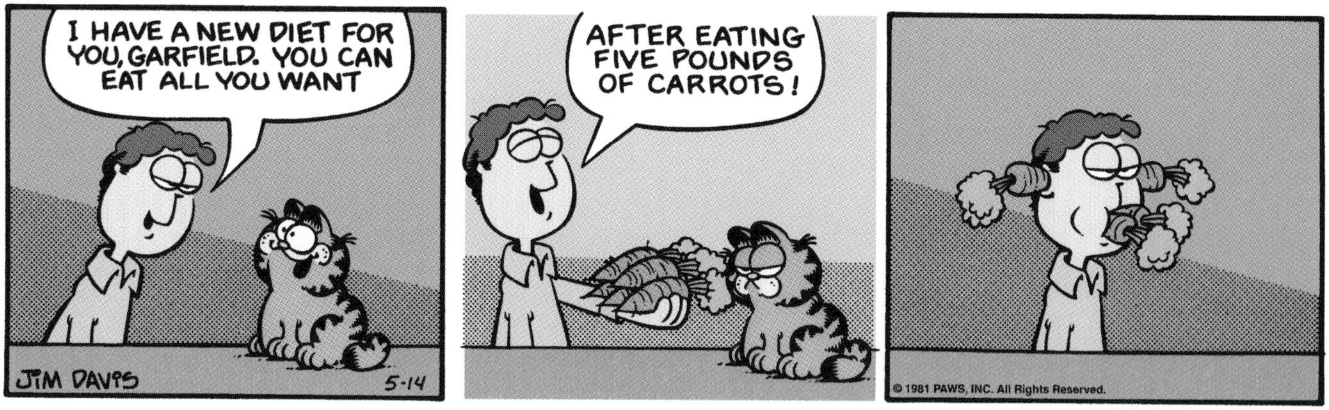
I HAVE A NEW DIET FOR YOU, GARFIELD. YOU CAN EAT ALL YOU WANT
AFTER EATING FIVE POUNDS OF CARROTS!
JIM DAVIS
5-14
© 1981 PAWS, INC. All Rights Reserved.

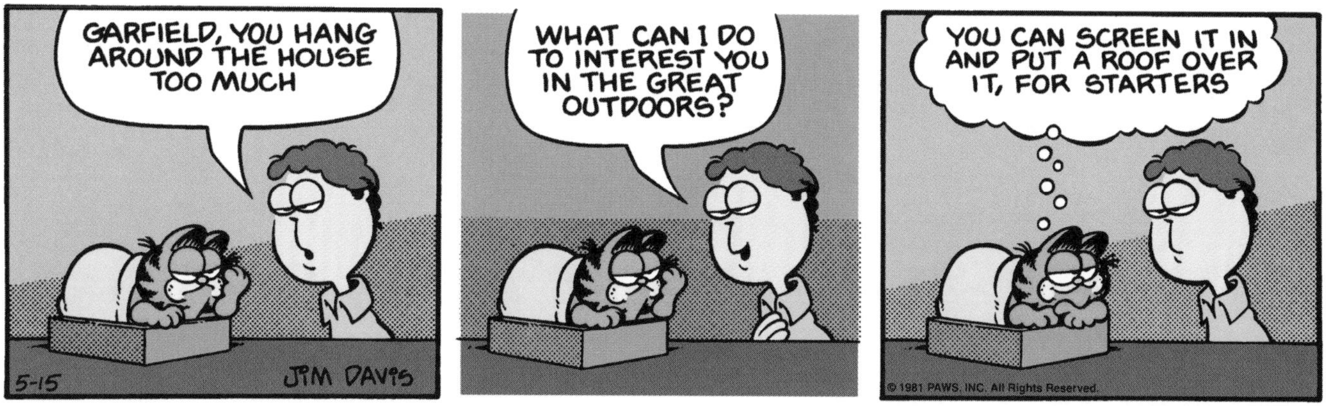
GARFIELD, YOU HANG AROUND THE HOUSE TOO MUCH
WHAT CAN I DO TO INTEREST YOU IN THE GREAT OUTDOORS?
YOU CAN SCREEN IT IN AND PUT A ROOF OVER IT, FOR STARTERS
5-15
JIM DAVIS
© 1981 PAWS, INC. All Rights Reserved.

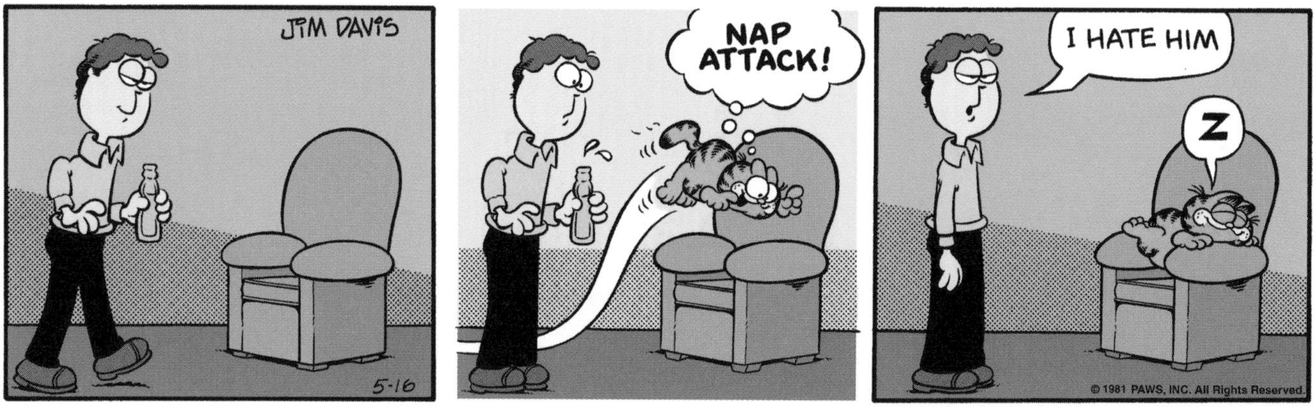
JIM DAVIS
5-16
NAP ATTACK!
I HATE HIM
Z
© 1981 PAWS, INC. All Rights Reserved.

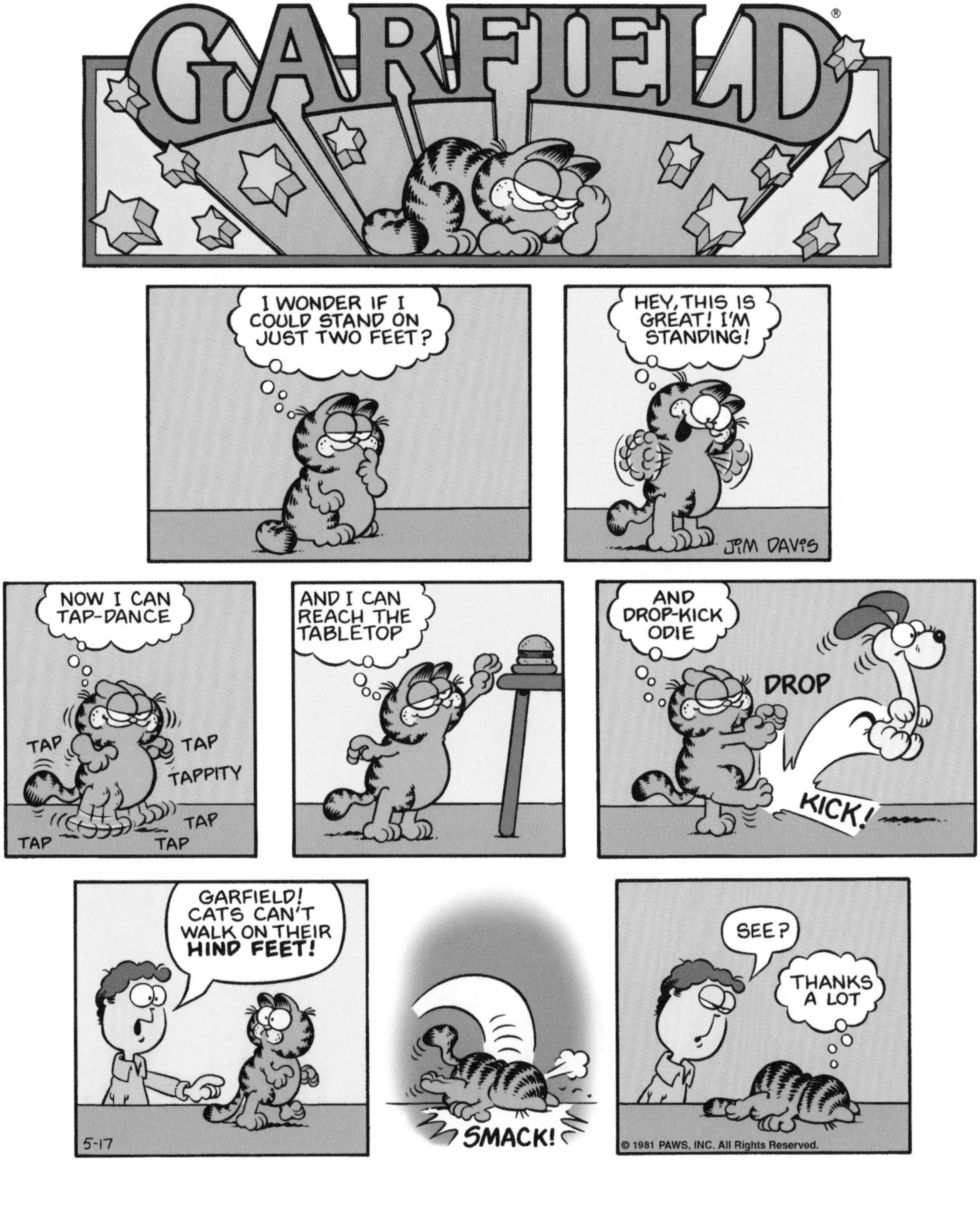
GARFIELD
I WONDER IF I COULD STAND ON JUST TWO FEET?
HEY, THIS IS GREAT! I'M STANDING!
JIM DAVIS
NOW I CAN TAP-DANCE
TAP
TAP
TAPPITY
TAP
TAP
TAP
AND I CAN REACH THE TABLETOP
AND DROP-KICK ODIE
DROP
KICK!
GARFIELD! CATS CAN'T WALK ON THEIR **HIND FEET!**
5-17
SMACK!
SEE?
THANKS A LOT
© 1981 PAWS, INC. All Rights Reserved.

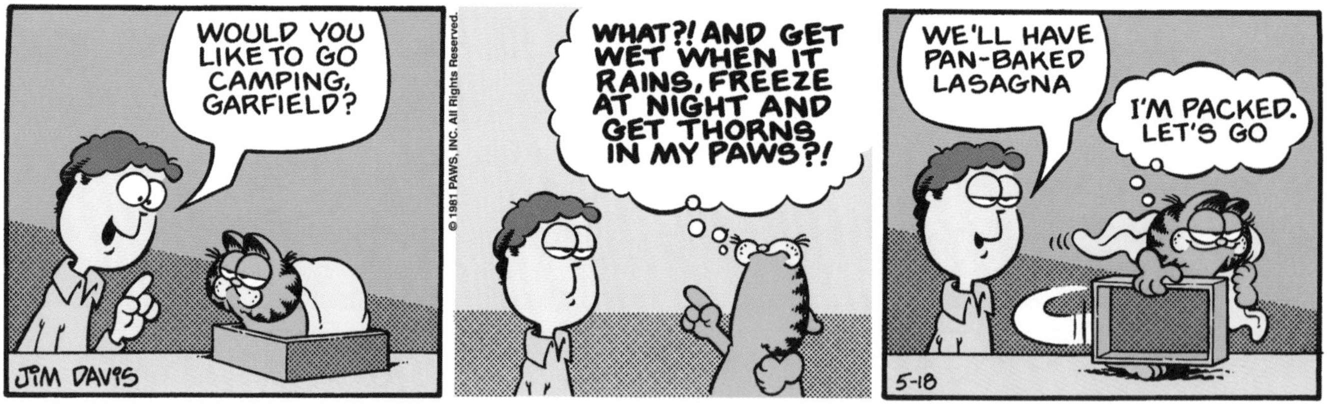
WOULD YOU LIKE TO GO CAMPING, GARFIELD?
JIM DAVIS
© 1981 PAWS, INC. All Rights Reserved.
WHAT?! AND GET WET WHEN IT RAINS, FREEZE AT NIGHT AND GET THORNS IN MY PAWS?!
WE'LL HAVE PAN-BAKED LASAGNA
I'M PACKED. LET'S GO
5-18

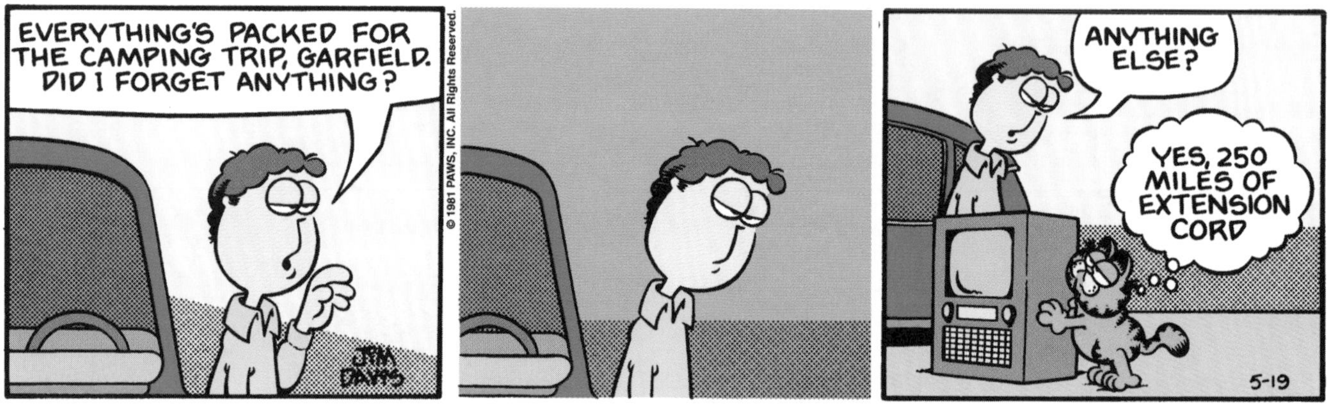
EVERYTHING'S PACKED FOR THE CAMPING TRIP, GARFIELD. DID I FORGET ANYTHING?
JIM DAVIS
© 1981 PAWS, INC. All Rights Reserved.
ANYTHING ELSE?
YES, 250 MILES OF EXTENSION CORD
5-19

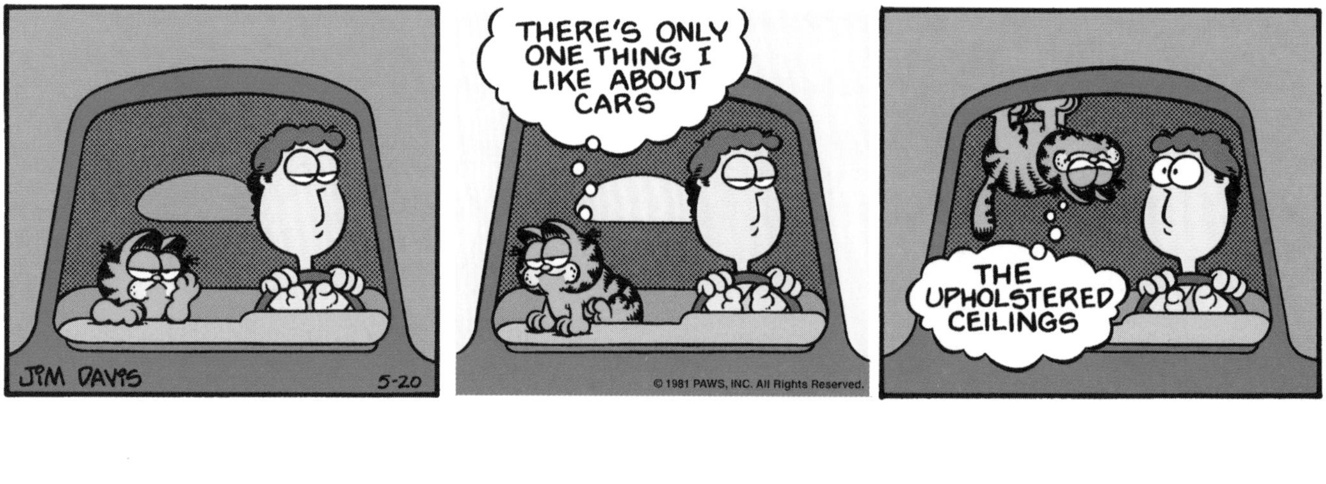
JIM DAVIS
5-20
THERE'S ONLY ONE THING I LIKE ABOUT CARS
© 1981 PAWS, INC. All Rights Reserved.
THE UPHOLSTERED CEILINGS

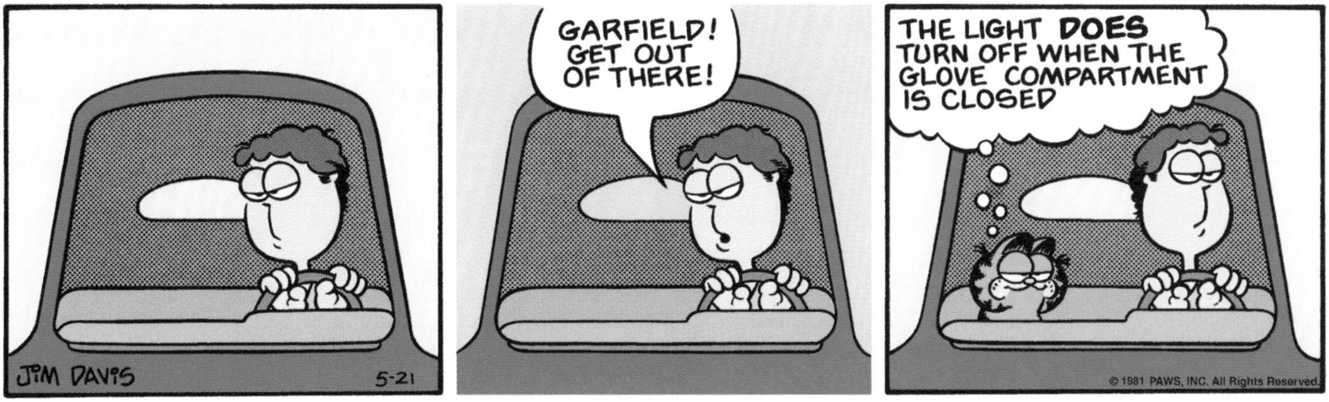
JIM DAVIS
5-21
GARFIELD! GET OUT OF THERE!
THE LIGHT **DOES** TURN OFF WHEN THE GLOVE COMPARTMENT IS CLOSED
© 1981 PAWS, INC. All Rights Reserved.

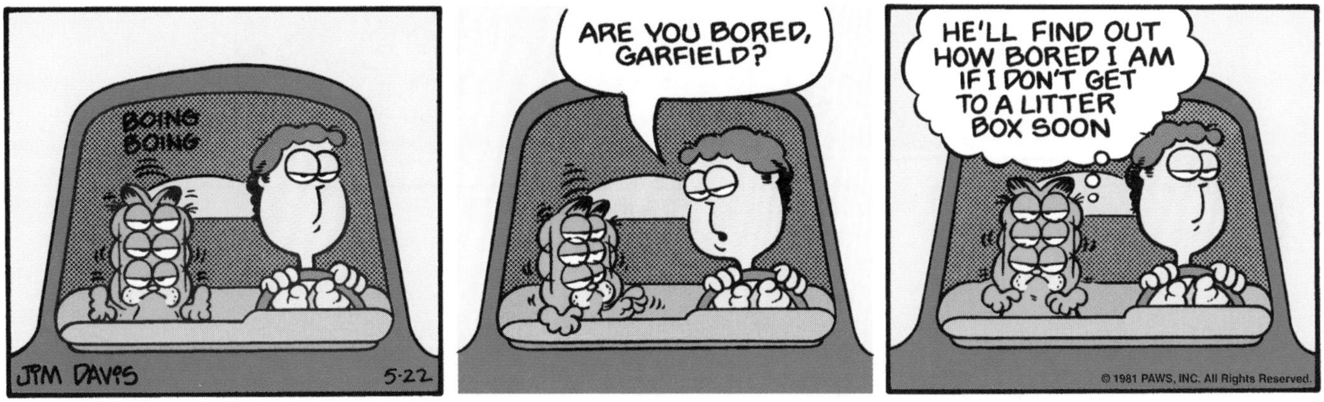
BOING BOING
JIM DAVIS
5-22
ARE YOU BORED, GARFIELD?
HE'LL FIND OUT HOW BORED I AM IF I DON'T GET TO A LITTER BOX SOON
© 1981 PAWS, INC. All Rights Reserved.

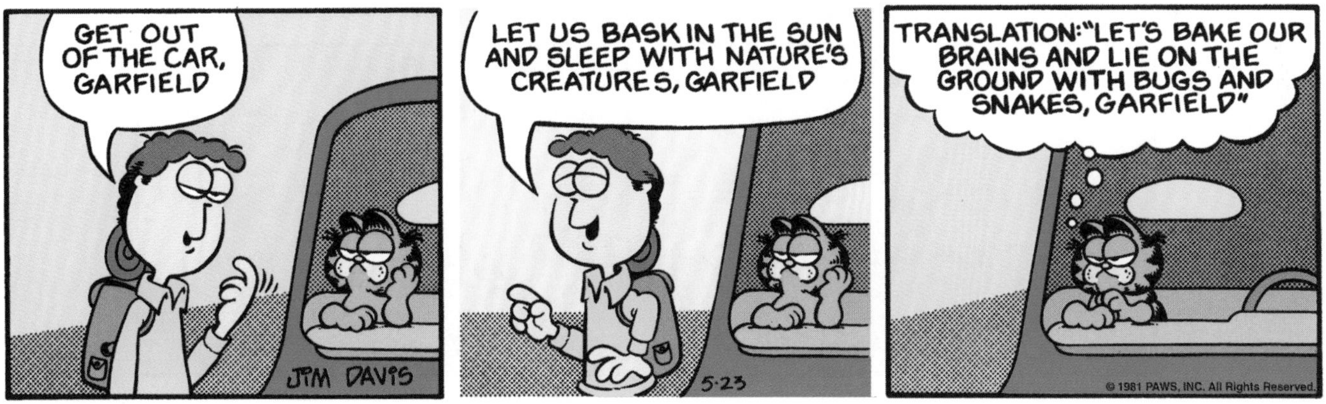
GET OUT OF THE CAR, GARFIELD
JIM DAVIS
LET US BASK IN THE SUN AND SLEEP WITH NATURE'S CREATURES, GARFIELD
5-23
TRANSLATION: "LET'S BAKE OUR BRAINS AND LIE ON THE GROUND WITH BUGS AND SNAKES, GARFIELD"
© 1981 PAWS, INC. All Rights Reserved.

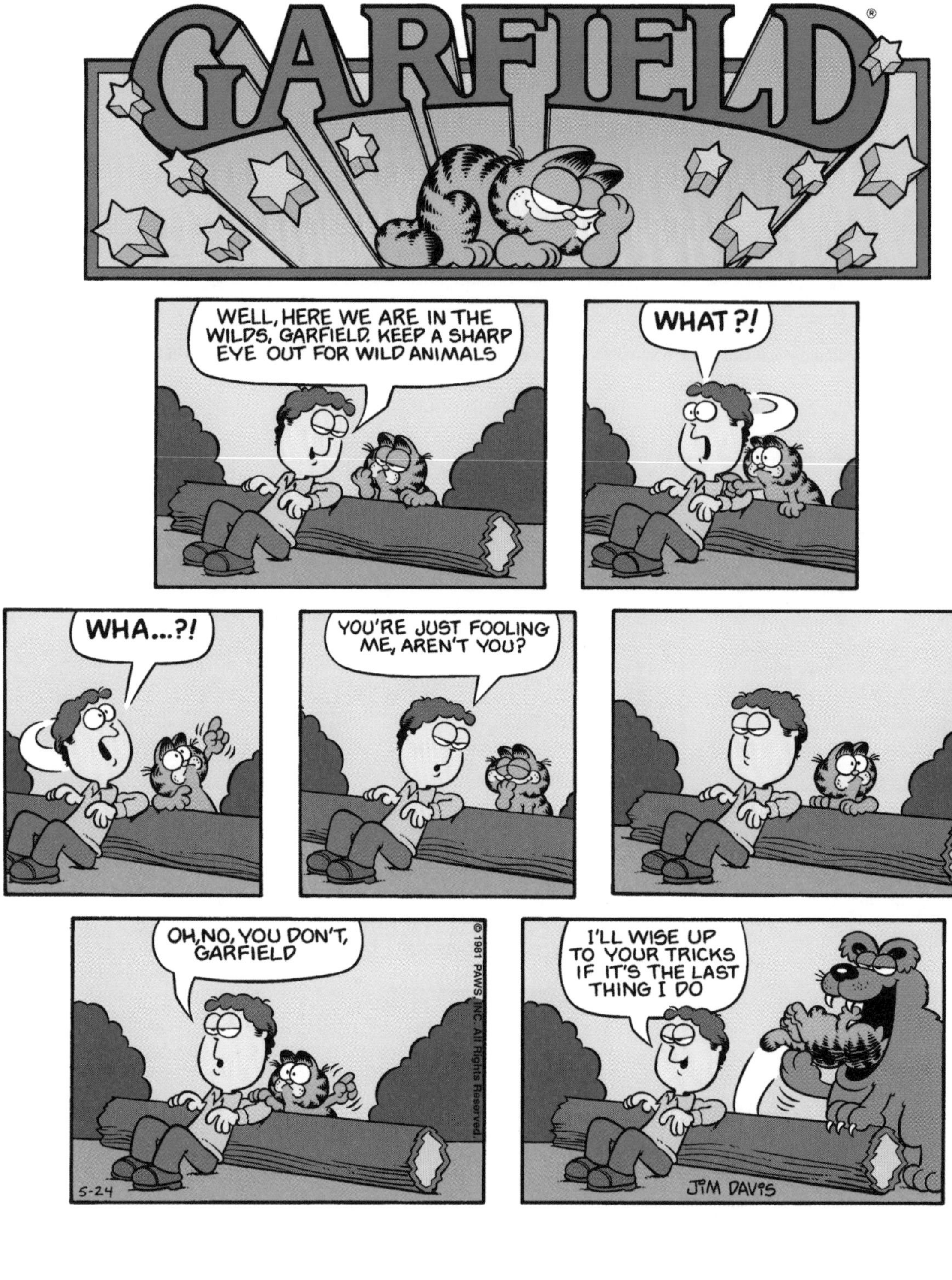
GARFIELD®
WELL, HERE WE ARE IN THE WILDS, GARFIELD. KEEP A SHARP EYE OUT FOR WILD ANIMALS
WHAT?!
WHA...?!
YOU'RE JUST FOOLING ME, AREN'T YOU?
OH, NO, YOU DON'T, GARFIELD
© 1981 PAWS, INC. All Rights Reserved.
5-24
I'LL WISE UP TO YOUR TRICKS IF IT'S THE LAST THING I DO
JIM DAVIS

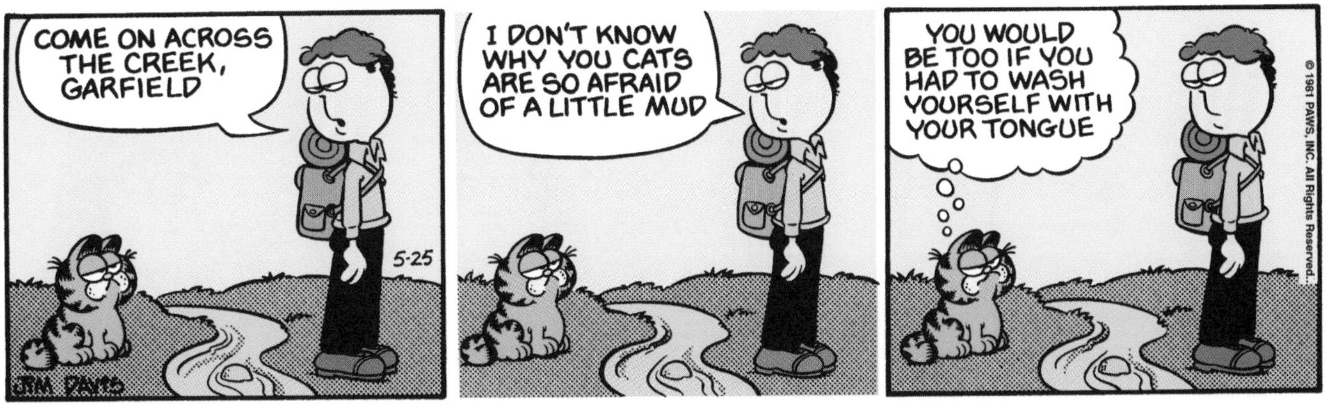
COME ON ACROSS THE CREEK, GARFIELD
JIM DAVIS
5-25
I DON'T KNOW WHY YOU CATS ARE SO AFRAID OF A LITTLE MUD
YOU WOULD BE TOO IF YOU HAD TO WASH YOURSELF WITH YOUR TONGUE
© 1981 PAWS, INC. All Rights Reserved.

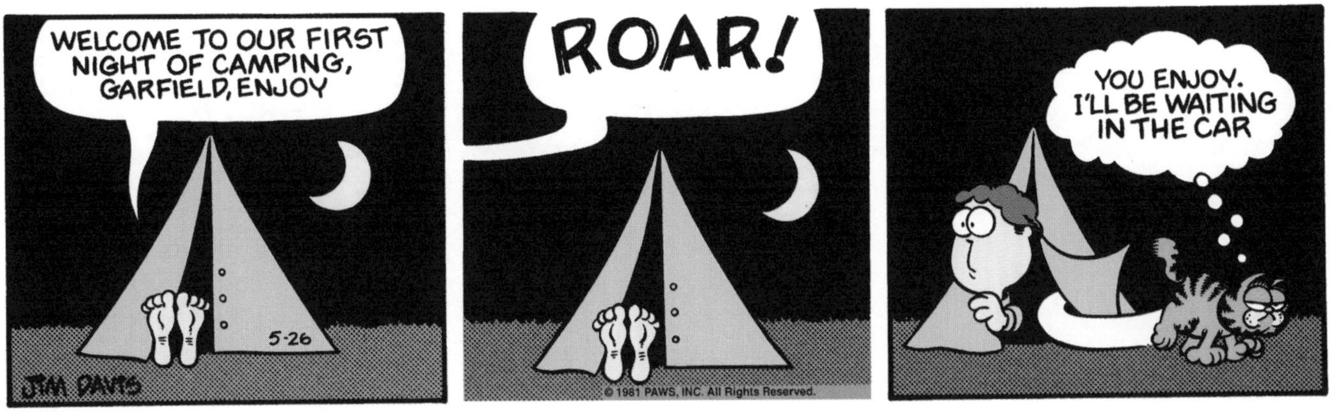
WELCOME TO OUR FIRST NIGHT OF CAMPING, GARFIELD, ENJOY
JIM DAVIS
5-26
ROAR!
© 1981 PAWS, INC. All Rights Reserved.
YOU ENJOY. I'LL BE WAITING IN THE CAR

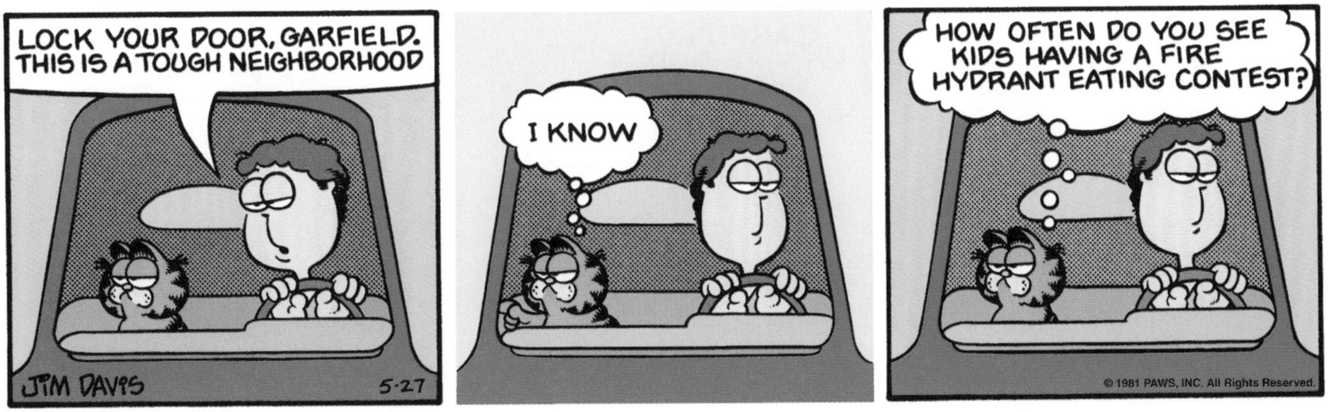
LOCK YOUR DOOR, GARFIELD. THIS IS A TOUGH NEIGHBORHOOD
JIM DAVIS
5-27
I KNOW
HOW OFTEN DO YOU SEE KIDS HAVING A FIRE HYDRANT EATING CONTEST?
© 1981 PAWS, INC. All Rights Reserved.

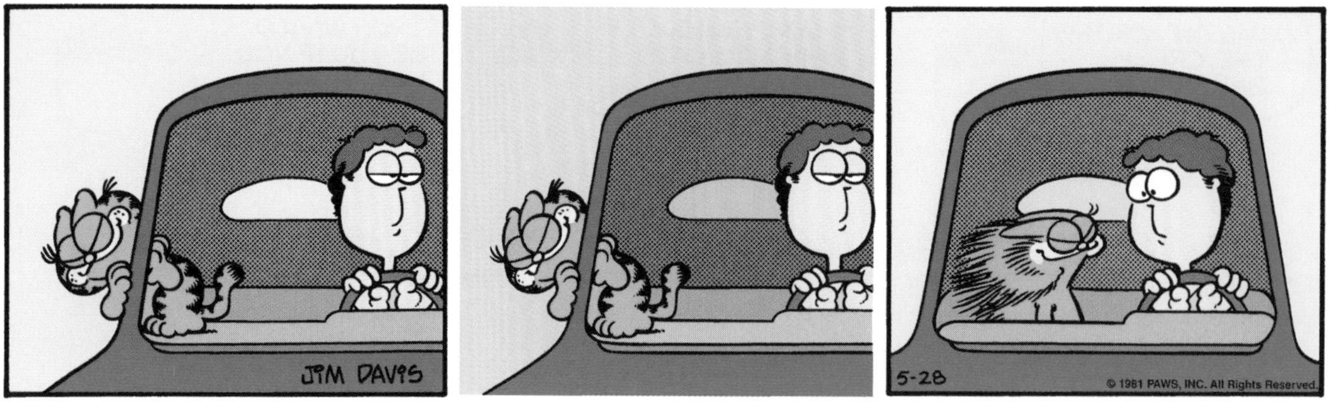
JIM DAVIS
5-28
© 1981 PAWS, INC. All Rights Reserved.

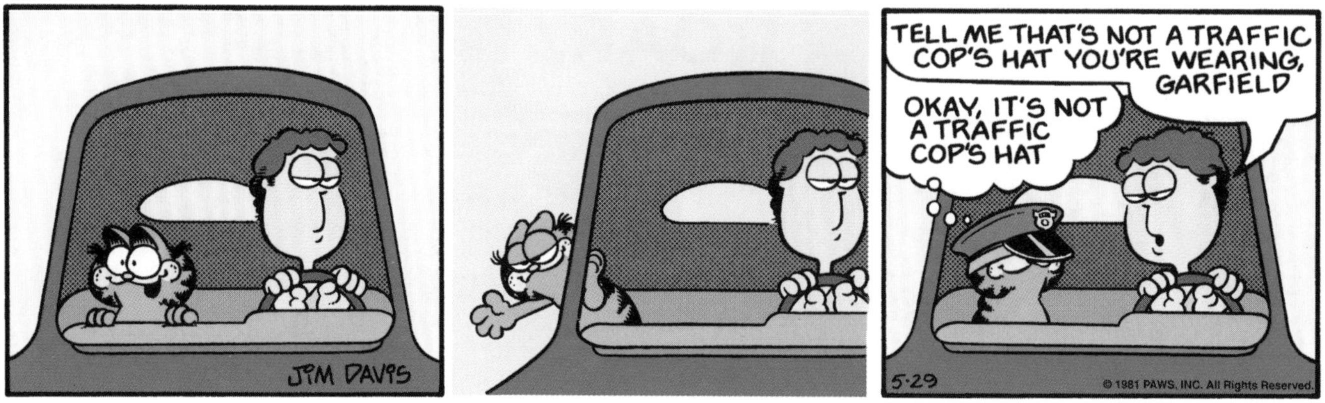
JIM DAVIS
TELL ME THAT'S NOT A TRAFFIC COP'S HAT YOU'RE WEARING, GARFIELD
OKAY, IT'S NOT A TRAFFIC COP'S HAT
5-29
© 1981 PAWS, INC. All Rights Reserved.

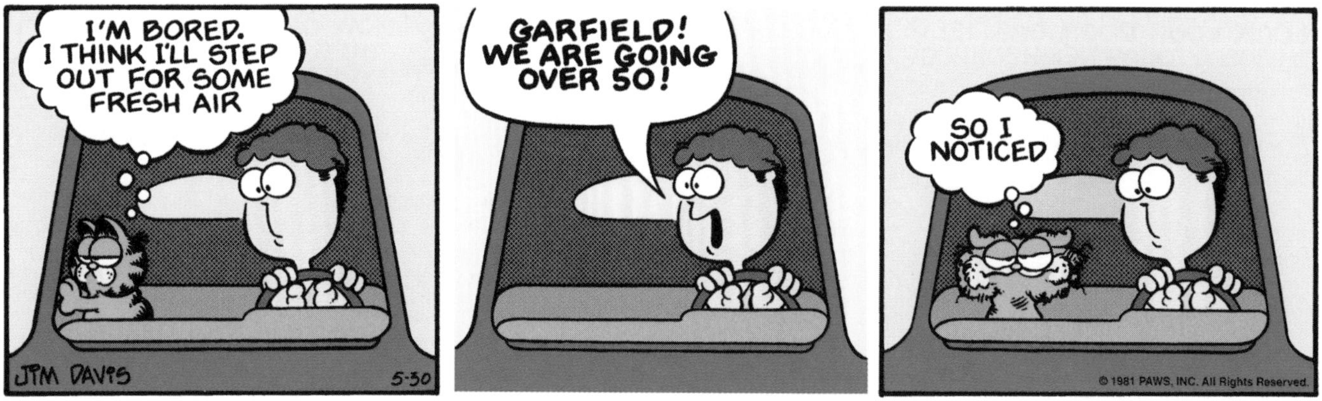
I'M BORED. I THINK I'LL STEP OUT FOR SOME FRESH AIR
JIM DAVIS
5-30
GARFIELD! WE ARE GOING OVER 50!
SO I NOTICED
© 1981 PAWS, INC. All Rights Reserved.

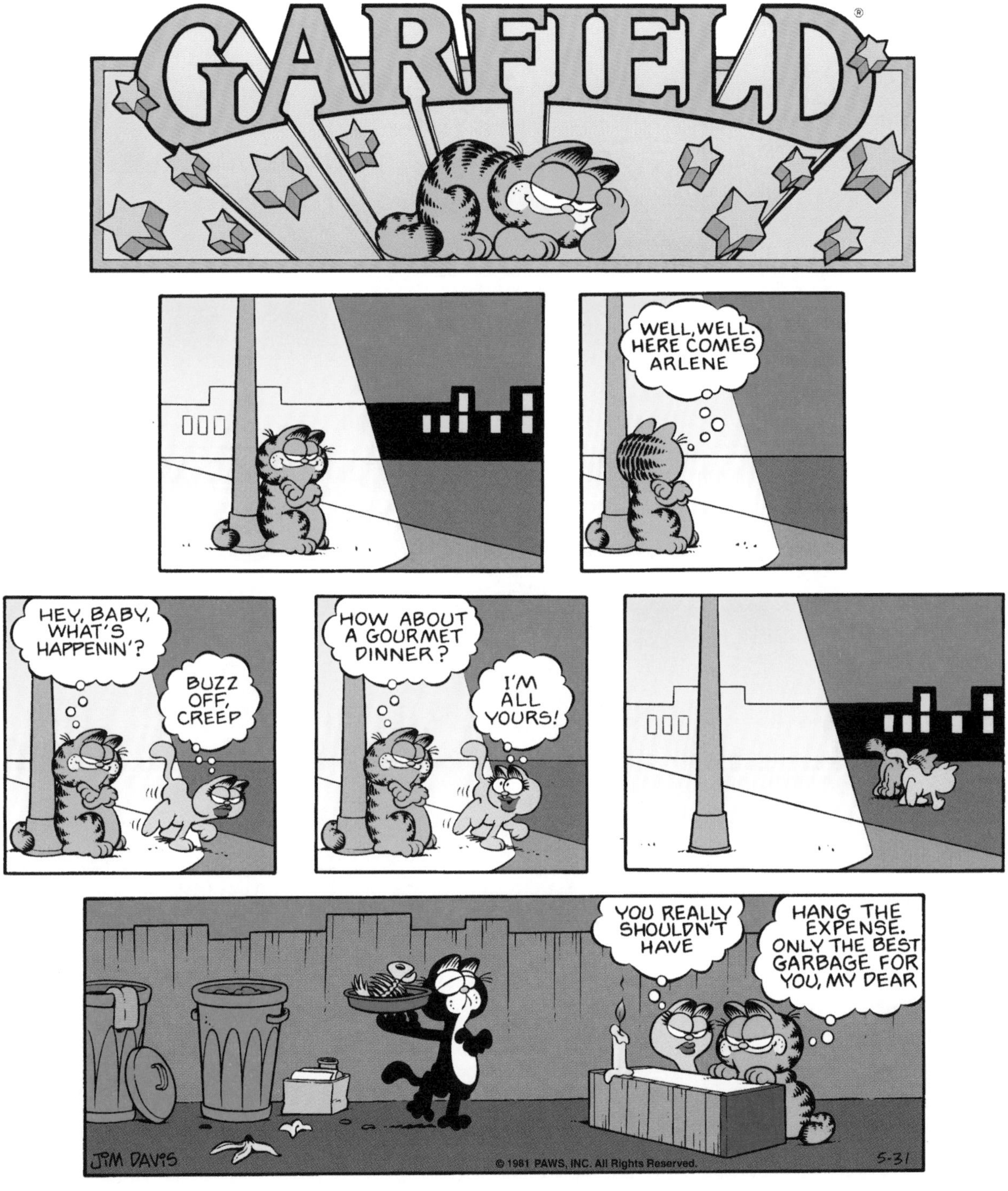
GARFIELD
WELL, WELL. HERE COMES ARLENE
HEY, BABY, WHAT'S HAPPENIN'?
BUZZ OFF, CREEP
HOW ABOUT A GOURMET DINNER?
I'M ALL YOURS!
YOU REALLY SHOULDN'T HAVE
HANG THE EXPENSE. ONLY THE BEST GARBAGE FOR YOU, MY DEAR
JIM DAVIS
© 1981 PAWS, INC. All Rights Reserved.
5-31

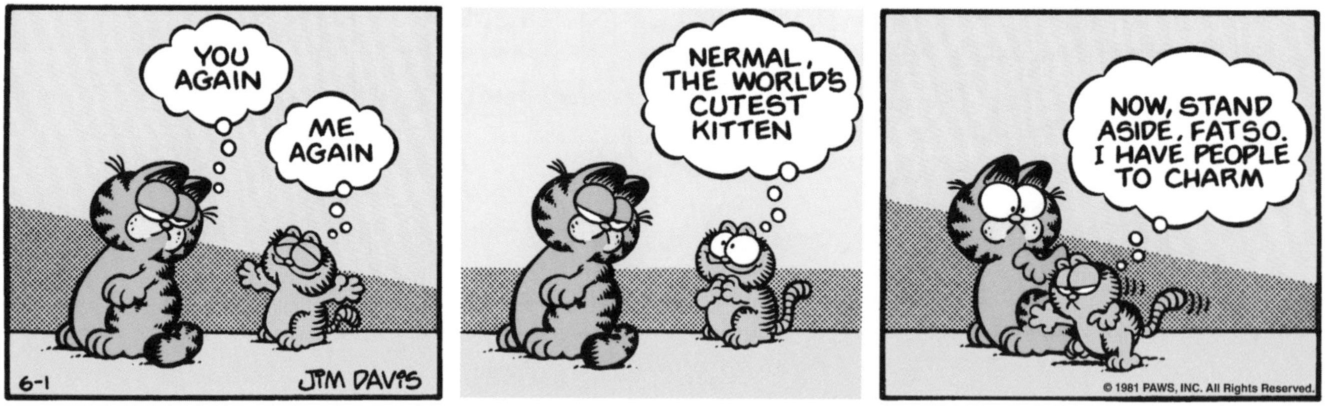
YOU AGAIN
ME AGAIN
6-1
JIM DAVIS
NERMAL, THE WORLD'S CUTEST KITTEN
NOW, STAND ASIDE, FATSO. I HAVE PEOPLE TO CHARM
© 1981 PAWS, INC. All Rights Reserved.

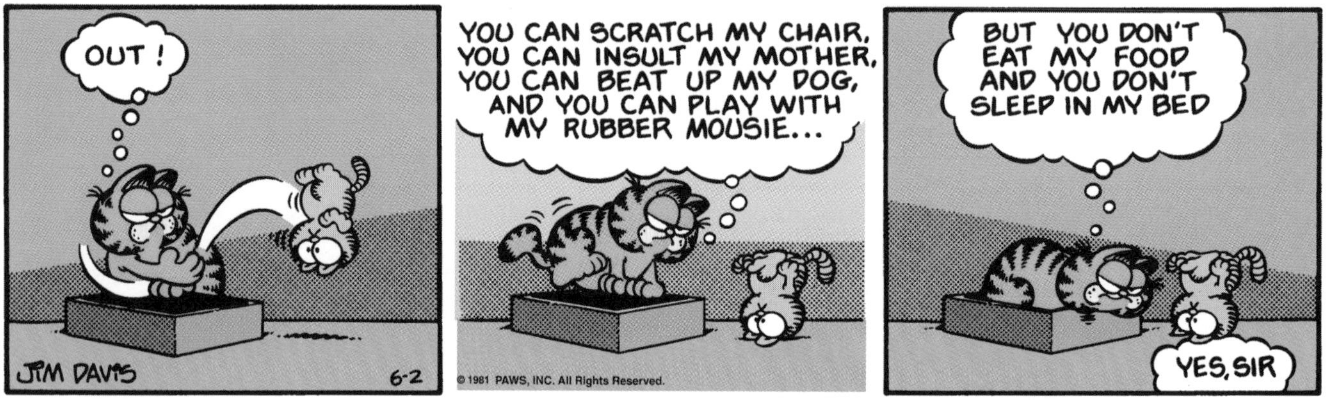
OUT !
JIM DAVIS
6-2
YOU CAN SCRATCH MY CHAIR, YOU CAN INSULT MY MOTHER, YOU CAN BEAT UP MY DOG, AND YOU CAN PLAY WITH MY RUBBER MOUSIE...
© 1981 PAWS, INC. All Rights Reserved.
BUT YOU DON'T EAT MY FOOD AND YOU DON'T SLEEP IN MY BED
YES, SIR

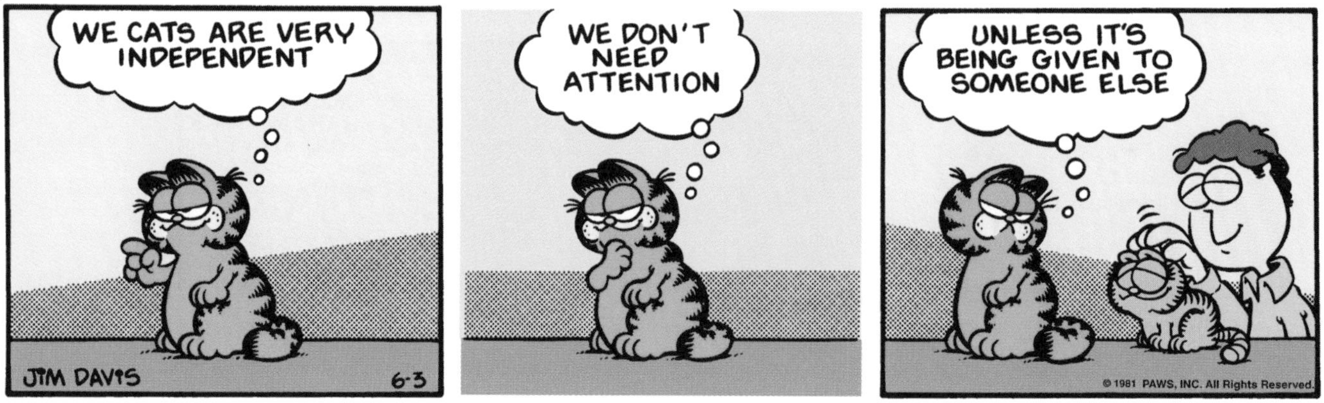
WE CATS ARE VERY INDEPENDENT
JIM DAVIS
6-3
WE DON'T NEED ATTENTION
UNLESS IT'S BEING GIVEN TO SOMEONE ELSE
© 1981 PAWS, INC. All Rights Reserved.

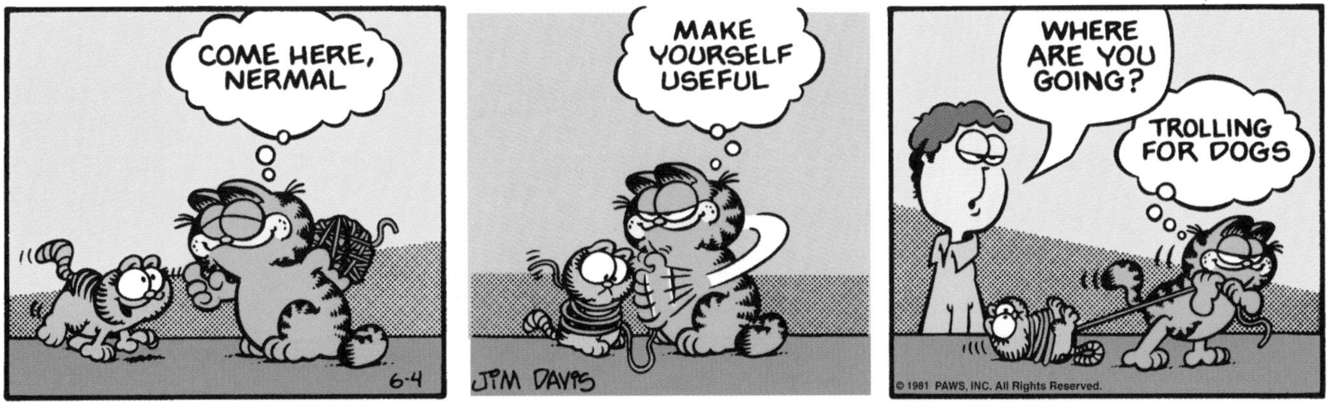
COME HERE, NERMAL
6-4
MAKE YOURSELF USEFUL
JIM DAVIS
WHERE ARE YOU GOING?
TROLLING FOR DOGS
© 1981 PAWS, INC. All Rights Reserved.

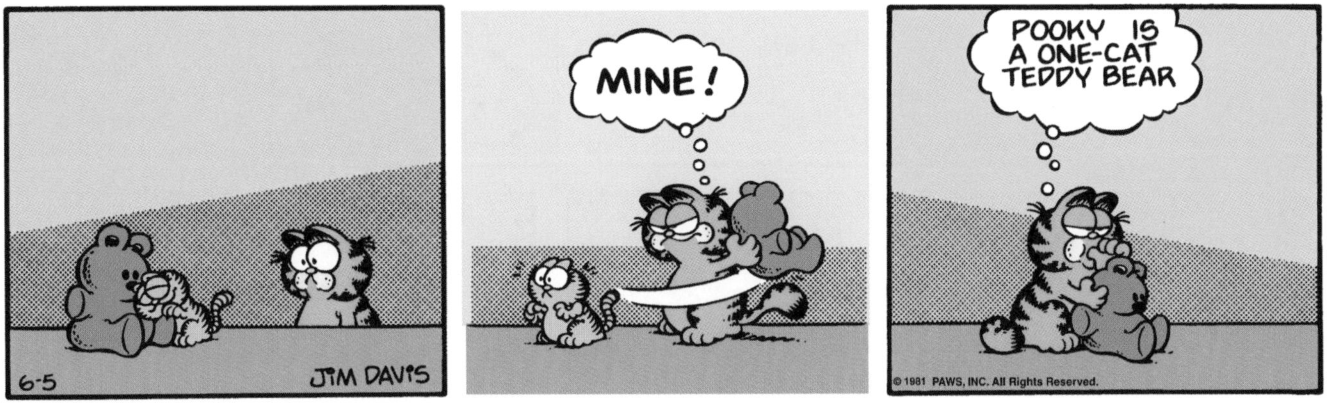
6-5
JIM DAVIS
MINE!
POOKY IS A ONE-CAT TEDDY BEAR
© 1981 PAWS, INC. All Rights Reserved.

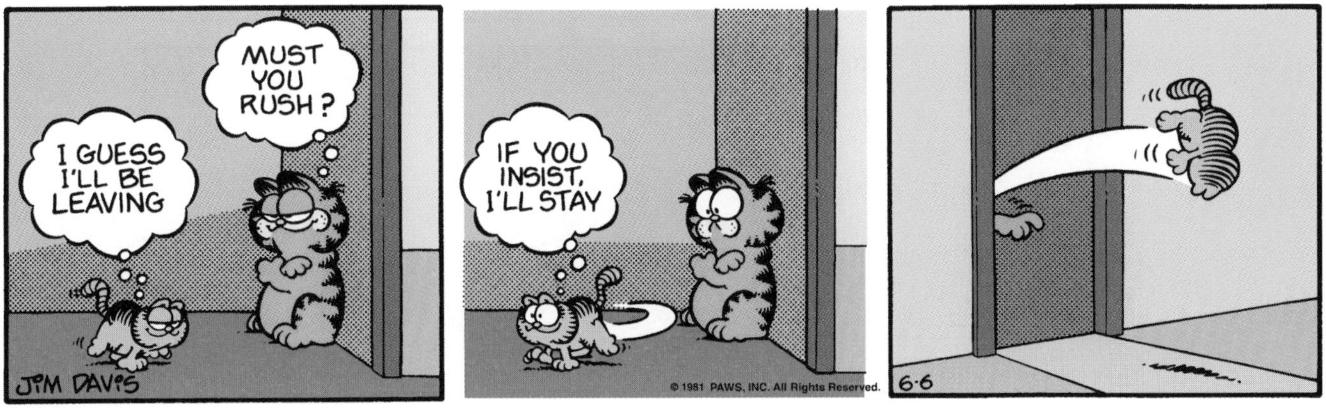
MUST YOU RUSH?
I GUESS I'LL BE LEAVING
JIM DAVIS
IF YOU INSIST, I'LL STAY
© 1981 PAWS, INC. All Rights Reserved.
6-6

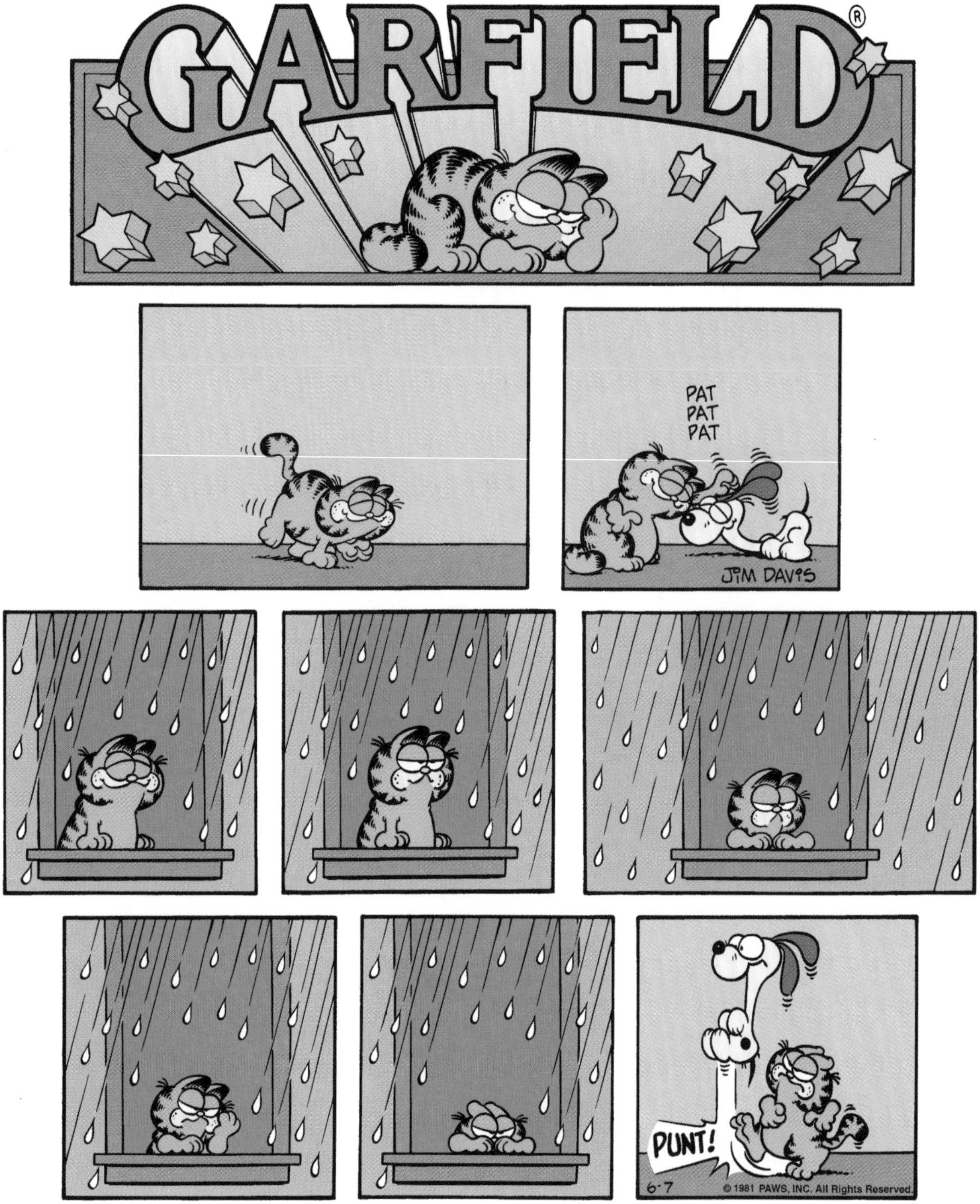
GARFIELD®
PAT
PAT
PAT
JIM DAVIS
PUNT!
6-7
© 1981 PAWS, INC. All Rights Reserved.

Garfield
eats his heart out

BY JIM DAVIS

Ballantine Books • **New York**

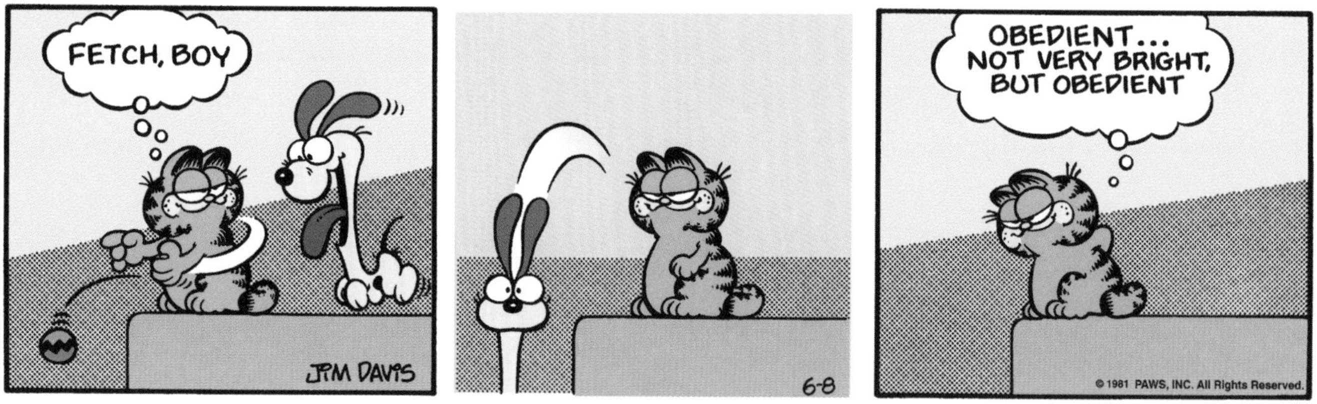
FETCH, BOY
JIM DAVIS
6-8
OBEDIENT... NOT VERY BRIGHT, BUT OBEDIENT
© 1981 PAWS, INC. All Rights Reserved.

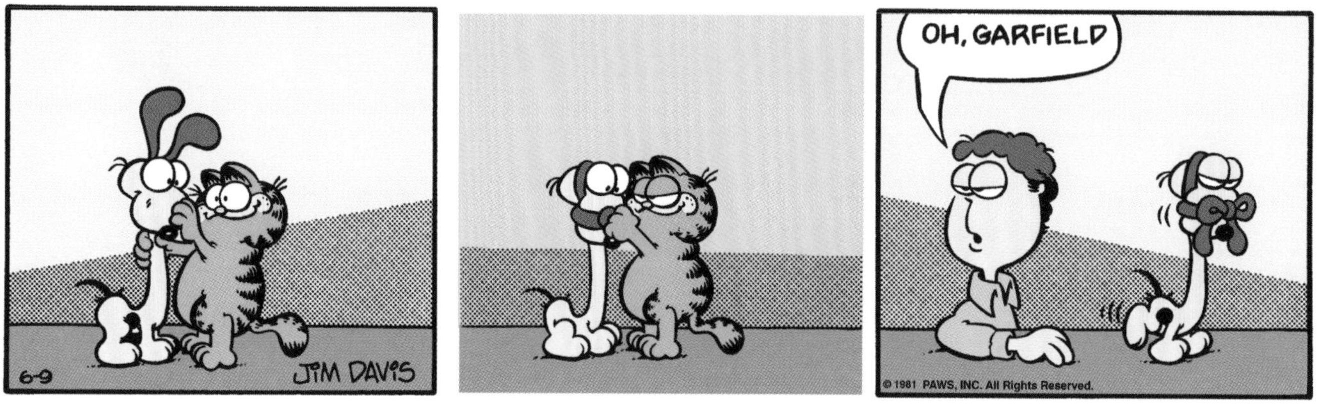
6-9
JIM DAVIS
OH, GARFIELD
© 1981 PAWS, INC. All Rights Reserved.

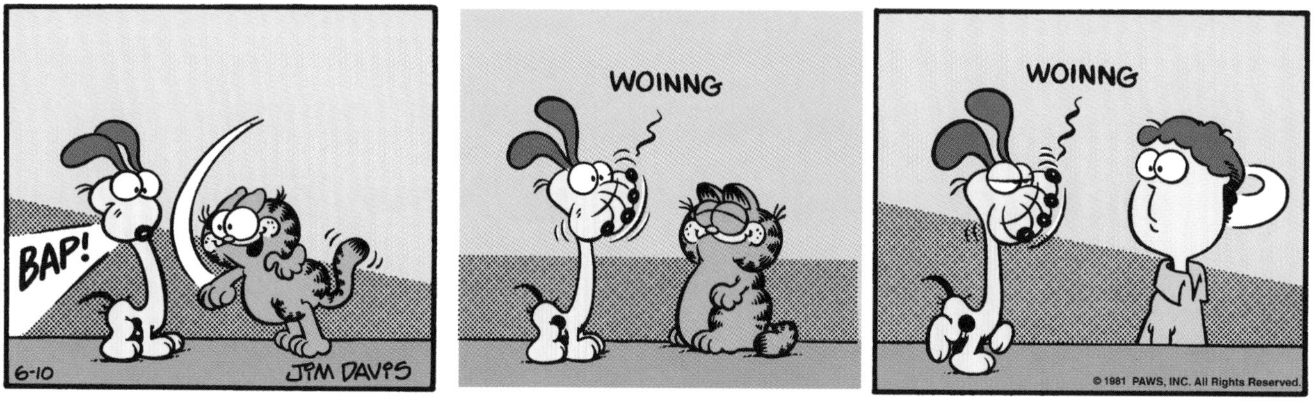
BAP!
6-10
JIM DAVIS
WOINNG
WOINNG
© 1981 PAWS, INC. All Rights Reserved.

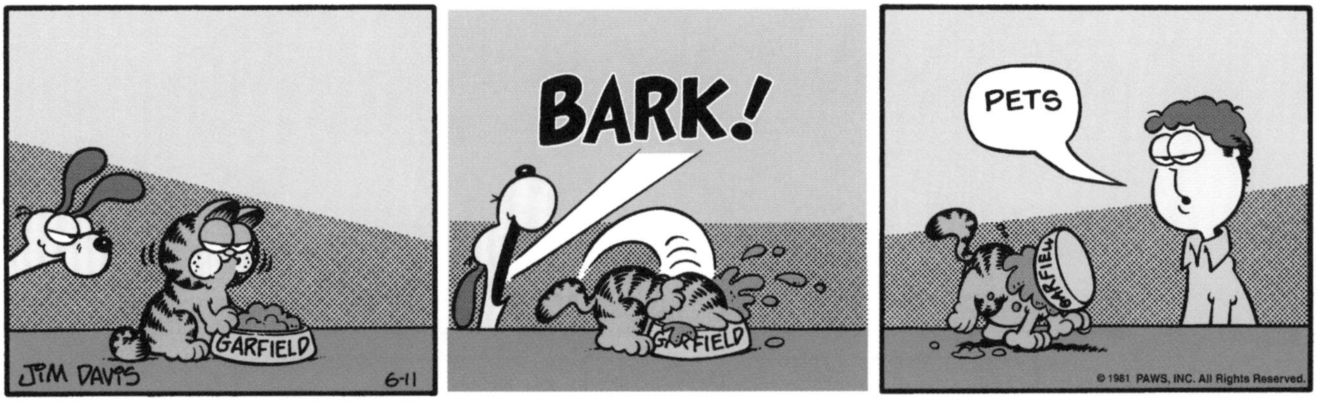
JIM DAVIS
6-11
BARK!
GARFIELD
PETS
© 1981 PAWS, INC. All Rights Reserved.

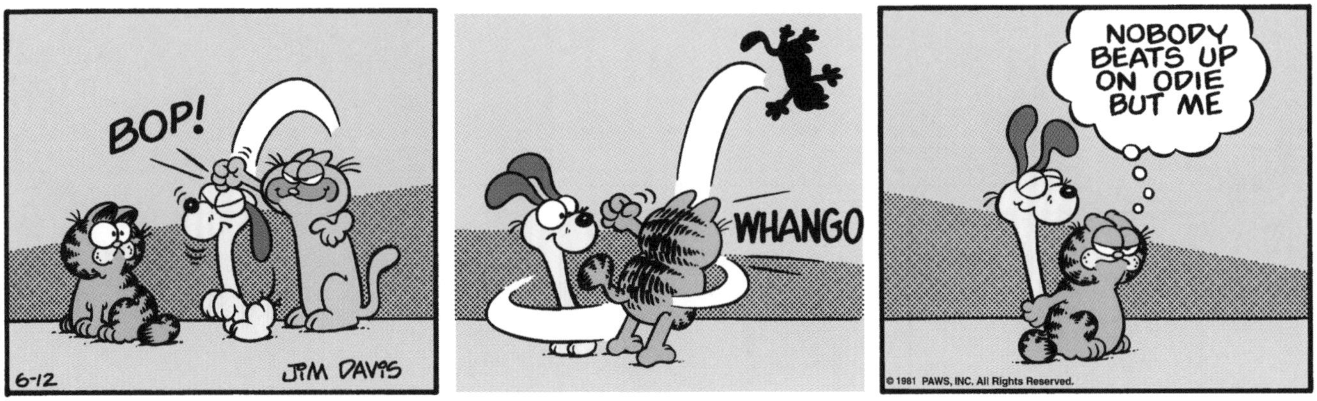
BOP!
6-12
JIM DAVIS
WHANGO
NOBODY BEATS UP ON ODIE BUT ME
© 1981 PAWS, INC. All Rights Reserved.

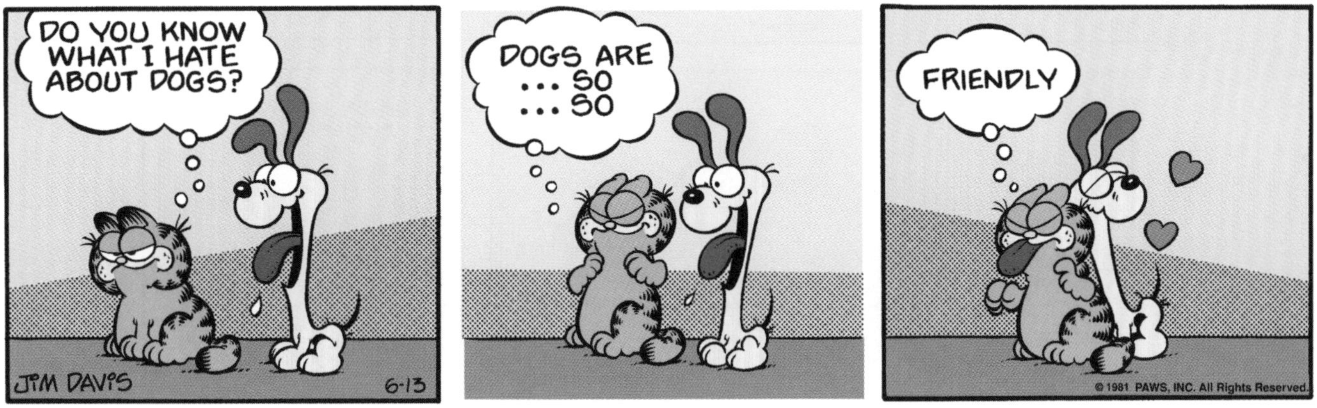
DO YOU KNOW WHAT I HATE ABOUT DOGS?
JIM DAVIS
6-13
DOGS ARE
... SO
... SO
FRIENDLY
© 1981 PAWS, INC. All Rights Reserved.

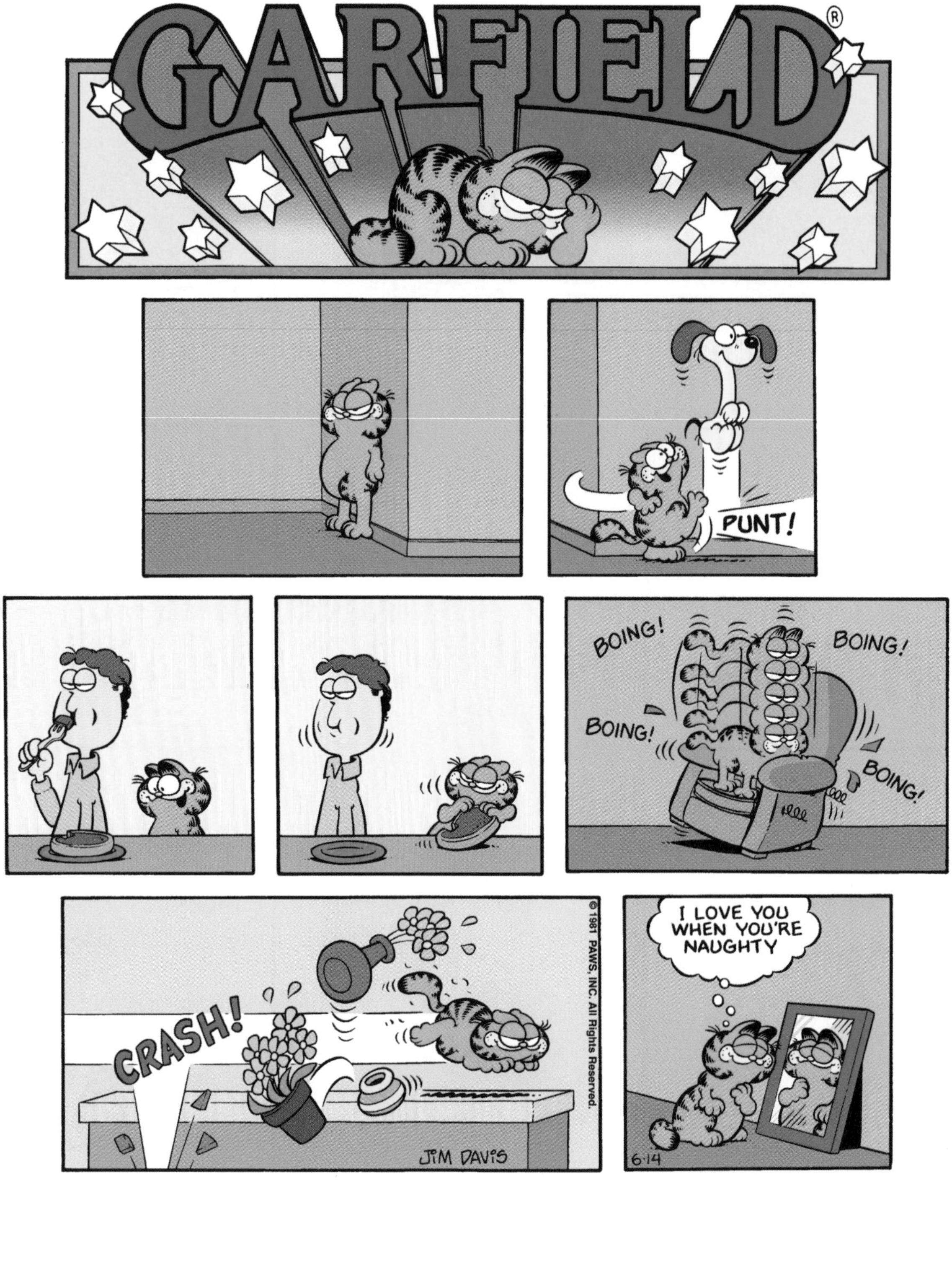
GARFIELD®
PUNT!
BOING!
BOING!
BOING!
BOING!
CRASH!
© 1981 PAWS, INC. All Rights Reserved.
JIM DAVIS
I LOVE YOU WHEN YOU'RE NAUGHTY
6·14

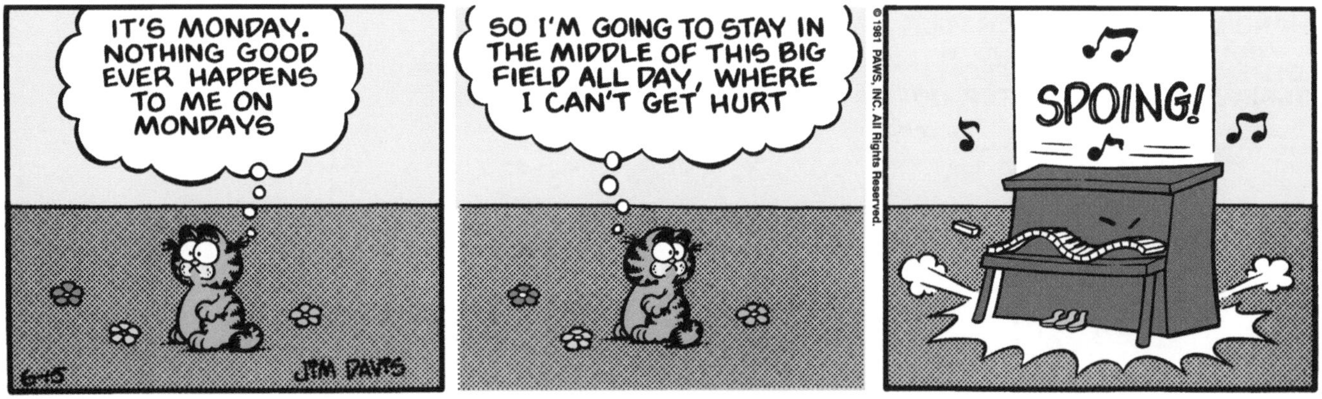
IT'S MONDAY. NOTHING GOOD EVER HAPPENS TO ME ON MONDAYS
6-15
JIM DAVIS
SO I'M GOING TO STAY IN THE MIDDLE OF THIS BIG FIELD ALL DAY, WHERE I CAN'T GET HURT
© 1981 PAWS, INC. All Rights Reserved.
SPOING!

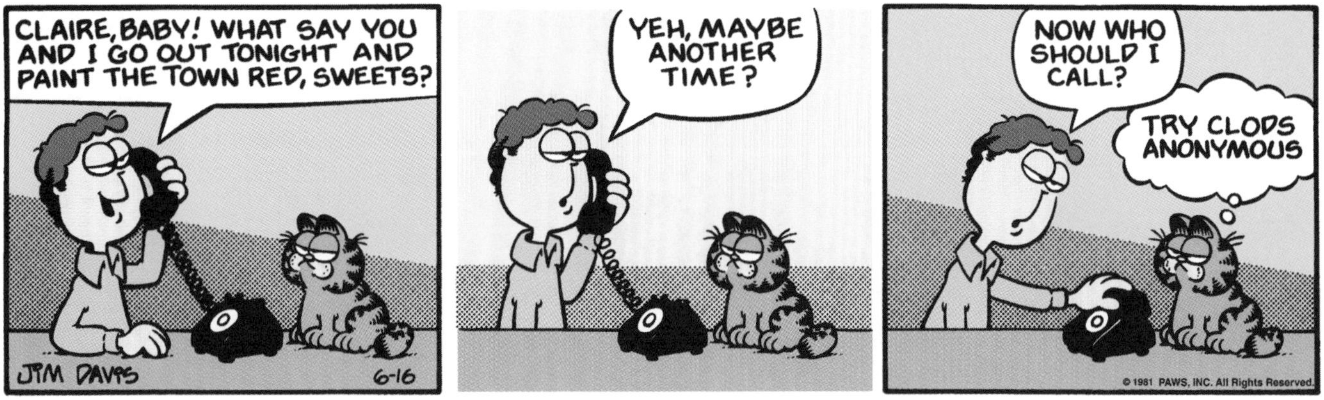
CLAIRE, BABY! WHAT SAY YOU AND I GO OUT TONIGHT AND PAINT THE TOWN RED, SWEETS?
JIM DAVIS
6-16
YEH, MAYBE ANOTHER TIME?
NOW WHO SHOULD I CALL?
TRY CLODS ANONYMOUS
© 1981 PAWS, INC. All Rights Reserved.

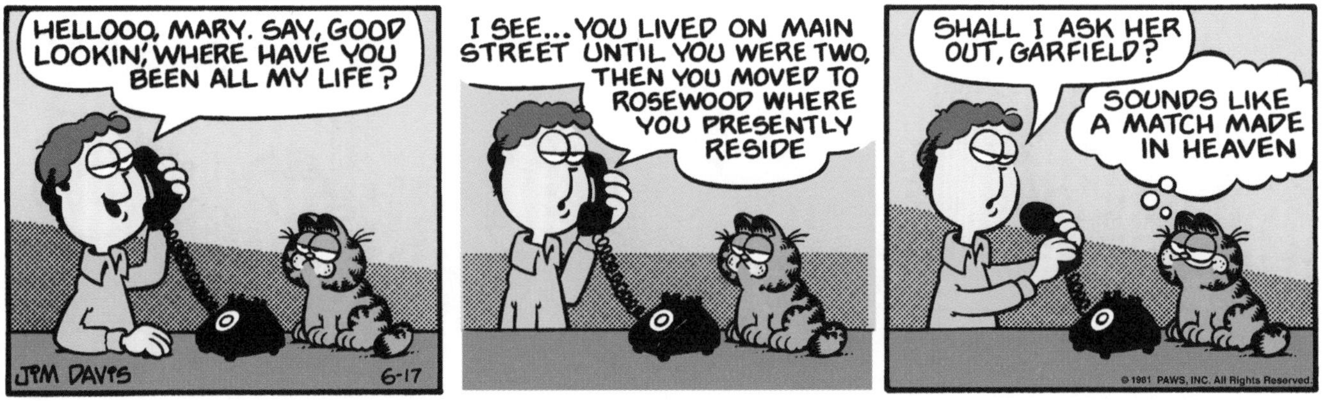
HELLOOO, MARY. SAY, GOOD LOOKIN', WHERE HAVE YOU BEEN ALL MY LIFE?
JIM DAVIS
6-17
I SEE... YOU LIVED ON MAIN STREET UNTIL YOU WERE TWO, THEN YOU MOVED TO ROSEWOOD WHERE YOU PRESENTLY RESIDE
SHALL I ASK HER OUT, GARFIELD?
SOUNDS LIKE A MATCH MADE IN HEAVEN
© 1981 PAWS, INC. All Rights Reserved.

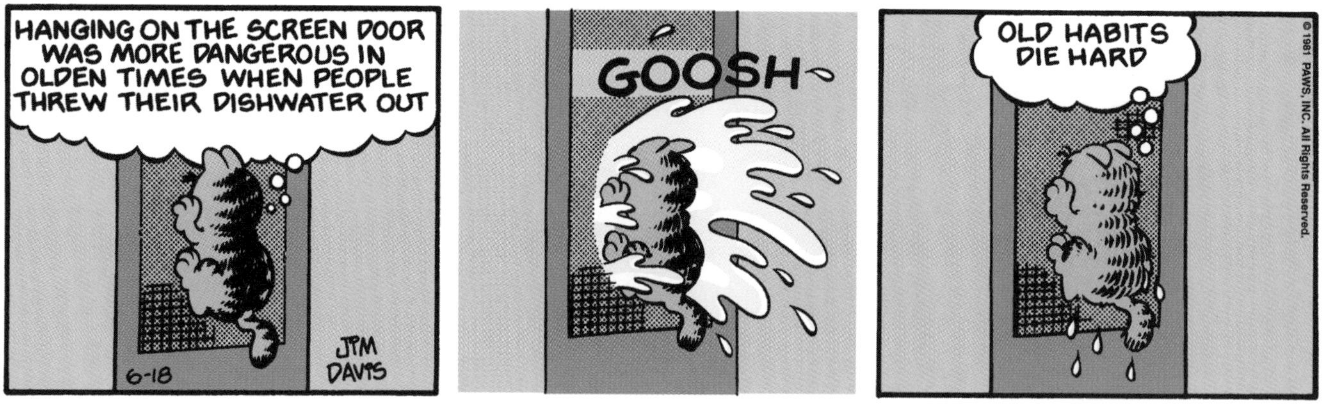
HANGING ON THE SCREEN DOOR WAS MORE DANGEROUS IN OLDEN TIMES WHEN PEOPLE THREW THEIR DISHWATER OUT
6-18
JIM DAVIS
GOOSH
OLD HABITS DIE HARD
© 1981 PAWS, INC. All Rights Reserved.

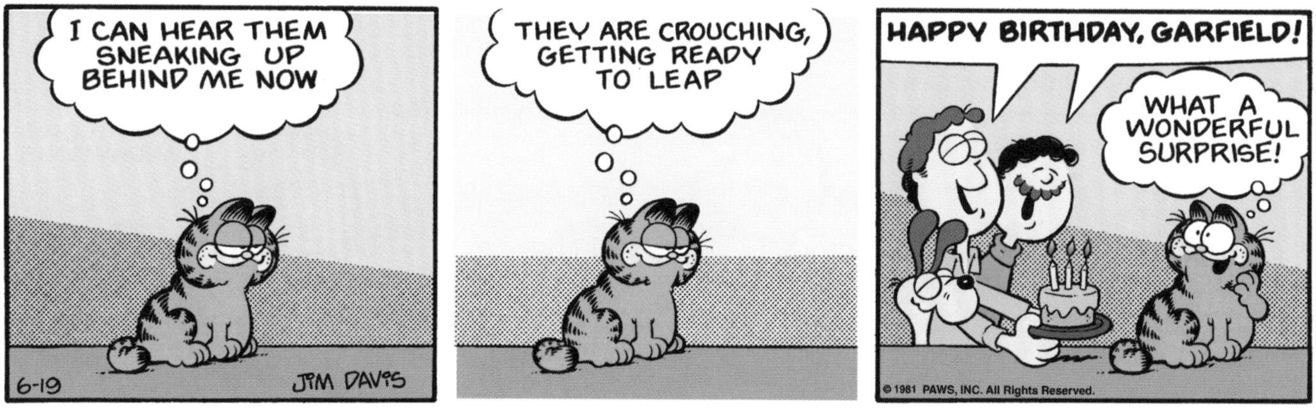
I CAN HEAR THEM SNEAKING UP BEHIND ME NOW
6-19
JIM DAVIS
THEY ARE CROUCHING, GETTING READY TO LEAP
HAPPY BIRTHDAY, GARFIELD!
WHAT A WONDERFUL SURPRISE!
© 1981 PAWS, INC. All Rights Reserved.

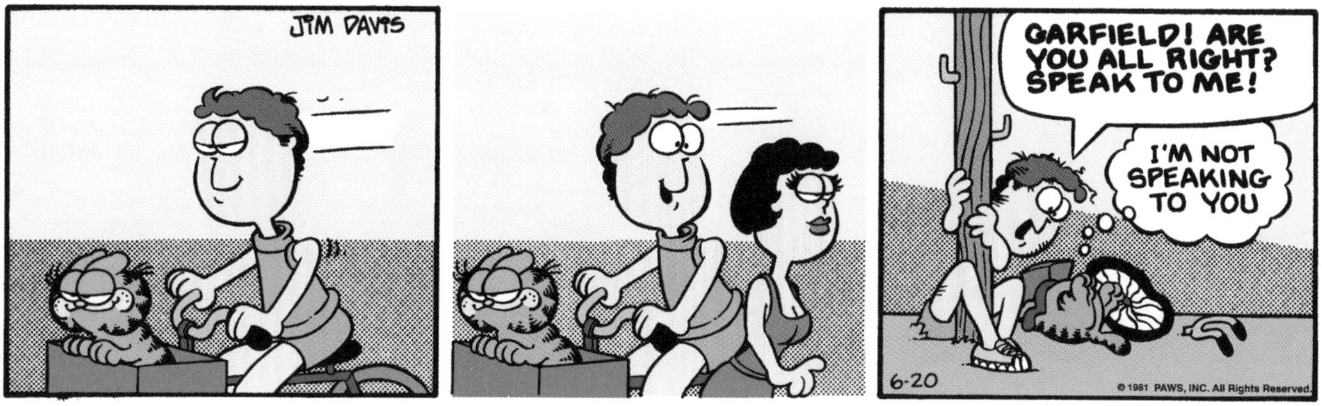
JIM DAVIS
GARFIELD! ARE YOU ALL RIGHT? SPEAK TO ME!
I'M NOT SPEAKING TO YOU
6-20
© 1981 PAWS, INC. All Rights Reserved.

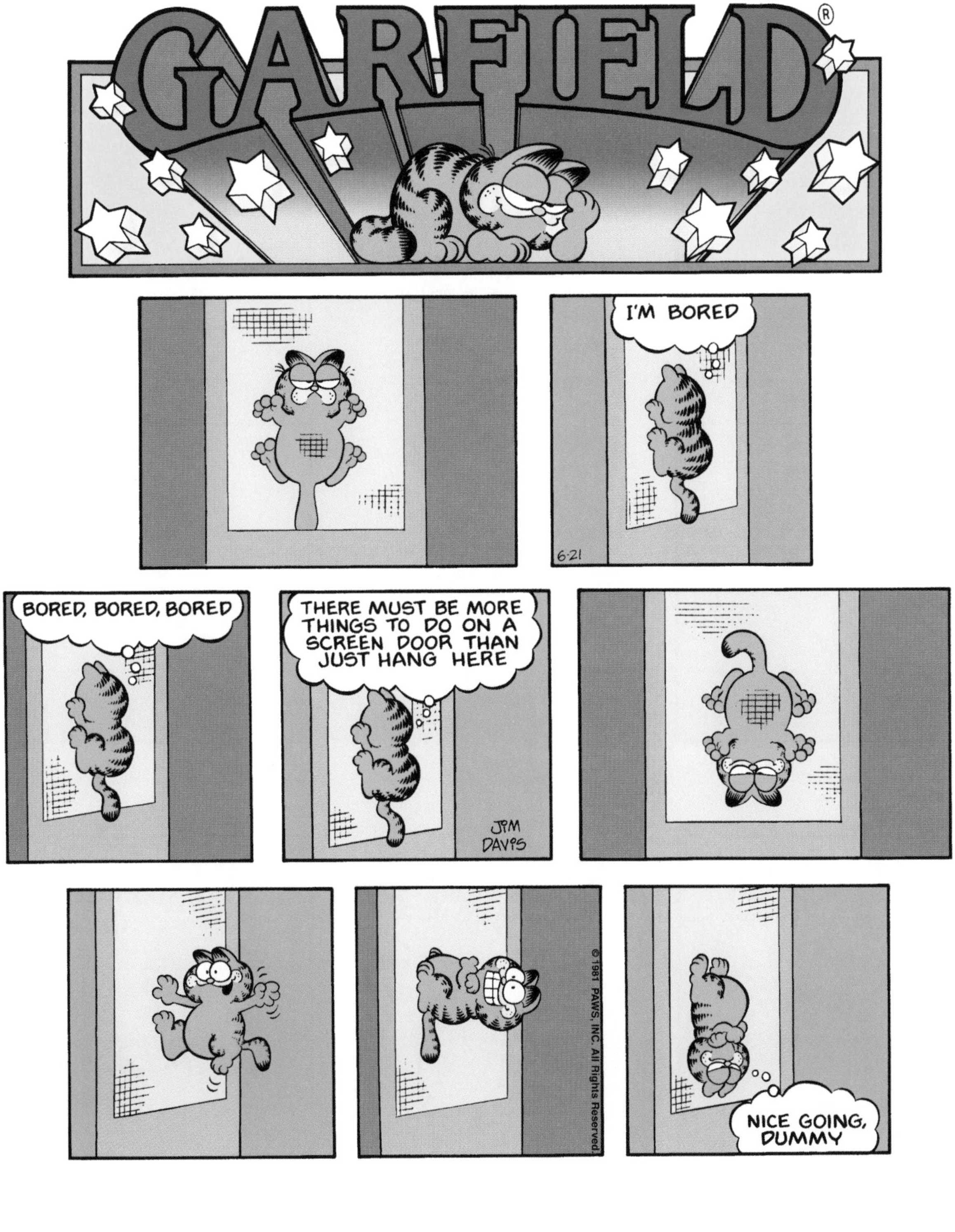
GARFIELD®
6·21
I'M BORED
BORED, BORED, BORED
THERE MUST BE MORE THINGS TO DO ON A SCREEN DOOR THAN JUST HANG HERE
JIM DAVIS
© 1981 PAWS, INC. All Rights Reserved
NICE GOING, DUMMY

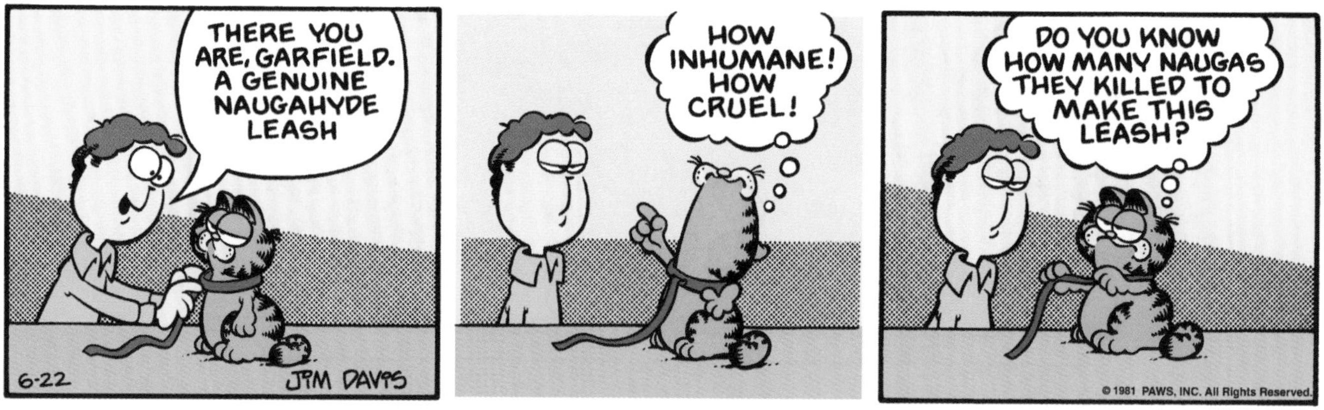
THERE YOU ARE, GARFIELD. A GENUINE NAUGAHYDE LEASH
HOW INHUMANE! HOW CRUEL!
DO YOU KNOW HOW MANY NAUGAS THEY KILLED TO MAKE THIS LEASH?
6-22
JIM DAVIS
© 1981 PAWS, INC. All Rights Reserved.

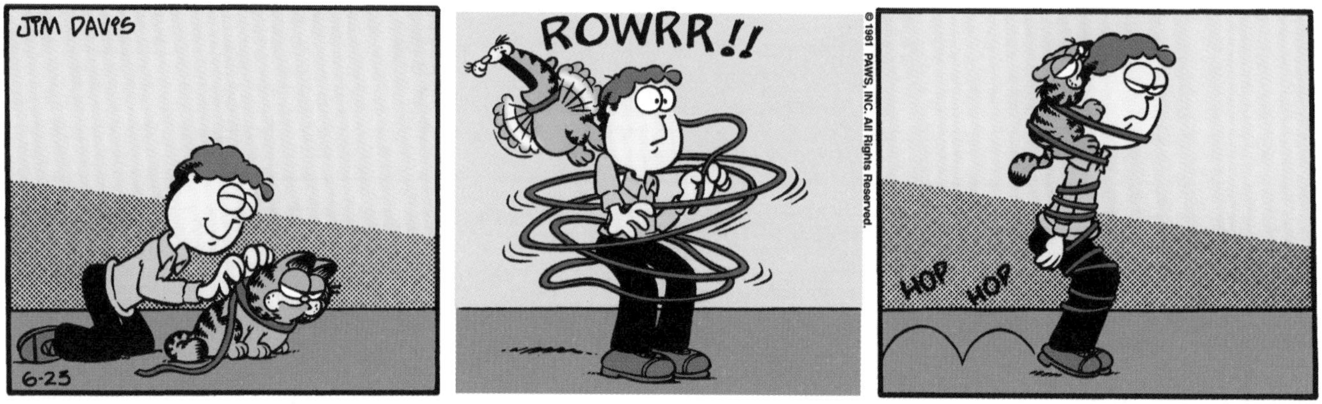
JIM DAVIS
6-23
ROWRR!!
© 1981 PAWS, INC. All Rights Reserved.
HOP
HOP

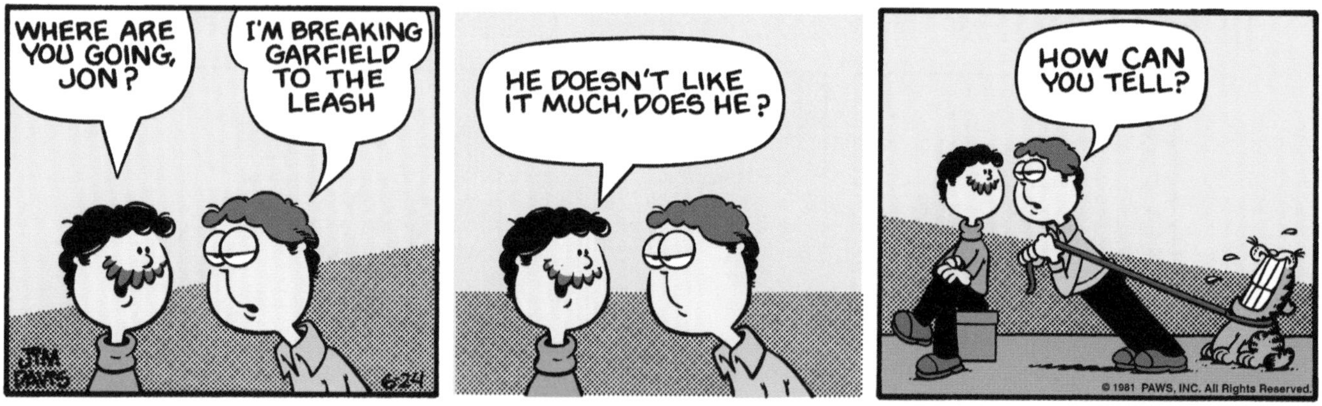
WHERE ARE YOU GOING, JON?
I'M BREAKING GARFIELD TO THE LEASH
JIM DAVIS
6-24
HE DOESN'T LIKE IT MUCH, DOES HE?
HOW CAN YOU TELL?
© 1981 PAWS, INC. All Rights Reserved.

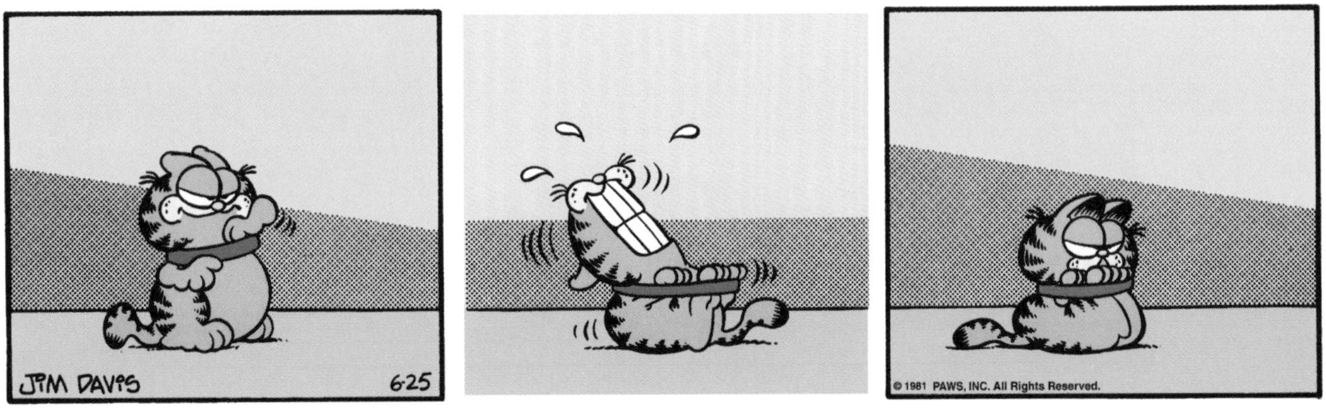
JIM DAVIS
6-25
© 1981 PAWS, INC. All Rights Reserved.

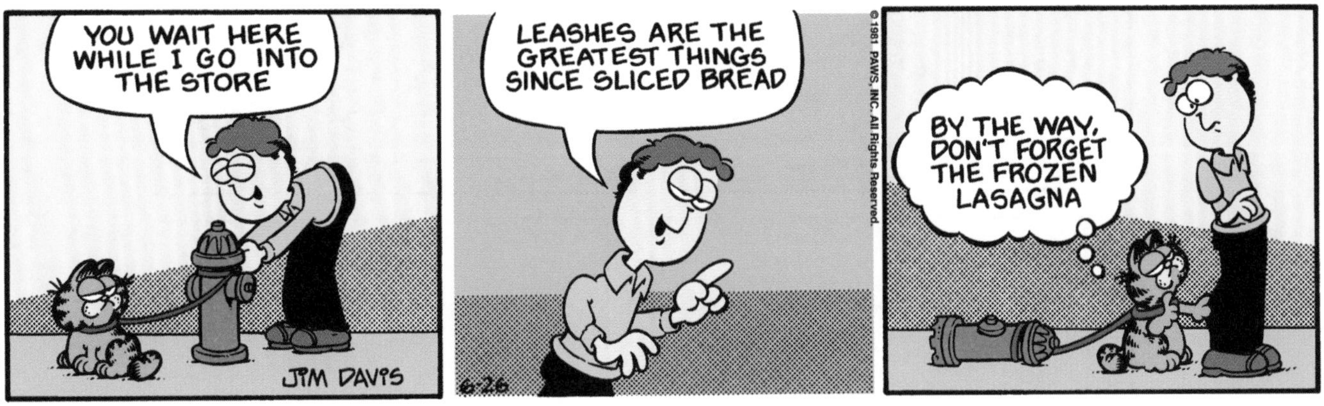
YOU WAIT HERE WHILE I GO INTO THE STORE
JIM DAVIS
LEASHES ARE THE GREATEST THINGS SINCE SLICED BREAD
6-26
© 1981 PAWS, INC. All Rights Reserved.
BY THE WAY, DON'T FORGET THE FROZEN LASAGNA

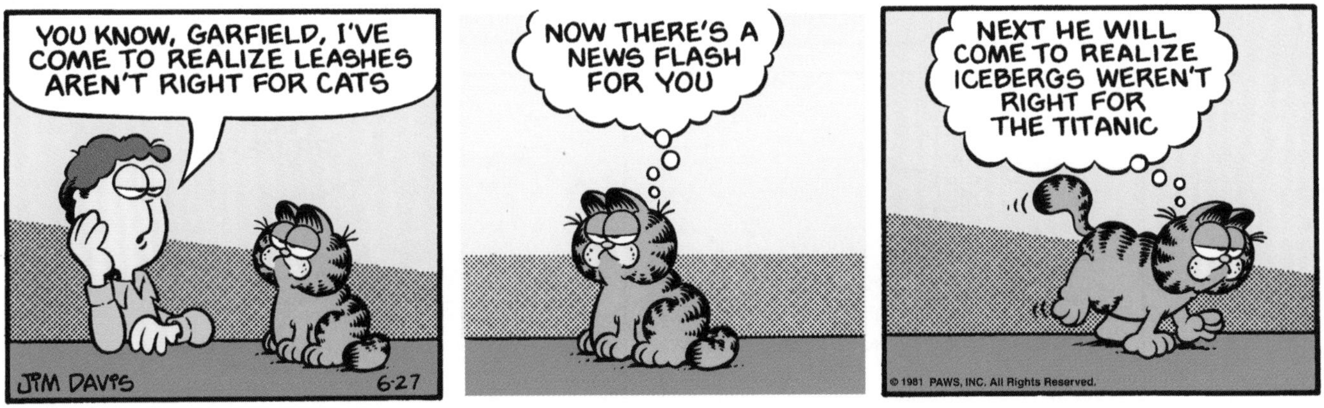
YOU KNOW, GARFIELD, I'VE COME TO REALIZE LEASHES AREN'T RIGHT FOR CATS
JIM DAVIS
6-27
NOW THERE'S A NEWS FLASH FOR YOU
NEXT HE WILL COME TO REALIZE ICEBERGS WEREN'T RIGHT FOR THE TITANIC
© 1981 PAWS, INC. All Rights Reserved.

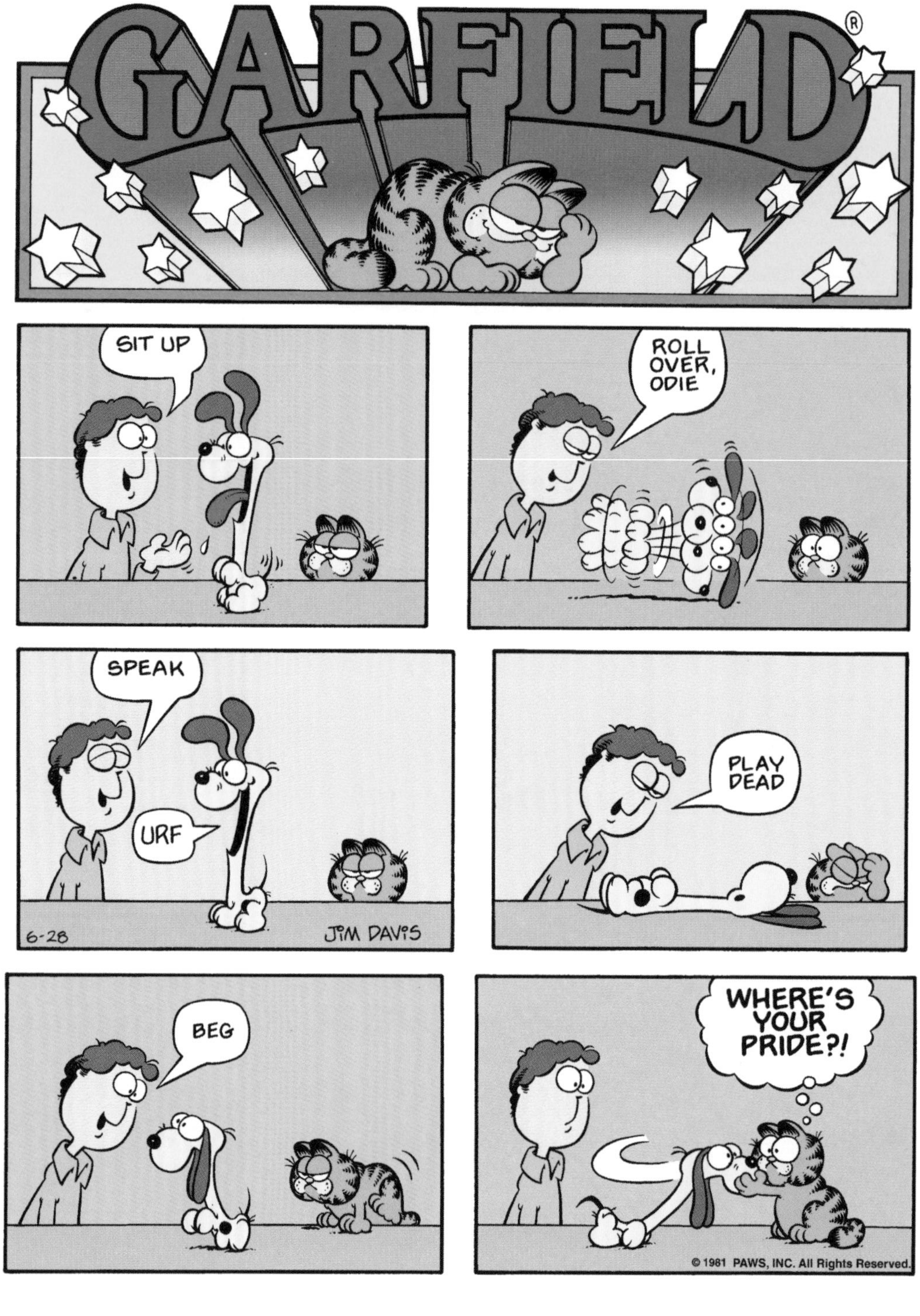
GARFIELD®
SIT UP
ROLL OVER, ODIE
SPEAK
URF
6-28
JIM DAVIS
PLAY DEAD
BEG
WHERE'S YOUR PRIDE?!
© 1981 PAWS, INC. All Rights Reserved.

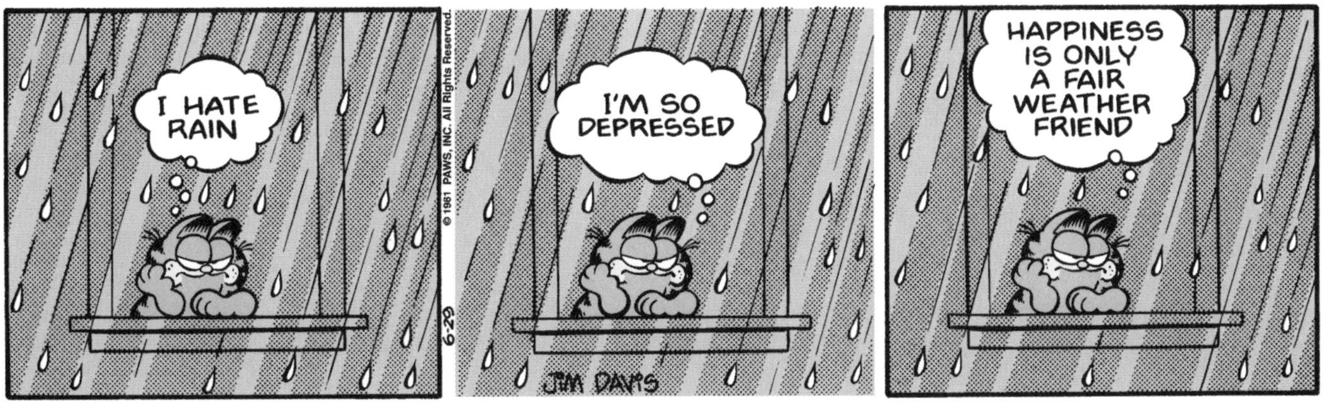
I HATE RAIN
© 1981 PAWS, INC. All Rights Reserved.
6-29
I'M SO DEPRESSED
JIM DAVIS
HAPPINESS IS ONLY A FAIR WEATHER FRIEND

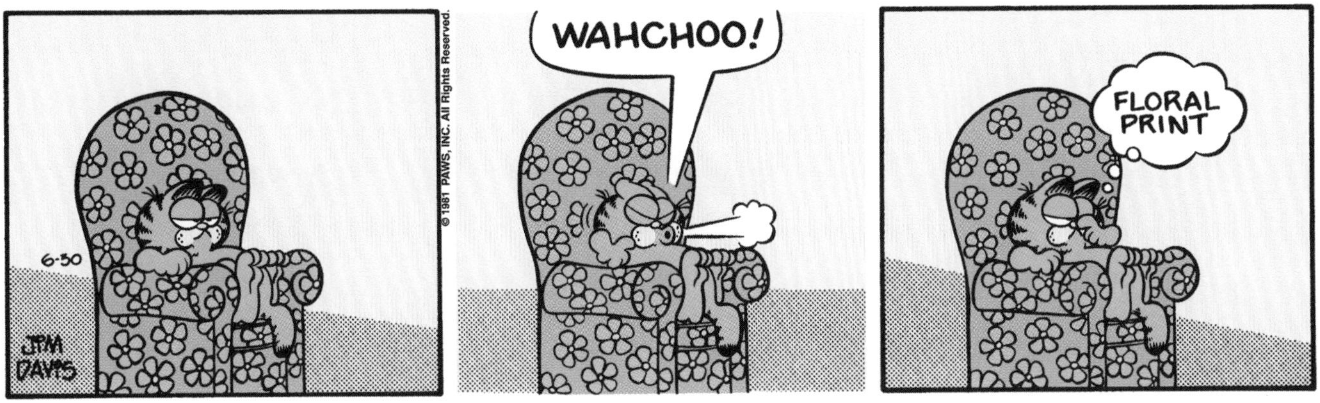
6-30
JIM DAVIS
© 1981 PAWS, INC. All Rights Reserved.
WAHCHOO!
FLORAL PRINT

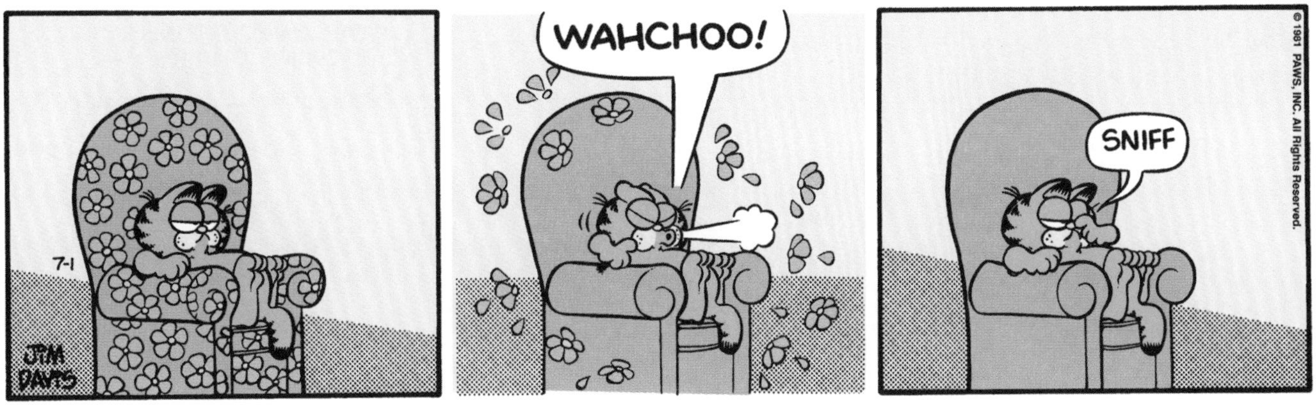
7-1
JIM DAVIS
WAHCHOO!
SNIFF
© 1981 PAWS, INC. All Rights Reserved.

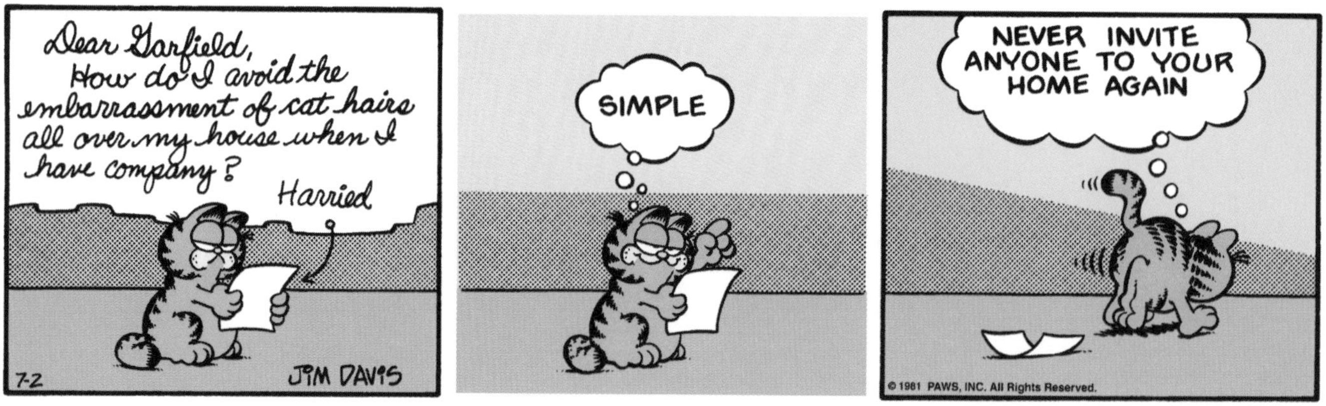
Dear Garfield,
How do I avoid the embarrassment of cat hairs all over my house when I have company?
Harried
7-2
JIM DAVIS
SIMPLE
NEVER INVITE ANYONE TO YOUR HOME AGAIN
© 1981 PAWS, INC. All Rights Reserved.

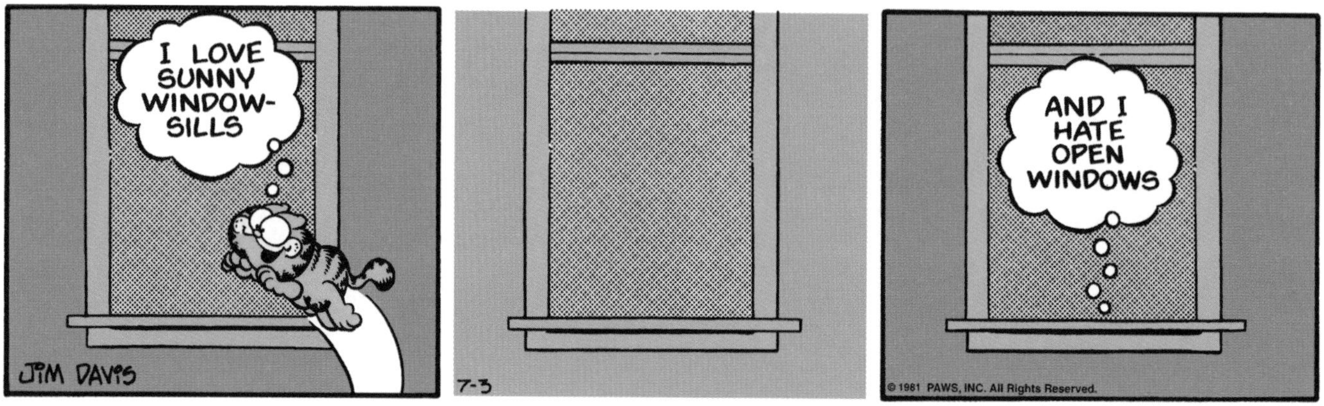
I LOVE SUNNY WINDOW-SILLS
JIM DAVIS
7-3
AND I HATE OPEN WINDOWS
© 1981 PAWS, INC. All Rights Reserved.

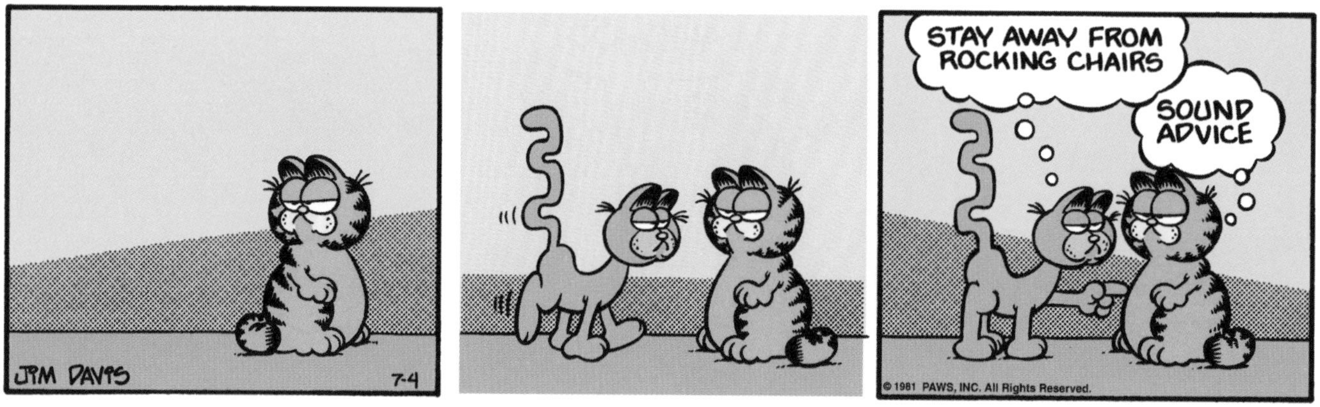
JIM DAVIS
7-4
STAY AWAY FROM ROCKING CHAIRS
SOUND ADVICE
© 1981 PAWS, INC. All Rights Reserved.

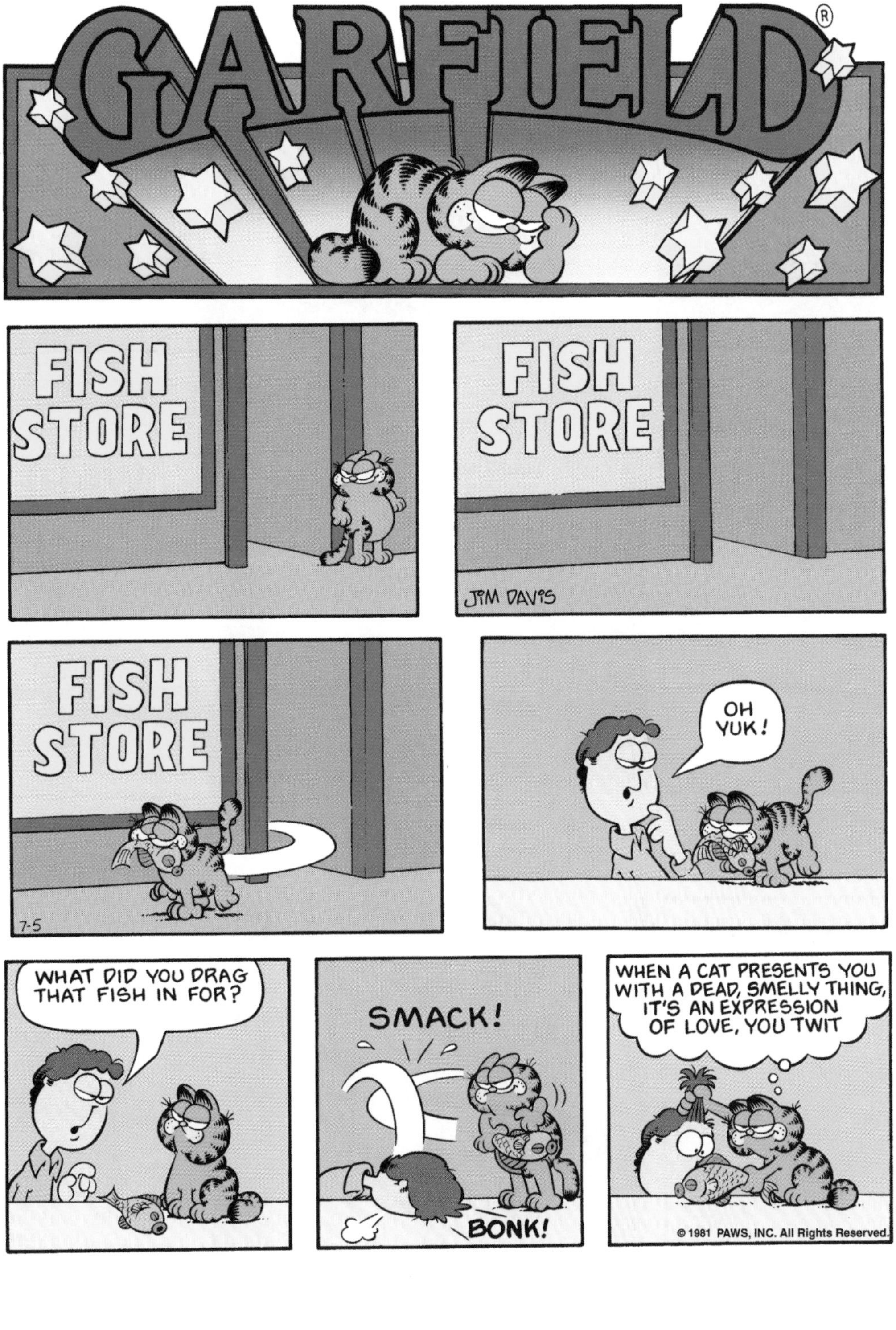
GARFIELD®
FISH STORE
FISH STORE
JIM DAVIS
FISH STORE
7-5
OH YUK!
WHAT DID YOU DRAG THAT FISH IN FOR?
SMACK!
BONK!
WHEN A CAT PRESENTS YOU WITH A DEAD, SMELLY THING, IT'S AN EXPRESSION OF LOVE, YOU TWIT
© 1981 PAWS, INC. All Rights Reserved.

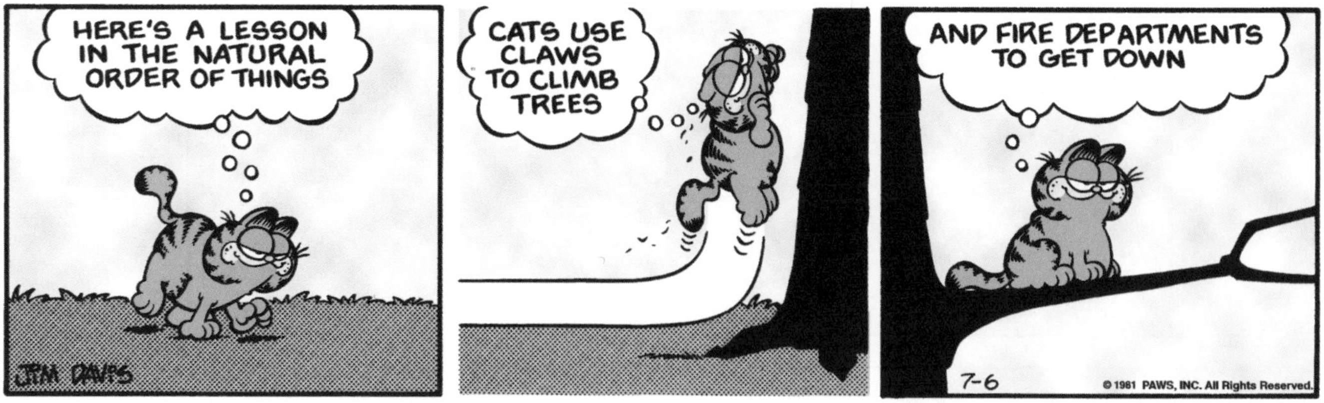
HERE'S A LESSON IN THE NATURAL ORDER OF THINGS
JIM DAVIS
CATS USE CLAWS TO CLIMB TREES
AND FIRE DEPARTMENTS TO GET DOWN
7-6
© 1981 PAWS, INC. All Rights Reserved.

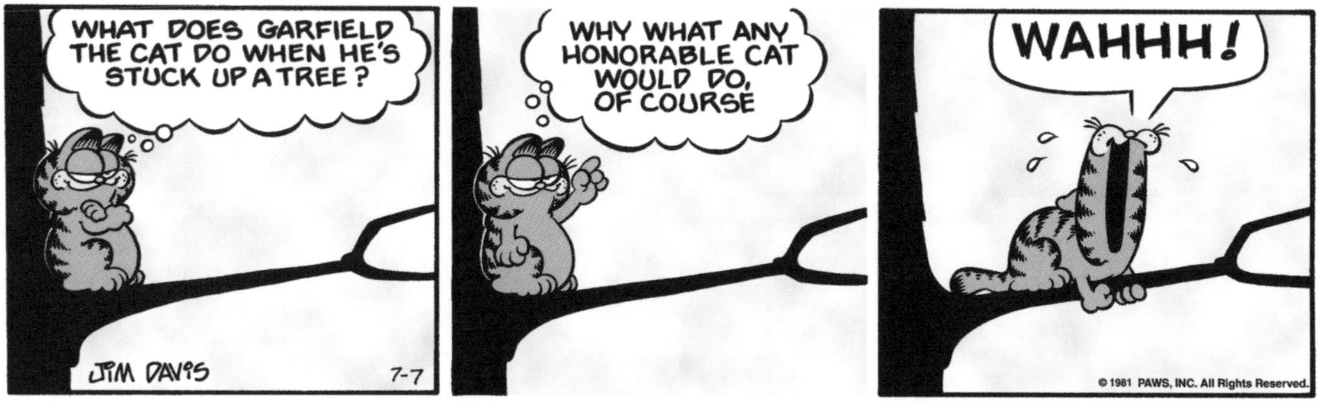
WHAT DOES GARFIELD THE CAT DO WHEN HE'S STUCK UP A TREE?
JIM DAVIS
7-7
WHY WHAT ANY HONORABLE CAT WOULD DO, OF COURSE
WAHHH!
© 1981 PAWS, INC. All Rights Reserved.

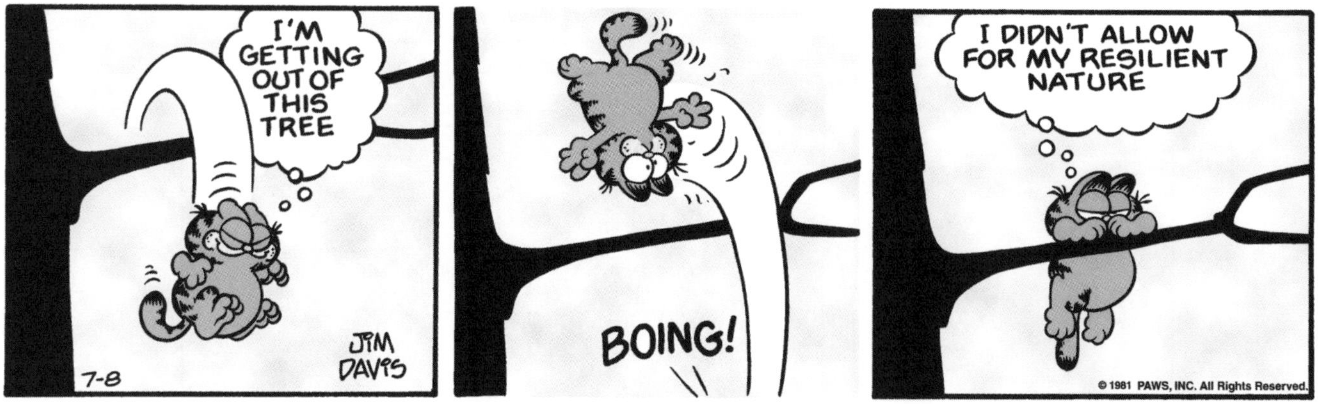
I'M GETTING OUT OF THIS TREE
JIM DAVIS
7-8
BOING!
I DIDN'T ALLOW FOR MY RESILIENT NATURE
© 1981 PAWS, INC. All Rights Reserved.

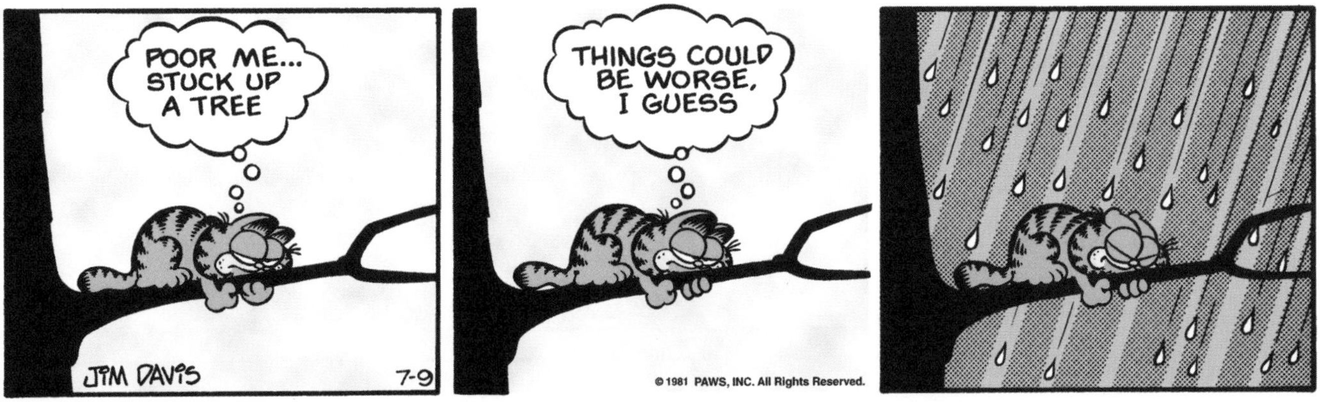
POOR ME... STUCK UP A TREE
JIM DAVIS
7-9
THINGS COULD BE WORSE, I GUESS
© 1981 PAWS, INC. All Rights Reserved.

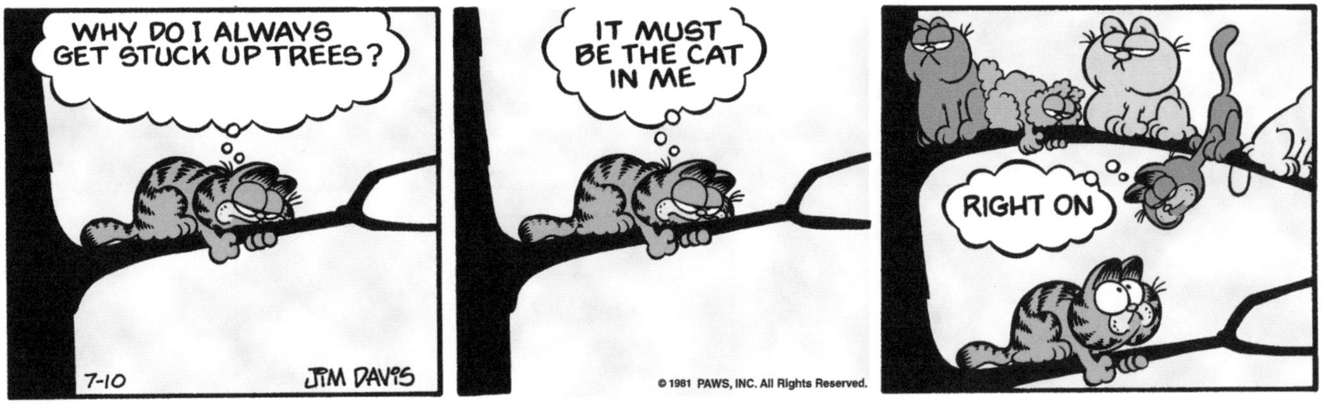
WHY DO I ALWAYS GET STUCK UP TREES?
7-10
JIM DAVIS
IT MUST BE THE CAT IN ME
© 1981 PAWS, INC. All Rights Reserved.
RIGHT ON

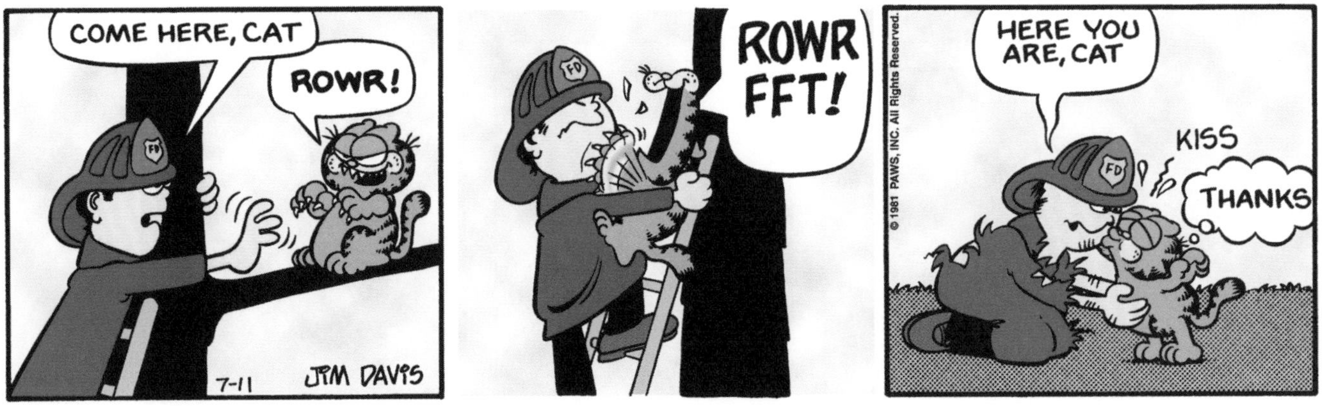
COME HERE, CAT
ROWR!
7-11
JIM DAVIS
ROWR FFT!
© 1981 PAWS, INC. All Rights Reserved.
HERE YOU ARE, CAT
KISS
THANKS

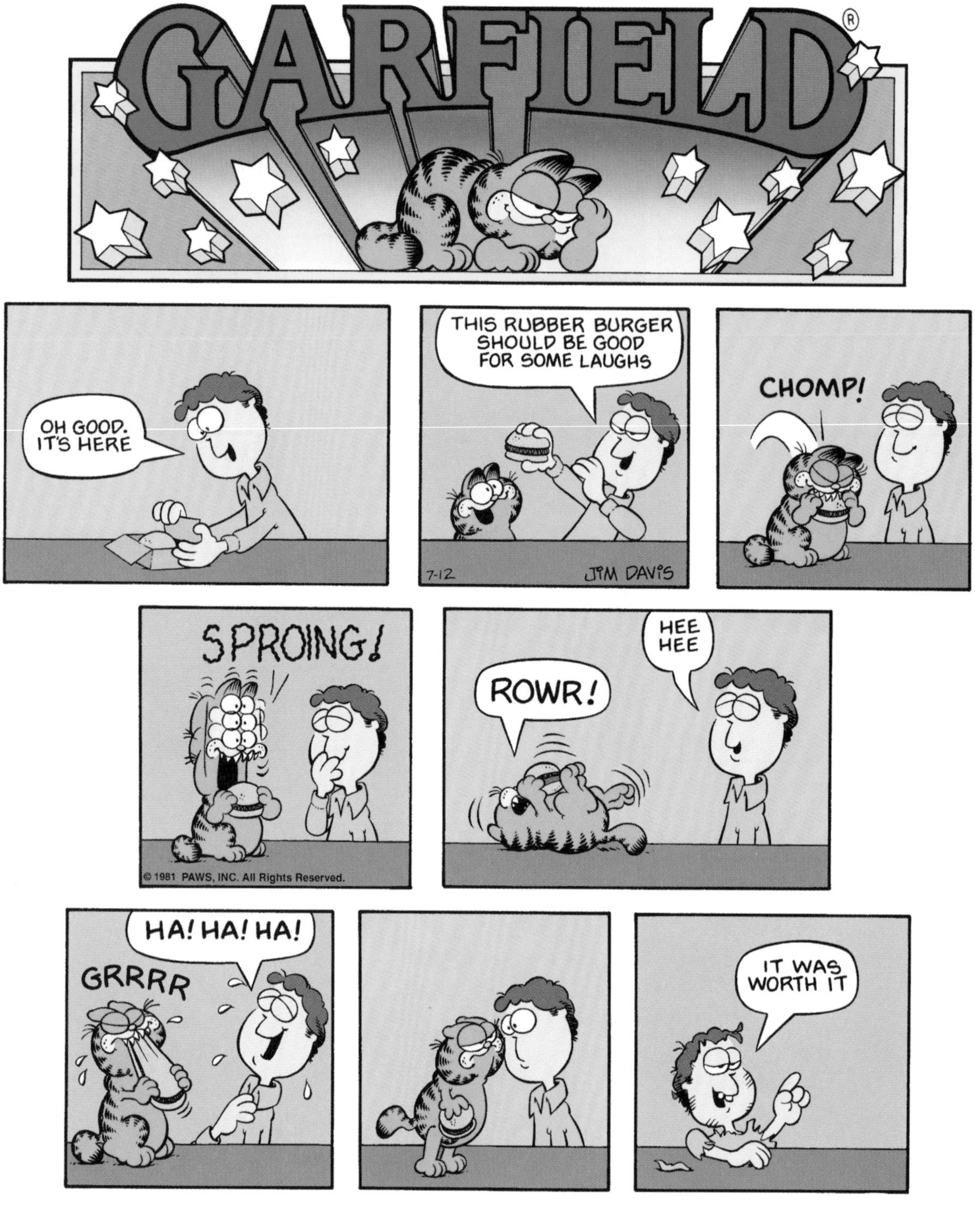
GARFIELD
OH GOOD. IT'S HERE
THIS RUBBER BURGER SHOULD BE GOOD FOR SOME LAUGHS
7-12
JIM DAVIS
CHOMP!
SPROING!
© 1981 PAWS, INC. All Rights Reserved.
ROWR!
HEE HEE
GRRRR
HA! HA! HA!
IT WAS WORTH IT

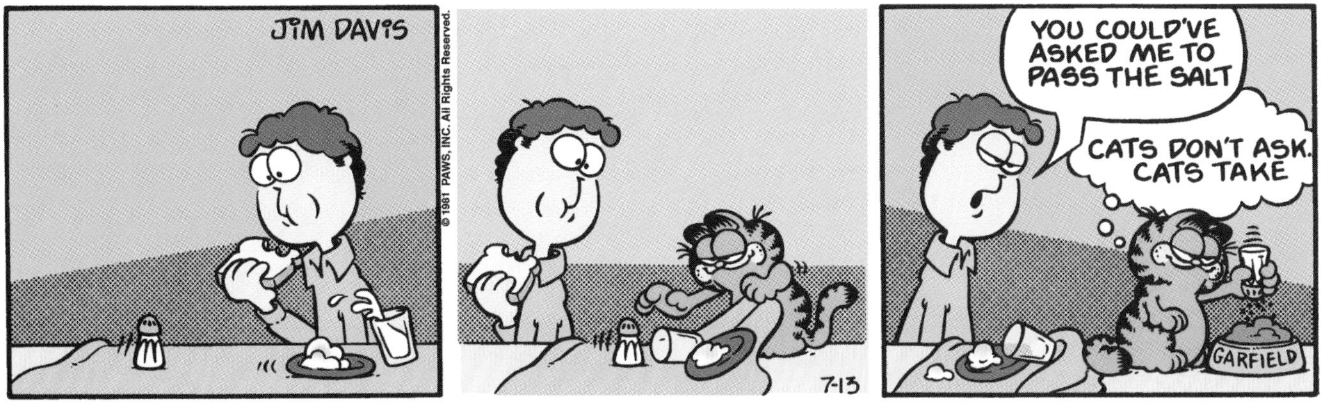
JIM DAVIS
© 1981 PAWS, INC. All Rights Reserved.
7-13
YOU COULD'VE ASKED ME TO PASS THE SALT
CATS DON'T ASK. CATS TAKE
GARFIELD

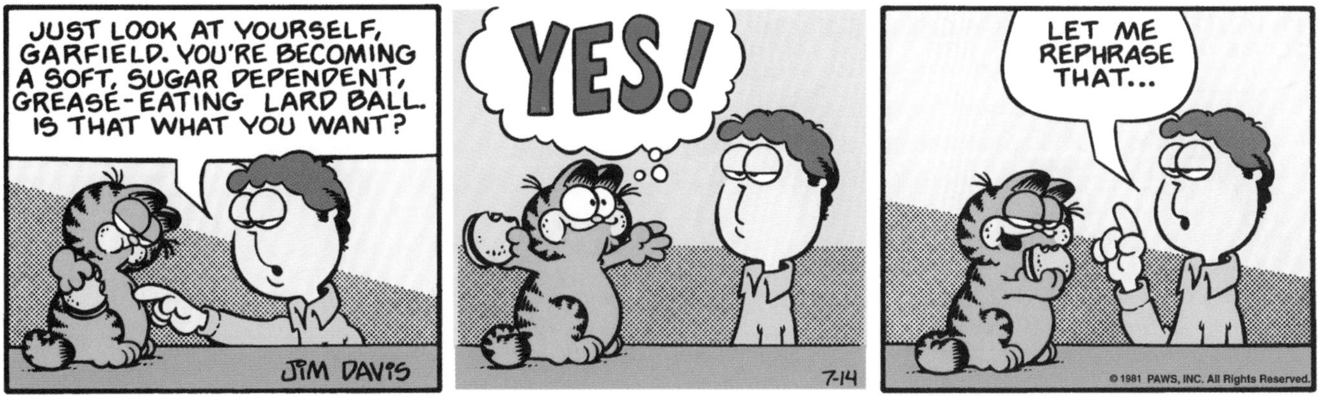
JUST LOOK AT YOURSELF, GARFIELD. YOU'RE BECOMING A SOFT, SUGAR DEPENDENT, GREASE-EATING LARD BALL. IS THAT WHAT YOU WANT?
JIM DAVIS
YES!
7-14
LET ME REPHRASE THAT...
© 1981 PAWS, INC. All Rights Reserved.

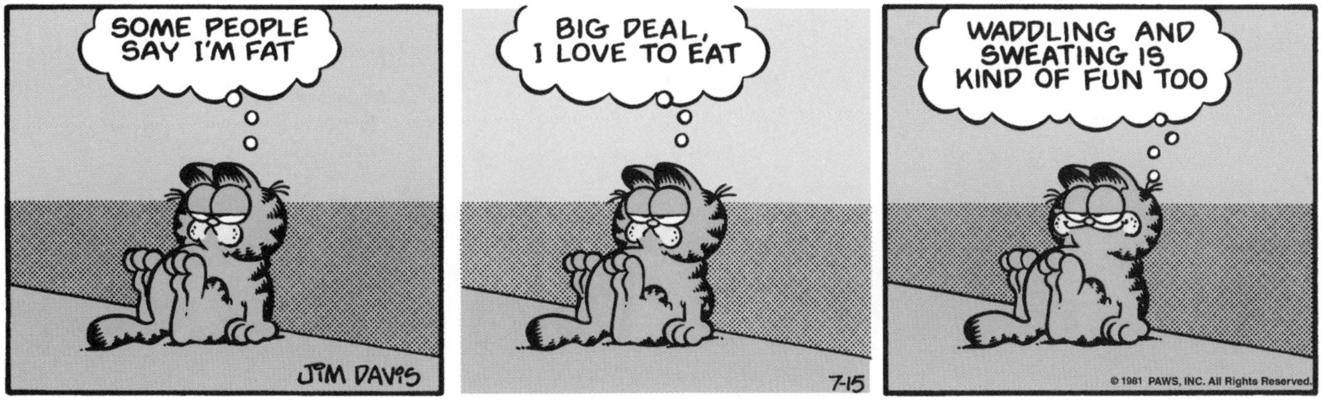
SOME PEOPLE SAY I'M FAT
JIM DAVIS
BIG DEAL, I LOVE TO EAT
7-15
WADDLING AND SWEATING IS KIND OF FUN TOO
© 1981 PAWS, INC. All Rights Reserved.

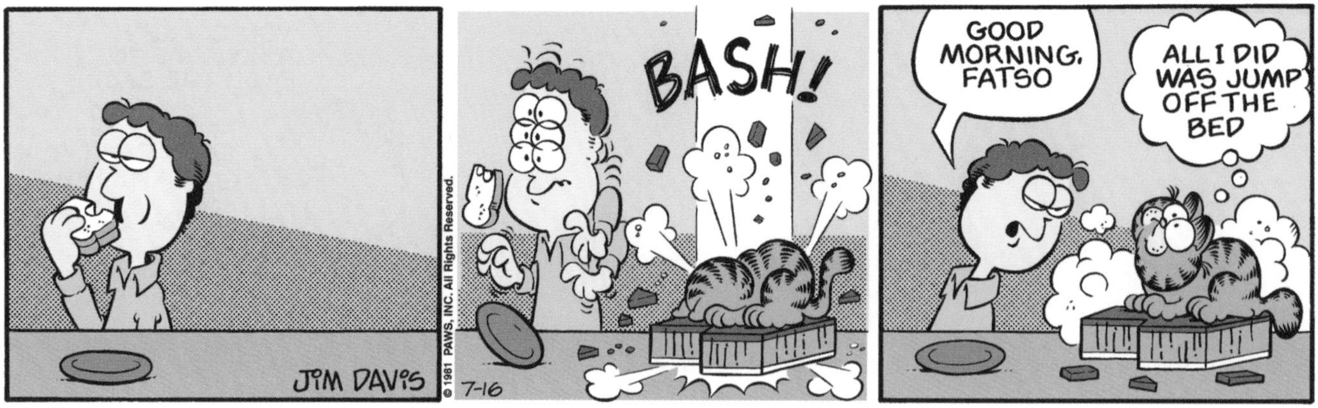
JIM DAVIS
© 1981 PAWS, INC. All Rights Reserved.
7-16
BASH!
GOOD MORNING, FATSO
ALL I DID WAS JUMP OFF THE BED

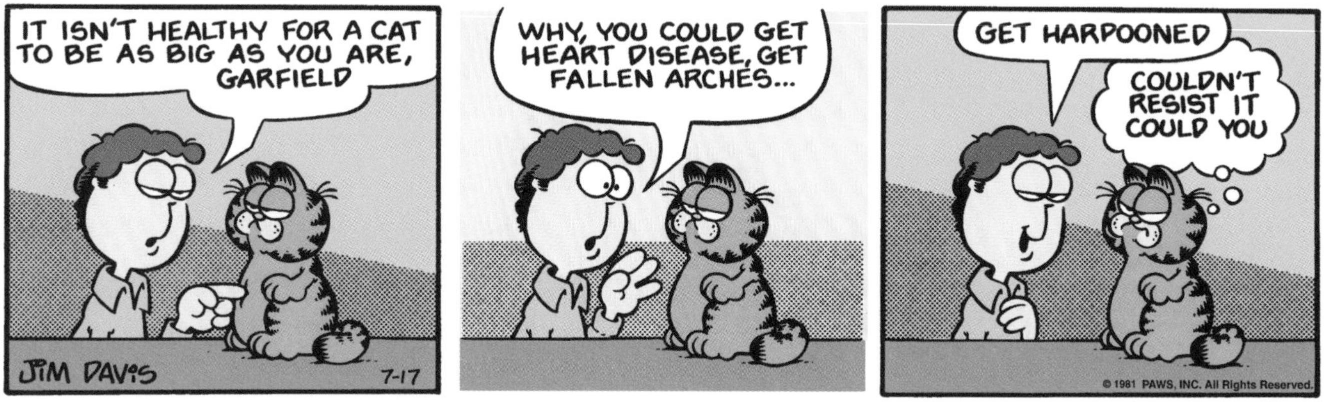
IT ISN'T HEALTHY FOR A CAT TO BE AS BIG AS YOU ARE, GARFIELD
JIM DAVIS
7-17
WHY, YOU COULD GET HEART DISEASE, GET FALLEN ARCHES...
GET HARPOONED
COULDN'T RESIST IT COULD YOU
© 1981 PAWS, INC. All Rights Reserved.

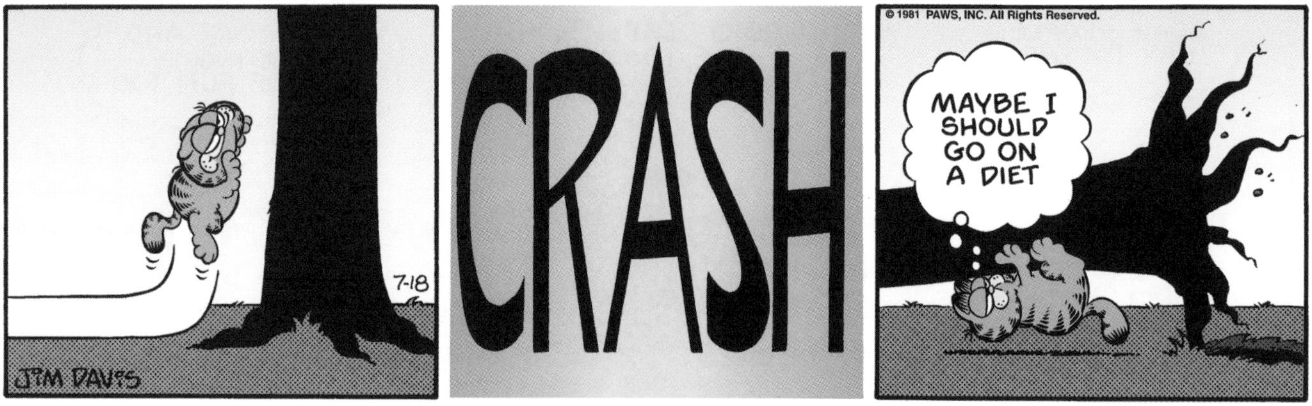
7-18
JIM DAVIS
CRASH
© 1981 PAWS, INC. All Rights Reserved.
MAYBE I SHOULD GO ON A DIET

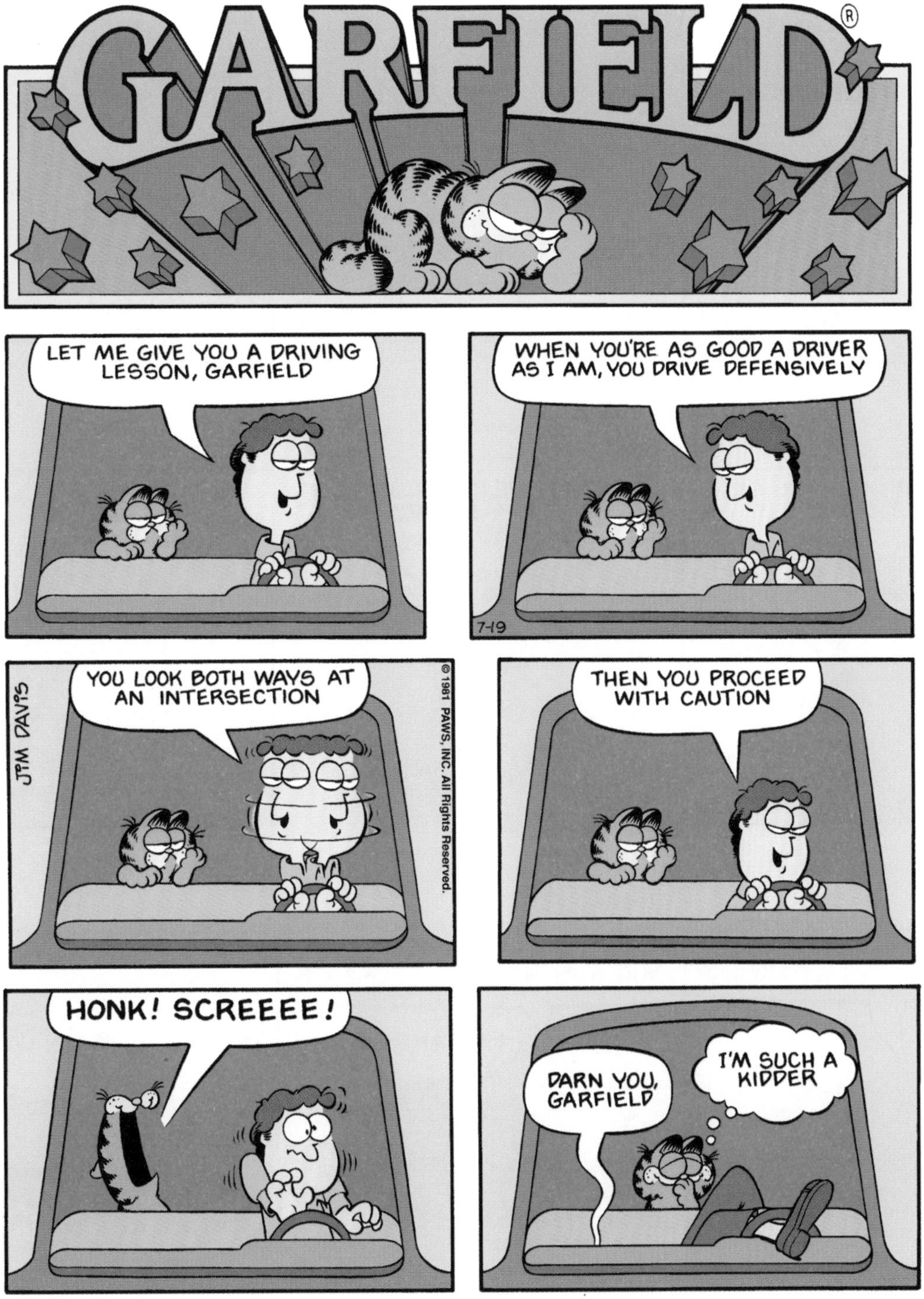
GARFIELD®
LET ME GIVE YOU A DRIVING LESSON, GARFIELD
WHEN YOU'RE AS GOOD A DRIVER AS I AM, YOU DRIVE DEFENSIVELY
7-19
JIM DAVIS
YOU LOOK BOTH WAYS AT AN INTERSECTION
© 1981 PAWS, INC. All Rights Reserved.
THEN YOU PROCEED WITH CAUTION
HONK! SCREEEE!
DARN YOU, GARFIELD
I'M SUCH A KIDDER

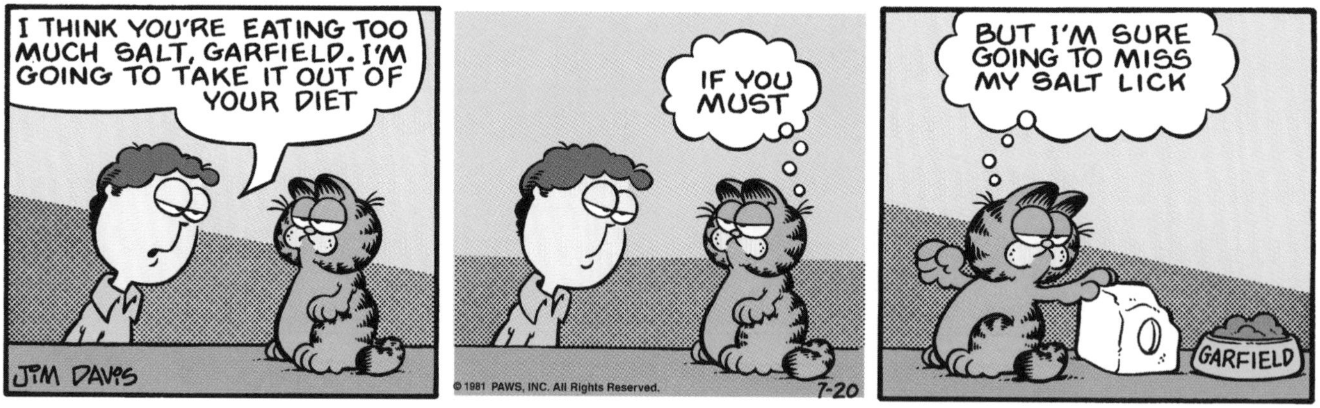
I THINK YOU'RE EATING TOO MUCH SALT, GARFIELD. I'M GOING TO TAKE IT OUT OF YOUR DIET
JIM DAVIS
IF YOU MUST
© 1981 PAWS, INC. All Rights Reserved.
7-20
BUT I'M SURE GOING TO MISS MY SALT LICK
GARFIELD

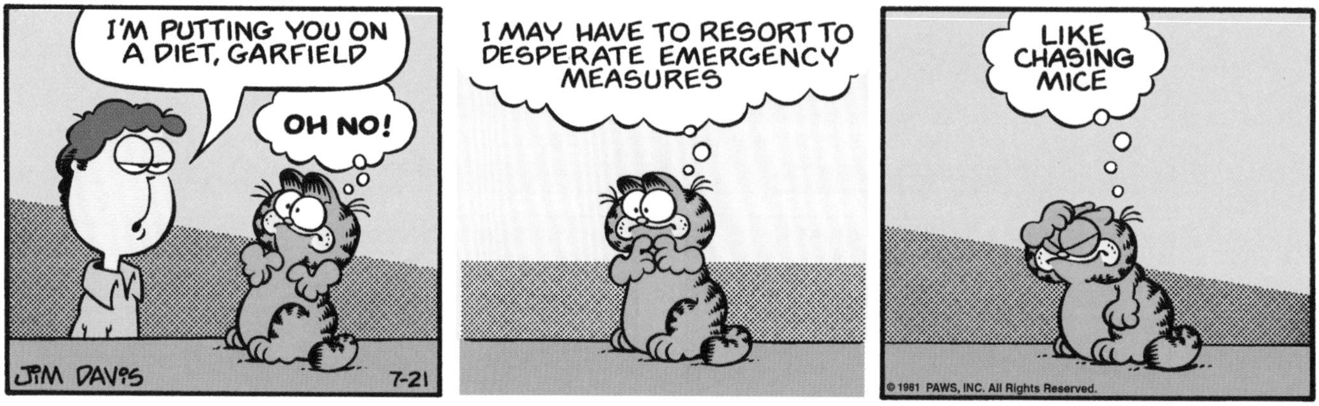
I'M PUTTING YOU ON A DIET, GARFIELD
OH NO!
JIM DAVIS
7-21
I MAY HAVE TO RESORT TO DESPERATE EMERGENCY MEASURES
LIKE CHASING MICE
© 1981 PAWS, INC. All Rights Reserved.

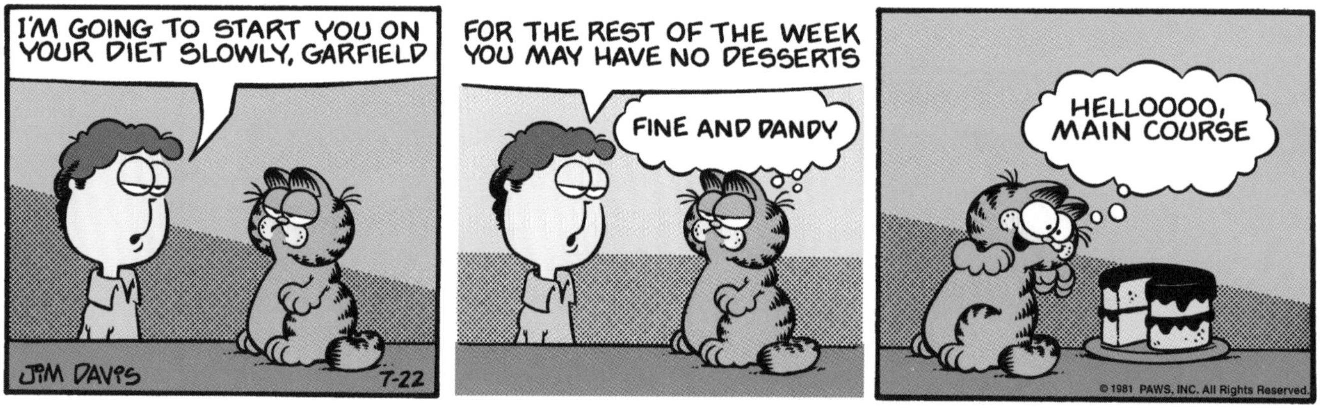
I'M GOING TO START YOU ON YOUR DIET SLOWLY, GARFIELD
JIM DAVIS
7-22
FOR THE REST OF THE WEEK YOU MAY HAVE NO DESSERTS
FINE AND DANDY
HELLOOOO, MAIN COURSE
© 1981 PAWS, INC. All Rights Reserved.

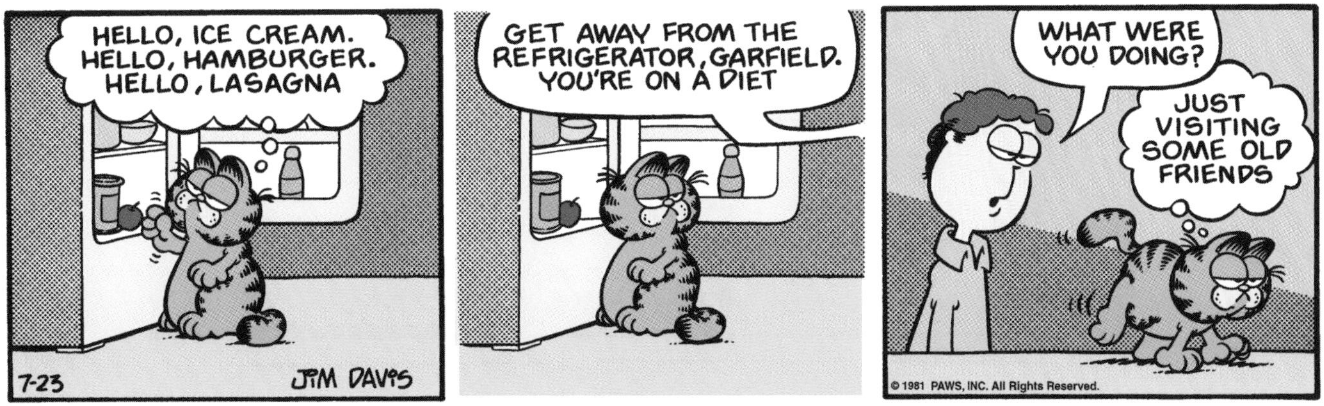
HELLO, ICE CREAM. HELLO, HAMBURGER. HELLO, LASAGNA
7-23
JIM DAVIS
GET AWAY FROM THE REFRIGERATOR, GARFIELD. YOU'RE ON A DIET
WHAT WERE YOU DOING?
JUST VISITING SOME OLD FRIENDS
© 1981 PAWS, INC. All Rights Reserved.

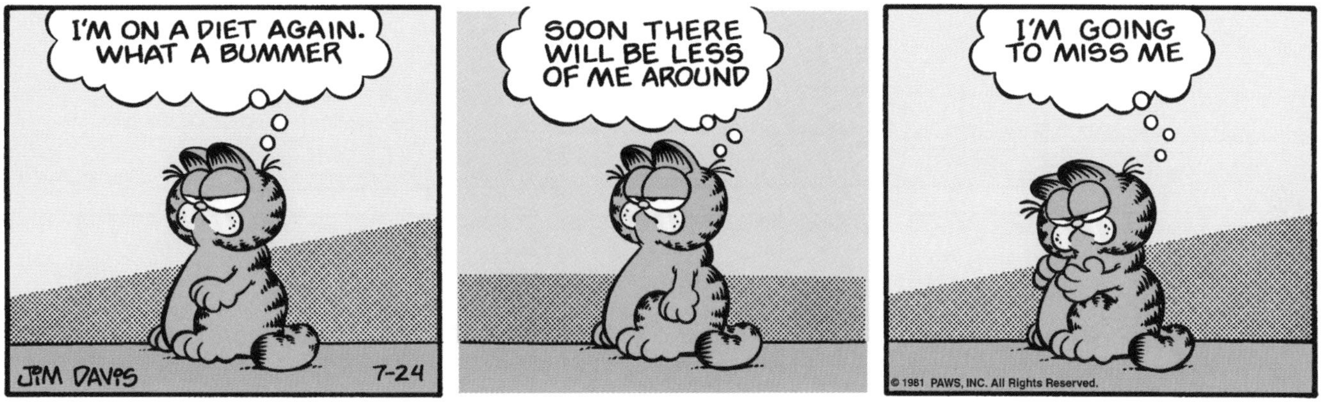
I'M ON A DIET AGAIN. WHAT A BUMMER
JIM DAVIS
7-24
SOON THERE WILL BE LESS OF ME AROUND
I'M GOING TO MISS ME
© 1981 PAWS, INC. All Rights Reserved.

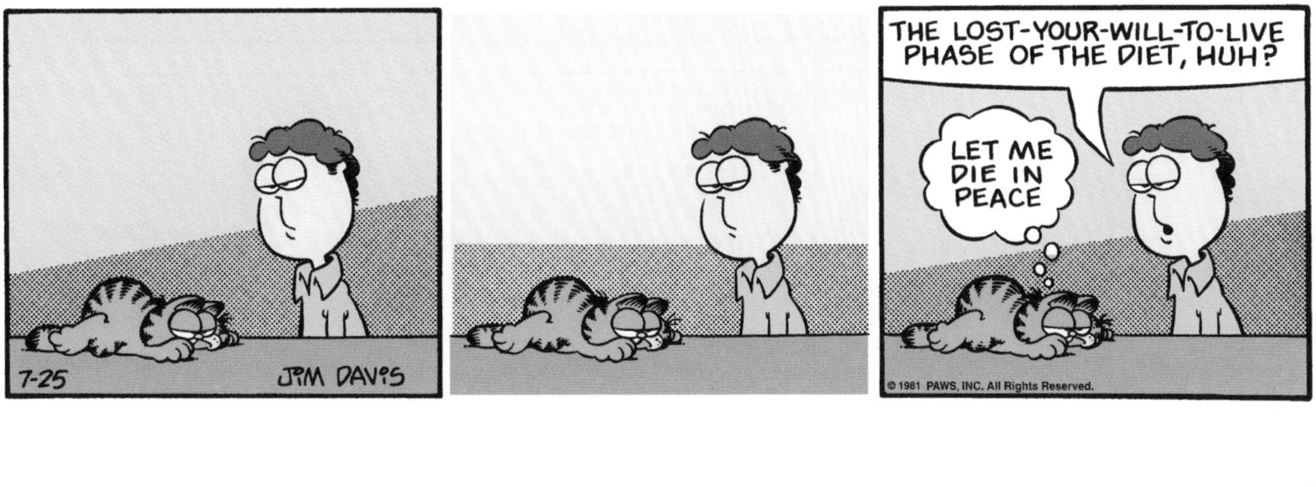
7-25
JIM DAVIS
THE LOST-YOUR-WILL-TO-LIVE PHASE OF THE DIET, HUH?
LET ME DIE IN PEACE
© 1981 PAWS, INC. All Rights Reserved.

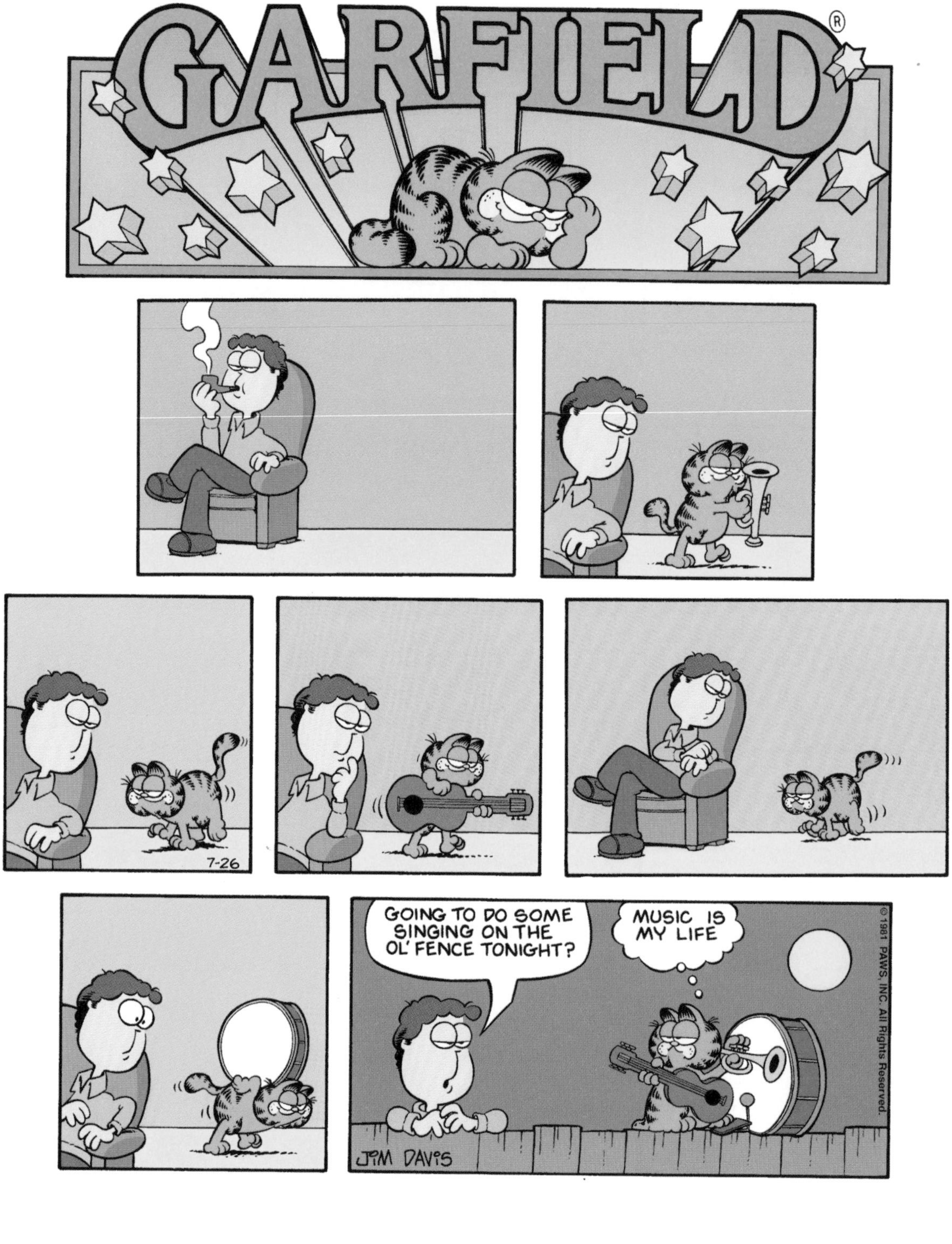
GARFIELD®
7-26
GOING TO DO SOME SINGING ON THE OL' FENCE TONIGHT?
MUSIC IS MY LIFE
JIM DAVIS
© 1981 PAWS, INC. All Rights Reserved.

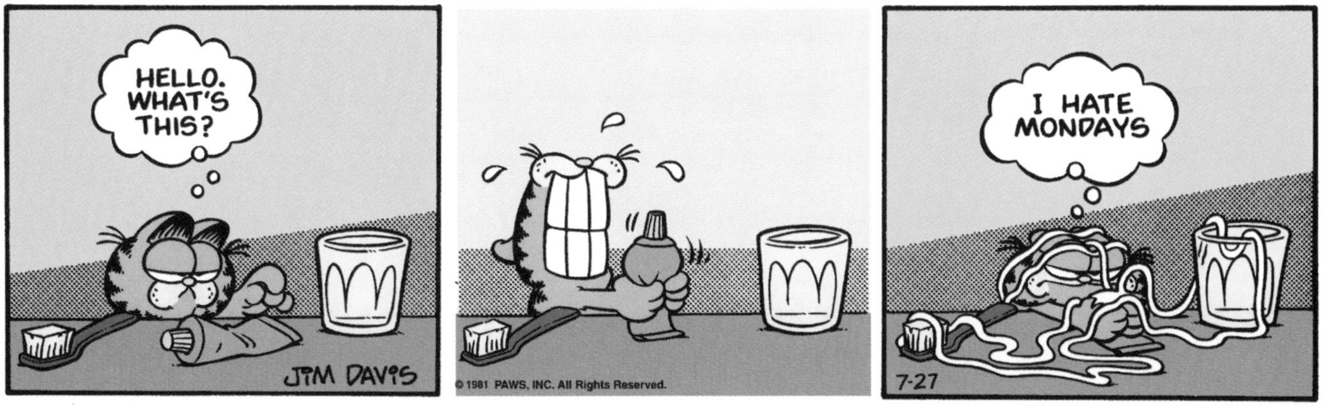
HELLO. WHAT'S THIS?
JIM DAVIS
© 1981 PAWS, INC. All Rights Reserved.
I HATE MONDAYS
7-27

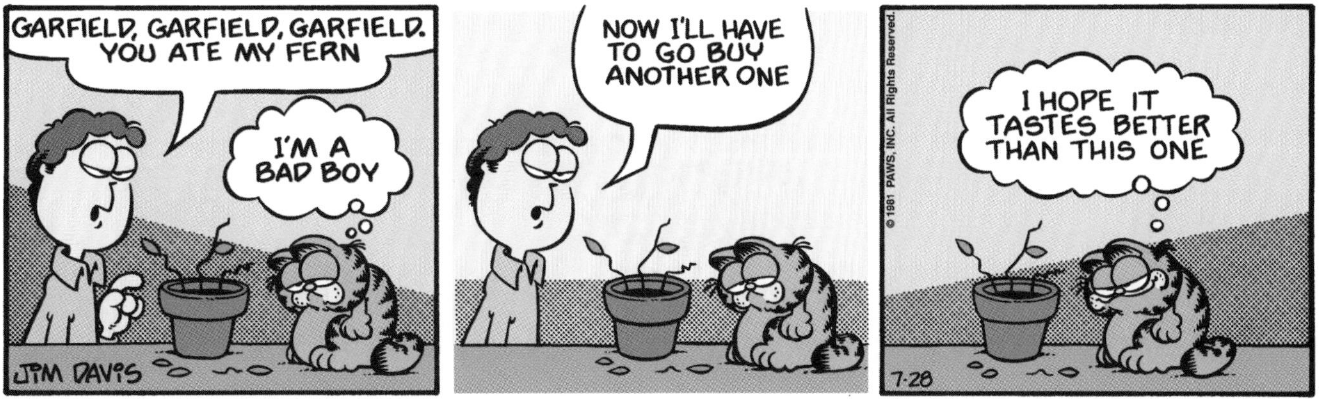
GARFIELD, GARFIELD, GARFIELD. YOU ATE MY FERN
I'M A BAD BOY
JIM DAVIS
NOW I'LL HAVE TO GO BUY ANOTHER ONE
© 1981 PAWS, INC. All Rights Reserved.
I HOPE IT TASTES BETTER THAN THIS ONE
7-28

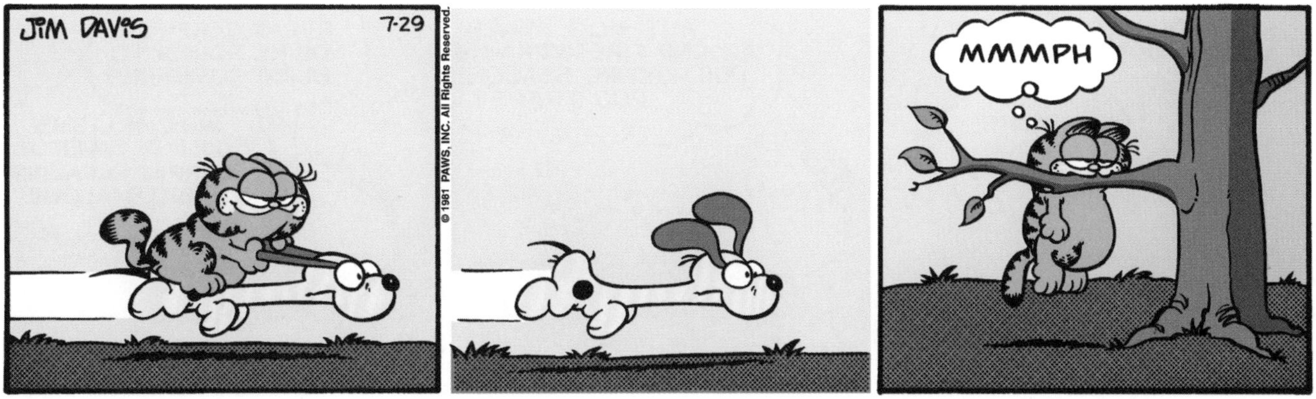
JIM DAVIS
7-29
© 1981 PAWS, INC. All Rights Reserved.
MMMPH

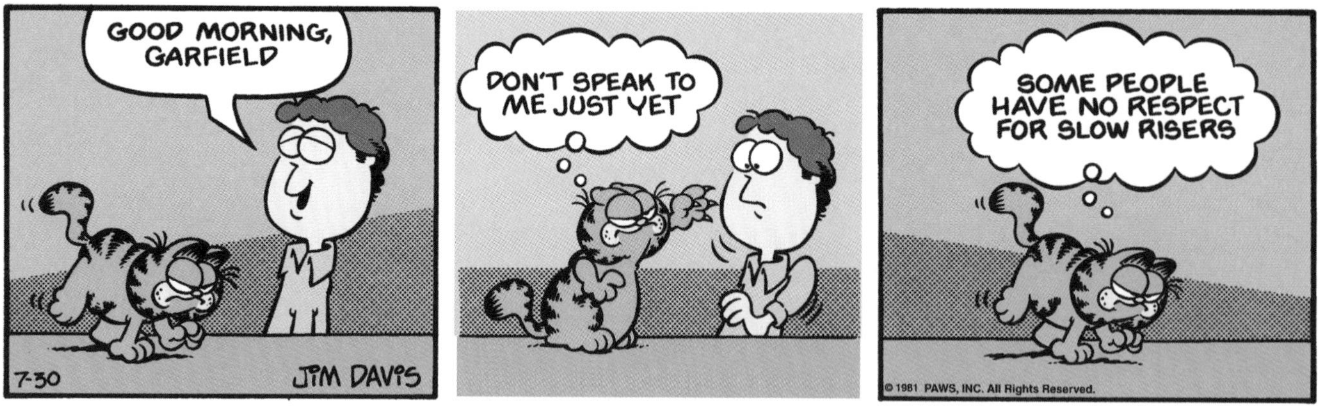
GOOD MORNING, GARFIELD
7-30
JIM DAVIS
DON'T SPEAK TO ME JUST YET
SOME PEOPLE HAVE NO RESPECT FOR SLOW RISERS
© 1981 PAWS, INC. All Rights Reserved.

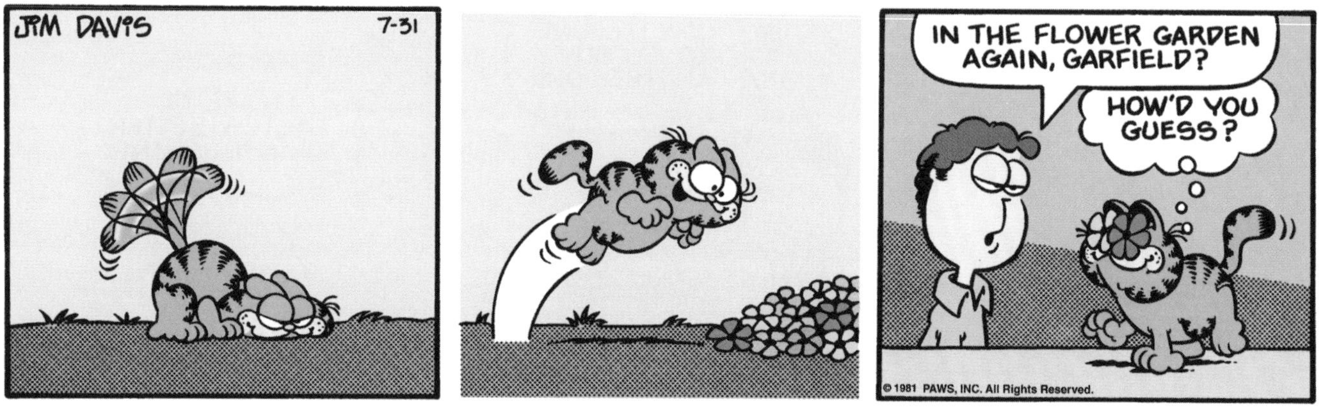
JIM DAVIS
7-31
IN THE FLOWER GARDEN AGAIN, GARFIELD?
HOW'D YOU GUESS?
© 1981 PAWS, INC. All Rights Reserved.

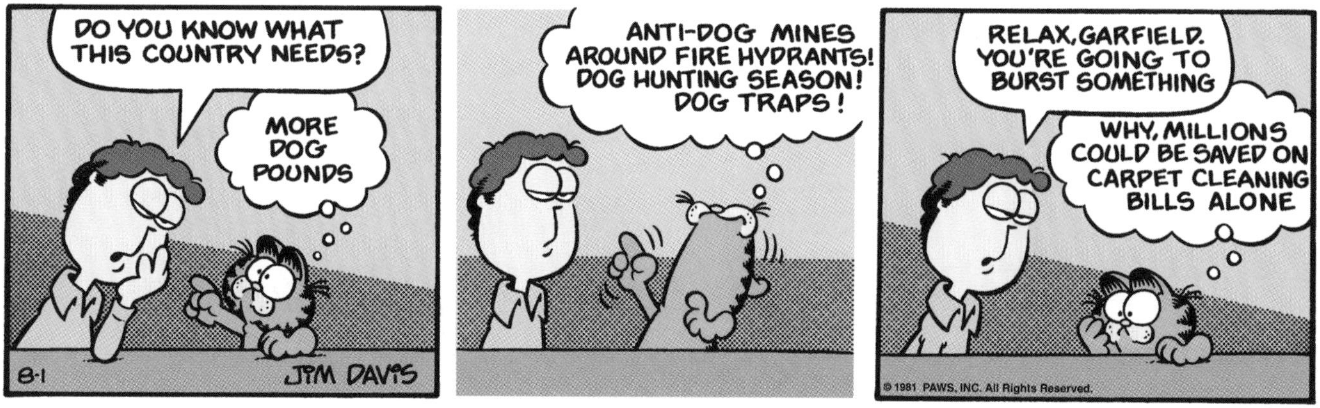
DO YOU KNOW WHAT THIS COUNTRY NEEDS?
MORE DOG POUNDS
8-1
JIM DAVIS
ANTI-DOG MINES AROUND FIRE HYDRANTS! DOG HUNTING SEASON! DOG TRAPS!
RELAX, GARFIELD. YOU'RE GOING TO BURST SOMETHING
WHY, MILLIONS COULD BE SAVED ON CARPET CLEANING BILLS ALONE
© 1981 PAWS, INC. All Rights Reserved.

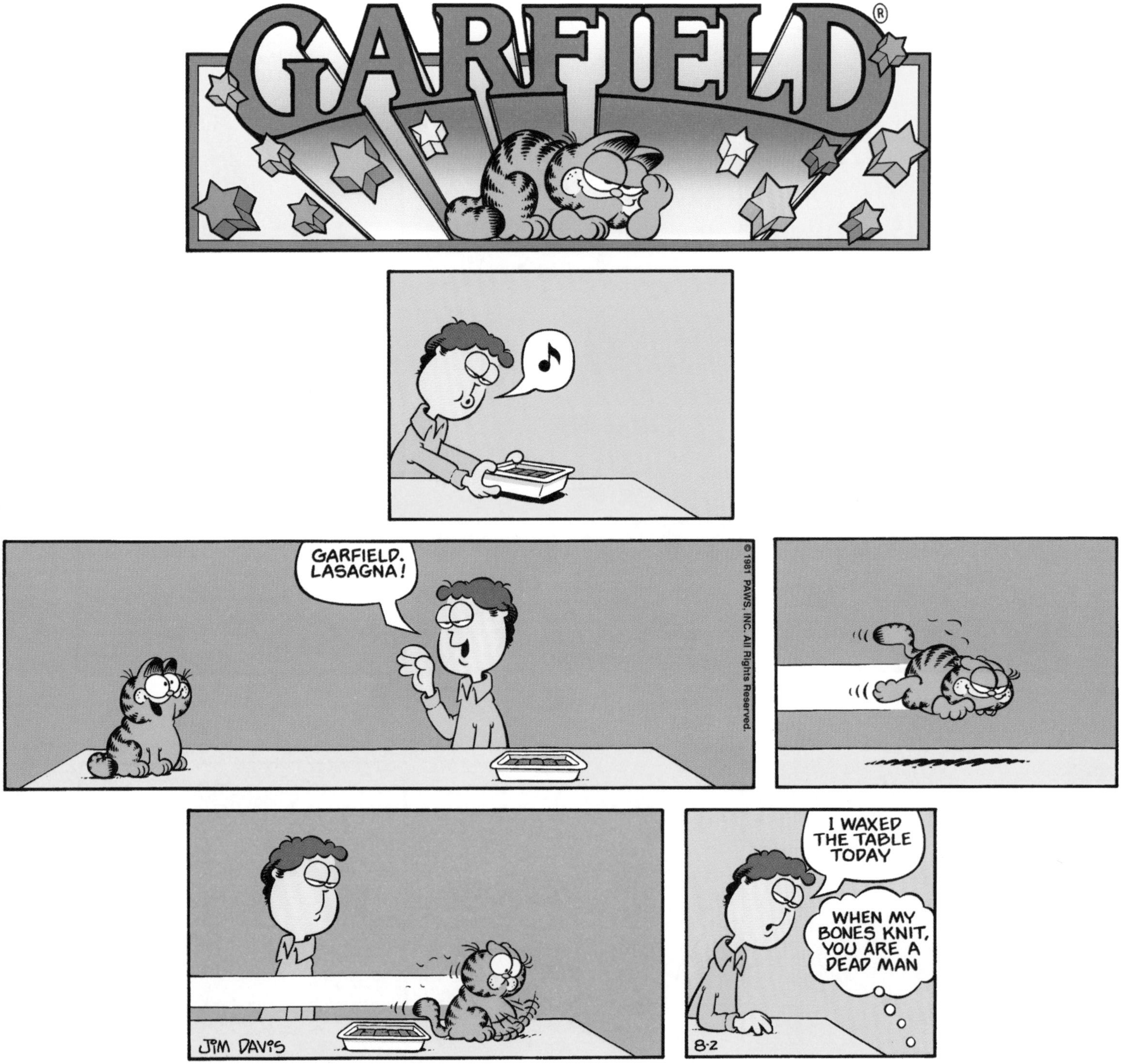
GARFIELD®
♪
GARFIELD. LASAGNA!
© 1981 PAWS, INC. All Rights Reserved.
JIM DAVIS
I WAXED THE TABLE TODAY
WHEN MY BONES KNIT, YOU ARE A DEAD MAN
8-2

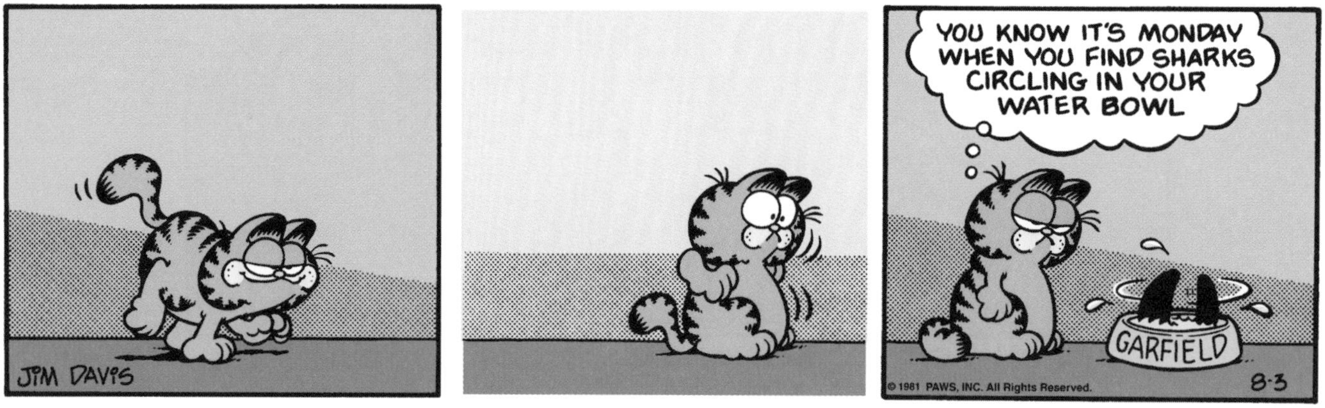
JIM DAVIS
YOU KNOW IT'S MONDAY WHEN YOU FIND SHARKS CIRCLING IN YOUR WATER BOWL
GARFIELD
© 1981 PAWS, INC. All Rights Reserved.
8-3

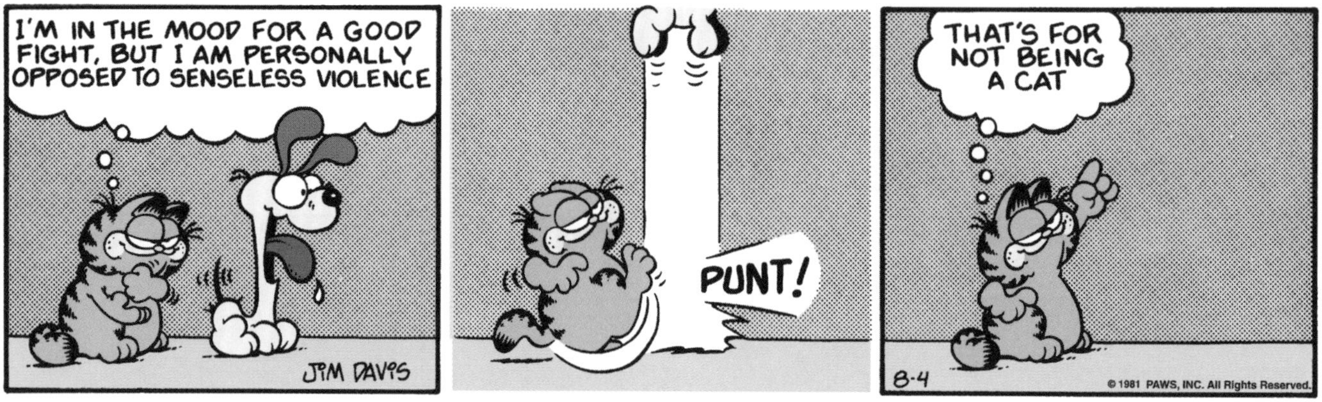
I'M IN THE MOOD FOR A GOOD FIGHT, BUT I AM PERSONALLY OPPOSED TO SENSELESS VIOLENCE
JIM DAVIS
PUNT!
THAT'S FOR NOT BEING A CAT
8-4
© 1981 PAWS, INC. All Rights Reserved.

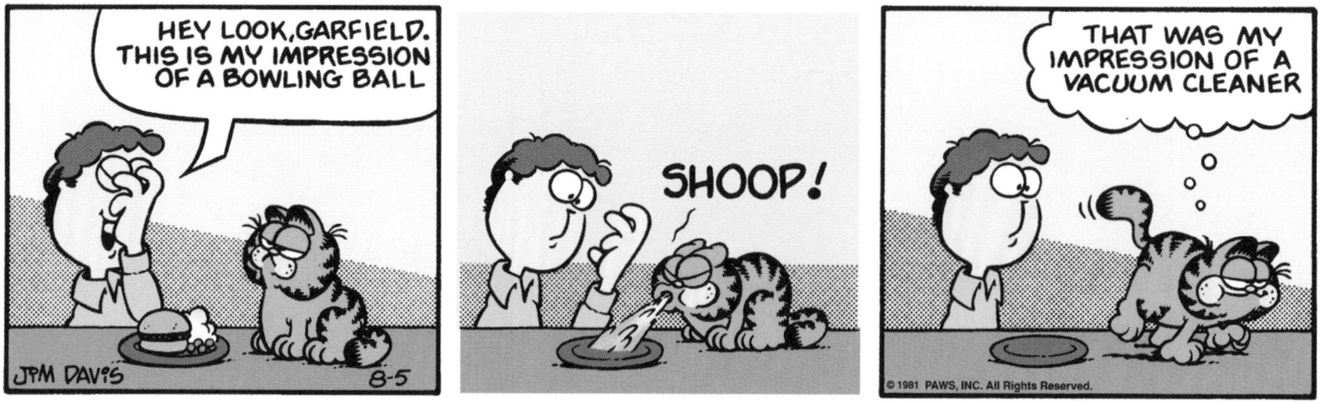
HEY LOOK, GARFIELD. THIS IS MY IMPRESSION OF A BOWLING BALL
JIM DAVIS
8-5
SHOOP!
THAT WAS MY IMPRESSION OF A VACUUM CLEANER
© 1981 PAWS, INC. All Rights Reserved.

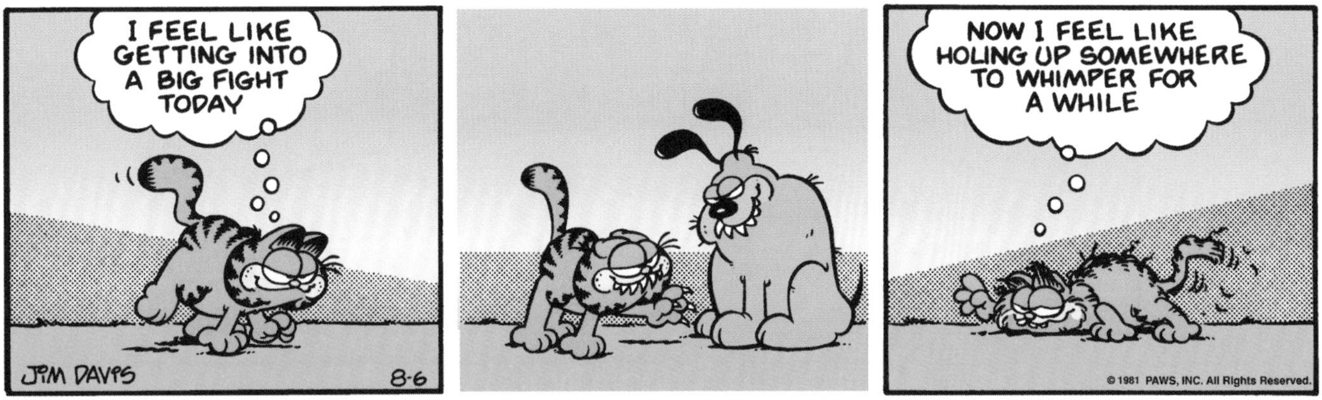
I FEEL LIKE GETTING INTO A BIG FIGHT TODAY
JIM DAVIS
8-6
NOW I FEEL LIKE HOLING UP SOMEWHERE TO WHIMPER FOR A WHILE
© 1981 PAWS, INC. All Rights Reserved.

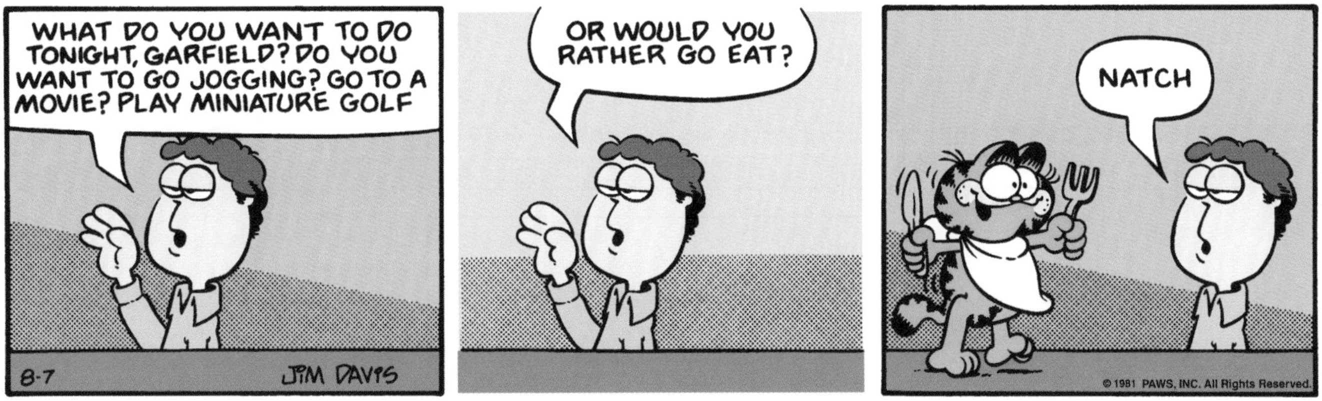
WHAT DO YOU WANT TO DO TONIGHT, GARFIELD? DO YOU WANT TO GO JOGGING? GO TO A MOVIE? PLAY MINIATURE GOLF
8-7
JIM DAVIS
OR WOULD YOU RATHER GO EAT?
NATCH
© 1981 PAWS, INC. All Rights Reserved.

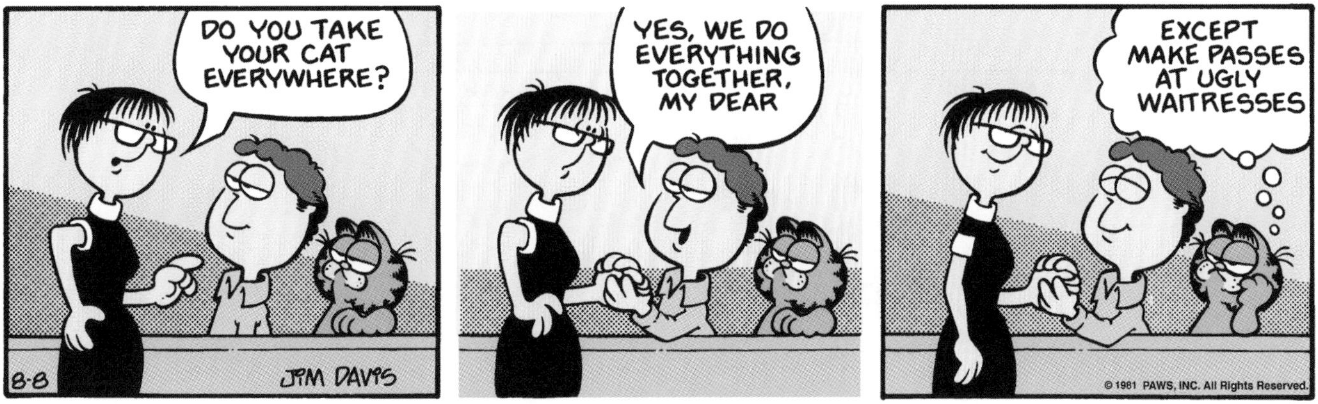
DO YOU TAKE YOUR CAT EVERYWHERE?
8-8
JIM DAVIS
YES, WE DO EVERYTHING TOGETHER, MY DEAR
EXCEPT MAKE PASSES AT UGLY WAITRESSES
© 1981 PAWS, INC. All Rights Reserved.

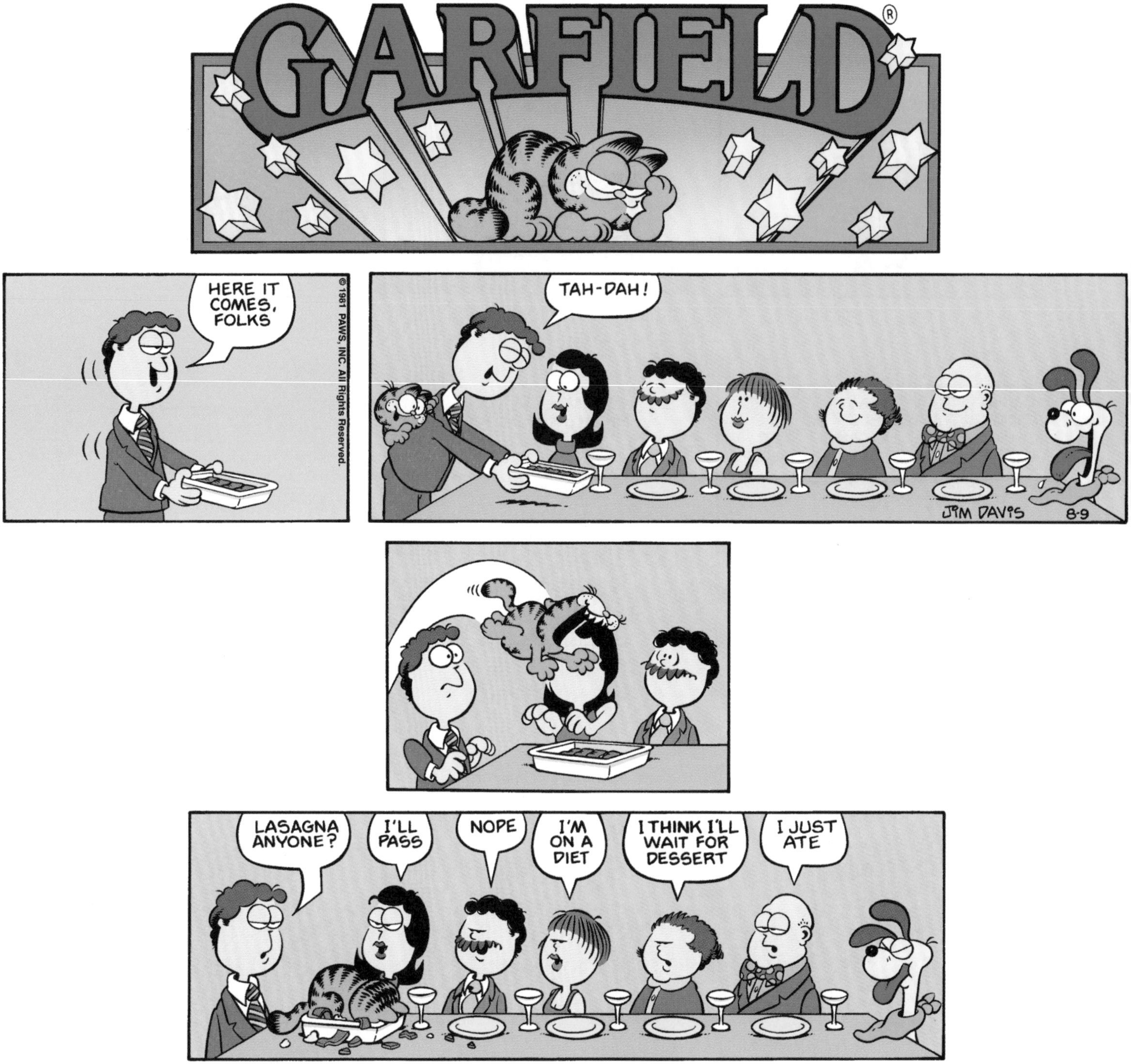
GARFIELD
HERE IT COMES, FOLKS
© 1981 PAWS, INC. All Rights Reserved.
TAH-DAH!
JIM DAVIS 8-9
LASAGNA ANYONE?
I'LL PASS
NOPE
I'M ON A DIET
I THINK I'LL WAIT FOR DESSERT
I JUST ATE

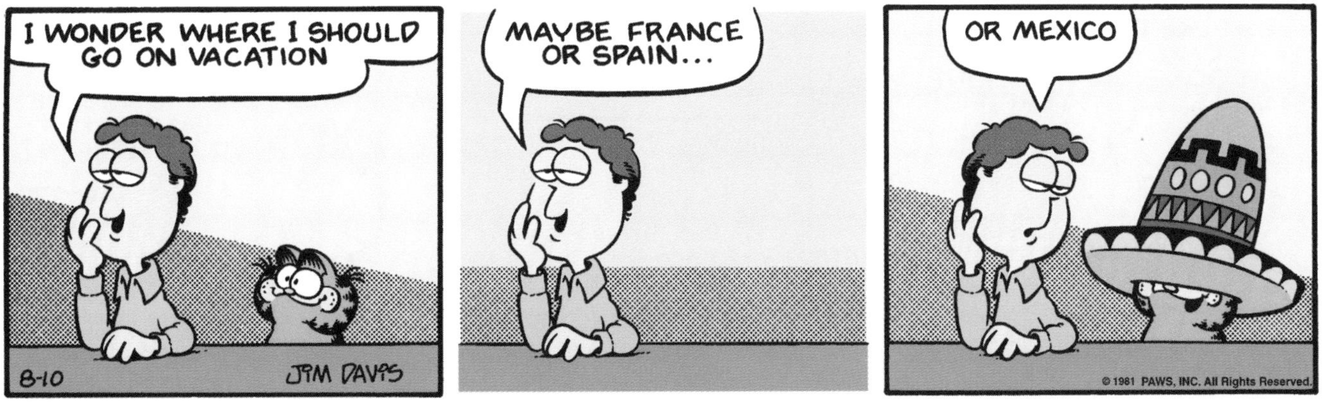
I WONDER WHERE I SHOULD GO ON VACATION
8-10
JIM DAVIS
MAYBE FRANCE OR SPAIN...
OR MEXICO
© 1981 PAWS, INC. All Rights Reserved.

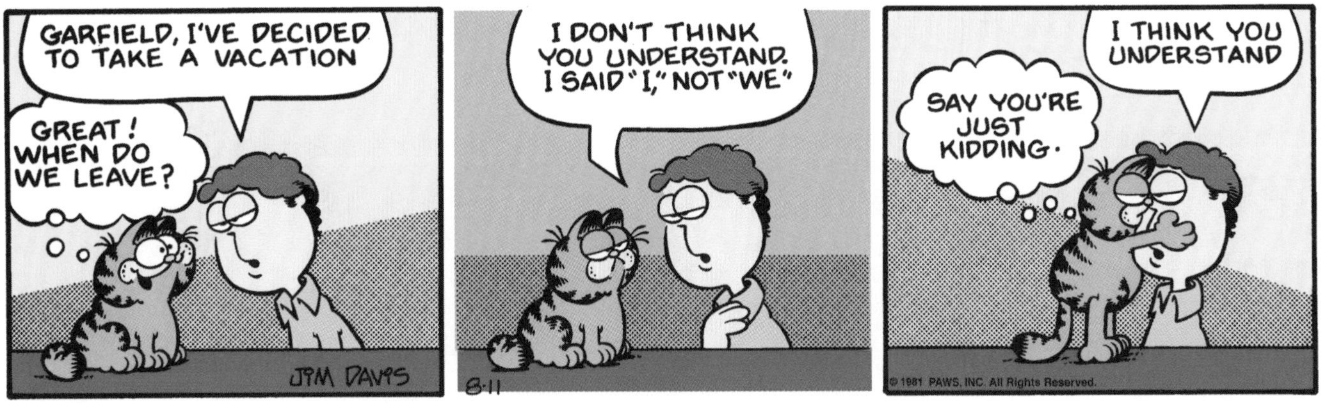
GARFIELD, I'VE DECIDED TO TAKE A VACATION
GREAT! WHEN DO WE LEAVE?
JIM DAVIS
I DON'T THINK YOU UNDERSTAND. I SAID "I," NOT "WE"
8-11
I THINK YOU UNDERSTAND
SAY YOU'RE JUST KIDDING.
© 1981 PAWS, INC. All Rights Reserved.

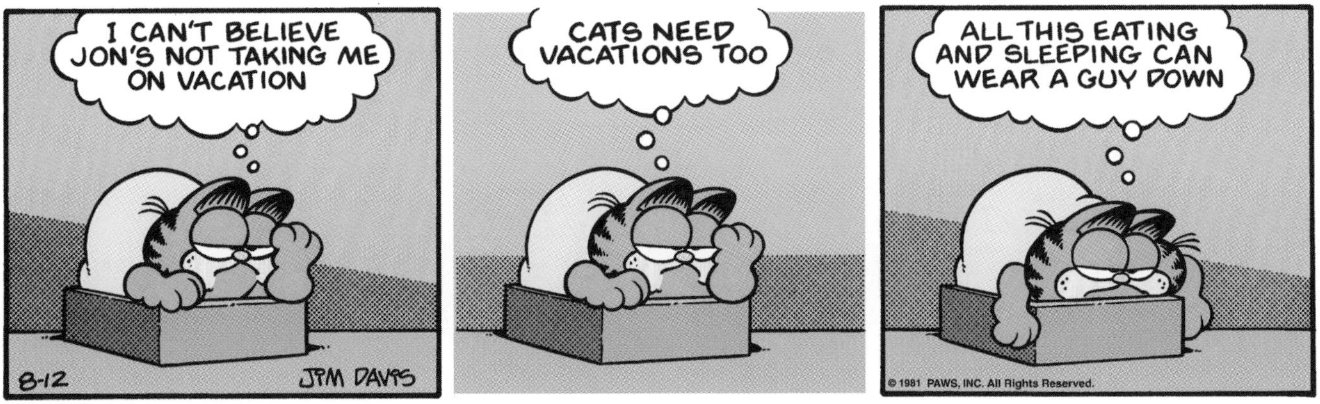
I CAN'T BELIEVE JON'S NOT TAKING ME ON VACATION
8-12
JIM DAVIS
CATS NEED VACATIONS TOO
ALL THIS EATING AND SLEEPING CAN WEAR A GUY DOWN
© 1981 PAWS, INC. All Rights Reserved.

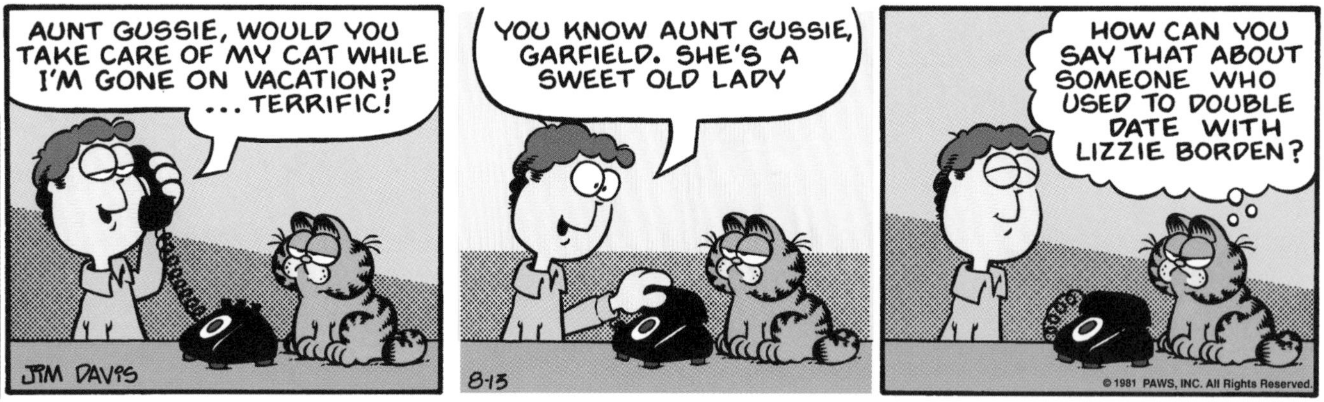
AUNT GUSSIE, WOULD YOU TAKE CARE OF MY CAT WHILE I'M GONE ON VACATION? ...TERRIFIC!
JIM DAVIS
YOU KNOW AUNT GUSSIE, GARFIELD. SHE'S A SWEET OLD LADY
8-13
HOW CAN YOU SAY THAT ABOUT SOMEONE WHO USED TO DOUBLE DATE WITH LIZZIE BORDEN?
© 1981 PAWS, INC. All Rights Reserved.

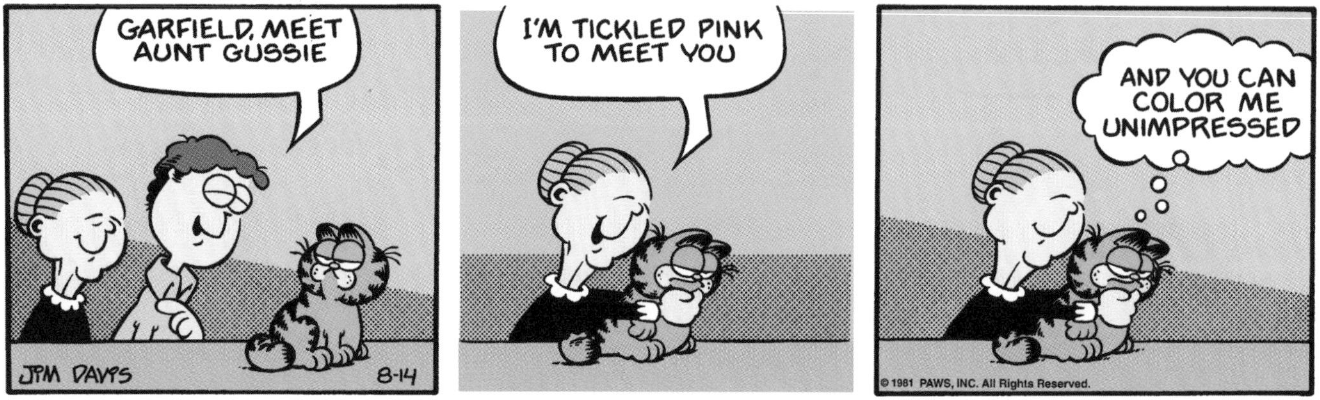
GARFIELD, MEET AUNT GUSSIE
JIM DAVIS
8-14
I'M TICKLED PINK TO MEET YOU
AND YOU CAN COLOR ME UNIMPRESSED
© 1981 PAWS, INC. All Rights Reserved.

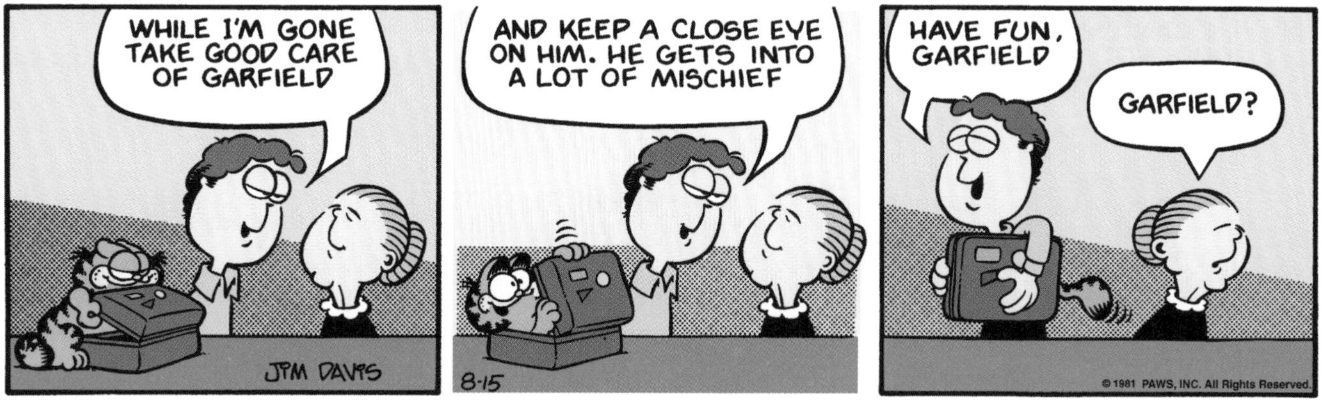
WHILE I'M GONE TAKE GOOD CARE OF GARFIELD
JIM DAVIS
AND KEEP A CLOSE EYE ON HIM. HE GETS INTO A LOT OF MISCHIEF
8-15
HAVE FUN, GARFIELD
GARFIELD?
© 1981 PAWS, INC. All Rights Reserved.

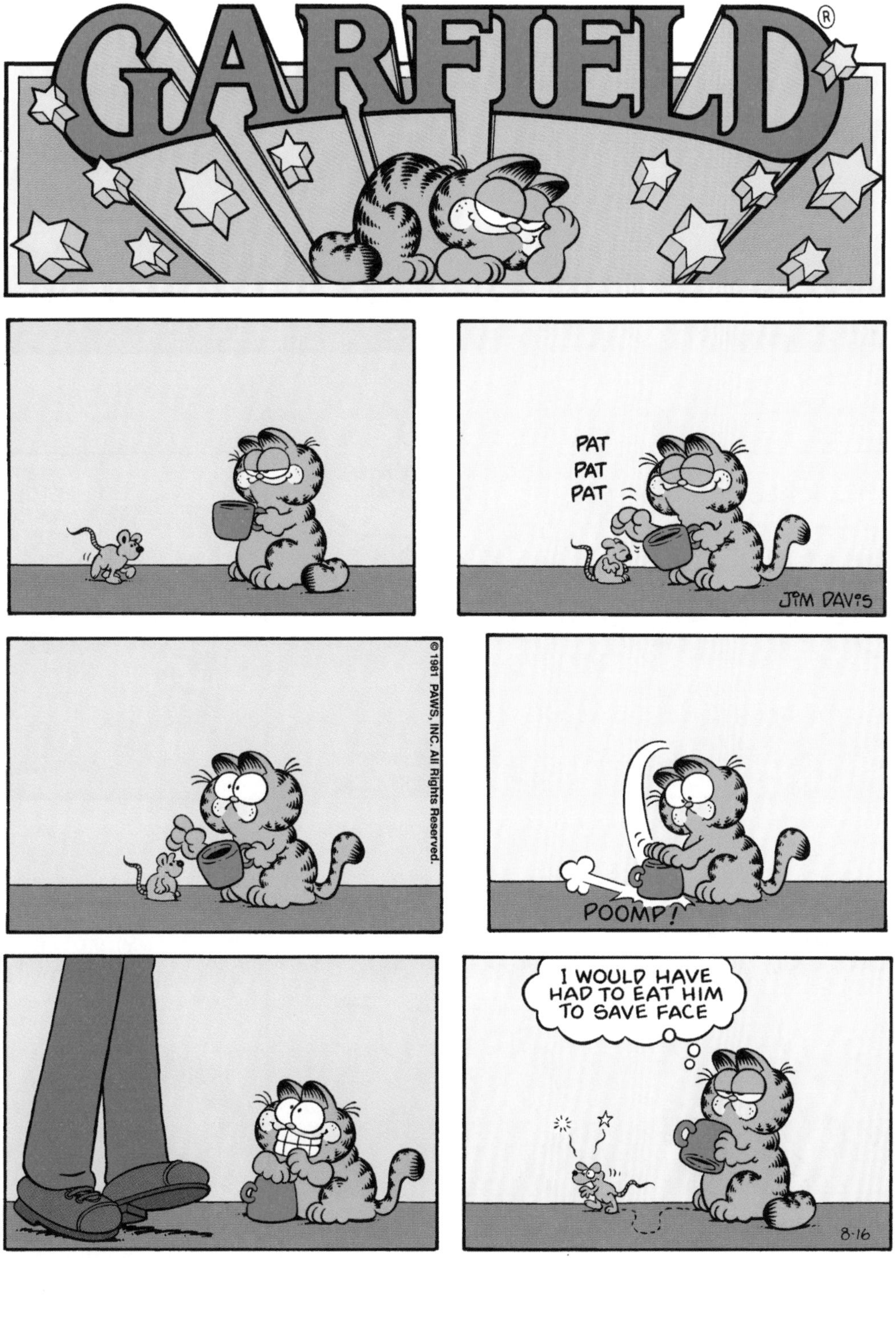

GARFIELD
PAT
PAT
PAT
JIM DAVIS
POOMP!
I WOULD HAVE HAD TO EAT HIM TO SAVE FACE
8-16

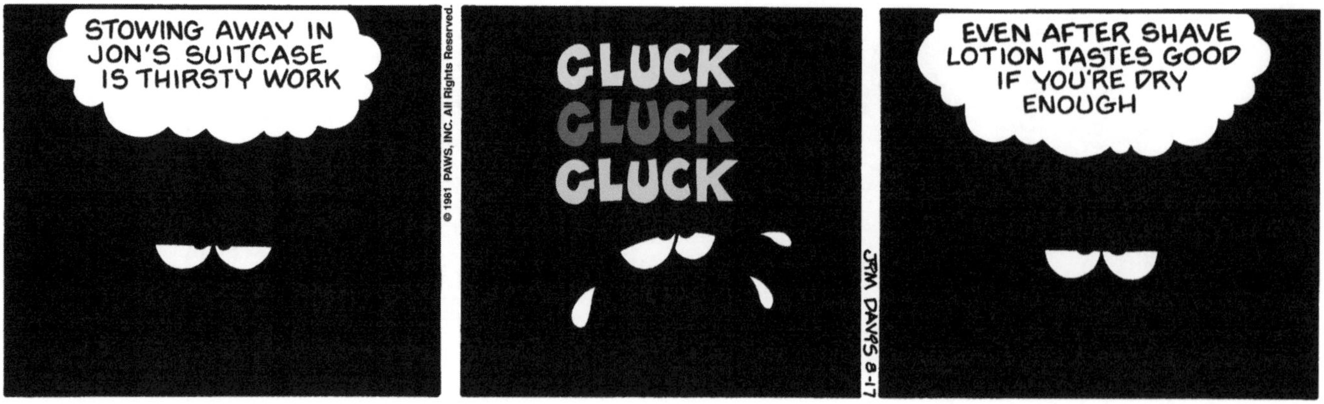
STOWING AWAY IN JON'S SUITCASE IS THIRSTY WORK
GLUCK
GLUCK
GLUCK
EVEN AFTER SHAVE LOTION TASTES GOOD IF YOU'RE DRY ENOUGH
© 1981 PAWS, INC. All Rights Reserved.
JIM DAVIS 8-17

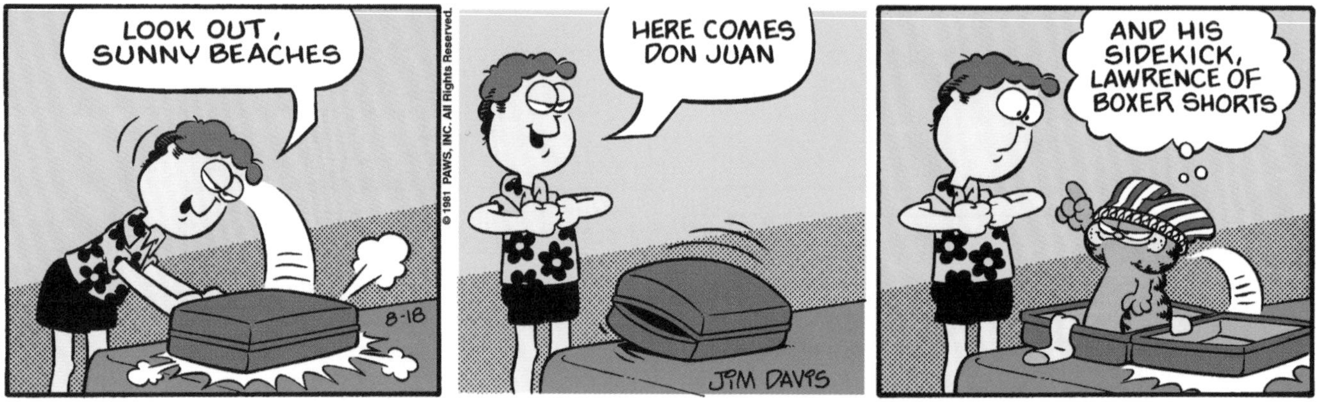
LOOK OUT, SUNNY BEACHES
8-18
HERE COMES DON JUAN
JIM DAVIS
AND HIS SIDEKICK, LAWRENCE OF BOXER SHORTS
© 1981 PAWS, INC. All Rights Reserved.

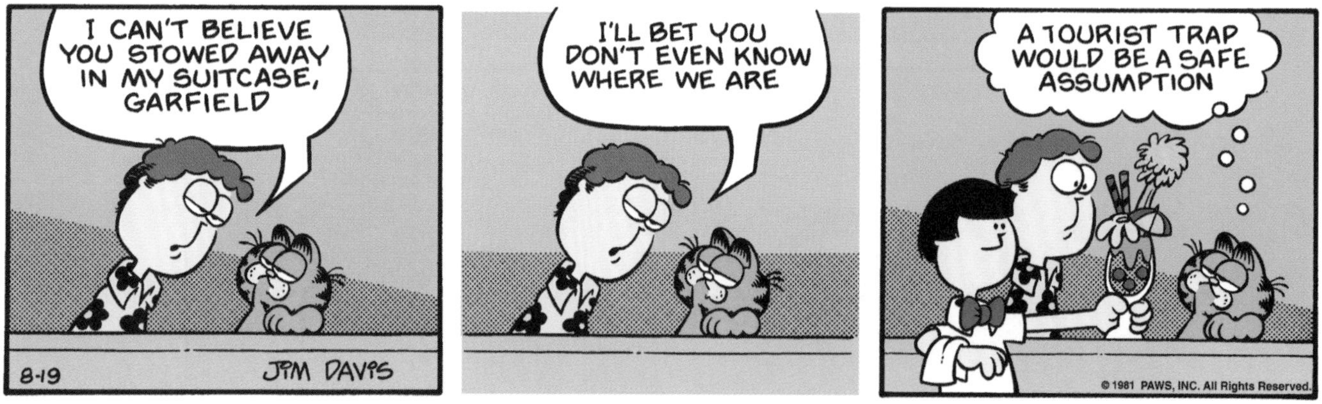
I CAN'T BELIEVE YOU STOWED AWAY IN MY SUITCASE, GARFIELD
8-19
JIM DAVIS
I'LL BET YOU DON'T EVEN KNOW WHERE WE ARE
A TOURIST TRAP WOULD BE A SAFE ASSUMPTION
© 1981 PAWS, INC. All Rights Reserved.

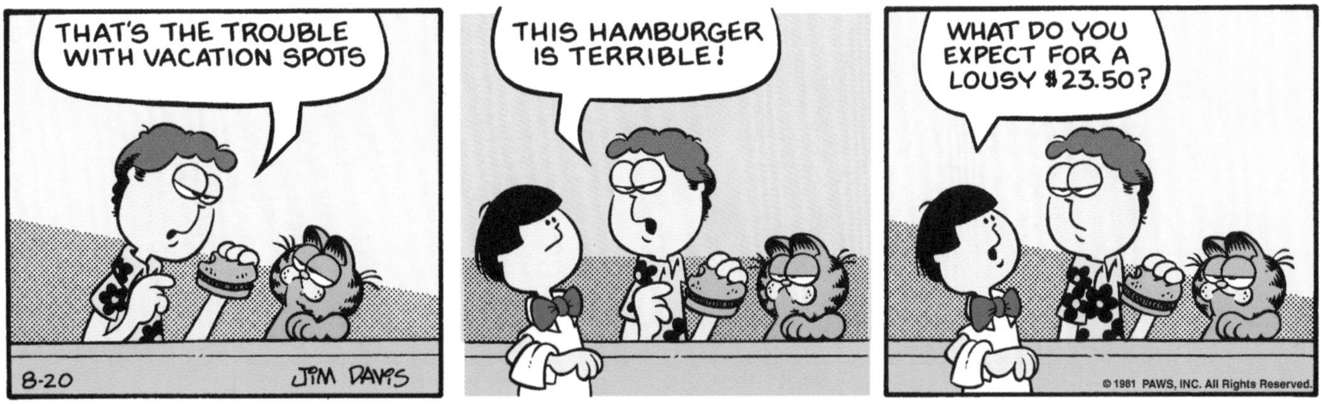
THAT'S THE TROUBLE WITH VACATION SPOTS
8-20
JIM DAVIS
THIS HAMBURGER IS TERRIBLE!
WHAT DO YOU EXPECT FOR A LOUSY $23.50?
© 1981 PAWS, INC. All Rights Reserved.

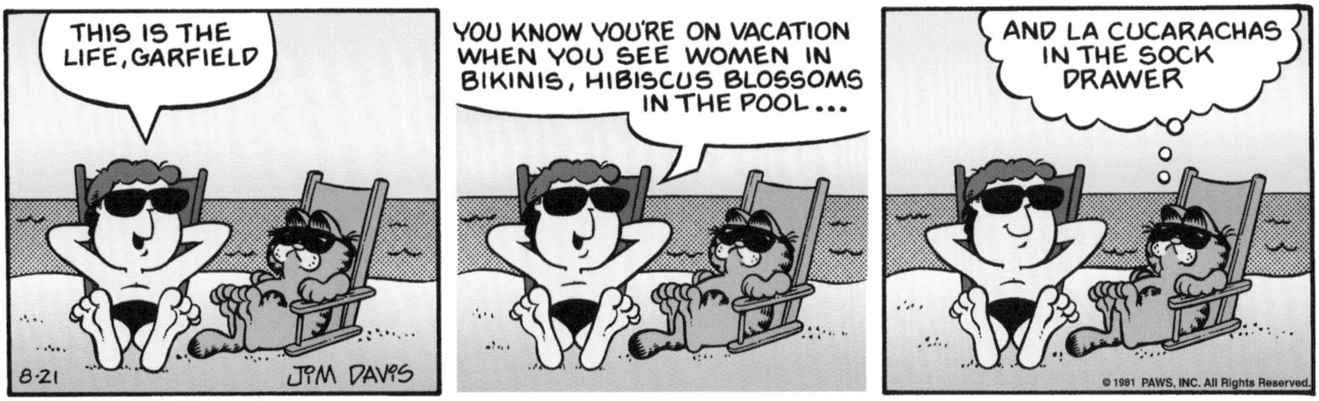
THIS IS THE LIFE, GARFIELD
8-21
JIM DAVIS
YOU KNOW YOU'RE ON VACATION WHEN YOU SEE WOMEN IN BIKINIS, HIBISCUS BLOSSOMS IN THE POOL...
AND LA CUCARACHAS IN THE SOCK DRAWER
© 1981 PAWS, INC. All Rights Reserved.

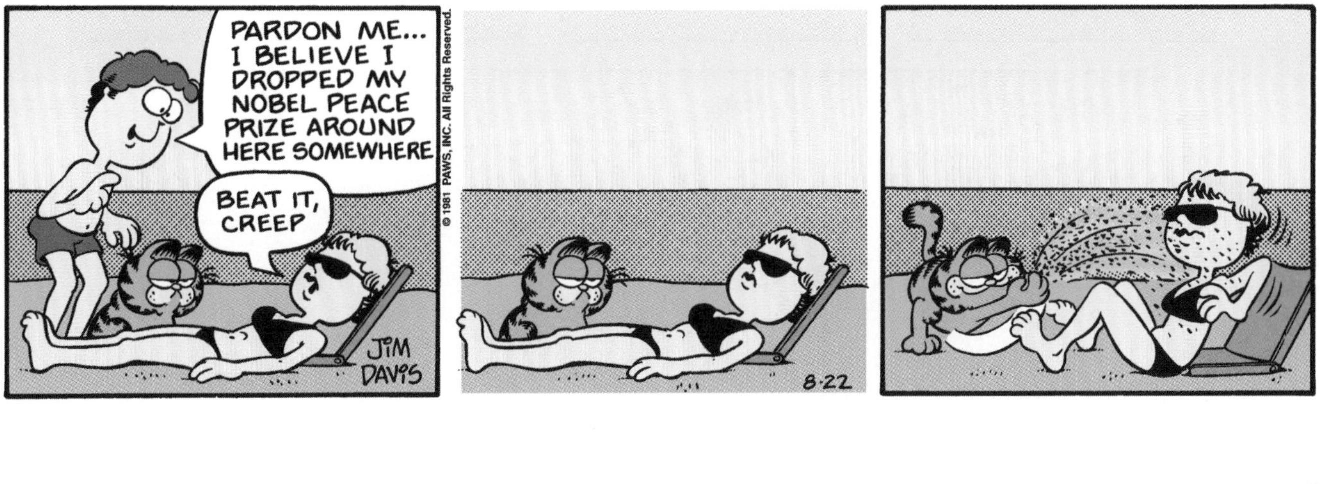
PARDON ME... I BELIEVE I DROPPED MY NOBEL PEACE PRIZE AROUND HERE SOMEWHERE
BEAT IT, CREEP
JIM DAVIS
© 1981 PAWS, INC. All Rights Reserved.
8-22

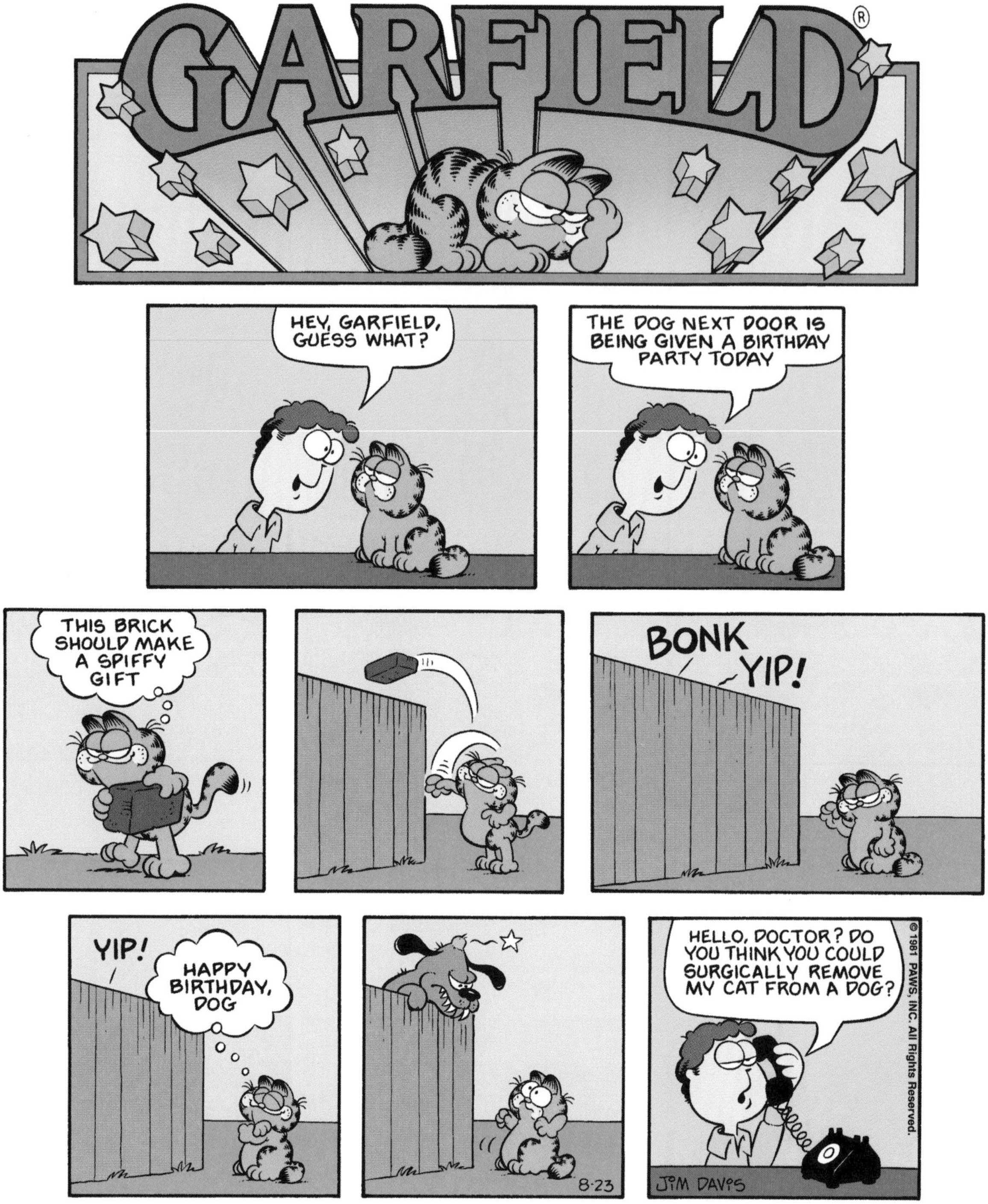
GARFIELD®
HEY, GARFIELD, GUESS WHAT?
THE DOG NEXT DOOR IS BEING GIVEN A BIRTHDAY PARTY TODAY
THIS BRICK SHOULD MAKE A SPIFFY GIFT
BONK
YIP!
YIP!
HAPPY BIRTHDAY, DOG
8-23
HELLO, DOCTOR? DO YOU THINK YOU COULD SURGICALLY REMOVE MY CAT FROM A DOG?
© 1981 PAWS, INC. All Rights Reserved.
JIM DAVIS

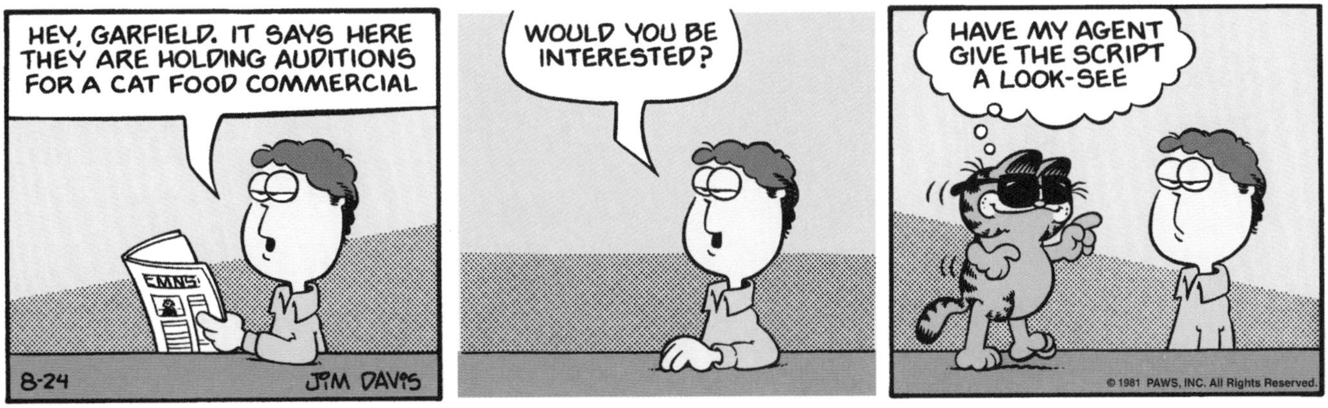
HEY, GARFIELD. IT SAYS HERE THEY ARE HOLDING AUDITIONS FOR A CAT FOOD COMMERCIAL
8-24
JIM DAVIS
WOULD YOU BE INTERESTED?
HAVE MY AGENT GIVE THE SCRIPT A LOOK-SEE
© 1981 PAWS, INC. All Rights Reserved.

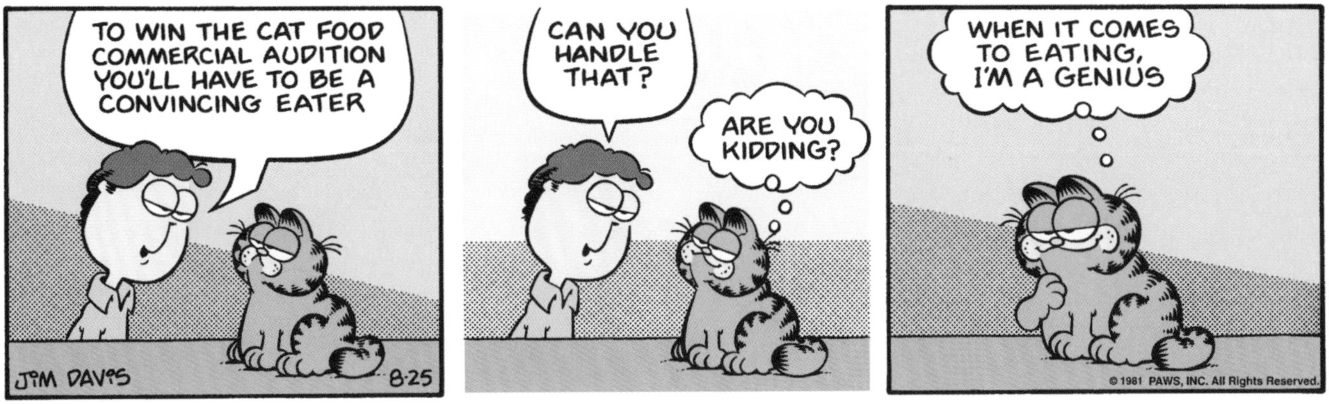
TO WIN THE CAT FOOD COMMERCIAL AUDITION YOU'LL HAVE TO BE A CONVINCING EATER
JIM DAVIS
8-25
CAN YOU HANDLE THAT?
ARE YOU KIDDING?
WHEN IT COMES TO EATING, I'M A GENIUS
© 1981 PAWS, INC. All Rights Reserved.

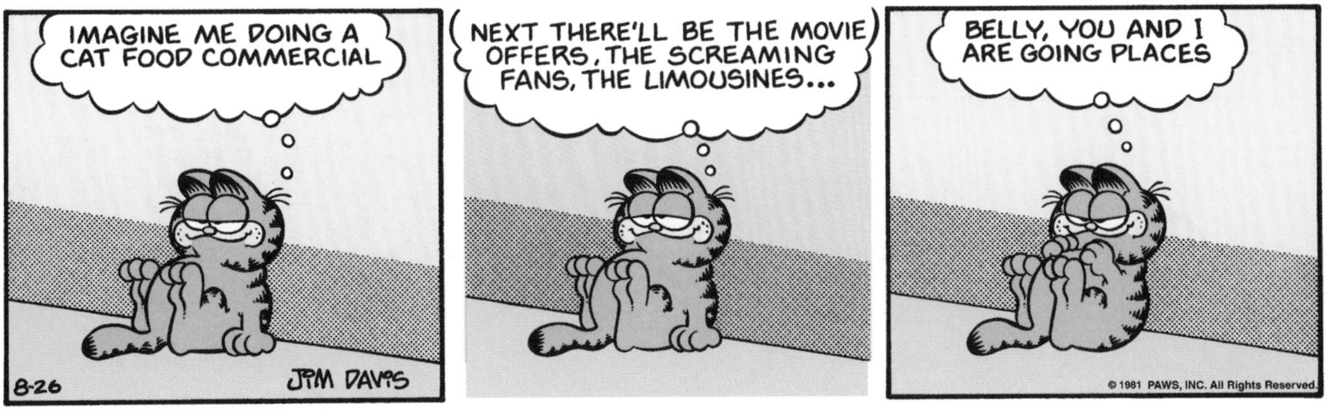
IMAGINE ME DOING A CAT FOOD COMMERCIAL
8-26
JIM DAVIS
NEXT THERE'LL BE THE MOVIE OFFERS, THE SCREAMING FANS, THE LIMOUSINES...
BELLY, YOU AND I ARE GOING PLACES
© 1981 PAWS, INC. All Rights Reserved.

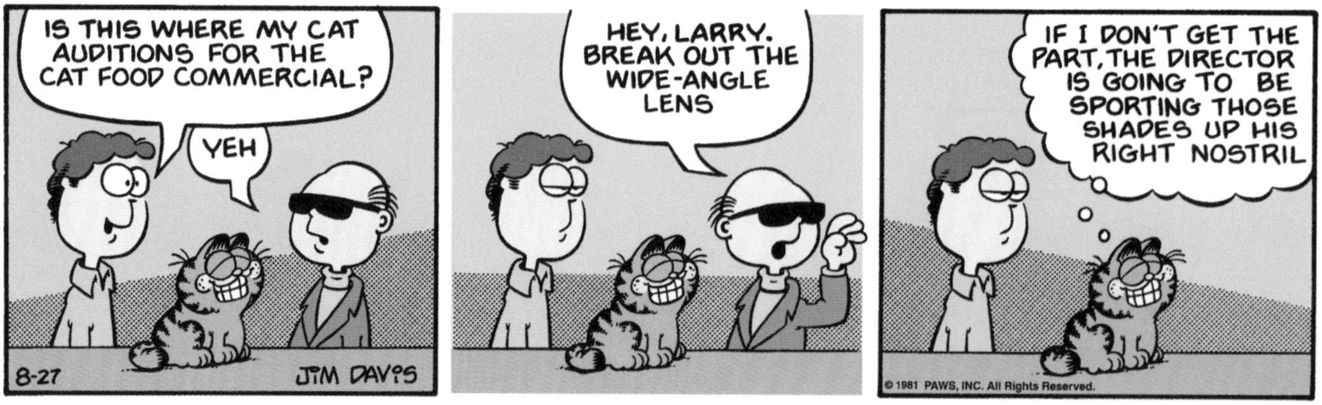
IS THIS WHERE MY CAT AUDITIONS FOR THE CAT FOOD COMMERCIAL?
YEH
HEY, LARRY. BREAK OUT THE WIDE-ANGLE LENS
IF I DON'T GET THE PART, THE DIRECTOR IS GOING TO BE SPORTING THOSE SHADES UP HIS RIGHT NOSTRIL
8-27
JIM DAVIS
© 1981 PAWS, INC. All Rights Reserved.

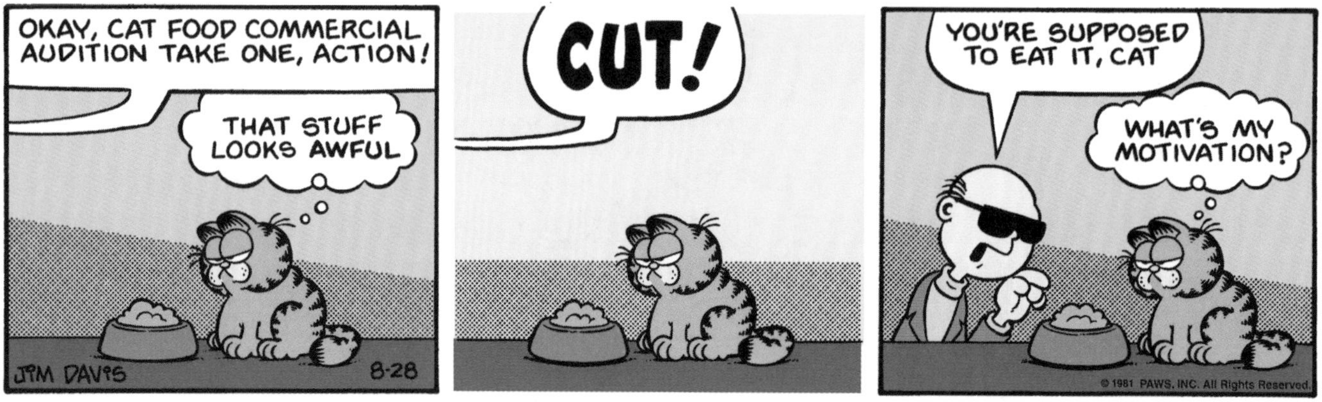
OKAY, CAT FOOD COMMERCIAL AUDITION TAKE ONE, ACTION!
THAT STUFF LOOKS AWFUL
JIM DAVIS
8-28
CUT!
YOU'RE SUPPOSED TO EAT IT, CAT
WHAT'S MY MOTIVATION?
© 1981 PAWS, INC. All Rights Reserved.

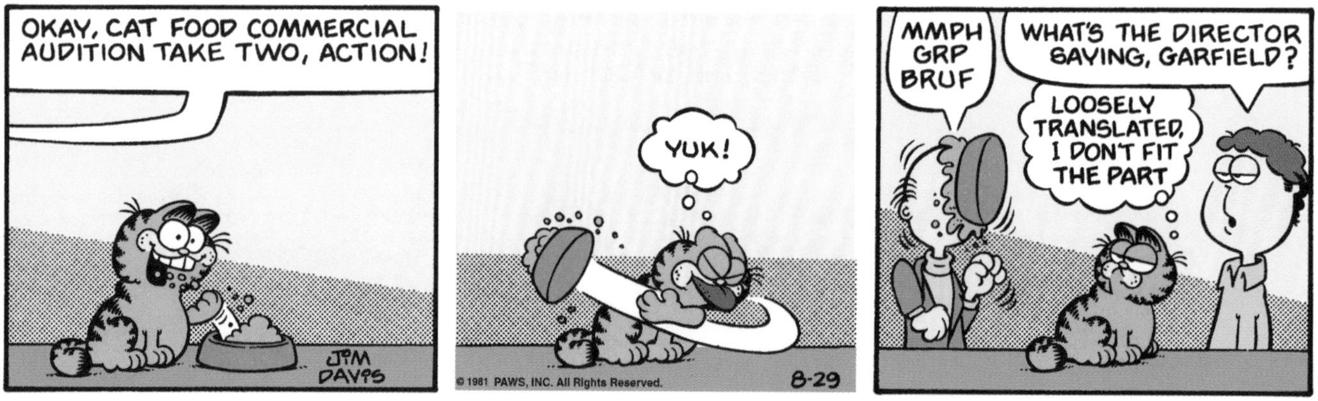
OKAY, CAT FOOD COMMERCIAL AUDITION TAKE TWO, ACTION!
JIM DAVIS
YUK!
© 1981 PAWS, INC. All Rights Reserved.
8-29
MMPH GRP BRUF
WHAT'S THE DIRECTOR SAYING, GARFIELD?
LOOSELY TRANSLATED, I DON'T FIT THE PART

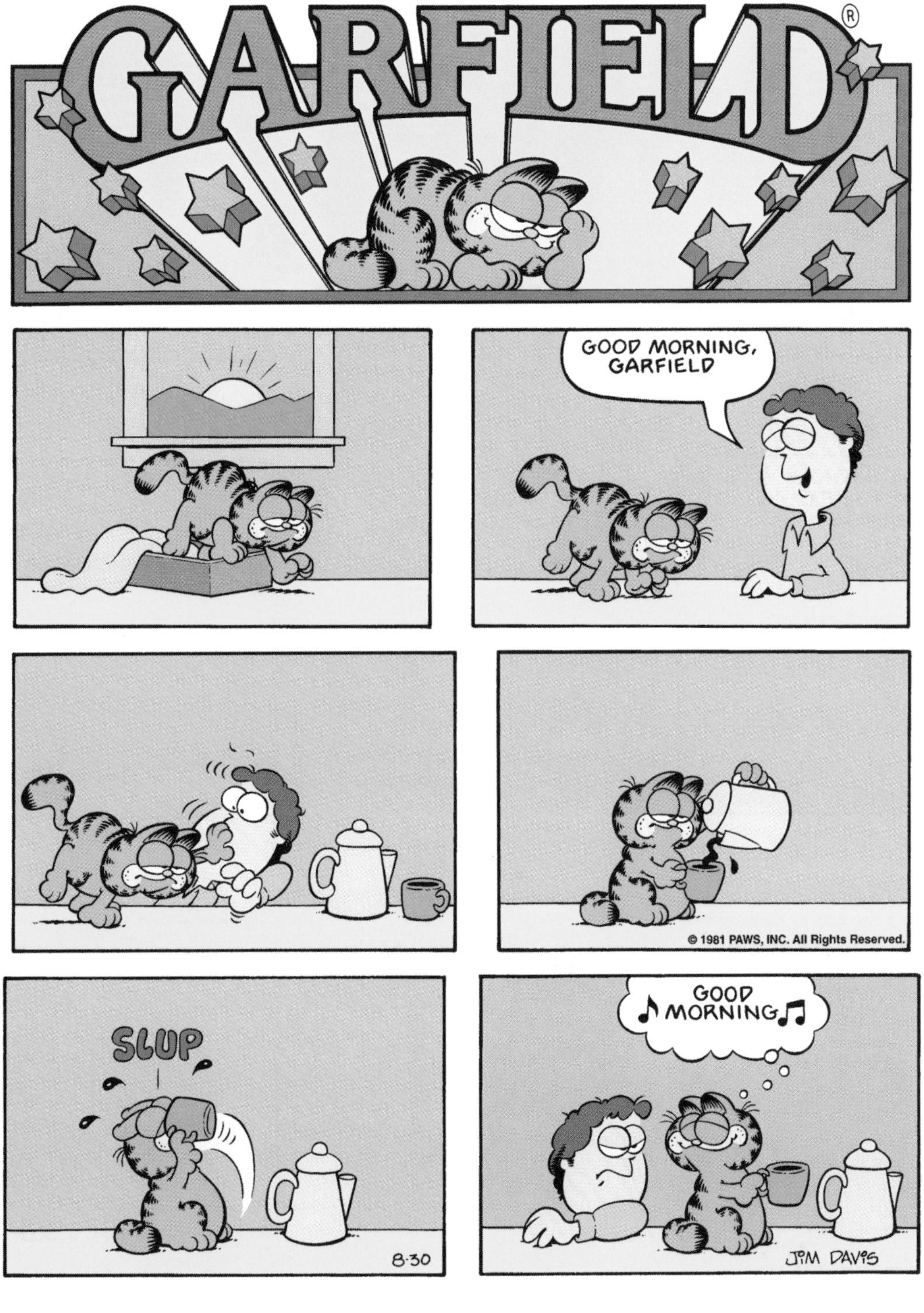
GARFIELD®
GOOD MORNING, GARFIELD
© 1981 PAWS, INC. All Rights Reserved.
SLUP
8-30
GOOD ♪MORNING♫
JIM DAVIS

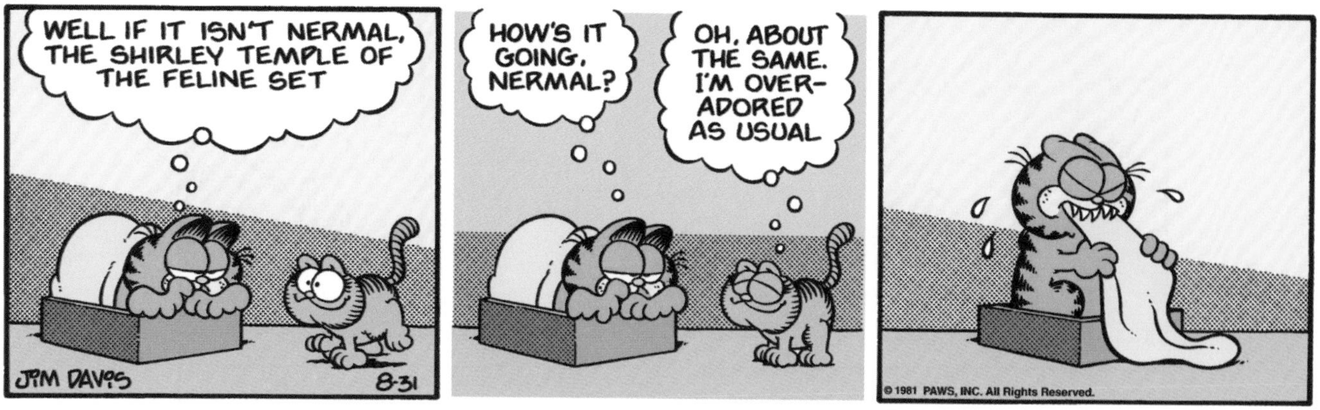
WELL IF IT ISN'T NERMAL, THE SHIRLEY TEMPLE OF THE FELINE SET
JIM DAVIS
8-31
HOW'S IT GOING, NERMAL?
OH, ABOUT THE SAME. I'M OVER-ADORED AS USUAL
© 1981 PAWS, INC. All Rights Reserved.

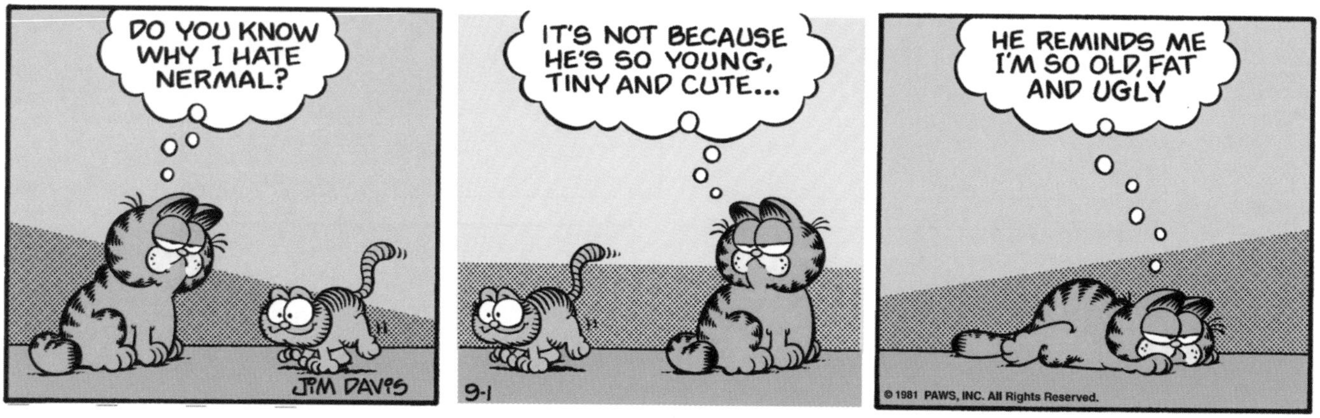
DO YOU KNOW WHY I HATE NERMAL?
JIM DAVIS
IT'S NOT BECAUSE HE'S SO YOUNG, TINY AND CUTE...
9-1
HE REMINDS ME I'M SO OLD, FAT AND UGLY
© 1981 PAWS, INC. All Rights Reserved.

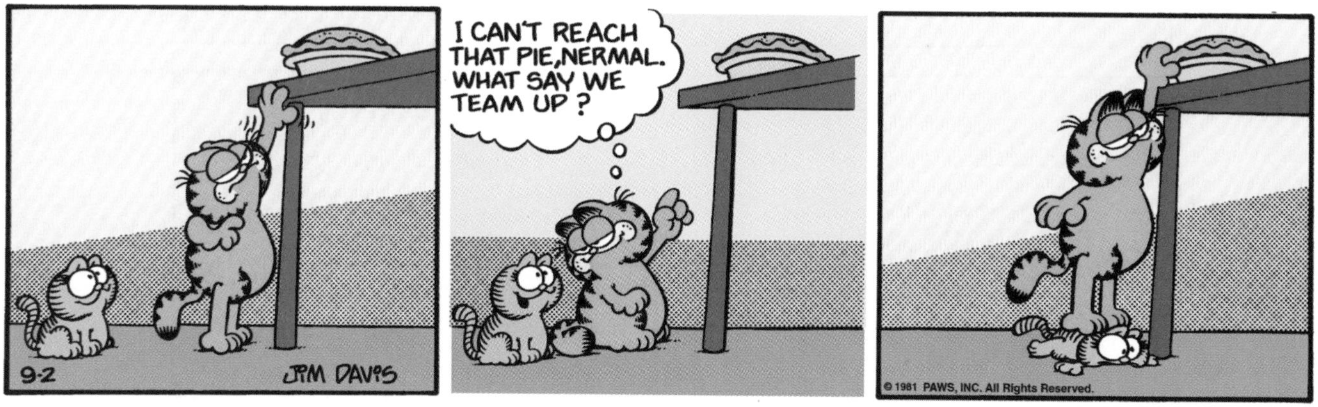
9-2
JIM DAVIS
I CAN'T REACH THAT PIE, NERMAL. WHAT SAY WE TEAM UP?
© 1981 PAWS, INC. All Rights Reserved.

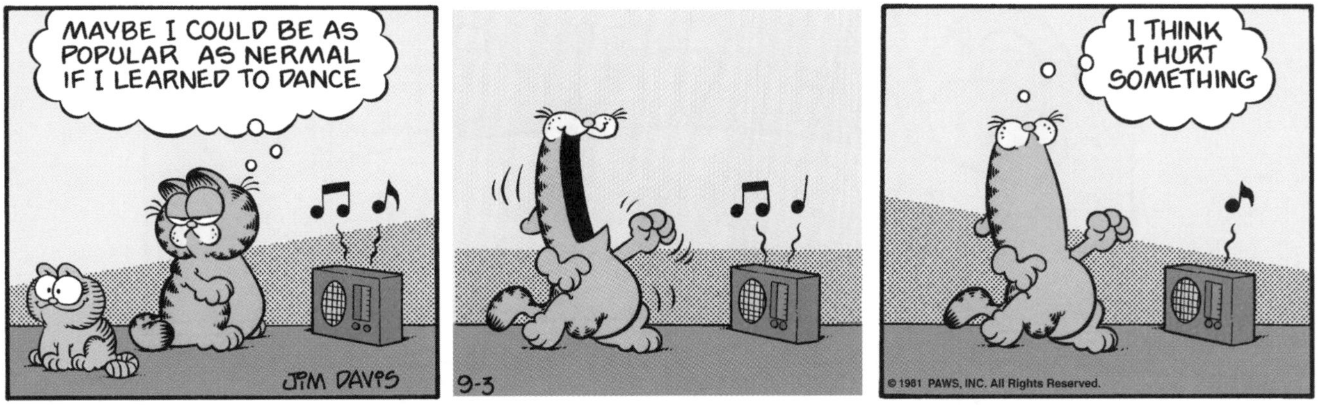
MAYBE I COULD BE AS POPULAR AS NERMAL IF I LEARNED TO DANCE
JIM DAVIS
9-3
I THINK I HURT SOMETHING
© 1981 PAWS, INC. All Rights Reserved.

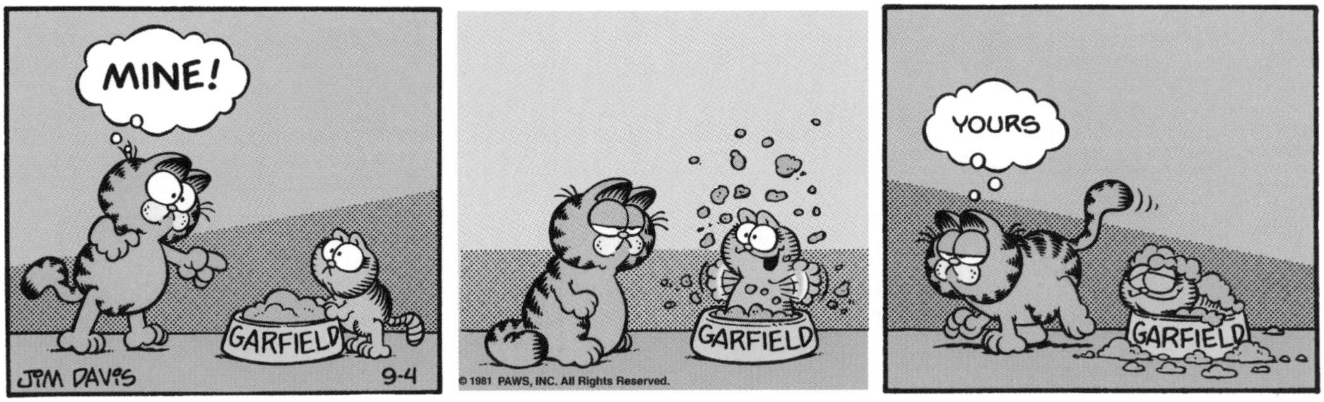
MINE!
GARFIELD
JIM DAVIS
9-4
GARFIELD
© 1981 PAWS, INC. All Rights Reserved.
YOURS
GARFIELD

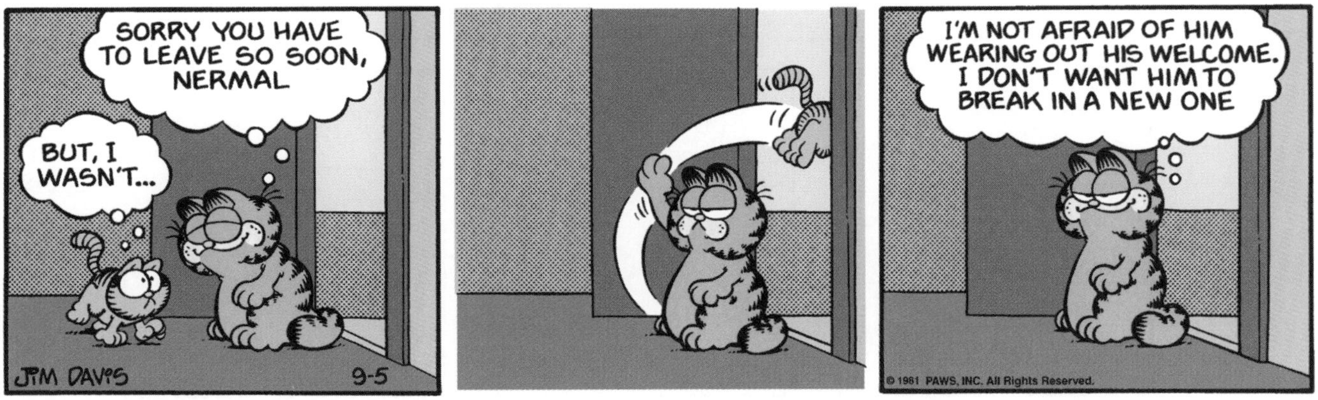
SORRY YOU HAVE TO LEAVE SO SOON, NERMAL
BUT, I WASN'T...
JIM DAVIS
9-5
I'M NOT AFRAID OF HIM WEARING OUT HIS WELCOME. I DON'T WANT HIM TO BREAK IN A NEW ONE
© 1981 PAWS, INC. All Rights Reserved.

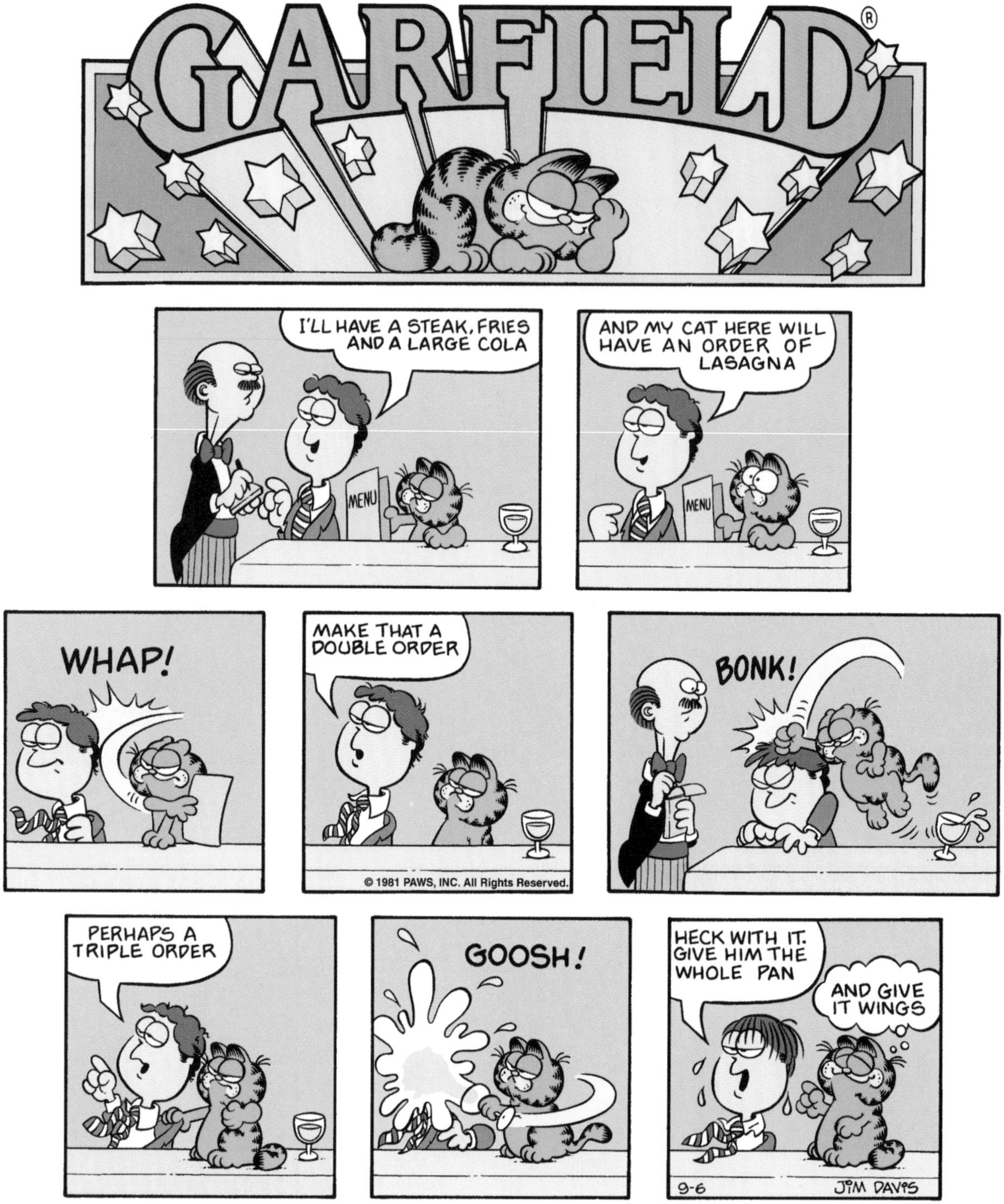
GARFIELD®
I'LL HAVE A STEAK, FRIES AND A LARGE COLA
MENU
AND MY CAT HERE WILL HAVE AN ORDER OF LASAGNA
MENU
WHAP!
MAKE THAT A DOUBLE ORDER
© 1981 PAWS, INC. All Rights Reserved.
BONK!
PERHAPS A TRIPLE ORDER
GOOSH!
HECK WITH IT. GIVE HIM THE WHOLE PAN
AND GIVE IT WINGS
9-6
JIM DAVIS

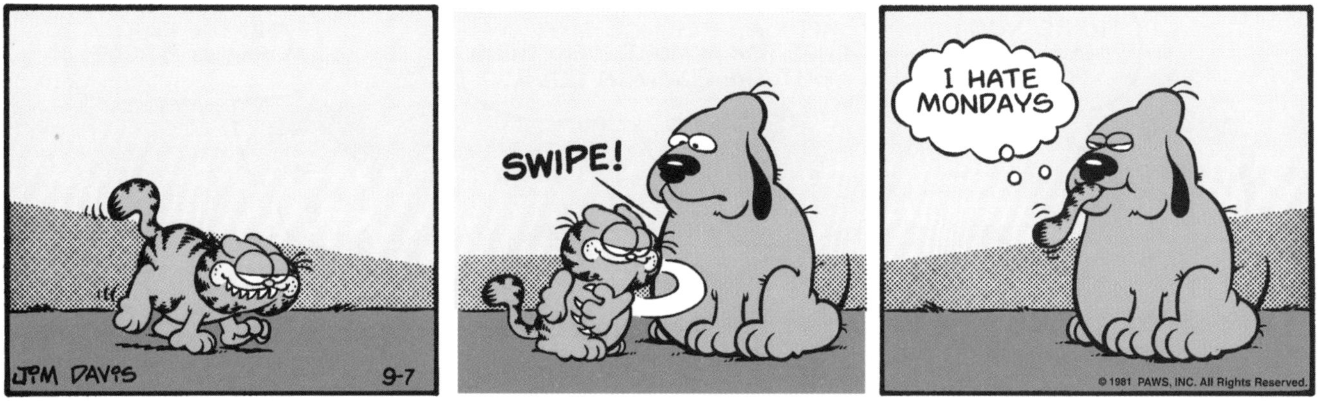
JIM DAVIS
9-7
SWIPE!
I HATE MONDAYS
© 1981 PAWS, INC. All Rights Reserved.

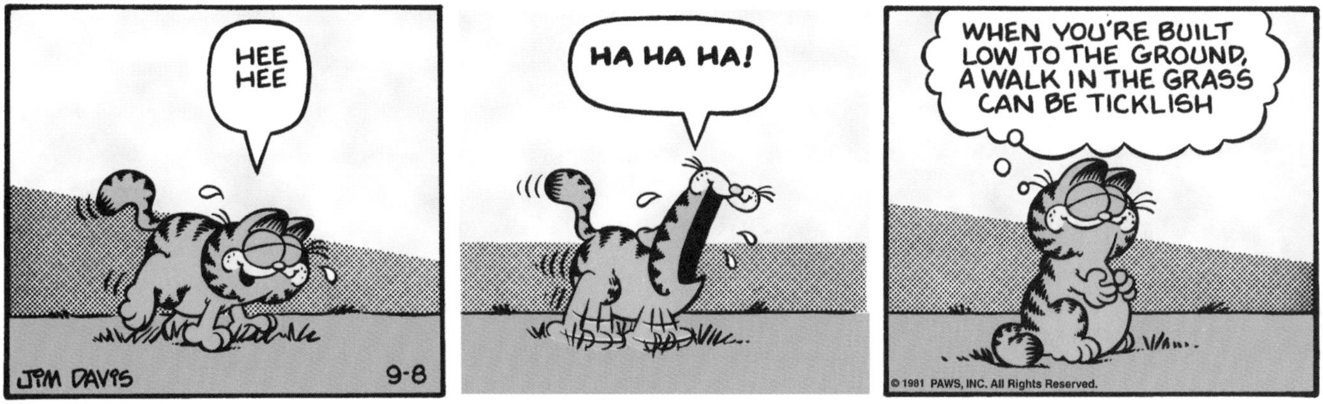
HEE HEE
JIM DAVIS
9-8
HA HA HA!
WHEN YOU'RE BUILT LOW TO THE GROUND, A WALK IN THE GRASS CAN BE TICKLISH
© 1981 PAWS, INC. All Rights Reserved.

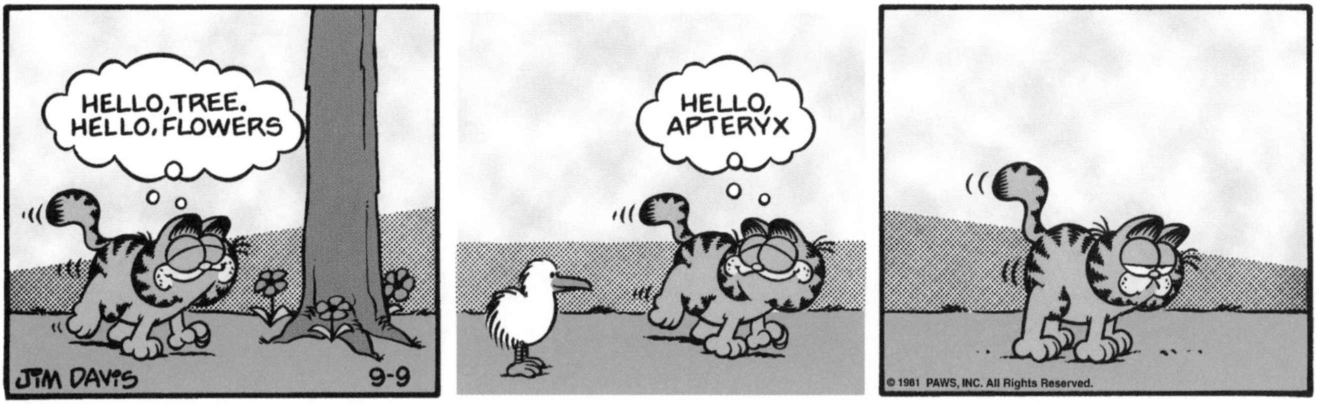
HELLO, TREE. HELLO, FLOWERS
JIM DAVIS
9-9
HELLO, APTERYX
© 1981 PAWS, INC. All Rights Reserved.

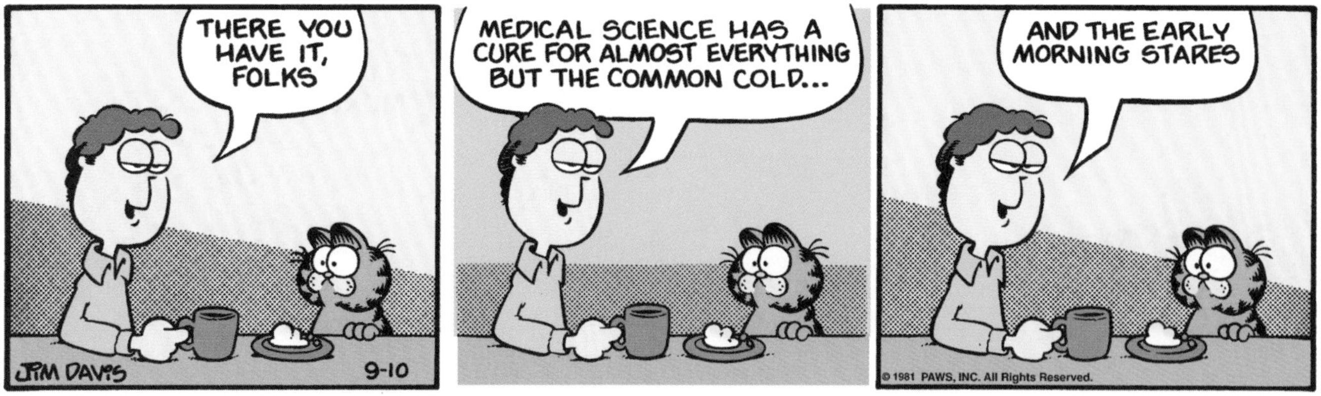
THERE YOU HAVE IT, FOLKS
JIM DAVIS
9-10
MEDICAL SCIENCE HAS A CURE FOR ALMOST EVERYTHING BUT THE COMMON COLD...
AND THE EARLY MORNING STARES
© 1981 PAWS, INC. All Rights Reserved.

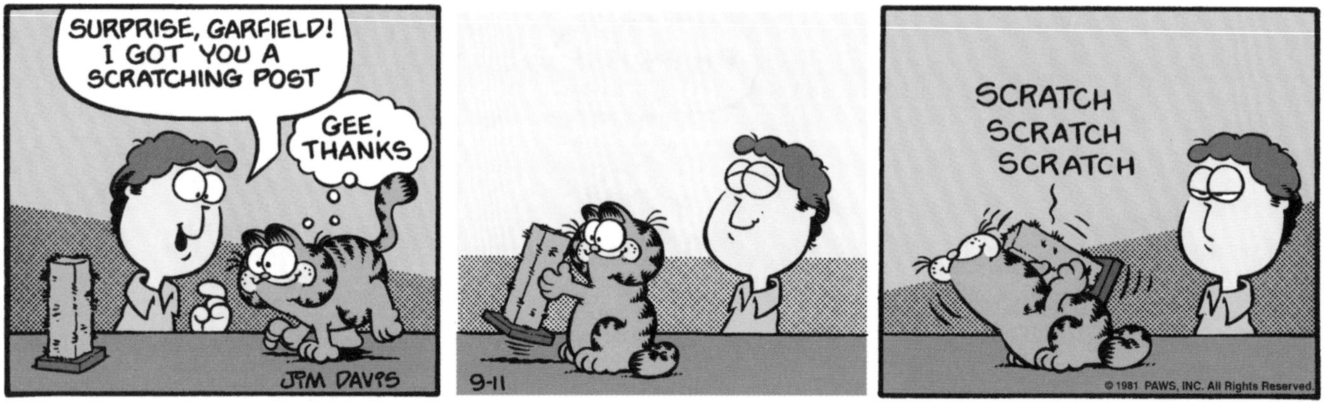
SURPRISE, GARFIELD! I GOT YOU A SCRATCHING POST
GEE, THANKS
JIM DAVIS
9-11
SCRATCH SCRATCH SCRATCH
© 1981 PAWS, INC. All Rights Reserved.

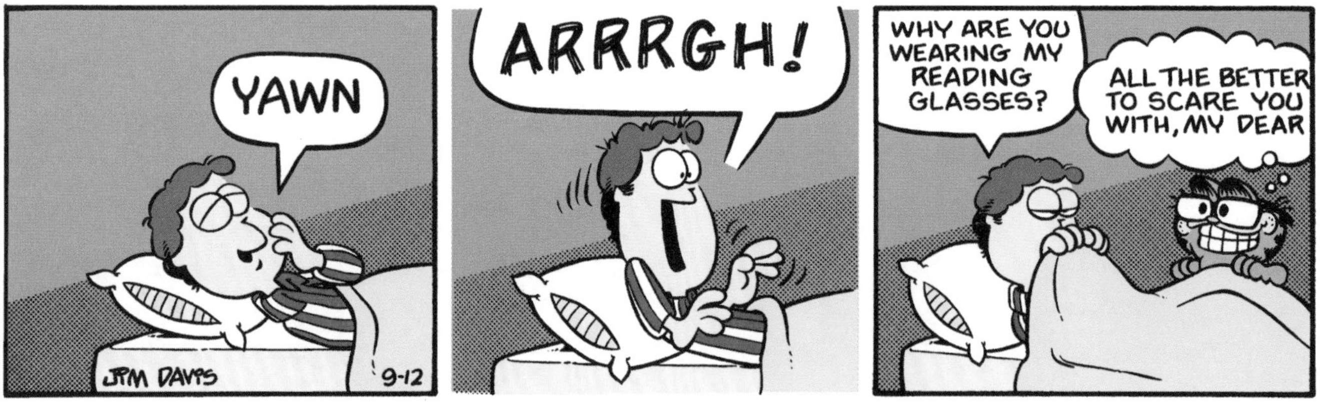
YAWN
JIM DAVIS
9-12
ARRRGH!
WHY ARE YOU WEARING MY READING GLASSES?
ALL THE BETTER TO SCARE YOU WITH, MY DEAR

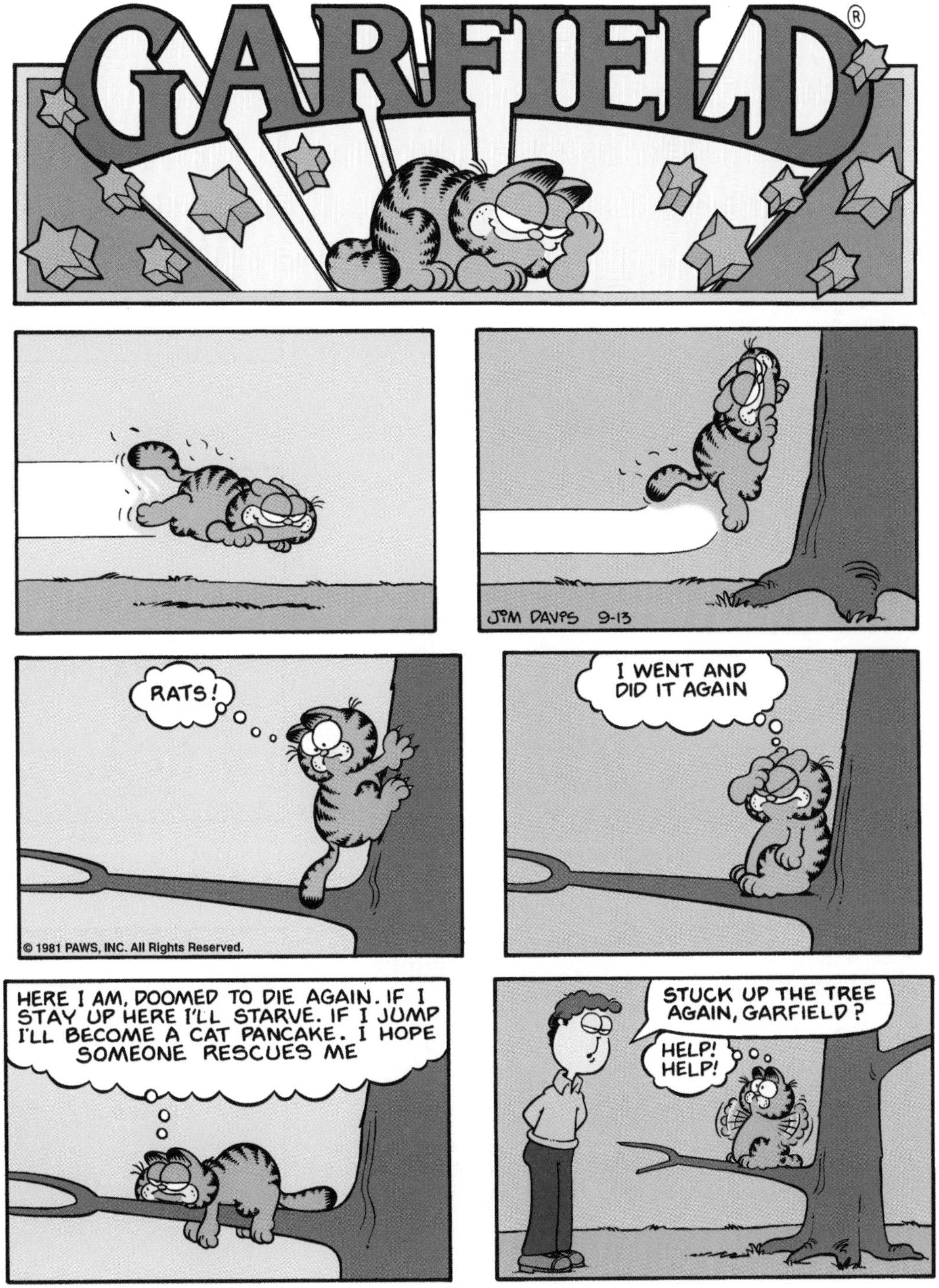
GARFIELD
JIM DAVIS 9-13
RATS!
I WENT AND DID IT AGAIN
© 1981 PAWS, INC. All Rights Reserved.
HERE I AM, DOOMED TO DIE AGAIN. IF I STAY UP HERE I'LL STARVE. IF I JUMP I'LL BECOME A CAT PANCAKE. I HOPE SOMEONE RESCUES ME
STUCK UP THE TREE AGAIN, GARFIELD?
HELP! HELP!

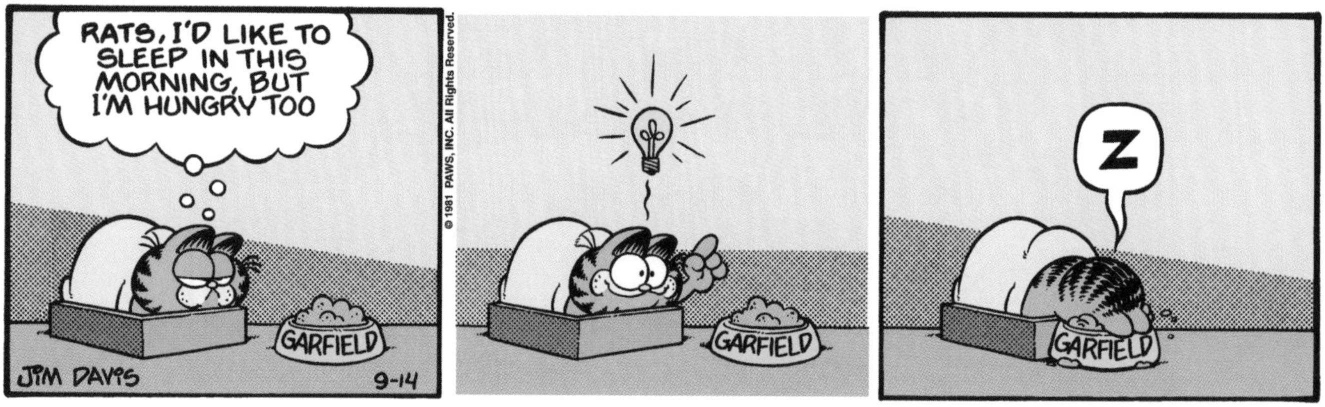
RATS, I'D LIKE TO SLEEP IN THIS MORNING, BUT I'M HUNGRY TOO
JIM DAVIS
9-14
GARFIELD
© 1981 PAWS, INC. All Rights Reserved.
GARFIELD
Z
GARFIELD

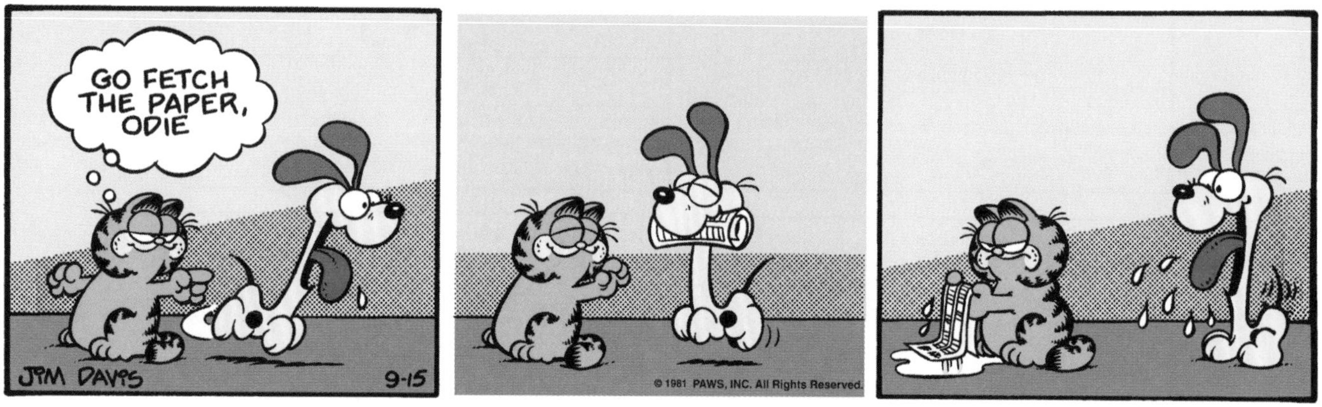
GO FETCH THE PAPER, ODIE
JIM DAVIS
9-15
© 1981 PAWS, INC. All Rights Reserved.

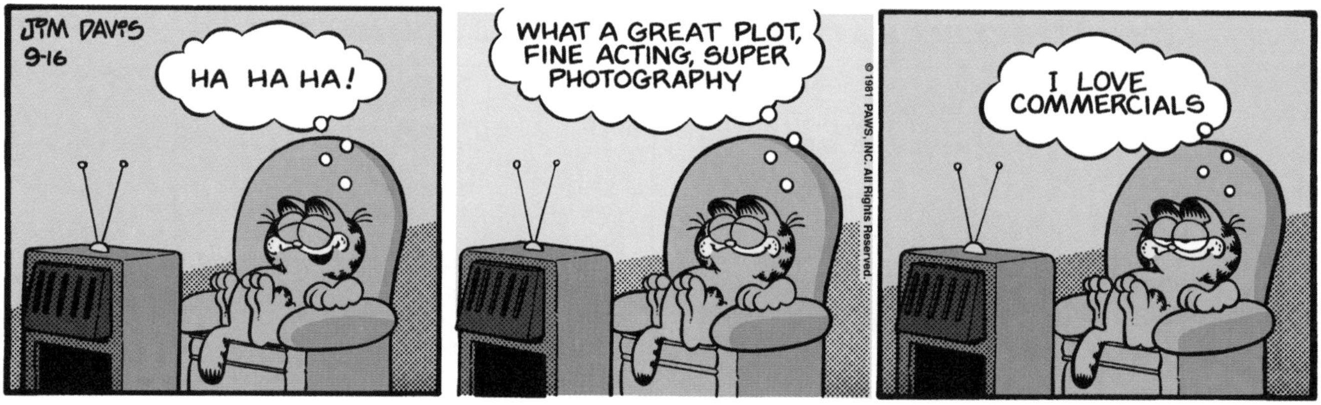
JIM DAVIS
9-16
HA HA HA!
WHAT A GREAT PLOT, FINE ACTING, SUPER PHOTOGRAPHY
© 1981 PAWS, INC. All Rights Reserved.
I LOVE COMMERCIALS

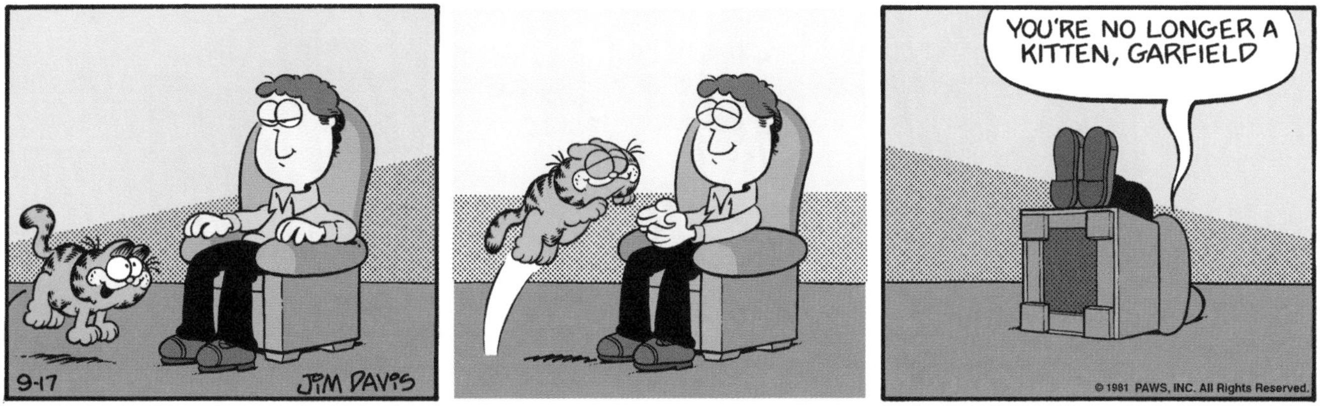
9-17
JIM DAVIS
YOU'RE NO LONGER A KITTEN, GARFIELD
© 1981 PAWS, INC. All Rights Reserved.

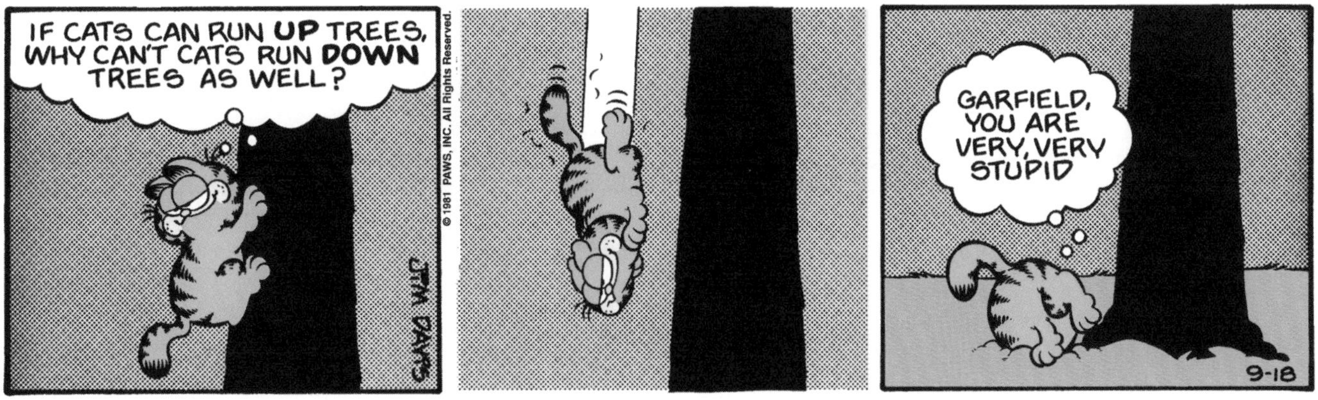
IF CATS CAN RUN **UP** TREES, WHY CAN'T CATS RUN **DOWN** TREES AS WELL?
JIM DAVIS
© 1981 PAWS, INC. All Rights Reserved.
GARFIELD, YOU ARE VERY, VERY STUPID
9-18

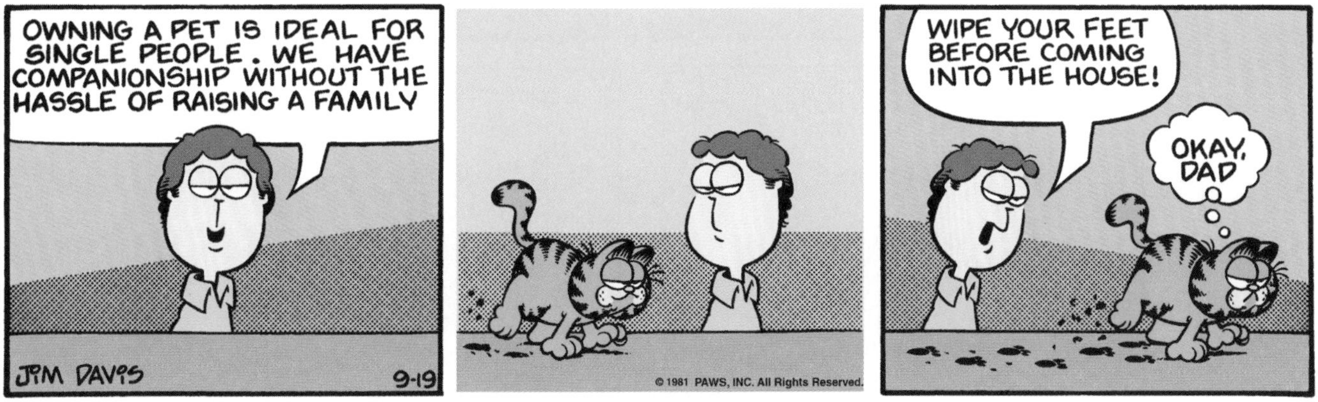
OWNING A PET IS IDEAL FOR SINGLE PEOPLE. WE HAVE COMPANIONSHIP WITHOUT THE HASSLE OF RAISING A FAMILY
JIM DAVIS
9-19
© 1981 PAWS, INC. All Rights Reserved.
WIPE YOUR FEET BEFORE COMING INTO THE HOUSE!
OKAY, DAD

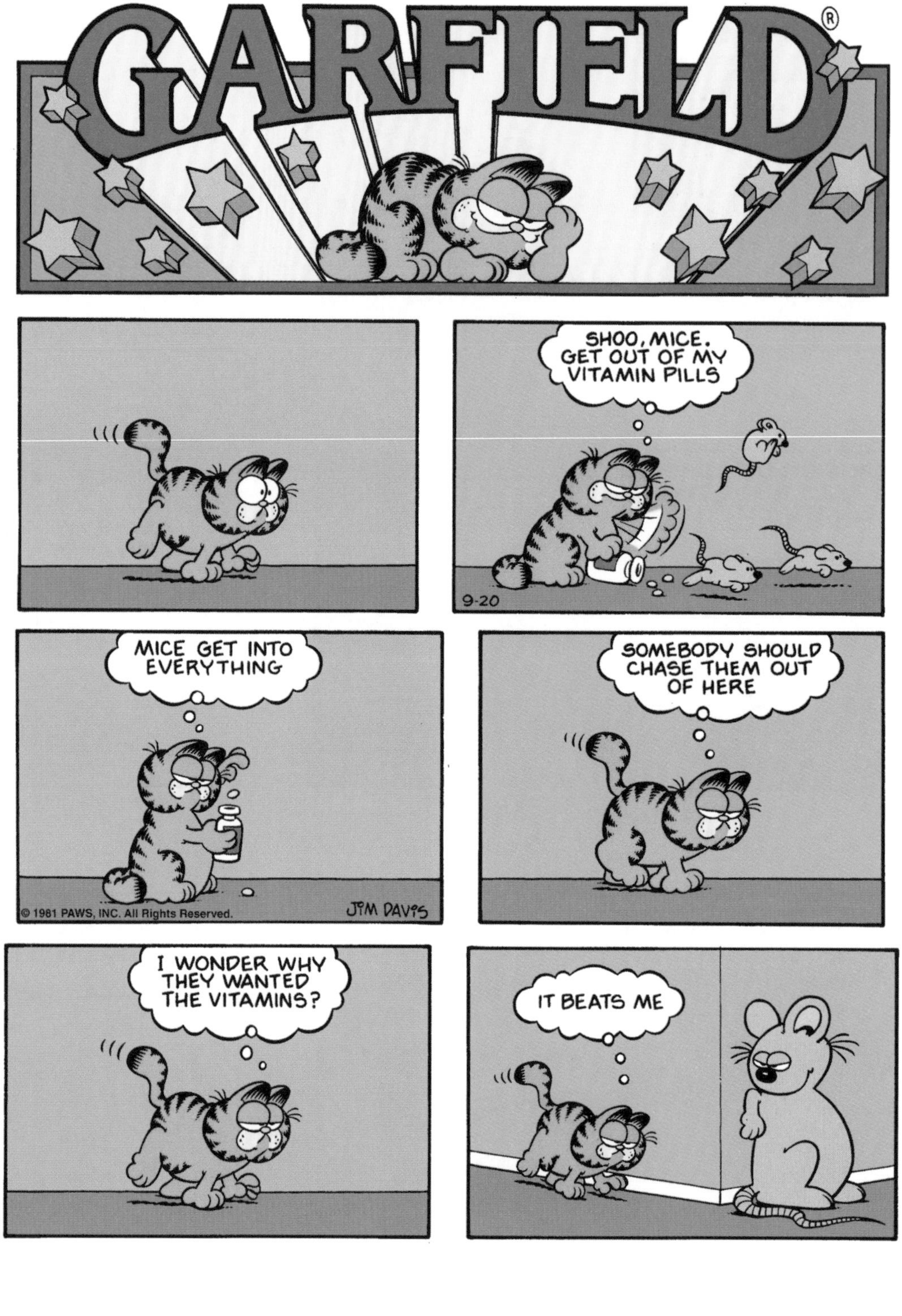
GARFIELD
SHOO, MICE. GET OUT OF MY VITAMIN PILLS
9-20
MICE GET INTO EVERYTHING
© 1981 PAWS, INC. All Rights Reserved.
JIM DAVIS
SOMEBODY SHOULD CHASE THEM OUT OF HERE
I WONDER WHY THEY WANTED THE VITAMINS?
IT BEATS ME

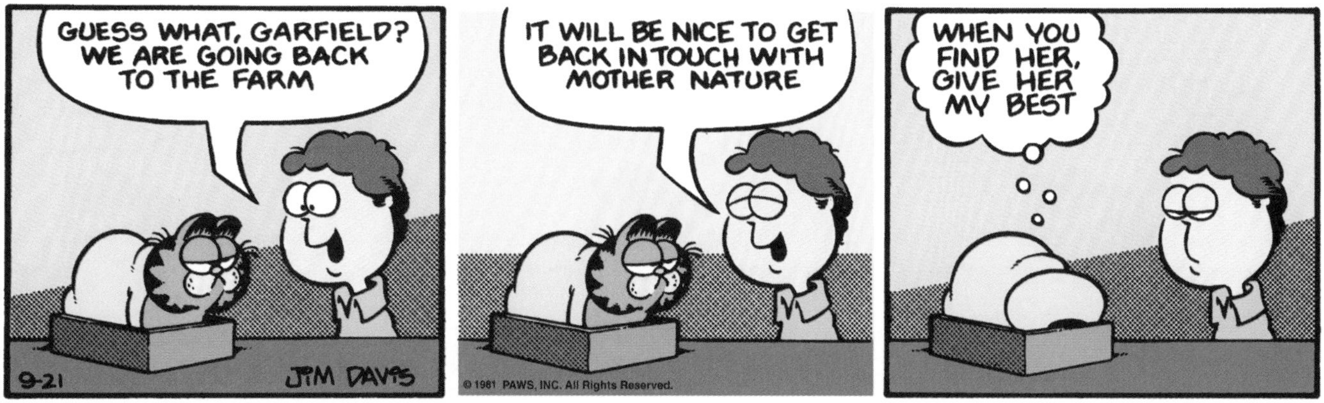
GUESS WHAT, GARFIELD? WE ARE GOING BACK TO THE FARM
9-21
JIM DAVIS
IT WILL BE NICE TO GET BACK IN TOUCH WITH MOTHER NATURE
© 1981 PAWS, INC. All Rights Reserved.
WHEN YOU FIND HER, GIVE HER MY BEST

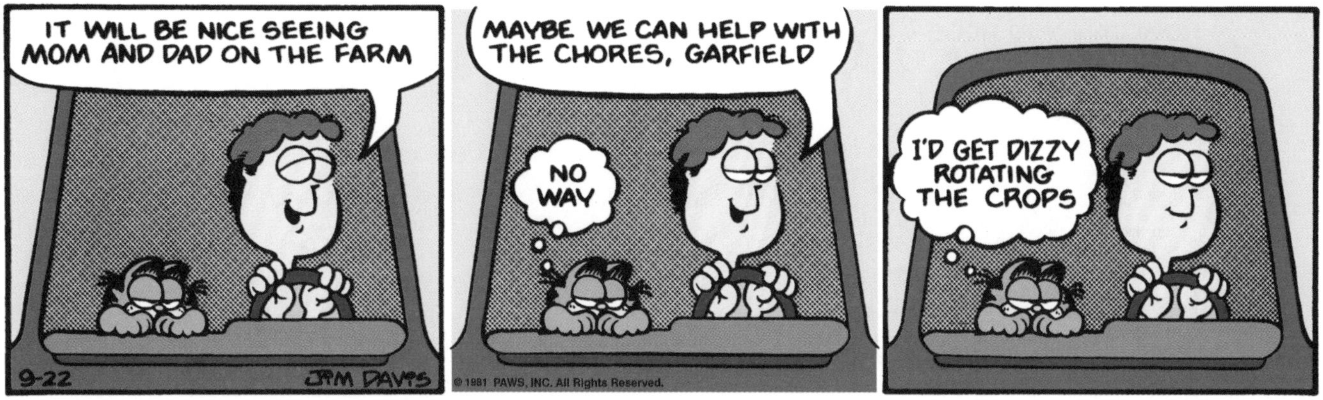
IT WILL BE NICE SEEING MOM AND DAD ON THE FARM
9-22
JIM DAVIS
MAYBE WE CAN HELP WITH THE CHORES, GARFIELD
NO WAY
© 1981 PAWS, INC. All Rights Reserved.
I'D GET DIZZY ROTATING THE CROPS

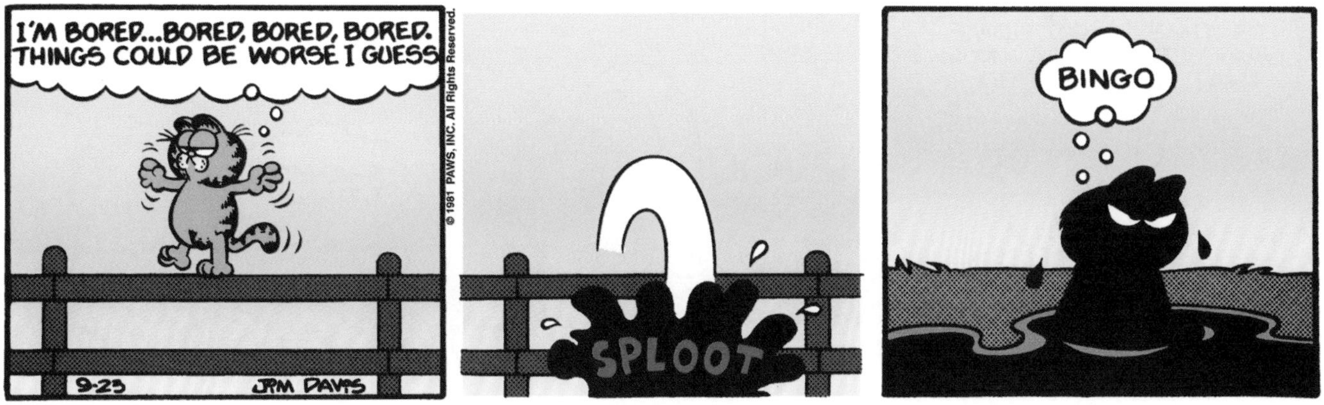
I'M BORED...BORED, BORED, BORED. THINGS COULD BE WORSE I GUESS
9-23
JIM DAVIS
© 1981 PAWS, INC. All Rights Reserved.
SPLOOT
BINGO

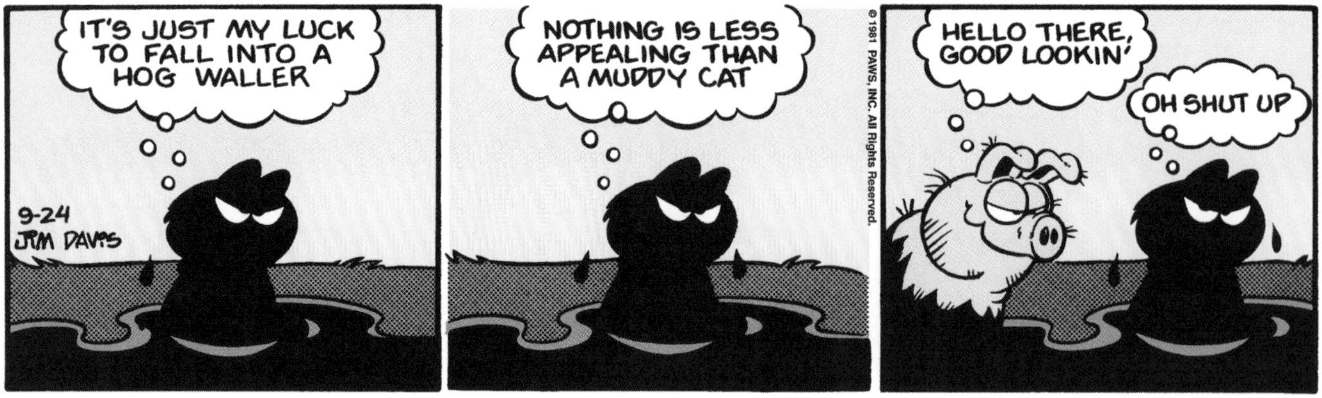
IT'S JUST MY LUCK TO FALL INTO A HOG WALLER
9-24
JIM DAVIS
NOTHING IS LESS APPEALING THAN A MUDDY CAT
© 1981 PAWS, INC. All Rights Reserved.
HELLO THERE, GOOD LOOKIN'
OH SHUT UP

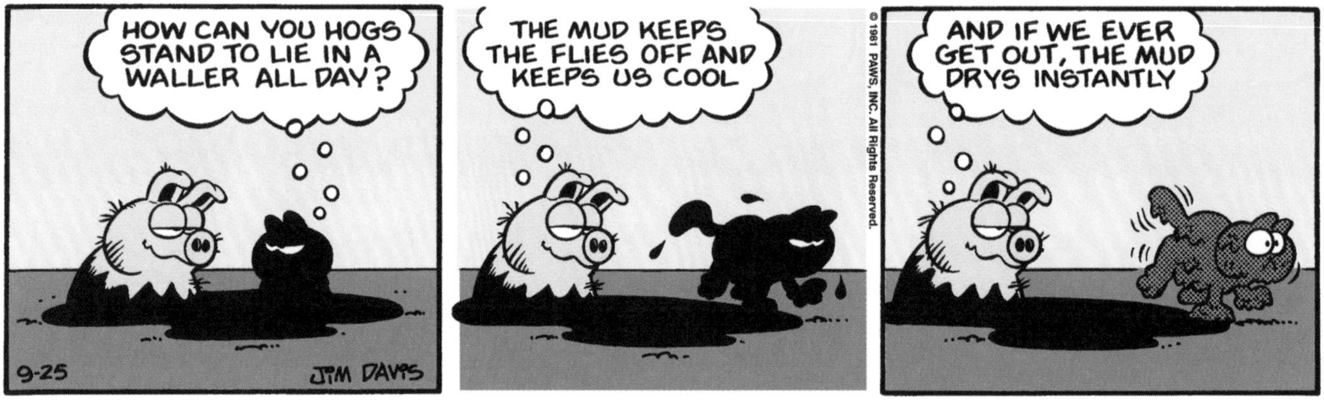
HOW CAN YOU HOGS STAND TO LIE IN A WALLER ALL DAY?
9-25
JIM DAVIS
THE MUD KEEPS THE FLIES OFF AND KEEPS US COOL
© 1981 PAWS, INC. All Rights Reserved.
AND IF WE EVER GET OUT, THE MUD DRYS INSTANTLY

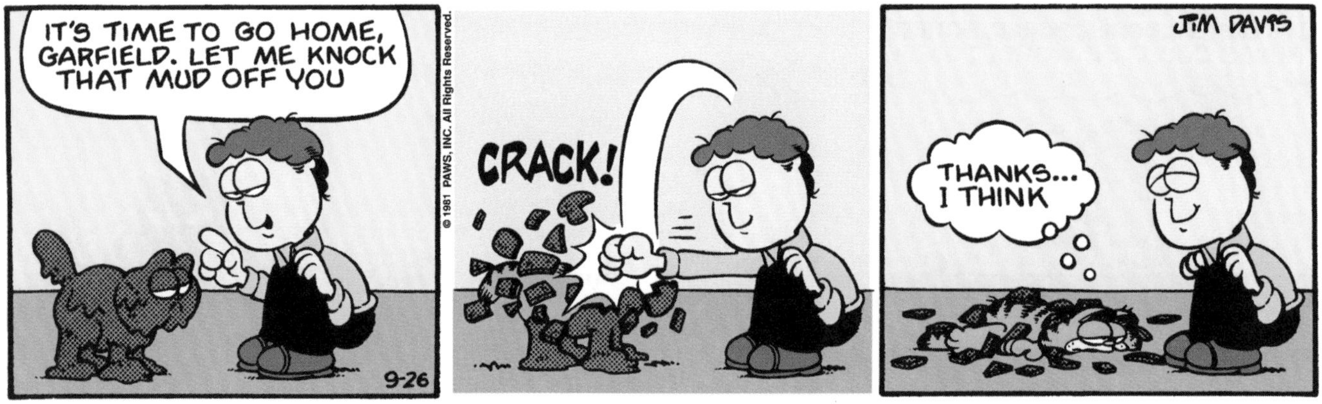
IT'S TIME TO GO HOME, GARFIELD. LET ME KNOCK THAT MUD OFF YOU
9-26
© 1981 PAWS, INC. All Rights Reserved.
CRACK!
JIM DAVIS
THANKS... I THINK

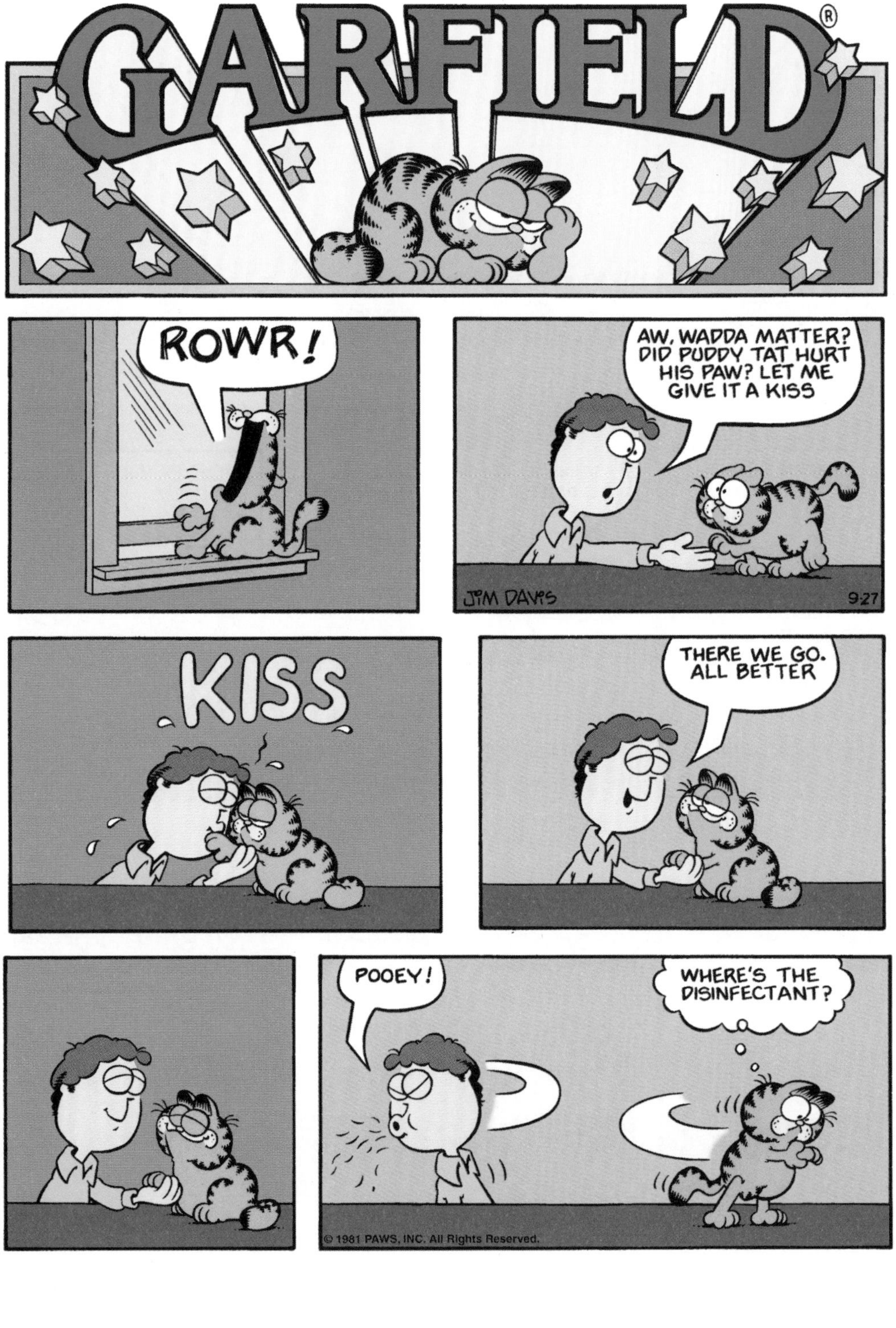
GARFIELD®
ROWR!
AW, WADDA MATTER? DID PUDDY TAT HURT HIS PAW? LET ME GIVE IT A KISS
JIM DAVIS
9·27
KISS
THERE WE GO. ALL BETTER
POOEY!
WHERE'S THE DISINFECTANT?
© 1981 PAWS, INC. All Rights Reserved.

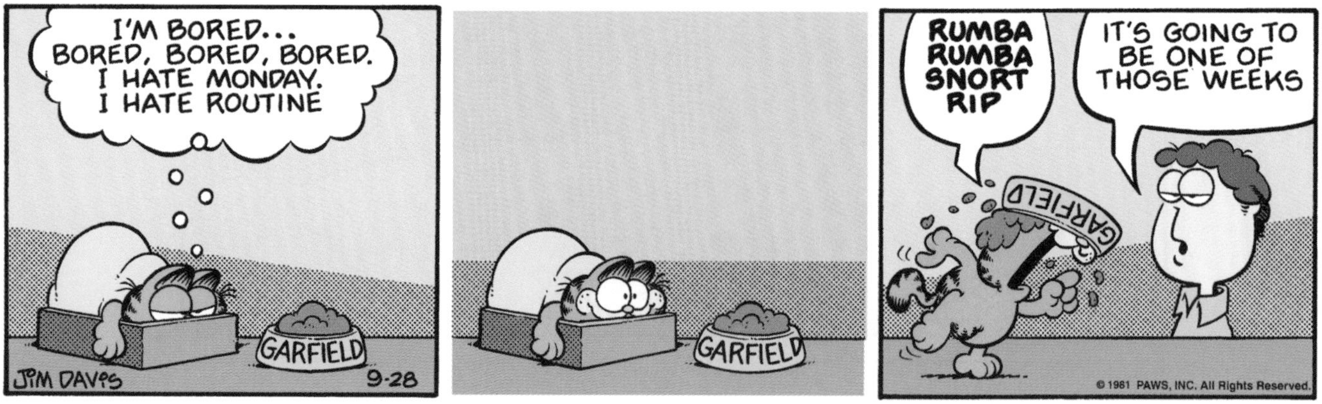
I'M BORED... BORED, BORED, BORED. I HATE MONDAY. I HATE ROUTINE
GARFIELD
JIM DAVIS
9-28
GARFIELD
RUMBA RUMBA SNORT RIP
IT'S GOING TO BE ONE OF THOSE WEEKS
GARFIELD
© 1981 PAWS, INC. All Rights Reserved.

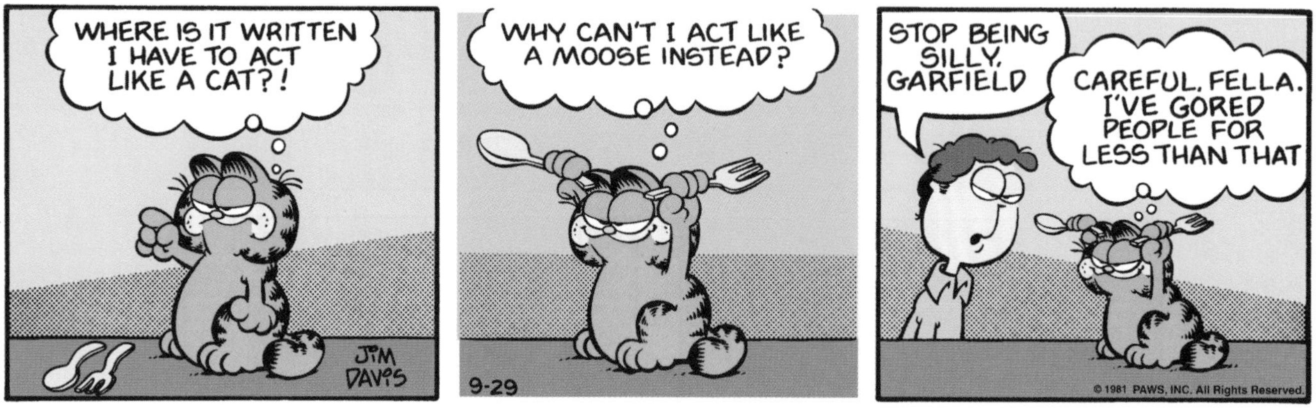
WHERE IS IT WRITTEN I HAVE TO ACT LIKE A CAT?!
JIM DAVIS
WHY CAN'T I ACT LIKE A MOOSE INSTEAD?
9-29
STOP BEING SILLY, GARFIELD
CAREFUL, FELLA. I'VE GORED PEOPLE FOR LESS THAN THAT
© 1981 PAWS, INC. All Rights Reserved.

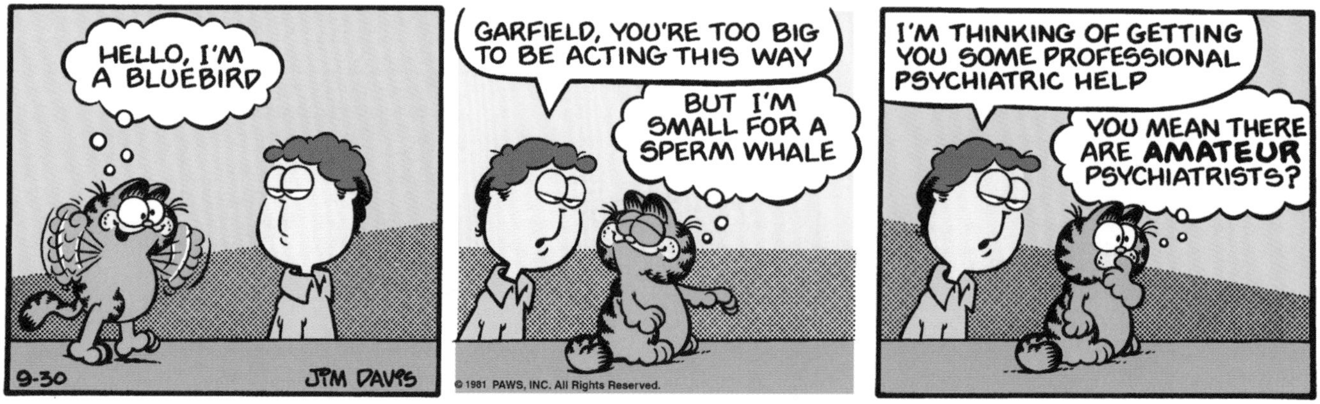
HELLO, I'M A BLUEBIRD
9-30
JIM DAVIS
GARFIELD, YOU'RE TOO BIG TO BE ACTING THIS WAY
BUT I'M SMALL FOR A SPERM WHALE
© 1981 PAWS, INC. All Rights Reserved.
I'M THINKING OF GETTING YOU SOME PROFESSIONAL PSYCHIATRIC HELP
YOU MEAN THERE ARE **AMATEUR** PSYCHIATRISTS?

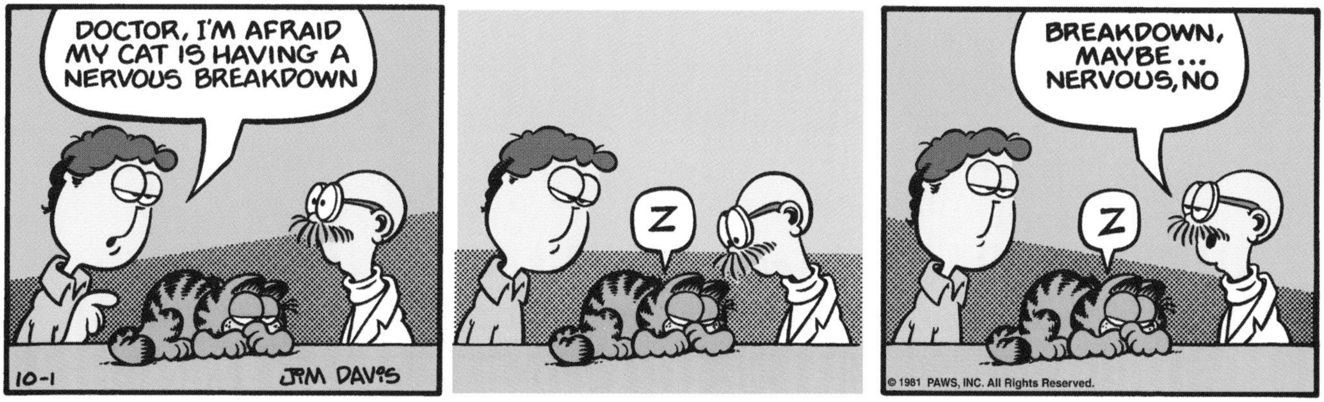
DOCTOR, I'M AFRAID MY CAT IS HAVING A NERVOUS BREAKDOWN
10-1
JIM DAVIS
Z
Z
BREAKDOWN, MAYBE... NERVOUS, NO
© 1981 PAWS, INC. All Rights Reserved.

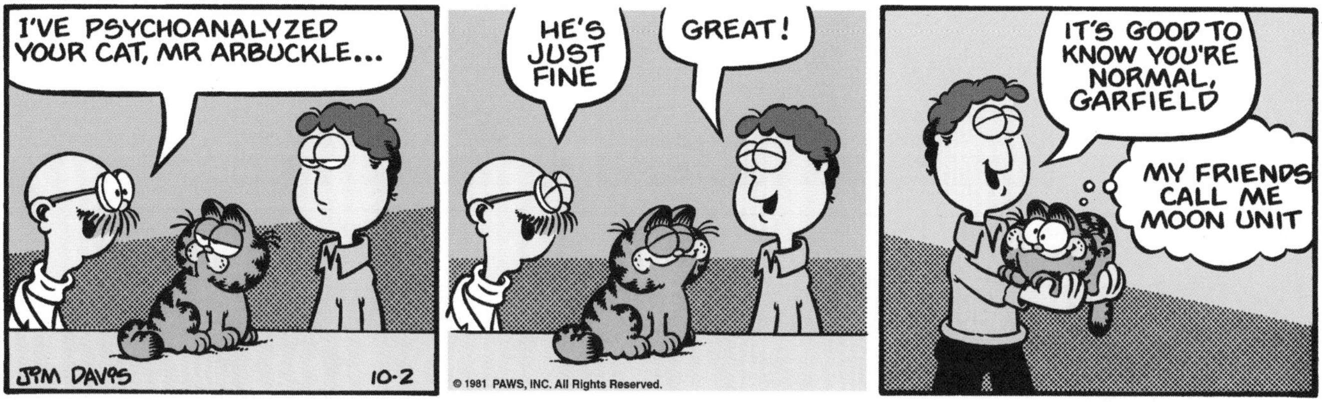
I'VE PSYCHOANALYZED YOUR CAT, MR ARBUCKLE...
JIM DAVIS
10-2
HE'S JUST FINE
GREAT!
© 1981 PAWS, INC. All Rights Reserved.
IT'S GOOD TO KNOW YOU'RE NORMAL, GARFIELD
MY FRIENDS CALL ME MOON UNIT

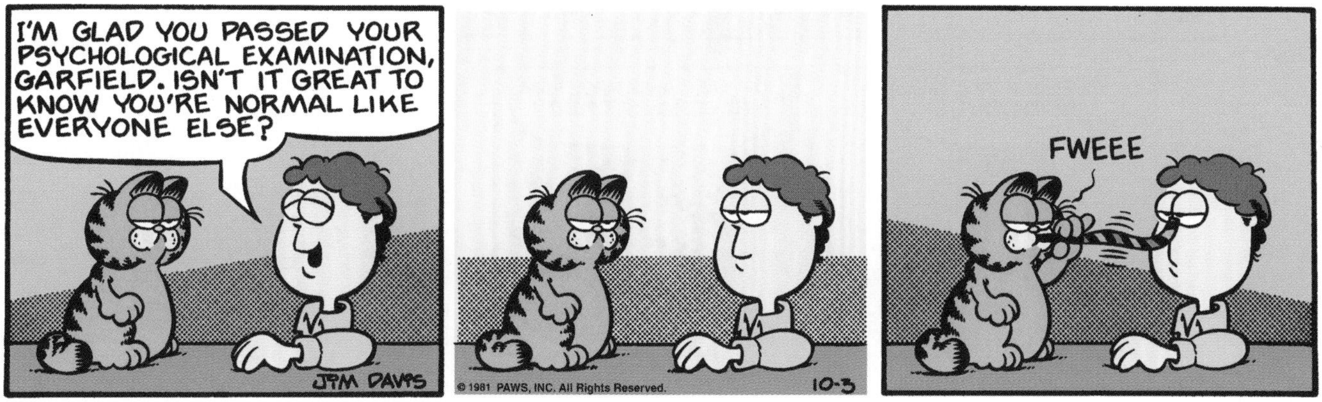
I'M GLAD YOU PASSED YOUR PSYCHOLOGICAL EXAMINATION, GARFIELD. ISN'T IT GREAT TO KNOW YOU'RE NORMAL LIKE EVERYONE ELSE?
JIM DAVIS
© 1981 PAWS, INC. All Rights Reserved.
10-3
FWEEE

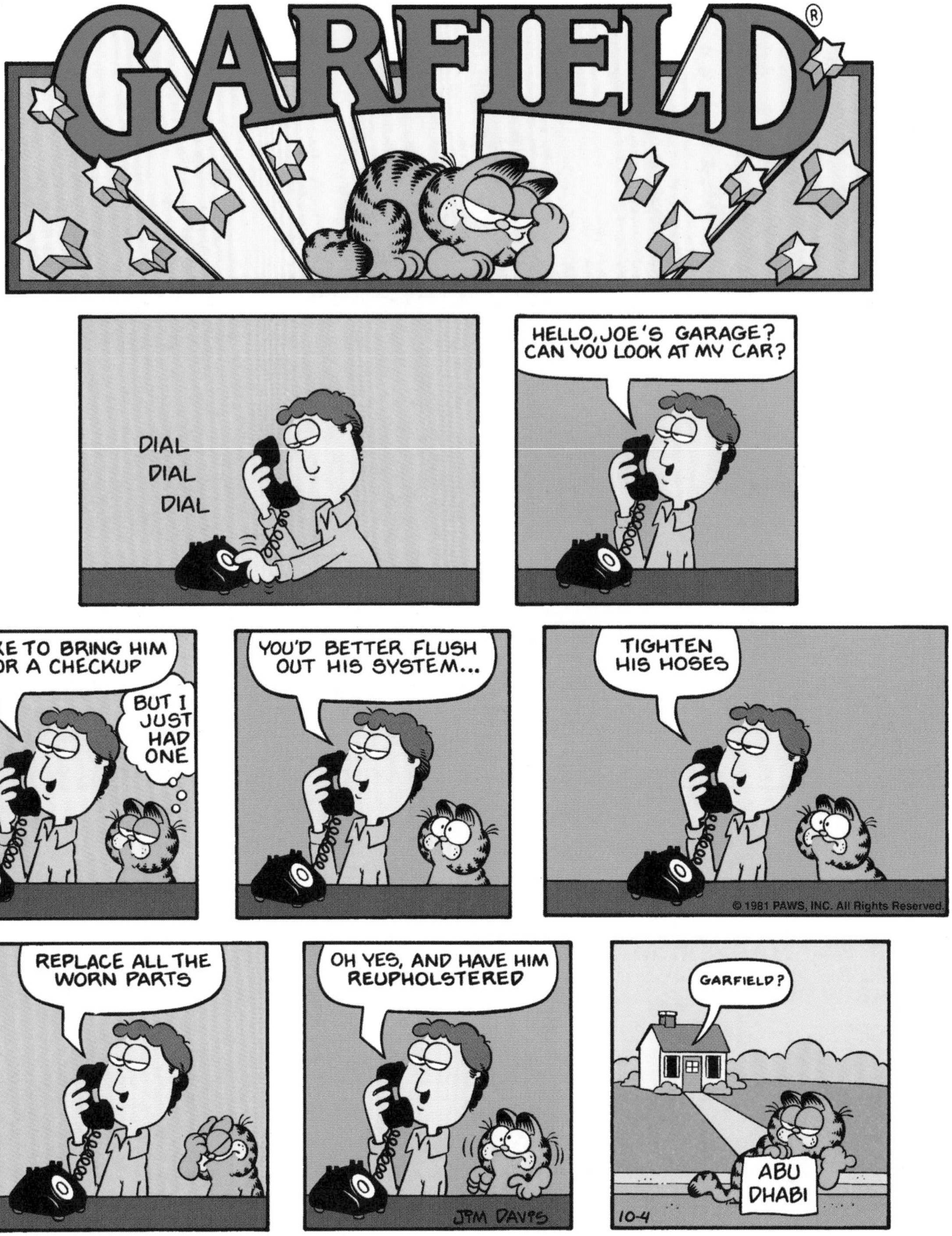
GARFIELD®
DIAL DIAL DIAL
HELLO, JOE'S GARAGE? CAN YOU LOOK AT MY CAR?
I'D LIKE TO BRING HIM IN FOR A CHECKUP
BUT I JUST HAD ONE
YOU'D BETTER FLUSH OUT HIS SYSTEM...
TIGHTEN HIS HOSES
© 1981 PAWS, INC. All Rights Reserved.
REPLACE ALL THE WORN PARTS
OH YES, AND HAVE HIM REUPHOLSTERED
JIM DAVIS
GARFIELD?
ABU DHABI
10-4

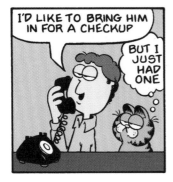

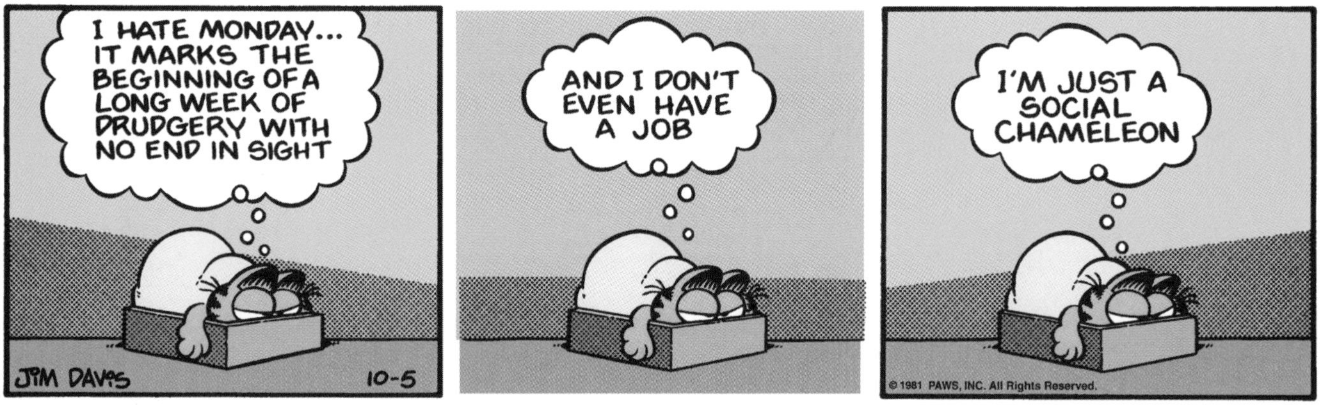
I HATE MONDAY... IT MARKS THE BEGINNING OF A LONG WEEK OF DRUDGERY WITH NO END IN SIGHT
JIM DAVIS
10-5
AND I DON'T EVEN HAVE A JOB
I'M JUST A SOCIAL CHAMELEON
© 1981 PAWS, INC. All Rights Reserved.

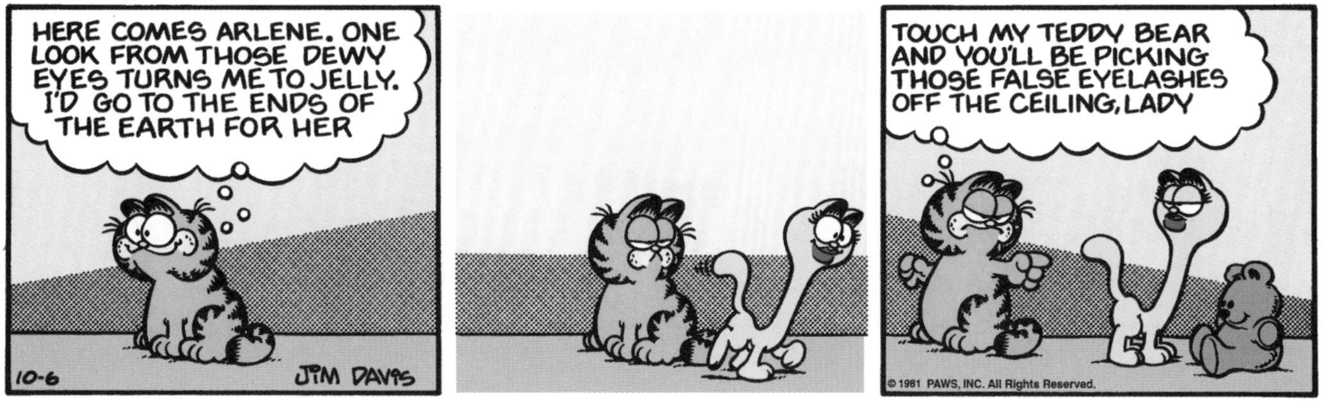
HERE COMES ARLENE. ONE LOOK FROM THOSE DEWY EYES TURNS ME TO JELLY. I'D GO TO THE ENDS OF THE EARTH FOR HER
10-6
JIM DAVIS
TOUCH MY TEDDY BEAR AND YOU'LL BE PICKING THOSE FALSE EYELASHES OFF THE CEILING, LADY
© 1981 PAWS, INC. All Rights Reserved.

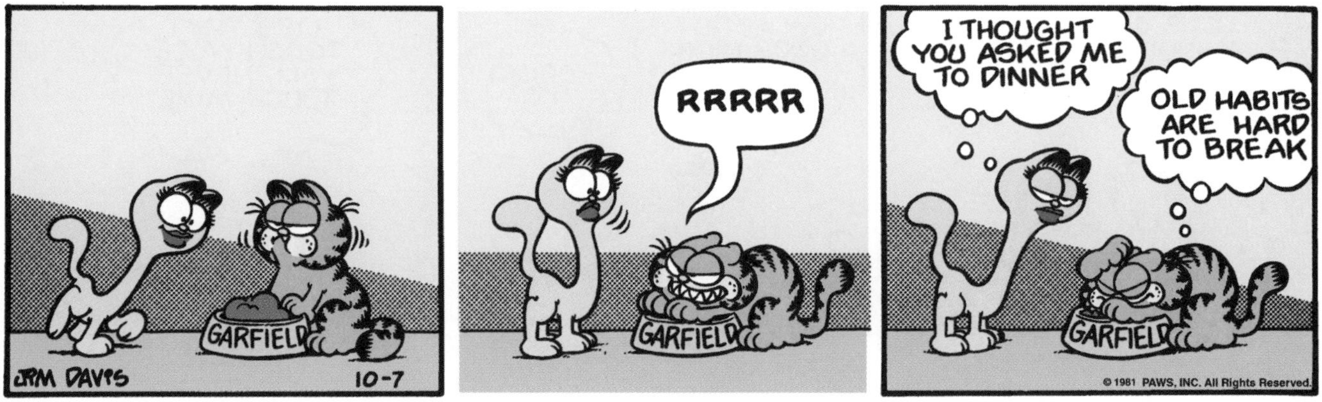
GARFIELD
JIM DAVIS
10-7
RRRRR
GARFIELD
I THOUGHT YOU ASKED ME TO DINNER
OLD HABITS ARE HARD TO BREAK
GARFIELD
© 1981 PAWS, INC. All Rights Reserved.

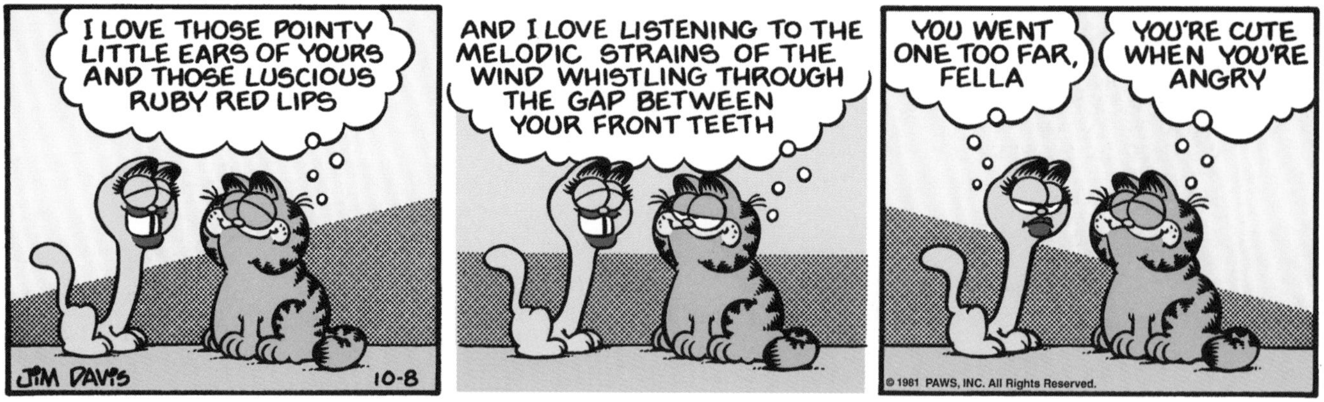
I LOVE THOSE POINTY LITTLE EARS OF YOURS AND THOSE LUSCIOUS RUBY RED LIPS
JIM DAVIS
10-8
AND I LOVE LISTENING TO THE MELODIC STRAINS OF THE WIND WHISTLING THROUGH THE GAP BETWEEN YOUR FRONT TEETH
YOU WENT ONE TOO FAR, FELLA
YOU'RE CUTE WHEN YOU'RE ANGRY
© 1981 PAWS, INC. All Rights Reserved.

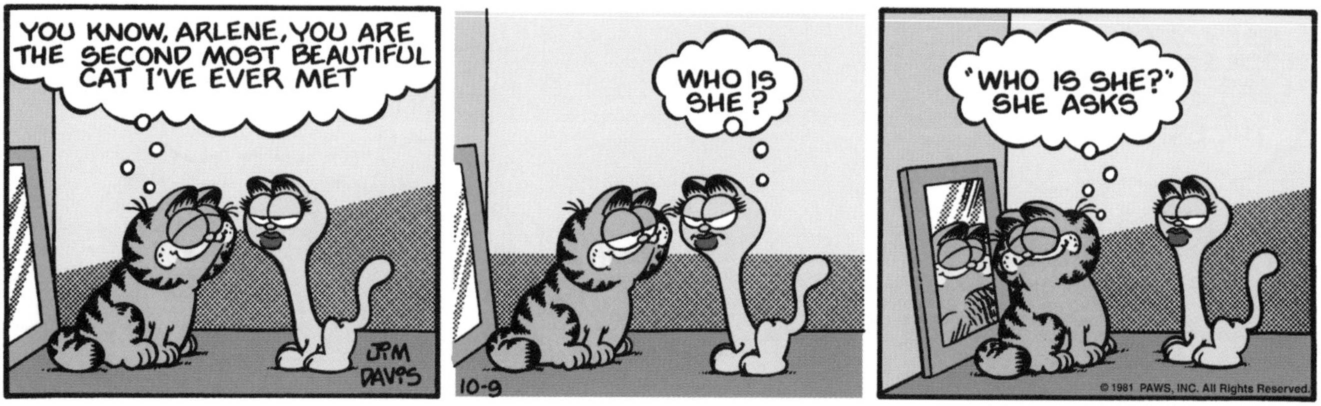
YOU KNOW, ARLENE, YOU ARE THE SECOND MOST BEAUTIFUL CAT I'VE EVER MET
JIM DAVIS
WHO IS SHE?
10-9
"WHO IS SHE?" SHE ASKS
© 1981 PAWS, INC. All Rights Reserved.

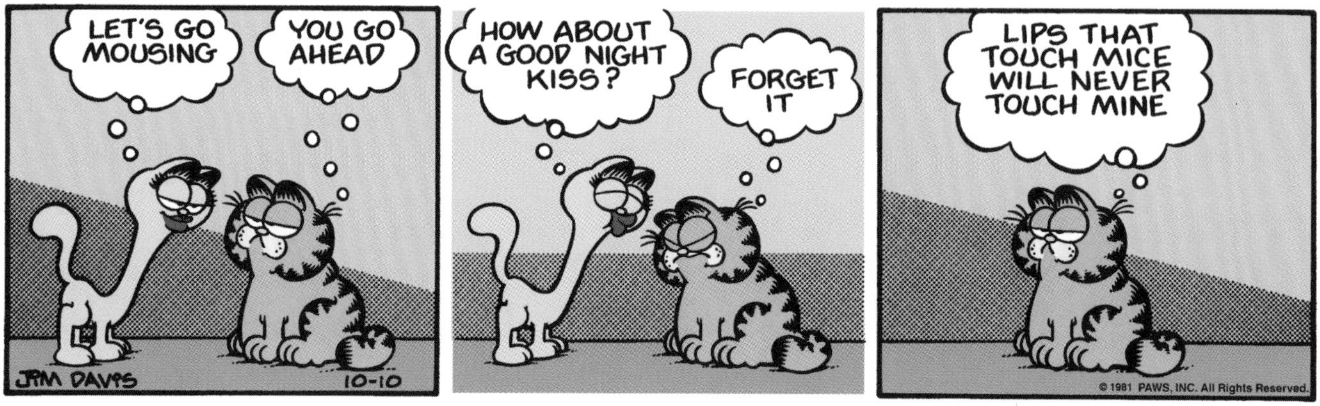
LET'S GO MOUSING
YOU GO AHEAD
JIM DAVIS
10-10
HOW ABOUT A GOOD NIGHT KISS?
FORGET IT
LIPS THAT TOUCH MICE WILL NEVER TOUCH MINE
© 1981 PAWS, INC. All Rights Reserved.

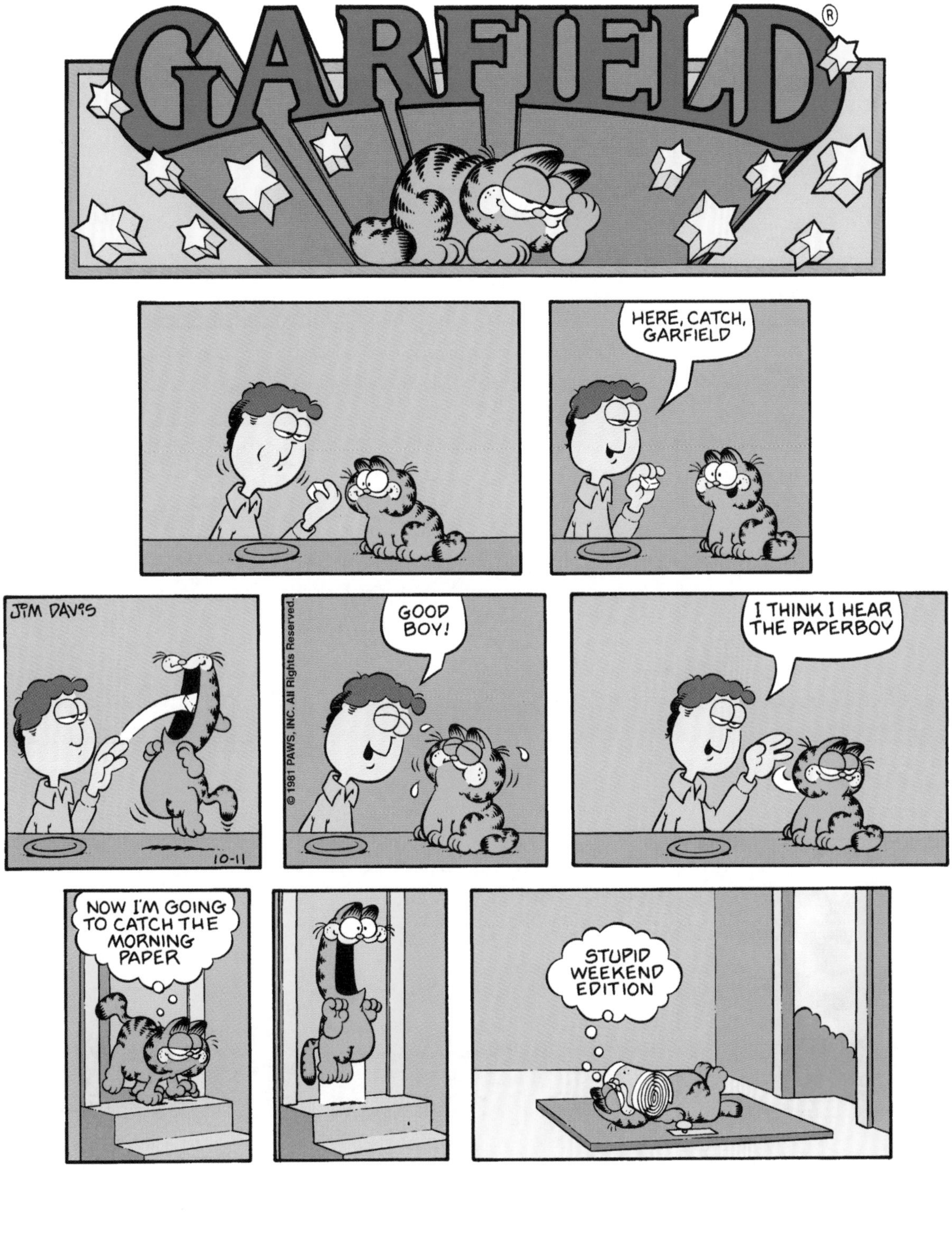
GARFIELD®
HERE, CATCH, GARFIELD
JIM DAVIS
10-11
© 1981 PAWS, INC. All Rights Reserved.
GOOD BOY!
I THINK I HEAR THE PAPERBOY
NOW I'M GOING TO CATCH THE MORNING PAPER
STUPID WEEKEND EDITION

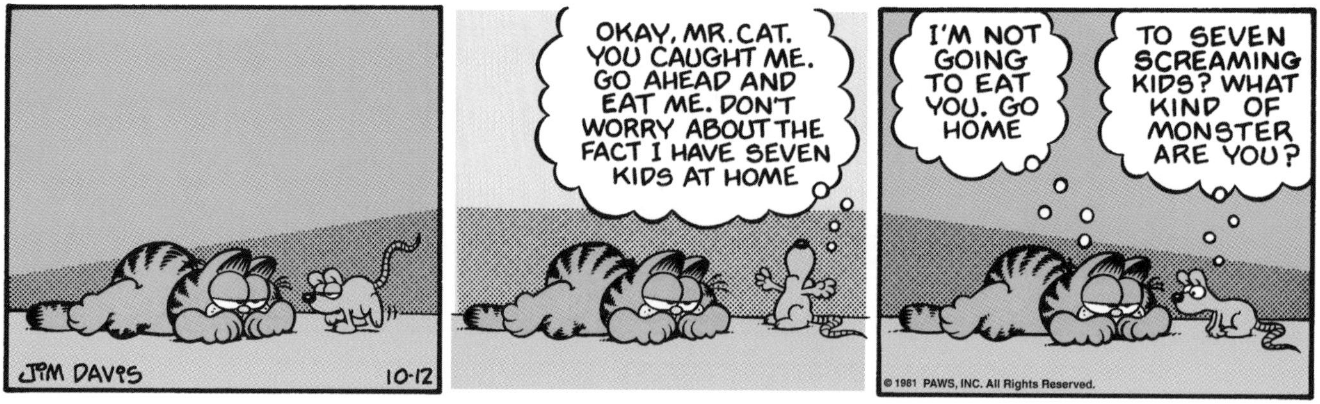
JIM DAVIS
10-12
OKAY, MR. CAT. YOU CAUGHT ME. GO AHEAD AND EAT ME. DON'T WORRY ABOUT THE FACT I HAVE SEVEN KIDS AT HOME
I'M NOT GOING TO EAT YOU. GO HOME
TO SEVEN SCREAMING KIDS? WHAT KIND OF MONSTER ARE YOU?
© 1981 PAWS, INC. All Rights Reserved.

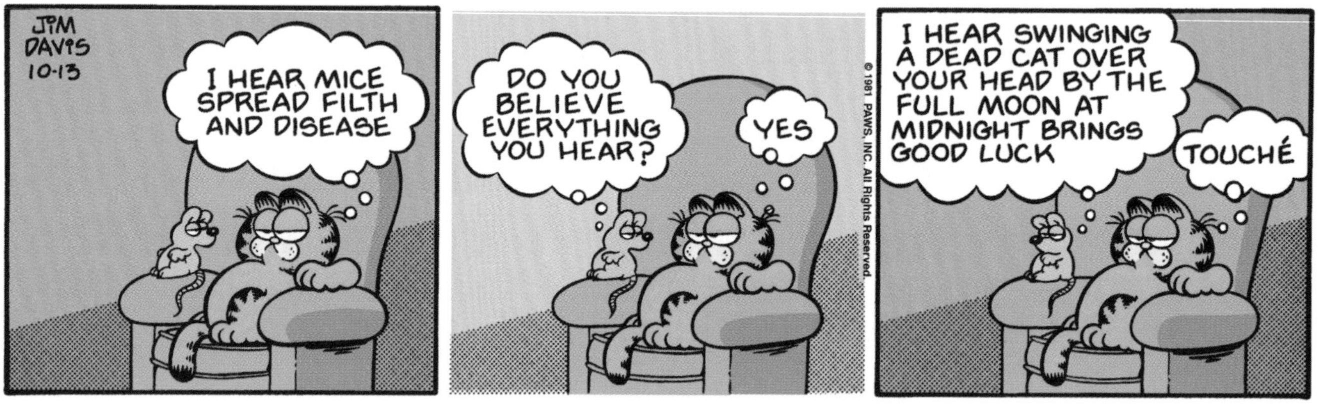
JIM DAVIS 10-13
I HEAR MICE SPREAD FILTH AND DISEASE
DO YOU BELIEVE EVERYTHING YOU HEAR?
YES
© 1981 PAWS, INC. All Rights Reserved.
I HEAR SWINGING A DEAD CAT OVER YOUR HEAD BY THE FULL MOON AT MIDNIGHT BRINGS GOOD LUCK
TOUCHÉ

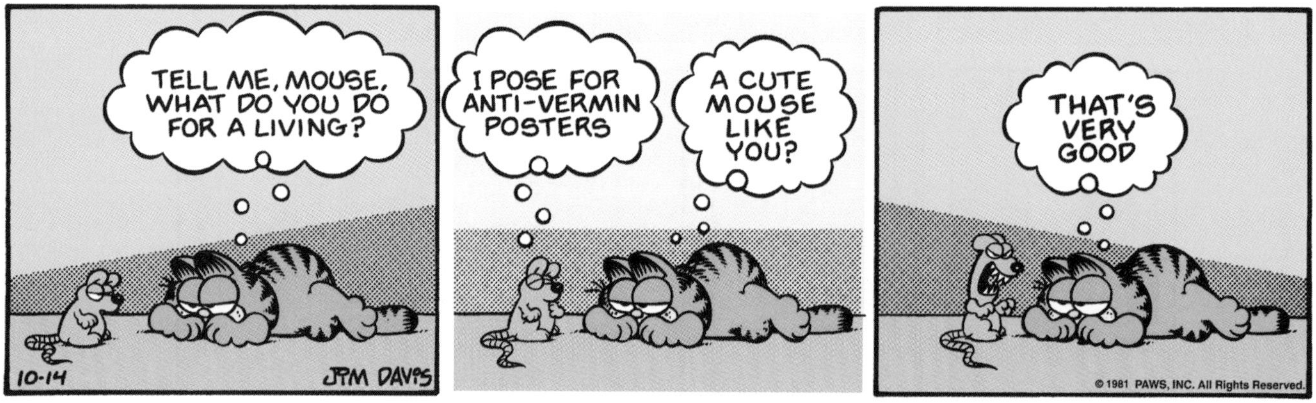
TELL ME, MOUSE, WHAT DO YOU DO FOR A LIVING?
10-14
JIM DAVIS
I POSE FOR ANTI-VERMIN POSTERS
A CUTE MOUSE LIKE YOU?
THAT'S VERY GOOD
© 1981 PAWS, INC. All Rights Reserved.

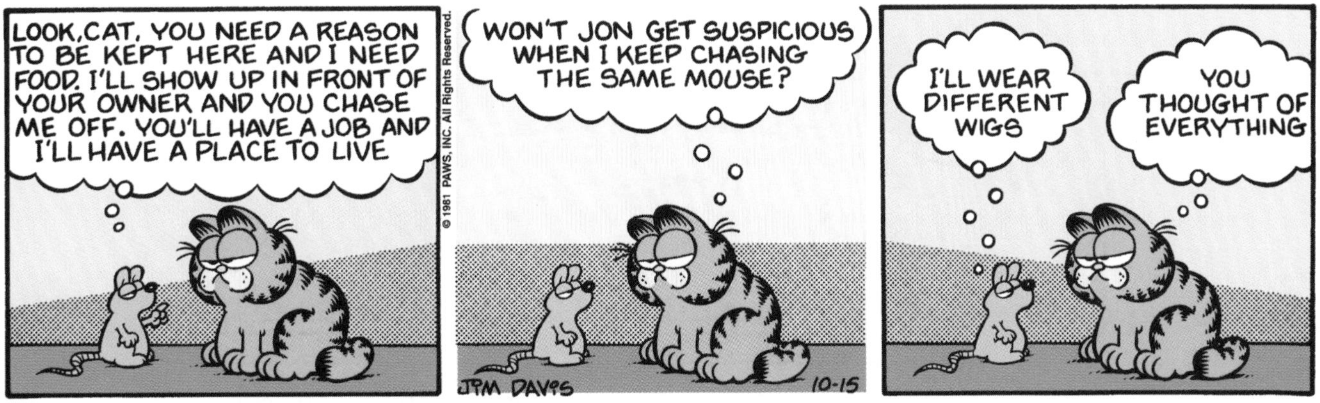
LOOK, CAT, YOU NEED A REASON TO BE KEPT HERE AND I NEED FOOD. I'LL SHOW UP IN FRONT OF YOUR OWNER AND YOU CHASE ME OFF. YOU'LL HAVE A JOB AND I'LL HAVE A PLACE TO LIVE
© 1981 PAWS, INC. All Rights Reserved.
WON'T JON GET SUSPICIOUS WHEN I KEEP CHASING THE SAME MOUSE?
JIM DAVIS
10-15
I'LL WEAR DIFFERENT WIGS
YOU THOUGHT OF EVERYTHING

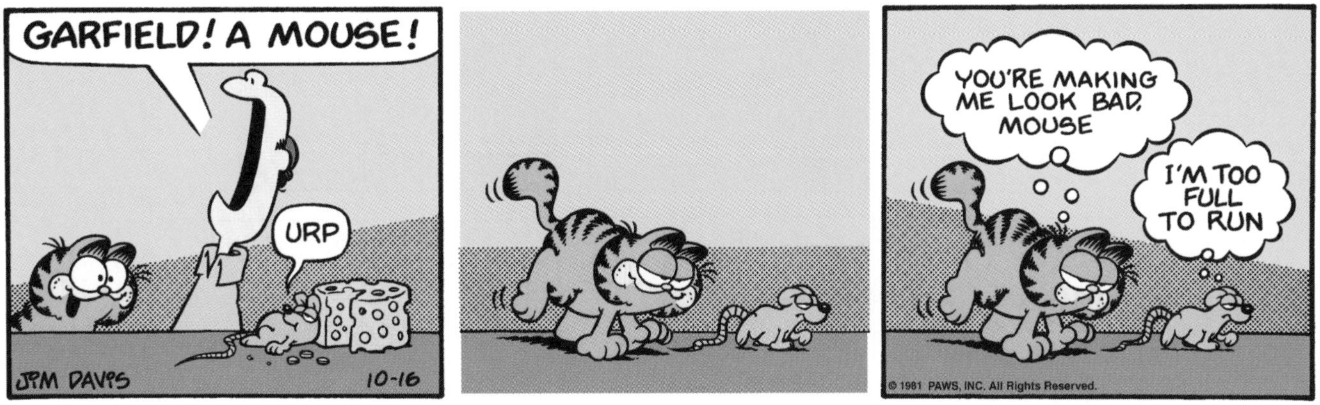
GARFIELD! A MOUSE!
URP
JIM DAVIS
10-16
YOU'RE MAKING ME LOOK BAD, MOUSE
I'M TOO FULL TO RUN
© 1981 PAWS, INC. All Rights Reserved.

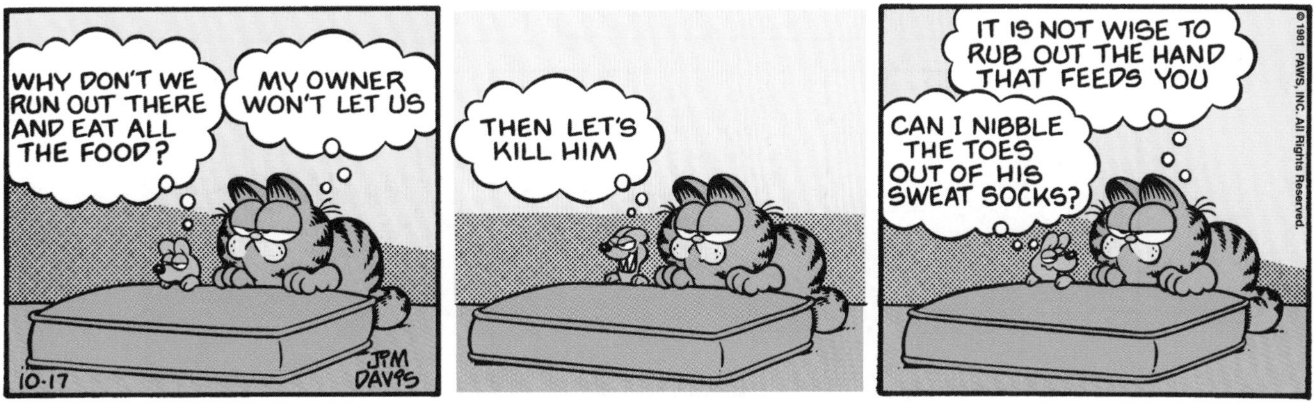
WHY DON'T WE RUN OUT THERE AND EAT ALL THE FOOD?
MY OWNER WON'T LET US
10-17
JIM DAVIS
THEN LET'S KILL HIM
IT IS NOT WISE TO RUB OUT THE HAND THAT FEEDS YOU
CAN I NIBBLE THE TOES OUT OF HIS SWEAT SOCKS?
© 1981 PAWS, INC. All Rights Reserved.

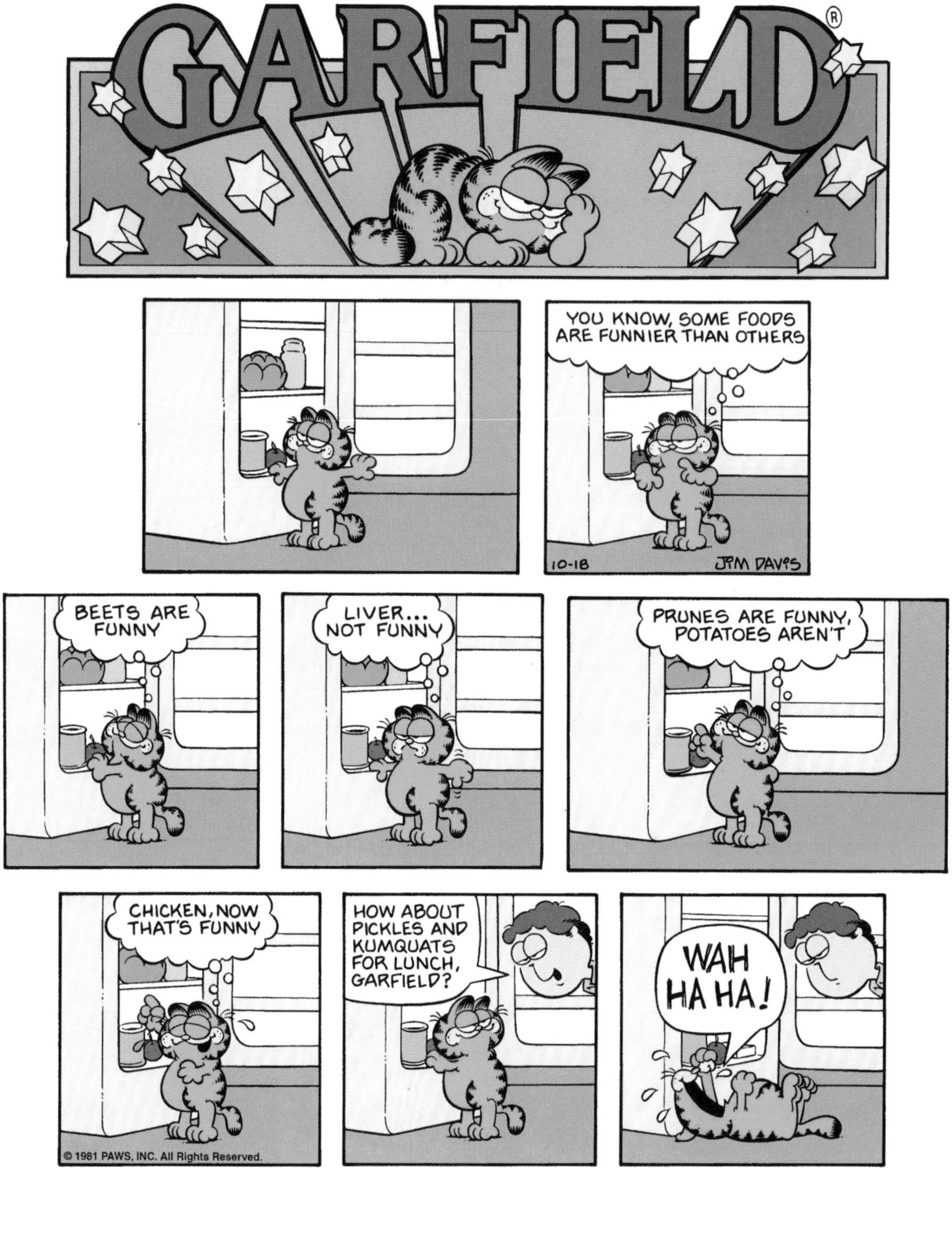
GARFIELD®
YOU KNOW, SOME FOODS ARE FUNNIER THAN OTHERS
10-18
JIM DAVIS
BEETS ARE FUNNY
LIVER... NOT FUNNY
PRUNES ARE FUNNY, POTATOES AREN'T
CHICKEN, NOW THAT'S FUNNY
© 1981 PAWS, INC. All Rights Reserved.
HOW ABOUT PICKLES AND KUMQUATS FOR LUNCH, GARFIELD?
WAH HA HA!

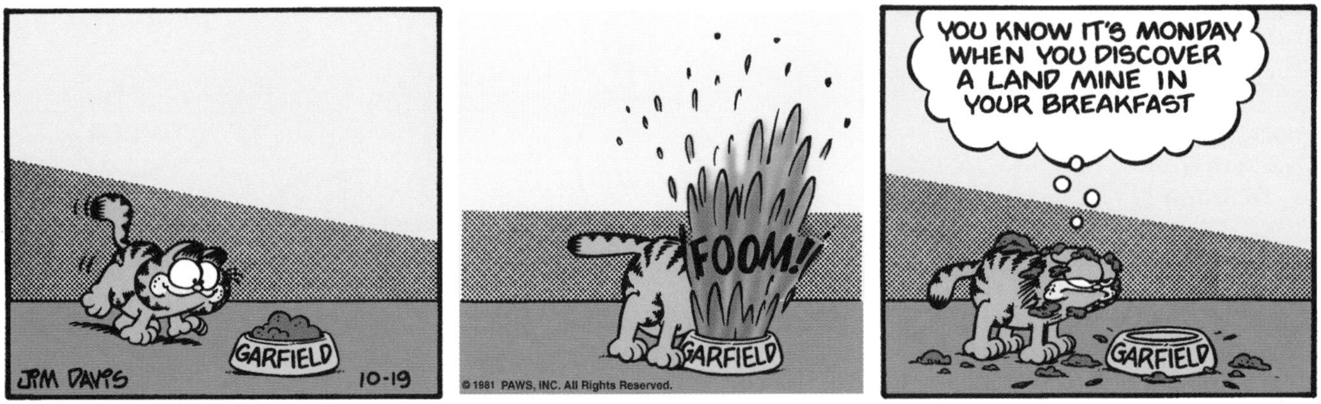
JIM DAVIS
10-19
GARFIELD
FOOM!!
GARFIELD
© 1981 PAWS, INC. All Rights Reserved.
YOU KNOW IT'S MONDAY WHEN YOU DISCOVER A LAND MINE IN YOUR BREAKFAST
GARFIELD

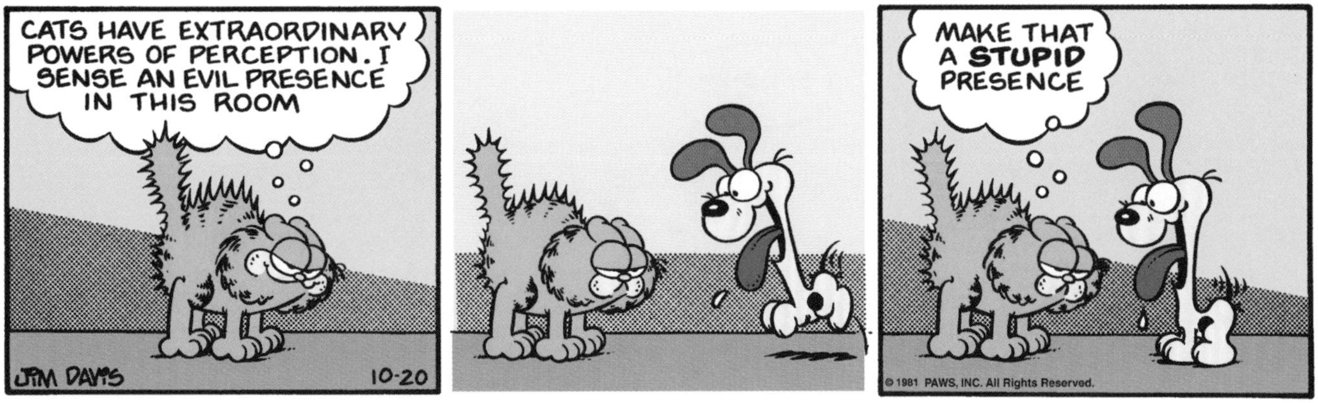
CATS HAVE EXTRAORDINARY POWERS OF PERCEPTION. I SENSE AN EVIL PRESENCE IN THIS ROOM
JIM DAVIS
10-20
MAKE THAT A **STUPID** PRESENCE
© 1981 PAWS, INC. All Rights Reserved.

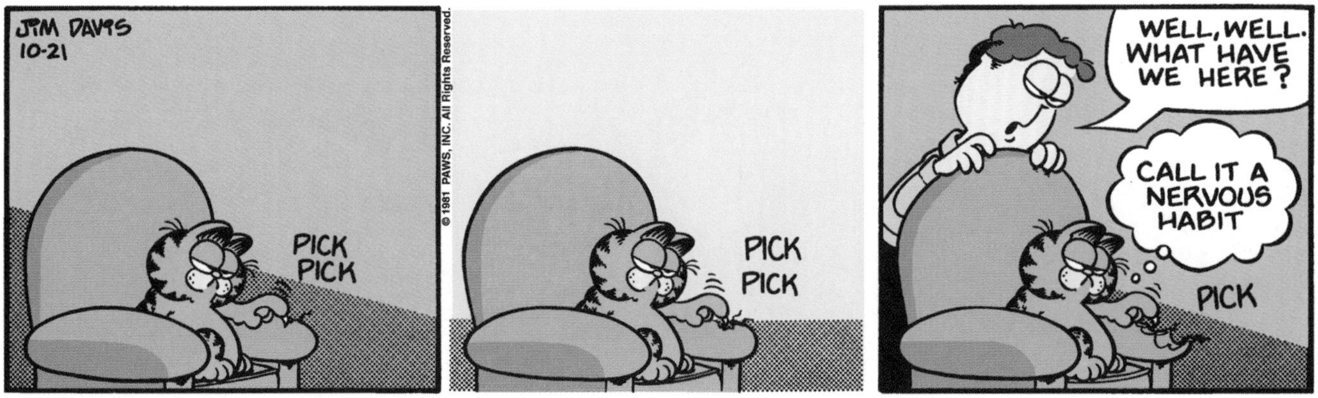
JIM DAVIS
10-21
PICK PICK
© 1981 PAWS, INC. All Rights Reserved.
PICK PICK
WELL, WELL. WHAT HAVE WE HERE?
CALL IT A NERVOUS HABIT
PICK

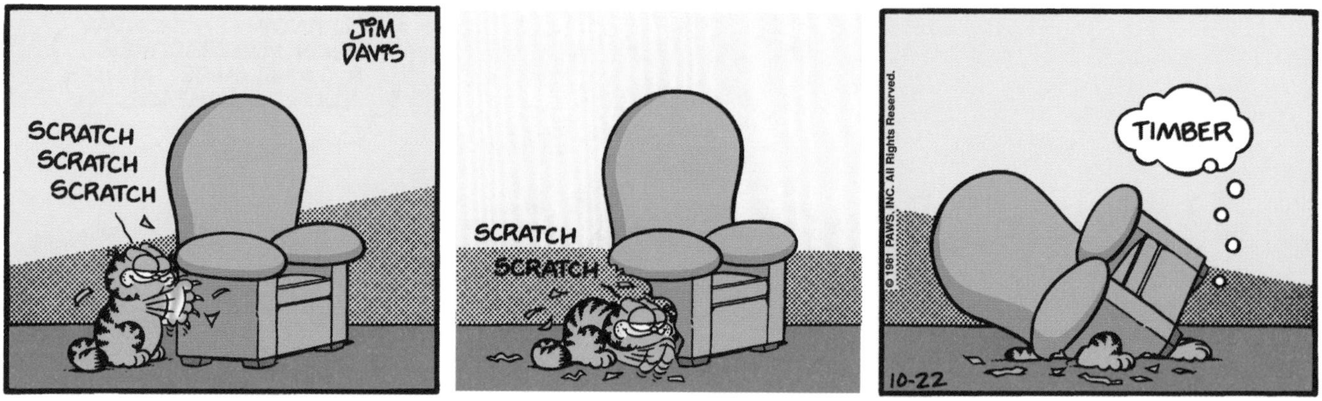
JIM DAVIS
SCRATCH SCRATCH SCRATCH
SCRATCH
SCRATCH
© 1981 PAWS, INC. All Rights Reserved.
TIMBER
10-22

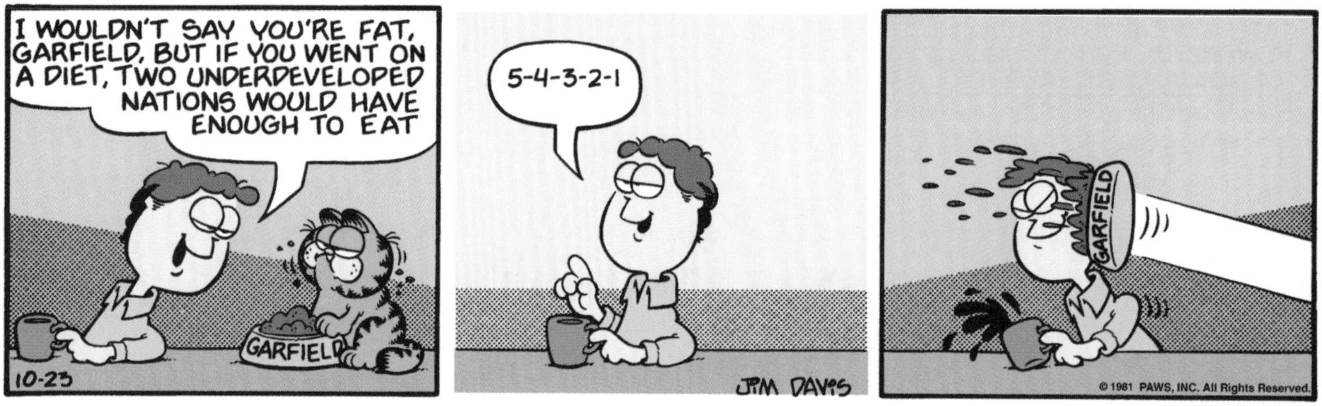
I WOULDN'T SAY YOU'RE FAT, GARFIELD, BUT IF YOU WENT ON A DIET, TWO UNDERDEVELOPED NATIONS WOULD HAVE ENOUGH TO EAT
GARFIELD
10-23
5-4-3-2-1
JIM DAVIS
GARFIELD
© 1981 PAWS, INC. All Rights Reserved.

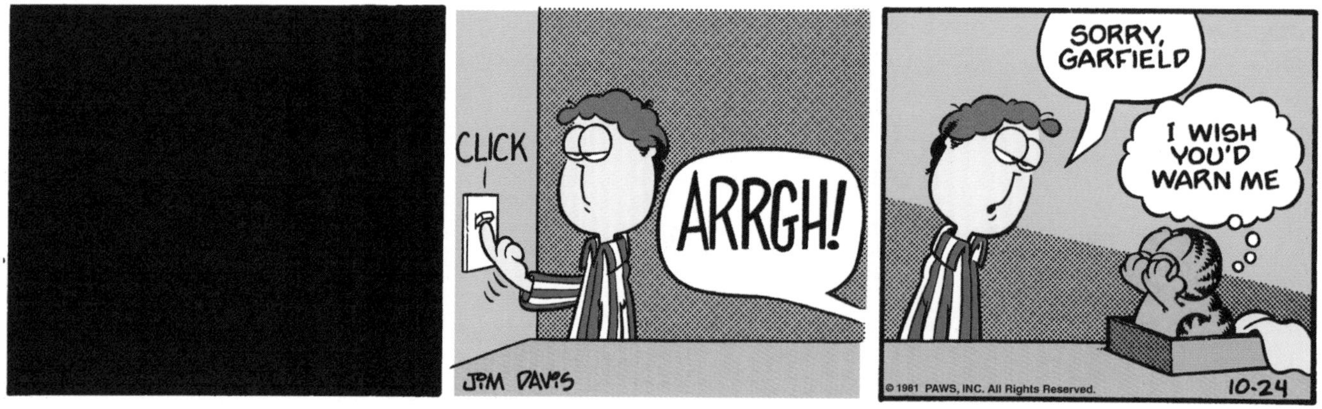
CLICK
ARRGH!
JIM DAVIS
SORRY, GARFIELD
I WISH YOU'D WARN ME
© 1981 PAWS, INC. All Rights Reserved.
10-24

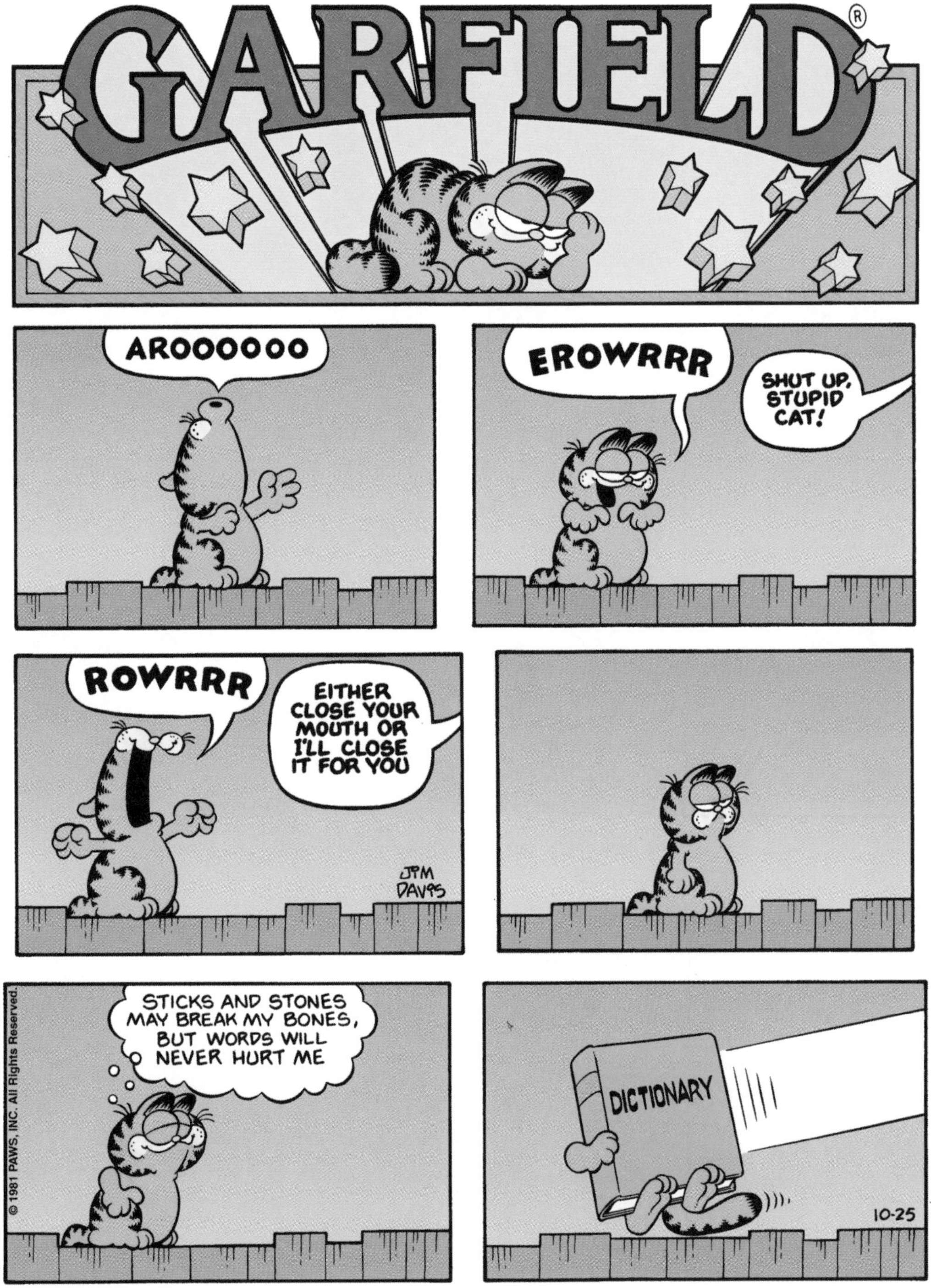
GARFIELD®
AROOOOOO
EROWRRR
SHUT UP, STUPID CAT!
ROWRRR
EITHER CLOSE YOUR MOUTH OR I'LL CLOSE IT FOR YOU
JIM DAVIS
STICKS AND STONES MAY BREAK MY BONES, BUT WORDS WILL NEVER HURT ME
DICTIONARY
10-25

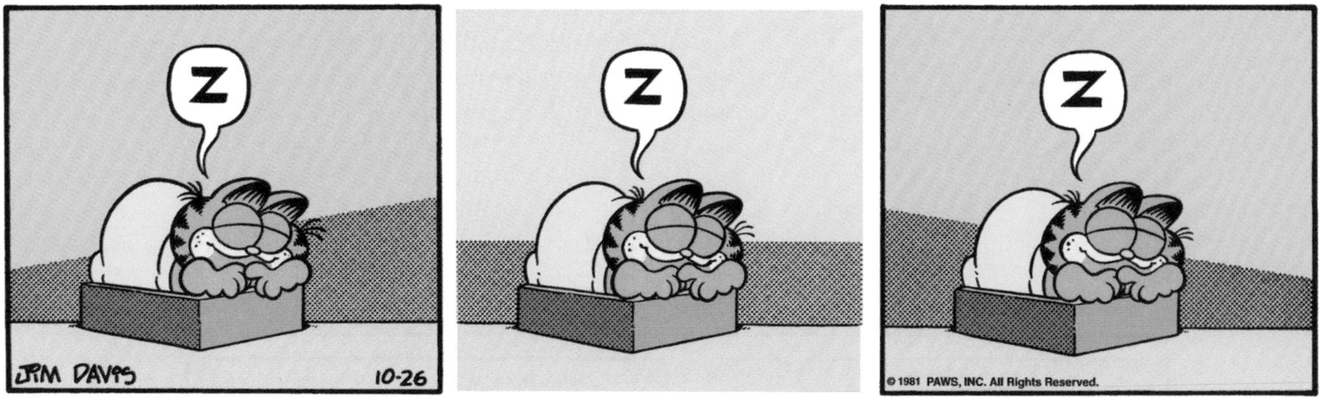
Z
JIM DAVIS 10-26
Z
Z
© 1981 PAWS, INC. All Rights Reserved.

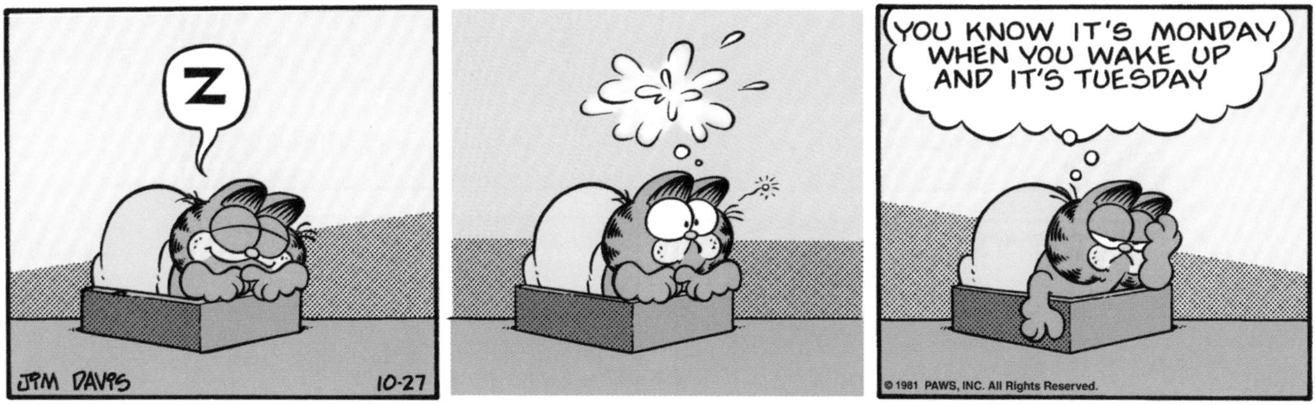
Z
JIM DAVIS 10-27
YOU KNOW IT'S MONDAY WHEN YOU WAKE UP AND IT'S TUESDAY
© 1981 PAWS, INC. All Rights Reserved.

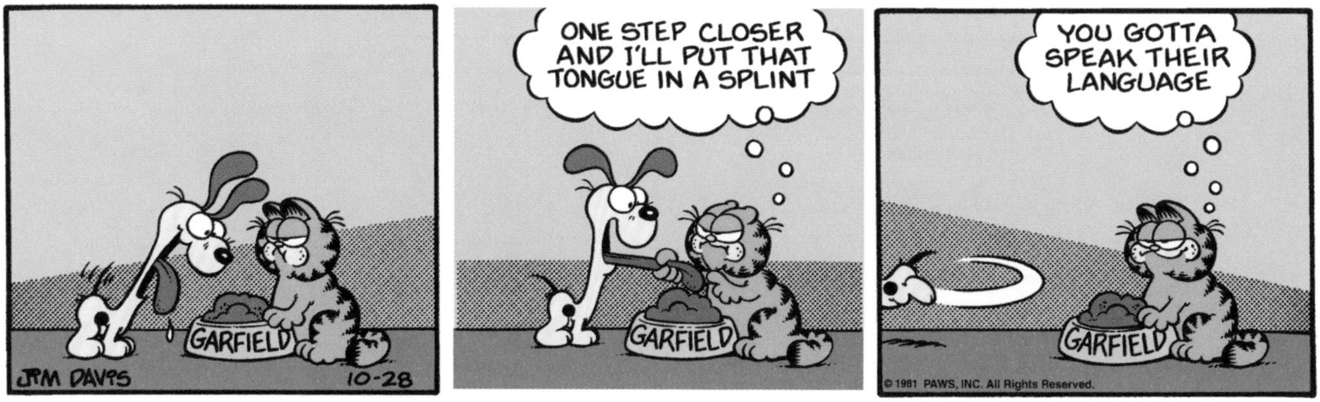
GARFIELD
JIM DAVIS 10-28
ONE STEP CLOSER AND I'LL PUT THAT TONGUE IN A SPLINT
GARFIELD
YOU GOTTA SPEAK THEIR LANGUAGE
GARFIELD
© 1981 PAWS, INC. All Rights Reserved.

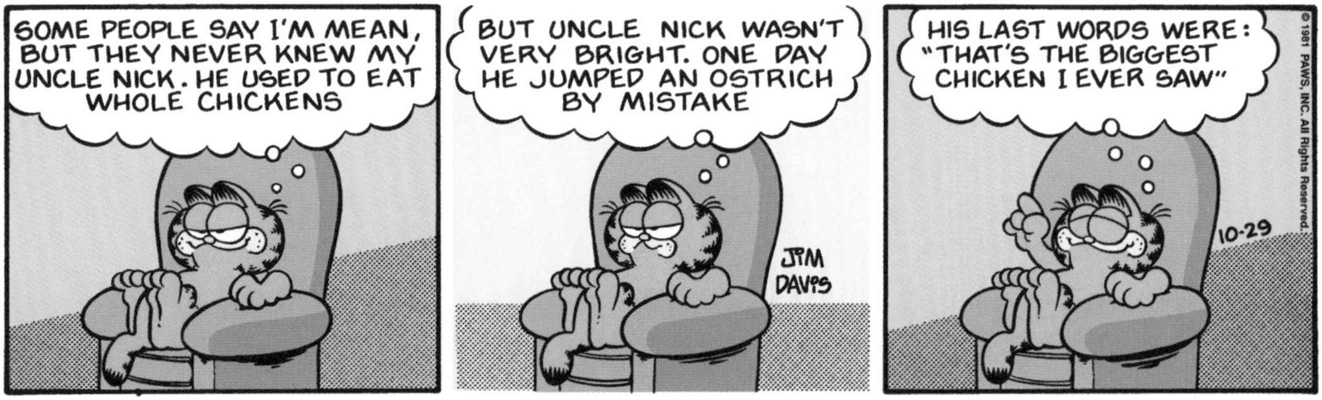
SOME PEOPLE SAY I'M MEAN, BUT THEY NEVER KNEW MY UNCLE NICK. HE USED TO EAT WHOLE CHICKENS
BUT UNCLE NICK WASN'T VERY BRIGHT. ONE DAY HE JUMPED AN OSTRICH BY MISTAKE
JIM DAVIS
HIS LAST WORDS WERE: "THAT'S THE BIGGEST CHICKEN I EVER SAW"
10-29
© 1981 PAWS, INC. All Rights Reserved.

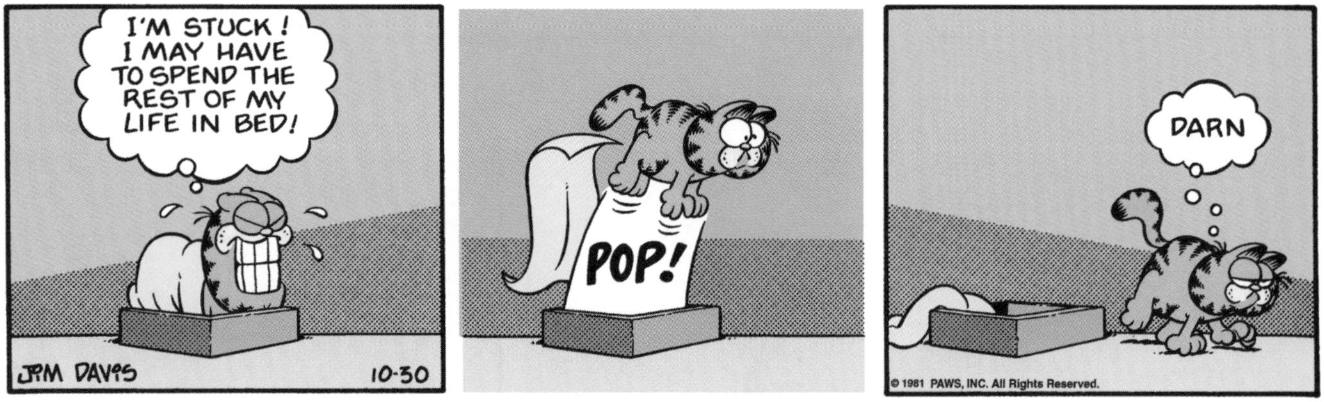
I'M STUCK! I MAY HAVE TO SPEND THE REST OF MY LIFE IN BED!
JIM DAVIS
10-30
POP!
DARN
© 1981 PAWS, INC. All Rights Reserved.

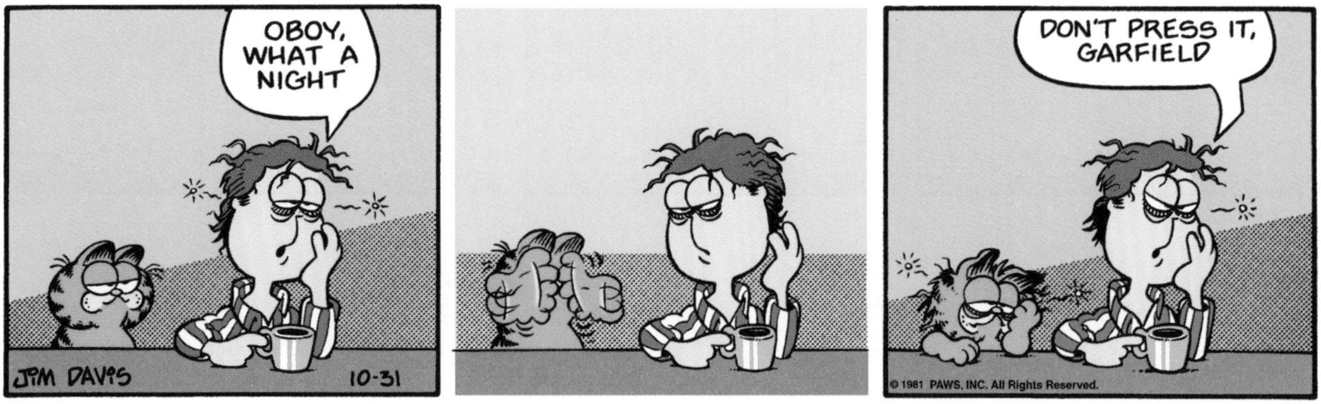
OBOY, WHAT A NIGHT
JIM DAVIS
10-31
DON'T PRESS IT, GARFIELD
© 1981 PAWS, INC. All Rights Reserved.

GARFIELD®
JIM DAVIS
11-1
CHUNG!
© 1981 PAWS, INC. All Rights Reserved.

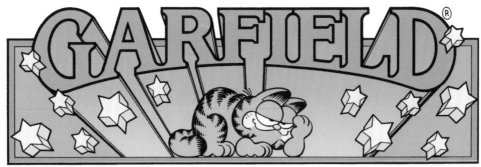

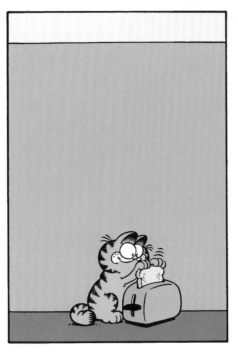

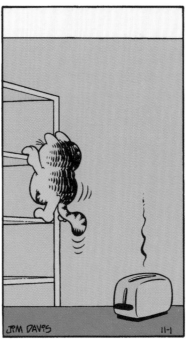

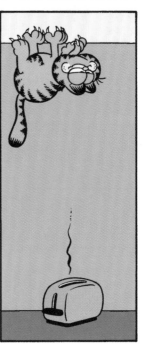

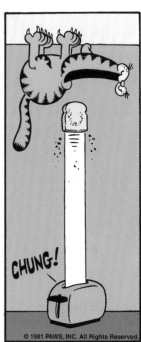

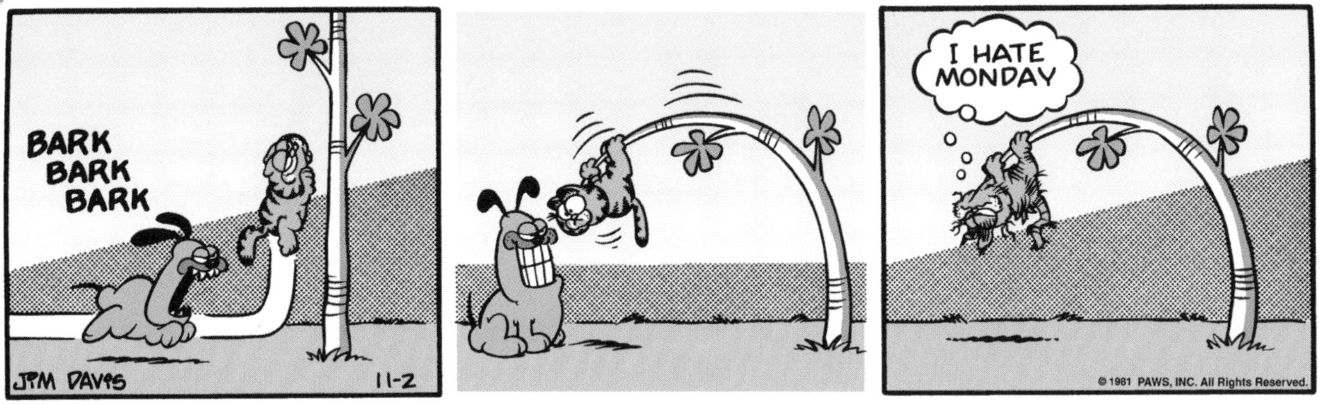
BARK
BARK
BARK
JIM DAVIS
11-2
I HATE MONDAY
© 1981 PAWS, INC. All Rights Reserved.

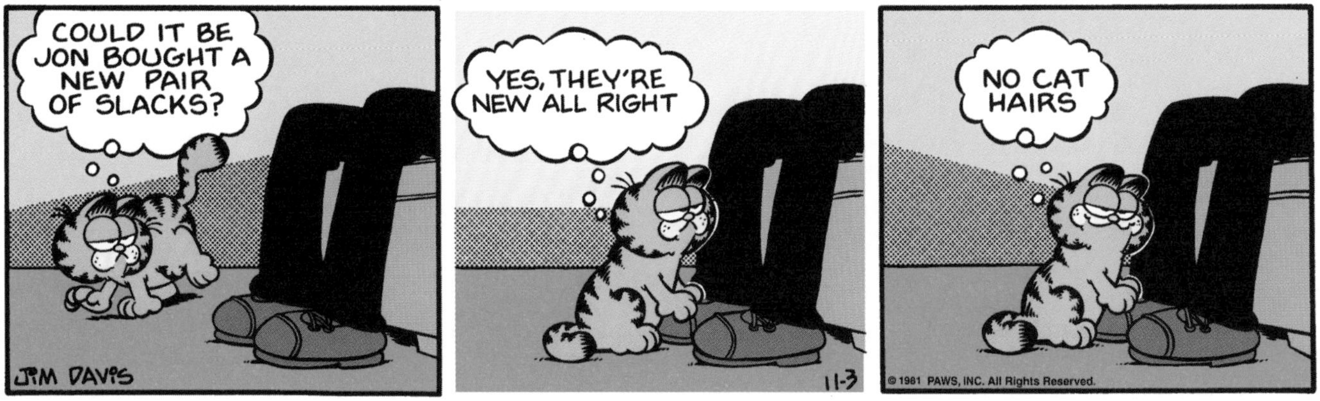
COULD IT BE JON BOUGHT A NEW PAIR OF SLACKS?
JIM DAVIS
YES, THEY'RE NEW ALL RIGHT
11-3
NO CAT HAIRS
© 1981 PAWS, INC. All Rights Reserved.

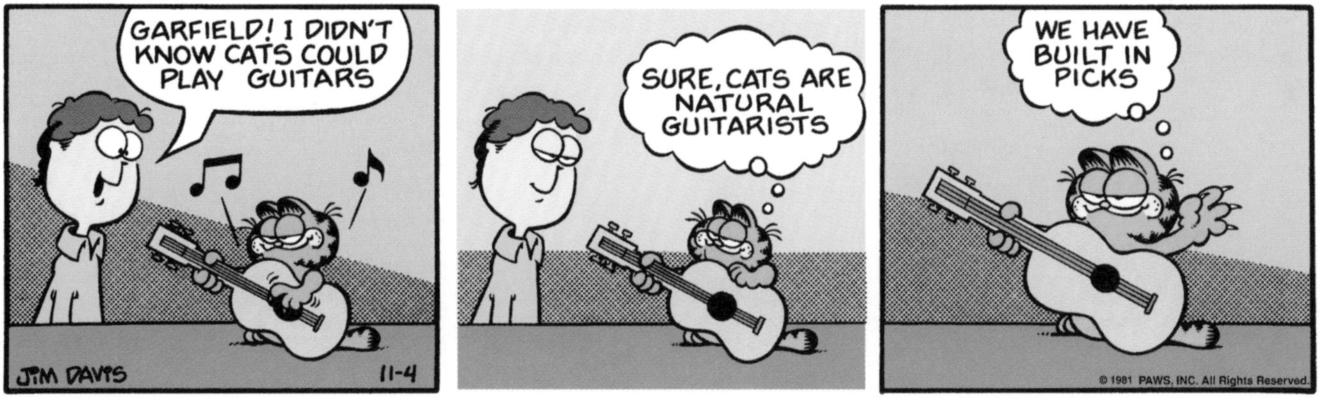
GARFIELD! I DIDN'T KNOW CATS COULD PLAY GUITARS
JIM DAVIS
11-4
SURE, CATS ARE NATURAL GUITARISTS
WE HAVE BUILT IN PICKS
© 1981 PAWS, INC. All Rights Reserved.

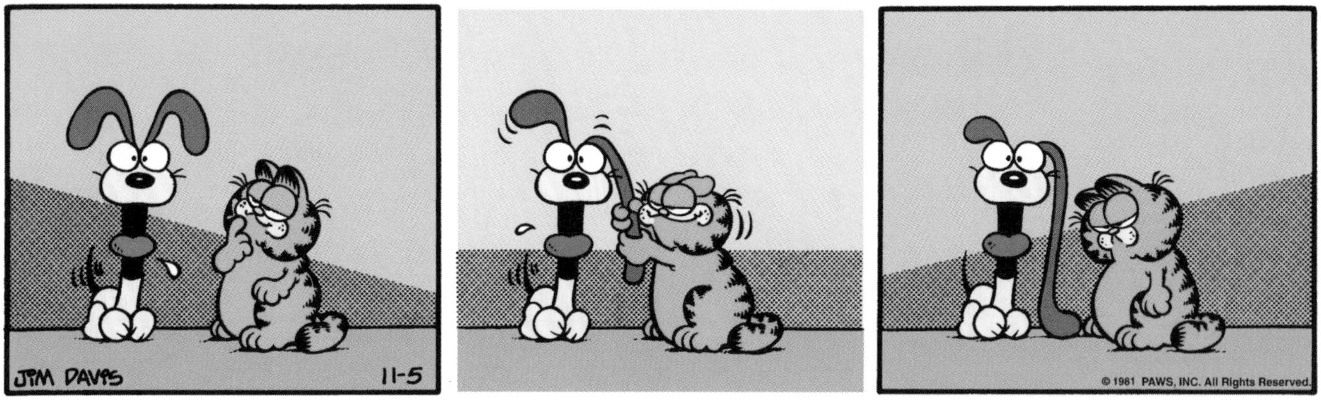
JIM DAVIS
11-5
© 1981 PAWS, INC. All Rights Reserved.

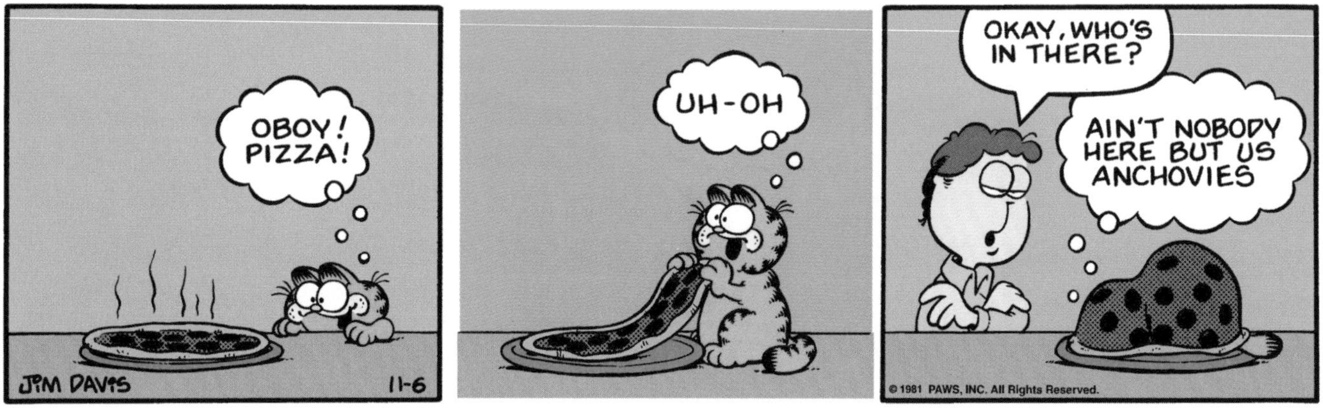
OBOY! PIZZA!
JIM DAVIS
11-6
UH-OH
OKAY, WHO'S IN THERE?
AIN'T NOBODY HERE BUT US ANCHOVIES
© 1981 PAWS, INC. All Rights Reserved.

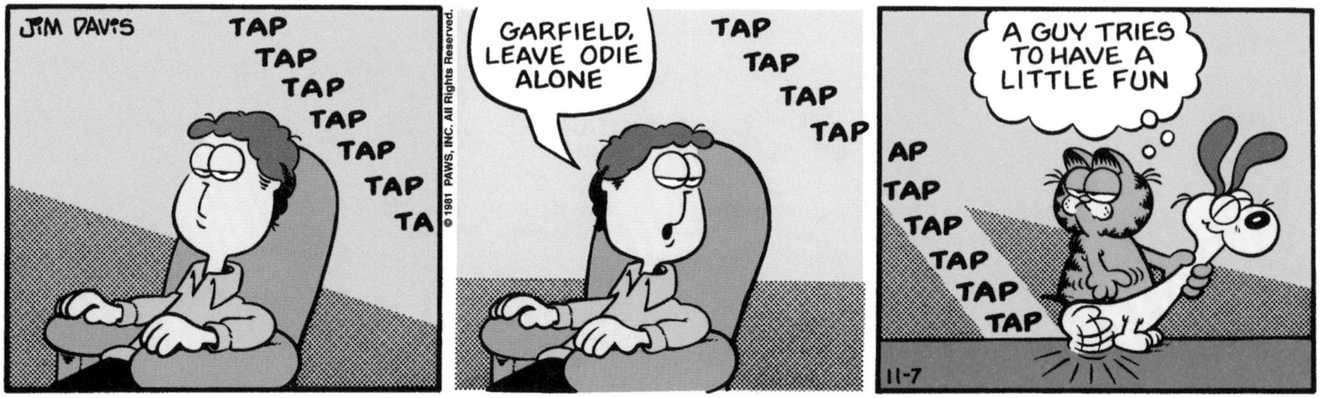
JIM DAVIS
TAP TAP TAP TAP TAP TAP TA
© 1981 PAWS, INC. All Rights Reserved.
GARFIELD, LEAVE ODIE ALONE
TAP TAP TAP TAP
A GUY TRIES TO HAVE A LITTLE FUN
AP TAP TAP TAP TAP TAP
11-7

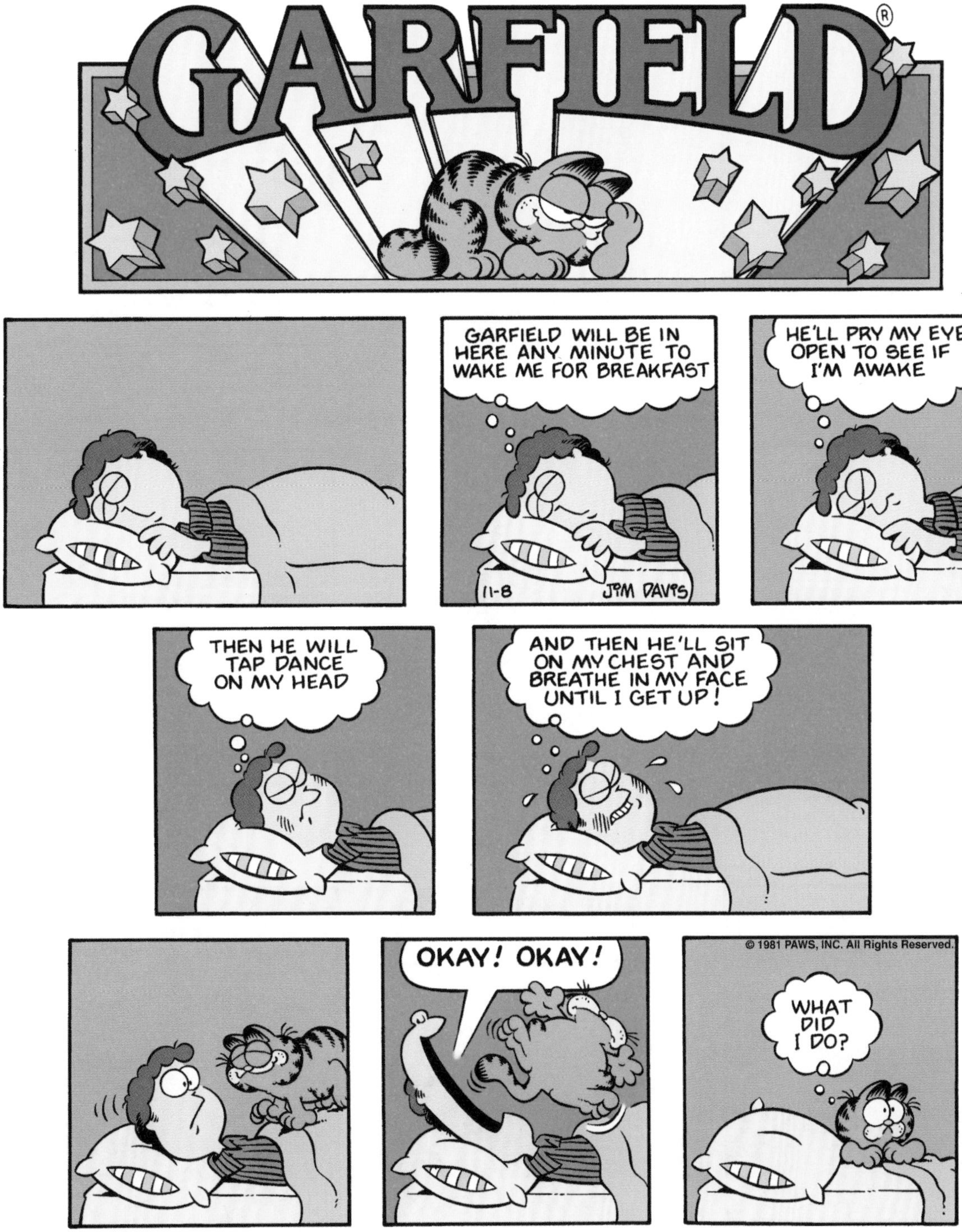
GARFIELD
GARFIELD WILL BE IN HERE ANY MINUTE TO WAKE ME FOR BREAKFAST
11-8
JIM DAVIS
HE'LL PRY MY EYE OPEN TO SEE IF I'M AWAKE
THEN HE WILL TAP DANCE ON MY HEAD
AND THEN HE'LL SIT ON MY CHEST AND BREATHE IN MY FACE UNTIL I GET UP!
OKAY! OKAY!
© 1981 PAWS, INC. All Rights Reserved.
WHAT DID I DO?

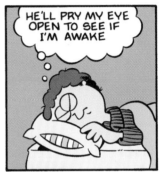

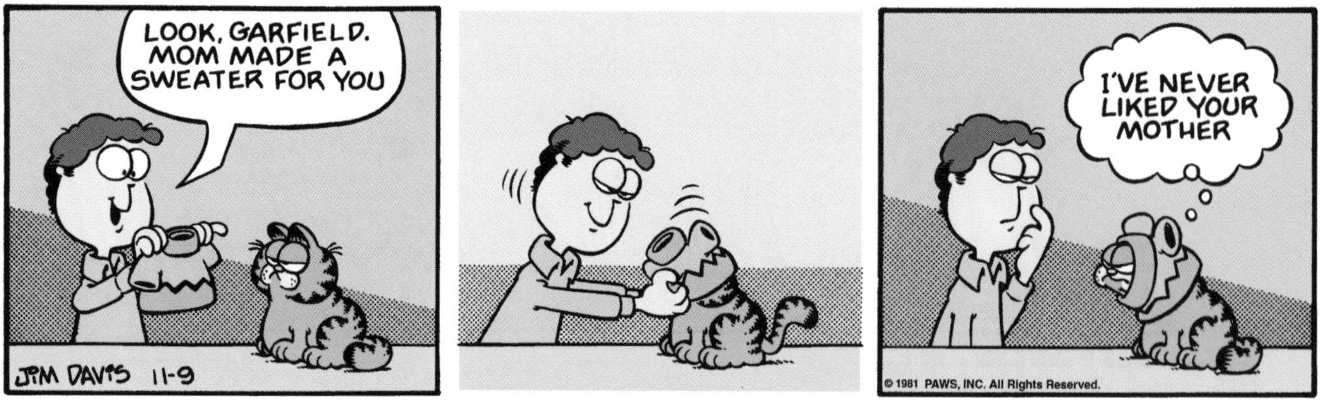
LOOK, GARFIELD. MOM MADE A SWEATER FOR YOU
JIM DAVIS 11-9
I'VE NEVER LIKED YOUR MOTHER
© 1981 PAWS, INC. All Rights Reserved.

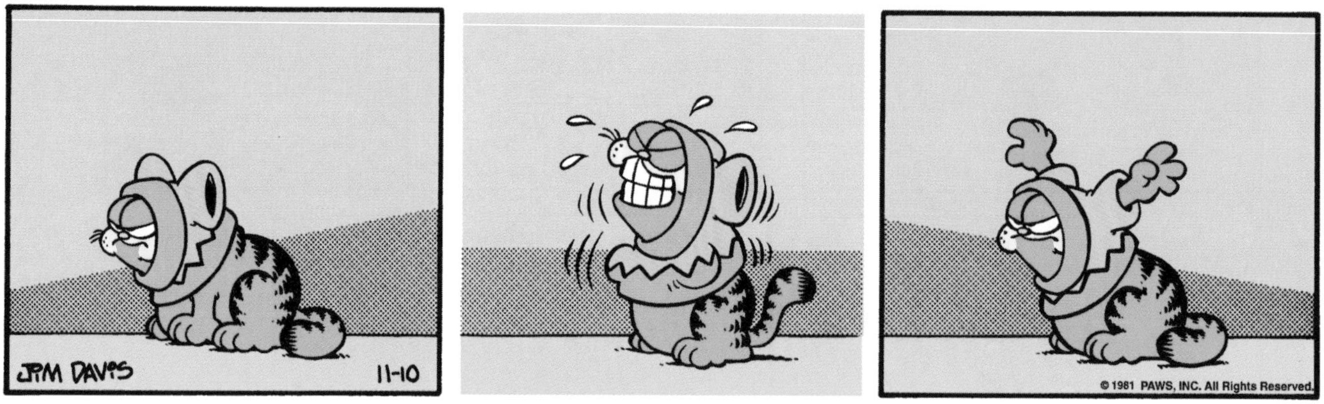
JIM DAVIS
11-10
© 1981 PAWS, INC. All Rights Reserved.

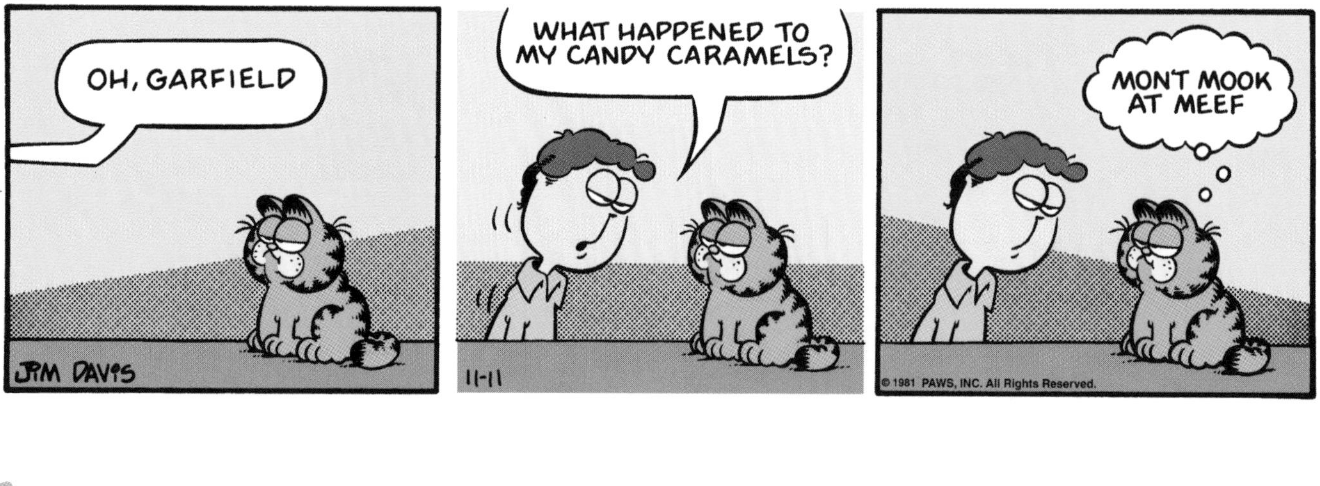
OH, GARFIELD
JIM DAVIS
WHAT HAPPENED TO MY CANDY CARAMELS?
11-11
MON'T MOOK AT MEEF
© 1981 PAWS, INC. All Rights Reserved.

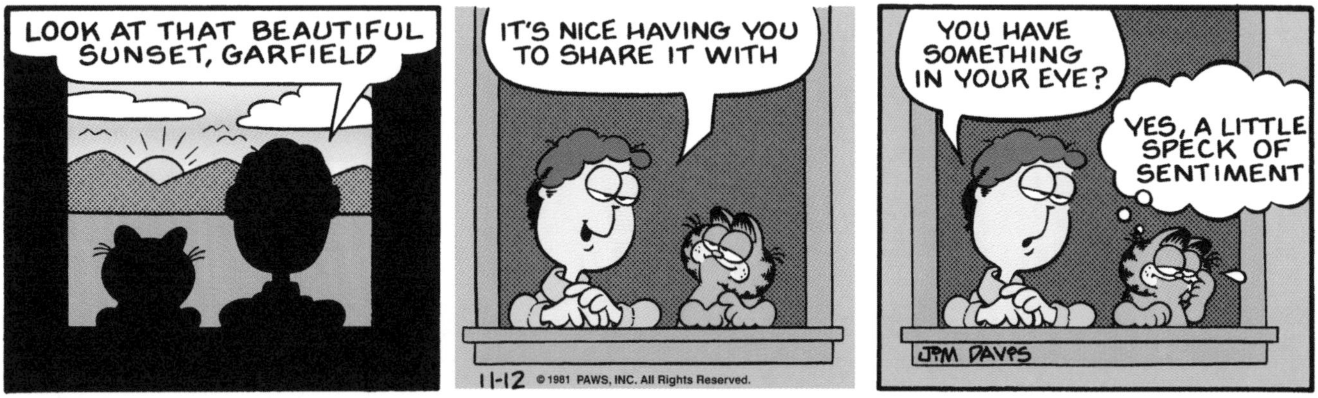
LOOK AT THAT BEAUTIFUL SUNSET, GARFIELD
IT'S NICE HAVING YOU TO SHARE IT WITH
11-12 © 1981 PAWS, INC. All Rights Reserved.
YOU HAVE SOMETHING IN YOUR EYE?
YES, A LITTLE SPECK OF SENTIMENT
JIM DAVIS

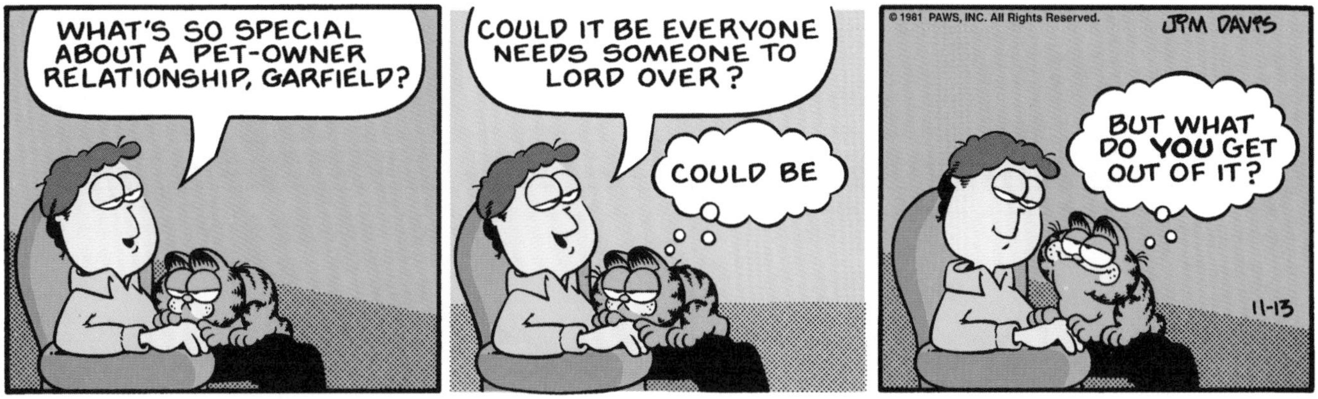
WHAT'S SO SPECIAL ABOUT A PET-OWNER RELATIONSHIP, GARFIELD?
COULD IT BE EVERYONE NEEDS SOMEONE TO LORD OVER?
COULD BE
© 1981 PAWS, INC. All Rights Reserved.
JIM DAVIS
BUT WHAT DO **YOU** GET OUT OF IT?
11-13

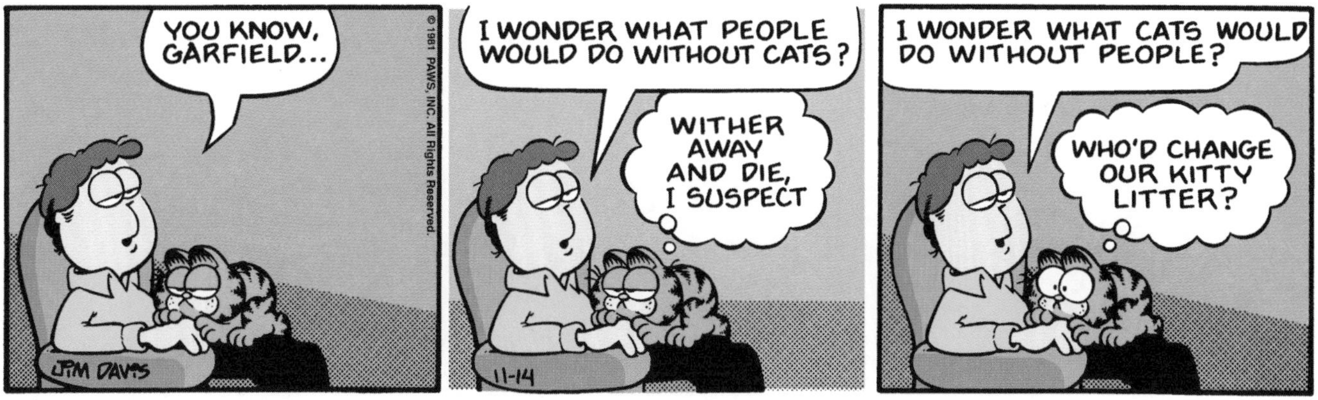
YOU KNOW, GARFIELD...
© 1981 PAWS, INC. All Rights Reserved.
JIM DAVIS
I WONDER WHAT PEOPLE WOULD DO WITHOUT CATS?
WITHER AWAY AND DIE, I SUSPECT
11-14
I WONDER WHAT CATS WOULD DO WITHOUT PEOPLE?
WHO'D CHANGE OUR KITTY LITTER?

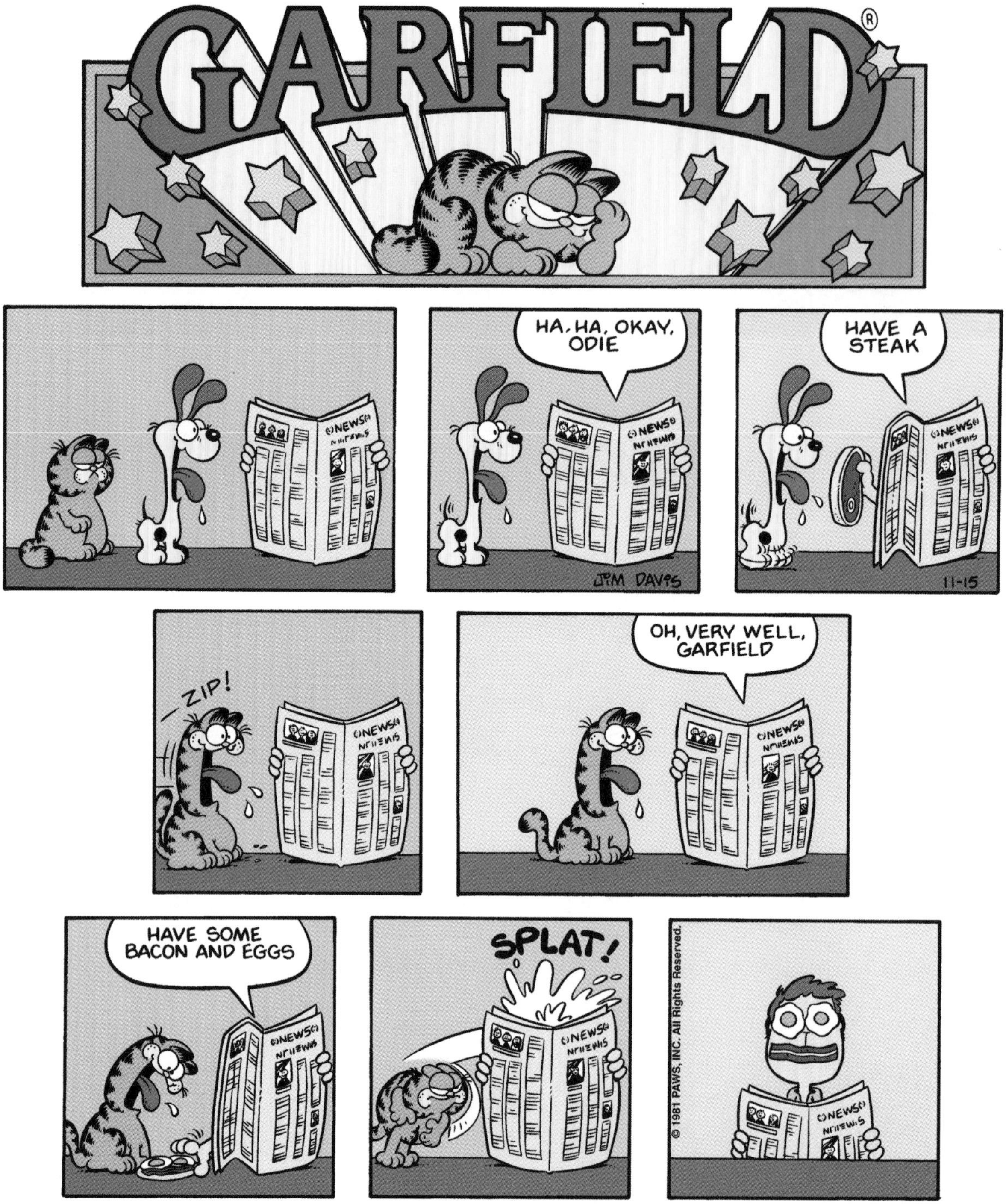
GARFIELD
HA, HA, OKAY, ODIE
HAVE A STEAK
JIM DAVIS
11-15
ZIP!
OH, VERY WELL, GARFIELD
HAVE SOME BACON AND EGGS
SPLAT!

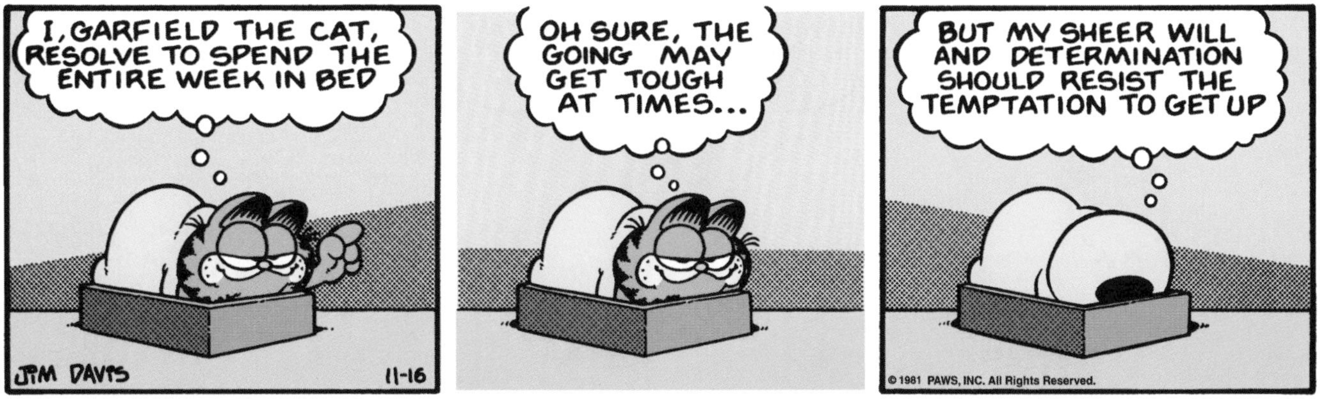
I, GARFIELD THE CAT, RESOLVE TO SPEND THE ENTIRE WEEK IN BED
JIM DAVIS
11-16
OH SURE, THE GOING MAY GET TOUGH AT TIMES...
BUT MY SHEER WILL AND DETERMINATION SHOULD RESIST THE TEMPTATION TO GET UP
© 1981 PAWS, INC. All Rights Reserved.

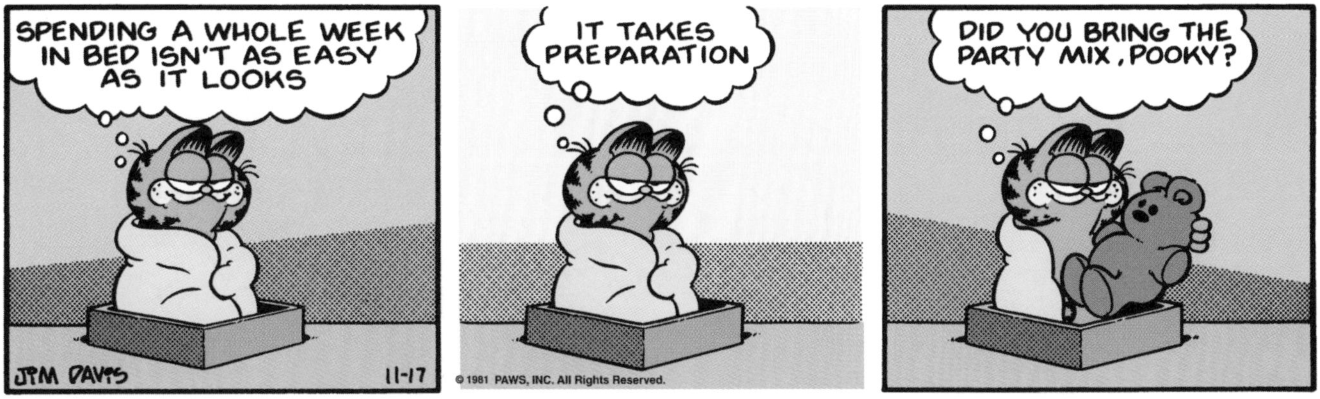
SPENDING A WHOLE WEEK IN BED ISN'T AS EASY AS IT LOOKS
JIM DAVIS
11-17
IT TAKES PREPARATION
© 1981 PAWS, INC. All Rights Reserved.
DID YOU BRING THE PARTY MIX, POOKY?

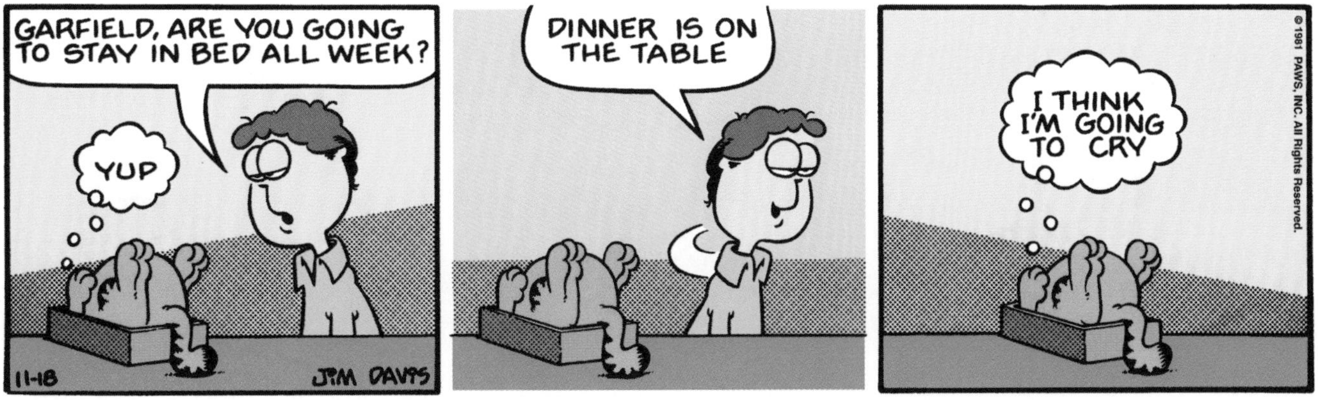
GARFIELD, ARE YOU GOING TO STAY IN BED ALL WEEK?
YUP
11-18
JIM DAVIS
DINNER IS ON THE TABLE
I THINK I'M GOING TO CRY
© 1981 PAWS, INC. All Rights Reserved.

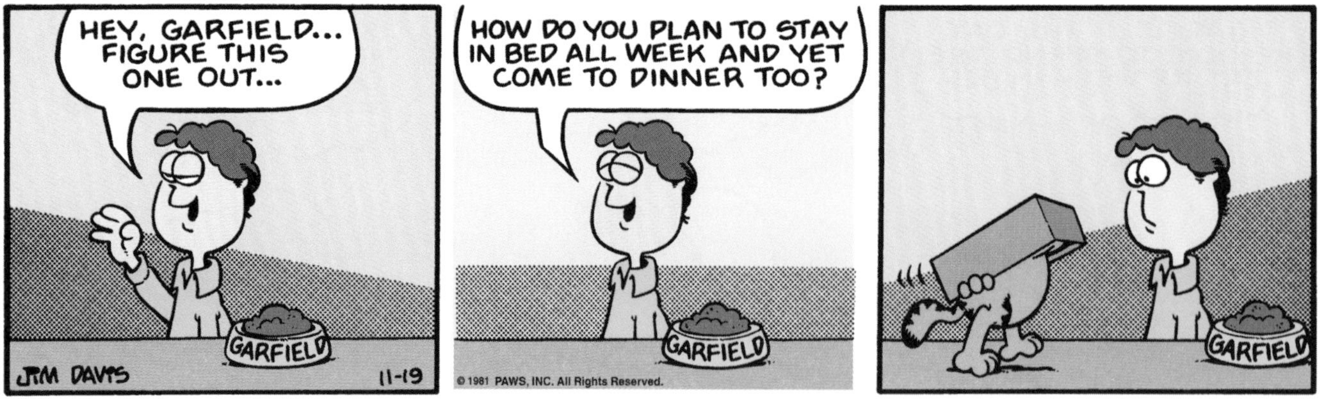
HEY, GARFIELD... FIGURE THIS ONE OUT...
GARFIELD
JIM DAVIS
11-19
HOW DO YOU PLAN TO STAY IN BED ALL WEEK AND YET COME TO DINNER TOO?
GARFIELD
© 1981 PAWS, INC. All Rights Reserved.
GARFIELD

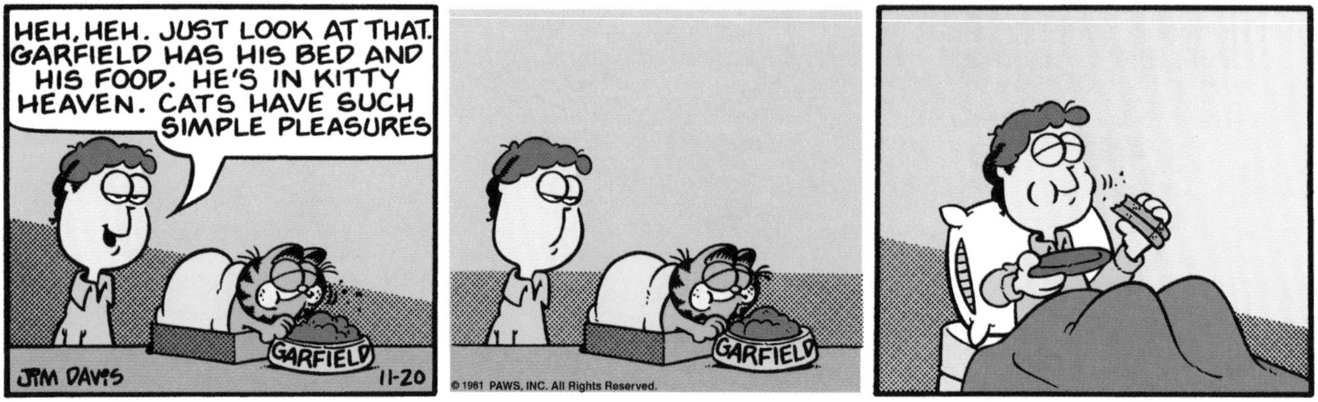
HEH, HEH. JUST LOOK AT THAT. GARFIELD HAS HIS BED AND HIS FOOD. HE'S IN KITTY HEAVEN. CATS HAVE SUCH SIMPLE PLEASURES
GARFIELD
JIM DAVIS
11-20
GARFIELD
© 1981 PAWS, INC. All Rights Reserved.

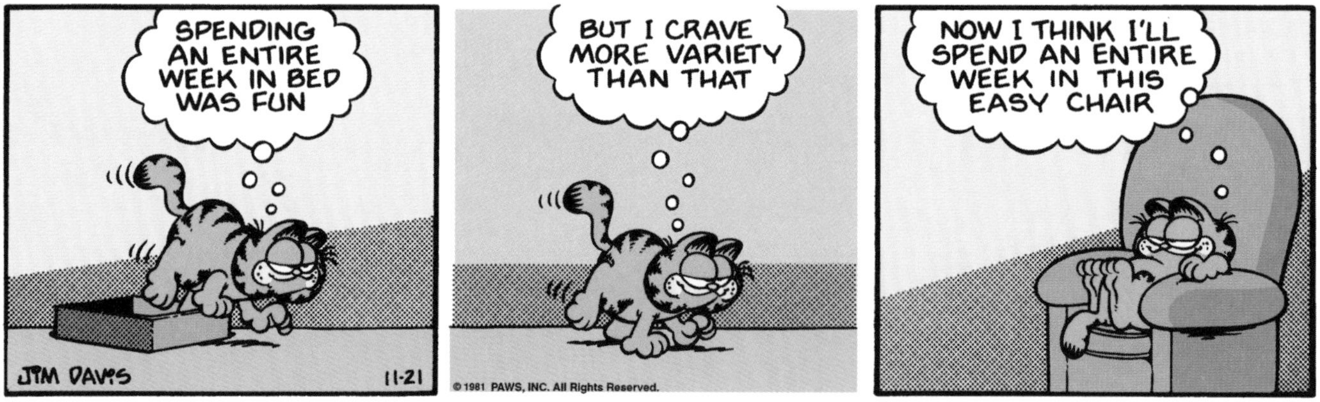
SPENDING AN ENTIRE WEEK IN BED WAS FUN
JIM DAVIS
11-21
BUT I CRAVE MORE VARIETY THAN THAT
© 1981 PAWS, INC. All Rights Reserved.
NOW I THINK I'LL SPEND AN ENTIRE WEEK IN THIS EASY CHAIR

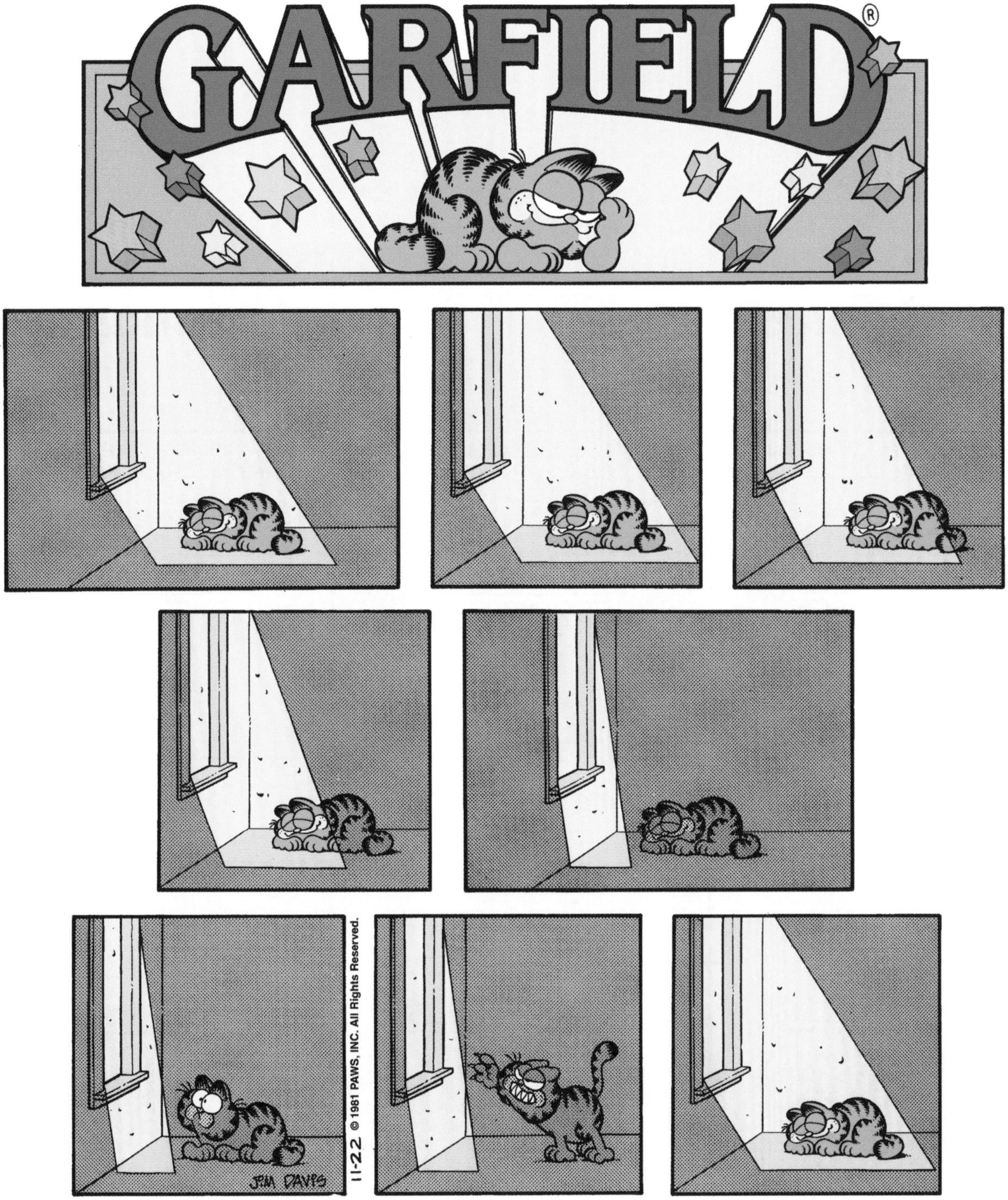
GARFIELD®
JIM DAVIS
11-22 © 1981 PAWS, INC. All Rights Reserved.

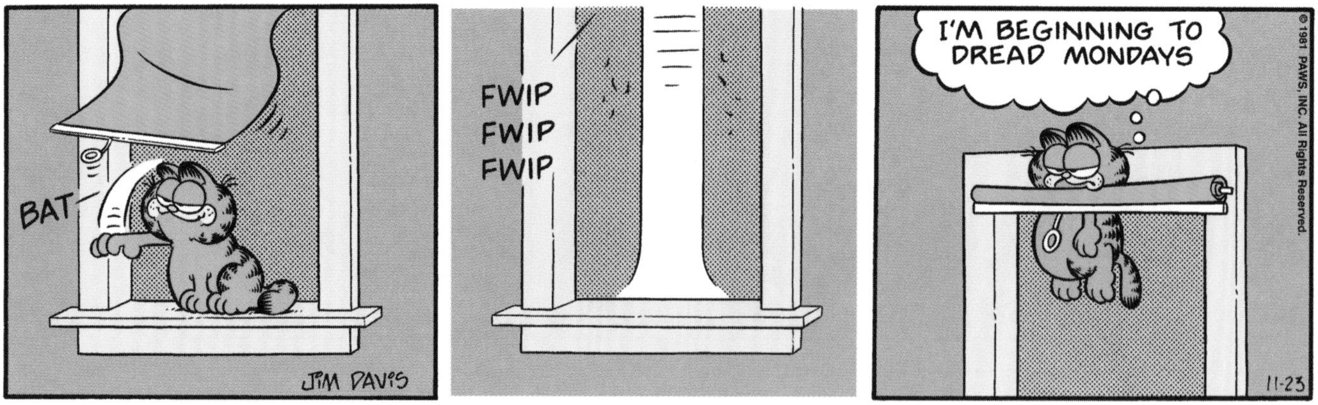
BAT
JIM DAVIS
FWIP
FWIP
FWIP
I'M BEGINNING TO DREAD MONDAYS
© 1981 PAWS, INC. All Rights Reserved.
11-23

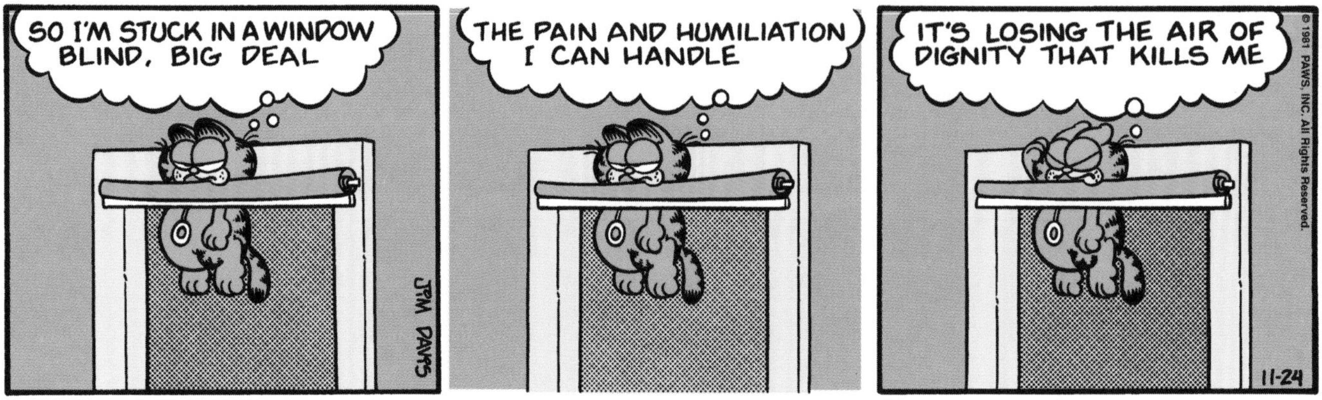
SO I'M STUCK IN A WINDOW BLIND. BIG DEAL
JIM DAVIS
THE PAIN AND HUMILIATION I CAN HANDLE
IT'S LOSING THE AIR OF DIGNITY THAT KILLS ME
© 1981 PAWS, INC. All Rights Reserved.
11-24

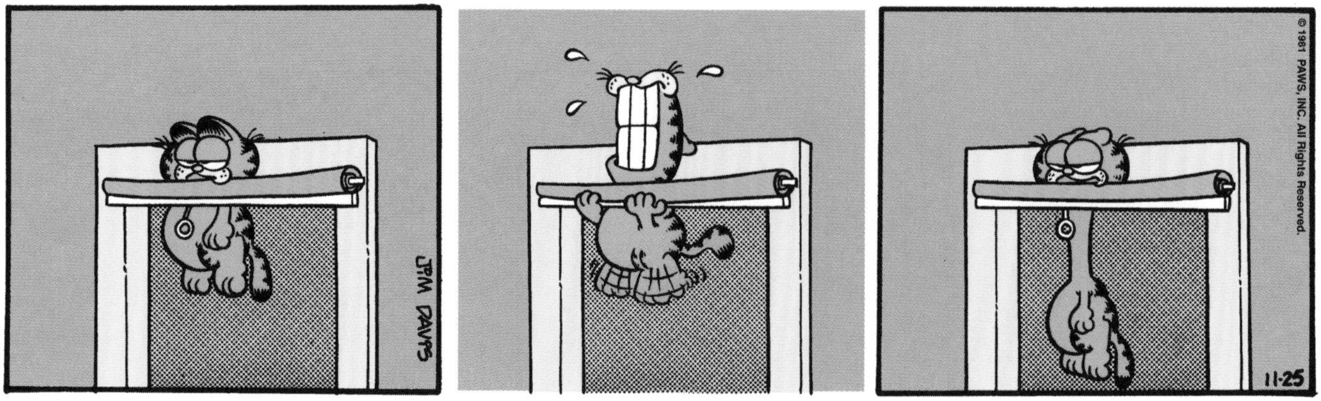
JIM DAVIS
© 1981 PAWS, INC. All Rights Reserved.
11-25

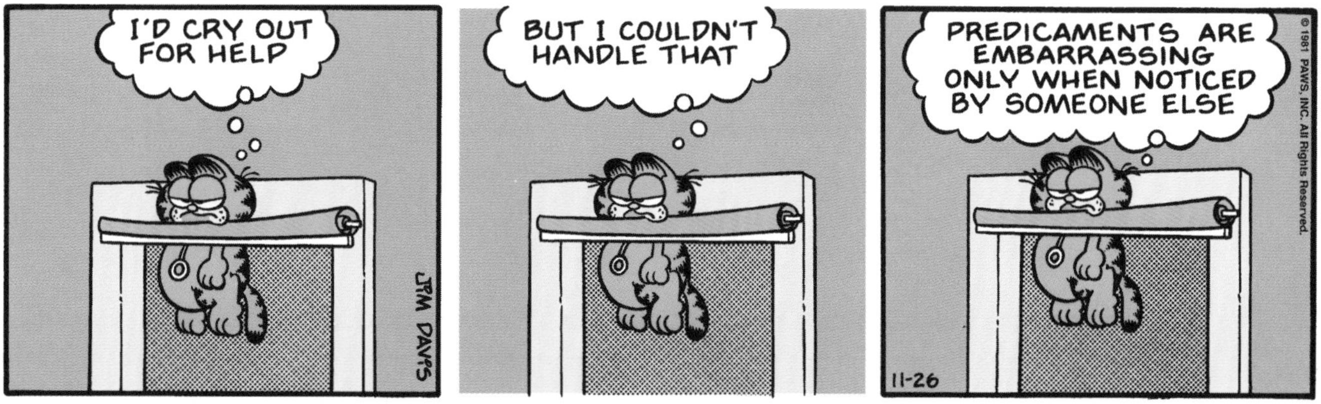
I'D CRY OUT FOR HELP
JIM DAVIS
BUT I COULDN'T HANDLE THAT
PREDICAMENTS ARE EMBARRASSING ONLY WHEN NOTICED BY SOMEONE ELSE
© 1981 PAWS, INC. All Rights Reserved.
11-26

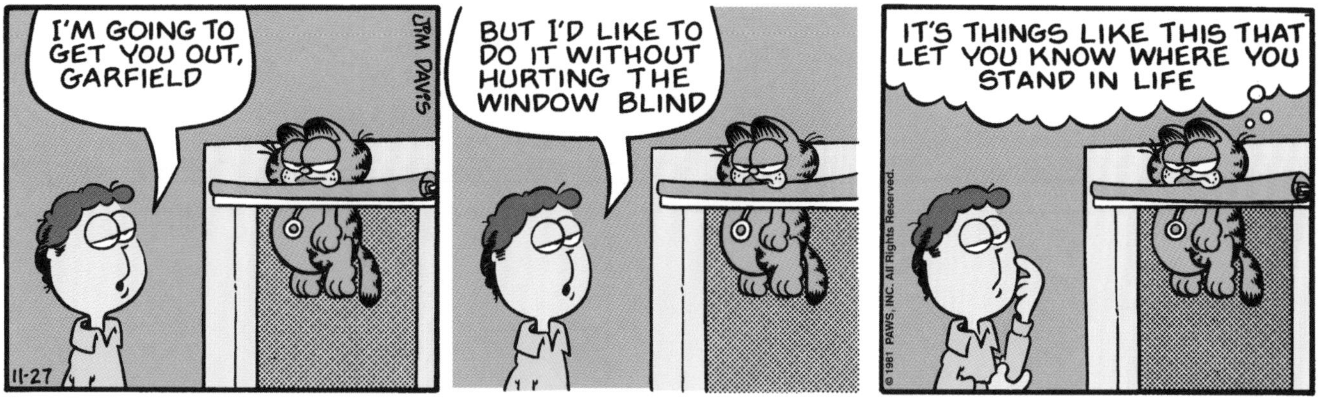
I'M GOING TO GET YOU OUT, GARFIELD
JIM DAVIS
11-27
BUT I'D LIKE TO DO IT WITHOUT HURTING THE WINDOW BLIND
IT'S THINGS LIKE THIS THAT LET YOU KNOW WHERE YOU STAND IN LIFE
© 1981 PAWS, INC. All Rights Reserved.

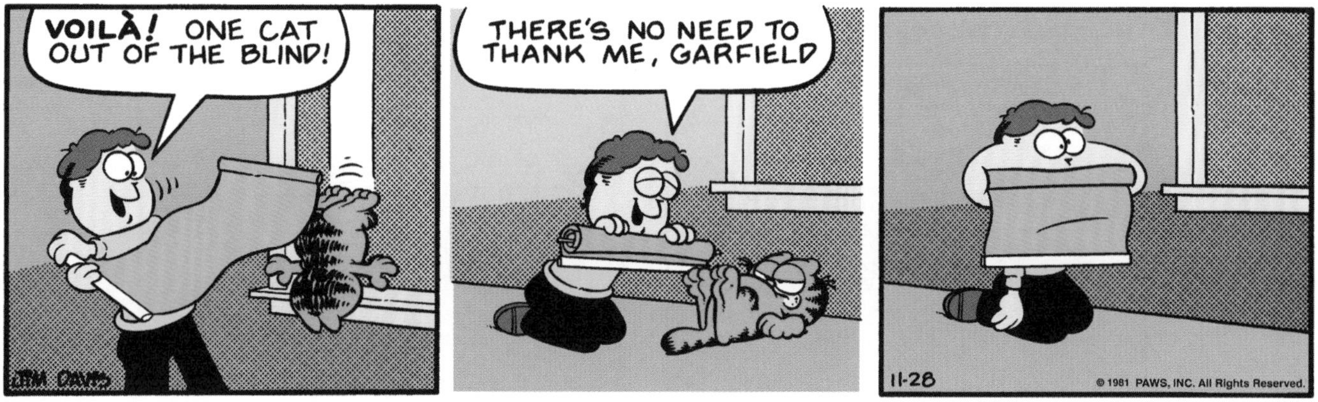
VOILÀ! ONE CAT OUT OF THE BLIND!
JIM DAVIS
THERE'S NO NEED TO THANK ME, GARFIELD
11-28
© 1981 PAWS, INC. All Rights Reserved.

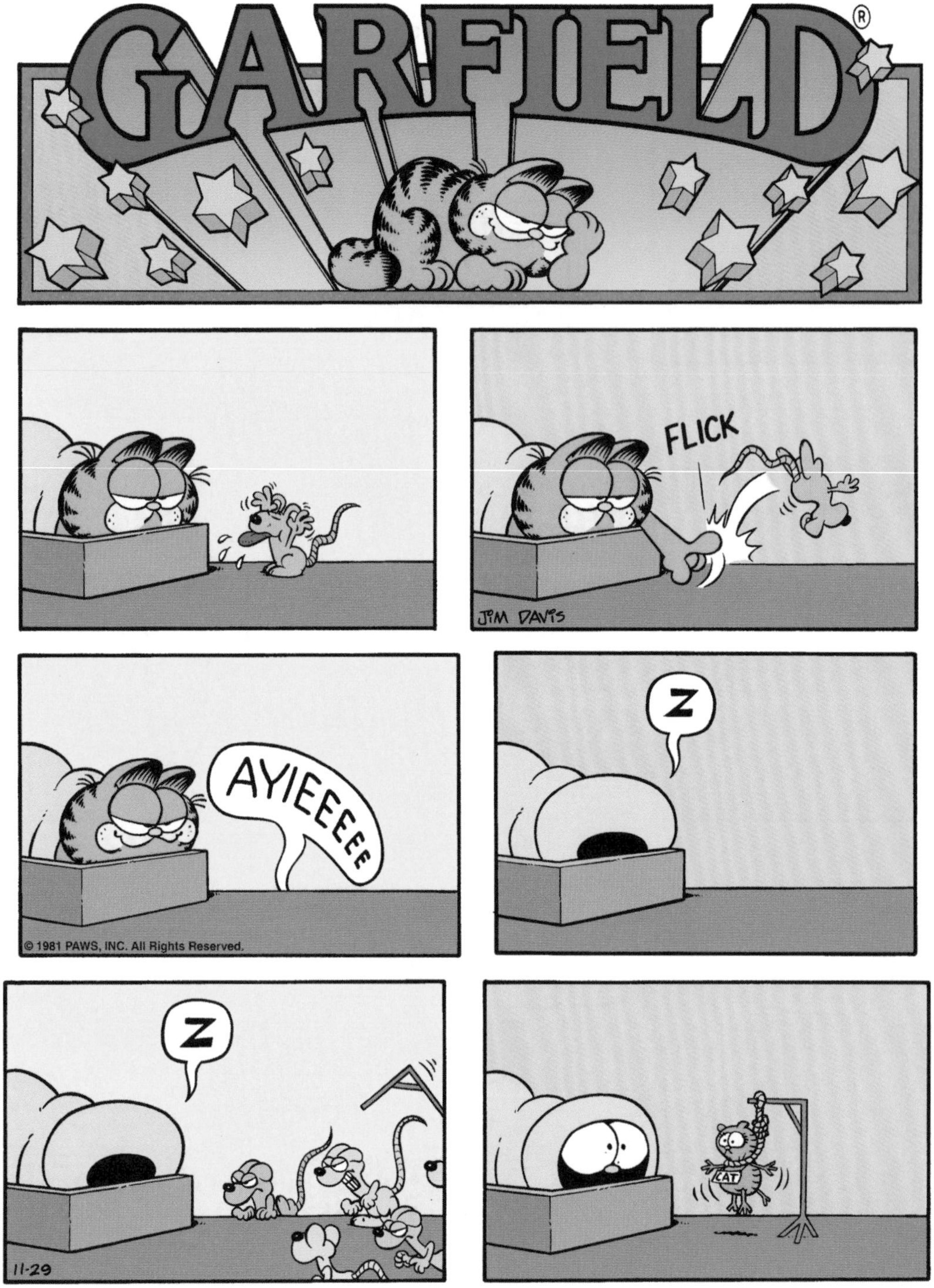
GARFIELD®
FLICK
JIM DAVIS
AYIEEEEEE
© 1981 PAWS, INC. All Rights Reserved.
Z
Z
11-29
CAT

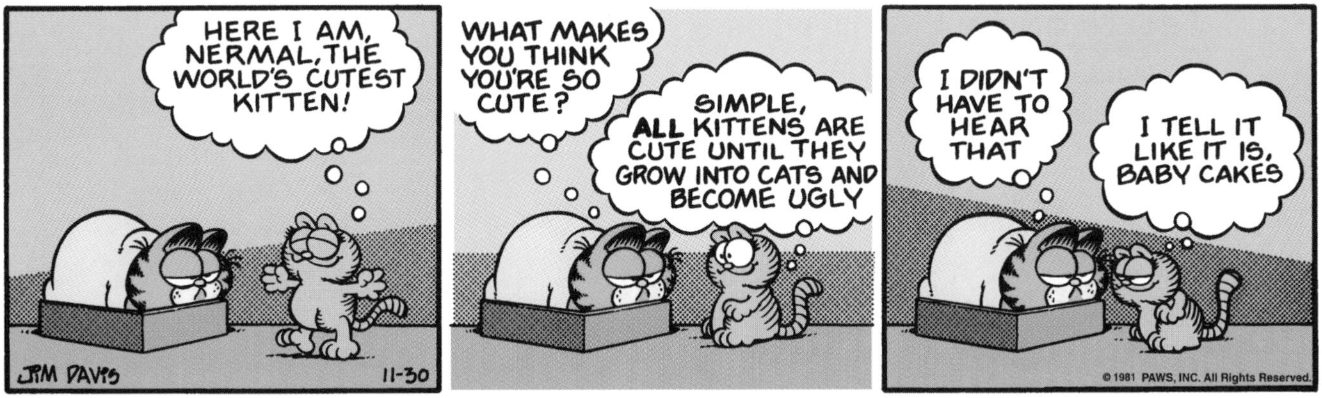
HERE I AM, NERMAL, THE WORLD'S CUTEST KITTEN!
JIM DAVIS
11-30
WHAT MAKES YOU THINK YOU'RE SO CUTE?
SIMPLE, **ALL** KITTENS ARE CUTE UNTIL THEY GROW INTO CATS AND BECOME UGLY
I DIDN'T HAVE TO HEAR THAT
I TELL IT LIKE IT IS, BABY CAKES
© 1981 PAWS, INC. All Rights Reserved.

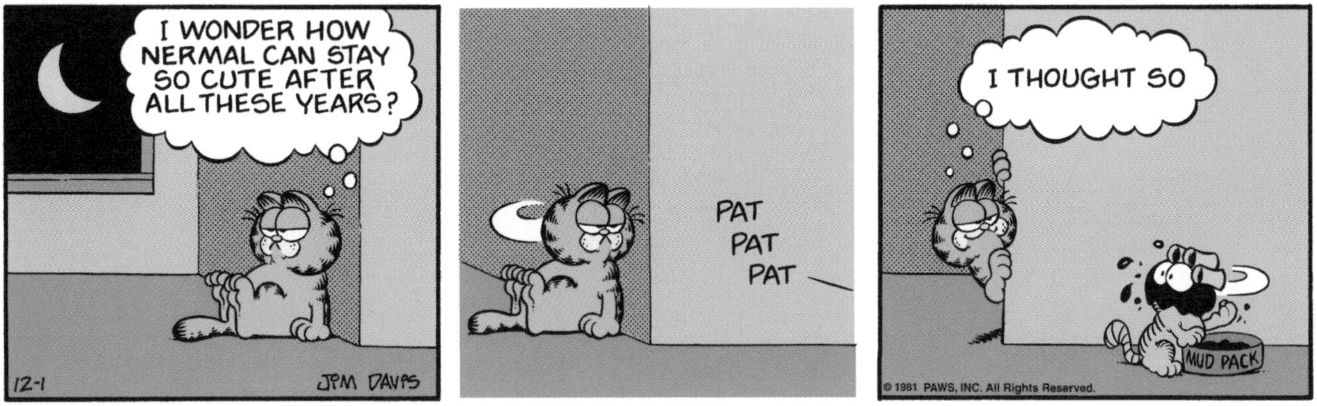
I WONDER HOW NERMAL CAN STAY SO CUTE AFTER ALL THESE YEARS?
12-1
JIM DAVIS
PAT PAT PAT
I THOUGHT SO
MUD PACK
© 1981 PAWS, INC. All Rights Reserved.

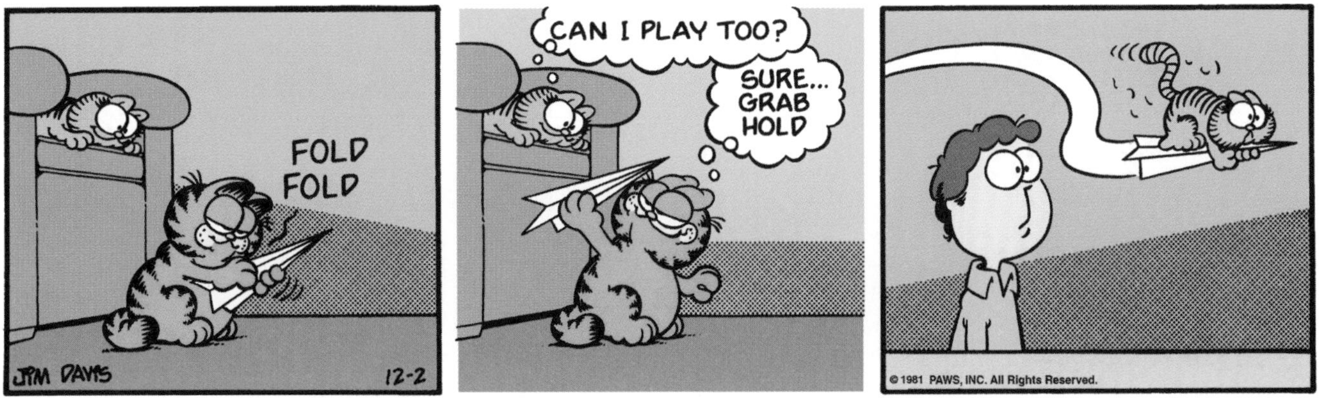
FOLD FOLD
JIM DAVIS
12-2
CAN I PLAY TOO?
SURE... GRAB HOLD
© 1981 PAWS, INC. All Rights Reserved.

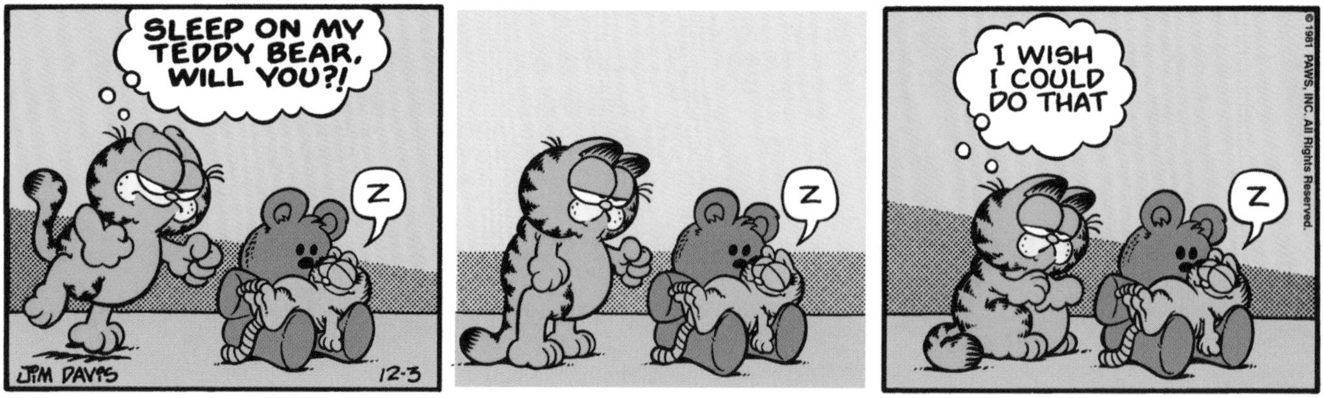
SLEEP ON MY TEDDY BEAR, WILL YOU?!
Z
JIM DAVIS
12-3
Z
I WISH I COULD DO THAT
Z

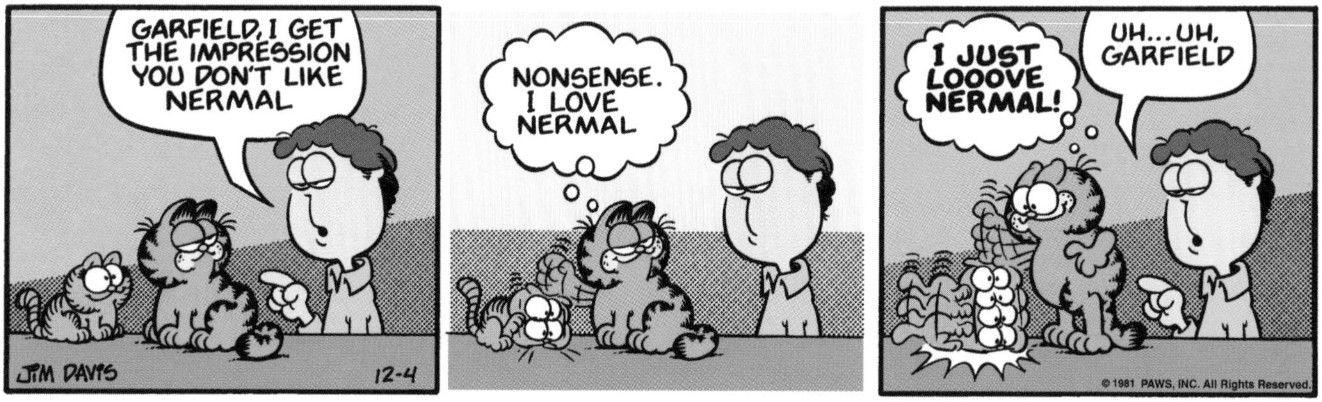
GARFIELD, I GET THE IMPRESSION YOU DON'T LIKE NERMAL
JIM DAVIS
12-4
NONSENSE. I LOVE NERMAL
I JUST LOOOVE NERMAL!
UH... UH, GARFIELD

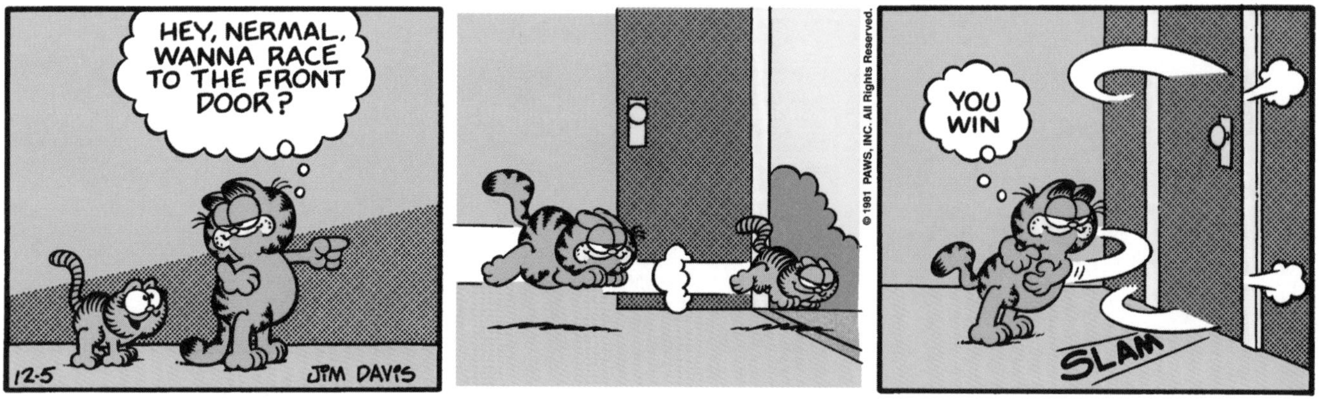
HEY, NERMAL, WANNA RACE TO THE FRONT DOOR?
12-5
JIM DAVIS
YOU WIN
SLAM

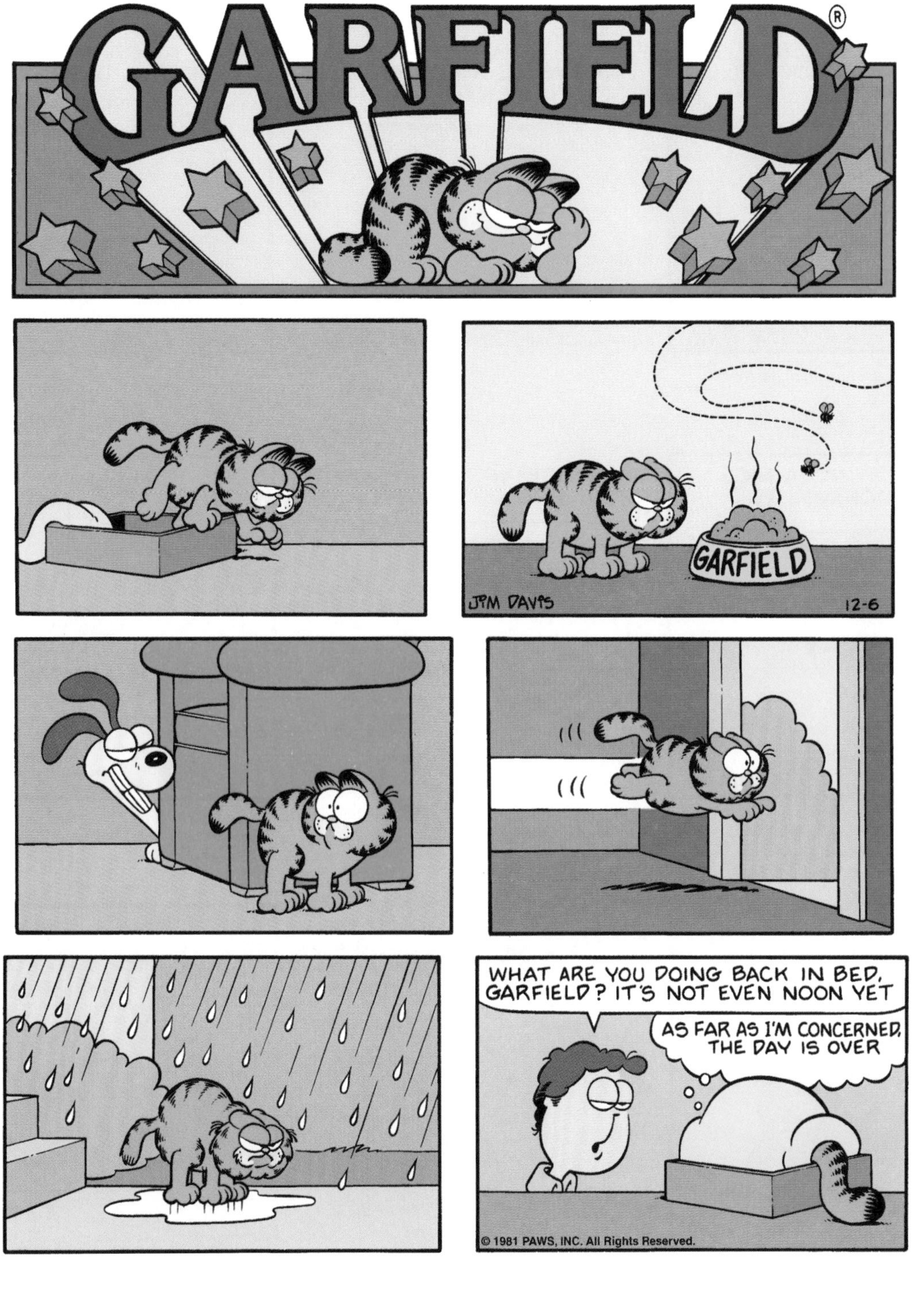
GARFIELD
GARFIELD
JIM DAVIS
12-6
WHAT ARE YOU DOING BACK IN BED, GARFIELD? IT'S NOT EVEN NOON YET
AS FAR AS I'M CONCERNED, THE DAY IS OVER
© 1981 PAWS, INC. All Rights Reserved.

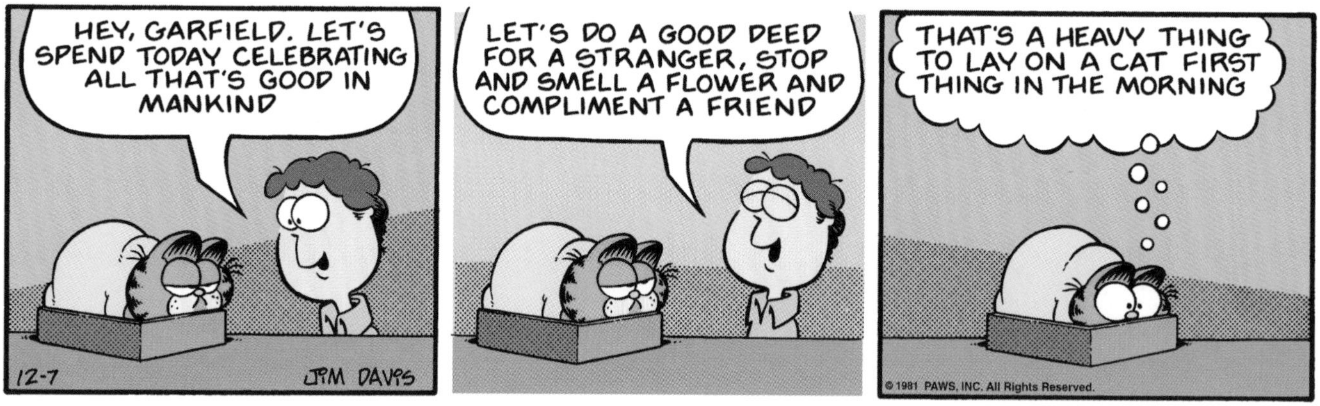
HEY, GARFIELD. LET'S SPEND TODAY CELEBRATING ALL THAT'S GOOD IN MANKIND
12-7
JIM DAVIS
LET'S DO A GOOD DEED FOR A STRANGER, STOP AND SMELL A FLOWER AND COMPLIMENT A FRIEND
THAT'S A HEAVY THING TO LAY ON A CAT FIRST THING IN THE MORNING
© 1981 PAWS, INC. All Rights Reserved.

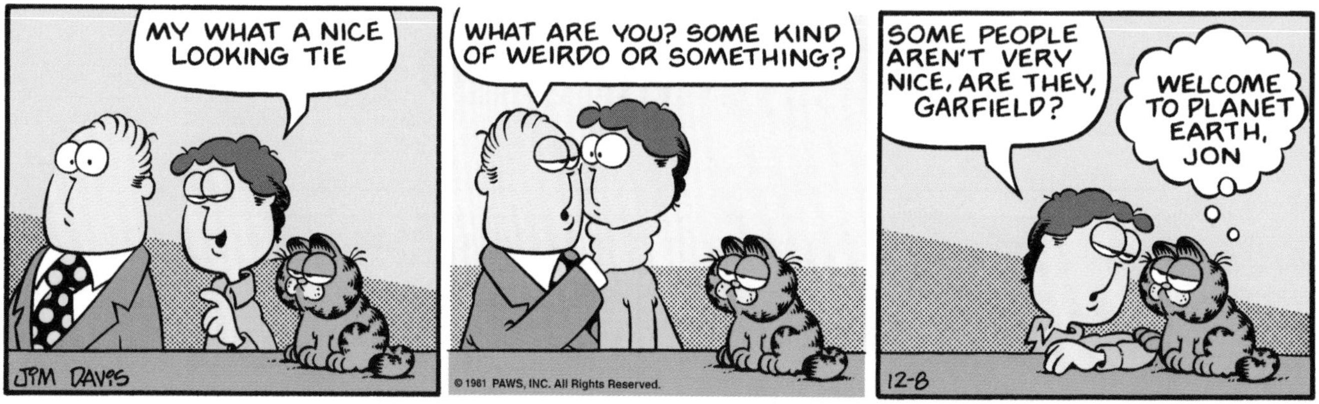
MY WHAT A NICE LOOKING TIE
JIM DAVIS
WHAT ARE YOU? SOME KIND OF WEIRDO OR SOMETHING?
© 1981 PAWS, INC. All Rights Reserved.
SOME PEOPLE AREN'T VERY NICE, ARE THEY, GARFIELD?
WELCOME TO PLANET EARTH, JON
12-8

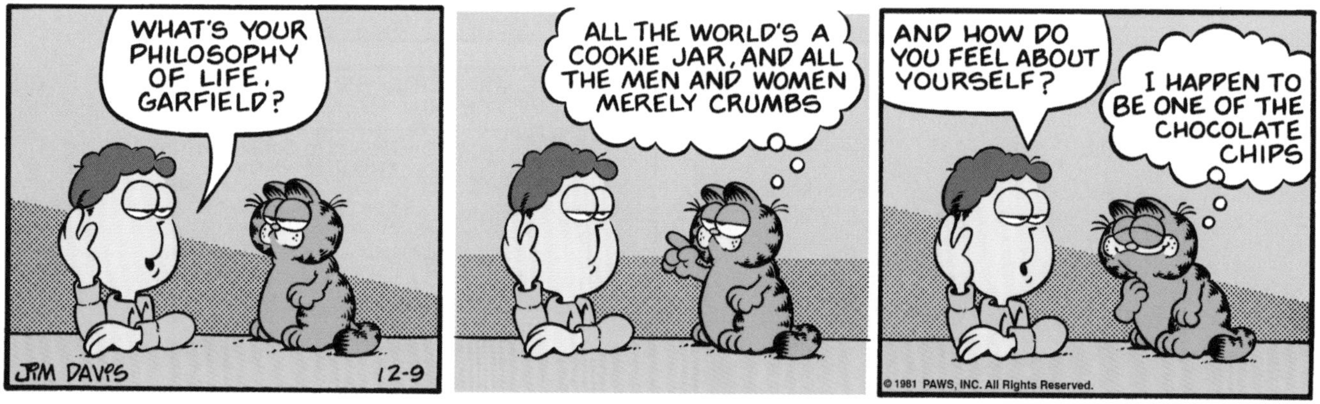
WHAT'S YOUR PHILOSOPHY OF LIFE, GARFIELD?
JIM DAVIS
12-9
ALL THE WORLD'S A COOKIE JAR, AND ALL THE MEN AND WOMEN MERELY CRUMBS
AND HOW DO YOU FEEL ABOUT YOURSELF?
I HAPPEN TO BE ONE OF THE CHOCOLATE CHIPS
© 1981 PAWS, INC. All Rights Reserved.

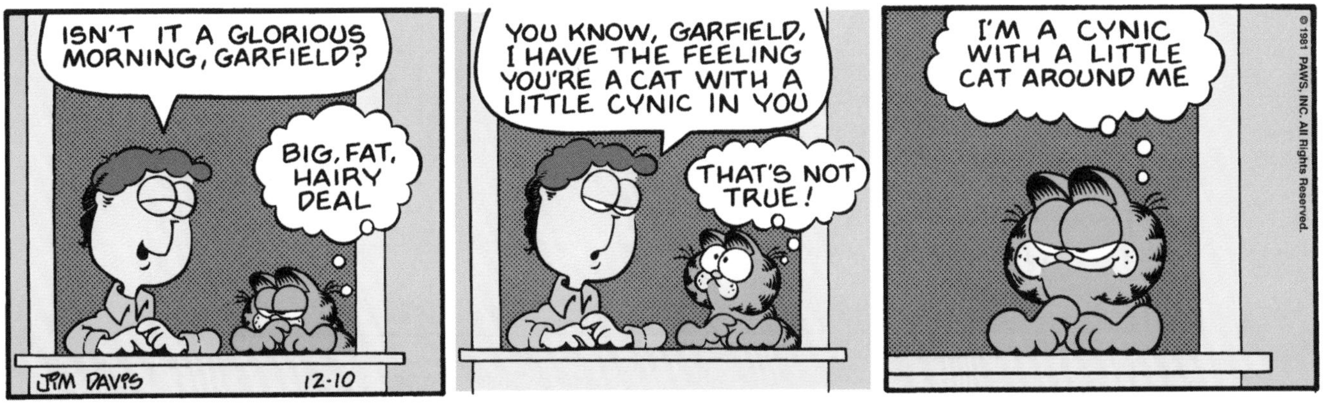
ISN'T IT A GLORIOUS MORNING, GARFIELD?
BIG, FAT, HAIRY DEAL
JIM DAVIS 12-10
YOU KNOW, GARFIELD, I HAVE THE FEELING YOU'RE A CAT WITH A LITTLE CYNIC IN YOU
THAT'S NOT TRUE!
I'M A CYNIC WITH A LITTLE CAT AROUND ME
© 1981 PAWS, INC. All Rights Reserved.

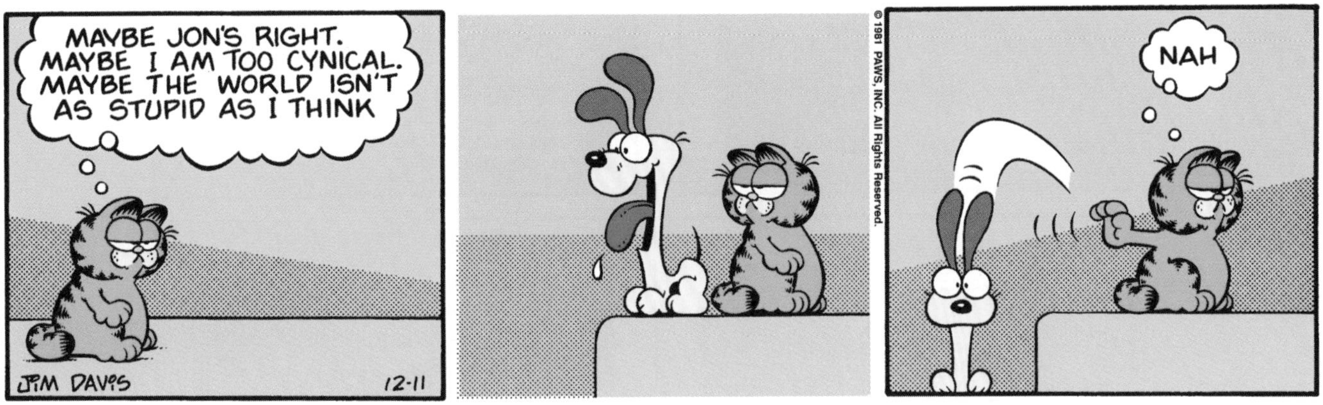
MAYBE JON'S RIGHT. MAYBE I AM TOO CYNICAL. MAYBE THE WORLD ISN'T AS STUPID AS I THINK
JIM DAVIS 12-11
© 1981 PAWS, INC. All Rights Reserved.
NAH

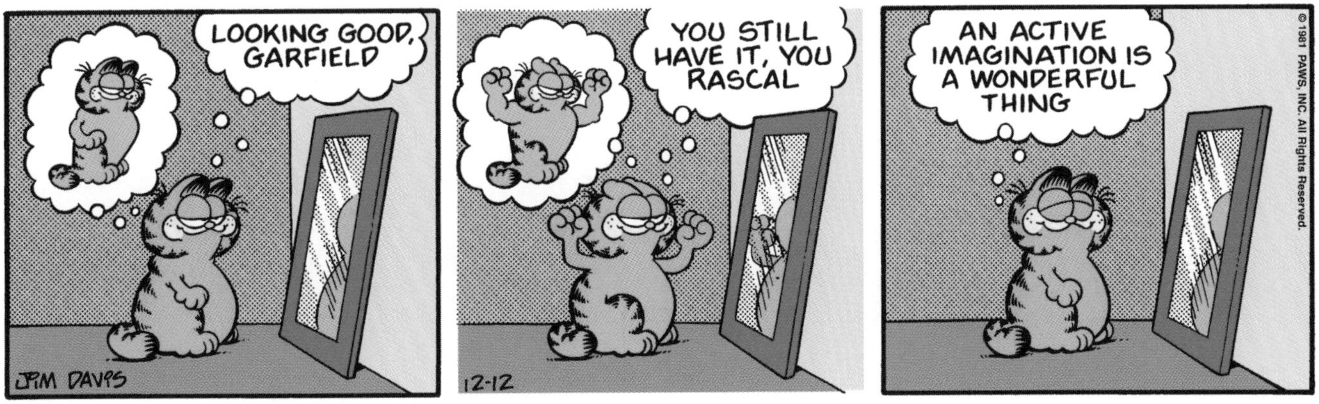
LOOKING GOOD, GARFIELD
JIM DAVIS
YOU STILL HAVE IT, YOU RASCAL
12-12
AN ACTIVE IMAGINATION IS A WONDERFUL THING
© 1981 PAWS, INC. All Rights Reserved.

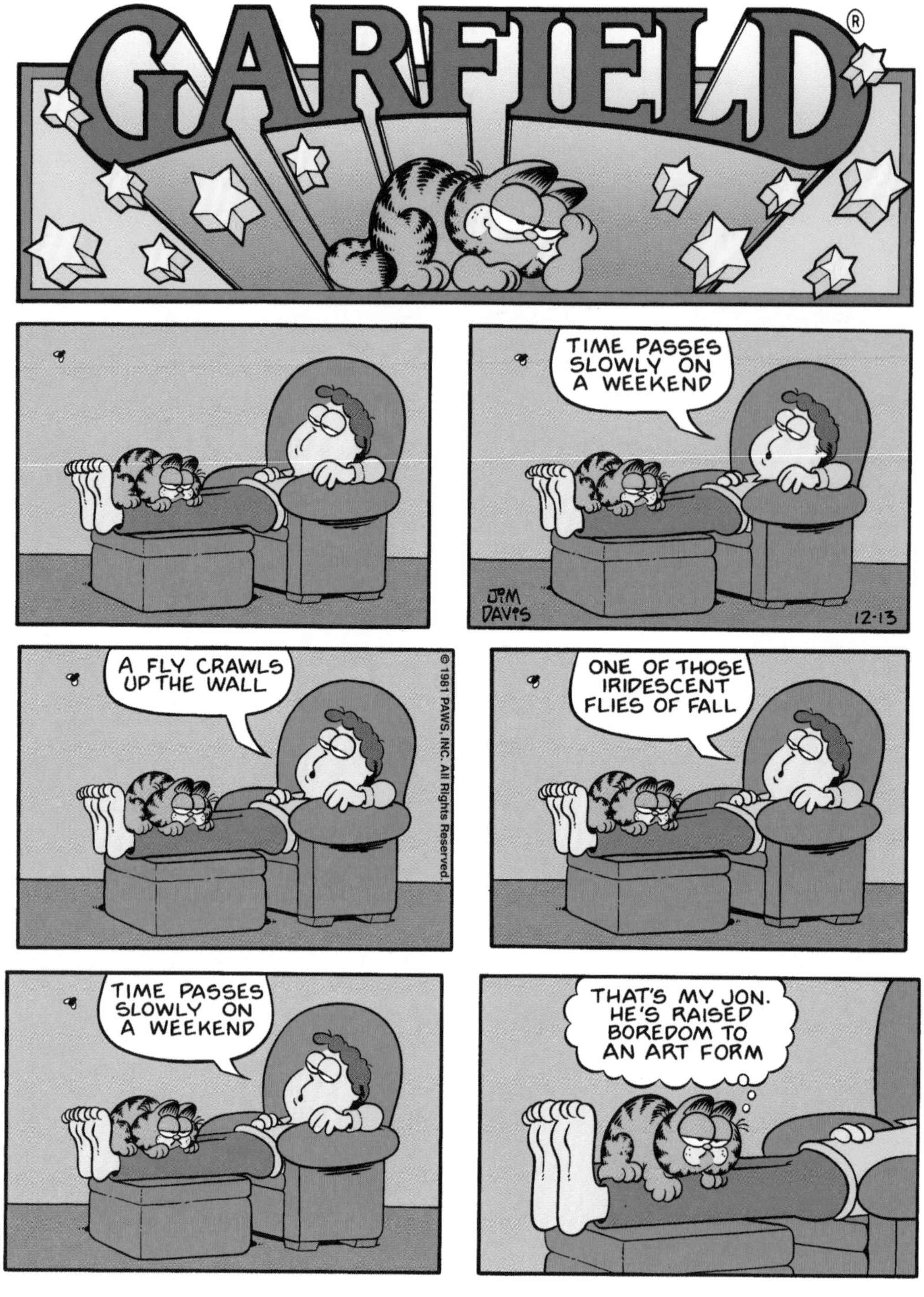
GARFIELD®
TIME PASSES SLOWLY ON A WEEKEND
JIM DAVIS
12-13
A FLY CRAWLS UP THE WALL
© 1981 PAWS, INC. All Rights Reserved.
ONE OF THOSE IRIDESCENT FLIES OF FALL
TIME PASSES SLOWLY ON A WEEKEND
THAT'S MY JON. HE'S RAISED BOREDOM TO AN ART FORM

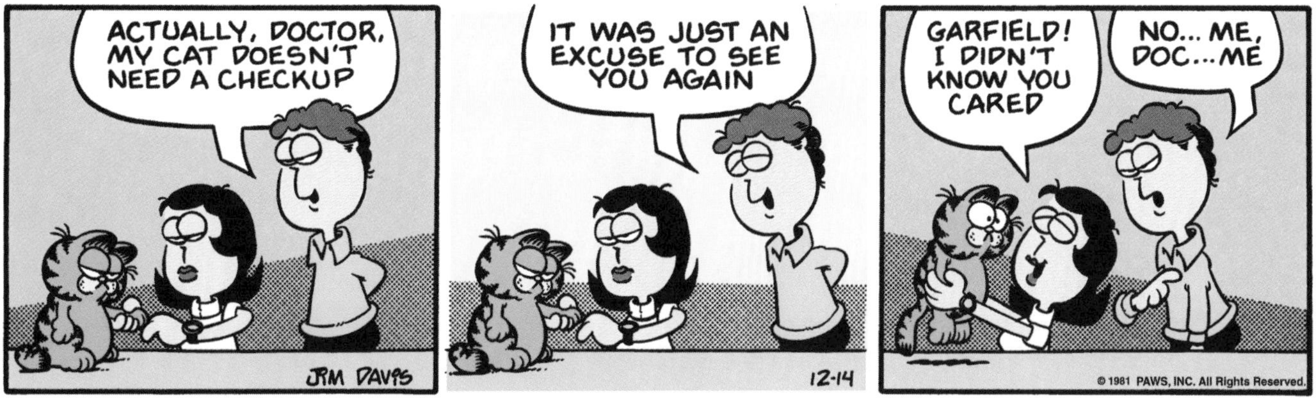
ACTUALLY, DOCTOR, MY CAT DOESN'T NEED A CHECKUP
JIM DAVIS
IT WAS JUST AN EXCUSE TO SEE YOU AGAIN
12-14
GARFIELD! I DIDN'T KNOW YOU CARED
NO... ME, DOC...ME
© 1981 PAWS, INC. All Rights Reserved.

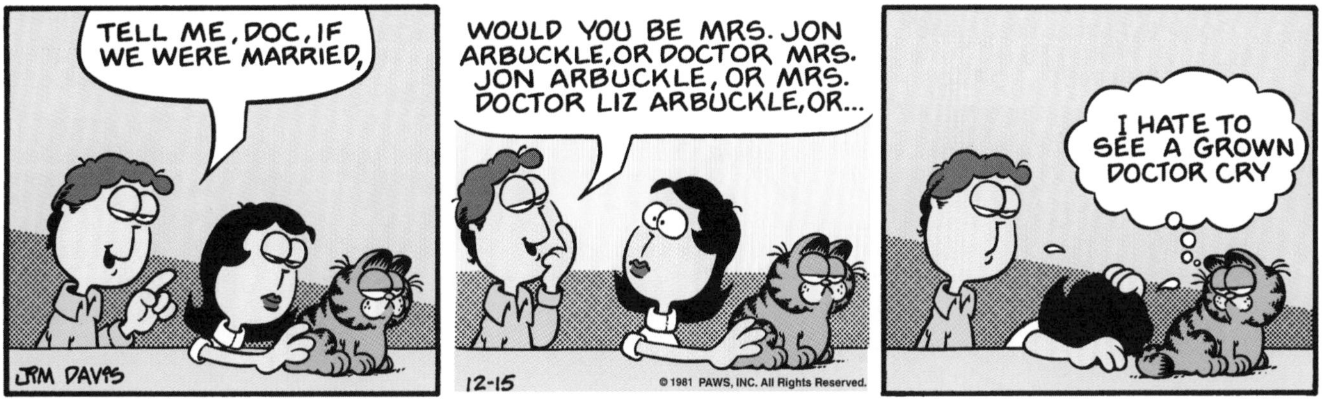
TELL ME, DOC, IF WE WERE MARRIED,
JIM DAVIS
WOULD YOU BE MRS. JON ARBUCKLE, OR DOCTOR MRS. JON ARBUCKLE, OR MRS. DOCTOR LIZ ARBUCKLE, OR...
12-15
© 1981 PAWS, INC. All Rights Reserved.
I HATE TO SEE A GROWN DOCTOR CRY

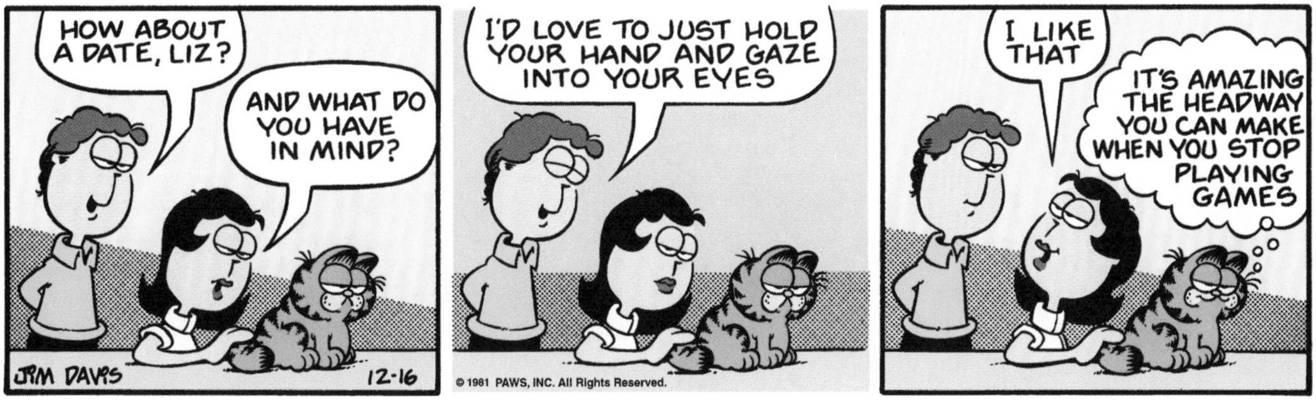
HOW ABOUT A DATE, LIZ?
AND WHAT DO YOU HAVE IN MIND?
JIM DAVIS
12-16
I'D LOVE TO JUST HOLD YOUR HAND AND GAZE INTO YOUR EYES
© 1981 PAWS, INC. All Rights Reserved.
I LIKE THAT
IT'S AMAZING THE HEADWAY YOU CAN MAKE WHEN YOU STOP PLAYING GAMES

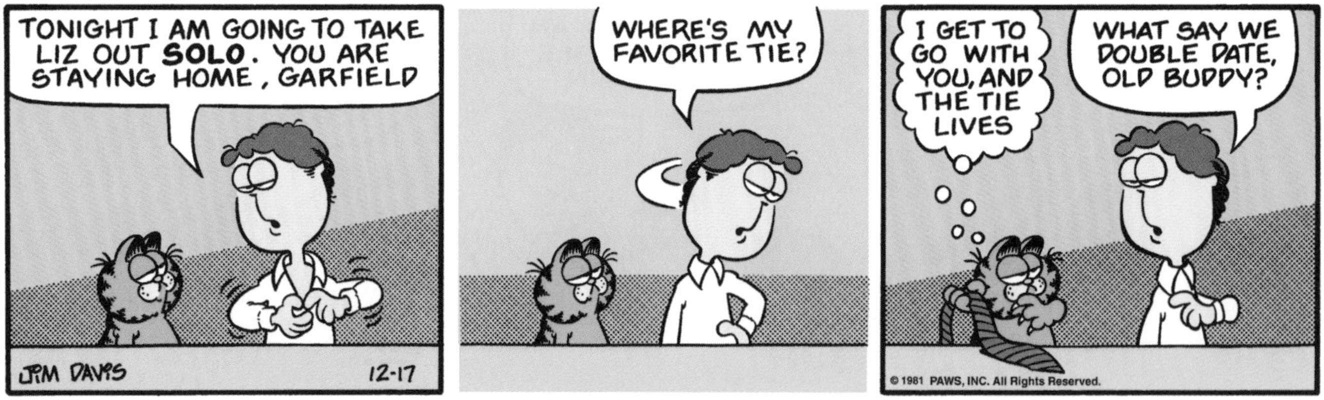
TONIGHT I AM GOING TO TAKE LIZ OUT **SOLO**. YOU ARE STAYING HOME, GARFIELD
JIM DAVIS
12-17
WHERE'S MY FAVORITE TIE?
I GET TO GO WITH YOU, AND THE TIE LIVES
WHAT SAY WE DOUBLE DATE, OLD BUDDY?
© 1981 PAWS, INC. All Rights Reserved.

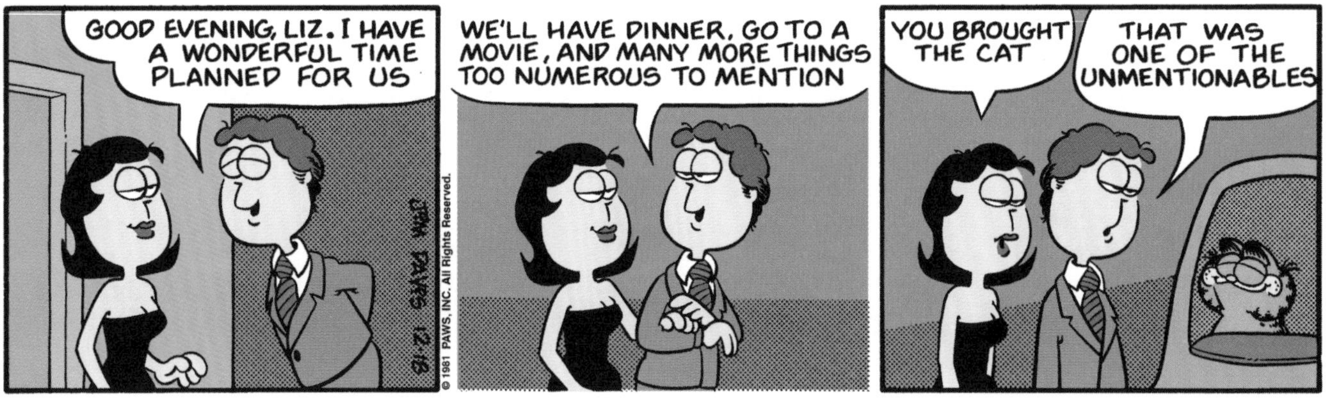
GOOD EVENING, LIZ. I HAVE A WONDERFUL TIME PLANNED FOR US
JIM DAVIS 12-18
© 1981 PAWS, INC. All Rights Reserved.
WE'LL HAVE DINNER, GO TO A MOVIE, AND MANY MORE THINGS TOO NUMEROUS TO MENTION
YOU BROUGHT THE CAT
THAT WAS ONE OF THE UNMENTIONABLES

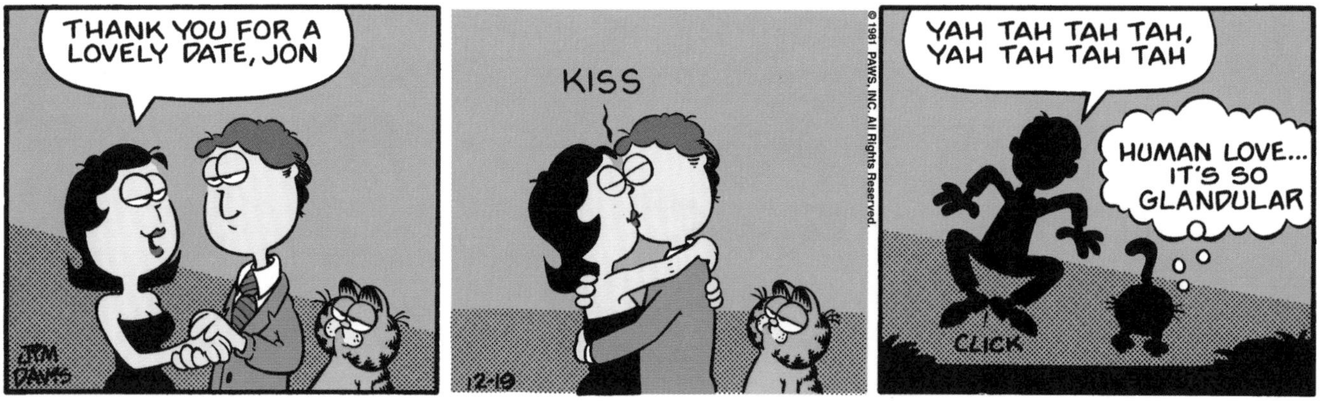
THANK YOU FOR A LOVELY DATE, JON
JIM DAVIS
KISS
12-19
© 1981 PAWS, INC. All Rights Reserved.
YAH TAH TAH TAH, YAH TAH TAH TAH
HUMAN LOVE... IT'S SO GLANDULAR
CLICK

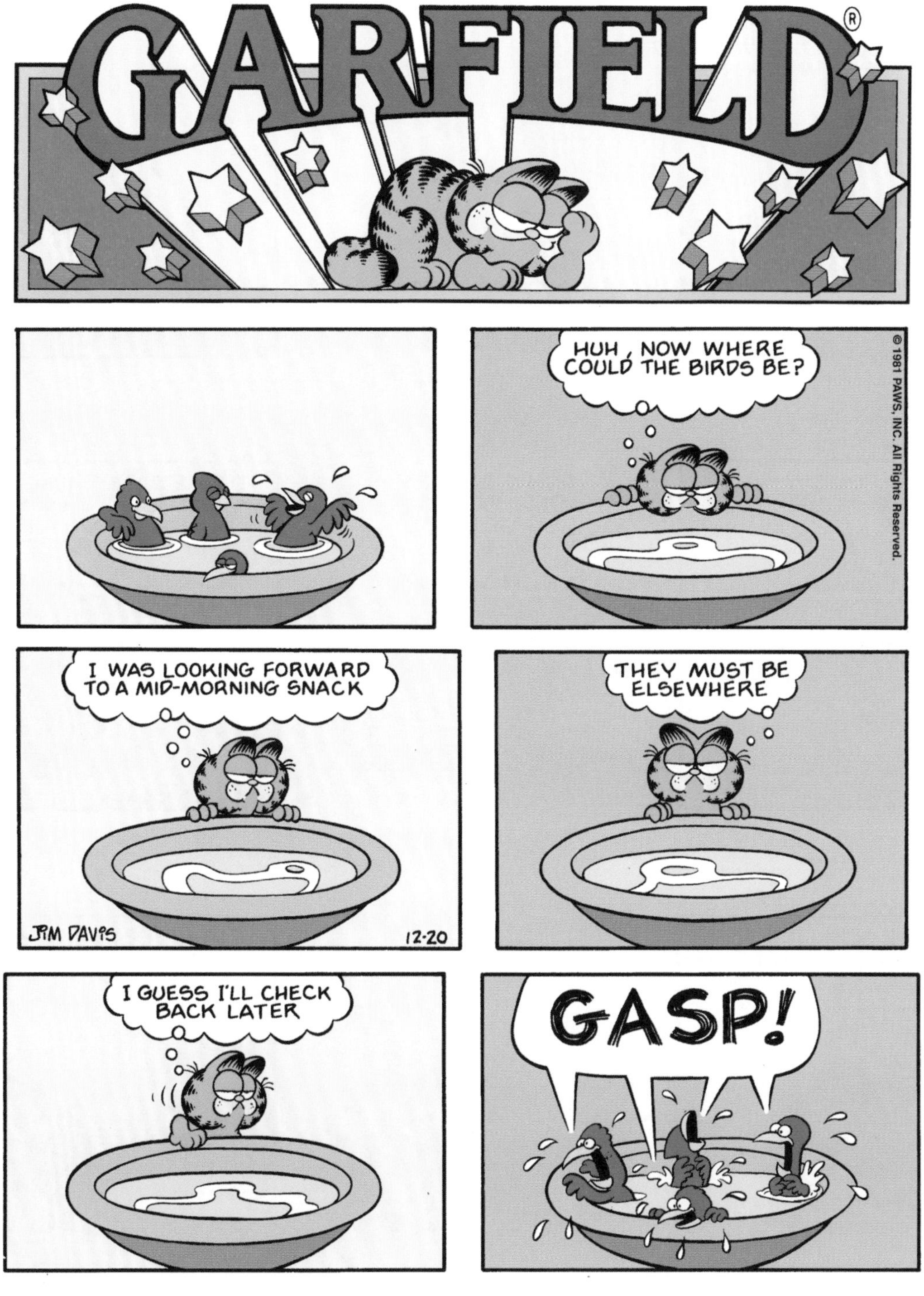
GARFIELD®
HUH, NOW WHERE COULD THE BIRDS BE?
© 1981 PAWS, INC. All Rights Reserved.
I WAS LOOKING FORWARD TO A MID-MORNING SNACK
JIM DAVIS
12-20
THEY MUST BE ELSEWHERE
I GUESS I'LL CHECK BACK LATER
GASP!

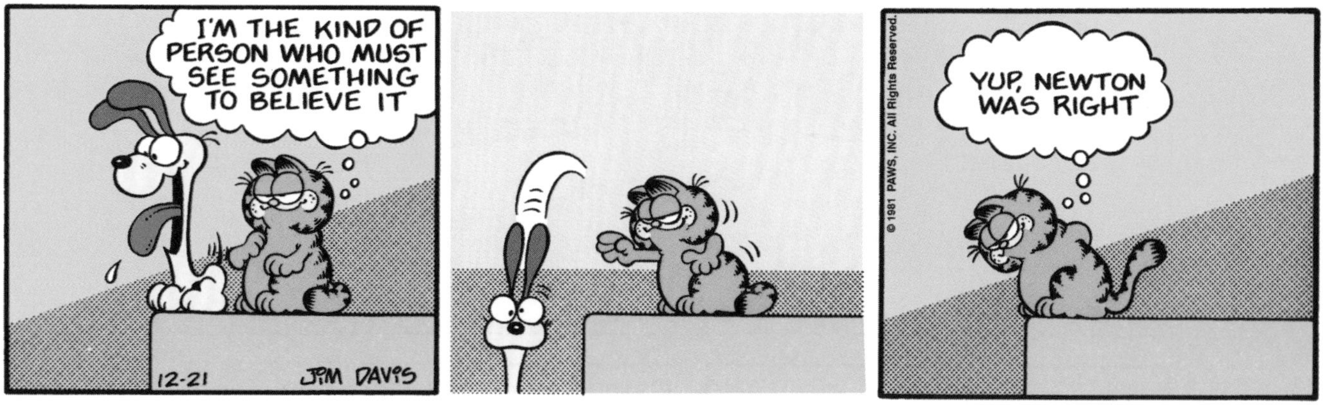
I'M THE KIND OF PERSON WHO MUST SEE SOMETHING TO BELIEVE IT
12-21
JIM DAVIS
© 1981 PAWS, INC. All Rights Reserved.
YUP, NEWTON WAS RIGHT

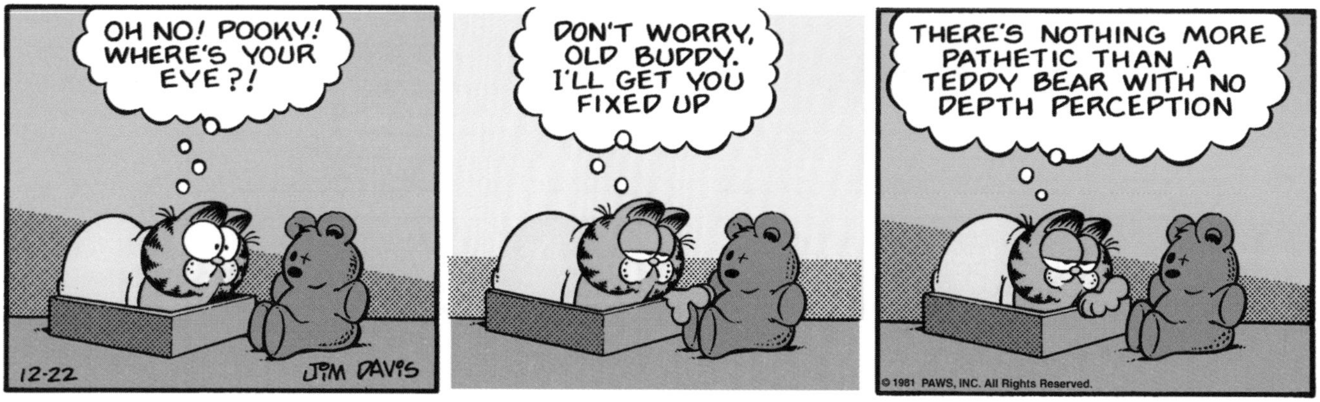
OH NO! POOKY! WHERE'S YOUR EYE?!
12-22
JIM DAVIS
DON'T WORRY, OLD BUDDY. I'LL GET YOU FIXED UP
THERE'S NOTHING MORE PATHETIC THAN A TEDDY BEAR WITH NO DEPTH PERCEPTION
© 1981 PAWS, INC. All Rights Reserved.

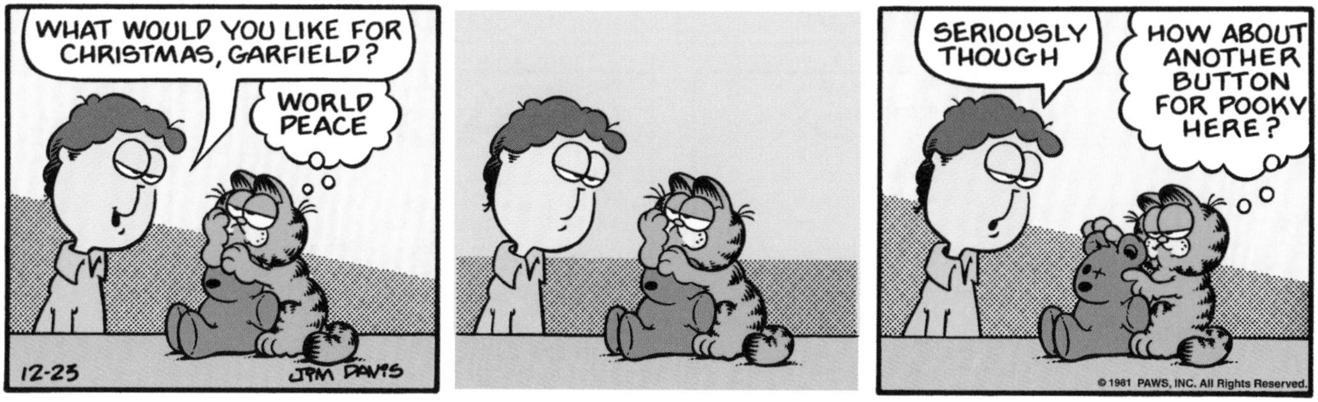
WHAT WOULD YOU LIKE FOR CHRISTMAS, GARFIELD?
WORLD PEACE
12-23
JIM DAVIS
SERIOUSLY THOUGH
HOW ABOUT ANOTHER BUTTON FOR POOKY HERE?
© 1981 PAWS, INC. All Rights Reserved.

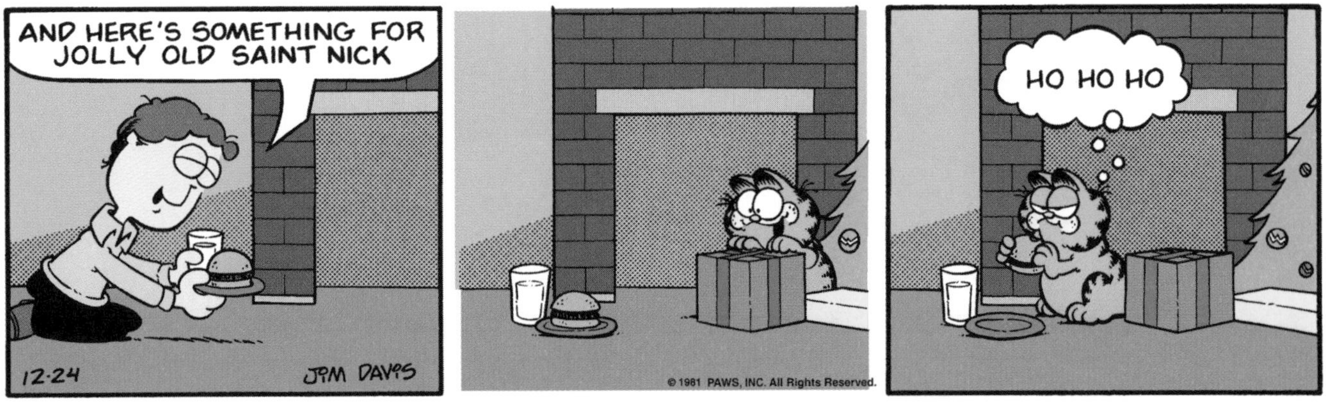
AND HERE'S SOMETHING FOR JOLLY OLD SAINT NICK
12-24
JIM DAVIS
© 1981 PAWS, INC. All Rights Reserved.
HO HO HO

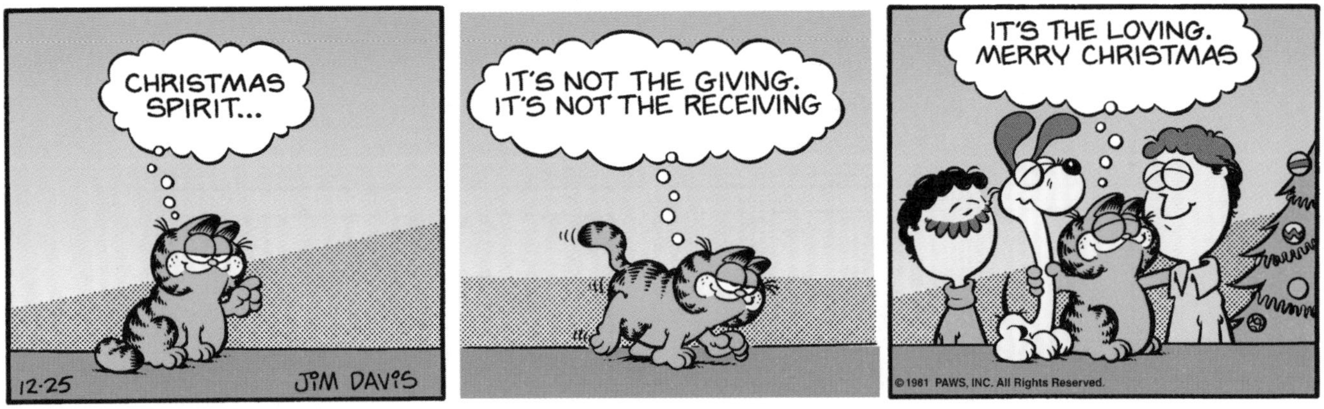
CHRISTMAS SPIRIT...
12-25
JIM DAVIS
IT'S NOT THE GIVING. IT'S NOT THE RECEIVING
IT'S THE LOVING. MERRY CHRISTMAS
© 1981 PAWS, INC. All Rights Reserved.

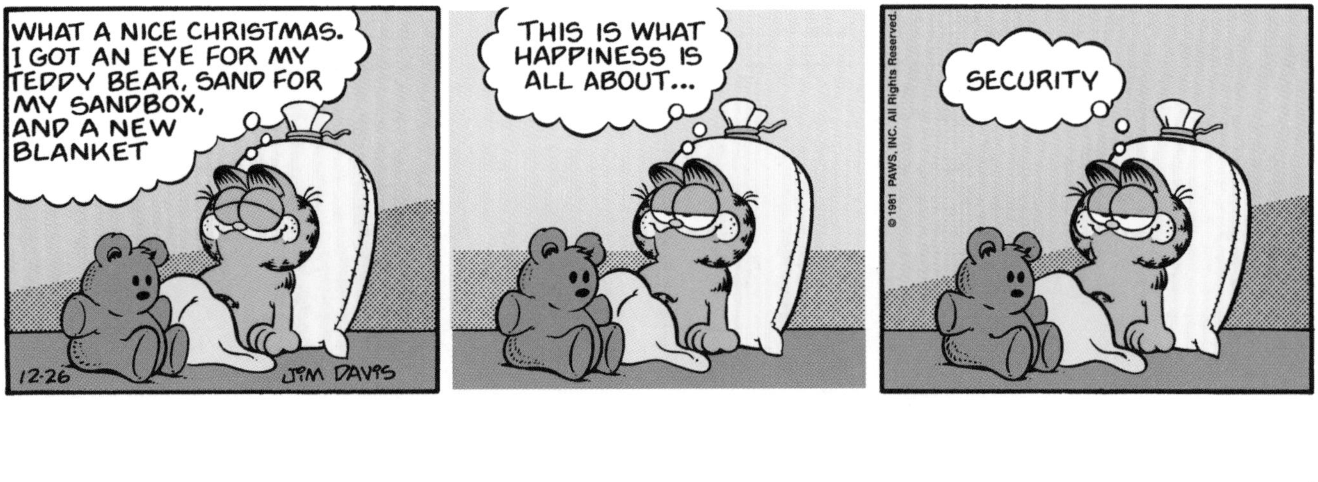
WHAT A NICE CHRISTMAS. I GOT AN EYE FOR MY TEDDY BEAR, SAND FOR MY SANDBOX, AND A NEW BLANKET
12-26
JIM DAVIS
THIS IS WHAT HAPPINESS IS ALL ABOUT...
© 1981 PAWS, INC. All Rights Reserved.
SECURITY

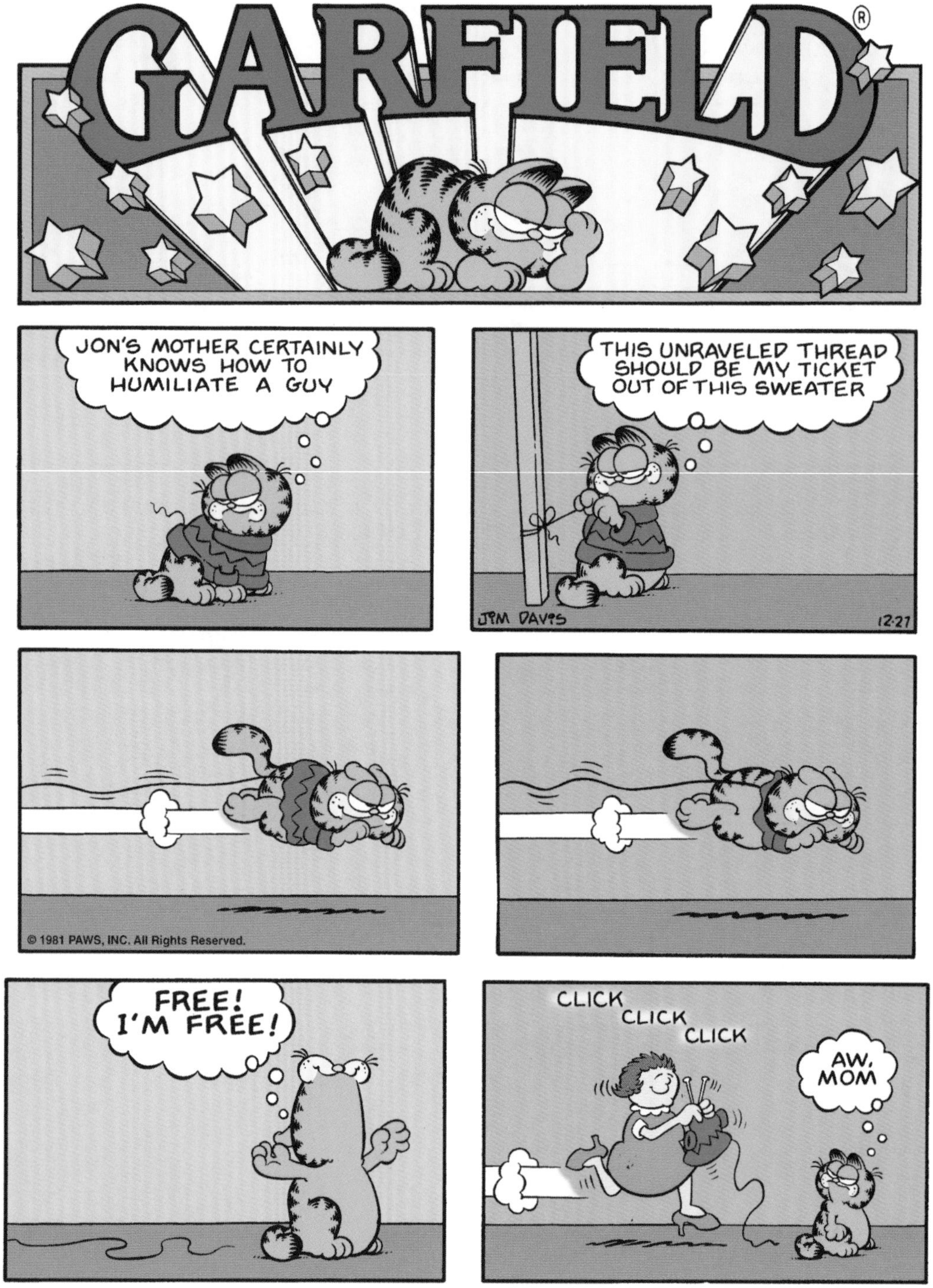
GARFIELD®
JON'S MOTHER CERTAINLY KNOWS HOW TO HUMILIATE A GUY
THIS UNRAVELED THREAD SHOULD BE MY TICKET OUT OF THIS SWEATER
JIM DAVIS
12-27
© 1981 PAWS, INC. All Rights Reserved.
FREE! I'M FREE!
CLICK
CLICK
CLICK
AW, MOM

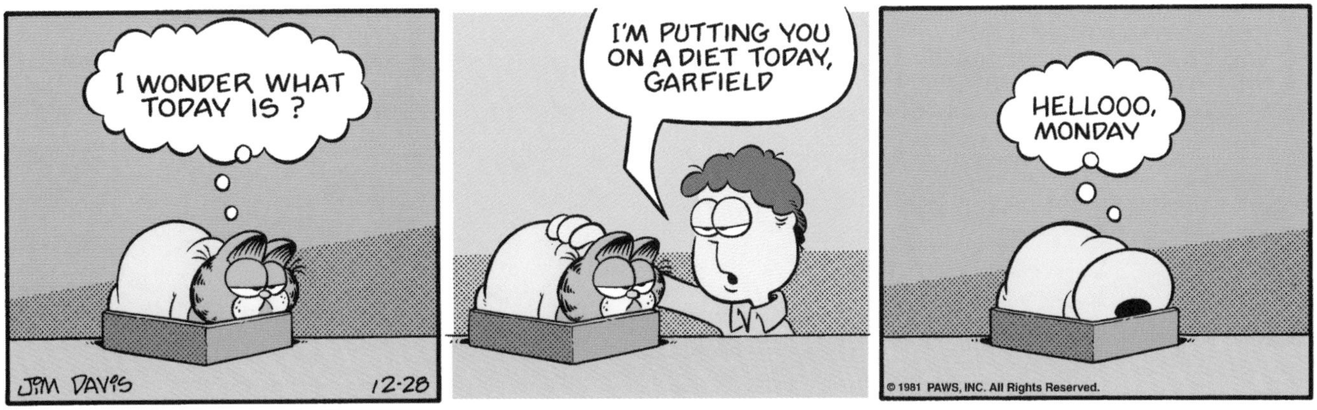
I WONDER WHAT TODAY IS ?
JIM DAVIS
12-28
I'M PUTTING YOU ON A DIET TODAY, GARFIELD
HELLOOO, MONDAY
© 1981 PAWS, INC. All Rights Reserved.

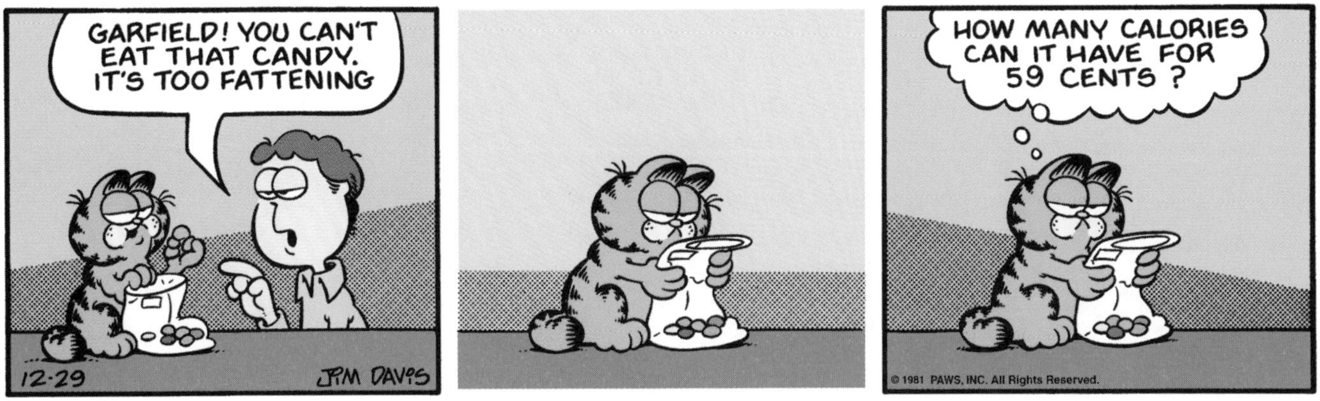
GARFIELD! YOU CAN'T EAT THAT CANDY. IT'S TOO FATTENING
12-29
JIM DAVIS
HOW MANY CALORIES CAN IT HAVE FOR 59 CENTS ?
© 1981 PAWS, INC. All Rights Reserved.

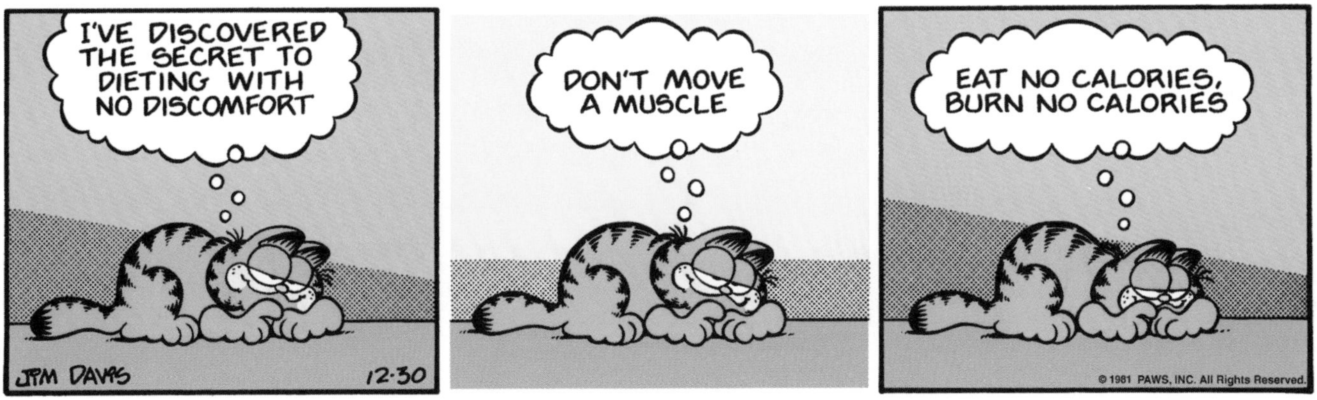
I'VE DISCOVERED THE SECRET TO DIETING WITH NO DISCOMFORT
JIM DAVIS
12-30
DON'T MOVE A MUSCLE
EAT NO CALORIES, BURN NO CALORIES
© 1981 PAWS, INC. All Rights Reserved.

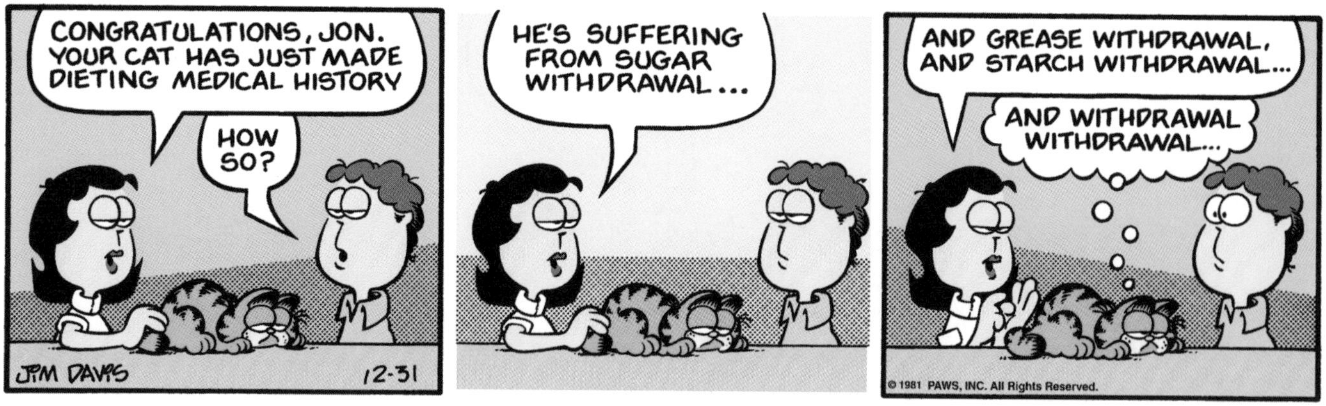
CONGRATULATIONS, JON. YOUR CAT HAS JUST MADE DIETING MEDICAL HISTORY
HOW SO?
JIM DAVIS
12-31
HE'S SUFFERING FROM SUGAR WITHDRAWAL...
AND GREASE WITHDRAWAL, AND STARCH WITHDRAWAL...
AND WITHDRAWAL WITHDRAWAL...
© 1981 PAWS, INC. All Rights Reserved.

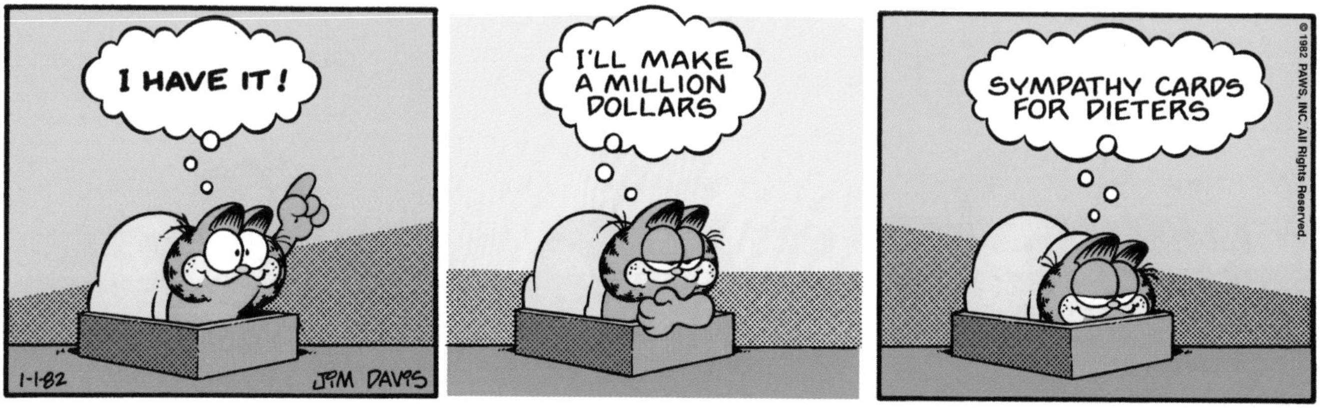
I HAVE IT!
1-1-82
JIM DAVIS
I'LL MAKE A MILLION DOLLARS
SYMPATHY CARDS FOR DIETERS
© 1982 PAWS, INC. All Rights Reserved.

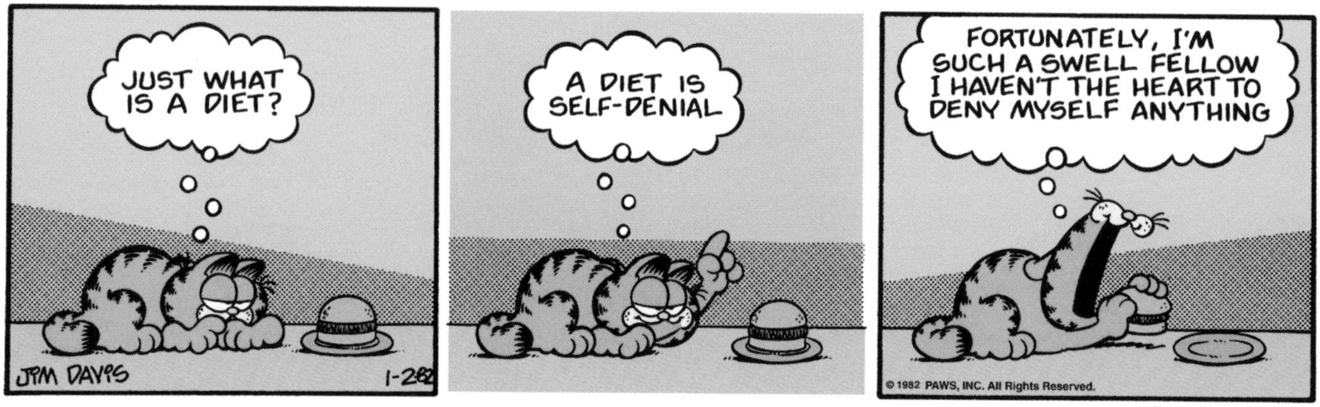
JUST WHAT IS A DIET?
JIM DAVIS
1-2-82
A DIET IS SELF-DENIAL
FORTUNATELY, I'M SUCH A SWELL FELLOW I HAVEN'T THE HEART TO DENY MYSELF ANYTHING
© 1982 PAWS, INC. All Rights Reserved.

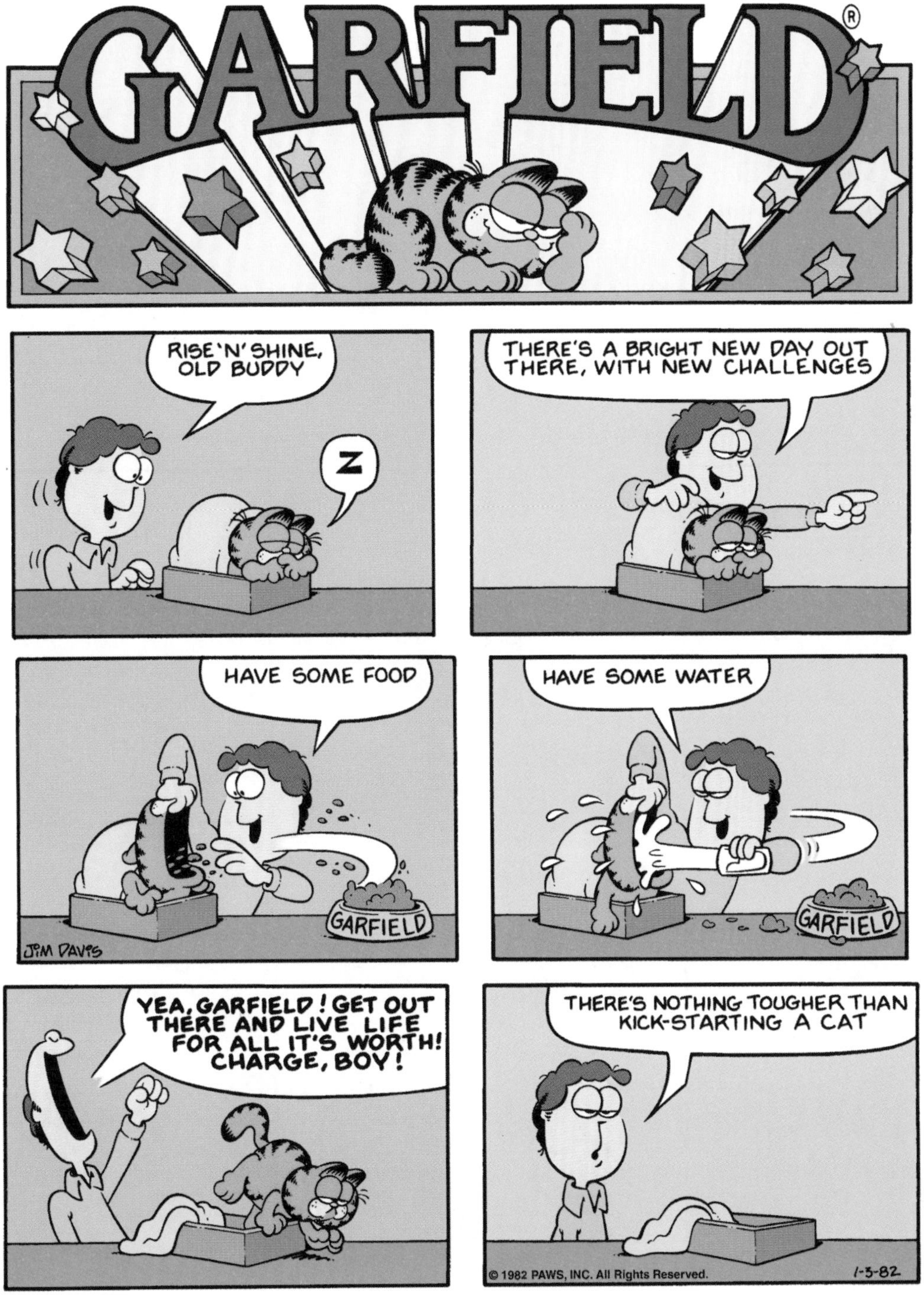
GARFIELD®
RISE'N' SHINE, OLD BUDDY
Z
THERE'S A BRIGHT NEW DAY OUT THERE, WITH NEW CHALLENGES
HAVE SOME FOOD
GARFIELD
JIM DAVIS
HAVE SOME WATER
GARFIELD
YEA, GARFIELD! GET OUT THERE AND LIVE LIFE FOR ALL IT'S WORTH! CHARGE, BOY!
THERE'S NOTHING TOUGHER THAN KICK-STARTING A CAT
© 1982 PAWS, INC. All Rights Reserved.
1-3-82

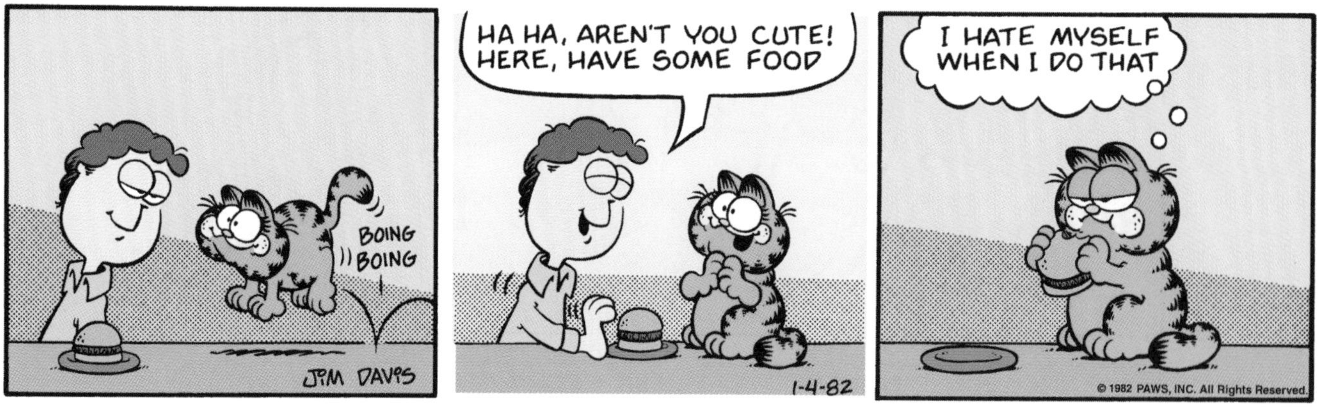
BOING
BOING
JIM DAVIS
HA HA, AREN'T YOU CUTE! HERE, HAVE SOME FOOD
1-4-82
I HATE MYSELF WHEN I DO THAT
© 1982 PAWS, INC. All Rights Reserved.

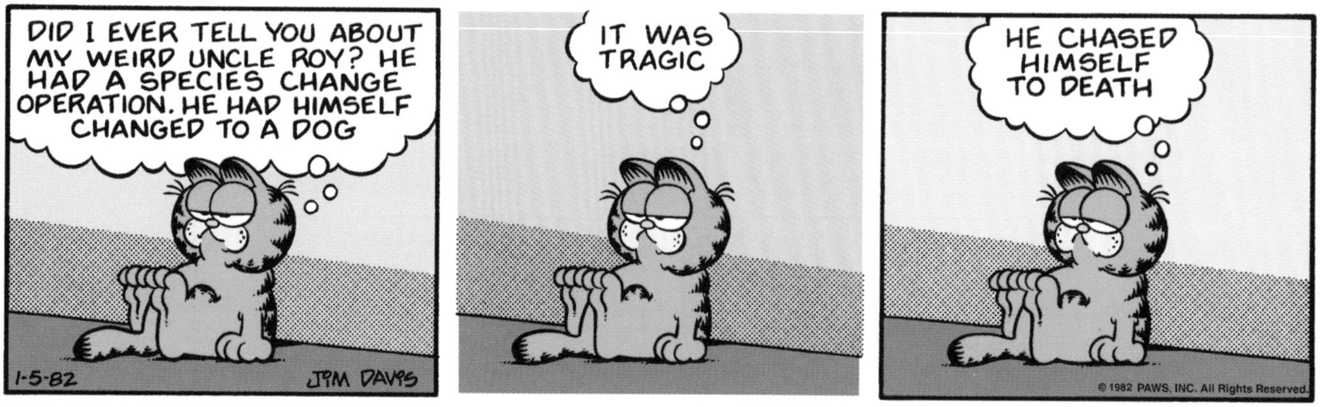
DID I EVER TELL YOU ABOUT MY WEIRD UNCLE ROY? HE HAD A SPECIES CHANGE OPERATION. HE HAD HIMSELF CHANGED TO A DOG
1-5-82
JIM DAVIS
IT WAS TRAGIC
HE CHASED HIMSELF TO DEATH
© 1982 PAWS, INC. All Rights Reserved.

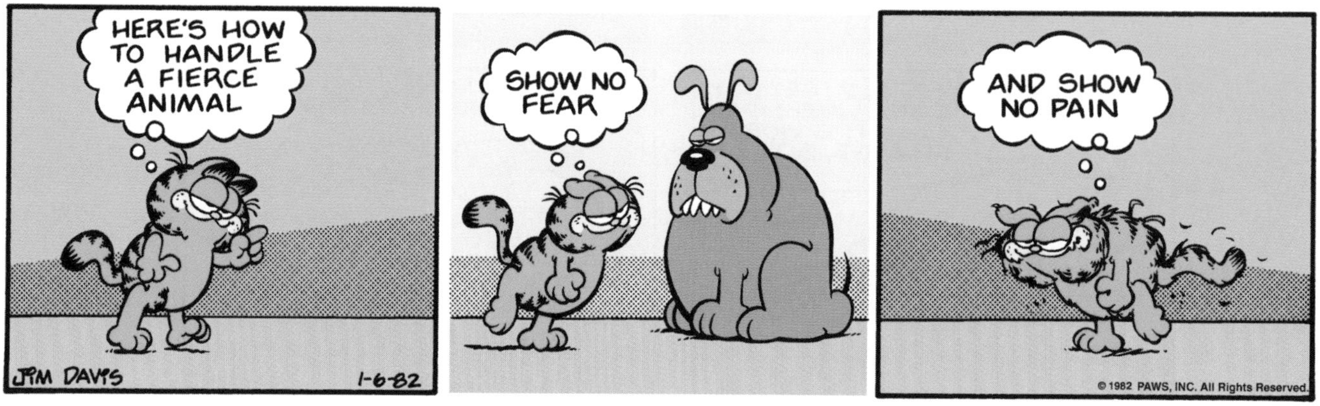
HERE'S HOW TO HANDLE A FIERCE ANIMAL
JIM DAVIS
1-6-82
SHOW NO FEAR
AND SHOW NO PAIN
© 1982 PAWS, INC. All Rights Reserved.

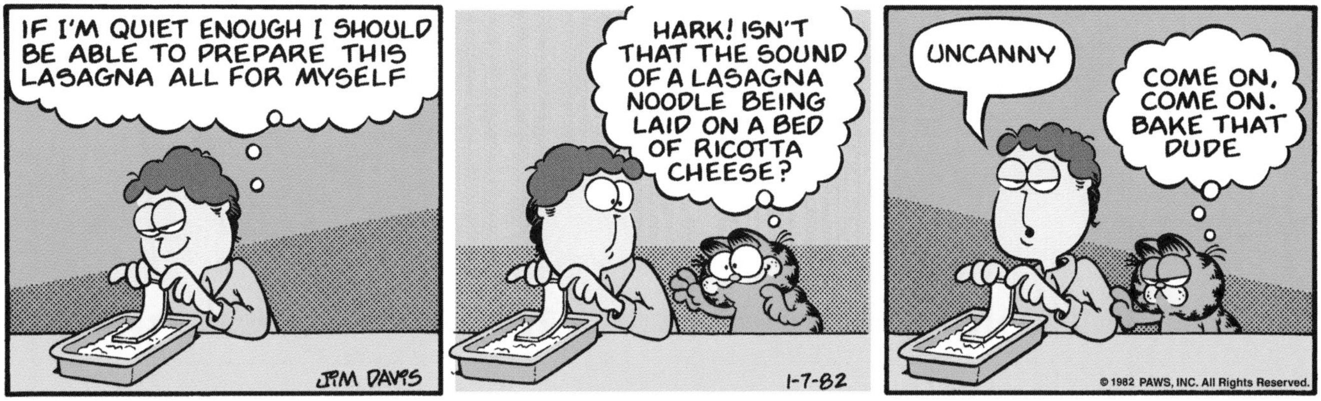
IF I'M QUIET ENOUGH I SHOULD BE ABLE TO PREPARE THIS LASAGNA ALL FOR MYSELF
JIM DAVIS
HARK! ISN'T THAT THE SOUND OF A LASAGNA NOODLE BEING LAID ON A BED OF RICOTTA CHEESE?
1-7-82
UNCANNY
COME ON, COME ON. BAKE THAT DUDE
© 1982 PAWS, INC. All Rights Reserved.

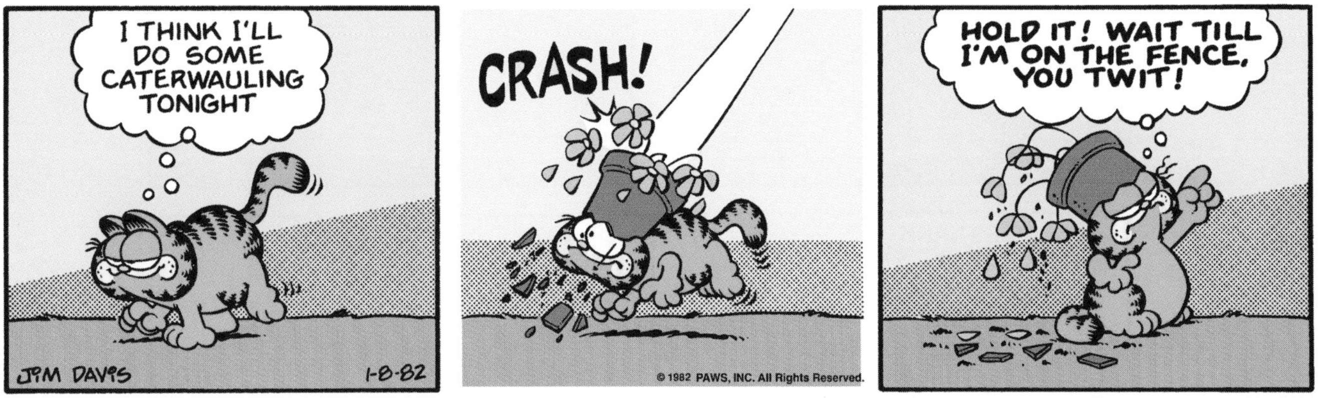
I THINK I'LL DO SOME CATERWAULING TONIGHT
JIM DAVIS
1-8-82
CRASH!
© 1982 PAWS, INC. All Rights Reserved.
HOLD IT! WAIT TILL I'M ON THE FENCE, YOU TWIT!

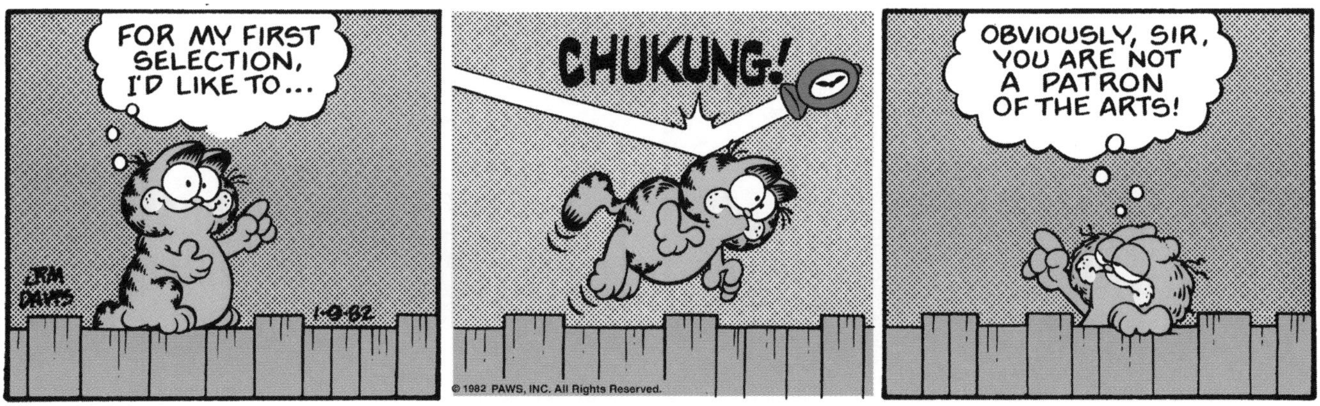
FOR MY FIRST SELECTION, I'D LIKE TO...
JIM DAVIS
1-9-82
CHUKUNG!
© 1982 PAWS, INC. All Rights Reserved.
OBVIOUSLY, SIR, YOU ARE NOT A PATRON OF THE ARTS!

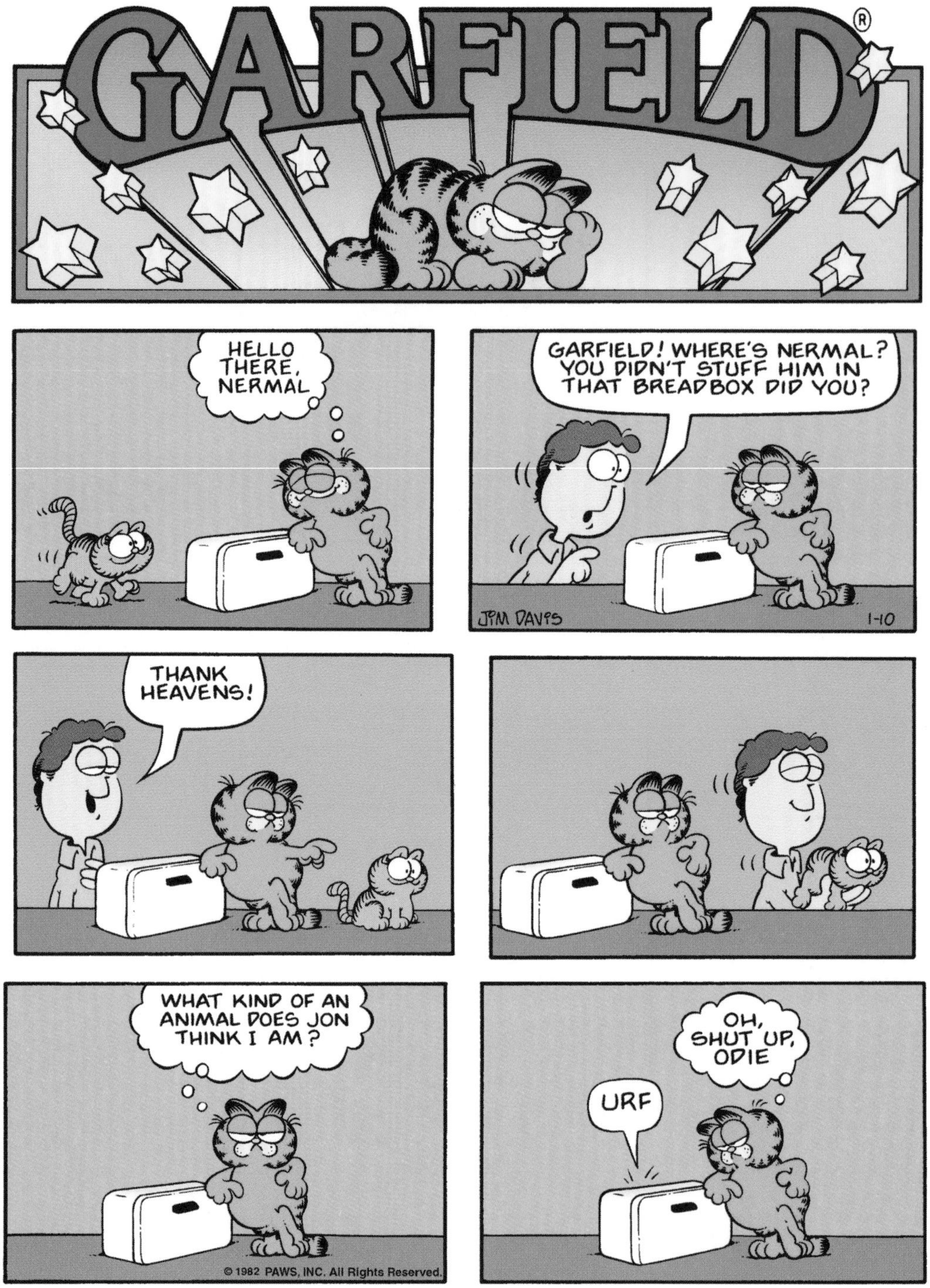
GARFIELD
HELLO THERE, NERMAL
GARFIELD! WHERE'S NERMAL? YOU DIDN'T STUFF HIM IN THAT BREADBOX DID YOU?
JPM DAVIS 1-10
THANK HEAVENS!
WHAT KIND OF AN ANIMAL DOES JON THINK I AM?
© 1982 PAWS, INC. All Rights Reserved.
URF
OH, SHUT UP, ODIE

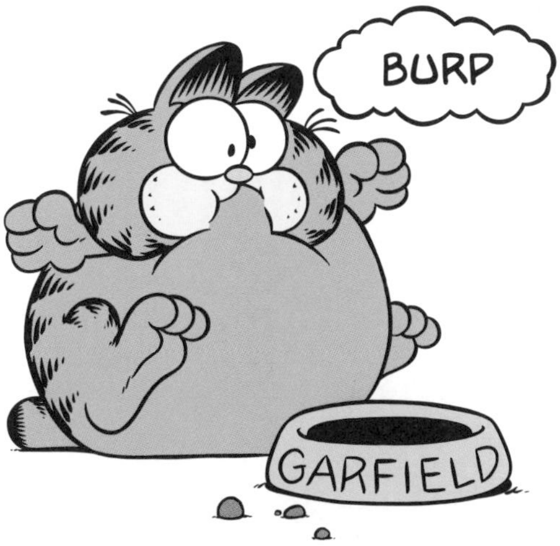
BURP
GARFIELD

GARFIELD DIET TIPS

1. Never go back for seconds—get it all the first time.
2. Set your scale back five pounds.
3. Never accept a candygram.
4. Don't date Sara Lee.
5. Vegetables are a must on a diet. I suggest carrot cake, zucchini bread, and pumpkin pie.
6. Never start a diet cold turkey (maybe cold roast beef, cold lasagna . . .).
7. Try to cut back. Leave the cherry off your ice cream sundae.
8. Hang around people fatter than you.

Garfield Goes Globetrotting

The GARFIELD strip appears worldwide.

Here's GARFIELD in English . . .

GARFIELD! DINNER!
JIM DAVIS
2-14
GARFIELD
I APPRECIATE YOUR PROMPTNESS, GARFIELD...
© 1981 PAWS, INC. All Rights Reserved.
BUT, NEXT TIME, OPEN THE DOOR!
OOPS

Spanish . . .

¡GARFIELD! LA COMIDA!
JIM DAVIS
2-14
GARFIELD
ME ALEGRO QUE HAYAS RESPONDIDO PRONTO
© 1981 PAWS, INC. All Rights Reserved.
PERO, ABRE LA PUER-TA LA PRÓXIMA VEZ
¡OH!

French . . .

GARFIELD! A TABLE!
JIM DAVIS
2-14
GARFIELD
CONTENT QUE TU OBÉISSES SI VITE, GARFIELD...
© 1981 PAWS, INC. All Rights Reserved.
...MAIS LA PROCHAINE FOIS, OUVRE LA PORTE!
AIE!

German . . .

GARFIELD! ESSEN!
JIM DAVIS
2-14
GARFIELD
ICH FREUE MICH ÜBER DEIN PROMPTES ER-SCHEINEN, GARFIELD
© 1981 PAWS, INC. All Rights Reserved.
ABER MACH NÄCHSTES MAL DIE TÜR AUF!
UPPS

Danish . . .

GARFIELD..SÅ ER DER MAD!
JIM DAVIS
2-14
GARFIELD
JEG SÆTTER STOR PRIS PÅ DU KOMMER, NÅR JEG KALDER, GARFIELD...
© 1981 PAWS, INC. All Rights Reserved.
...MEN ÅBN DØREN RØRST!!!
HOVSA!

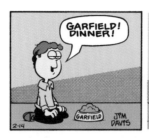

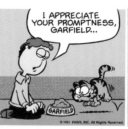

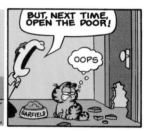

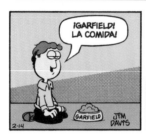

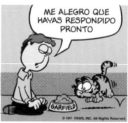

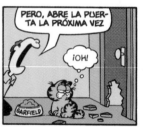

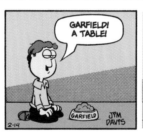

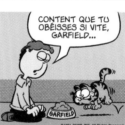

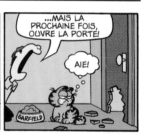

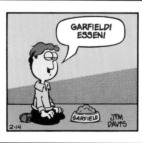

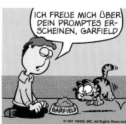

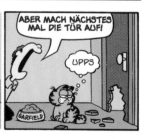

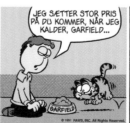

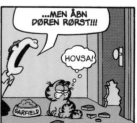